E

HANDBOOK OF
SERIOUS EMOTIONAL DISTURBANCE
IN CHILDREN AND ADOLESCENTS

HANDBOOK OF
SERIOUS EMOTIONAL DISTURBANCE
IN CHILDREN AND ADOLESCENTS

Edited by

Diane T. Marsh and Mary A. Fristad

John Wiley & Sons, Inc.

ISBN 0-471-39814-4

Printed in the United States of America.

10 9 8 7 6 5 4 3 2 1

Dedicated to the families that keep us grounded:

Rabe, Chris, Bonnie, Dan, Steve, and Trina
DTM
Joe, Elise, and Peter
MAF

Contributors

Jean Adnopoz, MPH
Yale Child Study Center
Yale University School of Medicine
New Haven, Connecticut

Anne Marie Albano, PhD
Child Study Center
New York University School of Medicine
New York, New York

Marie Armentano, MD
Massachusetts General Hospital Chelsea
Harvard Medical School
Boston, Massachusetts

Angela Arnold-Saritepe, PhD
Strong Center for Developmental
  Disabilities
University of Rochester Medical Center
Rochester, New York

Harriet S. Bicksler, MA
Pennsylvania Child and Adolescent
  Service System Program Training and
  Technical Assistance Institute
Harrisburg, Pennsylvania

Ronald T. Brown, PhD
College of Health Professions and
  Department of Pediatrics
Medical University of South Carolina
Charleston, South Carolina

Susanna Chang, PhD
Department of Psychiatry and
  Biobehavioral Sciences
University of California at Los Angeles
  School of Medicine
Los Angeles, California

James R. Cook, PhD
Department of Psychology
University of North Carolina at
  Charlotte
Charlotte, North Carolina

Valerie J. Cook-Morales, PhD
Department of Counseling and School
  Psychology
San Diego State University
San Diego, California

Adrienne Dixon, MS
Counseling Psychology Department
Gannon University
Erie, Pennsylvania

Gregory A. Fabiano, MA
Department of Psychology
State University of New York at
  Buffalo
Buffalo, New York

Wendy S. Freeman, PhD
Department of Psychology
University of Manitoba
Winnipeg, Manitoba

Mary A. Fristad, PhD, ABPP
Division of Child and Adolescent
  Psychiatry
The Ohio State University
Columbus, Ohio

John D. Gavazzi, PsyD, ABPP
Independent Practice
Mechanicsburg, Pennsylvania

Thomas J. Grundle, PhD
Aurora Health Care–Kenosha
  Behavioral Health Service
Kenosha, Wisconsin

Marsali Hansen, PhD, ABPP
Pennsylvania Child and Adolescent
  Service System Program Training and
  Technical Assistance Institute
Harrisburg, Pennsylvania

Kimberly Hoagwood, PhD
Office of the Director
National Institute of Mental Health
Bethesda, Maryland

Kristen E. Holderle, BA
Division of Child and Adolescent
  Psychiatry
The Ohio State University
Columbus, Ohio

Joseph D. Hovey, PhD
Department of Psychology
University of Toledo
Toldeo, Ohio

Kay Redfield Jamison, PhD
Department of Psychiatry
Johns Hopkins University School of
  Medicine
Baltimore, Maryland

Ryan P. Kilmer, PhD
Department of Psychology
University of North Carolina at
  Charlotte
Charlotte, North Carolina

Cheryl A. King, PhD
Department of Psychiatry
University of Michigan
Ann Arbor, Michigan

Linda K. Knauss, PhD
Institute for Graduate Clinical
  Psychology
Widener University
Chester, Pennsylvania

Ann Litzelman, MS
Pennsylvania Child and Adolescent
  Service System Program Training and
  Technical Assistance Institute
Harrisburg, Pennsylvania

Caroline Magyar, PhD
Director, Autism Spectrum Disorders
  Program
Strong Center for Developmental
  Disabilities
Department of Pediatrics
University of Rochester Medical
  Center
Rochester, New York

Diane T. Marsh, PhD
Department of Psychology
University of Pittsburgh at Greensburg
Greensburg, Pennsylvania

Susan L. McCammon, PhD
Department of Psychology
East Carolina University
Greenville, North Carolina

Deborah Megivern, MSW, PhD
George Warren Brown School of Social
  Work
Center for Mental Health Services
  Research
Washington University
St. Louis, Missouri

Carol T. Mowbray, PhD
School of Social Work
University of Michigan
Ann Arbor, Michigan

Robert A. Murphy, PhD
Yale Child Study Center
Yale University School of Medicine
New Haven, Connecticut

Joseph E. Nyre, PhD
Baylor Evaluation Services Center
Department of Educational Psychology
Baylor University
Waco, Texas

William E. Pelham Jr., PhD
Center for Children and Families
Department of Psychology
State University of New York at
    Buffalo
Buffalo, New York

John Piacentini, PhD
Child OCD, Anxiety, Tourette Disorders
    Program
Department of Psychiatry and
    Biobehavioral Sciences
University of California at Los Angeles
    School of Medicine
Los Angeles, California

Heather Ringeisen, PhD
Child and Adolescent Services Research
    Program
National Institute of Mental Health
Bethesda, Maryland

Michael C. Roberts, PhD
Clinical Child Psychology Program
University of Kansas
Lawrence, Kansas

Beatrice R. Salter, PhD
Independent Practice
Philadelphia, Pennsylvania

Nicole J. Setzer, PhD
Child Study Center
New York University School of Medicine
New York, New York

Amy E. Shaver, MA
Wright-Patterson Air Force Base
Dayton, Ohio

Tristram Smith, PhD
Strong Center for Developmental
    Disabilities
Department of Pediatrics
University of Rochester Medical Center
Rochester, New York

Ramon Solhkhah, MD
St. Luke's–Roosevelt Hospital Center
Columbia University College of
    Physicians and Surgeons
New York, New York

Shari Strauss, BS
School of Social Work
University of Michigan
Ann Arbor, Michigan

Katherine Tsatsanis, PhD
Child Study Center
Yale University
New Haven, Connecticut

Olivia N. Velting, PhD
Child Study Center
New York University School of Medicine
New York, New York

Eric M. Vernberg, PhD
Clinical Child Psychology Program
University of Kansas
Lawrence, Kansas

Fred R. Volkmar, MD
Child Study Center
Yale University
New Haven, Connecticut

Contents ————————————————————————

Section IV   Systems of Care

Foreword

Mental illness is devastating to anyone personally affected by it, but for those who are young it is particularly dreadful. At a time in life when the expectation of well-being is nearly universal, and when deviant behavior or poor psychological health is neither understood nor well-tolerated by friends, family, or teachers, emotional disturbances take a profound and painful toll. Mental illness, when it hits the young, is often pervasively destructive: It affects the ability to learn, remember, and to think coherently; it damages peer relationships at a time when they are most critical; and it removes pleasure from a time of life that is otherwise a remarkably rich period of delight and exploration.

Yet, as a society, we have for far too long overlooked, outright denied, or turned our back on mental illness in children and adolescents. This has resulted in an unconscionable level of unnecessary suffering and death, for mental illness is relatively common in adolescents, and far from rare in children. Suicide is responsible for more deaths in adolescents than AIDS, cancer, heart disease, stroke, and kidney disease *combined.* Parents, educators, religious leaders, and physicians need to be far more informed than they are and much more proactive. So, too, do mental health professionals.

It is fortunate that there is now an excellent text available, the *Handbook of Serious Emotional Disturbance in Children and Adolescents.* The editors, Diane Marsh and Mary Fristad, have done an outstanding job in putting together a book that so expertly covers the major areas of importance: clinical and scientific information about the disorders themselves (attention-deficit/hyperactivity disorder, obsessive-compulsive disorder, anxiety and mood disorders, psychosis, and substance abuse); research and training issues; and important information about the legal, educational, and primary care systems within which parents and patients are likely to find themselves. The editors have also made sure that the adolescents and college students who suffer from these illnesses have had a voice: Their first-hand accounts are included, as well.

No single book can capture everything there is to know about such complex problems, but this handbook is a terrific place to begin.

> Kay Redfield Jamison, PhD
> Professor of Psychiatry
> The Johns Hopkins School of Medicine

SECTION I

Introduction

Chapter 1

INTRODUCTION

DIANE T. MARSH AND MARY A. FRISTAD

The *Handbook of Serious Emotional Disturbance in Children and Adolescents* is designed to fill the need for a current and comprehensive resource that targets the most severe and persistent mental disorders of childhood and adolescence. The need for such a handbook is compelling. As indicated in the surgeon general's report on mental health (Satcher, 2000), one in five young people experience a diagnosable mental disorder during the course of a year. Approximately 5% have a serious emotional disturbance (SED) accompanied by extreme functional impairment that undermines their present lives and imperils their future.

The term *SED* serves as an umbrella term for certain diagnostic categories, including autistic and other pervasive developmental disorders, attention-deficit/hyperactivity disorder, schizophrenia, bipolar disorder, major depressive disorder, obsessive-compulsive disorder, and other severe anxiety disorders.

These disorders typically do not remit spontaneously, although effective psychosocial and psychopharmacological treatments are rapidly becoming available, with treatment outcomes comparable to those of adults. Yet at least two thirds of young people with a diagnosable mental disorder do not receive *any* mental health services at all, and many others are underserved (Satcher, 2000). The price of this neglect is unconscionable for these children and adolescents, for their often-desperate families, and for a society that is deprived of their contributions.

The challenges that accompany professional practice with the SED population are considerable. Many systems are involved in meeting the diverse needs of these children, adolescents, and families, including the mental health, educational, child welfare, juvenile justice, substance abuse, and primary health care systems. Thus, effective SED services require multisystemic coordination and collaboration. As Sybil Goldman (2000) has observed, many additional challenges mark the SED territory. Some of these challenges involve treatment access, including scarcity and fragmentation of services; racial, ethnic, and economic disparities in insurance coverage and treatment; financial barriers that discourage families from seeking or continuing services; inadequate assessment and diagnosis; poor public understanding about mental health concerns; and social stigma. Other challenges reflect the need for a sufficient supply of well-trained mental health professionals; for an adequate knowledge base to guide SED systems, services, and treatments; and for synergy among the worlds of system builders, clinicians, and researchers.

In spite of these challenges, there is now general agreement regarding the services that are needed for children and adolescents, as well as the way in which services should be delivered. A system of care must be driven by the needs and preferences of the child and family; must provide comprehensive, individualized, and flexible services; and must embody a community-based, culturally sensitive, and multisystemic approach. At the same time, stakeholders in child-serving systems are working to reduce the use of restrictive services, to enhance service integration and coordination, to reform mechanisms for financing services, and to increase cost-effectiveness and provider accountability. Another trend is the renewed emphasis on prevention and early intervention.

Assuming new roles on multidisciplinary teams, service providers can now offer an array of innovative and evidence-based child/adolescent, family, and community interventions. Such innovative interventions include intensive case management, crisis intervention and emergency services, in-home services such as family preservation and family support services, respite care, wraparound services, school-based-services, mentoring/coaching, therapeutic group and foster family care, and multisystemic interventions.

The *Handbook of Serious Emotional Disturbance in Children and Adolescents* delineates the SED territory and provides a comprehensive review of current SED theory, research, practice, and policy. The content has important implications for mental health practitioners and graduate students in all related disciplines, as well as administrators, system planners, policymakers, managed care organizations, educators, families, and mental health advocates. The distinguished contributors bring a wide range of expertise to the handbook, which is divided into four sections: section I: Introduction; section II: Practice, Research, and Training Issues; section III: SED Disorders; and section IV: Systems of Care.

In the introductory section, following this overview, we feature the voices of adolescents themselves, who convey their experience of SED with power and eloquence. They describe the impact of SED on their lives, share what has been helpful (and what has not), and offer suggestions for practitioners. In chapter 2, Harriet Bicksler offers a forum for four teenagers who have been diagnosed with a variety of emotional and behavioral disorders. In chapter 3, Carol Mowbray, Deborah Megivern, and Shari Strauss provide a retrospective look by college students at their high school experiences with SED.

Section II encompasses a wide range of practice, research, and training issues. In chapter 4, Heather Ringeisen and Kimberly Hoagwood delineate clinical and research directions for the treatment and delivery of children's mental health services. In chapter 5, Susan McCammon, James Cook, and Ryan Kilmer outline the process of integrating systems-of-care values into university-based training. Adrienne Dixon discusses culturally competent SED practice in chapter 6. In chapter 7, Marsali Hansen underscores the need for competence in children's mental health services. In the final chapter of this section, Linda Knauss examines supervisory issues related to the treatment of SED.

Section III explores specific SED disorders and their evidence-based treatments. In chapter 9, Tristram Smith, Caroline Magyar, and Angela Arnold-Saritepe describe autism spectrum disorders. Gregory Fabiano and William Pelham Jr. present a comprehensive treatment program for attention deficit/hyperactivity disorder in chapter 10. In chapter 11, Susanna Chang and John Piacentini examine obsessive-compulsive disorder and related disorders. Olivia Velting, Nicole Setzer, and Anne Marie Albano consider a range of anxiety disorders in chapter 12. In chapter 13, Mary Fristad, Amy Shaver, and Kristen Holderle provide a current perspective on mood disorders. Fred Volkmar and Katherine Tsatsanis discuss psychosis and psychotic conditions in chapter 14. In chapter 15, Joseph Hovey and Cheryl King analyze the spectrum of suicidal behavior, which is closely linked to SED disorders. Ramon Solhkhah and Marie Armentano address the problem of adolescent substance abuse and psychiatric comorbidity in chapter 16.

Section IV focuses on systems of care. In chapter 17, Thomas Grundle describes wraparound care and presents some exemplary programs. Jean Adnopoz explores home-based treatment for children with SED in chapter 18. In chapter 19, Robert Murphy examines mental health, juvenile justice, and law enforcement responses to youth psychopathology. Turning to the family system, in chapter 20, Marsali Hansen, Ann Litzelman, and Beatrice Salter offer an array of collaborative models for working with families that include a child with SED. Chapters 21 and 22 focus on the school system, beginning with a consideration of the home–school–agency triangle by Valerie Cook-Morales, who writes from the dual perspectives of a professional and a parent of a child with SED. Complementing that chapter is a discussion of school-based intensive mental health treatment by Eric Vernberg, Michael Roberts, and Joseph Nyre. In chapter 23, Ronald Brown and Wendy Freeman depict the role of the primary health care system in SED. Last, in chapter 24, John Gavazzi provides a primer on child and adolescent psychotropic medications for the nonprescribing mental health professional.

The future holds tremendous opportunity for children's mental health, as well as tremendous challenges. It is our hope that the science contained in this book becomes outdated within the decade, as new studies that provide clear clinical guidelines for the care of children with SED and their families are made available at an increasing rate. It is also our hope that the four areas represented in this book—namely, the voices of the children and families themselves; general practice, research, and training issues; specific knowledge regarding particular disorders; and systems of care—continue to advance together, with progress in each individual area enhancing progress in the remaining areas.

REFERENCES

Goldman, S. K. (2000, August). *Directions for child mental health: A comprehensive approach for the new millennium.* Presentation at the annual meeting of the American Psychological Association, Washington, DC.

Satcher, D. (2000). *Mental health: A report of the surgeon general. Chapter 3: Children and mental health* (pp. 124–219). Washington, DC: U.S. Public Health Service.

LISTENING TO THE VOICES OF ADOLESCENTS WITH SERIOUS EMOTIONAL DISTURBANCE

HARRIET S. BICKSLER

"I think I'm pretty normal," Nina said when I asked her how her illness has affected her life. That may be the most important point to remember when listening to adolescents with serious emotional disturbance. All adolescents want to be normal, to fit in with their peers, to do the same things that every other teenager likes to do. As I listened not only to Nina, but also to Michael, Savannah, and Markel tell their stories about their illnesses, I was struck by how much like other adolescents they all are.

Nina, Michael, Savannah, and Markel (not their real names) have all been diagnosed with a variety of emotional and behavioral disorders. They have all been hospitalized in psychiatric inpatient units at least once and have had significant contact with Pennsylvania's child and adolescent mental health system through outpatient, residential, partial hospitalization, wraparound, and other services. They have also participated as youth members of the planning committee for the youth track of Pennsylvania's annual children's interagency conference focusing on clinical best practice in children's mental health services. They have told their stories to two major audiences—first at the Pennsylvania conference and then at the annual convention of the American Psychological Association.

They are telling their stories again here as a reminder to mental health professionals that real children and adolescents are at the receiving end of their services. For this chapter, I personally interviewed each adolescent (one in person and three over the phone), and I had a copy of the transcript of their appearance at the APA convention in August 2000, where they were interviewed by Dr. Diane Marsh. I also heard each of them speak at our Pennsylvania conference. Three of them chose their own fictitious names for this chapter. (I chose the fourth fictitious name.) Their individual stories follow, after which I will conclude with a few summary observations. Keep in mind that their stories were current at the time of this writing, and their circumstances may have since changed.

NINA

Nina is 17 years old. Her parents divorced when she was 6 years old. She has one brother, two half sisters, and one half brother. She currently lives with a foster family—a mom, dad, brother, and sister.

Her parents' divorce triggered Nina's mental health problems. She lived with her mother, whom she blamed for the divorce. She had been very close to her father. Nina's anger toward her mother built up and eventually led to two suicide attempts that each resulted in hospitalization. Between ages 12 and 15 she was in and out of the hospital, a residential treatment facility, and a partial hospitalization program, and she attended emotional support classes at school. She also has been diagnosed with learning disabilities, including attention-deficit/hyperactivity disorder (ADHD). At one point she was diagnosed with bipolar disorder as well, although she is not sure about that diagnosis. She knows that sometimes she feels very depressed, and other times she feels energized and happy to be alive. She has lived with her foster family for almost 2 years and now attends regular classes as a junior at a public high school.

Family and cultural attachments are very important to Nina. She says that the most difficult aspect of her illness is not being with her family. "Even though they have done a lot to make me not want to be with them, they are still my family and I miss being with them," she says. She also misses the diversity of the city where she used to live and being with people of her own Hispanic culture. She describes herself as "louder" and more outspoken than others in the mostly white neighborhood where she lives with her foster family, and says that sometimes they do not understand her. She sees her birth mother a couple of times a year, but rarely sees her father, especially because he is currently in jail. "I don't want to talk to him while he is in jail," she notes.

Despite missing her birth family and culture, Nina has nothing but good things to say about her foster family. She especially appreciates living in a two-parent family where there is a strong bond between the husband and wife and their children. Nina says, "They are like my real parents. They make me realize what I didn't have with my own family, and now I understand what a real family feels like." Her foster family has been "100% and more" supportive. They are always on her side, understanding her and helping others to understand her, too. Her advice to other families is to offer the same kind of unconditional support to their children: "Whether you're yelling or screaming, just be there and understand them, even when they're saying they hate you."

Nina talks about how difficult it is to find friends who understand what it feels like to have mental health problems. People say things that can easily be offensive and sometimes talk about her behind her back, and it is often hard for her to function and do things the way everyone expects, not the way she wants to do them. She says she has one really good friend from whom she receives a lot of support.

Nina is not on any medication right now, although she has taken various antidepressants, as well as Ritalin. She believes the medications didn't really help her. She continues in therapy, however. When asked what has been most helpful about therapy and her relationships with mental health professionals, she mentions "having someone to talk to who understands me and translates what I say to others so they can understand, too." She is also adamant that "professionals should not jump around from job to job." Responding to a question about what has not been helpful, she is quick to criticize therapists who are "always leaving." She points out that it takes a long time to learn to trust a therapist, and she wishes she could have a single therapist for the entire duration of her therapy.

Her advice to kids with similar problems is to have faith and know that their mental health problems are not the end of the world. "Don't worry about what anyone else says. Believe in yourself—there can be no failure if you believe in yourself," she declares confidently. Nina plans to graduate from high school, and then she hopes to go to an art institute to pursue an art career based on her interests in photography, drawing, sketching, and painting.

MICHAEL

Michael is 17 years old and lives in a major metropolitan area with his mother and father and four siblings. He is the middle child—flanked by two older sisters and a younger brother and sister. He is a junior in high school and for 3 years has attended an approved private school that he likes.

Michael's mental health problems started when he was in the fourth grade. First he was diagnosed with attention-deficit/hyperactivity disorder (ADHD), then depression, then obsessive-compulsive disorder (OCD) and oppositional defiant disorder, and then he found out he had bipolar disorder as well. At one point Tourette's syndrome was also suspected. He describes himself as "inattentive, getting into lots of fights, hyperactive." "I knew I was hyper and I couldn't pay attention," he says. He has been hospitalized once and was in a partial hospitalization program for a while. Currently, he receives in-home treatment and services, mostly for OCD and bipolar, from a therapeutic staff support worker, a mobile therapist, and a behavioral specialist consultant (all positions that are part of his state's array of public behavioral health rehabilitation services, or *wraparound*).

Michael has attended private schools because he wasn't able to function in public schools and "teachers couldn't handle me." He has been frustrated by teachers who either don't know how to deal with kids like him or don't want to try: "One year you'll have a great teacher, the next year it will be the total opposite. One will work with you, the next one won't. It's like playing Ping-Pong." In public school, he didn't have any friends and often got into fights even though he tried to have friends. Michael still gets into fights at home; as he puts it, there is "lots of arguing and a little bit of physical fighting. Everybody gets tired of the fighting."

The most difficult thing, Michael says, is "being obsessive-compulsive and not being able to keep my mouth shut. I get myself in trouble. Things get taken away, like sports equipment, or I'm grounded. I use inappropriate language. I can't stop counting, or turning out lights." His problems mostly happen at home because he manages to control himself outside the house, and then he lets it all out when he gets home. He also knows that the repetitive actions characteristic of OCD increase when he's feeling particularly anxious about something. He says he experiences many of his symptoms on almost an hourly basis.

Michael's family has been very supportive, especially his parents. He suggests that families have to work together because "the kid can't do it himself." Families need to support each other, he says.

When it comes to therapists, the most helpful ones are those who stick around. Michael also likes therapists who "listen—really listen—and treat kids as though they are on the same level." Michael notes that just because they have experience (as clinicians, with other kids who have mental health problems, and so on) doesn't mean they have to talk down to kids like him. He also says that lots of therapists "try to put words in your mouth and make you sound like you said things you didn't. Then they tell your parents you said something you didn't." He talks positively about his mobile therapist and behavior specialist because they worked as a team and listened to him. But just as he felt he was starting to get better, the behavior specialist left because he had too many patients and had to drop some.

Michael advises other kids to take their medication. Even though he forthrightly declares, "Medications suck!" he knows he has to take them. He says he has been on lots of stuff that has not worked and has had adverse side effects. Right now he is taking Depakote and clonidine, but says only half jokingly that he thinks he's been on every medication in the *Physician's Desk Reference* (to go with what he hyperbolically calls his "5 million diagnoses").

Three years ago, Michael wrote about what it felt like to live with mental illness:

> I know I make it very hard to live with me. I make my sisters cry and don't exactly know why. They don't want to spend time with me because of the things I say to them. I don't mean to, but I can't help it. If I get too excited or too angry, I can't control what comes out of my mouth. I feel sad and guilty for making them sad, but it doesn't seem to help much. I wish I could change things and make the last several years completely different for my family and myself, but I can't. I'm sorry for that, but I am what I am and I wish people could just accept that. (Palan, 1998)

One of Michael's dreams for the future is to be a professional hockey player. He also wants to work in telecommunications, doing something like installing different kinds of systems. To qualify for that kind of work, he hopes to attend college and major in electrical engineering.

SAVANNAH

Savannah is the middle child of five and lives in a midsize city. She is 16 years old.

Midway through my interview with her, she told me to watch *Girl Interrupted,* a movie about a young woman who spent time in a psychiatric hospital in the 1960s— "That's my life, my friend and me. I'm Angelina Jolie and my friend is Winona Ryder" (the actresses in the movie). The comparison is somewhat apt. Savannah tells a rather dramatic story of police officers coming to her house because she was threatening to kill herself and her younger brother. Her older sister had called the police because "I tried to go after my sister." She was taken by police car to the hospital.

Savannah refers to her grandmother's death about 7 years ago when she was in the second grade as the beginning of her mental health problems. The permanence of that death settled in on Savannah several years later, and she became severely depressed. She has been hospitalized twice. The second time, she was discharged to a partial hospitalization program where she went to school for a year and a half. Her depression was so severe that she was unable to go outside and do the things that normal children do. With the help of therapy during the past 2 years, she has been able to go out in public more, including to a nearby city every 2 weeks for modeling classes, and she's back in public school.

Savannah's memories of the psychiatric hospital are unpleasant. She talks about one day when she felt no one was listening to her and her parents had not visited because they were told not to come. She lay on the floor and rubbed her chin and forehead on the carpet until the skin came off. She continues, "They put me on so many medications, with so many side effects, I don't remember being there half the time. I was freezing when everyone else was sweating. People thought I was high most of the time, even though I've never gone near any drugs."

She says one effect of her illness is more attention, but "I don't like that." On the other hand, she thinks her illness has brought her family closer together, especially her and her older brother. The transition back to public school has also been difficult: "Before this year, in the partial hospitalization program, everyone had the same problems at school. I could talk to someone when I needed to. Now I'm back in a large public school, people don't remember me, I can't talk to people as easily, and I have to be in classes at certain times." She feels shy and claustrophobic sometimes, and she has had some medical problems as well.

Savannah criticizes professionals who do not listen, or who just listen so they can write something down in their charts. "Listen while you write," she says. "Often, professionals won't ask if they're not sure what I'm talking about. I know they're not listening." Her first psychiatrist, however, stands out in her mind: "She was one of the nicest doctors you could ever meet. She really listened to my problems. There need to be more like her." She also speaks highly of the counselor in her partial program who helped her get through each day. Much of her day-to-day support, however, seems to come from friends and family.

Although Savannah does not like medications because of the side effects, she acknowledges that they have been helpful, and she is grateful for professionals who have prescribed medications that have worked. She expects she will be on some kind of medication the rest of her life.

Her advice to kids with similar problems is to answer all the questions professionals ask. "I didn't tell them everything, so I didn't really benefit." To parents, she says, "If you realize your kid is having a problem, listen." She thinks that families exhibit a lot of denial about problems until kids get in trouble with the law. "My father has definitely changed," she goes on. "Now he asks me if he thinks there is a problem. He also encourages me to try to be the best at anything I do."

Thanks to her father's encouragement and support, Savannah has been able to take modeling classes. She has other goals as well—to graduate from high school, to go to college, and to become a forensic scientist. She feels that she finally has control over her disability, and she's optimistic about her future. Savannah ended the interview with one word of advice to herself and others: "*Smile!*"

MARKEL

Markel is 21 years old and has lived all his life in a large city. He used to live with his mother, but now lives with and provides care for his grandmother, who has diabetes. He works as a message delivery person in the center of the city.

Markel was diagnosed with depression when he was 9 years old. He had difficulty concentrating in school, and a counselor suggested he see a therapist. He was first diagnosed with a learning disability, then depression. He also has struggled with his feelings of low self-esteem and has had difficulty getting along with his mother. Markel has tried to commit suicide four times—the first time when he was 12 and most recently when he was 18. His first hospitalization was at age 13, when he spent 3 months in a psychiatric unit.

Friendships have been difficult for Markel, and he often feels isolated from other people. He says, "I've never had any true friends and haven't been able to sustain a relationship because of my insecurities. I missed a lot of school activities, like the prom. I've felt stigma from other kids. I never had money to dress like other kids, and I wasn't popular." He says he's always afraid that people are talking about him and don't like him, and he feels "like I'm not an interesting person, and a disappointment to everyone." However, he actively tries to improve his situation and "show people that I'm not that weird of a person and include myself in conversations."

His illness has also affected his relationship with his mother and siblings. "I thought my mother loved my siblings more. I was always arguing with my mother, and they would get mad at me. It wasn't good for them to be around me all the time. My therapist decided I should live with my grandmother because there would be less turmoil. Sometimes my mother goes through depression as well, and she takes offense at things I do."

His grandmother and his music have been the most helpful to him. He likes to listen to music and write songs. He writes love songs and socially conscious songs. When asked what he does with the songs he writes, Markel said, "I just keep them. I'm too nervous to have anyone look at them or read them. I'm afraid I would be laughed at." He longs to find someone else with whom he can connect, talk to about his problems, and know the person will not laugh at him.

When it comes to professionals, Markel says that out of eight or nine therapists over the years, there have been only two with whom he has felt an instant connection. They are frank enough to point out exactly what is wrong and "help me see what I should do, get to the root of the problem, and help me see myself." Others would leave or resign just as he would feel he was getting close to them.

With some therapists, he felt like he was simply getting a long lecture, or they would talk to his mother more than listen to and talk with him. He suggests that professionals should not think of what they are doing as just a job, but "as though one of their own family members was going through the same situation." He adds, "Try to add a little humor, be down-to-earth, instead of trying to speak like a textbook." Markel still has a mobile therapist, although he does not see her very often anymore. He also says he does not think he ever actually had a bad therapist, but it has been hard to have to get attached to new people all the time.

Although he has taken a variety of medications, including Prozac, lithium, and Zoloft, he is no longer taking any medication. Instead, he tries to cope by going to church. Markel acknowledges that medication helped his depression "on the inside," and therapists helped him figure out what to do with his life "on the outside."

He wants to let other kids know that mental health problems are not their fault. "Just as some people are born to be short or tall," he says, "so some are born with depression genes." He advises others to take their medications because they can help them to live "a regular life." He asks parents to have patience and pray for kids like him. "Try not to have too high expectations," he says. "Help us find ourselves. Trust us to make the right decisions." He tells siblings not to judge or have negative feelings, to understand that even though parents may love all their children equally, some kids need more help.

Markel's care for his grandmother, who is diabetic, carries over into his hopes and dreams for the future. He does a lot of volunteer work and would like to work in a hospital, perhaps as an orderly where he can give personal attention to people. He isn't interested in a big car, lots of money, or a nice house. Instead, he says, "helping people, smiling—that's what's really important when it comes right down to it."

SUMMARY

Several common threads emerge from Nina, Michael, Savannah, and Markel's stories. First, each adolescent is extremely articulate in his or her own way, and each has a lot to say about his or her experiences in the mental health system. They are not shy about saying what they like and don't like about the way they have been treated in the system. Second, like all teenagers, they want people to listen to them—*really* listen. Third, they do not like "the revolving door" of therapists. Far too many therapists seem to come into and go out of children's lives at will—just when they need constancy, stability, and secure relationships. Often this isn't the fault of the therapists but rather reflects the systemic issue of low salaries and high turnover rates in public sector services. Nevertheless, according to these four adolescents, it is an issue that has a direct and negative impact on them.

Fourth, they want to be treated as "real people." They dislike therapists who talk past them to others in the room or who seem not really interested in them personally. For Nina, Michael, Savannah, and Markel, the best therapists are ones who treat them as individuals and for whom serving children and adolescents is much more than a job. Finally, Nina's claim that she is "pretty normal" rings true for all four, especially in their hopes and dreams for the future. Essentially, their goals are to settle down and have the kind of life that every normal person wants. In this they are no different from anyone else.

Pennsylvania's public mental health system is patterned after a federal National Institute of Mental Health initiative in the 1980s called the Child and Adolescent Service System Program (CASSP). As CASSP developed in Pennsylvania, the state formalized a set of principles for mental health services for children and adolescents with, or at risk for developing, severe emotional disturbance and their families. Treatment and services provided according to Pennsylvania's CASSP principles are (a) child-centered, (b) family-focused, (c) community-based, (d) multisystem, (e) culturally competent, and (f) least restrictive and least intrusive.

When I listen to Nina, Michael, Savannah, and Markel—just four of many adolescents with serious emotional disturbance—I hear their desire for these principles to be practiced on their behalf. Their message is consistent with a model of service delivery that does not pathologize children and adolescents and their families, but rather recognizes the individual strengths and needs of each child, works with the family in a genuine partnership, and treats each person with respect and dignity.

REFERENCE

Palan, P. (1998, June). One family's story of the effect of mental illness on the family. *PA CASSP Newsletter, 7*(2), 7–8.

Chapter 3

COLLEGE STUDENTS' NARRATIVES OF HIGH SCHOOL EXPERIENCES: COPING WITH SERIOUS EMOTIONAL DISTURBANCE

CAROL T. MOWBRAY, DEBORAH MEGIVERN, AND SHARI STRAUSS

Adolescents with serious emotional disturbance are rarely asked to tell others about their experiences in coping with teenage issues and a psychological disorder at the same time. This chapter offers readers the opportunity to listen to the voices of youths sharing their thoughts, opinions, and feelings about living with mental illness. The individuals who contributed to this chapter are currently attending college or are recent graduates, so their narratives are told retrospectively, as they contemplated their adolescent years.

Research has demonstrated that the transition to college from high school is especially challenging for adolescents with serious emotional disturbance. In contrast to students with other types of disabilities, students with emotional disturbances have the lowest high school completion rates (45%). A 1999 report by the U.S. Department of Education stated that high school students with emotional disturbances failed more courses, earned lower grade point averages, and missed more days of school than adolescents with any other disability. In a longitudinal study of youth with disabilities, Blackorby and Wagner (1996) found that between 3 and 5 years after high school completion, approximately 25% of those with serious emotional disturbance were enrolled in postsecondary school. Only students with mental retardation or multiple disabilities had lower postsecondary school attendance rates. In comparison, youths without a disability had postsecondary school enrollment rates of approximately 68%.

Despite the dismal outcomes for educational completion as documented here, other studies suggest that adolescents who experience mental illness can achieve success in higher educational environments. For example, Offer and Spiro (1987) found that approximately 10% of students entering college were experiencing emotional/behavioral problems that began in adolescence. Conclusions about what contributes to educational outcomes for these students, however, are difficult—there are just too few studies available with relevant information. Furthermore, the available studies use limited sources and perspectives. That is, in preparation for writing this chapter, we conducted a literature review using several standard psychological databases to locate articles written from the perspectives of adolescents or young adults with mental illness. No articles of this nature were located. We hope this chapter will provide an illuminating, alternative perspective on the high school experiences of students with mental illness, in retrospect, based on self-reported experiences of students now enrolled in college.

METHOD

Samples and Procedures

Focus group participants were recruited via e-mail invitation and word of mouth, asking for current or recently graduated college students who had experienced serious psychological problems starting in high school. A call for participants was sent out over e-mail lists for Mentality, a student organization that provides mental health education and awareness programming on college campuses. Mentality members from two Midwest universities passed the message on to appropriate groups and individuals in their communities. Interested students then contacted the third author, who arranged a date and location to hold the 90-minute focus group. There were 8 participants in the focus group—all women and all Caucasian. Participants were compensated $10 for their time.

Interviewed participants. Through the introductory subject pool at a large public university, students with mental illnesses were recruited for an in-depth study of college experiences of students coping with mental health problems. Selection was based on responses to a questionnaire administered at the beginning of their psychology class in which these students had responded affirmatively to at least one of the following: (1) having a history of significant psychological problems, (2) receiving psychological treatment during the past year, or (3) taking prescribed psychotropic medications during the past year. Of the 297 participants, 34 indicated they had high school experiences with mental illness. This subsample included 21 women (61.8%) and 13 men (38.2%), whose mean age at the time of the interview was 19.3 years ($SD = 1.13$ years), ranging from 18 to 21 years old. Students' racial/ethnic backgrounds were as follows: White ($n = 24$, 70.6%), African American (5, 14.7%), Latino (2, 5.9%), and Asian (3, 8.8%).

Primary psychiatric diagnoses were obtained through respondents' self-reports and included major depression ($n = 22$, 64.7%), bipolar disorder (7, 20.6%), anxiety disorder such as obsessive-compulsive disorder or panic disorder (4, 11.8%), and schizophrenia (1, 2.9%). The mean age of onset of psychiatric disorders was 12.3 years ($SD = 3.8$ years); thus, the majority of the respondents had been experiencing their psychiatric symptoms for more than 5 years.

All of these research respondents were interviewed using a semistructured interview guide. Each interview lasted from 1 to 2 hours and was audiotaped. Participants were compensated with partial credit toward the completion of requirements for the introductory psychology course.

THEMES

Themes were identified separately by each author. Following discussion, a consensus was reached on the five themes that characterized the majority of responses from the focus group participants and the interview sample. The themes are as follows:

1. The mentally ill are not us.
2. Friends can sometimes be helpful.
3. If mental illness doesn't exist, why would you need help for it?
4. Parental relationships: what helps, what hurts.
5. Good help is hard to seek and may be hard to find.
6. Advice to high school students experiencing mental illness.

Examples of these themes, as provided by focus group members and interviewed participants, follow.

1. *The mentally ill are not us.* In the focus group, participants were asked about attitudes toward mental illness in their high schools. They responded that *mental illness* was actually a little-used term. The concept of mental illness implied "crazy and psycho and people that don't have control of their minds." As one participant explained, "There's crazy homeless people and psycho girl who tried to kill herself and whatever, but there wasn't like 'the mentally ill.' Students might be overwhelmed and stressed out, but nobody would ever label themselves as having a mental illness." One woman said that even when she was diagnosed with depression, she didn't think of it as having a mental illness. Even a friend who was anxious and taking Xanax was not mentally ill. People were "in therapy" or people had "problems," but being mentally ill was like being "the other." "[There was] this huge dichotomy between being normal and being mentally ill. And it was a huge difference, a huge difference. And that idea just wasn't challenged and was only reinforced."

In high school, the students who did admit to having a mental illness were considered "weird" or "pitiful." For the most part, this was because they were seen as being too open about their symptoms, talking about their therapy or about how they cut themselves at lunch—or in other contexts where it just did not fit in. These students were seen as being overly dramatic and trying to get attention ("an ugly label"). One interviewee recalled that a sophomore in her high school had committed suicide, and the response of other students was, "That was so selfish of him, how could he do that?" In retrospect, participants recognized that these students really did need help: "I think they were honestly trying to get somebody to see how much pain they were in. I don't think they were, you know, in any way trying to be cool. . . . I think they were suffering." One of our focus group participants acknowledged that this description fit her. Most, however, said they were, "just hurting on the inside and feeling like they couldn't keep up with all of their work, or stressed out that they kept having to be perfect."

We asked the focus group members why there was this difference. Why did some students emphasize their symptoms, whereas others desperately tried to hide them? There were several explanations:

If you're in a lower social caste, you have less to lose if you just, you know, talk openly about things, inappropriately.

It was just plain desperation. Like they weren't getting *any* attention from *anyone.*

They weren't getting attention at home, they weren't getting attention from teachers . . . I know I got to some points, where, I mean, I felt like it didn't matter what I did, I felt like I was invisible. I felt like I could say anything, I could do anything, I could leave my arms bare with burn marks on them, and *nobody* said *anything.* Like, it didn't matter. . . . It was trying to get attention, and I just *wasn't* getting any.

Two people didn't have a very supportive home life, so this was the one place where they were, you know, crying out for help. . . . But they already had grouped themselves into like an outsider, a little stranger, less mainstream kind of a role in school, so this was more something that was expected of them.

Teachers who talked about their own problems reportedly got the same responses. One high school teacher had shared her past alcohol addiction, but "she just kind of made a joke out of it. . . . We didn't really discuss [it]." Another participant recalled having a teacher who was very depressed and had a breakdown in class. The response:

I don't remember sympathy. It was kind of like weird and then not talked about. The only thing that I remember other teachers saying was just, someone made a kind of remark about how she was pretty weak and whiny and pitiful.

One participant summed the attitudes up this way: "Private should be kept private. . . . You don't bring your problems into school, you just don't." Another said,

Like when something happened with a student, it was like all the teachers would whisper about it and there was nothing acknowledged ever in class. . . . It was like, maybe it will go away if we push it to the corner far enough, and so it kept it isolated, kept it in the closet.

An underlying fiction that seemed to contribute to not acknowledging serious mental health problems in school was the compelling drive to be "up." From the focus group:

You know you're supposed to be happy in this little world that is so privileged.

Because, like, if you weren't "up," if you didn't fit, then it's just, you didn't feel like you had a place. . . . And I knew I didn't feel right and that something wasn't right, but it didn't seem serious enough to warrant getting help.

Interviewed participants expressed similar sentiments: "I have learned to put on a good act," and "It was hard to deal with feeling very alone, and still have to function and behave, and not let anybody know. I didn't want anybody to know, so I had to pretend to be happy-go-lucky."

Thus, mental illness recognition in high school was minimal. Students who were seen by others or self-labeled as "mentally ill" were viewed as different, weird, and definitely "the other." This behavior was also true of students who themselves were experiencing symptoms of mental illness that had not yet been diagnosed.

2. *Friends can sometimes be helpful.* As participants spoke about their peers in high school, the general consensus was that existing friends were not supportive at the onset of a mental illness. Students often found that as they changed due to their illness, they no longer fit with their social cliques:

> All of the people I'd hung out with before were "scholarly," and caring about their grades and stuff. They didn't seem to accept me. . . . I was just so different that I could just feel me drifting away from every single one of my friends.

The attitudes and comments of friends made it clear that they did not like the change. As one student recalled, "I literally heard when I left the room once, like, 'Oh my God, here we go again, talking about how she's so different.' "

Even when students' friends accepted *who* they were, they did not necessarily accept the decision to get treatment. In an interview, one student recalled, "My friends back then just told me that I need to stop seeing a therapist because I'm getting brainwashed." One interview respondent had a very different experience, in that her high school friends "were so supportive for me, and they were there for me, and it was like this really showed how much people can really care about you."

Although most of the students in the focus group did feel a lack of support and acceptance in the social circles of which they were members at the onset of their illness, they experienced a wide range of support elsewhere among peers. One participant found that "as I drifted away from them [old friends], I started going, spending more time with people who [were] for some reason outcasted." These were the students who had been grouped and labeled as "the other." Another student said she "gravitated into a group of kids where it was kind of like a running joke that something had to be wrong with you to end up here."

Another participant "grew distant from all of my friends because I couldn't handle being with all of them and fell into my first boyfriend." This situation was manageable because it was a one-on-one interaction without the pressure of having to be funny and popular and "up" all of the time. Another student who was unable to find peer support expressed jealousy toward other focus group members who "were able to find a connection." She found that due to the small size of her school and the firmly established social cliques, she had no new group to turn to, and "when I became depressed I just fell inside myself." This was also true of some interview respondents—as one expressed, "Even if I told a friend, it didn't matter, because they didn't know, and they didn't understand. . . . It facilitated the withdrawal."

Having friends who were open about similar experiences with mental illness was positive in that it provided a somewhat greater sense of understanding regarding issues that might be affecting them. One interviewed respondent commented, "My best friend when I was younger had serious issues like that and has tried to kill herself numerous times, so I think that I was always kinda very aware of when things had gone too far." Students who did find friends with experiences similar to their own reported that they provided a new support:

> We accepted it, like we *saw* it, and we tried to take care of each other. . . . It was like, you know, you could overdose and people might joke about it, but at least it would be acknowledged, and you wouldn't be estranged. . . . If anything, people would be careful of you. . . . We were definitely in many cases the *only* people that we had.

Sometimes, friends' mere presence was an inadvertent support:

> There were always people at my house. I was never alone. And while I think that caused some problems, at the same time it made it really safe for me. I didn't have to worry about committing suicide; I was never alone to do it.

However, as respondents explained, friends were not adequately equipped to solve each others' problems.

> 'Cause we were 17, I mean, we didn't know how to take care of each other, but we were definitely the only ones *trying* to take care of each other, and like I said, it's probably not good we tried to take care of each other in some ways.

> I had one friend in high school who I could talk to and that was just the most therapeutic thing that I could have ever had—as long as it doesn't become like where two people could fall into the same trap again together.

This suggests that there was a risk in having friends with similar problems if students were not getting help elsewhere. Indeed, for those individuals who found new friends, sometimes these peers created additional problems for them: For example, the student whose boyfriend was her escape from unsympathetic friends dropped her, precipitating a major psychiatric breakdown. Furthermore, peers who were sympathetic and nonjudgmental often included students with drug, alcohol, and legal problems—causing additional difficulties for students with mental illness, such as addictions and contacts with the authorities. Although such supports did not solve the students' problems, they did help them recognize that they were not alone, that they did belong someplace, and that people were going to care about them.

3. *If mental illness doesn't exist, why would you need help for it?* In the focus group, we had to repeatedly probe to get information about the role of teachers, administrators, or staff in providing support to students with mental illness. Few positive examples were identified. For the most part, teachers reflected the attitude of the schools and were not interested in students' mental health problems.

> The teachers couldn't get that close with kids. . . . They would ask how you're doing, but they really didn't want to know because they might have to deal with it and they didn't want to. They wanted to go home. Three o'clock came around and they busted out of there.

One focus group participant stated, "Most of them [the teachers] didn't have any empathy, and most of them didn't have time to have empathy." Another participant said, "Teachers were just there to teach." And another offered this advice: "I think it would be very beneficial if they [teachers] knew more about emotional issues and how much they play a factor. . . . They think you can separate it, like separate your emotional problems from your academic performance."

In the focus group session, only two individuals identified *anyone* at their school who was helpful. One participant said she had told her counselor about a serious family problem that was causing her to miss school as she tried to cope with her feelings. The counselor responded that she had experienced a similar tragedy and empathized; she took the time to care. Another student described a school social worker whom many students with problems felt comfortable talking to. Among the 34 interviewed participants, 8 mentioned school staff involvement in their mental/emotional problems, either in terms of talking to parents or providing referral information. One young woman said that her school advisor (counselor) was the first person in whom she had ever confided about her bulimia.

In general, however, most high schools did not have social workers or psychologists (even upper-middle-class ones). Only two of the students interviewed were provided mental health services within their schools (one from a school social worker and the other from a school counselor). In many high schools, counselors had several hundred students assigned to them. Thus they functioned primarily as administrators, spending their time scheduling classes or processing college applications. One participant's high school had students who served as Peer Assistance Leaders; they were supposed to be available to other students to help with problems. However, their training never touched on mental health at all: "death and grieving . . . sex and pregnancy . . . but we never ever talked about depression." Some students thought that coaches might serve a support function for students on teams, but none had any personal experiences with this.

Several stories were offered in the focus group about how schools dealt with [unofficial] requests for accommodations. One participant was aware of a student in her high school who had a formal psychiatric diagnosis of clinical depression: "It took his father coming in with a psychiatrist's note and jumping up and down in the office" to get him a time-off excuse. We asked how other students in this school felt about that, and the reply was, "Oh, everybody else thought that he was a real fuck-up, 'cause, well, he was." One interviewed student needed to ask for accommodations from some of her teachers as she tried to keep up with school and cope with depression. However, she felt bad about asking, "And they would be nice about it . . . but I almost felt like I was abusing my condition. I was using it to my advantage . . . so that made me feel guilty." Another interviewed student said,

> Fortunately, I had teachers that would give me extensions and stuff, but it was just constantly like, "You're such a disappointment, I can't believe you're doing this—what's happening?" I think a lot of teachers, once they knew, just lost all expectations for me. Kinda like, she won't amount to anything or whatever.

One of the focus group participants talked about her experience in trying to drop a class 3 days after the deadline because her depression was becoming severe: "It was so awful because I was really slipping, and this was just too much . . . and they wouldn't hear it. The assistant principal, the principal, they couldn't have been more unhelpful about the whole thing. Or less understanding." The matter was resolved only when the student's parents intervened angrily; the school granted the request only after a doctor's note was supplied. Unfortunately, this was not the end of the problem:

> But, by then, I was a marked woman in that school. Nobody, like none of the teachers, treated me the same . . . because I was a troublemaker. And all because I was getting so depressed, and that was a problem. I had done so much for them. I had, you know, been a model student. I had worked so hard. And the one time I needed a break, they didn't give it to me. And how many students out there are gonna have my mother to come in and fight for them?

Another student was hospitalized for psychiatric problems. When she went back to high school, one of her teachers would not let her return to the classroom because he said she was too disruptive—but he provided no examples of problem behaviors.

Given these examples, it is understandable why most students did not turn to the high school for help: "The school was so unsafe that I can't imagine opening up to anyone at all." With the high school not wanting to help and friends not capable of helping, students often had to rely on their families.

4. *Parental relationships: what helps, what hurts.* Parents played significant roles for most participants and interviewees; however, the relationships described were both beneficial and detrimental. Focus group participants were asked to consider the sources of help and support they received, including family. While some familial problems were mentioned, these students largely felt that "really, really the most helpful things were my parents." Parents assisted these respondents as advocates in school settings where school officials were not always responsive. As one student said, "My mother was my savior. I mean, getting me out of class and fighting for me when I couldn't fight for myself."

Parents were mentioned by some interviewed students as among the first in their lives to notice the need for outside intervention:

> My parents would occasionally be banging down my door, like, "Open up!" and my mom had asked what they were going to do with me. Like, I'd sit in my room for hours on end. So I guess I was nonfunctioning. I'd just lie in bed and do nothing.

Although parents may have noticed problems, they also faced challenges trying to help. According to one interviewed student, "They noticed something wasn't quite right, but they didn't see a whole lot of me, either. I made myself really scarce." This respondent went on to say, "They asked me once, 'Are you thinking about killing yourself?' 'No.' That was luckily a time when I wasn't thinking about it."

Parental attitudes toward seeking help and mental health treatment settings varied. Some advocated treatment, even when their children were reluctant to participate. Others actively prevented help seeking by their children. Relevant to the former, parents were often mentioned by both focus group members and interviewed participants as treatment initiators. The pathway to professional help, according to one focus group member, was her mother: "She took me to the first psychiatrist I ever went to and she supported me when I said I don't like this psychiatrist, and she helped me find another one." Another interviewed student echoed this theme: "She [his mother] took me. Well, she asked me. By that time, I was a little older, and she asked me if I would feel uncomfortable if she took me to a psychiatrist, and I told her I was fine with it."

Parents' unfavorable views about mental health services also significantly affected many students. Several interviewed respondents indicated their parents were opposed to professional services. One said,

> I was seeing them [school-based mental health services] for a while, like maybe four or five months . . . just like randomly and I would go down there when I was feeling bad or having problems. But they really wanted to see me regularly in there and so I did, and that went on until my mother found out I was doing it and forbade me to do it anymore, so I stopped.

Her mother had, in fact, attributed the participant's suicide attempts to mental health treatment: "She [mother] said, 'Oh, like the problem is you're seeing counselors. . . . They put these ideas in your head.' "

Another student indicated that his family felt stigmatized by his getting mental health services:

> My parents were so opposed to me being in the hospital. They were so opposed to my therapy in the first place with my psychologist. They were always reminding me how much it costs and saying that they were taking it out of my college fund. "This is what you're doing. You're doing it to yourself." They wanted me out of the hospital as soon as possible. They hated the fact that I had to go to someone else. . . . They were ashamed that I had to miss school and that people had to know that I was in the psych ward.

Many of the respondents in the focus group and among those interviewed spoke both positively and negatively about mental illness in their families. For some, having a parent with a mental illness meant that their own emotional problems were "not so foreign." One focus group member shared with her mother, "Well, every time I was depressed, we always talked, me and my mom. We understood each other." Other focus group members felt less support from parents with mental illnesses, "Mine were not that helpful. Partly because they were dealing with their own shit, but partly because it was a way of life in my family." One respondent went further to say that her mother's bipolar illness led her to "never feel[ing] exactly safe around her."

As might be expected, families sometimes had turbulent relationships, including poor communication, not getting along, and even abuse. One interviewed participant said family relationships were strong at present, but around the time of the onset of his schizophrenia they were less so:

> I know I was a really hard person to deal with, but, uh, it just seems like they could have tried a little hard to just be nice and open up a little more. . . . It just didn't seem that they had the patience that I would hope for my parents to have with me.

Another interviewed participant initially thought her bipolar illness was solely a reaction to abuse: "My last year in high school, my mom finally took me to a therapist who was completely ineffectual. My dad was really abusive and I thought at the time that that must be the main problem."

Students acknowledged that some of their own behavior toward their parents was abusive; for example, "I just went crazy on my mom one night. I said so many mean things to her." Each student felt remorse in the present. One interviewed respondent said about her mother:

> Oh, Lord . . . I feel horrible for what I've done to her. She was supportive. She was in so much pain. I cannot believe what I've done to her, but she stuck with me. . . . I know she almost gave up on me, and then she didn't. I'm glad she didn't.

The reactions of family members to mental illness in the lives of their children were complex, ranging from advocacy and support to denial of symptoms and misunderstanding. Interestingly, those respondents who mentioned having a parent with a mental illness sometimes saw this reality as an asset. Nonetheless, many of the focus group participants and interviewees had dealt with strained relationships and even abuse. Although these problems may not have caused the mental illness they experienced, many of the young people felt that such relations were a contributing factor in their declining mental health.

5. *Good help is hard to seek and may be hard to find.* Focus group participants and interviewed respondents were asked to discuss their experiences with care providers (therapists, inpatient mental health workers, psychiatrists, etc.). Two focus group members and 12 interviewed participants said they had not received services until their late teens, after they left home to attend college. This may be partially attributed to lack of recognition of the severity of their symptoms, lack of societal norms about when to seek outside help for mental health problems, or stigma associated with recognition of one's mental illness, which may lead to beliefs such as, "I'm not sick enough to need help." One interviewed respondent stated,

> It's not like I had never heard of depression. . . . In theory, I knew what it was. I didn't know what was going on with me. I didn't term it *depression* or anything like that. I had no idea what was going on until afterward.

Another interviewed respondent described her resistance to accepting mental health services:

> Part of me doesn't want to admit to myself that I have depression. I believe what my mom says, "Oh, it's just a phase." Part of me is just like, I shouldn't use these services, because I don't really have depression. But then part of me is like, I was diagnosed. I did take medication.

For those who received services, there were mixed reactions. Five students who were hospitalized in a psychiatric ward felt the experience was "helpful," but one participant felt it was "traumatic." On the positive side, a focus group member described her experience with inpatient treatment: "I was in the hospital a couple of times, and every time, I felt like they cared. . . . It was like a safe haven. . . . I felt comforted and secure and like people really did care."

The interviewed student who felt that hospitalization was traumatic attributed this in part to the other patients' behavior:

> Nothing happened in the hospital. They put me on this drug, knocked me out for 8 hours, I sat in my room. . . . The other people there were just crazy. They would jump around, and like, hit people and just throw things. I was scared to be there, actually.

Receiving mental health treatment for the first time often means encountering many unknowns. One focus group member described her awkward entry into the mental health system:

> I didn't understand that you're supposed to have a psychiatrist and a therapist . . . that, like, your psychiatrist usually isn't a very good therapist, 'cause I'd go in there and I'd tell my psychiatrist about my problems and he'd be like, 'How's the medication working?' and I'm thinking, 'But what about my problems? You know, I didn't know they were just pretty much dispensing pills and making sure your levels were correct and everything.

Two individuals began treatment by seeing their family doctor for help. However, one respondent expressed concern about this:

> I went to my family doctor and she put me on Paxil. And I don't think that a family doctor is able to be a psychiatrist. And they shouldn't be. They don't have the knowledge, they don't have the time. You know, I think it was a mistake. . . . I needed the medication, but the follow-up and the regulation of it was not there.

Focus group members and interviewed respondents were asked about their experiences with psychotherapy, which yielded a wide variety of opinions from the 22 individuals who had therapy during their adolescence. One interviewed respondent said she was "not invested and didn't use it properly" because of her age and maturity level. Another felt that his symptoms, including paranoia, interfered with his ability to benefit from therapy:

> Definitely, my mental illness played a big role in me being scared of him, because I was thinking things. . . . I was almost scared to see my therapist back then because it felt like something strange was going on. . . . He just would not talk to me like a normal person. [He'd] talk to me like somebody trying to play with my head. . . . I'd say it was more scary than helpful. It's not scary anymore.

Other students reported that therapy was helpful and effective for improving their coping skills. One interviewed participant described the benefits he felt from therapy:

> Going through therapy my senior year was just breaking down a lot of those notions I had in my head. I don't know what to do. . . . There are many things I can do to help myself, and I just need to constantly review what I am doing to see what changes would make the situation better. But if it gets really out of my hands . . . or if I was really unable to do anything about what is going on, that's when I would turn to [mental health] services.

Psychotropic medications were important for many of the participants, although opinions varied widely among the 12 individuals who used medications during their adolescence. One interviewed respondent indicated that therapy was important, but only as a supplement to medications:

> What really helps me through is being on medication. My self-esteem is really high, and I have confidence in my abilities. I still cycle and do weird things, so the therapy helped me in terms of making me a better person, but less effectively in targeting the cyclothymia.

Although the importance of medication was stressed by some, ambivalence was apparent in others; for example, one focus group member stated, "With pills . . . like, do I feel good now? I'm not exactly sure. What am I supposed to feel like?" Taking psychotropic medication sometimes affected the self-concept of students, as one interviewee recalled:

> I was always anti-Prozac from the beginning, so I was so anxious to get off of it. It was just like a mental blockage, it was like I'm different from everybody else, and I'm, like, some depressed freak, and I need to take medication. I mean, I know it's just a mental thing, but I'd rather not think that I'm on medication because I'm depressed.

Young people received mixed messages from family and friends regarding medication usage. One respondent who experienced his onset of schizophrenia at age 16 describes his medication as "helpful," but at the same time has mixed feelings about using it. He went on to say that his parents and his doctor "made me take them," and that he wanted to "get off of them someday." This same respondent felt pressure from his friends *not* to take his medications, "My friends didn't really think I needed to be on medication, and at that time I didn't either."

A few focus group members and interviewed respondents felt that their questions about medications were not answered and their concerns were not addressed. One interviewed student felt no one would listen to him regarding the side effects of his medication:

> The medication had the weirdest side effects, and nobody believed I was having these side effects, which was making me mad. I think my mother thought I was suicidal. When they let me out of the hospital, she wouldn't let me out of her sight. She made sure I took that medication. But when she wasn't looking, it was flushed down the toilet, 'cause I couldn't get up in the morning.

Another respondent was dissatisfied with the way in which his psychiatrist educated him about medications:

> No one was dealing with my medications. . . . Then I started getting sick on Tofranil even though it was the minimum dosage. I was having side effects and I just ignored them because I was used to getting sick. I ignored them all summer. At the beginning of the year, I saw the man again, and he told me to stop the medication. "Stop it. You should have stopped it a long time ago. You should have told me." But he hadn't warned me about any of the side effects or anything.

Professional interventions for mental health were sought by two thirds of the young people who participated in the focus group and interviews. A sizable number of these students had not accessed services due to their own uncertainty about the "level of pain necessary to justify outside help." Stigma as a consequence of using professional services was mentioned by both those who sought services and those who did not. When these young people did seek services, the path to effective treatment was sometimes arduous. Lack of experience with service systems led to some confusion until service users were able to become savvy consumers, often through a process of trial and error. The majority of the participants did believe that services were beneficial and effective over the long term.

6. *Advice.* At the conclusion of the focus group, we asked participants whether, looking back on their experiences, they could offer any advice to current high school students. They commented that high school students who are experiencing symptoms of mental illness for the first time often feel as though they are alone in their struggles. All agreed that students should know, "Definitely that you aren't alone."

Another message was that suicide was not the way out. One student wisely remarked, "I would just tell them that suicide is a question but not an answer." Participants would remind students that in high school,

> You feel like there is only one way of living. . . . You're stuck in these social cliques, and this is how people see you. And you just can't imagine that there are so many other ways of living. . . . If you don't like that way and you feel stuck and it's causing you pain, that doesn't always have to be that way.

Participants agreed that students should "Get help . . . *talk* to *somebody* about it." They felt that it was very important to be open about problems because people cannot help you if they are not aware of how you are feeling. They also said that even though it was important to talk to friends, "They can't cure you." If problems become extreme, "I would tell them definitely seek some counseling."

At the beginning of the focus group, one participant said that "not being 'up' didn't seem like it was serious enough to warrant getting help." Coming back to this idea, another participant advised, "There's no sick-o-meter, you know. If you're in enough pain so that, well, you're in pain, then you're in enough pain to talk about it." They felt that it was important for students to realize that they do not have to have a crisis in order to seek help. Furthermore, "Nobody is as perfectly happy as you think . . . they're just not talking about it either."

High school students are making the transition from childhood to adulthood. Many times they want to prove that they are grown up by handling everything by themselves. However, "if you're trying to be like an independent, adult, healthy person, the way to be in control is to deal with it." Part of dealing with problems and taking control is to

> find a therapist and/or a psychiatrist if they need one and begin the process of getting help. . . . You might even be lucky that you're dealing with this when you are so that you don't develop [an] even more rampant disorder that diminishes your quality of life in your 20s or your 30s. . . . You can do the work now that will help you overcome what you're feeling and set you up for an even more happy and joyful life.

One participant wanted to make a general comment to everyone:

Our society does not deal with pain. We shove it as far away as possible. Feelings in general are scary things. I think we see that a lot with our parents' generation and just in this world. There's no time to deal with how you're feeling. And it really saddens me that problems progress and get out of control like they do because they aren't acknowledged.

Students in the focus group concluded that we should all take the time to recognize that "doing something positive is the way to take control of your life." If we deal with our grief and pain, maybe "they won't come back to haunt you in other ways."

DISCUSSION AND CONCLUSIONS

Respondents in the focus group and in the interview sample expressed many similar attitudes. One overriding conclusion is that attitudes toward mental illness and seeking help are extremely biased in high school settings—perhaps more so, in fact, than those reported in a recent national survey, which asked a large sample of Americans, "Have you ever felt that you were going to have a nervous breakdown?" and if so, "What did you do about it?" In answering the survey, 42% of respondents indicated they would seek out formal services (Swindle, Heller, Pescosolido, & Kikuzawa, 2000). Compared to the reports from our participants about seeking treatment for mental illness in high school, 42% is a large proportion.

Unfortunately, for comparison with our data, there is little quantitative information available about attitudes toward mental illness in high schools. For anecdotal information, a recent special issue of *The Journal of NAMI California* presented high school experiences of students and their parents describing how serious mental health problems were ignored (Martin, 2000) or attributed to personality flaws (Hawkins & Hawkins, 2000). Students with mental and emotional problems were disturbing to classroom teachers and were more likely to be expelled than considered for special education services (Forness & Kavale, 2000). One teacher wrote that her own daughter's death by suicide in high school eventually caused questions from her fifth-grade class. After she answered their questions, this mother-teacher was told she would be dismissed if she ever mentioned her daughter's death again. This school made no effort following the suicide to improve education and awareness regarding mental illness for students, teachers, or staff (Beal, 2000). Given such a climate of denial, it is little wonder that the response to cases of high school students who commit suicide is frequently, "We had no idea." Perhaps high school staff do not want to have any idea.

The respondents in our study consistently reported that their families definitely played a critical role in their mental health outcomes. Some students reported that their parents provided strong support and effective interventions; others said that their families contributed significantly to mental/emotional problems and prevented access to treatment. In either case, it was clear that families (parents and students) were not well informed about mental health problems. Families frequently had no information regarding the nature of mental illness, that having a mental illness is not a matter of shame, when you should seek help for a mental health problem, where you can get help, or what kinds of professionals provide various kinds of help. These results are congruent with literature that indicates many adults are not knowledgeable concerning effective mental health treatments (Jorm, 2000). Education and awareness about mental health problems are important for several reasons—not just related to accessing formal services. That is, our students indicated that they often went to friends for help—and many times got none or the wrong kind. As one respondent indicated, 17-year-olds are not really capable of helping each other. Clearly, more education is needed about the etiology of and treatment for mental health problems.

In terms of formal systems of care, it would seem that doctors might be able to help, because oftentimes families go to a doctor when a mental health problem arises. However, primary care providers lack information and resources necessary to provide mental health services or appropriate referrals. Furthermore, these providers, who spend an average of 13 minutes per visit, rarely have the time to conduct an adequate evaluation of their patients' mental health (LDI, 2000).

Schools, then, are left as the institutional structure that could provide identification and referrals. However, obviously they are not doing this. From incidents in the literature and the reports of our participants, high schools, unlike postsecondary institutions, seem unaware of the rights of students with psychiatric disabilities, probably because the special education process focuses primarily on students with developmental disabilities (DD), and this approach is not likely to work well for students with emergent mental illness, especially in the later years of high school. High schools also seem to have little in the way of resources for early identification and intervention, such as school social workers or psychologists. The available resources are devoted to students with DD in the special education system.

A recent *Report of the Surgeon General's Conference on Children's Mental Health* indicates that many families turn to schools for the mental health problems of their children and adolescents, but schools don't have the infrastructure to appropriately handle these problems. This is as true now as it was 20 to 30 years ago (U.S. Public Health Service, 2000). Other researchers have concluded that neither teachers nor administrators are trained in how to handle mental health issues of students (Doll, 1996). In contrast to the current situation, schools need to be emotionally healthy environments where every teacher and administrator takes ownership of students' mental health in addition to academic performance. But how do we make this happen? How do we fix a broken system? The changes needed appear to be so massive that they warrant a conjoint effort from professionals, family members, advocates, and students themselves. Some attention is being paid to the important roles that adolescents can play in planning their own services, perhaps actively participating in their own Individual Education Plan or wraparound planning team ("Roles for Youth," 2000). This handbook should provide methods and models for improvement so that in the future, school mental health will not be characterized by the dictum, "The private should be kept private."

REFERENCES

Beal, K. C. (2000). The place where Arlyn died. *The Journal of NAMI California, 11*(1), 4–7.
Blackorby, J., & Wagner, M. (1996). Longitudinal postschool outcomes of youth with disabilities: Findings from the National Transition Study. *Exceptional Children, 62*(5), 399–413.

Doll, B. (1996). Prevalence of psychiatric disorders in children and youth: An agenda for advocacy by school psychology. *School Psychology Quarterly, 11*(1), 20–47.

Forness, S. R., & Kavale, K. A. (2000). Inclusive practices and school discipline: Implications for children with mental illness. *The Journal of NAMI California, 11*(1), 66–68.

Hawkins, P., & Hawkins, R. (2000). A mother and daughter share their experiences. *The Journal of NAMI California, 11*(1), 11–13.

Jorm, A. F. (2000). Mental health literacy: Public knowledge and beliefs about mental disorders. *British Journal of Psychiatry, 177,* 396–401.

Leonard David Institute (LDI) of Health Economics. (2000, April). Children's mental health: Recommendations for research, practice and policy. *LDI Issue Brief, 5*(7), 1–4.

Offer, D., & Spiro, R. (1987). The disturbed adolescent goes to college. *Journal of American College Health, 35*(1), 209–214.

Martin, J. (2000). Caught between a rock and a hard place: How the school failed me. *The Journal of NAMI California, 11*(1), 8–10.

Roles for youth in systems of care. (2000, Fall). *Focal Point, 14*(2). Portland, OR: Portland State University, Regional Research Institute for Human Services.

Swindle, R., Heller, K., Pescosolido, B., & Kikuzawa, S. (2000). Responses to nervous breakdowns in America over a 40-year period. *American Psychologist, 55*(7), 740–749.

U.S. Department of Education. (1999). *Students with disabilities in postsecondary education: A profile of preparation, participation, and outcomes.*

U.S. Public Health Service. (2000). *Report of the Surgeon General's Conference on Children's Mental Health: A National Action Agenda.* Washington, DC: Government Printing Office.

SECTION II

Practice, Research, and Training Issues

Chapter 4 ───────────────────────────────

CLINICAL AND RESEARCH DIRECTIONS FOR THE TREATMENT AND DELIVERY OF CHILDREN'S MENTAL HEALTH SERVICES

HEATHER RINGEISEN AND KIMBERLY HOAGWOOD

This is a time of hopeful anticipation in children's mental health. The past several years have seen dramatic increases in our understanding of successful strategies for the identification and diagnosis of emotional and behavioral disorders in children, as well as in strategies for their treatment and service provision. Twenty years ago, treatments for children diagnosed with serious emotional disturbance (SED) consisted of services offered primarily in inpatient hospitals, residential centers, or outpatient centers; most of these treatment settings included limited family involvement. Since then, numerous alternative service delivery approaches have been developed for implementation in home, school, or health settings, and there has been a noted conceptual shift toward models of family inclusion in treatment.

In addition, recent reviews have identified a variety of efficacious treatments, including psychopharmacologic (Vitiello, Bhatara, & Jensen, 1999; Weisz & Jensen, 1999); psychosocial (Rogers, 1998; Weisz & Jensen, 1999); integrated community and prevention services (Burns, Hoagwood, & Mrazek, 1999); and school-based approaches (Rones & Hoagwood, 2000). We have learned that current treatments can successfully reduce symptoms of child psychopathology, improve adaptive functioning, and sometimes serve as a buffer to further long-term impairment. This is not to imply that the current knowledge base is complete or even sufficient. Information regarding children continues to lag behind the empirical evidence about adult mental illness and treatment. Nevertheless, important groundwork for further research in child mental health has been laid. And, even as new research findings emerge, the current knowledge has important implications for the ongoing provision of quality care. This chapter briefly examines some

───────────────

Note: The opinions and assertions contained in this chapter are the private views of the authors and are not to be construed as official or as reflecting the views of the Department of Health and Human Services or the National Institute of Mental Health.

clinical implications of what we have learned so far about children's mental health services and offers suggestions for future research directions.

The need for access to quality child mental health services is tremendous. It is estimated that 9% to 13% of children in the United States within any given year experience some form of a clinically significant mental disorder to a degree that warrants treatment (Friedman, Katz-Leavy, Manderscheid, & Sondheimer, 1996). A recent epidemiological study found that across 1 year, only one quarter of children with diagnosable mental disorders and significant functional impairment received any mental health services (Leaf et al., 1996). Given the pervasive nature of childhood mental disorders and the substantial number of children who do not access the mental health service delivery system, future research and clinical practice must take into consideration not only how to provide quality services, but also how to overcome barriers to treatment and to increase family engagement in the service delivery process.

A SUMMARY OF THE RESEARCH BASE

Engagement and Treatment Acceptability

Psychosocial and pharmacological treatments can be successful only if they reach those families in need. Unfortunately, research indicates that mental health services are often not accessed. Moreover, several years may pass between the time parents identify their child as having a problem and when they seek or receive services (Lardieri, Greenbaum, & Pugh, 1996). Dropping out of services is also relatively common among families of children with mental health problems. Of those children whose families seek outpatient mental health treatment, up to 40% to 60% may drop out of services prior to their formal completion (Kazdin, Holland, & Crowley, 1997). Moreover, these families typically do not use outpatient services for very long. Armbruster and Fallon (1994) indicate that the majority of children who enter outpatient treatment attend for only one or two sessions. Increasing evidence indicates that those children who are from especially vulnerable populations (e.g., children of single mothers, children living in poverty, minority children) and those with the most serious presenting problems are less likely to stay in treatment past the first session and more likely to discontinue services prematurely (Kazdin, 1993; Tuma, 1989).

Although many families do not receive care or choose to drop out of ongoing services, research indicates that efforts to enhance a family's service engagement can be successful. Two studies conducted by Szapocznik and colleagues have demonstrated decreased rates of premature treatment termination (Santisteban et al., 1996; Szapocznik et al., 1988). These researchers compared a typical family engagement strategy (a supportive and empathetic phone call to schedule a first appointment) to an enhanced strategy. In the enhanced engagement strategy, a therapist identified a caller's concerns about entering therapy and the concerns of other family members. If necessary, prior to the first appointment, the therapist made extra phone calls to respond to the concerns and helped the caller think about the therapy process in a way that would be more acceptable to all family members. Only 11% of the families in the enhanced engagement group failed to show up for their first appointment, and only 17% dropped out of treatment prematurely, compared to 57.7% and 41%, respectively, for the control group (Szapocznik et al., 1988). A similar telephone engagement intervention has been used among inner-city, primarily minority, families to increase attendance for initial mental health service appointments (McKay, McCadam, & Gonzales, 1996). Supplementing a telephone engagement strategy with an engagement-focused first interview (which included a discussion of the treatment process, professional roles, barriers to treatment, and mechanisms to overcome them) resulted in 25% more families continuing to keep scheduled intervention appointments compared to those who received the telephone intervention alone, and 16% more than those in the control group (McKay, Stoewe, McCadam, & Gonzales, 1998). These preliminary efforts to increase engagement are particularly noteworthy given the research that supports the importance of involving child caretakers in mental health treatment. For instance, family participation during and following day treatment hospitalizations (Kutash & Rivera, 1996) and inpatient hospitalizations (Pfeifer & Strzelecki, 1990) has been shown to be essential in obtaining and maintaining positive outcomes. Consequently, continued efforts to increase mental health service engagement and entry are necessary.

Access and consistent participation in mental health services are important for the families of children with emotional or behavioral problems; however, participating in any mental health service alone does not necessarily produce positive outcomes. Research suggests that the key to positive service outcomes for children may be access and engagement in *quality* mental health services (e.g., Weisz, Donenberg, Han, & Weiss, 1995). For the purposes of this chapter, we define *high-quality services* as those mental health interventions that have some empirical evidence to support their impact. The following sections will briefly describe examples of evidence-based treatments for use in outpatient, community, and school settings. These brief descriptions are meant to give clinicians an idea of the wide array of treatment approaches available to them that are supported by clinical research.

Empirically Supported Psychosocial Treatments

Summaries of experimental child psychotherapy intervention trials point to a consistent beneficial effect of treatment over no treatment (Casey & Berman, 1985; Kazdin, Bass, Ayers, & Rodgers, 1990; Weisz, Weiss, Alicke & Klotz, 1987; Weisz, Weiss, Han, Granger, & Morton, 1995); these effects are comparable to those found in adult psychotherapy (e.g., Smith & Glass, 1977). A similar analysis summarizing a less expansive literature on treatment effects of therapies conducted in clinical practice settings, as opposed to research settings, found almost no difference between treatment and no-treatment conditions (Weisz et al., 1995). In fact, the effect size was negative, falling well below the effects typically found in experimental studies. Consequently, the evidence suggests that psychosocial interventions for children can successfully reduce symptoms associated with childhood mental disorders when conducted in research-based settings; however, the impact of these therapies within clinical practice settings is as yet unknown.

In an effort to identify specific empirically supported psychosocial interventions for children, a special task force of the American Psychological Association (APA) modified adult treatment criteria previously set by the APA Society for Clinical Psychology (Chambless et al., 1996) for "well-established" and "probably efficacious" child treatments (Lonigan, Elbert, & Johnson, 1998). According to these criteria, treatments are to be supported by either group-design or single-subject experiments and clearly describe subject characteristics. "Well-established" treatments are required to have two or more studies that demonstrate their superiority to medication, placebo, or an alternative treatment; equivalence to an already established treatment; or nine single-subject case studies. "Well-established" treatments have been identified for attention-deficit/hyperactivity disorder, or ADHD (e.g., behavioral parent training, classroom behavior modification; see Pelham, Wheeler, & Chronis, 1998); conduct problems (e.g., parent training; see Brestan & Eyberg, 1998); and phobias (e.g., participant modeling, reinforced practice; see Ollendick & King, 1998).

"Probably efficacious" interventions are required to have two or more studies that demonstrate their superiority to wait-list control, one experiment meeting the criteria for a "well-established" treatment, or three single-case studies. "Probably efficacious" treatments have been identified for the treatment of depression (e.g., cognitive behavioral therapy; see Kaslow & Thompson, 1998) and anxiety disorders (e.g., cognitive behavioral therapy; see Ollendick & King, 1998); there are both "well-established" and "probably efficacious" treatments related to ADHD, conduct problems, and phobias. Current research on psychosocial interventions for autism, anorexia/bulimia, post-traumatic stress disorder, bipolar disorder, obsessive-compulsive disorder, panic disorder, and substance abuse has not yet met criteria for either "well-established" or "probably efficacious" treatments. Many of the aforementioned treatments will be described in more detail later in this book.

Integrated Community-Based Treatment

One criticism of empirically supported psychosocial interventions is their focus on specific disorders and their failure to address the multiple problems of children with serious emotional disturbance. Anywhere from 5% to 9% of children can be classified as "seriously emotionally disturbed" (Friedman et al., 1996). These children are most often served in several separate systems (e.g., child welfare, school, mental health, juvenile justice) and typically present for treatment with multiple diagnoses. This section will describe three evidence-based services that have been developed to intervene with just these children. These interventions have been designed as alternatives to institutional care. For the most part, they are not based within a clinician's office.

Because children with serious emotional disturbance often receive several different types of services to address their emotional and behavioral needs, case management can be an important aspect of treatment. Case management services often take the substantial burden of finding and connecting appropriate services from the primary caretakers, thus ensuring these services for children who might not otherwise have them. Many different forms of case management exist, although the two most widely researched include individual and team approaches. One individual model of case management is called *intensive case management* (ICM). In ICM, the case manager assesses individual service needs, plans and accesses appropriate treatment, coordinates mental health care, and advocates for the child and family. One study of ICM found that children with case managers had fewer psychiatric hospitalizations in the 2 years following case management services than in the previous 2 years without these services (Evans, Banks, Huz, & McNulty, 1994). Similar ICM-related reductions in inpatient hospitalizations were found for youths with substance abuse problems (Evans, Dollard, & McNulty, 1992). Among older children, the use of case managers within community-based interdisciplinary treatment teams has also been found to improve standard-practice foster care by reducing the number of placement changes and runaway episodes (Clarke, Prange, Lee, Stewart, McDonald, & Boyd, 1998). Multiple uncontrolled studies of case management services have been conducted within the context of wraparound care (for review, see Burns & Goldman, 1999). These studies indicate the potential for case management services to aid positive child adjustment, decrease negative behaviors, and increase stable community-living environments.

Children with serious or multiple comorbid mental disorders often have periodic placements in residential treatment facilities (e.g., group homes, inpatient psychiatric units). Of the potential residential placements for children with severe emotional disorders, therapeutic foster care is considered the least restrictive. In a therapeutic foster care environment, a child is placed in a home with foster parents who have received specialized training to work with children who have emotional or behavioral problems. Typically, only one child is placed in a home at a time and supervisors' caseloads are kept small. In addition to their extensive preservice training, therapeutic foster care parents receive substantial ongoing supervision and support. The primary treatment strategies used in the therapeutic foster home environment may be similar to those in residential treatment (e.g., behavior management), but they are provided individually in a family environment. These strategies are also often supplemented by more traditional mental health services (e.g., psychiatric medication monitoring, individual psychotherapy). Results from studies of therapeutic foster care demonstrate that it is an effective alternative to more restrictive types of residential placements. Treatment outcome studies indicate that children show decreases in aggressive behavior and increases in positive adjustment at the conclusion of placement (Chamberlain & Weinrott, 1990; Clarke et al., 1994). The empirical support for therapeutic foster care includes randomized controlled comparisons to usual community care (Chamberlain & Reid, 1991) and group homes (Chamberlain & Reid, 1998). Chamberlain and Reid (1991) compared treatment outcomes for youths from a state psychiatric hospital who were placed in either therapeutic foster care or usual community care. Those in therapeutic foster care demonstrated fewer reinstitutionalizations and faster behavioral improvement. Compared to group home placements, therapeutic foster home treatment also resulted in less frequent posttreatment incarcerations and criminal referrals and in more frequent parent or relative placements in the year following treatment among a group of chronic juvenile offenders (Chamberlain & Reid, 1998). In addition, this research has found therapeutic foster care to be less costly than these other residential placements.

Due to the substantial disruption of removing a child from his or her home and community for treatment or detention, several home-based service models have been developed. These models typically include comprehensive interventions that attempt to prevent an out-of-home placement. A rigorously studied home-based intervention is the multisystemic therapy (MST) model, originally designed for juvenile delinquents. It strives to identify and treat a youth's behavior problems directly in his or her family, peer, school, and neighborhood environments. The primary goal of MST is to develop independent skills among parents and youths with behavioral problems to cope with family, peer, school, and neighborhood problems through brief (3 to 4 months) and intense (sometimes daily) treatment (Schoenwald, Brown, & Henggeler, 2000). Treatment strategies integrate empirically based treatment approaches (e.g., behavioral parent training, cognitive behavior therapies, functional family therapy) to address youth problems across environmental contexts. Randomized trials of MST have demonstrated significant behavior change and reduced interactions with the juvenile justice system among its participants. A randomized comparison of MST to usual services for youth at risk of incarceration showed lower rates of recidivism and out-of-home placements 59 weeks after treatment and reduced arrest rates over 2 years posttreatment for the MST group (Henggeler, Melton, Smith, Schoenwald, & Hanley, 1993). Similar results were found when MST was compared to individual therapy for serious juvenile offenders (Borduin et al., 1995). An additional study comparing MST to emergency psychiatric hospitalization is finding that MST can safely reduce rates of psychiatric hospitalization and improve youth/family functioning (Henggeler et al., 1999; Schoenwald, Ward, Henggeler, & Rowland, 2000). The effects of MST have been further successfully demonstrated among juvenile sex offenders (Borduin, Henggeler, Blaske, & Stein, 1990) and abused or neglected children (Brunk, Henggeler, & Whelan, 1987).

Intensive case management, therapeutic foster care, and multisystemic therapy demonstrate that there are successful alternatives to lengthy inpatient treatment that help maintain a child within his or her community setting. Psychiatric hospitalizations and juvenile incarcerations are traumatic and costly for the child, family, and social care system. Given the particularly high financial expenses associated with psychiatric hospitalizations and incarcerations, findings related to the cost savings of these approaches are particularly noteworthy. As noted previously, these interventions are designed to aid children with serious emotional disturbances and consequently are characterized by small caseloads, extensive preservice training, and ongoing supervision. In fact, MST researchers now suggest that adequate supervision, therapist training, and institutional program support are key to successful MST outcomes (Schoenwald, Brown, & Henggeler, 2000).

Psychopharmacology

Research indicates that approximately 3.5 million child outpatient physician visits per year result in a psychotropic medication prescription (Jensen et al., 1999). Furthermore, prescription rates for child psychotropic medications are increasing, even in very young children (Zito et al., 2000). For many children with comorbid diagnoses and complex psychological difficulties, a combined pharmacological and psychosocial treatment approach is most commonly recommended. Consequently, it is important for child clinicians to understand the evidence base supporting psychotropic medication use with children. Weisz and Jensen (1999) recently reviewed evidence on the efficacy of child pharmacotherapy using criteria established for the International Psychopharmacology Algorithm Project (Jobson & Potter, 1995). By these criteria, a drug is considered efficacious if studied through random assignment and control group comparison and with replicated results in one or more similarly well-controlled studies. In addition, the National Institute of Mental Health (NIMH) recently commissioned six scientific reviews of published research on the safety and efficacy of psychotropic medications for children: the psychotropics (Greenhill, Halperin, & Abikoff, 1999); mood stabilizers and antimanic agents (Ryan, Bhatara, & Perel, 1999); the selective serotonin reuptake inhibitors, or SSRIs (Emslie, Walkup, Pliszka, & Ernst, 1999); tricyclic antidepressants (Geller, Reising, Leonard, Riddle, & Walsh, 1999); antipsychotic agents (Campbell, Rapoport, & Simpson, 1999); and other miscellaneous agents (Riddle et al., 1999). These reviews identified several psychotropic medications with empirical support for both childhood externalizing and internalizing disorders; some of these will be highlighted in the following paragraphs.

By far the most widely researched and commonly prescribed child psychotropic medications are the psychostimulants, which include methylphenidate (Ritalin). Over 200 studies have demonstrated the short-term efficacy of psychostimulant medication, primarily when compared to placebo, in reducing the off-task, hyperactive, impulsive, and sometimes aggressive behaviors associated with ADHD (Greenhill et al., 1999). Longer term studies of psychostimulants are less common, but continue to show efficacy and safety lasting up to 24 months. Controlled studies also support the efficacy of tricyclic antidepressants (e.g., imipramine) in treating adolescents diagnosed with ADHD (Geller et al., 1999), although their use is tempered by the availability of safer and easier to monitor medications. Many medications have been tested for conduct disorder and aggressive behavior, including antipsychotics, mood stabilizers, and anticonvulsants. Haloperidol (an antipsychotic) and carbamazepine (an anticonvulsant) have been shown to reduce aggressive behaviors in children and adolescents (Campbell et al., 1984), but multiple side effects accompanied their administration. Findings for the efficacy of lithium in reducing aggressive behavior are mixed (Campbell et al., 1984, 1995; Rifkin et al., 1997); consequently, lithium is not recommended in the primary treatment of aggression or conduct disorder. When weighing the combined results of medication effectiveness and associated side effects, the empirical evidence base for treating aggression and conduct disorder is weak.

Randomized, controlled studies have also compared the effects of psychotropic medications versus placebo in the treatment of internalizing disorders in childhood. For depression, the most commonly studied pharmacologic agents are the tricyclic antidepressants (or TCAs). Despite their study in 11 randomized, controlled studies, the TCAs have not demonstrated their effectiveness in treating childhood depression; consequently, TCAs are not currently recommended as a first line of treatment (Geller at al., 1999). Lately, newer and safer agents, such as the selective serotonin reuptake inhibitors (or SSRIs), are receiving more frequent study in the treatment of childhood depression. In the largest study of antidepressants in children, Emslie et al. (1997) tested fluoxetine versus placebo and found that over half of the study's participants were noted to have significantly benefited from fluoxetine, compared to only 33% showing benefit from placebo. In the only randomized, multisite, controlled trial of an SSRI for childhood anxiety disorders, fluvoxamine was found to be superior to placebo in treating children diagnosed with social phobia, separation anxiety, or generalized anxiety disorder (Vitiello, 2000). In addition, several pharmacologic agents have been shown to be efficacious (demonstrating greater symptom reduction compared to placebo) in the treatment of children and adolescents diagnosed with obsessive-compulsive disorder (OCD); these include the SSRIs and TCAs (Emslie et al., 1999; Geller at al., 1999).

Preliminary evidence supports the effective use of commonly prescribed adult medications for bipolar disorder and schizophrenia in children and adolescents. Lithium, the common first-line treatment for bipolar disorder in adults, has been shown to improve treatment outcomes in adolescents (Geller et al., 1998) and to reduce relapse rates when sustained over time (Strober, Morrell, Lampert, & Burroughs, 1990). Of clinical note, the safety precautions necessary with lithium require regular monitoring and consistent medical appointments. There is also evidence supporting the usefulness of antipsychotic medications for child/adolescent-onset schizophrenia; however, information on long-term effectiveness and safety is lacking (Weisz & Jensen, 1999).

Clinical psychotropic medication trials are desperately needed for many childhood mental disorders. Despite their the wide use, surprisingly few randomized controlled studies have been conducted (Weisz & Jensen, 1999). Often, medication choices and algorithms are based on individual practitioner experience or adult standards of care. In addition, proper medication selection is only one factor within successful pharmacological treatment. The recent NIMH multimodal treatment study for ADHD found that the delivery of stimulant medications within the context of this large, multisite study resulted in superior clinical outcomes compared to the delivery of similar medications within the community (MTA Cooperative Group, 1999). Research on the safety and efficacy of psychotropic medications is a necessary, but not sufficient, step in promoting the safe and effective use of psychotropic medications in children. Research must also explore the necessary practice behaviors, medication monitoring standards, and dosage regimens important for maximal treatment effectiveness.

School-Based Interventions

Between 70% and 80% of children who receive mental health services receive them in school; for many children the school system provides their only form of mental health treatment (Burns et al., 1995). Children identified in school as being in need of mental health services are more likely to actually enter treatment and receive services that are offered in the school system as opposed to within the community (Catron & Weiss, 1994). Several childhood disorders are associated with poor academic performance, learning disabilities, peer difficulties, or language delays. Although schools do not primarily focus on the delivery of mental health services, academic-related functional impairments and logistical accessibility make schools a logical and important point of intervention and service access for children with emotional or behavioral problems. However, we know surprisingly little about what is being provided within typical school-based mental health services and whether these services are effective.

Some empirically supported treatments for childhood behavior problems have been found to be effective in school settings. For instance, treatment outcome research has demonstrated that targeted classroom-based contingency management often reduces the incidence of disruptive behaviors in children diagnosed with ADHD (Pelham et al., 1998) and in children with other conduct problems (Brestan & Eyberg, 1998).

School-based contingency management strategies for children with disruptive behavior disorders may include a variety of interventions such as home-school behavior report cards, point reward systems for positive behaviors, or loss of desired privileges for negative behaviors. Contingency management also appears to successfully reduce aggression when implemented across entire classrooms. The Good Behavior Game, a classroom-based behavior management strategy for first-grade students, rewards students for their lack of negative disruptive behaviors during specific time periods (Dolan et al., 1993; Kellam, Rebok, Ialongo, & Mayer, 1994). At a 6-year follow-up, children rated as highly aggressive before the initial intervention continued to demonstrate lower rates of aggression than similar peers who did not receive the intervention (Kellam et al., 1994). Contingency management procedures can also be successfully implemented directly by classroom teachers. Behavioral consultation to teachers to help accommodate difficult classroom students has been found to reduce the number of special education referrals and placements, as well as to improve teacher reports of students' behavior problems (Fuchs, Fuchs, & Bahr, 1990).

School-based preventive interventions designed to target children at risk for emotional or behavioral problems also have been shown to successfully reduce symptoms and increase positive coping strategies. Cognitive group interventions to modify adolescents' depressive thinking styles have demonstrated a reduced risk for the development of full depression among group participants (Clarke et al., 1995). Similarly, a social problem-solving skills group intervention for elementary-age children reporting elevated depressive symptoms found reductions in reported depression even 1 year after the intervention (Gillham, Reivich, Jaycox, & Seligman, 1995). Further evidence demonstrates that school-based preventive interventions can reduce the risk for conduct problems. Successful interventions typically involve multiple components targeting classroom, home, and peer environments. For instance, the Linking the Interests of Families and Teachers (LIFT) program includes parent training, social skills training, a playground behavioral program, and regular communication between teachers and parents. This program has been shown to reduce aggressive playground behaviors, decrease negative family interactions during a problem-solving task, and increase teacher reports of social behaviors and positive peer interactions among participating elementary-school students (Reid, Eddy, Fetrow, & Stoolmiller, 1999). Participating students were less likely to demonstrate inattentive, impulsive, overactive, and disruptive behaviors in the classroom even 3 years after the program was completed. Similarly, the FAST (Family and Schools Together) Track program, which targets aggressive kindergarten students, has been shown to reduce oppositional and aggressive behavior as well as the use of special education services among participants (Conduct Problems Prevention Research Group, 1999). Fast Track consists of parent training, home-visit and case management activities, social skills training, academic tutoring, and classroom behavior management.

School-based research on interventions for children with emotional or behavior problems demonstrates efficacious individual, classroomwide, and targeted preventive interventions (Rones & Hoagwood, 2000); however, there continues to be a critical need for increased mental health research within the school system, especially for interventions that target the most common childhood mental health problems (i.e., anxiety, depression, ADHD). Furthermore, many of the evidence-based school interventions have been tested in very academic-like studies. Research on the implementation of school-based interventions initiated or conducted directly by school personnel is more rare and desperately needed.

Potentially Ineffective Treatments

The current identification of empirically supported treatments for children has to date focused on the accumulation of supportive findings without an established procedure for dealing with null or even negative results (Weisz & Hawley, 1998). Equally important, treatments can be identified that consistently fail to show an effect on symptoms across empirical studies, or possibly lead to worse outcomes. This section will highlight some clinical interventions without empirical support as well as some with empirical evidence of detrimental effects.

The surgeon general's report on youth violence (U.S. Department of Health and Human Services, 2001) estimates that many of the services provided to delinquent juveniles have little or no evidence base. Worse yet, a recent study indicated that peer, group-based interventions may actually increase behavior problems among high-risk adolescents (Dishion, McCord, & Poulin, 1999). Examples of these peer group interventions include group counseling sessions run and supervised by clinicians as well as summer camps. The authors suggest that these groups may serve as "deviancy training," whereby maladaptive behaviors are promoted through the positive reinforcement (e.g., laughter, attention, and interest in deviant behavior) that occurs among teens in the groups. Dishion et al. (1999) found evidence of increased substance abuse, delinquent behaviors, and violence among youths participating in these groups compared to youths not participating in the groups. Consequently, for youths with a history of delinquent behavior, these well-intentioned interventions may actually exacerbate the very behavior problems that brought them into treatment in the first place. Occasionally, some treatment may not be better than no treatment at all.

Despite their prevalent use in mental health settings, there is little empirical justification for the use of nonbehavioral psychotherapies for the treatment of disruptive behavior disorders (Weisz et al., 1995). For instance, in their review of effective treatments for ADHD, Pelham et al., (1998) found *no* empirical studies testing the efficacy of many psychosocial treatments commonly used for ADHD, such as individual therapy and play therapy. And, although there have been controlled treatment outcome studies for cognitive therapy (e.g., self-instructions, self-monitoring, self-reinforcement) to treat children diagnosed with ADHD, these studies generally show no clinical or academic benefits of the treatment (e.g., Abikoff & Gittelman, 1985). Given the supporting evidence of the positive effects of behavioral interventions with disruptive behavior disorders, it does not appear warranted at this time to provide nonbehavioral interventions to these youths and their families.

Finally, a common treatment for children with complex emotional and behavioral problems is the therapeutic group home. Group homes are located within the community, and children typically attend local schools. Each home normally serves 5 to 10 children, many of whom are involved in the child welfare or juvenile justice systems. Existing research does indicate that children placed in group homes show improvement while they are in the home; however, the limited research available indicates that these changes are often not maintained after the child is returned to the community (Kirigin, Braukmann, Atwater, & Wolf, 1982). Residential treatment centers and inpatient hospitals also appear to improve outcomes shortly after discharge, but findings are mixed about whether these gains are sustained (e.g., Greenbaum et al., 1996). Further, only two controlled clinical trials of residential treatment centers or hospitals have been conducted; both studies demonstrated improved or equivalent outcomes for the alternative intervention (Schoenwald, Ward, Henggeler, & Rowland, 2000; Winsberg, Bialer, Kupietz, Botti, & Balka, 1980).

Long-term outcomes for residential facilities are likely related to the extent of appropriate services and support after discharge (e.g., Wells, 1991). These findings are particularly troubling because inpatient treatment consumes a large portion of child mental health resources, almost 33% of the total child and adolescent treatment expenditures, or $3.9 billion (Ringel & Sturm, 2001). Considering its costs, it is surprising that inpatient hospitalization has the weakest evidence base among child mental health service models. Nevertheless, many children with severe emotional or behavioral problems will require periodic stabilization and perhaps inpatient hospitalization. Crisis stabilization is often important for these youths, and residential or inpatient facilities are successful in helping to stabilize children at imminent risk for further harm. However, without adequate aftercare services and community support, these youths remain at high risk for rehospitalization. Many children placed in these environments have histories of multiple out-of-home placements and consequently carry a poor prognosis. For these children, it will be especially critical to study different aftercare plans following stabilization and discharge from a more restrictive placement.

CLINICAL IMPLICATIONS

Intensify Outreach and Engagement Efforts

There are many barriers to seeking or consistently receiving mental health care for families of children with emotional or behavioral problems. First, children and adolescents do not typically refer themselves for treatment; referrals are often made by their parents, schools, courts, or social service system. Not surprisingly, in a survey that asked parents about reasons for service termination, the most commonly endorsed response was "child did not want to come back" (Gould, Shaffer, & Kaplan, 1985). Furthermore, families may not seek mental health services for their children or may drop out early from treatment for many reasons; these include the stigma associated with using mental health services, lack of information regarding available services, and inaccessible locations (e.g., Acosta, 1980). Kazdin and colleagues (1997) were able to identify three primary areas involved in families quitting mental health services prematurely: stressors and obstacles associated with treatment (e.g., cost, transportation); perceptions that treatment was not relevant; and a poor relationship with the therapist. On one hand, clinicians sometimes have little control over the stigma associated with mental health problems and over financial or transportation hurdles to receiving care. On the other hand, additional factors apparently important to treatment engagement, such as treatment relevance and the therapeutic relationship, are directly a part of the clinician's responsibility. Mental health providers should be aware of the barriers and hardships associated with mental health service access and use for families. As much as possible, outreach to families in need should include, but not end with, efforts to help families initiate services. Additional ongoing strategies to engage families in the treatment process will likely be equally important.

Increase Awareness and Incorporation of Evidence-Based Treatments and Service Delivery Models

The contrast between findings of psychotherapy effect in general practice versus in experimental studies raises the question of whether commonly used child mental health services in practice are achieving maximal success. Despite recognized limitations to empirically supported psychosocial treatments, the positive treatment outcomes for commonly referred disorders of childhood and adolescence (i.e., ADHD, specific phobias, depression) are noteworthy. Empirically supported interventions tend to be manualized, goal-oriented, and behavioral or cognitive-behavioral in nature. Although a strict adherence to specific manualized treatments in clinical practice may be difficult, flexible adherence to their guiding principles and components should not be. As we await findings of empirically supported treatment outcomes in real-world settings, it seems reasonable to recommend that training opportunities in empirically supported interventions, particularly cognitive-behavioral therapy for internalizing disorders and behavioral parent training for child externalizing disorders, be made available to students and practicing clinicians to assist in the treatment process. Similar to psychosocial intervention practice, there are noted barriers within the primary care and psychiatric settings for using research-derived medication monitoring and diagnostic assessment procedures. However, efforts should be made to expand clinicians' use of evidence-based medication practices and monitoring.

Discontinue Ineffective Interventions

The fact that existing and sometimes commonly used child mental health services may not be effective, or may potentially be harmful, highlights the importance of empirically based treatments. Well-intentioned clinicians may not be using the most effective approach with their clients, or in some cases may be doing harm. Based on existing research evidence, practices such as group peer-based interventions for juvenile delinquents should be discouraged, as should traditional individual psychotherapy approaches for children with disruptive behavior disorders. Furthermore, group home placements or hospitalizations should ideally be used for only brief periods of crisis stabilization and be accompanied by efforts to increase family support and aftercare services. An increased awareness of residential treatment alternatives and community-based support services within the local community would enable practicing and future clinicians to consider every option prior to extensive out-of-home placements for their child and adolescent clients. When available, clinicians should attempt to seek training in empirically based interventions, their limits, and appropriate use. While recognizing that empirical justification for the treatment of some disorders remains insufficient, it is critical that practicing clinicians familiarize themselves with the existing evidence to support or disprove their practice choices.

Broaden Knowledge of Diverse Service-Sector Care Opportunities

As noted previously, children typically receive mental health services in a variety of service systems. These include, but are not limited to, schools, primary care settings, child welfare systems, and sometimes the juvenile justice system. Successful interventions to address children's emotional and behavior problems will likely be intrinsically tied to the child's family, peer, school, and community environments. Given this, child mental health services should include the availability of a continuum of care that includes a variety of professionals. Child mental health practitioners must become acquainted with the multiple systems within which a particular child operates and fit intervention recommendations within the context of that child's care system and other service needs. If possible, child-oriented mental health clinicians should seek training and experience in school consultation and collaboration. Furthermore, clinicians should become aware of the role that other service providers (e.g., probation officers, social workers) may play in their client's comprehensive treatment.

FUTURE RESEARCH DIRECTIONS

Closing the Gap Between Research and Practice

Research has documented differences in the efficacy of treatment strategies tested outside of typical clinical settings and treatments conducted within these practice settings (e.g., Weisz et al., 1995). For instance, those psychosocial treatment strategies found to be most effective in meta-analyses are most often cognitive-behavioral (or behavioral) in nature, rely on specific methods, and have provisions for treatment structure through manuals or fidelity-monitoring procedures; meanwhile, those strategies employed by the majority of clinicians in practice are eclectic and blend various therapeutic strategies and approaches (Weisz et al., 1995). Differences between research and real-world practice do not exist only for psychosocial treatments, but also for psychotropic medication practices. In the recent multisite treatment study of ADHD, medication-monitoring procedures in the experimental condition of the recently conducted multisite treatment study of ADHD included 30-minute-per-month meetings with the child's physician, higher maximum medication dosages, and ongoing contact with the child's teacher, whereas children who received medication in the community treatment-as-usual (TAU) condition had lower dosages and much less (and briefer) contact with their physicians (MTA Cooperative Group, 1999).

This gap between research and practice exists for a variety of reasons. First, the degree of control needed to preliminarily test an intervention's efficacy typically controls for those factors common within real-world practice settings. These factors may, in fact, turn out to be important moderators or mediators of the treatment's effects. For instance, efficacy research often designs and tests interventions for single-disorder populations (excluding those with comorbid conditions) with a single target treatment strategy. In inner-city mental health clinics, Weisz, Huey, and Weersing (1998) found that children often entered treatment with an average of 3.5 different diagnoses. Similarly, although medication efficacy studies typically tend to focus on single-disorder populations and with one target medication, polypharmacy and disorder comorbidity are common within clinical practice. Efficacy studies are necessary to establish the basic parameters of a treatment's impact, but they are hardly sufficient for answering questions about the extent to which a treatment will exert that impact under conditions of typical clinical practice. For these kinds of questions, effectiveness studies are needed. The challenge for future research is to take interventions shown to produce positive outcomes in experimental studies and study those modifications necessary for their successful implementation in typical practice settings (Hoagwood, Hibbs, Brent, & Jensen, 1995).

Practice Research to Facilitate Transportability and Sustainability

As our knowledge of evidence-based treatments for children grows, so does the impetus for these strategies to be incorporated into existing service settings. As previously noted, children receive mental health services in a variety of service sectors. Unfortunately, very little research has been conducted to examine the characteristics of these settings or the types of services typically provided within them. All service settings have unique organizational structures, personnel, and client caseloads that will likely influence their incorporation of modified, different, or completely new mental health treatment strategies or service models. It is likely that the successful dissemination of innovative treatments for children's mental health will need to happen in an individualized fashion that incorporates strategies appropriate for the selected service sector.

Practicing clinicians are very familiar with the preparation necessary to select and present an appropriate treatment to clients based on their individual needs and presenting situation. A similar selection and presentation process will likely be necessary for service-sector dissemination efforts. Indeed, studies that examine barriers to the provision of mental health services or evidence-based practices find different factors at work within various practitioners and service settings. For instance, Reid, Vasa, Maag, and Wright (1994) examined barriers to the provision of services for children diagnosed with ADHD in schools. Teachers indicated that the primary impediments were lack of time to administer specialized interventions, lack of training, and class sizes too large to focus on individualized interventions. Like teachers, primary care physicians also note time and training as barriers to following evidence-based practice guidelines for ADHD; however, physicians additionally cite cost and lack of reimbursement as major hurdles to the provision of behavioral assessments and treatment (Hoagwood, Kelleher, Feil, & Comer, 2000). Finally, when psychotherapists are asked why they do not use "empirically supported treatments," they report unique concerns about the rigidity of manualized treatments that limit the flexibility they see as key to their practice (Barlow, Levitt, & Bufka, 1999).

Additional research is needed to examine the complex contextual factors at work within various practice settings (e.g., organizational structure, practitioner characteristics and attitudes, client preferences) that may impede or facilitate the incorporation of empirically based mental health services. This research is a necessary part of the dissemination process and should be incorporated to evaluate the transportability of certain interventions into specific settings. This same type of information may also be used to modify evidence-based interventions to facilitate their incorporation into practice. The poor fit between a particular dissemination strategy and a targeted practice setting will not likely lead to independent service implementation and will be even less likely to result in ongoing sustainability of these new or modified strategies.

Integrating Research on Service Structure, Efficacy, and Quality

Mental health services research has examined which types of treatments are beneficial to children as well as how best to structure the delivery of services. Research on the efficacy of individual treatments has traditionally focused on reducing target symptoms and associated impairments. As noted throughout this chapter, this research has led to the discovery of multiple interventions that reduce the problems associated with specific emotional or behavioral disorders. At the same time, research on the structure of mental health services for children has focused primarily on the provision of a *continuum of care*. This research specifically aims to address the needs of children with serious emotional disturbance who most often interact with multiple, and often fragmented, service systems. The continuum-of-care, or system-of-care, model integrates a range of services (outpatient, residential, and intermediate) within a community environment.

Two randomized controlled trials of this model have been conducted (Bickman, 1996; Bickman, Noser, & Summerfelt, 1999). Compared to another community treating children as usual, a continuum-of-care program in Fort Bragg, North Carolina, led to greater continuity in care, greater access to mental health services, more client satisfaction, and more children treated in less restrictive settings. This research demonstrated that mental health systems can be structured in a way to improve access to care and to aid in keeping children within their communities for treatment. These are important outcomes and ones typically not examined in psychosocial or pharmacological efficacy research. Unfortunately, the Fort Bragg continuum-of-care site also showed no significantly different improvement in clinical outcomes compared to the community treatment, and it was more expensive (Bickman, 1996).

A study by Glisson and Hemmelgarn (1998) that investigated organizational factors related to the delivery of child mental health services also failed to show the benefit of greater interorganizational coordination on child welfare outcomes. However, this study did demonstrate the positive effects of intraorganizational factors, such as a positive organizational climate (e.g., the perceived sense of well-being gained from working within a certain environment), on positive child client outcomes. This finding is particularly striking given the lack of attention paid to intraorganizational factors within both efficacy and systems structure research. Taken together, these various lines of child mental health research point to hopeful directions for the future. They document successful strategies for improving the content and quality of child mental health treatments, and they suggest improvements for the way in which these services are delivered within each type of organizational environment. Mental health system changes may need to be linked to efficacious clinical care to maximize improvements for children and families. Further, quality of care is likely enhanced by a positive organizational climate.

Theory-Driven Treatment Development

Research on how to take what we know about tested treatments into real-world service settings is very important, but so is research that attempts to improve on current interventions or to create new ones. The past several years have noted multiple risk factors for the onset of specific emotional or behavioral problems, particularly disruptive behavior disorders. Unfortunately, very few of these documented risks have been translated into targets for intervention (or prevention). One notable exception is the psychosocial treatment-development process for conduct problems. Research has long demonstrated an association with deviant peers, inadequate parental monitoring, and harsh parental punishment styles as risk factors for the development of conduct disorders (Loeber & Farrington, 1998; Patterson, Reid, & Dishion, 1992). These risk factors have been targeted for intervention development, and specific services have been designed that successfully help to manage these risks (e.g., parent training, strategies to increase parental monitoring). However, a wealth of risk factor research remains to be incorporated into future intervention development. Moreover, we often have a limited understanding of what makes existing evidence-based interventions work.

There are likely certain key factors (e.g., goal-driven, skill development, therapeutic relationship) in current evidence-based practices that are critical to the change process; however, few efforts in child treatment research have attempted to identify these factors. A traditional measurement focus on treatment outcomes has shed little light on why these interventions produce certain effects. The incorporation of treatment process measures linked to outcome measures will aid in the identification of critical intervention components. The intervention development process ideally should be grounded in theory and previous research findings to hypothesize why a particular strategy would be important for use in a targeted situation and why it might be expected to produce change in specific symptoms or behaviors.

Looking Beyond Symptom-Based Outcomes

Rosenblatt (1993) stated simply that children should be "at home, in school and out of trouble." Anecdotal reports from parents often confirm that they would like the same thing. In addition to the symptoms of their emotional or behavioral problem, children with serious emotional disturbances often also have deficits in other important areas, such as intellectual and educational functioning or social and adaptive skills. Furthermore, these children have often been exposed to other major life stressors or losses, such as divorce, separation, death, exposure to violence in their communities, or abuse and neglect. Likely due to the interaction of their life experiences, symptoms, and functional impairments, children with emotional or behavioral problems may have problematic relationships with parents, peers, or teachers. Child treatment outcome studies have traditionally focused on the reduction of target symptoms (e.g., decreased inattentive behaviors) and less on functional outcomes (e.g., increased positive peer

relationships). However, symptom reduction without concordant increases in functioning are likely less meaningful. Ideally, treatment would additionally result in
decreased perceptions of family burden associated with the child's emotional disturbance. Future treatments and tests of their efficacy or effectiveness should be designed
to target multiple domains of functioning and symptom reduction.

Incorporation of Strategies to Increase Access and Engagement

For obvious reasons, mental health practitioners focus on those clients who enter their
offices; however, research indicates that these children represent only a small portion
of those in need of treatment. Those who do not attend scheduled appointments or
who never seek services may in fact be those children with the most severe emotional
disturbance and from the most vulnerable populations. A clear disparity exists in the
access to mental health treatment services, particularly among rural and ethnic minority populations. Research should not stop at simply documenting the disparities. A few
studies have demonstrated the success of relatively simple engagement strategies in
increasing initial treatment attendance (McKay et al., 1996, 1998; Santisteban et al.,
1996; Szapocznik et al., 1988). However, these strategies appear slightly less successful
at decreasing the likelihood of premature treatment dropout (e.g., McKay et al.,
1998). Continued research on such strategies is critical: The creation of newer and better mental health services will do nothing unless these services reach the children who
need them. A future research challenge becomes one of focusing not solely on the
development of new interventions, but on new treatments that incorporate strategies
for client engagement and ongoing involvement in treatment. Research on the effectiveness of mental health services should additionally be evaluated in terms of its
responsiveness to client needs and ability to engage those typically unreached by existing service delivery systems.

CONCLUSIONS

For most of the 20th century, child mental health treatment was framed by conceptual
principles that positioned it within traditional psychiatric or psychological models,
whereas many children with severe mental health problems were being identified (and
sometimes served) outside the traditional mental health care system. Children with
mental health needs represent a large portion of the children in both the child welfare
and the juvenile justice systems (U.S. Public Health Service, 2000). Furthermore, many
children with behavioral or emotional problems are identified by their school and/or
primary care physician rather than by a psychiatrist or psychologist (Burns et al.,
1995). Many of these children then receive some mental health services at school, and
often only from the school. In addition, we know that these children are not the only
ones in need of support. The parents of children with mental health problems are
often highly stressed or may have psychological difficulties of their own (e.g., Lahey et
al., 1988; Breen & Barkley, 1988). Furthermore, to make interventions with children
even more complicated, children are in a constant state of change by nature of their
ongoing development; this change substantially impacts the meaning of their symp-

tom presentations and course of treatment (Jensen & Hoagwood, 1997). These factors are unique to the lives of children and make critical the need for a developmental model of children's mental health services that conceptualizes the child as functioning *within* a system.

In the recently released surgeon general's call to action for children's mental health (U.S. Public Health Service, 2000), child social and emotional functioning is conceptualized as an integral part of a child's overall development. This development is further viewed as intrinsically tied to the child's family, peer, school, and community environments. These environmental factors are no less influential for the development of positive mental health than is physical well-being. Moreover, they are likely critical in the ultimate development of positive functional outcomes for children with emotional or behavioral problems. Given this, successful child health, and mental health, services must include the availability of a continuum-of-care possibilities. Ideally, appropriate care options then can be accessed based on level of need and problem severity. These multiple and varied care options require a diverse range of professionals. Child mental health practitioners must become acquainted with the multiple systems within which a particular child operates and fit intervention recommendations within the context of that child's care system and other service needs. Child mental health researchers must likewise incorporate a comprehensive knowledge of service systems, within and outside of traditional mental health systems, into the development and transfer of effective assessment and treatment strategies. Substantial opportunities exist to share resources among the various child health care systems and professionals. Such efforts will ultimately have the greatest potential for increasing the helpfulness of child mental health services.

This is a time of exponential growth in the knowledge of treatment and service effectiveness for children with emotional or behavioral problems. Although there is ample room for growth in the understanding of how best to incorporate this research into daily practice, enough evidence exists to suggest new avenues for treatment and service delivery by clinicians, as well as fresh attention to issues of clinical relevance by researchers. This pursuit will depend on a heightened awareness and communication among clinicians and scientists. Practicing and future clinicians should increase their knowledge of evidence-based practices; practicing and future researchers should increase their knowledge of clinical service delivery systems. Only through the mutual reciprocation of practice to research and of research to practice can we expect to advance the truly useful knowledge of what works in children's mental health and expect this knowledge to in turn be applied in clinical settings.

REFERENCES

Abikoff, H., & Gittelman, R. (1985). Hyperactive children treated with stimulants: Is cognitive training a useful adjunct? *Archives of General Psychiatry, 42,* 953–961.

Acosta, F. X. (1980). Self-described reasons for premature termination of psychotherapy by Mexican-American, Black American and Anglo-American patients. *Psychological Reports, 47,* 435–443.

Armbruster, P., & Fallon, T. (1994). Clinical, sociodemographic, and systems risk factors for attrition in a children's mental health clinic. *American Journal of Orthopsychiatry, 64,* 577–585.

Barlow, D. H., Levitt, J. T., & Bufka, L. (1999). The dissemination of empirically supported treatments: A view to the future. *Behaviour Research and Therapy, 37*(Suppl. 1), S147–S162.

Bickman, L. (1996). A continuum of care: More is not always better. *American Psychologist, 51,* 689–701.

Bickman, L., Noser, K., & Summerfelt, W. T. (1999). Long-term effects of a system of care on children and adolescents. *Journal of Behavioral Health Services and Research, 26,* 185–202.

Borduin, C. M., Henggeler, S. W., Blaske, D. M., & Stein, R. (1990). Multisystemic treatment of adolescent sexual offenders. *International Journal of Offender Therapy and Comparative Criminology, 35,* 105–114.

Borduin, C. M., Mann, B. J., Cone, L. T., Henggeler, S. W., Fucci, B. R., Blaske, D. M., & Wilson, R. A. (1995). Multisystemic treatment of serious juvenile offenders: Long-term prevention of criminology and violence. *Journal of Consulting and Clinical Psychology, 63,* 569–578.

Breen, M. J., & Barkley, R. A. (1988). Child psychopathology and parenting stress in girls and boys having attention-deficit disorder with hyperactivity. *Journal of Pediatric Psychology, 13,* 265–280.

Brestan, E. V. & Eyberg, S. M. (1998). Effective psychosocial treatments of conduct-disordered children and adolescents: 29 years, 82 studies, and 5,272 kids. *Journal of Child Clinical Psychology, 27,* 180–189.

Brunk, M., Henggeler, S. W., & Whelan, J. P. (1987). A comparison of multisystemic therapy and parent training in the brief treatment of child abuse and neglect. *Journal of Consulting and Clinical Psychology, 55,* 311–318.

Burns, B. J., Costello, E. J., Angold, A., Tweed, D., Stangl, D., Farmer, E., & Erkanli, A. (1995). Children's mental health service use across service sectors. *Health Affairs, 14,* 147–159.

Burns, B. J., & Goldman, S. K. (Eds.). (1999). *Promising practices in wraparound for children with serious emotional disturbance and their families; Systems of care: Promising practices in children's mental health* (1998 series, Vol. 4). Washington, DC: Center for Effective Collaboration and Practice, American Institutes for Research.

Burns, B. J., Hoagwood, K., & Mrazek, P. (1999). Effective treatment for mental disorders in children and adolescents. *Clinical Child and Family Psychology Review, 2,* 199–254.

Campbell, M., Adams, P. B., Small, A. M., Kafantaris, V., Silva, R., Shell, J., Perry, R., & Overall, J. (1995). Lithium in hospitalized aggressive children with conduct disorder: A double-blind and placebo-controlled study. *Journal of the American Academy of Child and Adolescent Psychiatry, 34,* 445–453.

Campbell, M., Rapoport, J. L., Simpson, G. M. (1999). Antipsychotics in children and adolescents. *Journal of the American Academy of Child and Adolescent Psychiatry, 38,* 537–545.

Campbell, M., Small, A. M., Green, W. H., Jennings, S., Perry, R., Bennett, W., & Anderson, L. (1984). Behavioral efficacy of haloperidol and lithium carbonate: A comparison in hospitalized aggressive children with conduct disorder. *Archives of General Psychiatry, 41,* 650–656.

Casey R. J., & Berman, J. S., (1985). The outcome of psychotherapy with children. *Psychological Bulletin, 98,* 388–400.

Catron, T., & Weiss, B. (1994). The Vanderbilt School-Based Counseling Program. *Journal of Emotional and Behavioral Disorders, 2,* 247–253.

Chamberlain, P., & Reid, J. (1998). Comparison of two community alternatives to incarceration for chronic juvenile offenders. *Journal of Consulting and Clinical Psychology, 4,* 624–633.

Chamberlain, P., & Reid, J. (1991). Using a specialized foster care community treatment model for children and adolescents leaving the state mental hospital. *Journal of Community Psychology, 19,* 266–276.

Chamberlain, P., & Weinrott, M. (1990, January–February). Specialized foster care: Treating seriously emotionally disturbed children. *Children Today,* 24–27.

Chambless, D. L., Sanderson, W. C., Shohman, V., Bennett Johnson, S., Pope, K. S., Crits-Cristoph, P., Baker, M., Johnson, B., Woody, S. R., Sue, S., Beutler, L., Williams, D. A., & McMurry, S. (1996). An update on empirically validated therapies. *The Clinical Psychologist, 49,* 5–18.

Clarke, G., Hawkins, W., Murphy, M., Sheeber, L., Lewinsohn, P., & Seeley, J. (1995). Targeted prevention of unipolar depressive disorder in an at-risk sample of high school adolescents: A randomized trial of a group cognitive intervention. *Journal of the American Academy of Child and Adolescent Psychiatry, 34,* 312–321.

Clarke, H. B., Prange, M., Lee, B., Boyd, L. A., McDonald, B. A., & Stewart, E. S. (1994). Improving adjustment outcomes for foster children with emotional and behavioral disorders: Early findings from a controlled study on individualized services. *Journal of Emotional and Behavioral Disorders, 2,* 207–218.

Clarke, H. B., Prange, M., Lee, B., Stewart, E., McDonald, B., & Boyd, L. (1998). An individualized wraparound process for children in foster care with emotional/behavioral disturbances: Follow-up findings and implications from a controlled study. In M. Epstein, K. Kutash, & A. Duchnowski (Eds.), *Outcomes for children and youth with behavioral and emotional disorders and their families* (pp. 513–542). Austin, TX: PRO-ED Publishing.

Conduct Problems Prevention Research Group (1999). Initial impact of the FAST Track prevention trial for conduct problems: II. Classroom effects. *Journal of Consulting and Clinical Psychology, 67,* 648–657.

Dishion, T. J., McCord, J., & Poulin, F. (1999). When interventions harm: Peer groups and problem behavior. *American Psychologist, 54,* 755–765.

Dolan, L., Kellam, S., Brown, C., Werthamer-Larsson, L., Rebok, G., Mayer, L., Laudolff, J., Turkkan, Ford, C., & Wheeler, L. (1993). The short-term impact of two classroom-based preventive interventions on aggressive and shy behaviors and poor achievement. *Journal of Applied Developmental Psychology, 14,* 317–345.

Emslie, G. J., Rush, A. J., Weinberg, W. A., Kowatch, R. A., Hughes, C. W., Carmody, T., & Rintelmann, J. (1997). A double-blind, randomized, placebo-controlled trial of fluoxetine in children and adolescents with depression. *Archives of General Psychiatry, 54,* 1031–1037.

Emslie, G. J., Walkup, J. T., Pliszka, S. R., & Ernst, M. (1999). Nontricyclic antidepressants: Current trends in children and adolescents. *Journal of the American Academy of Child and Adolescent Psychiatry, 38,* 517–528.

Evans, M. E., Banks, S. M., Huz, S., & McNulty, T. L. (1994). Initial hospitalization and community tenure outcomes of intensive case management for children and youth with serious emotional disturbance. *Journal of Child and Family Studies, 3,* 225–234.

Evans, M. E., Dollard, N., & McNulty, T. L. (1992). Characteristics of seriously emotionally disturbed youth with and without substance abuse in intensive case management. *Journal of Child and Family Studies, 1,* 305–314.

Friedman, R., Katz-Leavy, J., Manderscheid, R., & Sondheimer, D. (1996). *Prevalence of serious emotional disturbance in children and adolescents' mental health* (DHHS Publication No. SMA 96-3098, pp. 71–89). Washington, DC: U.S. Government Printing Office.

Fuchs, D., Fuchs, L., Bahr, M. (1990). Mainstream assistance teams: A scientific basis for the art of consultation. *Exceptional Children,* 128–139.

Geller, B., Cooper, T. B., Sun, K., Zimermann, B., Razier, J., Williams, M., & Heath, J. (1998). Double-blind and placebo-controlled study of lithium for adolescent bipolar disorders with secondary substance dependency. *Journal of the American Academy of Child and Adolescent Psychiatry, 37,* 171–178.

Geller, B., Reising, D., Leonard, H. L., Riddle, M. A., & Walsh, B. T. (1999). Critical review of tricyclic antidepressant use in children and adolescents. *Journal of the American Academy of Child and Adolescent Psychiatry, 38,* 513–516.

Gillham, J., Reivich, K., Jaycox, L., & Seligman, M. (1995). Prevention of depressive symptoms in school children: Two-year follow-up. *Psychological Science, 6,* 343–351.

Glisson, C., & Hemmelgarn, A. (1998). The effects of organizational climate and interorganizational coordination on the quality of outcomes of children's serviced systems. *Child Abuse and Neglect, 22,* 401–421.

Gould, M. S., Shaffer, D., & Kaplan, D. (1985). The characteristics of dropouts from a child psychiatry clinic. *Journal of the American Academy of Child Psychiatry, 24*(3), 316–328.

Greenbaum, P. E., Dedrick, R. F., Kutash, K., Brown, E. C., Larieri, S. P., & Pugh, A. M.

(1996). National adolescent and child treatment study (NACTS): Outcomes for children with serious emotional and behavioral disturbance. *Journal of Emotional and Behavioral Disorders, 4*, 130–146.

Greenhill, L. L., Halperin, J. M., & Abikoff, H. (1999). Stimulant Medications. *Journal of the American Academy of Child and Adolescent Psychiatry, 38*, 503–512.

Henggeler, S. W., Melton, G. B., Smith, L. A., Schoenwald, S. K., & Hanley, J. H. (1993). Family preservation using multisystemic treatment: Long-term follow-up to a clinical trial with serious juvenile offenders. *Journal of Child and Family Studies, 2*, 283–293.

Henggeler, S. W., Rowland, M. D., Randall, J., Ward, D. M., Pickrel, S. G., Cunningham, P. G., Miller, S. L., Edwards, J., Zealberg, J. J., Hand, L. D., & Santos, A. B. (1999). Home-based multisystemic therapy as an alternative to the hospitalization of youths in psychiatric crisis: Clinical outcomes. *Journal of the American Academy of Child and Adolescent Psychiatry, 38*, 1331–1339.

Hoagwood, K., Hibbs, E., Brent, D., & Jensen, P. (1995). Introduction to the special section: Efficacy and effectiveness in studies of child and adolescent psychotherapy. *Journal of Consulting and Clinical Psychology, 63*, 683–687.

Hoagwood, K., Kelleher, K. J., Feil, M., & Comer, D. M. (2000). Treatment services for ADHD: A national perspective. *Journal of the American Academy of Child and Adolescent Psychiatry, 39*, 198–206.

Jensen, P. S., Bhatara, V. S., Vitiello, B., Hoagwood, K., Feil, M., Burke, L. B. (1999). Psychoactive medication prescribing practices for U.S. children: Gaps between research and clinical practice. *Journal of the American Academy of Child and Adolescent Psychiatry, 38*, 557–565.

Jensen, P., & Hoagwood, K. (1997). The book of names: *DSM-IV* in context. *Development and Psychopathology, 9*, 231–249.

Jobson, K. O., & Potter, W. Z. (1995). International Psychopharmacology Algorithm Project report. *Psychopharmacology Bulletin, 31*(3), 457–459, 491–500.

Kaslow, N. J. & Thompson, M. P. (1998). Applying the criteria for empirically supported treatments to studies of psychosocial interventions for child and adolescent depression. *Journal of Child Clinical Psychology, 27*, 146–155.

Kazdin, A. E. (1993). Premature termination from treatment among children referred for antisocial behavior. *Journal of Clinical Child Psychology, 31*, 415–425.

Kazdin, A. E., Bass, D., Ayers, W. A., & Rodgers, A. (1990). Empirical and clinical focus of child and adolescent psychotherapy research. *Journal of Consulting and Clinical Psychology, 58*, 729–740.

Kazdin, A. E., Holland, L., & Crowley, M. (1997). Family experiences of barriers to treatment and premature termination from child therapy. *Journal of Consulting and Clinical Psychology, 65*, 453–463.

Kellam, S., Rebok, G., Ialongo, N., Mayer, L. (1994). The course and malleability of aggressive behavior from early first grade into middle school: Results of a developmental epidemiology-based preventive trial. *Journal of Child Psychology, Psychiatry, and the Allied Disciplines, 35*, 259–281.

Kirigin, K. A., Braukmann, C. J., Atwater, J. D., & Wolf, M. M. (1982). An evaluation of teaching-family (achievement place) group homes for juvenile offenders. *Journal of Applied Behavior Analysis, 15*, 1–16.

Kutash, K., & Rivera, V. R. (1996). *What works in children's mental health services: Uncovering answers to critical questions.* Baltimore, MD: Paul H. Brookes.

Lahey, B. B., Piacentini, J. C., McBurnett, K., Stone, P., Hartdagen, S., & Hynd, G. (1988). Psychopathology in the parents of children with conduct disorder and hyperactivity. *Journal of the American Academy of Child and Adolescent Psychiatry, 27*, 163–170.

Lardieri, S., Greenbaum, P. E., & Pugh, A. M. (1996, February). *Parent reports of problem behavior onset among children and adolescents with serious emotional disturbances.* Paper presented at the ninth Annual System of Care Research Conference, Tampa, FL.

Leaf, P. J., Alegria, M., Cohen, P., Cohen, P., Goodman, S. H., Horwitz, S. M., Hoven, C. W.,

Narrow, W. E., Vaden-Kiernan, M., & Regier, D. A. (1996). Mental health service use in the community and schools. Results from the four-community MECA study. *Journal of the American Academy of Child and Adolescent Psychiatry, 35,* 889–897.

Loeber, R., & Farrington, D. P. (Eds.). (1998). *Serious and violent juvenile offenders: Risk factors and successful interventions.* Thousand Oaks, CA: Sage Publications.

Lonigan, C. J., Elbert, J. C., & Johnson, S. B. (1998). Empirically supported psychosocial interventions for children: An overview. *Journal of Child Clinical Psychology, 27,* 138–145.

McKay, M. M., McCadam, K., & Gonzales, J. J. (1996). Addressing the barriers to mental health services for inner city children and their caretakers. *Community Mental Health, 32,* 353–361.

McKay, M. M., Stoewe, J., McCadam, K., & Gonzales, J. (1998). Increasing access to child mental health services for urban children and their caretakers. *Health and Social Work, 23,* 9–15.

MTA Cooperative Group (1999). A 14-month randomized clinical trial of treatment strategies for attention-deficit/hyperactivity disorder. *Archives of General Psychiatry, 56,* 1073–1086.

Ollendick, T. H. & King, N. J. (1998). Empirically supported treatments for children with phobic and anxiety disorders. *Journal of Child Clinical Psychology, 27,* 156–167.

Patterson, G., Reid, J., & Dishion, T. (1992). *A social interactional approach: Vol. 4. Antisocial boys.* Eugene, OR: Castalia.

Pelham, W. E., Wheeler, T., & Chronis, A. (1998). Empirically supported psychosocial treatments for attention-deficit/hyperactivity disorder. *Journal of Child Clinical Psychology, 27,* 190–205.

Pfeifer, S. I., & Strzelecki, S. C. (1990). Inpatient psychiatric treatment of children and adolescents: A review of outcome studies. *Journal of the American Academy of Child and Adolescent Psychiatry, 29,* 847–854.

Reid, J., Eddy, M., Fetrow, R., & Stoolmiller, M. (1999). Description and immediate impacts of a preventive intervention for conduct problems. *American Journal of Community Psychology, 27,* 483–517.

Reid, R., Vasa, S., Maag, J., & Wright, G. (1994). An analysis of teachers' perceptions of attention deficit-hyperactivity disorder. *Journal of Research and Development in Education, 27*(3), 195–202.

Riddle, M. A., Bernstein, G. A., Cook, E. H., Leonard, H. L., March, J. S., & Swanson, J. M. (1999). Anxiolytics, adrenergic agents, and naltrexone. *Journal of the American Academy of Child and Adolescent Psychiatry, 38,* 546–556.

Rifkin, A., Karajgi, B., Dicker, R., Perl, E., Boppana, V., Hasan, N., & Pollack, S. (1997). Lithium treatment of conduct disorders in adolescents. *American Journal of Psychiatry, 154,* 554–555.

Ringel, J. S., & Sturm, R. (2001). National estimates of mental health utilization and expenditures for children in 1998. *Journal of Behavioral Health Services and Research, 28*(3), 319–333.

Rogers, S. J. (1998). Empirically supported comprehensive treatments for young children with autism. *Journal of Child Clinical Psychology, 27,* 168–179.

Rones, M., & Hoagwood, K. (2000). *School-based mental health services: A research review.* Unpublished manuscript.

Rosenblatt, A. (1993). In home, in school and out of trouble. *Journal of Child and Family Studies, 2,* 275–282.

Ryan, N. D., Bhatara, V. S., & Perel, J. M. (1999). Mood stabilizers in children and adolescents. *Journal of the American Academy of Child and Adolescent Psychiatry, 38,* 529–536.

Santisteban, D. A., Szapocznik, J., Perez-Vidal, A., Kuartines, W. M., Murray, E. J., & La-Perriere, A. (1996). Efficacy of intervention for engaging youth and families into treatment and some variables that may contribute to differential effectiveness. *Journal of Family Psychology, 10,* 35–44.

Schoenwald, S. K., Brown, T. L., & Henggeler, S. W. (2000). Inside multisystemic therapy: Therapist, supervisory, and program practices. *Journal of Emotional and Behavioral Disorders, 8,* 113–127.

Schoenwald, S. K., Ward, D. M., Henggeler, S. W., & Rowland, M. D. (2000). MST vs. hospitalization for crisis stabilization of youth: Placement and service use 4 months post-referral. *Mental Health Services Research, 2,* 3–12.

Smith, M. L., & Glass, G. V., (1977). Meta-analysis of psychotherapy outcomes studies. *American Psychologist, 32,* 752–760.

Strober, M., Morrell, W., Lampert, C., & Burroughs, J. (1990). Relapse following discontinuation of lithium maintenance therapy in adolescents with bipolar I illness: A naturalistic study. *American Journal of Psychiatry, 147,* 457–461.

Szapocznik, J., Perez-Vidal, A., Brickman, A. L., Foote, F. H., Santisteban, D., & Hervis, O. (1988). Engaging adolescent drug abusers and their families in treatment. A strategic structural systems approach. *Journal of Consulting and Clinical Psychology, 56,* 552–557.

Tuma, J. M. (1989). Mental health services for children. *American Psychologist,* 188–189.

U.S. Department of Health and Human Services. (2001). *Youth Violence: A Report of the Surgeon General—Executive Summary.* Rockville, MD: Author, Centers for Disease Control and Prevention, National Center for Injury Prevention and Control; Substance Abuse and Mental Health Services Administration, Center for Mental Health Services; and National Institutes of Health, National Institute of Mental Health.

U.S. Public Health Service. (2000). *Report of the Surgeon General's Conference on Children's Mental Health: A National Action Agenda.* Washington, DC: Author.

Vitiello, B. (2000). *A multi-site double-blind placebo-controlled trial of fluvoxamine for children and adolescents with anxiety disorders.* Presentation at the 40th annual meeting of the New Clinical Drug Evaluation Unit (NCDEU), Boca Raton, FL.

Vitiello, B., Bhatara, V. S., Jensen, P. S. (1999). Current knowledge and unmet needs in pediatric psychopharmacology. *Journal of Abnormal Child Psychology, 22,* 560–568.

Weisz, J. R., Donenberg, G. R., Han, S. S., & Weiss, B. (1995). Bridging the gap between laboratory and clinic in child and adolescent psychotherapy. *Journal of Consulting and Clinical Psychology, 63,* 688–701.

Weisz, J. R., & Hawley, K. M. (1998). Finding, evaluating, refining and applying empirically supported treatments for children and adolescents. *Journal of Clinical Child Psychology, 27,* 206–216.

Weisz, J. R., Huey, S. J., & Weersing, V. R. (1998). Psychotherapy outcome research with children and adolescents. *Advances in Clinical Child Psychology, 20,* 49–90.

Weisz, J. R., & Jensen, P. S. (1999). Efficacy and effectiveness of child and adolescent psychotherapy and pharmacotherapy. *Mental Health Services Research, 1,* 125–158.

Weisz, J. R., Weiss, B., Alicke, M. D., & Klotz, M. L. (1987). Effectiveness of psychotherapy with children and adolescents: A meta-analysis for clinicians. *Journal of Consulting and Clinical Psychology, 55*(4), 542–549.

Weisz, J. R., Weiss, B., Han, S. S., Granger, D. A., & Morton, T. (1995). Effects of psychotherapy with children and adolescents revisited: a meta-analysis of treatment outcome studies. *Psychological Bulletin, 117,* 450–468.

Wells, K. (1991). Placement of emotionally disturbed children in residential treatment: A review of placement criteria. *American Journal of Orthopsychiatry, 61,* 339–347.

Winsberg, B. G., Bialer, I., Kupietz, S., Botti, E., & Balka, E. B. (1980). Home versus hospital care of children with behavior disorders. *Archives of General Psychiatry, 37,* 413–418.

Zito, J. M., Safer, D. J., dosReis, S., Gardner, J. F., Boles, M., & Lynch, F. (2000). Trends in the prescribing of psychotropic medications to preschoolers. *Journal of the American Medical Association, 283,* 1025–1060.

Chapter 5

INTEGRATING SYSTEMS-OF-CARE VALUES INTO UNIVERSITY-BASED TRAINING

SUSAN L. MCCAMMON, JAMES R. COOK, AND RYAN P. KILMER

Epidemiological data from 1996 indicate that approximately 21% of U.S. children ages 9 to 18 met criteria for a diagnosable mental or addictive disorder associated with at least *minimal* impairment in functioning at home, in school, or with peers. When diagnostic criteria required *significant* functional impairment, the estimate reached 11%, which translates into 4 million youth. The estimate dropped to 5% when *extreme* functional impairment was the criterion (U.S. Department of Health and Human Services, 1999).

Children and youth with the most pronounced difficulties (i.e., those with severe emotional disturbances, or SED), typically evidence problems across multiple domains—at school, in the home, in their communities, and with friends. These children require the involvement of multiple services and systems to address their needs in such areas as mental health, education, special education, child welfare, health, substance abuse, vocational programming, and juvenile justice (Stroul & Friedman, 1986b). Despite the clear needs of these children and their families, their situations have been further complicated historically because many have either not been able to access care or have not received appropriate services (Stroul & Friedman, 1986b). For instance, Knitzer (1982) noted that approximately two thirds of children and youth with SED do not receive the services they need. Moreover, Stroul and Friedman (1986b) reported that many other children with SED were receiving inappropriate or excessively restrictive care. A more recent study reported that only 1 in 5 children with a serious emotional disturbance was treated through mental health specialty services, with the majority of these children receiving no services at all (Burns et al., 1995).

OVERVIEW OF SYSTEM-OF-CARE PRINCIPLES

In 1984, following multiple convergent reports suggesting the need for coordinated systems of care that would provide a range of services to children and families, for individual and group advocacy efforts, and for the appropriation of funds for a federal children's mental health initiative, the National Institute of Mental Health (NIMH) launched the Child and Adolescent Service System Program (CASSP; Stroul & Friedman, 1986b). The goal of the CASSP program, currently under the auspices of the Center for Mental Health Services (CMHS) of the Substance Abuse and Mental Health Services Administration, U.S. Department of Health and Human Services, is to assist in the development of systems of care for children and youth with SED (Stroul & Friedman, 1986b).

Early on, CASSP initiated efforts intended to further define the system-of-care concept (i.e., addressing its components, guiding principles, and reach), resulting in Stroul and Friedman's (1986a) influential monograph, *A System of Care for Severely Emotionally Disturbed Children and Youth.* Stroul and Friedman (1986b) provide a conceptual framework for a system of care and define it as follows:

> A system of care is a comprehensive spectrum of mental health and other necessary services which are organized into a coordinated network to meet the multiple and changing needs of children and adolescents with severe emotional disturbances and their families. (p. 3)

Stroul and Friedman (1986b) emphasize that the system of care "represents a philosophy about the way in which services should be delivered to children and their families" and that the actual components and configuration may vary across states and communities (p. xxii).

According to Stroul and Friedman (1986b), this philosophy is guided by three core values. First, the system of care must be *child centered* and *family focused* (i.e., the needs of the child and family must dictate the nature of the services provided), and there must be a commitment to adapt services to the child and family instead of expecting them to conform to an existing model, program, or configuration. Second, although services for those with SED have traditionally been limited to state hospitals, training schools, and other restrictive institutional care facilities, the system of care should be *community based* so that children are served via a network of services provided in less restrictive, more normative environments within, or close to, the child's home community. Thus, the locus of services and management and decision-making responsibility rest at the community level. Finally, the system of care should be *culturally competent,* with agencies, programs, and services that are responsive and sensitive to the diverse cultural, racial, and ethnic differences and special needs of the populations they serve, ensuring that children and families are served within their own unique and specific contexts.

In addition to these core values, Stroul and Friedman (1986b) delineate a number of guiding principles that reflect components of the philosophy, including the importance of individualized services, the least restrictive environments for service provision, well-integrated and coordinated care, the rights of children, and early identification and intervention for children with emotional disturbances (see Stroul & Friedman, 1986b, for a detailed description and discussion of these principles). Essentially, this framework is informed by the notion that the needs of children and youth with SED cannot effectively be met solely by the services available through the mental health system; rather, an array of mental health and other systems, reflecting multiple agencies, disciplines, and services, must work in concert to care for and optimally address the needs of these children and their families (Stroul & Friedman, 1986b).

EFFECTIVENESS OF THE SYSTEM OF CARE

The Comprehensive Community Mental Health Services for Children and Their Families Program provides grants to states, communities, territories, and Native American Indian tribes to improve and expand their system of care (SOC) to meet the needs of an estimated 4.5 to 6.3 million children with SED and their families (*Annual Report to Congress,* 1998). To date, through the 67 local systems of care that have received federal funding, 40,000 children and families have participated in SOC services (Holden, Friedman, & Santiago, 2001). Activities within this program have had two foci: (a) the development of infrastructure (e.g., the organizational arrangements and procedures to support the interventions and approaches to services) and (b) service delivery (*Annual Report to Congress,* 1998).

With the expanding adoption and implementation of the system-of-care philosophy and approach, efforts have been made to research this innovative model for mental health service provision. Most notably, a large-scale, longitudinal evaluation is being conducted nationally by MACRO International to determine the effectiveness of the SOC approach, assessing progress in child and family outcomes and exploring the system's impact on children with SED and their families (*Annual Report to Congress,* 1998). Clinical and functional outcome data were collected on a sample ($n = 200–400$) of the children and families for whom data were available at intake, 6 months, and 1 year. According to the 1998 report to Congress, summarizing data from the 3rd year of the national evaluation, preliminary findings showed notable improvements for children who were in services for at least 1 year. Outcomes included a reduction in behavioral and emotional problems (as measured by the Child Behavior Checklist [CBCL]; Achenbach, 1991), improvement in clinical functioning (measured by the Child and Adolescent Functional Assessment Scale [CAFAS]; Hodges, 2000), improvement in school attendance and performance, and reductions in law enforcement contacts. In addition, residential stability improved.

Some localities have reported dramatically significant program outcomes. For instance, the Crossroads Program of San Mateo County, California, reported a 61% reduction in the number of crimes committed by 101 youths on probation in the 12 months after entry into the program compared to the 12 months prior to entry (*Annual Report to Congress,* 1997). Furthermore, according to the report to Congress, since the 1995 inception of the ACCESS program in Alexandria, Virginia, residential placements for children with SED were reduced by over 48%, from 27 to 14. The report also cites Vermont's Families First Program, which provides crisis services for children who have been abused or neglected or who are characterized as delinquent or "unmanageable." Program evaluators reported that it costs an average of $18,334 per year to support a child placed in the custody of the state, whereas the average cost of serving a child in Families First is $600, representing an average savings of $17,734.

It should be noted that not all studies have documented cost savings and results superior to "usual care." Bickman's analyses of the Fort Bragg Continuum of Care (1996) and of the Stark County, Ohio, system of care (1997) did not find superior clinical outcomes (functioning and symptoms) compared to usual care. Data collection has just been completed for a study of three grantee and three comparison communities similar in demographics but differing in service delivery models. This will allow comparison between the outcomes in communities with a funded SOC grant and communities that do not have such grants (Holden et al., 2001). Further research is necessary for a compelling demonstration of the approach's efficacy. Important research tasks include the identification of what it is about clinical services that leads to better outcomes and the determination of the essential elements in a continuum of care (Hoagwood, 1997).

Current studies are under way to particularly assess the inclusion of an evidence-based treatment for selected children served within a CMHS-funded SOC; sustainability of SOC functioning following the completion of a funded demonstration project; and a study designed, conducted, analyzed and interpreted by a team of family members organized by the Federation of Families for Children's Mental Health (Holden et al., 2001). The creation of a principle-based SOC may be the necessary infrastructure for the provision of treatment, and providing evidence-based interventions probably is necessary as well (Burns, 2001). As De Carolis (2001) observed, the CMHS system-of-care initiative was designed to address the significant challenges presented by children with serious emotional disturbance to themselves, their families, and their communities. Perhaps, fueled by this increased federal investment over the past 15 years, mental health professionals can apply these principles of care to better serve these groups and to be more effective partners.

This chapter will now address (a) the need to update the training of mental health professionals working with children to enable them to function with a system-of-care approach; (b) state–community linkages that may facilitate new approaches to training; (c) movements in higher education that accord with updated approaches to training in mental health; (d) methods of integrating system-of-care values into university training, including curricula, teaching strategies, and applied research opportunities; and (e) the multiple and varied challenges involved for both service providers and universities in incorporating new training models.

NEED FOR UPDATED TRAINING OF CHILD MENTAL HEALTH PROFESSIONALS

There have been several recent calls for the training and education of human service workers to catch up with the changes of the past 15 years in the nature of treatment approaches, social context of needy populations, and operation of contemporary service delivery systems (Meyers, Kaufman, & Goldman, 1999; Macht & Whyte, 1999). The lack of adequate numbers of well-trained child mental health professionals has been identified as the "missing link in child mental health reform" (Hanley & Wright, 1995). Indeed, a 1992 survey of members of the Southern Human Resource Development (HRD) Consortium for Mental Health revealed that the vast majority of respondents (80%) believed their states lacked sufficient staff to implement community-based services for children (Pires, 1996).

There is also concern that traditional treatment efforts are largely inadequate in meeting the needs of children with serious emotional problems and their families. These children and families often have problems that are more severe and intense than in past decades, requiring assessment and intervention on multiple levels to address clinical needs within their social contexts (Roberts & Sobel, 1999). As Roberts and Sobel (1999) noted, today's new trainee is not likely to be working with toilet training issues or mild disobedience, but is more apt to be attempting to help a child or adolescent with multiple problems that require ecological intervention with family, school, juvenile justice, peer, and medical systems.

Although public colleges and universities supply most of the staff for these service systems and have an important responsibility to see that curricula and practica are relevant to public system needs, they are not seen as meeting this responsibility. A majority of respondents (71%) in the HRD study attributed the lack of staff preparation to the irrelevance of university curricula to state priority areas (Pires, 1996). Unfortunately, the situation has not improved markedly in the years since that study. Recently, universities were characterized as "ineffective and largely unchangeable for the delivery of high quality education and training needed in today's behavioral healthcare work" (The Santa Fe Summit on Behavioral Health, 2000). In fact, psychologists have been warned that if they do not adjust their training models to better fit emerging service-delivery models and marketplace realities, they risk becoming marginalized among child and adolescent mental health services providers (Task Force on Professional Child and Adolescent Psychology, 1998).

Medical care has also been criticized. It has been characterized as fragmented and directed toward meeting institutional efficiencies and provider preferences rather than fulfilling the complex needs of patients and families, especially those with chronic illness ("Moving Toward a New Health Care Model," 1999). Growing out of the needs of children with disabilities and their families, there has been an educational movement to introduce family-centered concepts into medical education and residency programs ("A View to the Future," 1999). Many patients and families today are seeking collaboration in the delivery of health care and a partnership approach with their health care providers. Innovations in medical education have included a focus on coordinating care for children with special needs, taking the perspective of family members, and promoting family resiliency ("Innovations in Medical Education," 1999).

Likewise, social work education has required revamping. Partnerships have been forged with public human service agencies to prepare social workers for contemporary family-centered practice. A job analysis conducted by the American Association of State Social Work Boards (1996) observed the changes in social work practice in the prior 10 years and noted an increasing focus on case management of multiservice delivery. The Council on Social Work Education began an initiative in 1992 to develop and expand the curricula and practica in social work education programs to make them more relevant to public sector practice (Zlotnik, 1997). Public agencies in the 1990s have struggled to "address rising caseloads, poorly trained staff, class action lawsuits, and the increasingly complex problems of families and children" (p. 18). Zlotnik observed that in the new century it is important to focus on the role of social work education in preparing frontline practitioners competent in delivering and evaluating family-focused, community-based services (including new modes of service delivery).

In 1999, the surgeon general's report on mental health (U.S. Department of Health and Human Services) urged mental health professionals to develop culturally competent services that transcend mental health's traditional "focus on the 'identified client' to embrace the community, cultural, and family context of a client" (p. 186). Community- and neighborhood-based social networks can provide important resources to help people cope with difficulties and improve their life circumstances. "A key to the success of mental health programs is how well they use and are connected with established, accepted, credible community supports" (p. 186). Partnerships with neighborhoods, faith communities, and other local groups must be developed, and these partnerships need to emphasize and build on the community's strengths. Enlisting community residents in solving problems that affect community residents, including those with severe emotional problems, is a key strategy that is alien to many mental health professionals. To function effectively in a system of care, mental health professionals need to learn how to build collaborative partnerships among diverse community groups. As one important starting point, the concept of "client" must expand to include the community and its various components.

Higher education's programs to train professionals are organized within departments that prepare students in a specific discipline based on standards set by national professional organizations and state licensing boards (Roberts, Rule, & Inocenti, 1998). Newer skills and competencies that are important in contemporary practice but not typically emphasized in mental health training programs or internships include issues of diversity and cultural responsiveness in assessment and intervention; interprofessional relationships and collaboration across multiple disciplines and service-delivery systems; empirically supported intervention strategies; program monitoring and evaluation and outcome assessment; systems intervention and evaluation; family support; and comprehensive strategies for addressing social issues affecting children, adolescents, and families (Roberts, Erickson, et al., 1998; Task Force on Professional Child and Adolescent Psychology, 1998). Clearly, it is time for universities to make sure that students across the range of disciplines that address needs of children with emotional disturbances and their families are trained in ways that enable them to work with families and other professionals to serve the multiple needs of the diverse set of clients within a system of care.

STATE–UNIVERSITY LINKAGES

Part of the stimulus for professional preparation programs to equip students to serve in changing service-delivery systems has come from potential employers—the state agencies responsible for operating and staffing the service systems. "There is a critical need for state and local officials, providers, parents, other key stakeholders, and university representatives to come together to address child workforce concerns and explore common ground for addressing them" (Pires, 1996, p. 295). Some believe that state leaders have not done enough to engage and support university efforts to meet public sector demands (Pires, 1996), but there have been some notable exceptions involving, for instance, alliances between state departments of mental health and educators in the mental health professions. These state–university collaborations have often focused on training in psychiatry (Moore & Sanchez, 1988; Talbott & Robinowitz, 1986). Moreover, in 1988 the National Institute of Mental Health announced the availability of funds for clinical and services research through a mechanism called the Public-Academic Liaison (PAL) for Research on Serious Mental Disorders (Bevilacqua, 1991). The PAL concept, which involves formal partnerships between the universities and the state or local service providers, has been further developed in North and South Carolina with the development of multidisciplinary PALs to improve public mental health services (Behar, 1995; Bray & Bevilacqua, 1993; Hernandez, Lineberger, & Baimbridge, 1992). In these initiatives, academic faculty have participated in providing public mental health system service and consequently developed curricula and placements to enhance student skills, and they have participated in collaborative research aimed at improving service delivery in the public sector. Other state mental health administrators, as in Pennsylvania (the Pennsylvania Child and Adolescent Service System Program Training and Technical Institutes, which is affiliated with Pennsylvania State University), have linked with universities for training initiatives (Meyers et al., 1999). To our knowledge, the North Carolina PAL council is currently the most comprehensive PAL network. It involves most of the UNC-system universities and a community college. The programs, developed within the university and college departments, widely involve the faculty, courses, and programs of participating units. We hope that this integration of SOC principles and practices into the fabric of the participating universities will contribute to the sustainability of this initiative.

Initiated in 1994, within one of the CMHS-funded Comprehensive Community Mental Health Services for Children and Their Families Program sites, a linkage was formalized between the Child and Family Services Section of the North Carolina Department of Mental Health, Developmental Disabilities, and Substance Abuse Services; service systems from Pitt, Edgecombe, and Nash Counties; and East Carolina University. Subsequently, North Carolina developed two additional CMHS-funded initiatives and linked them with other universities and the community college system. The resulting PAL council now includes partners from the state Child and Family Services Section; service providers; family advocates; and university faculty from East Carolina University, University of North Carolina (UNC) at Greensboro, UNC at Charlotte, Appalachian State University, Sandhills Community College, UNC at Chapel Hill, and Western Carolina University. (For a description of the initial project, see chapter 5 in Meyers et al., 1999.) Our participation in the North Carolina (NC) PAL initiative and our attempts to update training efforts at each of our respective universities has informed our writing of this chapter.

HIGHER EDUCATION MOVEMENTS COMPATIBLE WITH UPDATING MENTAL HEALTH PROFESSIONAL TRAINING

The development of a professional workforce that can fit into the roles specified by a system-of-care approach requires nontraditional training components. Professionals need to work effectively with other disciplines, families, and informal supports in the community, requiring a familiarity with the strengths and weaknesses of these groups, knowledge of their languages (including professional jargon), and a genuine appreciation of the contributions they can make. Training content needs to be different as well, because needed interventions extend beyond the individual child and family level. Organizations need to change, as do communities, since the degree to which children and families are successful is largely dependent on how well the community provides various supports for families. Thus, professionals need to learn how to help these organizations and communities change how they operate.

Although this training is nontraditional, there are educational movements consistent with and supportive of the development of professionals able to function and assume leadership roles within systems of care. Although grants and contracts have provided initial support for our work to date, these support sources are time-limited. Therefore, we have identified contemporary educational movements compatible with our goals as vehicles for sustaining our curriculum reform efforts. The first of these movements is the growing emphasis on *service learning,* or *civic engagement,* which places emphasis on students becoming engaged in the community so they can better learn to function and effect positive changes within it. A second movement is the series of efforts to develop *interprofessional education programs* that involve different disciplines in teaching and learning about complex human problems. The third movement is the development of *university–community partnerships* that may center on service learning, interprofessional education, applied research, or other common interests. Each of these movements will be described, and suggestions will be provided regarding ways that these movements can be used to develop training that supports systems of care.

Service Learning

Experiential education emphasizes learning through personal experience. Service learning is one type of experiential education in which students are involved in organized community service that addresses local needs while developing their academic skills. In 1971, the National Society for Experiential Education (NSEE), formerly called the National Society for Internships and Experiential Education, was created to support the development and expansion of experiential education programs in schools (NSEE, 2000).

Although federal support for service and service learning dates back to the 1930s and the Civilian Conservation Corps, the development of the Corporation for National Service in 1993 has spurred service-learning programs through Learn and Serve grants and funding for state and local service learning and community service organizations. Greater public support for and attention to service learning has resulted from a number of national summits and conferences on service that have attracted bipartisan presidential support (Corporation for National Service, 2000).

Universities have also recognized the importance of service learning and have developed the Campus Compact, which now has over 500 member colleges and universities. Started by the presidents of 23 universities, Campus Compact originally focused on student volunteer service, but more recently has shifted its emphasis to include service learning and the integration of service into college curricula (Campus Compact, 2000).

Interdisciplinary/Interprofessional Education

A second significant movement in training to address complex social problems is the focus on interprofessional education. This movement (also called *interdisciplinary* or *multiprofessional education*) has recognized that traditional department/discipline-based training programs are limited in their ability to address complex problems (Schorr & Schorr, 1989). More integrative solutions do not require the creation of a new discipline, but rather new ways for practitioners in existing disciplines to work together effectively (Short, 1997). Thus, interprofessional education engages a group of students or workers from different educational backgrounds in the process of learning together and working together to address complex human problems (Brandon & Knapp, 1999; Goble, 1994). This can involve preservice education, in which teams of university faculty collaborate to teach courses that involve students from different disciplines, addressing particular topics such as child abuse, policy analysis, or chemical dependency. Some interprofessional courses are designed to help students discover the human service field in which they have most interest; others are designed to help developing professionals learn to appreciate and most effectively use the strengths of professionals from other disciplines. Interprofessional education efforts can also include continuing education, in which professionals are cross-trained to develop an understanding of the ways other professionals approach problems. Casto (1994) has suggested that students progress through a series of stages in their ability to work together, from sensitivity through openness, engagement, and cooperation.

Commonly, interprofessional education efforts are combined with community service integration efforts. Thus, community agencies often serve as learning laboratories for the interprofessional education preservice or inservice students. Service learning, then, is often a critical component of interprofessional education, with students working in teams in the community to provide integrated services to clients.

There have been a number of national and international efforts to foster interprofessional education. Since 1973, Ohio's Commission on Interprofessional Education and Practice has linked practitioners and academics from such professions as education, law, medicine, nursing, public administration, and theology. Out of this grew the National Consortium on Interprofessional Education and Practice in 1985. Currently, over 60 institutions of higher education are in the process of enacting interprofessional reforms (Briar-Lawson, 1998). Notable interprofessional efforts have been developed at the University of Southern California, the University of Washington, and Baylor University, among others (Casto, 1994). In addition, the World Health Organization has developed a position paper on multiprofessional education in health (WHO Study Group, 1988), the United Kingdom's Council for the Advancement of InterProfessional Education (CAIPE) has worked to develop collaborative practice among health care professionals since 1987, and the *Journal of Interprofessional Practice* was created in 1988 to serve as an outlet for scholarly work on collaborative practice (Goble, 1994).

University–Community Partnerships

Partnerships between universities and communities are quite varied, frequently including service learning as a significant component. Interprofessional education efforts, when they are paired with community agencies and organizations that provide opportunities for applying learning in integrative settings, almost always involve some university–community partnerships. Yet, community–campus partnerships can also be quite extensive, going far beyond service learning and interprofessional education into the realm of applied research and community and economic development.

Some universities have long histories of partnerships with communities. In particular, cooperative extension services at land grant universities have for many years provided a range of services and research expertise to communities, including the National Children, Youth and Families at Risk (CYFAR) initiative, which supports community-based programs in all states for at-risk children and their families (Cooperative State Research, Education, and Extension Service; CSREES, 2000). In addition, University Affiliated Programs (UAPs), housed in research universities in every state, work with people with developmental disabilities, their families, state and local government agencies, and community providers to provide training, technical assistance, service, and research (American Association of University Affiliated Programs, 2000). The Department of Housing and Urban Development's Office of University Partnerships supports university–community partnerships, and its University Partnerships Clearinghouse disseminates information about universities' contributions to local community revitalization efforts (U.S. Department of Housing and Urban Development, 2000). More recently, the Community-Campus Partnership for Health (CCPH) was founded in 1996 to foster health-promoting partnerships between communities and educational institutions (Community-Campus Partnerships for Health, 2000).

Community–university partnerships have commonly evolved in universities nestled in deteriorated urban neighborhoods, where the university was compelled by some combination of moral and civic responsibility, economic reality, or community pressure to mobilize the university's resources to help improve the surrounding community. However, universities have increasingly seen the benefits of broad partnerships that can (a) improve training through service learning opportunities, (b) assist in the development of research projects addressing important community issues, and (c) generate political and social support for the university through the assistance provided to the community (Cox, 2000). Furthermore, partnerships can help a university shape its mission to better serve the surrounding community.

These three movements are each quite consistent with the development of better trained professionals who can function effectively within systems of care. Partnerships between universities and communities are critically needed to develop better training and better systems of care. Current movements to develop and expand service learning, interprofessional education, and broad-based partnerships can be marshaled to address the needs of children with severe emotional problems and their families. The values inherent in these movements are highly consistent with the values expressed by proponents of systems of care. Consequently, it is important to draw on them to strengthen training that can improve services for children and families.

METHODS OF INTEGRATING SOC VALUES INTO UNIVERSITIES

To successfully train a new workforce that is competent to function collaboratively with other professionals and parents and that will be able to incorporate SOC values into practice, it is crucial to find ways to integrate the values and practices into the ongoing training in a variety of disciplines. This section describes some of the strategies that the PAL efforts in North Carolina have undertaken to integrate SOC values and principles into training. Although the examples come primarily from psychology, it is important to note that a wide range of disciplines can be and have been involved in curriculum development efforts. Psychology, social work, special education, counseling, and nursing are among the likely suspects in efforts to address the needs of children with severe emotional disturbances, but criminal justice, medicine, recreation, education, performing and visual arts, communication, marketing, sociology, public administration, and other disciplines can make important contributions to the development of systems of care to serve children and families. Furthermore, faculty members and practitioners in each of these disciplines can be found who are interested in addressing the needs of children and who recognize that they require additional knowledge and skills for dealing with children with special needs.

Four main strategies have been used to integrate SOC values into university cultures: (a) integration of the content into existing courses, (b) development of new courses and programs, (c) involvement of parents and professionals in teaching, and (d) development of applied research and evaluation projects. Each of these strategies is described here, using examples from our experience in North Carolina.

Integration Into Existing Courses

Knowledge and skills needed for these new model services can be readily infused into existing courses and programs without significant disruption of the extant curricula. For example, at the undergraduate level, the concepts, goals, and practices of a system of care can be incorporated into psychology coursework ranging from Child/Developmental Psychopathology to Adjustment, from Community Psychology to topics in treatment, from Abnormal Psychology to practica. Other disciplines, including social work, education, counseling, special education, sociology, and nursing can also easily incorporate the guiding ideas or practical ideas of a system of care into their offerings. For other disciplines, such as music therapy or recreational therapy, basic information on ways to meet the needs of families, issues of cultural competence, family involvement, behavioral management, and appreciation for and understanding of other disciplines can help increase the broader community capacity for dealing with children with severe emotional disturbance and their families. We have found, for example, that arts teachers (in schools or community groups) frequently have daily contact with special needs children. These teachers receive very little or no training in dealing with these children or in working with their parents, so they often welcome the opportunity to receive preparation or instruction.

Concepts related to a system-of-care philosophy can be included in both course syllabi and class requirements (e.g., exams, research papers) as well as integrated throughout course curriculum via lectures, class discussions and exercises, articles (e.g., describing wraparound services, working with families, promoting wellness), and case presentations. For instance, in courses that include psychological disorders as a prominent topic area (e.g., Abnormal Psychology, Child Psychopathology, Adjustment), an early class exercise could involve the presentation of various scenarios, or minicases, with posed questions centering around what is abnormal or disordered, what circumstances raise concerns, and what students would do if they were professionals meeting with the family. Such discussions can facilitate the introduction of issues involving context and individual differences and can lay the groundwork for the consideration of important values such as cultural competence and an appreciation and understanding of diversity. Efforts could also be made to direct student attention to the child and family's strengths and competencies as well as their difficulties.

As another means of introducing primary components of the system-of-care philosophy, discussions of the process of treatment and desired qualities or characteristics in a treatment provider may be transitioned into a larger consideration of the SOC approach. For example, students can be asked, "If you were looking for a therapist, what kinds of qualities would you want? What would you look for, and what would be important in your work with the service provider?" Following a general discussion, one could later pose more pointed questions, contrasting system-of-care values with more traditional approaches (e.g., "If you were a parent of a child experiencing difficulties, which would you prefer—to be included in treatment planning and a part of the decision-making process for your child and family, or would you rather I hand you a plan to sign that I, your caseworker, and a few other professionals developed? To which circumstance would you likely be most receptive? Do you want someone who is going to dictate to you and your family the plan for your treatment?") Such inquiries can help guide the discussion, addressing the need for an approach that is respectful, inclusive, and sensitive to issues of diversity, and underscoring the need for caregivers and families to have input into service planning, service goals, and decision making. Role-playing these scenarios also can help students understand how families feel when treated in different ways.

Other discussions or lectures can emphasize ways to identify and build on the strengths of children, families, and communities, and to expose students to intervention and treatment approaches used to meet the needs of children and families, as well as to introduce strategies for the prevention of maladaptation and the promotion of wellness. Specific lecture topics may include values and guiding principles of the system-of-care philosophy; issues of cultural competence; early intervention, prevention, and wellness enhancement, including a consideration of successful programs; the impact of children's difficulties (e.g., SED) on the family system; the role of parents and professionals in the system of care; and the process of treatment. Furthermore, in smaller, upper-level undergraduate courses, exercises and role plays can also be used to demonstrate treatment team meetings or the dynamics contributing to the need for a new approach. Guest speakers (e.g., caregivers, professionals) can describe their personal experiences and share their insights to help make the material real and germane for the students.

Graduate-level courses, with their emphasis on skill building and training, can even more actively integrate the material and expose students to these new ideas in greater depth. For instance, in courses with an applied, or service, learning thrust, students can learn, firsthand, strategies for coordinated service delivery and early intervention. In addition to readings, discussions, or lectures to introduce system-of-care components in their classes, instructors of group practicum courses in assessment or treatment can, for example, build the values and principles directly into their supervision, assignments, and course exercises. Student cases can be discussed, with a focus on child-centered, family-focused practice, addressing the unique strengths, needs, and issues involved in a given case. Relatedly, faculty can facilitate the development of student skills in engaging parents and families as participants in treatment planning and delivery, and they can help students consider the specific nature of their cases and tailor individualized recommendations in their report writing. Warren (1994) and Wasow (1994) offer suggestions for training clinicians to work with families.

Developing New Courses and Programs

Integrating SOC content into core curricula of training programs has been our main strategy to expose the greatest possible number of students and faculty to relevant values, core concepts, and skills. We hope this helps to sustain our initiative. However, we have also developed new, elective courses. Although these courses do not reach as many students, the students who enroll in them have the opportunity for greater depth of exposure and application of SOC content and skills.

At most of our North Carolina PAL campuses, these new courses have included an interdisciplinary course focusing on collaborative practice in systems of care, and field practica provide an opportunity to work collaboratively. The development of one of the interdisciplinary SOC courses (including the syllabus and issues involved in the coteaching of it), is described elsewhere (Dosser, Handron, McCammon, Powell, & Spencer, 2001). At the East Carolina University and the UNC-Greensboro campuses, the course is offered by a multidisciplinary faculty team (psychology, social work, nursing, child development, and family relations), which includes parents as faculty team members. The course often serves as a focal point for gathering SOC literature and training materials and for the university and parent faculty to work together. As parents prepare course materials and become familiar with campus, they often make themselves available as speakers or resources to additional classes. Practicum settings in which SOC skills are learned and rehearsed have offered the service and energy of students to community initiatives. In return, the students have received supervised experience in community settings. For example, at UNC-Greensboro, a newly developed practicum at Mary's House permits students to assist in providing family-centered care in an interdisciplinary setting to women who have substance abuse problems and their children. The WE CARE Too program pairs East Carolina University Recreational Therapy students with families of children with special needs at the local Boys and Girls Club. This practicum within a skills course was developed to integrate SOC principles into the provision of recreational therapy services (Groff, Spencer, & McCammon, in press). Evaluation of this program has found that, across a semester, students became more realistic about their skill levels and about developing programs that could be implemented in a community setting.

Involvement of Parents and Professionals in Teaching

It is important for teaching professionals in mental health–related fields to recognize that the parents and families of children with special needs may be among their most valuable community-based partners. Strickland (1997) noted the importance of professionals who are not only interprofessionally trained, but also family centered. Unfortunately, traditional training programs have done little to prepare professionals to work collaboratively with family members (Jivanjee & Friesen, 1997); the movement of expanded family roles in systems of care has outstripped professional training and practice (Friesen & Stephens, 1998). Our educational programs need to help students and trainees to view parents not simply as causal agents of their children's mental health problems or as targets for behavior change and parent training, but to consider the needs, strengths, resources, and circumstances of the families with whom they work and collaborate with them within a partnership model.

We include this approach in assigned readings and class lectures and discussions in our teaching, and we have also found the use of the Parents in Residence model to be especially effective. In the North Carolina PAL initiatives, we have developed variations of the Parents in Residence (PIR) concept, in which parents of youth with mental health concerns work together with university faculty to develop the content of university curricula and coteach classes and workshops. (The development of the PIR at East Carolina University is described by Osher, deFur, Nava, Spencer, and Toth-Dennis, 1999.) Parents offer their experiences as caregivers and as consumers attempting to navigate service systems, thus providing valuable information for service providers in training. The modeling of parent-professional partnerships by the PIR in the course is also important, helping to bring the lecture and reading material into a real-life context for students. In evaluating the impact of parent involvement in a graduate social work class at the University of Connecticut, Johnson found that students were less blaming of parents following the module in which parents taught (McCammon, Johnson, Groff, Spencer, & Osher, 2001). Students also increased their endorsement of openly sharing information with parents, validating statements about parents, valuing psychotropic medication for children and adolescents, and offering specific instructions for coping with behaviors of the children (McCammon et al., 2001). At East Carolina University, we have found similar results in an interdisciplinary graduate course cotaught by a parent. Students have evaluated the course, and especially the parent involvement, very favorably over a number of semesters. The university faculty and the parents have greatly benefited from the partnership as well, with faculty finding their base of knowledge enriched and expanded and parents being affirmed by their reception from students and by the prospect of influencing professionals in training.

Applied Research and Evaluation

Although universities continue to claim that the dissemination of knowledge is their primary function, faculty are more likely to be rewarded for efforts to create new knowledge. At larger, doctoral-granting institutions especially, research and scholarly work is often the primary basis for faculty promotion, tenure, compensation, and status. Partnerships that fail to recognize this fact can have significant difficulties engaging faculty, especially junior faculty who need to demonstrate research productivity simply to survive as academicians. Thus, if system-of-care values and principles are to be successfully incorporated into university cultures, it is important to identify mechanisms for faculty members to develop research projects that can simultaneously advance knowledge, provide needed training, and serve families in systems of care.

Systems of care yield multiple and varied opportunities for research. First, as with any relatively new approach to treatment, studies are needed to evaluate the impact and efficacy of the model under a range of circumstances. This is particularly true in a system of care, because broad principles and values are prescribed, but the specific methods for addressing needs are not. Furthermore, relatively little research has been conducted to identify the relative benefits of particular modes of treatment in a system-of-care approach.

Research possibilities are particularly extensive and accessible in communities where community mental health system funds have been used to develop systems of care. Comprehensive data sets are collected and maintained for the ongoing SOC national evaluation, and these data can be made available to universities working in partnership with the communities. In some communities, university faculty or staff have participated in the system-of-care project's data collection. For example, the Multiagency Integrated System of Care in Santa Barbara County linked with the University of California at Santa Barbara School of Education. Students in the joint counseling/clinical/school psychology doctoral program assist in evaluating the service program. They also help to communicate the evaluation results, creating a feedback loop that informs staff training and service provision (Meyers et al., 1999). At several universities this has permitted the identification of relevant research questions for both faculty and students (theses, dissertations) using these data. Notably, many communities have found it particularly important to develop applied research efforts to assess change, because the national evaluation is not designed to provide detailed feedback to local sites.

The variables of interest for applied research and evaluation in systems of care cut across several levels of analysis. Improvement in the functioning of targeted children in systems of care is clearly important. However, since the SOC's goal is to provide family-focused services, the impact on the entire family, including siblings, is also meaningful and relevant. Siblings, for example, may be at elevated risk because they share risk factors with the child experiencing problems and are influenced by that child's impact on the family. That is, in the context of coping with the identified child's needs and difficulties, siblings may experience decreased parental attention and may be subjected to increased family turmoil and other stresses. Children vary in their response to such risk factors; some siblings adapt successfully and do well at home and at school, whereas others experience problems. Enhancing understanding of the relationship between childhood risk and individual differences in adjustment, particularly those factors and processes that contribute to healthy adaptation in the face of adversity (i.e., resilience) can provide useful knowledge in the education and training of service providers, policymakers, and parents about how best to meet the needs of these children and families and offer preventive interventions for at-risk children, youth, and families. At a more systemic level of analysis, the nature and methods of collaboration across service providers, families, and informal supports could significantly influence the outcomes of children and families. Consequently, it may be important to assess the degree to which these system changes (i.e., inclusion of caregiver and family in service planning, interdisciplinary collaboration, organizational support for the new model, and new interorganizational relationships) are occurring and their relationship to changes at the child and family level.

The development of research projects addressing these levels of analysis in systems of care should, as much as possible, adopt a participatory research philosophy to remain consistent with the guiding principles of systems of care. Parents and service providers have important roles to play in the development of questions to be answered, hypotheses to be tested, and variables of interest. They are also often quite eager to receive prompt reports and feedback about the impact of an intervention program or other services on children, families, and the system. In a study conducted by the second and third author examining risk and resilience among siblings of target children in a system of care, caregivers and service providers were engaged in the project from the outset, helping develop research questions and the procedures for data collection, participant recruitment, and data interpretation. Parents were our strongest allies in conducting the study, because they had observed differences among their own children and wanted to know not only *how* siblings were doing but *why,* given that they viewed these siblings as frequently overlooked by them and service providers in light of the child with SED's needs. The local family advocacy group benefited from an unforeseen outcome of the research—the study helped them access parents with SED children whom they had not yet been able to contact. Moreover, they were interested in obtaining information about and from these parents, as they believed such information could support their advocacy efforts on behalf of the families (Kilmer & Cook, 2001). Such experiences underscore the need for researchers to invest time at the front end of research, cultivating relationships with consumer groups and developing the partnerships that enable the research effort to meet multiple needs.

CHALLENGES IN INSTITUTIONALIZING NEW TRAINING MODELS

Although the needs for and benefits of university training in systems-of-care principles and practices are quite clear, there are many challenges and obstacles for developing successful partnerships and implementing new training models in universities. Significant obstacles exist on both sides of the campus–community divide. For instance, universities can be extremely slow to change because of rigid bureaucratic structures and faculty who may be detached from current practice. Among professionals, many service providers prefer to adhere to traditional methods that are known and comfortable for them and their organizations.

Service Provider Challenges

Unfortunately, change among practicing service providers moves slowly. Not only are professionals bound in some ways by the training they received, perhaps many years ago, but also by the institutional contexts in which they work. In a discussion of a community model for physician, educator, and parent collaboration for children with developmental and behavioral disorders, collaborative barriers included interdisciplinary process problems, lack of appropriate education, professional role confusion, difficulty in knowing how to involve parents, and difficulties from the use of terminology (Ulrey, Hudler, Marshall, Wuori, & Cranston, 1987).

New roles for professionals are required, altering the relationships professionals have had with families and other professionals. This change may be uncomfortable, and it requires training that many organizations are reluctant to provide. Often, professionals are busy responding to crises and are overwhelmed by the ongoing demands of their agencies and clients. Those who have been working for many years may have seen many unsuccessful attempts to improve service provision, leading them to give up hope that change in their organizations is possible. In addition, allowing families to have greater decision-making power and responsibility can be threatening to professionals, who feel accountable for decisions made and their consequences. In a national survey of programs serving youth with serious emotional disturbances, the use of an interagency team approach was identified as the factor that most contributes to the success of individualized programs. However, the report noted the greatest challenge to their implementation is the need to reeducate and change the attitudes of providers trained in traditional component-based thinking (MacFarquhar, Dowrick, & Risley, 1993). Finally, even if they desire change, many individuals and organizations do not know how to successfully break out of traditional models.

University Challenges

Although service providers have many difficulties effecting significant change in their practice, changes in training can be even more difficult. As McCroskey (1998, p. 5) has indicated, "Although many faculty members think of themselves as ahead of the times, institutions of higher education take their roles as protectors of traditional wisdom very seriously and are notoriously slow to respond to contemporary shifts in thinking." Universities are structured by specialized disciplines and subdisciplines, and publishing in conjunction with others from the same discipline is the most highly rewarded. While interdisciplinary work is often viewed as important, organizational structures and rewards seldom support interdisciplinary work. In addition, accrediting bodies often require narrowly defined training and supervision that limits contact with professionals from other disciplines. This can lead to a disciplinary arrogance that interferes with professionals' ability to work effectively with other disciplines. Furthermore, the integration of service, teaching, and research that can be very effective in community partnerships is not the most effective way for university faculty to build reputations and publish, because publication outlets tend to focus more on research findings.

If we are to successfully integrate training in systems of care into training that will create an able, effective workforce, significant institutional support will be required from universities and service providing agencies (Short, 1997). Improved evaluative criteria will be needed to help assess how changes in training are related to changes in student knowledge and skills and subsequent changes in service delivery and child and family outcomes. However, these changes are not likely to be made at the university if service providers do not (a) demand that these changes occur and (b) support the changes in their own agencies so that they can serve as learning laboratories for students. If students and service providers view this as strong theory but not applicable to and supported in practice, then it will not take place.

Partnerships between universities, service providers, and families and family advocacy groups are critical to the development of effective systems of care to ensure that the values and principles are enacted. Universities can help ensure that the newly trained workforce of the coming years is able to function effectively in a system of care. However, this training cannot occur without the support of university administrations, service providers, parents, and accrediting bodies all working in concert.

REFERENCES

Achenbach, T. M. (1991). *Manual for the child behavior checklist and 1991 profile.* Burlington: University of Vermont, Department of Psychiatry.

American Association of State Social Boards. (1996, September/October). *Continuing education = continuing competence* (5, p. 2). Culpepper, VA: Author.

American Association of University Affiliated Programs. (2000). Retrieved from www.aauap .org/aauapbrochure0799.htm

Annual report to Congress on the evaluation of the comprehensive community mental health services for children and their families program. (1997). Atlanta, GA: Macro International Inc.

Annual report to Congress on the evaluation of the comprehensive community mental health services for children and their families program. (1998). Atlanta, GA: Macro International Inc.

Behar, L. (1995). Implementing and monitoring case management: A state agency perspective. In B. J. Friesen & J. Poertner (Eds.). *From case management to service coordination for children with emotional, behavioral, or mental disorders: Building on family strengths.* Baltimore: Brookes.

Bevilacqua, J. D. (1991). The NIMH public-academic liaison (PAL) research initiative: An update. *Hospital and Community Psychiatry, 42,* 71.

Bickman, L. (1996). A continuum of care: More is not always better. *American Psychologist, 51,* 689–701.

Bickman, L., Summerfelt, W. T., & Noser, K. (1997). Comparative outcomes of emotionally disturbed children and adolescents in a system of services and usual care. *Psychiatry Services, 48,* 1543–1548.

Brandon, R. N., & Knapp, M. S. (1999). Interprofessional education and training: Transforming professional preparation to transform human services. *The American Behavioral Scientist, 42,* 876–891.

Bray, J. D., & Bevilacqua, J. J. (1993). A multidisciplinary public-academic liaison to improve public mental health services in South Carolina. *Hospital and Community Psychiatry, 44,* 985–990.

Briar-Lawson, K. (1998). Community collaboration and service integration: Models and challenges. In McCroskey, J. & Einbinder, S. D., *Universities and communities: Remaking professional and interprofessional education for the next century.* Westport, CT: Praeger.

Burns, B. J. (2001). Commentary on the special issue on the national evaluation of the comprehensive community mental health services for children and their families program. *Journal of Emotional and Behavioral Disorders, 9,* 71–76.

Burns, B. J., Costello, E. J., Angold, A., Tweed, D., Stangl, D., Farmer, E. M., & Erkanli, A. (1995). Children's mental health service use across service sectors. *Health Affairs, 14,* 147–159.

Campus Compact. (2000). Retrieved from www.compact.org/about/

Casto, M. (1994). Interprofessional work in the USA: education and practice. In A. Leathard (Ed.), *Going inter-professional: Working together for health and welfare.* London and New York: Routledge.

Community-Campus Partnerships for Health (2000). Retrieved from www.futurehealth.ucsf .edu/ccph.html

Cooperative State Research, Education, and Extension Service (CSREES). (2000). Retrieved from www.4h-usa.org/4h/cyfar/intro.htm

Corporation for National Service. (2000). Retrieved from www.cns.gov

Cox, D. (2000). Developing a framework for understanding university-community partnerships. *Cityscape: A Journal of Policy Development and Research, 5*(1). Retrieved from www .huduser.org/periodicals/cityscpe/vol5num1/ch1.html

De Carolis, G. (2001). Introduction to special issue. *Journal of Emotional and Behavioral Disorders, 9,* 2–3.

Dosser, D. A., Jr., Handron, D. S., McCammon, S. L., Powell, J. Y., & Spencer, S. S. (2001). Challenges and strategies for teaching collaborative interdisciplinary practice in children's mental health care. *Families, Systems, & Health, 19,* 65–82.

Friesen, B. J., & Stephens, B. (1998). Expanding family roles in the system of care: Research and practice. In M. H. Epstein, K. Kutash, & A. Duchnowski (Eds.). *Outcomes for children and youth with emotional and behavioral disorders and their families: Programs and evaluation best practices* (pp. 231–259). Austin, TX: PRO-ED.

Goble, R. (1994). Multi-professional education in Europe: An overview. In A. Leathard (Ed.), *Going inter-professional: Working together for health and welfare.* London and New York: Routledge.

Groff, D., Spencer, S., & McCammon, S. (in press). Building a system of care: Partnering with public agencies to provide recreational therapy to children with emotional/behavioral problems and their families. *Trends in Therapeutic Recreation Programming.* Arlington, VA: NTRS.

Hanley, J. H., & Wright, H. (1995). Child mental health professionals: The missing link in child mental health reform. *Journal of Child and Family Studies, 4*(4), 383–388.

Hernandez, J. T., Lineberger, H. P., & Baimbridge, T. (1992). Development of an innovative child and youth mental health training and services delivery project. *Hospital and Community Psychiatry, 43,* 375–379.

Hoagwood, K. (1997). Interpreting nullity: "The Fort Bragg experiment—A comparative success or failure? *American Psychologist, 52,* 546–550.

Hodges, K. (2000). *The child and adolescent functional assessment scale (CAFAS) self-training manual.* Available from: Kay Hodges, 2140 Old Earhart Road, Ann Arbor, MI 48105.

Holden, E. W., Friedman, R. M., & Santiago, R. L. (2001). Overview of the national evaluation of the comprehensive community mental health services for children and their families program. *Journal of Emotional and Behavioral Disorders, 9,* 4–12.

Innovations in medical education. (1999, Fall). *Advances in Family-Centered Care, 5*(1), 6–12.

Jivanjee, P. R., & Friesen, B. J. (1997). Shared expertise: Family participation in interprofessional training. *Journal of Emotional and Behavioral Disorders, 5,* 205–211.

Kilmer, R. P., & Cook, J. R. (February, 2001). *Risk and resilience: Adjustment of siblings of children with serious emotional disturbances.* Poster session presented at the 14th Annual Research Conference: A System of Care for Children's Mental Health: Expanding the Research Base, Tampa, FL.

Knitzer, J. (1982). *Unclaimed children: The failure of public responsibility to children and adolescents in need of mental health services.* Washington, DC: Children's Defense Fund.

MacFarquhar, K. W., Dowrick, P. W., & Risley, T. R. (1993). Individualizing services for seriously emotionally disturbed youth: A nationwide survey. *Administration and Policy in Mental Health, 20*(3), 165–174.

Macht, J., & Whyte, D. A. (1999). Human services: History and recent influences. In H. S. Harris & D. C. Maloney (Eds.), *Human services: Contemporary issues and trends* (2nd ed.). Boston: Allyn & Bacon.

McCammon, S. L., Johnson, H. C., Groff, D., Spencer, S., Osher, T. W. (2001). Topical discussion overview: The power of parent-professor partnerships. In Newman, C. (Ed.), *A System of Care for Children's Mental Health: Expanding the Research Base, 9th Annual Conference Proceedings.* Tampa, FL: University of South Florida, Florida Mental Health Institute, Research and Training Center for Children's Mental Health.

McCroskey, J. (1998). Remaking professional and interprofessional education. In J. McCroskey & S. D. Einbinder, *Universities and communities: Remaking professional interprofessional education for the next century.* Westport, CT: Praeger.

Meyers, J., Kaufman, M., Goldman, S. (1999). *Promising practices: Training strategies for serving children with serious emotional disturbance and their families in a system of care; Systems of care: promising practices in children's mental health* (1998 series, Vol. 4). Washington, DC: Center for Effective Collaboration and Practice, American Institutes for Research.

Moore, J. D., & Sanchez, A. M. (1988). *Innovation in collaboration: Vignettes of state/university collaboration to improve mental health systems.* Boulder, CO: Western Interstate Commission for Higher Education Mental Health Program.

Moving toward a new health care model. (1999, Fall). *Advances in Family-Centered Care 5,*(1), 2–4.

National Society for Experiential Education. (2000). Retrieved from www.nsee.org/

Osher, T., deFur, E., Nava, C., Spencer, S., & Toth-Dennis, D. (1999). New roles for families in systems of care. *Systems of care: Promising practices in children's mental health* (1998 series, Vol. 1). Washington, DC: Center for Effective Collaboration and Practice, American Institutes for Research.

Pires, S. (1996). Human resource development. In B. Stroul (Ed.), *Children's mental health: Creating systems of care in a changing society.* Baltimore: Brookes.

Roberts, M. C., Erickson, M. T., LaGreca, A. M., Russ, S. W., Vargas, L. A., Carlson, C. I., Friedman, R. M., Lemanek, K. L., Schroeder, C. S., & Wohlford, P. F. (1998). A model for training psychologists to provide services for children and adolescents. *Professional Psychology: Research and Practice, 29,* 239–299.

Roberts, R. N., Rule, S., & Innocenti, M. S. (1998). *Strengthening the family-professional partnership in services for young children.* Baltimore: Brookes.

Roberts, M. C., & Sobel, A. B. (1999). Training in clinical child psychology: Doing it right. *Journal of Clinical Child Psychology, 28,* 482–489.

The Santa Fe Summit on Behavioral Health (2000, March 15–18). Changing the actions, strategies & behaviors of clinicians, consumers, families, & organizations: The critical role of education and training. Summary of Dialogue Groups.

Schorr, L. B., & Schorr, D. (1989). *Within our reach: Breaking the cycle of disadvantage.* New York: Anchor Books.

Short, R. J. (1997). Education and training for integrated practice: Assumptions, components and issues. In R. J. Illback, C. T. Cobb, & H. M. Joseph (Eds.), *Integrated services for children and families: Opportunities for psychological practice.* Washington: American Psychological Association.

Strickland, B. (1997). Applying lessons learned: Family-centered, interprofessional education and practice. In K. K. Bishop, M. S. Taylor, & P. Arango (Eds.), *Partnerships at work: Lessons learned from programs and practices of families, professionals and communities.* Burlington, VT: Partnerships for Change.

Stroul, B. A., & Friedman, R. M. (1986a). A system of care for children and youth with severe emotional disturbances. Washington, DC: Georgetown University Child Development Center, CASSP Technical Assistance Center.

Stroul, B. A., & Friedman, R. M. (1994; 1986b). A system of care for children and youth with severe emotional disturbances (revised edition). Washington, DC: Georgetown University Child Development Center, CASSP Technical Assistance Center.

Talbott, J. A., & Robinowitz, C. B. (1986). *Working together: State-university collaboration in mental health.* Washington, DC: American Psychiatric Press.

Task force on child and adolescent professional psychology. (1998, October 19). Report of the Task Force on Child and Adolescent Professional Psychology to the Board of Professional Affairs. Executive Summary. Washington, DC: American Psychological Association.

Ulrey, G., Hudler, M., Marshall, R., Wuori, D., & Cranston, C. (1987). A community model for physician, educator, and parent collaboration for management of children with developmental and behavioral disorders. *Clinical Pediatrics, 26*(5), 235–239.

U.S. Department of Health and Human Services. (1999). *Mental health: A report of the Surgeon General (chap. 3: Children and mental health).* Rockville, MD: Author, Substance Abuse and Mental Health Services Administration, Center for Mental Health Services, National Institutes of Health, National Institute of Mental Health.

U.S. Department of Housing and Urban Development. (2000). Office of University Partner-
    ships, www.oup.org/about/about.html
A view to the future. (1999, Fall). *Advances in Family-Centered Care, 5*(1), 19–20.
Warren, N. J. (1994). Training psychiatry residents and psychology interns to work with families
    of the seriously mentally ill. In H. R. Lefley & M. Wasow (Eds.), *Helping families cope with
    mental illness* (pp. 295–308). New York: Harwood Academic Publishers.
Wasow, M. (1994). Training future clinicians to work with families. In H. R. Lefley & M. Wasow
    (Eds.), *Helping families cope with mental illness* (pp. 277–293). New York: Harwood Aca-
    demic Publishers.
World Health Organization (WHO). (1988). *Learning together to work together for health.*
    Geneva: WHO.
Zlotnik, J. L. (1997). *Preparing the workforce for family-centered practice: Social work education
    and public human services partnerships.* Alexandria, VA: Council on Social Work Education.

Chapter 6

CULTURALLY COMPETENT PRACTICES WITH CHILDREN AND YOUTH WHO HAVE SERIOUS EMOTIONAL DISTURBANCE

ADRIENNE DIXON

Jose Rodriguez, a 7-year-old Puerto Rican male, was referred to outpatient services by his school counselor in light of his aggression toward peers, oppositional and defiant behavior, and school avoidance.* The counselor indicated that Jose often refused to complete class and homework assignments, experienced difficulty remaining focused and on task, and was failing most of his academic subjects. At the time of referral, Jose lived at home with his biological parents, Jose Sr. and Maria, and his 10-year-old sister, Marisol.

During the intake interview, Maria reported that her son's behavior problems had recently escalated in school and at home and that he had begun to experience enuretic and encopretic episodes. Jose Sr., who spoke only Spanish, was unable to participate in the interview, which was conducted in English. Jose himself said he had difficulty sleeping at night and sometimes heard voices telling him they wanted to harm his family. He appeared to be excessively anxious and fearful, describing nightmares that featured a "strange man" who planned to kill him while he slept.

Before moving to the United States 3 years ago, the Rodriguez family had lived with Maria's parents and worked on the family farm. Their move was precipitated by the death of Maria's father, who had been a beloved family patriarch. Because of Jose Sr.'s inability to speak, read, or write English, the family spoke only Spanish at home. The children spoke both English and Spanish, although their English was not yet completely fluent. Maria had attended English as a second language (ESL) classes at a local community center. Since moving from Puerto Rico, Jose Sr. had experienced difficulty finding stable employment because of the language barrier and his lack of trade experience. As a result, Maria had become the primary provider in the home, working as a full-time housekeeper for a local hotel.

---

*Although the Rodriguez family is fictional, this vignette portrays some actual experiences of a diverse family.

Jose was assigned to a European American female counselor, whose preliminary diagnoses were attention-deficit/hyperactivity disorder and oppositional defiant disorder. Jose's initial treatment plan focused on his attention problems, sleeping difficulties, enuretic and encopretic episodes, and oppositional behavior in school. Weekly individual sessions were scheduled for Jose; neither school consultation nor family sessions were planned. After Jose had attended three sessions, Maria contacted the therapist to terminate treatment, indicating that Jose refused to return. In fact, both parents felt excluded from their son's treatment, which they did not consider helpful.

Several months later, in response to pressure from Jose's school counselor, Maria again contacted the clinic to request services, reporting that her son's behavioral and academic problems had worsened significantly. Following another evaluation, Jose was referred to a partial hospitalization program and assigned to a bilingual and bicultural Latino therapist. In addition to individual sessions with Jose, the revised treatment plan included family sessions and school consultation. Now able to communicate in his primary language, Jose began to express his fears and discuss his concerns. During family sessions, the therapist learned that Jose Sr. was experiencing major problems in adjusting to life in the United States. Moreover, he had been very close to his deceased father-in-law and was troubled by the altered family circumstances.

Jose Sr. also expressed great concern about his inability to meet his family's financial needs. Of necessity, his wife had become the family breadwinner, a role reversal that threatened his sense of manhood. Jose Sr. told the therapist that he experienced difficulty sleeping and often watched television late at night. Pacing the floors, he frequently spoke to his deceased father-in-law and shared his distress. Other members of the family sometimes heard him tell his father-in-law that he wanted God to take all of them to join him.

Consulting with the school counselor, the therapist learned that although Jose spoke English, he had difficulty processing information and integrating what was happening in the classroom. As a result, he felt overwhelmed and frustrated much of the time. Jose told the therapist that it didn't seem to matter how hard he tried; he always seemed to be in trouble. The counselor also discovered that Jose was often teased by the other children about his language and academic problems. During one of his individual sessions, Jose mentioned that he sometimes heard his father speaking to his deceased grandfather and assumed it was normal to communicate with people who were not present.

During joint sessions, the therapist helped the family to understand the cultural issues they faced, to adapt to their new environment, and to accept their altered family structure. Specific therapeutic foci included the move to an urban setting from a very rural farm environment and the alterations in marital roles. With renewed hope for the future, Jose Sr. began to attend the ESL classes at the community center and to follow through on the therapist's referral to a local vocational program. The counselor also assisted Jose's parents in understanding his academic problems and helping him with his school work. One session included Jose's classroom teacher, who offered to have a bilingual aide work with him. The teacher also referred Jose for an evaluation of his academic problems.

As the Rodriguez family developed the skills and confidence to succeed in their new environment, they experienced less distress and a greater sense of personal and family satisfaction. Gradually, the family began to welcome the challenges and opportunities associated with their move to a new country. Individual and family sessions continued for a year, as did periodic consultation with the school counselor. Many of Jose's problems appeared to be reactive to the psychosocial stress experienced by his family, including the language barrier, his father's adjustment problems, and the altered family structure. With family and school support, Jose's behavioral and academic functioning improved, although he continued to experience significant anxiety and depression. He also reported that he still sometimes heard the voices at night and insisted that they were real.

During the final family session, Maria told the therapist that she felt the family could solve their own problems now, thanks to the services they had received. Following discharge from the partial program, Jose was referred to outpatient services, where he continued to attend individual sessions. A psychiatric consult was scheduled to clarify the nature of Jose's "voices" and to consider the use of medication for his persistent anxiety and depression. In addition to Jose's individual therapy, the bilingual outpatient therapist planned to meet regularly with his parents and to consult with the school counselor on an as-needed basis. With the support of the mental health and school systems, the Rodriguez family felt hopeful about their future.

AN INCREASINGLY DIVERSE SOCIETY

The Rodriguez family is among the increasing number of racial and ethnic minorities in the United States. Indeed, as documented in a barrage of statistics, American society is becoming progressively more diverse (Sue & Sue, 1999). Based on immigration patterns, for instance, the U.S. Census Bureau (2000) reports that the number of residents born outside the country has increased significantly since the last census count. These demographic shifts have had a significant impact on our communities, work environments, and schools. These shifts have important implications for the mental health field, as well. Professionals in all disciplines continue to search for effective strategies for evaluating and treating culturally, ethnically, and linguistically diverse populations. This search is hampered by poor understanding of the diverse groups represented within the United States and of the clinical implications of this diversity.

The challenge of providing culturally competent services to a diverse and multicultural population is further complicated by the incongruent worldview and value orientations of clinicians who predominately espouse Westernized cultural beliefs systems. To facilitate effective treatment outcomes, it is essential that therapists be sensitive to differences among diverse populations and offer interventions that are congruent with clients' values. Practitioners need to recognize that clients' social and cultural experiences influence many aspects of their behavior, as well as the core interpersonal interactions that define the therapeutic relationship. Equally important are clinicians' cultural heritage and experience, which serve as a template for interpreting the behaviors and interactions of the children and families with whom they work. Similarly, because the supervisory relationship has considerable impact on supervisees and their clients, the supervisor's cultural expectations and competencies are also important.

In exploring the parameters of culturally competent practice, this chapter considers the following topics: cultural worldviews and conceptual models, ethnocultural and personality development, psychopathology and culture, professional practice with diverse children and families, assessment and intervention, training and supervision, and implications for serious emotional disturbance.

CULTURAL WORLDVIEWS AND CONCEPTUAL MODELS

Culture determines how group-shared patterns of social interactions, values, beliefs, perceptions, behaviors, and roles are manifested (Barth, 1969; Ogbu, 1981). Culture also defines how individuals meet their basic needs, resolve their problems, and cope with their crises. Reflecting cultural variations in lifelong development and personal identity, there are significant differences in attitudinal and behavioral patterns across cultures (Whiting & Whiting, 1975). The concept of *worldview* captures these cultural phenomena.

In fact, cultural and professional worldviews are a central aspect of culturally competent practice. *Worldview* is a framework that imparts meaning to one's world. Ibrahim (1985) describes worldview as an overall philosophy of life that reflects our experiences within specific social, cultural, and environmental domains. Worldview, which derives from such cultural variables as family membership and racial or ethnic identity, consists of specific attitudes, values, beliefs, opinions, assumptions, and concepts. Our worldview has a profound impact on the way we think, make decisions, behave, and assign meaning to interactions and events. As children are growing up, their worldview mediates their interpretation of the world and their relationships with others.

Likewise, professional worldviews—or conceptual models—influence the responses of clinicians, including their perceptions, thoughts, attitudes, and beliefs, as well as their interpretation of personality, interactions, and behavior. In the clinical encounter, professional models function as a filter for client communications, often determining what is heard and how it is construed. When therapists work with diverse populations, their models may undermine their ability to understand and respond appropriately to clients. Differences between the worldviews of practitioners and clients are likely to have a significant impact on professional practice, particularly if clinicians base their interpretations on their own worldview rather than those of the child and family. During cross-cultural exchanges, differing worldviews can result in conflict and misunderstanding.

Many current psychological and counseling models reflect a predominantly Eurocentric perspective (Atkinson, Morten, & Sue, 1998; Ivey, Ivey, & Simek-Morgan, 1993; Katz, 1985; Parham, 1993; Ponterato & Casas, 1991; Sue, Arredondo, & McDavis, 1992; Sue & Sue, 1990). Culture-bound models do not reflect worldview differences across cultures and therefore provide an inappropriate framework for working with diverse clients. As Sue (1995) has pointed out, Western values and beliefs may be considered antagonistic or controversial among people with different cultural experiences and beliefs. Most professional models provide an inappropriate framework for understanding culture-bound behavior and meeting the needs of culturally diverse systems.

Often, these models assume that psychological constructs offer universal explanations of human behavior, yet such explanations may not apply to all children and families. In fact, although human nature can be conceptualized in universal terms, the meaning assigned to children's behaviors or symptoms is largely determined by the cultural context. Namely, the child's environment assigns specific meaning to universal behavior and defines what is normal and abnormal.

In addition, current conceptual models often endorse a one-dimensional view of human behavior that ignores other important characteristics. For instance, many popular models embody Westernized beliefs that emphasize the individual's ability to make decisions based on an internalized locus of control rather than external forces. Discounting external factors, this individual-centered worldview minimizes the role of cultural experience, which in fact plays an important role in all aspects of functioning. More generally, professional models frequently ignore the cultural, social, and political context of personality.

Clearly, professional practice requires models of counseling and psychotherapy that incorporate the worldviews of culturally diverse children and families. The use of such multidimensional models encourages therapists to recognize group differences in behavior, ideas, values, and beliefs; to acknowledge the importance of cultural variables; to focus on difference rather than deviation; and to emphasize the strengths of children and families. Indeed, such models are essential for effective practice, which is characterized by accurate diagnoses, helpful interventions, and culturally appropriate treatment plans. Moreover, appreciation of diversity can help practitioners to minimize the potentially negative impact of conflicting worldviews on therapeutic alliances with clients.

ETHNOCULTURAL AND PERSONALITY DEVELOPMENT

Children develop both as individuals and as members of families and cultures. In fact, their ethnocultural and personality developmental processes are intertwined, and group membership is a key factor in both personal and cultural identity. Group membership promotes the development of personal identity and provides individuals with a sense of security and belonging based on their cultural, ethnic, and linguistic context. Culture shapes the very essence of our experiences and interactions with others. For instance, culture supplies filters for understanding the world, influences our interactions and perceptions of behavior, and promotes shared meaning and mutual perspectives among group members (Diller, 1999). Defining our sociocultural orientation, culture governs the interpretation and integration of environmental and interpersonal encounters.

Children's development of personal identity—their emerging sense of themselves as distinct individuals—is mediated by their status as members of families and cultural groups, as well as by such cultural variables as race, ethnicity, and gender. Group membership also influences the acquisition, expression, and interpretation of behavior. Cultural groups reinforce certain behaviors, a practice that affects personality development throughout the life span. Because culture imbues behavior and relational patterns with specific meaning, it also plays a central role in the emergence and interpretation of abnormal behavior and processes.

Children's socialization begins in infancy with their family members and primary caregivers. Children gradually begin to develop their sense of personal identity based on membership within the family system, later expanding their identity to incorporate membership in the larger sociocultural system. As members of families and cultures, children learn from a very early age that there are specific rules and norms regarding appropriate and inappropriate interactions with society. They manifest these cultural mandates in their relational patterns, their personality, and their psychological processes. Ultimately, individuals learn to function both as unique individuals and as members of particular cultural groups.

Ethnocultural development is closely related to the processes of acculturation and assimilation, which are central to the experience of many culturally diverse individuals in the United States. *Acculturation* refers to the extent to which the child and family have adopted the values, beliefs, and practices of the host culture. *Assimilation* is the degree to which they maintain traditional values and beliefs. In working with a given child and family, clinicians must be sensitive to their level of acculturation and assimilation, as well as the impact of these processes on their worldview.

Although debate continues regarding the relative impact of nature and nurture on specific psychological variables, there is general agreement that children's psychological development is profoundly shaped by the environment in which they are reared. Personality is not merely a function of genetic or biological components, but also of cultural beliefs and experiences. Indeed, personality is a culture-specific construct that develops within a particular sociocultural context. Various cultural groups espouse different worldview and value orientations, which in turn influence personality traits and characteristics. As a result, personality not only develops differently in various ethnic and cultural groups; it is also expressed differently.

Through socialization, children become increasingly aware of cultural differences. They gradually learn how to relate to others who are culturally both similar and different. Culture provides a blueprint for interpreting the behavior of others and for distinguishing between normal and abnormal behavior based on particular cultural nuances. Thus, various cultural groups may conceptualize pathology in quite different ways.

PSYCHOPATHOLOGY AND CULTURE

Counseling services are provided to ethnic populations largely by practitioners who are culturally different from their clients. Yet psychopathology and its behavioral manifestations have contextual meaning within specific cultural frameworks, which has important implications for professional practice. Working with diverse clients, clinicians need to understand the meanings assigned by the culture and the family to various behaviors, interactions, and psychological processes. Furthermore, cultural norms define optimal psychological functioning within a particular environment.

Children learn specific patterns of interacting, engaging, thinking, and processing within their unique cultural worlds. Because behavior is learned within a particular social context, the manifestations of illness and discomfort are culturally imprinted. Moreover, cultural beliefs and attitudes determine child-rearing practices, which play an important role in normal and abnormal development. In fact, the very definition of abnormal behavior is closely tied to the cultural context, as is the presence or absence of certain behaviors.

The family's response to the child's behavior is also influenced by the family's cultural background. For instance, the family's beliefs about illness are closely tied to the family's worldview. Likewise, cultural values and assumptions significantly influence the help-seeking behaviors of families, which tend to model those endorsed by their cultural system (Ibrahim, 1985; Ivey et al., 1993, Sue & Sue, 1977). Working with culturally diverse children and families, therapists can learn about their cultural norms and values, their illness models, and their interpretation of specific behaviors.

Listening to the stories of diverse families, practitioners can gain insight into their lives, their values, and their goals. Learning from families, clinicians will develop a better understanding of the child as emerging from a particular culture. At the same time, such dialogues will enhance the family's sense of feeling understood and culturally validated within the therapeutic relationship (Sue, 1992).

PROFESSIONAL PRACTICE WITH DIVERSE CHILDREN AND FAMILIES

Effective professional practice with families depends on the establishment of collaborative partnerships designed to build on the strengths and expertise of all parties; to respect the needs, concerns, and priorities of families; to promote a sense of family mastery; and to develop mutually acceptable treatment plans. Cross-cultural therapeutic relationships pose particular challenges in achieving these objectives. In professional practice with families that are ethnically, racially, and linguistically diverse, differences in the life experiences and cultural backgrounds of practitioners and clients may undermine the therapeutic alliance and adversely affect all aspects of therapy.

Risks associated with cultural incongruence include communication problems, unsatisfactory interactions between clinicians and clients, inability to share meaning and establish mutual goals for treatment, and differing perceptions, values, and beliefs. These risks are increased when clinicians themselves have limited multicultural experience or lack understanding of cultural diversity. If such problems cannot be resolved, there is the risk of premature termination, with the loss of potential therapeutic benefits.

When working with culturally diverse children and families, clinicians can take steps to promote family engagement and minimize potential problems. Initially, practitioners must be aware of the cultural context of professional practice. They need to understand the role that culture plays in individual development, family dynamics, and psychopathology. Equally important, therapists should develop an appreciation of culturally appropriate coping strategies, belief systems, and practices, all of which may be inherently different from those of the dominant culture. Culturally competent practice is fostered by familiarity with and openness to various worldview and cultural orientations. Understanding of diverse worldviews can also help clinicians avoid subjecting clients to culturally related stressors, such as professional models and practices that conflict with their traditional values and beliefs (Sue, 1995).

Practitioners need to recognize that abnormal behavior is manifested within a particular cultural context and reflects the child's unique worldview. In fact, behavior that is labeled abnormal by the mainstream culture may be a normal expression within the child's primary culture. Cultural differences can also color the interpretation of clinical interactions and observations. When assessment and intervention are guided by dominant cultural values, there is the risk of misunderstanding and misinterpretation that subsequently can result in misdiagnosis and inappropriate treatment.

An appreciation of diversity allows therapists to enter the worlds of culturally different families and to participate in their cultural systems. Practitioners need to validate the distinct cultural heritage and experiences of the child and family. Participation and validation increase the likelihood of reciprocal understanding, effective communication, and shared meaning. In an atmosphere of mutual understanding and respect, cross-cultural exchanges can guide the therapeutic process, alleviate distress, and assist the child and family in beginning a journey toward optimal functioning.

Clinicians can model and promote constructive communication. Effective communication with diverse families involves listening attentively, responding empathically, speaking clearly and directly, and keeping messages brief and straightforward. These clients may have culturally specific patterns of verbal and nonverbal communication that are manifested a variety of ways, including eye contact, physical distance, body movements, and emotional expression.

Closely related to culture, language plays an important role in clinical settings. For some clients, the ability to identify and express concerns in their primary language is critical. When services are not delivered in the family's primary language, poor language proficiency may limit their ability to express themselves during assessment and treatment. Under these circumstances, linguistic limitations may be a source of tremendous stress for children and families. Language problems increase the likelihood that interactions and information will be misinterpreted. For example, culturally diverse families may have difficulty understanding and defining the difference between normal and abnormal developmental processes.

As a corrective to inappropriate conceptual models, clinicians can employ multidimensional conceptual models that incorporate an array of cultural variables. Implementing a multicultural approach to clinical practice, practitioners will be better able to understand the worldviews of diverse children and families, to address their needs, and to recognize their strengths. Working with these clients, therapists must be able to move continuously between their own cultural perspective and that of the family. As clinicians gain insight into the cultural context of symptoms, there is less risk that the child's behavior will be over- or underpathologized. Likewise, there is increased likelihood of shared understanding of the child's psychological problems and of mutual agreement regarding the treatment plan. In short, practitioners are encouraged to meet clients where they are.

ASSESSMENT AND INTERVENTION

In order to serve diverse populations effectively, practitioners must be trained in culturally competent skills for conducting assessments, formulating case conceptualizations, selecting treatment strategies, and implementing interventions. Because psychological problems and their behavioral manifestations develop in specific sociocultural settings, clinicians need to apply a multicultural lens when undertaking evaluations. Similarly, understanding the relationship that culture plays in child development can assist therapists in arriving at an accurate diagnosis and providing beneficial interventions. Clearly, the process of culturally competent assessment necessarily involves a consideration of the client's worldview.

Psychopathology in children must be evaluated from both developmental and sociocultural perspectives. Namely, psychological problems can be understood only when they are viewed as occurring in a particular setting and within a certain developmental context. Because abnormal behavior reflects a specific culture and its worldview, traditional means of assessment may be inappropriate when used with the culturally different child and family. Moreover, the use of culturally encapsulated conceptual models and traditional assessment instruments increases the likelihood that the behavior of diverse children will be misunderstood, overpathologized, or misdiagnosed. Traditional approaches often fail to consider the norms that define normal and abnormal within a particular culture, although behavior that is labeled abnormal by the mainstream culture may in fact be a normal expression within the child's primary culture. Accordingly, when making decisions about psychopathology, clinicians need knowledge of children's social, cultural, and ethnic history.

Children are products of their family systems as well as their larger sociocultural system. Through socialization, they internalize social norms that guide their behavior and develop cultural frameworks for operating in their world. In evaluating the behavior of diverse children, clinicians need to consider the norms and rules of the child's particular culture or subculture. When a child's behavior or interactions deviate from mainstream social norms, therapists are cautioned not to assume that the deviation represents abnormality or pathology. In order to evaluate children's behavior, they need to obtain relevant information from primary cultural brokers and family members. Such information can help practitioners understand how the child is expected to behave in a particular culture and evaluate whether the child's behavior is incongruent with the family's worldview.

Clinicians must be able to understand universal behavioral patterns and how these patterns may be manifested in particular cultural settings. For instance, although psychological problems are present in all groups, there may be cultural variations in the manifestation of symptoms of depression and other disorders, in the behavioral and emotional patterns that are often the focus of psychotherapeutic services, and in definitions of what is considered impairment in social skills, attention, and intellectual functioning. Accordingly, assessment of possible psychological problems and impairments necessitates a consideration of the sociocultural context in which they occur.

To enhance their understanding of the cultural context of the child and family, Ramirez (1991) recommends that practitioners undertake a comprehensive, culturally oriented life history. He emphasizes that therapists cannot understand children's personality without exploring their developmental history and their cultural and cognitive styles. Ramirez also underscores the importance of multicultural development; namely, the degree to which children experience diversity, learn from their experiences, and begin to develop their own cultural filters. He observes that the number and types of barriers to development, such as stereotypes or discriminatory behaviors and attitudes, also contribute to the child's diversity.

A comprehensive ethnocultural assessment of child psychopathology examines the historical background and cultural context of the child, as well as relevant developmental processes. Such an assessment entails explicit and detailed information from primary culture brokers and family members. Other important sources of information include teachers, peers, and community members, all of whom may influence the child's behavioral manifestation of psychological problems. An ethnocultural assessment requires the clinician to be familiar with the practices, beliefs, attitudes, and norms of specific cultural groups. When working with diverse clients, this cultural context is crucial in obtaining an accurate understanding of behavior and a clear diagnostic picture.

Culture is manifested through a wide array of personal, family, kinship, and community variables, including age, gender, place of birth, socioeconomic status, educational status, nationality, racial history, ethnic identity, sociopolitical background, and language (Pedersen, 1991). Accordingly, ethnocultural assessments should incorporate a full range of psychosocial and cultural factors, including the family's immigration and migration patterns, as well as their acculturation and assimilation experiences. Results of such an evaluation can provide insight into the extent to which diverse clients continue to espouse traditional values and beliefs or have integrated new values and beliefs from the host culture. Other important considerations include their learning and communication styles, their culturally specific behaviors, and their beliefs about spirituality, childrearing, and other relevant matters. Culturally related psychosocial stressors should also be explored, including the family's experiences with racism and discrimination, as well as their employment and housing history.

In addition, cultural considerations play an important role in the interpretation of clinical interactions and observations. For example, there are cultural differences in such characteristics as voice tone, eye contact, language, proximity, and expression of feelings (Ryan & Hendricks, 1989). Misinterpretation of verbal and nonverbal cues can result in misdiagnosis and inappropriate treatment. Working with diverse children and families, practitioners need to acknowledge the importance of clients' worldviews during the therapeutic exchange and modify interventions to match their needs. Effective cross-cultural services are congruent with the child's language, the culture's behavioral norms and values, and the sanctions of family members.

TRAINING AND SUPERVISION

In light of the immigration patterns and growing diversity within the United States, practitioners will be increasingly faced with children and families from various cultural backgrounds. In response to these demographic changes, culturally competent training and supervision will assume greater importance. Working with diverse clients, clinicians must be flexible and sensitive to the sociocultural context of professional practice. Reflecting this emphasis on culturally competent practice, the current *Diagnostic and Statistical Manual* (American Psychiatric Association, 1994) provides a cultural formulation designed to assist clinicians in the evaluation and assessment of culturally specific syndromes.

Both training and supervision can promote the delivery of culturally competent services to racially, ethnically, and linguistically diverse children and families. The mental health field has increasingly recognized the importance of developing curricula that incorporate multicultural counseling competencies. In response, graduate programs across all mental health disciplines are working to address this need. However, although many academic courses and textbooks have begun to incorporate cultural diversity and multicultural themes into professional training, these perspectives rarely infuse the overall curriculum (Sue & Sue, 1999).

The *Code of Ethics* of the American Counseling Association (1995) underscores the importance of developing culturally appropriate competencies and skills. The code focuses on the following areas: (a) personal development, (b) case conceptualization, and (c) skills and interventions. In a multicultural world, clinicians need to consider alternatives to traditional conceptual models and learn a variety of verbal and nonverbal helping responses that can enhance their skills when working with diverse clients. They must also be willing to consider their own attitudes, worldviews, and biases, as well as alternative conceptualizations of client concerns and behaviors. Ultimately, culturally competent practice must be driven by consumer-held values and beliefs.

In the contemporary world, all mental health practitioners need to be familiar with the parameters of cultural competence. Indeed, diversity training is critical for preparing practitioners to work in cross-cultural settings. Such training must include both didactic instruction and experiential encounters that facilitate sensitivity to cultural differences and promote the development of services that are congruent with the particular worldviews and values of clients.

Clinicians also need to recognize personal biases and assumptions that may affect the therapeutic relationship (Pedersen, 1988, 1991). For instance, therapists must be aware of their own cultural worldview, which can have a significant impact on their relationships with clients and on their ability to appreciate clients' perspectives. In addition, practitioners must learn to identify their personal values, norms, and beliefs, as well as their theoretical orientations and ideologies, which can also influence the therapeutic process in important ways. When applied to diverse clients, as noted, the Eurocentric cultural orientations of clinicians may result in inappropriate assessment, incorrect diagnosis, and ineffective treatment.

Acknowledging the potential impact of their own cultural identity, practitioners should seek opportunities to expand their multicultural experiences. Greater personal awareness and exposure to diverse cultures will enhance the ability of clinicians to work in meaningful ways with various systems and clients, to better understand diverse children and families, and to design and implement treatment plans that are culturally relevant and congruent with the values and beliefs of clients.

Supervision can also increase the prospects for culturally competent practice. Watkins (1995) has noted that although supervision can take place in a wide array of settings, the process remains largely the same. Namely, the supervisor provides guidance and direction in order to enhance the supervisee's clinical knowledge and practice. As Bernard and Goodyear (1992) point out, supervision involves a relationship between a senior member of a profession and a junior member of the same profession. The relationship serves to enhance the professional development of the junior professional and may focus on a wide range of professional issues, such as theoretical orientation, treatment, values, and beliefs regarding human nature. Deriving from their professional and life experiences, the values and beliefs of both parties affect the supervisory and therapeutic processes.

Supervision assists clinicians in interpreting client behaviors within the context of the therapeutic relationship. Because therapy is also delivered within a cultural context, however, this latter context has a major impact on the attribution of meaning to client behaviors and interactions, on the quality of the therapeutic relationship, and on the supervision process. Through supervision, therapists can learn to make use of information regarding cultural dynamics and to use that information in selecting appropriate techniques, strategies, and interventions for diverse populations.

Culturally competent supervision assists practitioners in understanding the potential impact of cultural differences on the therapeutic process and in developing shared meaning with children and families, particularly members of diverse groups. Supervision can provide the supervisee with greater understanding of individual intrapsychic and interpersonal phenomena, as well as of the relationship of these phenomena to larger social systems. The worldviews of the child and family strongly influence their perception of therapy. Likewise, the clinician's worldview affects the perception and interpretation of the child's behavior. The worldviews of both clients and therapists can have a significant impact on the clinical process and on the family unit. During supervision, the supervisor can help the supervisee to understand the role of cultural variables in the therapeutic process, to recognize the client's group membership and cultural identity, and to place the needs of children and families within their larger sociocultural system.

Multicultural experiences can assist clinicians in understanding the behavioral expectations and nuances of particular cultures, the cultural and cognitive schemas of diverse children and families, and the cultural frameworks of both clients and themselves. Supervision can encourage practitioners to develop an appreciation for the primary social system of children and families, to conceptualize clients in terms of their own cultural perceptions and worldviews rather than those of the dominant culture, to support their cultural frameworks, and to negotiate various cultural frameworks in the course of clinical practice.

There have been some efforts to specify the parameters of culturally competent practice. For example, Arredondo (1984) has emphasized the importance of cross-cultural awareness, counseling theory and techniques, assessment and diagnosis, and research skills. Sue et al. (1992) have mentioned practitioners' awareness of their own cultural values, of the client's worldview, and of culturally appropriate interventions and strategies. The supervisor's task is to facilitate the development and implementation of cultural competencies by highlighting the diversity of interpersonal styles, relational patterns, and cultural expectations, as well as the ethnic and cultural background of particular clients.

The ultimate goal of supervision is to promote the competence and growth of the clinician in a manner that improves treatment outcomes for children and families. With that goal in mind, the supervisory process may focus on the acquisition of knowledge and skills, the development of trust and shared meaning, or the dynamics of the supervisory relationship (Sue et al., 1992). Thus, supervision offers therapists the opportunity to expand their own experience and expertise and to benefit from supervisory relationship itself. In fact, the quality of the supervisory relationship is likely to have a significant impact on the supervisee's ability to provide effective services.

Several factors can affect the supervisory process. These include (a) the supervisor's cultural frame of reference, (b) the client's cultural frame of reference, (c) the clinician's frame of reference, (d) the clinician's experience, (e) the theoretical orientation of both the supervisor and clinician, (f) the clinician's learning style, and (g) the cultural dynamics and characteristics of the client. Other important factors include differences in power and worldview. An imbalance of power always exists in supervisory and therapeutic relationships; this imbalance may be amplified by racial and cultural differences. Differences in cultural worldviews can also undermine the supervisory process, as can problems in the supervisor–supervisee relationship.

The concept of shared meaning, which is central to both supervisory and therapeutic processes, highlights the significance of mutual understanding and agreement (Kaiser, 2000). Shared meaning is important in the clinician's interpretation of verbal and nonverbal client behaviors and in the supervisor's assessment and interpretation of the clinician's behavior, skills, and techniques. Because mutual understanding is fundamental to effective communication and information processing, clashes in values, attitudes, and beliefs can adversely affect the quality of care. Clinical outcomes are enhanced when shared meaning has been achieved between the clinician and client and between the supervisor and supervisee (the *triad* concept). As well, mutual understanding increases the likelihood that diverse children and families will be encouraged to define their own problems and that practitioners will accurately interpret their worldview.

Working with the supervisee, the culturally competent supervisor seeks to promote the acquisition of cultural knowledge and the translation of that knowledge into attitudes and actions. The following suggestions can assist clinicians in delivering culturally competent services (American Psychological Association, 1993):

- Understand the role that culture, ethnicity, and race play in the social, psychological, and economic development of ethnically and culturally diverse populations.
- Understand that social, economic, and political factors significantly influence the psychosocial, political, and economic development of ethnically and culturally diverse clients.
- Help clients to understand, maintain, and resolve their own sociocultural identification.
- Understand the interaction of culture, gender, and sexual orientation, as well as the impact of this interaction on the behavior of clients.

In summary, practitioners who wish to achieve cultural competence are encouraged to seek out educational and training opportunities that can increase their understanding of diverse populations; to attend to the historical, cultural, social, and psychological experiences of diverse groups; and to recognize their personal limitations when working with culturally diverse populations.

SERIOUS EMOTIONAL DISTURBANCE

This chapter generally focuses on cultural competence, which has important implications for the full range of mental health problems. It is important to note, however, that neglect of the cultural context poses particular risks when clinicians are working with children who have the most severe and persistent mental disorders. As reported by the surgeon general (Satcher, 2000), at least 5% of our children and adolescents have a serious emotional disturbance (SED) and extreme impairment that undermines their ability to function at home, in school, and in the community.

The diagnoses subsumed under SED include autistic and other pervasive developmental disorders, attention-deficit/hyperactivity disorder, schizophrenia, bipolar disorder, major depressive disorder, obsessive-compulsive disorder, and other severe anxiety disorders. Although an array of effective psychosocial and psychopharmacological treatments are now available, with treatment outcomes comparable to those of adults, at least two thirds of young people with a diagnosable mental disorder receive *no* mental health services at all (Satcher, 2000).

Cultural competence is of critical importance in working with clients with SED. Because SED disorders are severe and persistent, and because they generally do not remit spontaneously, the absence of effective treatment can have catastrophic long-term consequences for these children and their families. Moreover, as noted in the surgeon general's report, cultural differences exacerbate the general problem of access to appropriate mental health services. Although culturally appropriate services have been designed, they are not widely available. Not surprisingly, minority parents are therefore far less likely than mainstream parents to seek assistance for their children from professionals and agencies. In one study (McMiller & Weisz, 1996), two thirds of minority parents initially did not seek mental health services for their children, turning instead to family and community contacts. When they do receive professional services, diverse families may find services incongruent with their cultural worldview, insensitive to their concerns, and unresponsive to their needs.

CONCLUSION

Although psychological principles are based on individual differences, the field of psychology has become a science of the mean and mode. For the most part, the uniqueness of individuals and groups has been minimized in a social system that emphasizes conformity to dominant cultural norms, a perspective that is perpetuated by those in power, who set the standard for what is normal and desirable behavior (Ramirez, 1991). This relative disregard of diversity has a pervasive impact on all aspects of society, including the mental health field.

Historically, mental health practitioners have failed to consider culture-specific patterns of behavior and personality in designing assessment instruments and intervention strategies. Because they largely ignore cultural variables, traditional approaches to assessment and treatment are often inappropriate for diverse children and families. Moreover, there is insufficient appreciation for the impact of culture on psychological disorders, help-seeking behaviors, and access to professional services.

Additional problems include the pervasive use of culturally encapsulated models and practices with diverse clients and the lack of respect for their values and beliefs. Under these circumstances, diverse families may avoid seeking professional services because they anticipate that their needs will not be met; and these families may prematurely terminate treatment that fulfills this expectation. Without question, this absence of culturally appropriate services has devastating consequences for these children, for their families, and for society at large.

A multicultural approach reduces the risk that diverse families will avoid seeking professional services for their children or will find such services unresponsive to their needs. Such an approach encourages the integration of cultural differences, recognizes the impact of culture on lifelong development, respects the unique communication patterns and symbols of particular groups, acknowledges the impact of culture on psychological problems and their behavioral expression, and enhances the likelihood of positive outcomes among diverse clients.

Culturally appropriate training and supervision can prepare practitioners to manage the dynamics of difference. With regard to clinical services, it is clear that one size does not fit all. Rather than a homogeneous mass, humans are unique beings who have different life experiences, cultures, and worldviews. Because individuals perceive and approach the world differently, they also respond to treatment in idiosyncratic ways. Our communities are rapidly changing to accommodate the increasing number of diverse families. Responding to these changes, we must design mental health services that can address their needs.

There is increasing agreement that cultural competence is an essential prerequisite for effective practice in cross-cultural settings (Cross, Bazron, Dennis, & Isaacs, 1989). Some progress has been made in providing training and supervisory experiences that prepare clinicians to work with racially, ethnically, and linguistically different children and families. As well, efforts are currently under way to expand culturally appropriate services and to conduct research that validates and clarifies the role of cultural variables in clinical practice. We have indeed come a long way; however, we still have a long way to go.

REFERENCES

American Counseling Association. (1995). *Code of ethics in standards of practice.* Alexandria, VA: Author.

American Psychiatric Association. (1994). *Diagnostic and statistical manual of mental disorders* (4th ed.). Washington, DC: Author.

American Psychological Association. (1993). Guidelines for providers of psychological services to ethnic, linguistic, and culturally diverse populations. *American Psychologists, 48,* 45–48.

Arredondo, P. (1984). Bilingual counseling training project. In J. Axelson (Ed.), *Counseling and development in a multicultural society* (3rd ed., p. 61). Pacific Grove, CA: Brooks/Cole.

Atkinson, D. R., Morten, G., & Sue, D. W. (1998). *Counseling American minorities* (5th ed.). Boston: McGraw-Hill.

Barth, F. (1969). Introduction. In F. Barth (Ed.), *Ethnic groups and boundaries* (pp. 3–38). Boston: Little, Brown.

Bernard, J. M., & Goodyear, R. K. (1992). *Fundamentals of clinical supervision.* Boston: Allyn & Bacon.

Cross, T. L., Bazron, B. J., Dennis, K. W., & Isaacs, M. R. (1989). *Towards a culturally competent system of care.* Washington, DC: Georgetown University Child Development Center.

Diller, J. V. (1999). *Cultural diversity: A primer for the human services.* Belmont, CA. Brooks/Cole.

Ibrahim, F. (1985). Effective cross-cultural counseling and psychotherapy: A framework. *The Counseling Psychologist, 13,* 625–638.

Ivey, A. E., Ivey, M. B., & Simek-Morgan, L. (1993). *Counseling and psychotherapy: A multicultural perspective.* Boston: Allyn & Bacon.

Kaiser, T. L. (2000). *Supervisory relationships: Exploring the human element.* Pacific Grove, CA: Brooks/Cole.

Katz, J. (1985). The social political nature of counseling. *The Counseling Psychologist, 13,* 615–624.

McMiller, W. P., & Weisz, J. R. (1996). Help-seeking preceding mental health clinic intake among African-American, Latino, and Caucasian youths. *Journal of the American Academy of Child and Adolescent Psychiatry, 35,* 1086–1094.

Ogbu, J. U. (1981). Origins of human competencies: A cultural ecological perspective. *Child Development, 52,* 413–429.

Parham, T. A. (1993). White researchers conducting multi-cultural counseling research: Can their efforts be "mo betta?" [Reaction]. *The Counseling Psychologist, 21,* 240–256.

Pedersen, P. B. (1988). *A handbook for developing multicultural awareness.* Alexandria, VA: American Association of Counseling and Development Press.

Pedersen, P. B. (1991). Multiculturalism as a fourth force in counseling [Special issue]. *Journal of Counseling and Development, 70.*

Ponterotto, J. G., & Casas, J. M. (1991). *Handbook of racial/ethnic minority counseling research.* Springfield, IL: Charles C. Thomas.

Ramirez, M. (1991). *Psychotherapy and counseling with minorities: A cognitive approach to individual and cultural differences.* New York: Pergamon Press.

Ryan, A. S., & Hendricks, C. O. (1989). Culture and communication: Supervising the Asian and Hispanic social workers. *The Clinical Supervisor, 7,* 27–140.

Satcher, D. (2000). *Mental health: A report of the surgeon general.* Washington, DC: U.S. Public Health Service.

Sue, D. W. (1992). The challenge of multi-culturalism: The road less traveled. *American Counselor, 1,* 7–14.

Sue, D. W. (1995). Toward a theory of multicultural counseling and therapy. In J. A. Banks & C. A. M. Banks (Eds.), *Handbook of research on multicultural education* (pp. 647–649). New York: Macmillan.

Sue, D. W., Arredondo, P., & McDavis, R. J. (1992). Multicultural competencies and standards: A call to the profession. *Journal of Counseling and Development, 70*(4), 477–486.

Sue, D. W., & Sue, D. (1977). Barriers to effective cross-cultural counseling. *Journal of Counseling Psychology, 24,* 420–429.

Sue, D. W., & Sue, D. (1990). *Counseling the culturally different: Theory and practice.* New York: John Wiley & Sons.

Sue, D. W., & Sue, D. (1999). *Counseling the culturally different: Theory and practice* (3rd ed.). New York: John Wiley & Sons.

U.S. Census Bureau. (2000). *Population estimates program, population division.* Washington, DC: U.S. Government Printing Office.

Watkins, L. E., Jr. (1995). Psychotherapy supervision in the 1990s: Some observations and reflections. *American Journal of Psychotherapy, 49,* 468–581.

Whiting, B. B., & Whiting, J. W. (1975). *Children on six cultures: A psychocultural analysis.* Cambridge, MA: Harvard University Press.

Chapter 7

THE NEED FOR COMPETENCE IN CHILDREN'S PUBLIC MENTAL HEALTH SERVICES

MARSALI HANSEN

Human resource development in children's public mental health services has become a national crisis. The rapid expansion of new service delivery models (see section IV) has not been followed by equally rapid advances in the clinical preparation of the workforce. Sufficient numbers of children's mental health workers are not available, current educational programs do not yet address the skills required by the new service delivery models, and changes in children's mental health policy are not yet reflected in workforce preparation. Many child-serving systems, including children's mental health services, have begun to articulate the specific knowledge, skills, and values required for workforce competency as a foundation for the needed changes in education and training.

Major changes in children's mental health services in the public sector arose from the national recognition that children with severe emotional disturbance (SED) were not being adequately served in their communities. Preliminary changes are often recognized as a response to Jane Knitzer's (1982) seminal work, *Unclaimed Children,* and the subsequent federal initiative that became known by the acronym CASSP (Child and Adolescent Service System Program). Initial efforts focused on the development of integrated systems of care, with intense attention on implementing interagency collaboration and incorporating active parent involvement and advocacy into the delivery systems. Children with SED were identified as experiencing difficulties in several areas, including the school, the home, and the community. An individualized case-based approach was developed to create a more collaborative interface with all child-serving systems, including juvenile justice, education, protective services, child welfare, and mental retardation, as well as mental health. Much of the attention of policymakers was directed toward creating this seamless, multidisciplinary service system and developing programs that would provide a "comprehensive array of services" (Stroul & Friedman, 1986). This approach resulted in the concept now known as *systems of care* and the current federal systems-of-care agenda.

Within these new service models, human resource development was directed both toward developing a highly skilled workforce of case managers and toward empowering parents to become advocates for their children and families and to navigate the process of receiving services in such complex systems (Pires, 1997). Specific governing values and principles were generated and identified in the process of developing these service models; these were integrated into federal, state, and local policy. These principles and values were recognized as being necessary if this seamless system of care was to be implemented effectively, and they were also integrated into the structure of the service delivery models themselves.

Among the beliefs presented, for example, was the principle that caseworkers cannot function as advocates without knowing and addressing the individual characteristics of the children they work with and without careful collaboration with parents. Parents cannot be empowered to collaborate in communities without careful acknowledgment of, assessment of, and attention to the impact of their culture and the culture of the community on service delivery. Children are best integrated into communities when their family continuously interfaces with the agencies and the community members themselves. Removal of children from communities often prolongs the need for services because transitional services are needed when the children return. The more restrictive and intrusive the intervention, the more transitional adjustment is required. A much-cited example of the types of value structures that were generated is presented by Stroul and Friedman (1986):

VALUES AND PRINCIPLES FOR THE SYSTEM OF CARE

Core values

1. The system of care should be child-centered and family-focused, with the needs of the child and family dictating the types and mix of services provided.
2. The system of care should be community-based, with the locus of services as well as management and decision-making responsibility resting at the community level.
3. The system of care should be culturally competent, with agendas, programs, and services that are responsive to the cultural, racial, and ethnic differences of the populations they serve.

Guiding principles

1. Children with emotional disturbances should have access to a comprehensive array of services that address the child's physical, emotional, social, and educational needs.
2. Children with emotional disturbances should receive individualized services in accordance with the unique needs and potentials of each child and guided by an individualized service plan.
3. Children with emotional disturbances should receive services within the least restrictive, most normative environment that is clinically appropriate.
4. The families and surrogate families of children with emotional disturbances should be full participants in all aspects of the planning and delivery of services.
5. Children with emotional disturbances should receive services that are integrated, with linkages between child-serving agencies and programs and mechanisms for planning, developing, and coordinating services.
6. Children with emotional disturbances should be provided with case management or similar mechanisms to ensure that multiple services are delivered in a coordinated and

therapeutic manner and that they can move through the system of services in accordance with their changing needs.

7. Early identification and intervention for children with emotional disturbances should be promoted by the system of care in order to enhance the likelihood of positive outcomes.

8. Children with emotional disturbances should be ensured smooth transitions to the adult service system as they reach maturity.

9. The rights of children with emotional disturbances should be protected, and effective advocacy efforts for children and youth with emotional disturbances should be promoted.

10. Children with emotional disturbances should receive services without regard to race, religion, national origin, sex, physical disability, or other characteristics, and services should be sensitive and responsive to cultural differences and special needs. (Stroul & Friedman, 1986, p. vii)

A similar example that reflects a statewide policy effort was generated and adopted by the Commonwealth of Pennsylvania's Office of Mental Health and Substance Abuse Services (OMHSAS; Pennsylvania State CASSP, 1995):

CORE PRINCIPLES, PA CHILD AND ADOLESCENT SERVICE SYSTEM PROGRAM

Pennsylvania's Child and Adolescent Service System Program (CASSP) is based on a well-defined set of principles for mental health services for children and adolescents with or at risk of developing severe emotional disorders and their families. These principles, variously expressed since the beginning of CASSP, can be summarized in six core statements. When services are developed and delivered according to the following principles, it is expected that they will operate simultaneously and not in isolation from each other.

1. Child-centered

    Services are planned to meet the individual needs of the child, rather than to fit the child into an existing service. Services consider the child's family and community contexts, are developmentally appropriate and child-specific, and also build on the strengths of the child and family to meet the mental health, social and physical needs of the child.

2. Family-focused

    Services recognize that the family is the primary support system for the child. The family participates as a full partner in all stages of the decision-making and treatment planning process, including implementation, monitoring and evaluation. A family may include biological, adoptive and foster parents, siblings, grandparents and other relatives, and other adults who are committed to the child. The development of mental health policy at state and local levels includes family representation.

3. Community-based

    Whenever possible, services are delivered in the child's home community, drawing on formal and informal resources to promote the child's successful participation in the community. Community resources include not only mental health professionals and provider agencies, but also social, religious and cultural organizations and other natural community support networks.

4. Multi-system

    Services are planned in collaboration with all the child-serving systems involved in the child's life. Representatives from all these systems and the family collaborate to define the goals for the child, develop a service plan, develop the necessary resources to implement the plan, provide appropriate support to the child and family, and evaluate progress.

5. Culturally competent

Culture determines our world view and provides a general design for living and patterns for interpreting reality that are reflected in our behavior. Therefore, services that are culturally competent are provided by individuals who have the skills to recognize and respect the behavior, ideas, attitudes, values, beliefs, customs, language, rituals, ceremonies and practices characteristic of a particular group of people.

Note: Pennsylvania's cultural competence initiative has focused specifically on African Americans, Latinos, Asian Americans and Native Americans who have historically not received culturally appropriate services.

6. Least restrictive/least intrusive

Services take place in settings that are the most appropriate and natural for the child and family and are the least restrictive and intrusive available to meet the needs of the child and family.

All such sets of principles are intended to be incorporated at all levels of service formulation and delivery and to serve as the value base for sets of core competencies. Similar sets of values are included in most other child-serving systems, such as the person-centered planning of the mental retardation system and the balanced and restorative justice focus of the juvenile justice system.

Subsequent evaluations of these system-of-care programs resulted in serious and complex questions regarding their effectiveness compared to that of traditional approaches (Bickman, Summerfelt, & Foster, 1996). Careful examination of the programs' implementation generated questions regarding the ability of all staff members to integrate the core values into their treatment approaches and the delivery of services. The evaluators specifically challenged the treatment delivered by the clinicians who implemented the 44 systems-of-care programs and the consistent integration of the staff's fundamental clinical training with the values and principles of the new projects.

Although the development of programmatic designs for systems of care may have progressed, results of outcome studies fail to demonstrate significant differences in the progress of the children themselves when compared to children receiving services in more traditional delivery systems (Pires, 1997). The need for clinicians to integrate new perspectives, values, and principles into their own clinical practice is a challenge that has resulted in further requests for specific workforce competencies. Mental health practitioners must integrate expectations for quality in clinical practice with the application of systems-of-care values and newly developed systems-of-care delivery models. The interface between traditional training, knowledge, skills, and values and the current expectations placed on clinicians by children's public mental health and systems-of-care models is being recognized with increasing concern. In 1998, the American Psychological Association (APA)'s Task Force on Child and Adolescent Professional Psychology to the Board of Professional Affairs explored the matter of expectations for professional child and adolescent psychologists. Among the task force's charges were to "identify issues in the pre and post-doctoral education and training of professional child and adolescent psychology," and to "prioritize and recommend to the Practice Directorate means to broaden, expand, and solidify the practice of child and adolescent psychology, including inter-directorate coordination" (Tharinger et al., 1998).

After extensive review and discussion, one of the three specific summary recommendations stated:

> Promote increased awareness of: (a) the changes to psychological practice with children and families that have occurred; (b) the existing and new competencies and skills that psychologists will need to maintain and expand public and private practice opportunities and leadership in the face of these changes; and (c) the need for these practice competencies and skills to be sensitive to and integrated with the knowledge base and issues of concern within the practice, education, science, and public interest communities. (Tharinger et al., 1998, p. 31)

Subsequently, Surgeon General David Satcher held a national conference to address concerns in children's mental health services, and the APA was an active participant. One of the specific goals identified at the conference was to "train frontline providers to recognize and manage mental health issues and educate mental health providers in scientifically proven prevention and treatment services" (U.S. Surgeon General, 2000, p. 5). Robert Friedman, a participant both on the APA task force and at the surgeon general's conference, stated during the proceedings:

> Children's mental health is largely divided, not just between the practitioner community and the research community, but also among the practitioner community, the evidence-based intervention community and the systems of care community. Each has much to offer, but there is a gulf between them that needs to be reduced. (Friedman, 2000).

Competencies are one effort to narrow this gulf through the development of an integrated approach to best practice with systems of care and input from the evidenced-based intervention community and the practitioner community.

One review examined the content of sets of competencies available to children's mental health professionals practicing in the public sector (Goldman & De La Cruz Irvine, 1997). A panel of 27 experts reviewed a sample of 22 documents. Generally, these documents were criticized for failing to integrate the various disciplines and child-serving systems, a fundamental value of the changes in policy. Competencies were reviewed for their inclusion of values, attitudes, knowledge, and skills. Of these four areas, 10 of the 22 addressed all four. The panel expressed concern that competencies were inadequately included in higher education training programs and in the practice by professionals in the field. Disciplines identified as having formalized sets of competencies applicable for children with mental health concerns in the public sector included child and adolescent psychiatry, social work, child welfare, school psychology, and mental health counseling—but not, as yet, psychology, although the APA is currently expressing a need for such a focus, as noted.

One of the noted disciplines that has expressed a commitment to competencies and generated specific efforts is school psychology. The National Association of School Psychologists (NASP) has prepared a set of competencies. These competencies reflect the standards for training and field placement required for credentialing school psychologists. Upon careful review, the distinction between "competencies" and professional guidelines and standards becomes blurred in such documents. For example, guidelines for course content, applied experiences, and performance expectations are included. Specific knowledge, skills, and values are not distinguished from general areas of content.

The challenge to the disciplines is to integrate current values and trends in policy into competencies for best practice, particularly the efforts to increase collaboration and partnership at all levels of clinical practice. Service delivery systems have changed, as have the fundamental models of practice, to a more collaborative rather than discipline-specific and expert-based approach. Integrating these changes through the credentialing process while retaining the unique contributions and skills of each discipline requires vigilance. General course expectations and professional guidelines often fail to specify what the professional needs to know and believe in order to provide the best possible service within the current context of children's mental health.

Child psychiatry has also developed a specific set of clinical competencies that is quite elaborate and incorporates many of the system-of-care principles. This set of core competencies, developed by the American Academy of Child and Adolescent Psychiatry's Workgroup on Training and Education, is organized into knowledge, skills, and values in specific clinical areas. One example comes from the section on systems-based care:

> Treatment of children and adolescents with psychiatric problems is undertaken in the context of multiple, complex systems. The most important competencies in systems-based care are
>
> • Works in a mutually respectful, culturally competent manner with systems of care including various family compositions and extended family,
> • Demonstrates a working knowledge of the diverse systems involved in treating children and adolescents,
> • Integrates multiple systems of care in treatment planning,
> • Effectively collaborates in developing a shared treatment plan and,
> • Advocates for children and adolescents in various systems of care. (Cuffe and Sylvester, 2000, p. 1)

The section on knowledge of this set of competencies for systems-based care includes the following item regarding the mental health system:

MENTAL HEALTH SYSTEM

• Has working knowledge of available services in the community, both public and private.
• Understands the use of home, school, and other community-based treatments such as family preservation, intensive case management.
• Assesses patients for the level and intensity of care required.
• Explains the role of community-based treatment and their appropriate use to supervisors. (Cuffe & Sylvester, 2000, p. 2)

Organizations and agencies within other child-serving systems that provide or monitor services in the public sector have begun to explore the need for sets of specific expectations for public sector practitioners. The developers of training programs for both child welfare caseworkers and probation officers have actively sought to base them on competence training. Many children with SED are served in these systems, and a qualified workforce contributes to their overall well-being. These groups often describe *competencies* as the specific tasks required to perform a job, based on a thorough analysis of each specific position. Therefore, these efforts may appear far more prescriptive and specific than the content requirements for training that have been set out within individual disciplines and specialties.

As noted from these examples, *competencies* most frequently refers to the three components of knowledge, skills, and values needed to perform a task or provide a service. Sets of competencies that have been developed within the children's public mental health system frequently reflect system-of-care policies and the core values and principles that have been adopted by CASSP. The knowledge component often integrates and applies didactic material from multiple disciplines and settings. Skills remain the greatest challenge and the area most frequently addressed only in general terms or in terms of disciplinary standards (one noted exception is in the field of child psychiatry). Skills are where knowledge and values are integrated in practice; clear specifications are needed if the competencies are to be useful for the improvement of the workforce. In addition, though these competencies integrate knowledge across disciplines and service systems, rarely is the integration of new knowledge and values with fundamental clinical best-practice standards specifically addressed.

In 1999, the Child, Adolescent, and Family branch of the Center for Mental Health Services in the Substance Abuse and Mental Health Services Administration (SAMHSA) published a series of monographs, *Promising Practices in Children's Mental Health*. Volume 5 of the series addresses training strategies, including core competencies (Meyers, Kaufman, & Goldman, 1999). The monograph highlights the perspective of competence, with various definitions, but generally meaning a shared perspective of doing the right thing for the right reason at the right time. The authors emphasize the view that competence is not necessarily acquired through training but also requires personal characteristics such as flexibility, common sense, problem-solving ability, and compassion. Two examples of comprehensive sets of core competencies are provided. These two sets are also cited as exemplary models by the Child, Adolescent, and Family panel of the Mental Health Managed Care and Workforce Training Project previously described (Goldman & De La Cruz Irvine, 1997).

Trinity College's set of core competencies is the basis for the college's master's program in community mental health. The core competencies were developed by experts in the field and reviewed nationally. The materials highlight the specific knowledge, skills, and values required to function within a community-based system of care for children and adolescents with SED. The skills incorporate the fundamental best practice of community mental health with the values and expectations articulated in systems-of-care documents. One example from those competencies follows:

I. Demonstrates respect for children and adolescents experiencing a serious emotional disturbance and their families.

    A. Uses language and behavior which consistently respects the dignity of children and adolescents experiencing a serious emotional disturbance and behavioral problems.

      1. Written materials

      2. Verbal communications

  B. Demonstrates holistic understanding of children and adolescents experiencing a serious emotional disturbance and their families.

      1. Stages and milestones in basic child, adolescent, and adult development

      2. Basic needs for food, shelter, clothing, affiliation, and dignity

      3. Individual strengths, interests and capabilities

      4. Impact of serious emotional disturbance on self and on family expectations

  C. Involves child or adolescent in all aspects of service planning and support activities.

      1. Invites and fosters expression of child/youth goals and preferences

      2. Assists child/youth and family in reaching mutually agreeable goals

      3. Provides support and resources as needed to facilitate involvement of child/youth

  D. Provides information as needed.

      1. Provides information about serious emotional and behavioral problems, medications, services and resources

      2. Provides information about target symptoms, possible side effects, anticipated problems, other contingencies

      3. Provides referrals to appropriate resources as needed (Meyers et al., 1999, p. 85)

The second set of core competencies cited by Meyers et al. (1999) was developed and adopted by the Commonwealth of Pennsylvania. These core competencies are designed to address the specific integration of system-of-care values, professional standards of practice, and models of clinical best practice across mental health disciplines. As the professions cry out for models of core competencies, Pennsylvania's document serves as an example of a comprehensive effort to present the expectations for best practice for children and adolescents with SED and their families. Such a model can serve as a foundation for other efforts within disciplines, professions, and child-serving systems, and for other statewide approaches.

Pennsylvania's initial work on developing core competencies was funded by a federal CASSP grant. New models of service delivery had proliferated, the state had accepted the CASSP principles as values to be demonstrated throughout children's mental health services, and policy experts were becoming increasingly concerned by the lack of general knowledge within the workforce about children's needs or serious emotional disturbance. The state hired a small staff and developed the Pennsylvania CASSP Training and Technical Assistance Institute. A workgroup of state-based and nationally recognized experts convened to generate specific expectations for clinical best practice within the state, under the coordination and leadership of the current author.

The names of the individuals are worth noting for the depth and breadth of their expertise in work with families, SED, and serious mental illness. These leaders in the field included Carol Anderson, nationally known for her many books on family therapy and for generating the psychoeducational model for treating families with a member with schizophrenia; Marion Lindblad-Goldberg, an internationally known family therapist and currently the director of the Philadelphia Child and Family Therapy Training Center; Diane Marsh, nationally known expert in the area of serious mental illness and families, and coeditor of this volume; Sherry (Harbaugh) Peters, a policy expert from the state, who trained extensively in family systems with Virginia Satir; and Catherine Gray, a longtime family advocate and mother of a son with schizophrenia.

Child, Family and Community Core Competencies (Hansen et al., 1999) was written to serve as the foundation for university-based curriculum and continuing education curriculum within the state. The specificity of the document is far greater than that of other nationally recognized sets of standards and competencies. Included are the clinical fundamentals that most seasoned clinicians recognize as crucial but which may seem so obvious that they are rarely discussed. The competencies were reviewed by more than 75 participants, including representatives from higher education, state and local government, parent groups and family members, all child-serving systems, providers, and all mental health professions. The institute strove to be inclusive and avoid divisiveness. It intended to create a document that residents of the state would embrace. Recommendations for additions were incorporated whenever they added to the comprehensiveness of the document. The document is intended to be meta-theoretical; comments from the reviewers suggested these efforts were successful, as not one reviewer noted any theoretical bias and many reviewers added substantive material.

Pennsylvania's core competencies are organized in three categories consistent with systems-of-care and CASSP core values. The first section, Child Core Competencies, focuses on values of being "child-centered" and "individualized." This section is by far the most specific. Expectations that include values, knowledge, and skills are stated for each age group, and ages are divided at approximately 3-year intervals, from birth to age 21. Subcategories within age groups include such topics as social development, cognitive development, emotional development, physical development, the cultural context, impairment and risk of impairment, assessment, interventions, and legal and ethical issues. Two examples follow regarding the knowledge and skills needed related to a child's emotional development, one from the *Infant and Toddler Book* (ages 0 to 2) and one from the *Early Teen Book* (ages 12 to 14):

100-1-C. EMOTIONAL DEVELOPMENT (AGES 0–2)

1. Professionals will be able to demonstrate general knowledge of:
   a. The range of infant and toddler temperaments
   b. Factors affecting temperament, such as over-stimulation
   c. The development of emotional regulation and the role of parents in its development
2. Professionals will be able to demonstrate the willingness to implement the following skills:

a. Ability to recognize when a child's intensity or lack of intensity exceeds the normal range and to help the parent develop strategies to cope with either extreme as well as strategies for helping the infant/toddler better modulate his or her expression of affect

b. Ability to provide parental support and interventions to increase the "goodness of fit" between the infant/toddler and the caregiver

c. Ability to conduct and write a mental status examination on an infant/toddler

d. Ability to identify concerns about developmental delay, disruption and deviation

e. Ability to assist parents in developing strategies to help their infant/toddler learn to regulate his or her affect, including helping the infant/toddler learn self-soothing abilities and the toddler to learn behavioral control when upset

f. Ability to differentiate normal separation concerns from separation anxiety (Hansen et al., 1999, pp. 16–17)

100-V-C.   EMOTIONAL DEVELOPMENT (AGES 12–14)

1. Professionals will be able to demonstrate general knowledge of the emotional issues of this age group, particularly the extreme fluctuations between the needs for dependence, supervision and independence, as well as privacy and "equal rights with parents."

2. Professionals will be able to demonstrate the willingness to implement the following skills:

   a. Ability to differentiate among and tolerate the extreme range of moods of this age group

   b. Ability to remain calm in provocative interactions with teens from this age group

   c. Ability to formulate interventions that address the emotional concerns of these teens and allow for their expression of emotion

   d. Ability to engage teens in treatment

   e. Ability to discuss emotionally charged issues (Hansen et al., 1999, p. 41)

Following is an example from the *Pre-Teen Book* (ages 9 to 11) of the knowledge and skills needed related to legal and ethical issues:

100-IV-I.   PROFESSIONAL, LEGAL AND ETHICAL ISSUES

1. Professionals will be able to demonstrate general knowledge of

   a. The scope of legal and ethical issues for parents including custody issues, paternity suits, child abuse and conservatorships

    b. The role of clinicians in the process

    c. The role of family and grandparents

    d. Confidentiality and exceptions to confidentiality, such as duty to warn and potential harm to self and others

    e. The civil and legal rights of children with disabilities

2. Professionals will be able to demonstrate the willingness to implement the following skills with children and families.

    a. Ability to maintain strict professional boundaries, refrain from dual relationships (multiple roles) and uphold the ethical standards in all interactions with children and families in accordance with good clinical standards

    b. Ability to implement a variety of therapeutic interventions and match the approach with the needs of the child and family

    c. Ability to use supervision and consultation productively to improve the quality of treatment

    d. Ability to provide quality documentation in a timely manner

    e. Ability to demonstrate the accepted role of confidentiality and its limitations with children and their families (Hansen et al., 1999, p. 39)

Finally, the following is an example from the *Teen Book* (ages 15 to 17) of the knowledge and skills needed related to cultural competence:

100-VI-E.   THE CULTURAL CONTEXT

1. Professionals will be able to demonstrate general knowledge of the needs and functioning of teens within their cultural context including an awareness of variations in the following areas:

- Developmental expectations
- Caregiving expectations
- Sources of support
- Role of extended family
- Development of sexuality and sexual identity
- Development of cultural/ethnic identity with the context of the family
- Role of peer groups
- Expected parental response to teen distress
- Gender roles for parenting of teens
- The role of spirituality and religion
- The cultural variability in expectations for independent functioning, including caregiving expectations
- The sources of support available to adolescents from different cultures

2. Professionals will be able to demonstrate the willingness to implement the following skills:

   a. Ability to connect with teens from various cultural groups

   b. Ability to recognize stereotyping and racist perceptions of teens from various cultural groups

   c. Ability to address racism and stereotyping with the teen

   d. Ability to recognize the role of the teen within the extended family

   e. Ability to identify and appreciate the strengths of teens from various cultural groups

   f. Ability to develop the teen's social and community awareness skills within the cultural and geographic context

   g. Ability to provide services to teens from multiple cultures

   h. Ability to recognize areas that are culturally sensitive to teens

   i. Ability to assess the following:
      • Sources of support
      • Cultural strengths
      • The role of the extended family and the diverse range of family configurations
      • How culture affects gender roles
      • The cultural perception of the role of the father, mother and grandparents

   j. Ability to facilitate the development of the teen's social and community skills within the cultural and geographic context

   k. Ability to identify and encourage culturally appropriate parenting techniques and styles within the family's own cultural context

   l. Ability to ensure transition to and help with connections to referral sources outside the culture, helping both the family and the referral source in transition

   m. Ability to assist parents when cultural practices differ from local, state or federal regulations

   n. Ability to reinforce the formulation of cultural identity without stereotyping when working with teens

   o. Ability to identify cultural strengths and formulate culturally appropriate interventions

   p. Ability to help parents formulate an appropriate range of freedom for their teens within the environmental, social and cultural contexts (taking into account factors such as neighborhood violence) (Hansen et al., 1999, pp. 49–50)

The second section, Family Core Competencies, integrates best-practice models for working with families while articulating systems-of-care efforts to move from an "expert model" to a "partnership" approach. The intent of this section is to identify competencies for all individuals who work with families within the context of children's mental health services. Additional skills and competencies would be expected of individuals who identified themselves as family therapists. The following example is taken from the subsection on intervention skills:

F. Professionals will be able to demonstrate the following skills related to severe psychiatric disorders:

1. Ability to recognize the symptoms of severe psychiatric disorders, such as autism and other developmental disorders, schizophrenia, major depressive disorder, bipolar disorder and obsessive-compulsive disorder

2. Ability to recognize the need for a psychiatric referral

3. Ability to prepare the family for the referral

4. Ability to collaborate with a psychiatrist and treatment team

5. Ability to educate the family regarding severe psychiatric disorder and its treatment

6. Ability to assist the family in supporting the treatment plan

7. Ability to assist families in coping with the symptoms of severe psychiatric disorders, including hallucinations, delusions, disorganized thinking or speech, bizarre behavior, negative symptoms, severe depression, sharp mood swings, self-destructive or violent behavior, and severe anxiety

8. Ability to assist the family in recognizing the signs of impending relapse and in developing an early intervention plan (Hansen et al., 1999, p. 67)

The third section of the document, Community Core Competencies, reflects expectations of interagency collaboration (particularly at the local level), familiarity with community culture and resources, and the ability to integrate knowledge and skills in community mental health service with the core values of CASSP and systems of care. An example of expectations for familiarity with agencies follows, from the subsection on knowledge of community systems:

300-1-D. CHILD WELFARE/CHILDREN, YOUTH AND FAMILIES

1. Professionals will be able to demonstrate the ability to locate information on the following aspects of the community child welfare system:

a. How and when to access the system

b. What populations are served

c. The administrative structure and the division of labor

d. The philosophical orientation

e. The history

f. The funding structure

    g. Programs available, including entitlement programs, housing, family preservation, family support, shelters (women/children; homelessness/abuse), residential, therapeutic group homes, foster care

    h. The structure of the system's collaborative process

    i. Requirements of the Child Protection Act regarding mandated reporting of suspected abuse

    j. Family support groups (Hansen et al., 1999, pp. 72–73)

An example of skills for collaborating within the community follows, from the subsection on skills related to community systems:

300-II-B. DEVELOPING AND USING COMMUNITY RESOURCES

1. Professionals will be able to demonstrate the willingness to implement the following skills:

    a. Ability to discuss, explain and clarify county, regional or community profiles that include the following:

- Location, size and population
- Percentage of rural, suburban and urban populations
- Municipalities (cities, boroughs, townships)
- The cultural or ethnic composition and cultural biases
- The economic base
- Strengths and sources of pride
- Problems and limitations
- Community violence/community response to violence

    b. Ability to discern what community resources might be helpful in specific situations and how to access them; e.g., transportation

    c. Ability to establish contact and credibility with appropriate people within community systems, organizations and groups

    d. Ability to identify informal community leaders and cultural brokers and to access them

    e. Ability to conduct community, interagency and intra-agency meetings

    f. Ability to facilitate interagency collaboration, and develop and implement interagency service plans while participating in collaborative efforts of other systems

    g. Ability to identify the least restrictive settings in the community that will meet the child's and family's needs

    h. Ability to explore all possible resources in the community

    i. Ability to use the strengths of the community (as identified through working with the family) in developing a plan of care

j. Ability to be flexible and explore creative plans that address the culture-specific needs of children and families

k. Ability to identify advocates and collaborate with families and advocates (Hansen et al., 1999, p. 78)

A summary of all three components of Pennsylvania's core competencies is included in the appendix to this chapter.

In Pennsylvania, there are currently several efforts underway to integrate the core competencies with existing training and education programs. For example, the competencies are beginning to be integrated with the Ethical Standards of Human Service Professionals for the preparation of human service workers in community college programs. Such an effort would address concerns regarding the large proportions of interventions and services provided by individuals who have not earned a bachelor's degree.

In addition, the Community section of the core competencies is serving as the foundation for a cross-systems effort among mental health, juvenile justice, drug and alcohol services, child welfare, and medical assistance agencies to help increase access to services for children identified as dependent or delinquent. Pennsylvania's core competencies are also serving as a foundation for revising a master of social work training program within a nationally recognized school of social work.

At the national level, efforts are focusing on the widely recognized crisis in children's mental health—a crisis that includes concerns about recruitment and retention as well as the recognition that the workforce is poorly prepared to address the needs of children with SED. These efforts embrace core competencies as a foundation for future developments. Training initiatives on many fronts are starting with sets of specific clinical expectations for individuals who work with children with SED. These expectations (or competencies), when combined and integrated with professional standards, serve as a foundation for curriculum revisions that will better prepare students for their positions in the workforce.

Competencies also serve as a set of expectations to assist the current workforce in identifying necessary standardized continuing education programs that will address specific needs. These competencies can also serve parents and parent advocates. Catherine Gray, the parent advocate coauthor of Pennsylvania's core competencies, commented as she reviewed numerous revisions, "I wish I had had this when my son was in the system. I would have known what I could have expected from the people who worked with him. If he had only had people with these skills . . ." (author's personal conversation). What better service can any document provide than to improve the services to children with SED and their families?

APPENDIX: CHILD, FAMILY AND COMMUNITY CORE COMPETENCIES SUMMARY

The *Child, Family and Community Core Competencies* document as a whole answers the questions of what professionals should know about children, families, and communities and what skills they should have in order to provide competent services and treatment. This section is an overview of the general competencies expected from professionals who provide services to children and families within Pennsylvania's CASSP framework. The section is divided into the same three categories as the more specific knowledge and skill competencies outlined earlier in this chapter. All of the knowledge requirements and skills that are named in these summaries are addressed in detail later in the document.

100.   CHILD COMPETENCIES

The *child-centered* CASSP principle states: "Services are planned to meet the individual needs of the child, rather than to fit the child into an existing service. Services consider the child's family and community contexts, are developmentally appropriate and child-specific, and also build on the strengths of the child and family to meet the mental health, social and physical needs of the child." The following summary of the "Child Core Competencies" lists the general skills necessary to demonstrate the clinical application of this principle.

1. Professionals will be able to view the child and family from the perspective of the child.
2. Professionals will be familiar with developmental expectations for children within the social, emotional, cognitive and physical domains.
3. Professionals will be able to recognize when children's behavior exceeds the range of "normal variability/expectation" within these domains.
4. Professionals will know how to conduct informal assessments of functioning within these domains and how to use information provided by formal assessments of these domains.
5. Professionals will know how and when to intervene to address behavior of concern to the parent and or child.
6. Professionals will recognize the range of mental health problems and be able to institute appropriate and effective interventions and referrals.
7. Professionals will have knowledge of and be sensitive to cultural strengths and differences.
8. Professionals will be able to implement services that incorporate cultural strengths.
9. Professionals will demonstrate their cultural sensitivity in their interactions with children and families.
10. Professionals will be aware of specific risks to children—biological, psychological and sociocultural—and be able to identify the severity of these risks with specific families and children.
11. Professionals will be familiar with current psychiatric diagnostic criteria and the etiology and frequency of childhood disorders including severe psychiatric disorders.
12. Professionals will be able to use this knowledge of psychiatric diagnosis in their work with specific children and families and be able to individualize and personalize their approach.
13. Professionals will be familiar with professionally recognized and current practices for work with children and families and be able to implement these approaches appropriately.
14. Professionals will identify and use interventions that are compatible with the culture of children and families.
15. Professionals will know professional standards of conduct and specific concerns within these standards that apply to children.
16. Professionals will have skills to communicate and document their assessments and interventions.

17. Professionals will be able to recognize children in crisis and intervene appropriately and effectively in a manner that includes the family as partners.
18. Professionals will be able to identify the least restrictive and intrusive service and intervene in a manner that incorporates this awareness.

200. FAMILY COMPETENCIES

The *family-focused* CASSP principle states: "Services recognize that the family is the primary support system for the child. The family participates as a full partner in all stages of the decision-making and treatment planning process, including implementation, monitoring and evaluation. A family may include biological, adoptive and foster parents, siblings, grandparents and other relatives, and other adults who are committed to the child. The development of mental health policy at state and local levels includes family representation." The following summary of the "Family Core Competencies" lists the general knowledge and skills that will demonstrate whether professionals are working respectfully and competently in partnership with families.

1. Professionals will be familiar with the functions of a family and the potential impact and mutual influences of a child's emotional concerns and mental health problems on these functions.
2. Professionals will be familiar with the characteristics of the family, including structure, organization, dynamics, development and functioning.
3. Professionals will be familiar with the experiences and needs of families that have a child with a specific concern or disorder, including severe psychiatric disorders.
4. Professionals will be familiar with family risk factors, including life events within the family, life events in the social cultural context, and difficulties in the family and extended family system.
5. Professionals will possess fundamental family assessment skills including the ability to prioritize, identify strengths, establish partnership in the assessment process, and recognize the multiple characteristics of individual families including cultural factors.
6. Professionals will possess fundamental family intervention skills, including contacting the family, connecting with the family, establishing a treatment contract, helping the family meet their needs, and helping the family develop adaptive patterns of functioning.
7. Professionals will be able to provide services in a culturally respectful manner.
8. Professionals will be able to intervene to prevent crisis and to intervene when crises occur.
9. Professionals will be able to provide appropriate referral and collaboration.
10. Professionals will be able to appropriately address issues involved with medication.
11. Professionals will be able to provide collateral and collaborative family counseling in an appropriate and professionally sound manner.
12. Professionals will be able to intervene with couples and refer when appropriate.
13. Professionals will be aware of professional codes of ethics and conduct and be able to behave in a professional manner consistent with these codes.

300. COMMUNITY COMPETENCIES

The *community-based* CASSP principle states: "Whenever possible, services are delivered in the child's home community, drawing on formal and informal resources to promote the child's successful participation in the community. Community resources include not only mental health professionals and provider agencies, but also social, religious and cultural organizations and other natural community support networks." In addition and closely related, the *multi-system* CASSP principle states: "Services are planned in collaboration with all the child-serving systems involved in the child's life. Representatives from all these systems and the family collaborate to define the goals for the child, develop a service plan, develop the necessary resources to implement the plan, provide appropriate support to the child and family, and evaluate progress." The following summary of the "Community Core Competencies" identifies areas of competency for professionals who are expected to demonstrate the knowledge and skills for delivering services that use community resources and coordinate among all the systems involved in the child's life.

1. Professionals will be knowledgeable about formal government systems.
2. Professionals will be knowledgeable of other formal community and private child- and family-serving systems.
3. Professionals will have the ability to describe the range of mental health systems of care.
4. Professionals will have the ability to describe and recognize differences in community mental health, private sector provision, and facility-based services.
5. Professionals will have the ability to develop a county/regional profile.
6. Professionals will have the ability to assist families in the use of appropriate resources.
7. Professionals will have the ability to engage and maintain collaboration with formal and informal systems and resources.
8. Professionals will have the ability to collaborate with families in accessing the least restrictive and least intrusive interventions and services.
9. Professionals will have the ability to identify cultural strengths in a community and intervene in a culturally competent manner from the perspective of the child's community.
10. Professionals will have the ability to identify the child's and family's perspective of community.
11. Professionals will have the ability to assist the family to be effective advocates for themselves and their child in multiple systems. (Hansen et al., 1999, pp. 11–14)

REFERENCES

Bickman, L., Summerfelt, W. T., & Foster, M. (1996) Research on systems of care: Implications of the Fort Bragg evaluation. In B. Stroul (Ed.), *Children's mental health: Creating systems of care in a changing society* (pp. 337–354). Baltimore, MD: Paul H. Brookes.

Cuffe, S., & Sylvester, C. (2000, August). *Core competencies for child and adolescent psychiatry.* Paper presented at the meeting of the Core Competency Project of the Workgroup on Training and Education of American Academy of Child and Adolescent Psychiatry, Washington, DC.

Friedman, R. (2000). *At the Core Competency Project of the Workgroup on Training and Education of American Academy of Child and Adolescent Psychiatry.* Washington, DC: American Academy of Child and Adolescent Psychiatry.

Goldman, S. K., & De La Cruz Irvine, M. (1997). *Report of the Child and Adolescent Panel for the Mental Health Managed Care and Workforce Training Project.* Washington, DC: Georgetown University, Child Development Center.

Hansen, M., Anderson, C., Gray, C., Harbaugh, S., Lindblad-Goldberg, M., & Marsh, D. T. (1999). *Child, family and community core competencies.* Harrisburg, PA: Pennsylvania CASSP Training and Technical Assistance Institute.

Knitzer, J. (1982). *Unclaimed children: The failure of public responsibility to children and adolescents in need of mental health services.* Washington, DC: Children's Defense Fund.

Meyers, J., Kaufman, M., & Goldman, S. (1999). Promising practices: Training strategies for serving children with serious emotional disturbance and their families in a system of care. In *Systems of care: Promising practices in children's mental health* (Vol. 5). Washington, DC: Center for Effective Collaboration and Practice, American Institutes for Research.

Pennsylvania State Child and Adolescent Service System Program Advisory Committee. (1995). *Core principles: Pennsylvania Child and Adolescent System Program.* Harrisburg, PA: Office of Mental Health and Substance Abuse Services.

Pires, S. A. (1997). Human resource development. In B. Stroul (Ed.) *Children's mental health: Creating systems of care in a changing society* (pp. 281–297). Baltimore, MD: Paul H. Brookes.

Stroul, B., & Friedman, R. (1986). *A system of care for children and youth with severe emotional disturbances* (Rev. ed). Washington, DC: Georgetown University Child Development Center, National Technical Assistance Center for Children's Mental Health.

Tharinger, D., Friedman, B., Hughes, J., La Greca, A., Silverstein, L., Vargas, L., & Willis, D. (1998). *Report of the Task Force on Child and Adolescent Professional Psychology to the Board of Professional Affairs.* Washington, DC: American Psychological Association.

U.S. Surgeon General. (2000). *Report of the surgeon general's conference on children's mental health: A national action agenda.* Washington, DC: U.S. Department of Health and Human Services.

Chapter 8

SUPERVISORY ISSUES RELATED TO TREATING CHILDREN WITH SERIOUS EMOTIONAL DISTURBANCE

LINDA K. KNAUSS

Supervision is the primary professional training model for mental health clinicians (Alonzo, 1985), and providing supervision is a key task for many clinicians. Although most mental health professionals begin their career as supervisees, the ways in which they are influenced during this period play a crucial role in their professional development (Pope & Vasquez, 1991). This chapter covers supervisory issues related to treating children with serious emotional disturbance (SED).

First, the following section sets the stage for working with children with SED by describing the process of supervision. This includes the definition of *supervision,* the essential elements of a successful supervisory relationship, and the goals of supervision. Although working with children with SED presents many dilemmas, several challenging situations are discussed. In addition, the impact of cultural competence on the supervisory relationship is presented. There are many ways to provide supervision, from cotherapy to case presentations. The advantages and disadvantages of the modalities of supervision are evaluated, along with the attributes of good supervisors and good supervision.

When supervising individuals who are providing services to children with SED, it is important to ensure that clinicians include the family, focus on the reason for referral, establish goals for treatment, and recognize when it is time for termination. Supervisors also need to be able to recognize and resolve issues of parallel process, which are especially prevalent when working with at-risk children and adolescents. Since home-based services are a preventive strategy for multiproblem, at-risk families, a model of supervision of in-home services is presented. Finally, supervision is identified as an important component in preventing burnout when working with children with SED. The importance of supervision is stressed as part of the lifelong learning process. The success of supervision depends on the effective integration of all of these elements.

WHAT IS SUPERVISION?

Supervision has been defined as "an intensive, interpersonally focused relationship in which one person is designated to facilitate the development of therapeutic competence in the other person(s)" (Loganbill, Hardy, & Delworth, 1982, p. 4). Supervision is the process that develops out of the relationship between a supervisor and a supervisee, and is a developmental process that occurs over time. In supervising a less experienced therapist, the supervisor may initially assume a more directive, hierarchical style to meet the beginner's needs for structure and immediate knowledge. However, as the supervisee gains competence and deserves more autonomy, the supervisor must shift to a more collaborative, less hierarchical role. Supervisors become ineffective when they do not shift their role from that of expert to that of collaborative partner, an accommodation that acknowledges the supervisee's increased expertise.

With a more experienced therapist, mutual discussion can help a supervisor gauge the optimal levels of intensity, interaction, and autonomy. Both inexperienced and experienced therapists and their supervisors are responsible for ultimately developing a collaborative learning alliance (Lindblad-Goldberg, Dore, & Stern, 1998). The parameters of the supervisory relationship must be clearly defined and understood by both parties. A supervisory relationship should be ongoing and should occur within a consistent time frame. The goal of supervision is the clinical socialization of the therapist, as evidenced by knowledge, clinical skills, and ethical public practice (Bernard & Goodyear, 1992).

THE SUPERVISORY RELATIONSHIP

Supervisors need to maintain clear boundaries between professional development and personal growth or therapy. The supervisor must ensure that the supervisee is neither encouraged nor allowed to become the supervisor's therapy patient. Some forms of supervision may share aspects of some forms of therapy. Sometimes supervisees, in the course of supervision, become aware of personal concerns, psychological problems, or behavioral difficulties that might benefit from therapy. If supervisees decide to seek treatment for these matters, they should consult a therapist with whom they have no dual relationship (Pope & Vasquez, 1998).

A supervisor has the responsibility for both the client and the professional growth of the supervisee. However, the client's welfare must always be primary. The supervisor must ensure that no aspect of the training process jeopardizes the client. Supervisors are responsible for the clinical services provided by individuals functioning under their supervision. Any conflicts between a supervisor and a supervisee regarding the best course of treatment must be promptly, honestly, and comprehensively addressed. Both individuals may avoid addressing such conflicts because they are ill at ease with conflict or authority issues (Pope & Vasquez, 1998). The fact that the supervisor is in a position of authority and evaluation raises the issues of power and hierarchy in the supervisory relationship. Because the supervisor's job is to impart expert knowledge, make judgments on the supervisee's performance, and act as a gatekeeper in the profession (Holloway, 1995), the supervisor's position is by definition a hierarchical one.

If conflicts between a supervisor and supervisee are not adequately addressed, both the supervision and the therapy will suffer. Such conflicts are often recreated in the relationship between a supervisee and a client. In the same way, the dynamics of the relationship between a supervisee and a client are often acted out in the supervisor–supervisee relationship. It is important to recognize that this is a normal part of the supervisory process (Pope & Vasquez, 1998).

Supervision requires the same competence that assessment, therapy, and consultation require. It is also important that the supervisor be trained, knowledgeable, and skilled in the practice of supervision (Stoltenberg & Delworth, 1987). Supervisors must also be competent in the approaches used to assess and treat the client. Thus, a supervisor whose training and practice are exclusively with adults should not be supervising child or family interventions (Pope & Vasquez, 1998).

When a supervisor and a supervisee begin working together, it often takes time to establish a positive relationship and an open, honest context in which the therapist's skills can be evaluated. Supervisors are responsible for assessing and evaluating the competence, skills, and professional development of their supervisees. In initial supervisory meetings, supervisees should be encouraged to discuss what they perceive to be their strengths and the areas where they feel competent, as well as to identify areas in which they need help to grow or learn.

During subsequent evaluation sessions, supervisors and supervisees can explore the progress made in meeting these goals (Boyd-Franklin & Bry, 2000). Just as parents who feel accused, blamed, and judged by family workers tend to blame and scapegoat their children and adolescents, therapists who feel blamed and unsupported by their supervisors tend to be harsh in judging or diagnosing the clients and families they treat (Boyd-Franklin, 1989).

Supervisees are also entitled to timely feedback. Koocher and Keith-Spiegel (1998) indicate that lack of timely feedback is the most common basis of ethics complaints regarding supervision. Although supervisors must, at times, prevent unsuitable or unqualified individuals from becoming therapists, reflecting a responsibility to future clients who might be harmed by incompetent or unscrupulous practice, this must also be done in a way that is not excessively hurtful to the supervisee (Pope & Vasquez, 1998).

Clients whose therapists are being supervised also have a right to information about the supervisory arrangements. They should know that the clinical services they are receiving are being formally supervised. Also, clients should know if their therapist is a student. Clients should know the identity of the supervisor and should have access to the supervisor. Supervisors have a duty to clients to truly supervise the services that are being provided. Because supervisors are responsible for the services of anyone under their supervision, any failure on the part of the supervisee is presumed to be a failure on the part of the supervisor.

Another important aspect of supervision has to do with the availability of the supervisor. If a client has an emergency, supervisees need to know how to reach supervisors promptly. Other important considerations include whether the supervisor is available for phone supervision between scheduled sessions; whether the supervisor can be reached during late-night hours, on weekends, or on holidays; whether there are adequate preparations for supervisor absences—both planned and unanticipated; and whether the supervisee has options for securing necessary help if the supervisor is unavailable during a crisis (Pope & Vasquez, 1998).

With regard to the supervisory process, it is very important that the supervisor and supervisee honestly confront their reactions to each other and to their work together. The purpose is to evaluate what each has gained from the other. Disappointment, anger, and hurt as well as attentiveness, support, and creativity need to be acknowledged. Therapeutic interventions take place in the context of intense and intimate relationships. Whether these relationships are helpful or hurtful depends on fulfilling responsibilities with regard to power, trust, and caring (Pope & Vasquez, 1998).

SUPERVISORY GOALS

Once the supervisory relationship has been defined, it is important to establish goals. Often, the goals of supervision parallel the goals of the therapeutic process. The goals of supervision are also situationally dependent and differ depending on whether the treatment is individual or family therapy and whether the clients are adults, children, or families. However, the numerous goals and skills identified in the literature generally fit into five broad areas: counseling or therapeutic skills, case conceptualization, professional role, emotional awareness, and self-evaluation (Holloway, 1995).

Supervision of *counseling skills* includes communication patterns; empathy; personalization; techniques of counseling, such as symptom prescription, desensitization, and reinforcement; and any of the specific skills that the supervisor identifies as both fundamental to counseling knowledge and relevant to a particular trainee. The task of counseling skills focuses on what action to take with the client (Holloway, 1995).

Case conceptualization involves the supervisor and supervisee understanding the client's history and presenting problem and then developing a conceptual framework for how to proceed. In conceptualizing a case, the supervisor strives to have the trainee understand the client's behavior and then connect it to theoretical bases of knowledge. Supervision sessions usually consist of a discussion of the client's situation, the counseling relationship, and the course of the therapeutic process, leading to the formulation of a diagnosis and treatment plan.

Professional role relates to how trainees use appropriate external resources for their clients; apply principles of professional and ethical practice; learn tasks of record keeping, procedure, and appropriate interprofessional relationships; and participate in the supervisory relationship (Holloway, 1995). Sometimes learning how to be a supervisee, what to ask for, and what to expect is the most challenging task of training. The supervisory relationship allows trainees to gain an understanding of their own interpersonal style and the impact of this style on clients. Attention to both the boundaries and responsibilities of the supervisor and supervisee roles is essential to an effective supervisory relationship. Thus, it is often necessary to focus on the context of the supervisory situation without becoming sidetracked into a discussion of the client.

Holloway (1995) defines *emotional awareness* as the supervisee's self-awareness of feelings, thoughts, and actions that result from working with the client and the supervisor. Both intra- and interpersonal awareness are relevant to therapy and supervision.

Not only are a supervisee's responses to the client important, but his or her emotional responses in the supervisory relationship may have important implications for his or her work with clients. The reenactment of the emotional dynamic of the supervisory relationship is often referred to as *parallel process.*

Self-evaluation is a critical skill in the field of mental health service delivery. Learning the limits of one's competence and effectiveness is particularly important in a field in which much of the work is done confidentially and with only the client as a witness. Even when a therapist is being supervised, the supervisor still depends on the supervisee to contribute the data to the supervision session. It is important that supervisors model effective self-evaluation. Supervisors can highlight the process of self-evaluation by encouraging a supervisee to focus on what happened in the session and to assess the effect on the client rather than making a judgment about the supervisee's behavior.

SUPERVISORY CHALLENGES AND DILEMMAS

Working with children and adolescents, especially when they are struggling with SED, creates many challenges to the supervisory relationship. What is defined as a clinical challenge is unique to each therapist's self-perception regarding what to do in a particular session, with a specific client or family, presenting with a particular problem and their own idiosyncrasies. Therapy always involves making quick decisions in response to the verbal and nonverbal feedback that occurs in every clinical encounter. This decision-making process is influenced by the self-knowledge of therapists and the skills they bring to the clinical transaction. Also, the constraints of a given treatment context need to be considered. The therapist's challenge then becomes the supervisor's challenge, because the therapeutic system always includes the client or family, the therapist (or therapists if a team is involved), the supervisor, and their interrelationships (Lindblad-Goldberg, et al., 1998).

One dilemma that can occur with a new or inexperienced supervisee is when and how to use confrontation. In the initial stages of treatment, the need to be respected and appreciated by clients may result in positive consequences. It can facilitate joining and lead to the development of a good initial therapeutic alliance. However, if later on no change is occurring or there is a major therapeutic impasse around a treatment issue, the challenge for the supervisee and the supervisor is to identify the impasse and explore the issues getting in the way for both the client or family and the clinician in the process of producing change (Boyd-Franklin & Bry, 2000). Even experienced clinicians may encounter a dilemma when they have worked hard to establish a therapeutic bond with a client or family but fear that a confrontation will disrupt this therapeutic alliance. However, timing, sensitivity, and the framing of the intervention are crucial to both the clinical and the supervisory process (Boyd-Franklin & Bry, 2000).

Supervisors also need to be able to expand a supervisee's style of contact and intervention when faced with personal clinical challenges. The clinical challenges experienced by therapists are the responses they make when confronted by the events of a therapy session. Knowing how to respond to a client's feedback or the feedback of an entire family as well as one's internal reactions is central to relationship building, assessment, and treatment. An effective supervisor must be sensitive to the therapist's struggle to overcome the anxiety of doing therapy. Anxiety is especially high during initial sessions between a therapist and client or family. Also, anxiety increases in relation to the number of clients or family members in the room. Sometimes the therapist's efforts to reduce anxiety may be counterproductive to relationship building. It is the supervisor's responsibility to contain the trainee's anxiety in response to what the client or family presents by providing feedback that alters the therapist's affective, cognitive, or behavioral responses. These alterations should then shift the client or family's reactions to the therapist (Lindblad-Goldberg et al., 1998). These are only a few of the challenges and dilemmas that confront supervisors when working with children and adolescents who have SED. However, the most valuable interactions are those that teach supervisees how to think and react in difficult situations.

CULTURAL COMPETENCE IN SUPERVISION

Cultural competence is a central task in the supervision process. With the increasing diversity in the United States, therapists are constantly faced with new clients from cultures different from their own (Gibbs & Huang, 1998). This will lead to an increased likelihood of cross-cultural and cross-racial treatment (Comas-Diaz & Griffith, 1998; McGoldrick, Giordano, & Pearce, 1996). As more ethnic minority therapists and supervisors enter the field, there is also an increased likelihood of cross-cultural or cross-racial supervision (Helms & Cook, 1999). Twenty-five years ago there was very little awareness that minority status in this country, which seemed to be only a political issue, would also impact the process of therapy and supervision (Bernard & Goodyear, 1992). Current professional journals in mental health have begun to reflect the needs of racial and ethnic minorities. However, this task has just begun.

Cultural knowledge, consciousness raising, and challenging the myth of sameness are all important supervisory issues. The most valuable component of supervision appears to be an open and honest dialogue between a supervisor and supervisee about their attitudes toward their own ethnic group and others they serve. Supervisors must feel comfortable themselves in raising these issues with supervisees, if the supervisees are to feel comfortable in exploring these issues with their clients and families (Boyd-Franklin & Bry, 2000). The most serious problem encountered in this regard is the assumption that everyone is working with a shared belief system and that there is no problem.

Hunt (1987) was one of the first authors to document supervisory issues for Black and White therapists working with Black clients. However, her comments have relevance for many multicultural situations. The most difficult aspect of therapy with Black clients is establishing the relationship. Even a Black trainee needs to acquire the knowledge base about intra- and interracial cultural norms that shape racial identity. Racial identity can be as much an issue for the Black therapist or supervisee as it is for the Black client. How supervisees handle their own racial identity determines how they view their clients. Black trainees' understanding of the therapy process and their willingness to be open with a supervisor, even a Black supervisor, is in part a function of their comfort with their own racial identity.

Supervisees need practice in working through difficult interactions. They need to know how to acquire information about clients' perceptions and attitudes toward them and about the clients' intragroup beliefs (if the supervisee and client share the same ethnic group). Moreover it is important to determine the client's cultural mindset about seeking help from a mental health professional.

There are also several multicultural pitfalls to be avoided. For example, minority supervisees are often considered experts regarding all clients of their cultural group when working with a White supervisor. Although the minority perspective is certainly valuable, to assume that the supervisee understands all clients of that culture is another form of prejudice (Bernard & Goodyear, 1992). Also, when a minority supervisee works with a White supervisor, the supervisor may lean on the supervisee's insights more than is usual or appropriate. If a supervisor has not worked with many minority supervisees, the supervisor often will not know what to expect in supervision. However, the supervisor should seek consultation from a minority-group colleague rather than turn to the supervisee for consultation (Bernard & Goodyear, 1992).

Another problem is that racial stereotyping can challenge White supervisees' confidence in a supervisor of color. They may assume that supervisors of color have had less exposure to White clients and therefore can not adequately supervise White clients' therapy (McGoldrick, Almeida, Preto, & Bibb, 1999). Similarly, assumptions about expertise and knowledge base affect how referrals are made to supervisees. Often referrals are made to supervisees of the same race or culture, so Black clients are assigned to Black therapists, Latino clients to Latino therapists, and so forth. However, it is naive to assign clients in this way. Within the Latino culture, a Cuban client may be less satisfied with a Puerto Rican therapist than with a European American therapist unless language is a major factor, and an Asian client may prefer a White therapist because of the close-knit Asian American community.

Also, supervisees' experiences will be limited if they only work with clients of their cultural or social group. Thus, White clinicians often receive client referrals from a broader range of social and ethnic and class backgrounds than therapists of color. This type of case assignment can also be considered another form of discrimination and cultural stereotyping. It raises the question of whether clinicians and supervisors of color are valuable only when they work with their own kind (McGoldrick et al., 1999). Bernard and Goodyear (1992) cite an example of an African American trainee who said that when a Black client was referred to him in the university counseling center, he had to prove to clients that he was competent because they assumed they were assigned to him because he was Black and that he was not good enough to see White clients. It is this type of conclusion that can be drawn when race is made an obvious focus, but not discussed.

The supervisor's role in developing transcultural therapists is extremely important. If the supervisor can help supervisees explore their interracial and intercultural beliefs and attitudes, then there is a better chance for mental health professionals to serve multicultural clients (Hunt, 1987). However, in spite of some recent progress in this area, more efforts still need to be made.

MODALITIES OF SUPERVISION

How does a supervisor know what the supervisee is doing? There are a variety of supervisory modalities that fall along a continuum from most to least intrusive. At the most intrusive end of the continuum, the supervisor is closest to the therapeutic encounter and interacts directly with the therapists or the therapists and clients. In these situations, the supervisor takes an active role in assessing, intervening, and evaluating the immediate situation (Anderson, Rigazio-DiGilio, & Kunkle, 1995). These modalities include cotherapy, direct consultation with clients, in-home supervision, and interactive supervision from behind a one-way mirror (the bug-in-the-ear technique).

In the middle of this continuum are the modalities that lack the opportunity for immediate feedback, but still provide raw data. These are the modalities of audiotape and videotape. At the other end of the continuum are case conferences, therapy notes, and discussions between a supervisor and supervisee. In these modes of supervision, the data are first interpreted and then reported by therapists in the way they describe the case. The therapist alone assesses, intervenes, and evaluates clinical progress. The supervisor knows the clients only through the supervisee's frame of reference (Anderson et al., 1995).

There are advantages and disadvantages to each modality. Cotherapy enables supervisees to provide immediate intervention to clients and offers direct modeling for supervisees, but it may take longer for supervisees to become involved in the therapy process than if they were working alone or even with a peer. Also, it may impede the client from seeing the supervisee in a professional role. In-home supervision is a relatively new modality, as are in-home services for children and adolescents. In this model, the supervisor and possibly other team members accompany the therapist to the client's home for home-based supervision of home-based services. There are several advantages to this technique. For example, the supervision takes place in the same location as the intervention; the supervisor can observe the supervisee's style and the client's reaction to the therapist's style; and through consultation during breaks in the therapy session, the supervisor can influence the outcome of the session. One challenge presented by this model is overcoming the family's resentment of the therapeutic process and the intrusion into their home. Another is ensuring that the family does not look to the supervisor as the primary therapist and thereby undermine the work of the supervisee (Zarski, Sand-Pringle, Greenbank, & Cibik, 1991).

Live supervision behind a one-way mirror can help supervisees correct mistakes and avoid getting stuck (McGoldrick, 1982). Supervisors sometimes call the supervisee on the telephone in the therapy room, communicate using a bug in the ear, call the supervisee out for consultation, or enter the therapy room directly. These interruptions can disrupt the session's flow (Liddle, Davidson, & Barnett, 1988) and cause supervisees increased anxiety. Oppenheimer (1998) wrote about her own experience being supervised from behind a one-way mirror. She said she found it difficult to carry on with the session and at the same time pay attention to the expert's advice. After 20 minutes, she wanted to select another profession. Although not all supervisees have this experience of one-way mirror supervision, it is important not to let supervisees feel overly criticized or demeaned by this process.

Audiotaping and videotaping provide supervisors with the raw data of therapy without the need to respond to the immediate therapeutic encounter. Supervisors and supervisees can review the tapes and conceptualize what occurred and also save the session for future reference (Whiffen, 1982). Tapes can be stopped for discussion during review, and supervisees can be asked what they were thinking or feeling at a particular point during a session (Breunlin, Karrer, McGuire, & Cimmarusti, 1988). In addition to some clients or families refusing audiotaping or videotaping, at least until trust has been established with the therapist (Boyd-Franklin & Bry, 2000), some supervisees are so anxious about being taped that they do not focus on the therapy session.

Case presentations based on notes or the supervisee's memory provide an opportunity for discussing, analyzing, planning, and addressing issues related to the development of a professional role. It can also be useful to examine the supervisee's use of self in therapy and supervision. The major limitation is that the supervisor must rely extensively on the perspective of the supervisee (Biggs, 1988; Prichard, 1988).

The continuum of supervision from most to least direct supervisory participation is also not intended to be a developmental continuum. Thus, it would be incorrect to assume that beginning supervisees need the supervisor to be in the room, whereas more advanced supervisees should make case presentations. In fact, more advanced supervisees may be more likely to be more creative, thus requiring closer supervision. In spite of the extensive use of the preceding modalities in supervision, little empirical data exist to document which modality is the most effective (Anderson et al., 1995), or which modality best fits a specific training or supervisory situation.

ATTRIBUTES OF GOOD SUPERVISION AND GOOD SUPERVISORS

Anderson, Schlossberg, and Rigazio-DiGilio (2000) surveyed supervisees in 52 Commission on Accreditation for Marriage and Family Therapy Education accreditation and candidacy-training programs. The supervisees were asked to describe their best and worst supervision experiences in terms of the context of training and supervision, the perceived personal attributes of the supervisor, and specific behaviors of the supervisor during supervision.

With regard to the supervision modality used, supervisees' best experiences were more likely to involve live supervision as the primary source of supervisory data, and worst experiences more often included reliance on verbal reports. Review of videotapes as a supervisory modality was relatively evenly distributed between best and worst experiences. In addition, best supervision experiences were longer in duration, involved more weekly contact, included more frequent contacts per week, and addressed a greater number of cases per supervisory session in comparison to worst experiences. The amount of contact appeared to outweigh the supervisor's theoretical orientation or level of experience, because these factors did not differentiate between the best and worst experiences. Supervision in best experiences was also more likely to balance personal growth with the development of technical skills.

This study indicated that in interactions between supervisors and supervisees, best experiences included providing feedback in a straightforward manner, accepting mistakes, and encouraging experimentation. Poor experiences were characterized by avoiding communication, emphasizing supervisees' shortcomings, and supervisors' preoccupation with their own problems. Overall, an open supervisory environment and supervisors who communicated respect, support, and encouragement were highly valued. In contrast, less valued supervisors were authoritarian or demeaning, encouraged unthinking conformity, failed to accept divergent viewpoints, and devalued supervisees. It is important for supervisors to realize that these behaviors do not contribute to effective learning experiences for supervisees. It is also valuable to acknowledge the variables that supervisees identify as contributing to negative experiences so that they can be eliminated through improved training of supervisors.

SUPERVISION OF TREATMENT FOR CHILDREN WITH SED

Mental health treatment for children with SED takes place in a variety of settings, including inpatient facilities, residential treatment facilities, schools, and outpatient clinics. More recently, home-based family therapy has been designed as a preventive intervention for multiproblem, at-risk families. The purpose of home-based family therapy is to improve functioning and prevent institutional placement of at-risk children or adolescents (Zarski et al., 1991).

Regardless of the setting in which treatment takes place, there are a number of supervisory issues that are common to working with children. These include the importance of working with the family and all relevant parties, the need to focus on the referral question, the need to establish clear and attainable treatment goals, and the importance of termination issues. Supervisors also need to be able to recognize and resolve issues of parallel process.

It is especially important not to work with children in isolation. Children are most often part of a family unit, whether it is their biological family, adoptive family, or foster family. Because children spend far more time with their family than with a therapist, it is essential to include family members in the therapeutic process. This needs to occur in two ways. Namely, practitioners can gather data from the family about the child's behavior and progress since the last treatment session, and can partner with the family in the therapeutic process, thereby making them "deputy therapists" to carry on the work of therapy during the week. This can also be a more effective way of encouraging a family to interact differently with a child or adolescent than confronting this issue directly. Once children are old enough to attend school, which is a major part of their lives, teachers or other relevant school personnel should be included in the therapeutic process when appropriate. This is not to say that they should be in every session, or even in any session, but at the least their input and feedback should be solicited through consultation. Supervisees will benefit from including discussion of all relevant parties in their work with children and adolescents rather than only reviewing material about the child or adolescent, per se. Although supervisees may be concerned about the limits of confidentiality with this model, at the beginning, it is necessary to explain the value of collaboration through the informed consent process.

Supervisors should also discuss with trainees their sense of normal family functioning. Because there is a wide variety of family patterns and interactions, it will be helpful for supervisors to be aware of the assumptions their trainees may be making and to expand their definition if necessary. This is also an opportune time to discuss racial, cultural, or ethnic issues that may be relevant to the trainee's cases.

It is also important that the supervisor help the supervisee establish the goals for treatment. It will be helpful for supervisees to have a plan of how each therapy session contributes to the overall goal. In establishing treatment goals, the importance of obtaining a thorough family history should not be overlooked. This is valuable in identifying family patterns that may need to be targeted for change and can also high-light parents' experiences that may be influencing their behavior with their children. Thus, it is easier to be empathic and therapeutic with a harsh mother whose own parents made her kneel on glass when she seems overly punitive with her child. It is also sometimes necessary for supervisors to help supervisees focus or refocus on the referral question when they become overwhelmed by the multiple problems of at-risk children and their families. Beginning therapists can feel compelled to "fix everything" or try to make a client or family conform to a preconceived notion of functioning rather than focusing on the family's needs through the referral question.

The perspective of the supervisor is especially valuable in this respect, as well as in situations when supervisees become so involved in the details of a session that they lose sight of the overall objective. At these times, they may even be working at cross-purposes to the overall goal of treatment. For example, new trainees sometimes look for an easy solution to a difficult problem. Supervisors can help them to see the complexity of cases and to work in a positive way with parents. Although parents may seem like an easy and available target for blame, blaming parents may result in premature termination of therapy as well as a reluctance to seek help in the future.

Supervisors can help supervisees recognize when termination is appropriate. This is not only true for treatment in general, but can also be applied to individual sessions. After describing a particularly disastrous therapy session in which an adolescent displayed many out-of-control behaviors, a supervisee was astonished when she was asked by the supervisor why she did not just end the session? This demonstration of limit setting would have been far more useful in this case than a discussion of the need for rules or the importance of therapy. Changing the supervisee's mind-set about ending a session made a lasting impression, and this particular supervisee has since frequently commented on how helpful this has been in her subsequent work.

Termination of therapy should be an issue throughout the treatment process and should take place when the referral issue has been resolved, not necessarily when every problem is solved. However, when the referral issue has been resolved, there may be other problems that the family would like to address. For example, a child's behavior problem may be resolved, but the parents want to improve their relationship or develop better communication skills. Further treatment can always be discussed. It is also important for clients to know at the beginning of treatment whether the intervention is time limited, due to the requirements of a brief therapy model, insurance policy requirements, or other practical reasons. When therapy is time limited, it is crucial that treatment goals be clear and attainable and that termination be an issue in every therapy session.

Another supervisory issue is the ability to recognize and intervene when a supervisee replicates the problems and symptoms of clients during supervision. This has been referred to as *parallel process* (Deering, 1994). When working with a rebellious, acting-out adolescent, this occurs when the supervisee begins to test the supervisor's limits and challenges his or her authority. In response, the supervisor demonstrates how to handle the situation. Parallel process can work in the opposite direction when aspects of the supervisory relationship are mirrored in the client–therapist relationship (Doehrman, 1976).

According to Deering (1994), certain situations seem particularly prone to parallel process. By being aware of these situations, supervisors can recognize and intervene in this process more quickly. One situation, as just mentioned, is when adolescents test limits and challenge the therapist's authority, causing the therapist to challenge the supervisor. Another is the tendency of supervisees to cancel supervision sessions when clients miss sessions. Although supervisees may feel they have nothing to discuss, it is usually an important time to meet for supervision to identify the cause of the missed sessions.

Dealing with children in therapy who have strong dependency needs may result in supervisees seeking magical solutions, immediate feedback, and advice or unusual levels of emotional support. Similarly, a supervisee working with a client who has an obsessive-compulsive or anorexic disorder and relies on intellectualization will tend to discuss these cases in an intellectualized fashion in supervision. There are also some cases that never seem to be discussed in supervision. Because children who internalize their symptoms do not demand as much attention as children who externalize their symptoms, they also do not command as much focus in supervision. However, this should be a signal that these cases do need supervisory attention. Thus, an adolescent who has a conduct disorder and who is shoplifting and therefore breaking parole requirements may make a new trainee more anxious and therefore more panicked about seeking supervision than a teen who is restricting food intake but who is not below critical weight.

Approaches to supervision need to alternate between concentrating on cases in which the supervisee has questions or concerns and reviewing all of a supervisee's cases. A general review of cases may not highlight issues that need follow-up from previous weeks and does not allow for any in-depth focus on a particular theme or problem. On the other hand, if the supervisee always knew which cases to take to supervision, then supervision might not be necessary. The job of the supervisor is to oversee all of the supervisee's cases and to create sufficient opportunity so that problem areas become apparent. Although supervisees should seek supervision when they know they are having difficulty, this may be the time they are most likely to avoid supervision.

The first step in confronting and resolving parallel process is to recognize it when it occurs (Deering, 1994). The most common signs are atypical behavior by the trainee, such as being late or missing supervision sessions, sudden changes in the supervisory relationship, and therapeutic impasses (Sigman, 1989). Once parallel process is identified, the next step is to intervene. It may not be necessary to confront the process if supervisors can handle it skillfully and promote resolution by changing the way they interact with the supervisee. This is preferred if the supervisory relationship is new or uncertain. Directly confronting this process works best when there is a strong alliance between the supervisor and the trainee (Deering, 1994). Supervisors can either ask their supervisee what may be going on in the relationship between the two of them, or supervisors can describe their own experiences with the process and ask if it is similar to the supervisee's experience with the client. Sometimes, as supervisees describe their feelings toward the supervisor, there is a gradual recognition of the similarity to the process with the client (Deering, 1994).

Identifying and resolving these issues can be a powerful learning experience for both the supervisor and the supervisee. The supervisor can vicariously experience the supervisee's struggle, and the supervisee achieves a deeper understanding of the client's experiences (Sigman, 1989). The supervisor and supervisee can then work together toward a common goal.

SUPERVISION OF IN-HOME SERVICES

Home-based family therapy programs are growing rapidly in the United States (Kaplan, 1986; Maluccio, Fein, & Olmstead, 1986; Norman, 1985). Advantages of these programs include generally high satisfaction with services, and reduced rates of institutional placement have been reported (Frawley, 1986; Reid, Kagan, & Schlosberg, 1988). Families receiving home-based intervention enter therapy in crisis: the crisis of a child or adolescent at risk of placement outside the home in a residential or psychiatric facility. The initial goal of therapy is crisis stabilization.

Zarski et al. (1991) developed an in-home approach to supervision based on feedback from therapists, such as, "The family is not the same when I see them in their home." In-home supervision allows for the creation of an optimal learning situation in which a supervisor can encourage a therapist's autonomy in the context of a structured learning environment. The in-home supervisor can take advantage of the home environment to observe the interaction between the therapist and family and can intervene with the therapist to change that interaction. This in-home approach to supervision includes four distinct phases: the session preceding in-home supervision; the in-home supervision session; the exit of the supervisor and team following the session; and the next home-based therapy session.

During the presession, the home-based team and the supervisor define an overall strategy for the session and clarify the rules of the session, such as whether the team will take a break during the session. The supervisor and supervisees then clarify session-specific goals for the family and the therapist or team. Also during this period, the supervisor helps the therapist work with the family if there is resentment about the in-home supervision session. It is important that the family members know that the supervisor is a part of the treatment team.

In the supervised in-home session, it is important that the supervisor maintain the flexibility to move around during the session. Also, family members may hear the supervisor communicate an intervention to a therapist. The supervisor's decision to intervene will be based on the urgency and the importance of the intervention and on the consequence if the intervention is not carried out (Liddle, 1988).

Following the in-home supervised session, the supervisor meets with the team to discuss whether it accomplished what it set out to do. Also, did the therapist implement the supervisor's interventions, and did this have the desired effect? Finally, the supervisor should connect this session to the overall treatment process and the supervisee's development.

In-home family therapy lends itself to a type of flexibility that is possible, but seldom realized, in traditional outpatient treatment. Although structure and boundaries are certainly needed, sessions can range from 30 minutes to 2 or 3 hours and can take place several times per week if needed. In addition, family members can be seen individually or in various combinations (mother and children, siblings, etc.) during the same session with a minimum amount of inconvenience. Therapists who provide in-home services are more likely to meet with school personnel and to have meetings in the school or even at a parent's place of work if warranted. In the case of parents who are divorced or separated, it is also valuable to meet in both homes and to include any stepparents. Through this model, as much as a year of therapy can be compressed into several months. It is truly a model to provide the service that is needed where and when it is needed.

The in-home approach to supervision is a supervisory approach for training therapists working with high-risk families in their home environment (Zarski et al., 1991). Due to the mobility of the therapists, flexibility in scheduling, and high-risk nature of the clients, this is more difficult than supervising traditional outpatient family therapists. Framo (1979) recognized the need for family therapy supervisors to update their methods in response to contemporary service delivery models. In-home family therapy supervision is consistent with current trends in service delivery.

SUPERVISION CAN PREVENT BURNOUT

Many clinicians find that after their training experience ends, so does supervision. However, work with children with SED and their families can be overwhelming, demanding, and draining. In home-based family treatment, and in all multisystem work, even experienced clinicians need ongoing clinical case supervision and consultation (Boyd-Franklin & Bry, 2000). This can be helpful in allowing a therapist to stand back from a complex family or problem and to analyze the situation. Regular case discussions are helpful and sharpen the clinical skills of all therapists. Although supervision is not just for students or trainees, many clinicians benefit from peer consultation once training has ended. Consultation differs from supervision because in consultation, clinicians do not give up their independent authority. Clinicians can accept or reject the opinion of the consultant. It is common for therapists who work with such a difficult population to have occasional doubts about their work. Such practitioners may benefit significantly from consultation with other staff members or from participation in a group of clinicians who can share experiences and exchange ideas. A number of ethics writers (Koocher & Keith-Spiegel, 1998; Pope & Vasquez, 1991, 1998) stress the need to maintain ongoing consultation or supervision throughout one's career.

Through supervision, therapists can keep improving their skills and update their knowledge of recent developments in the field. They can also learn specialized skills or techniques in this way. For example, supervision can be used to learn new, evidence-based methods of treatment. The supervisory relationship is often a place to discuss professional growth and development. This can provide an incentive for further growth and training (Boyd-Franklin & Bry, 2000). Further education as well as career plans should be discussed with supervisees. Discussing long-term and short-term career goals with supervisees in a supportive atmosphere can boost morale and energize clinicians who work in difficult situations. Thus, supervision is important for clinicians at all levels of experience. It provides necessary support in a very demanding treatment process.

CONCLUSION

Supervision is the primary professional training model for mental health clinicians. Within the supervisory relationship, the supervisor is responsible for both the client and the professional growth of the supervisee. Good supervision is especially crucial when working with children with SED. This is because children with SED often have multiple problems and may also be members of families with multiple problems. Good supervision can help keep the therapist focused and maintain attainable treatment goals rather than becoming overwhelmed by the task. In addition, children with SED can undermine therapists in their efforts. Good supervision prevents therapists from doing things in therapy that are counterproductive. In general, good supervision increases therapists' confidence and helps them to be more effective in their work. Supervision can take many forms, from in-home supervision sessions to case discussions. Supervisors face many challenges in their work, including the need to recognize and intervene when supervisees replicate the problems and symptoms of their clients during supervision. Although there is no single definition of good supervision, elements of good supervision include communicating respect, support, and encouragement, and balancing personal growth with the development of technical skills. Overall, professional growth that can be facilitated by supervision is a lifelong process.

REFERENCES

Alonzo, A. (1985). *The quiet profession: Supervisors of psychotherapy.* New York: Macmillan.

Anderson, S. A., Rigazio-DiGilio, S. A., & Kunkle, K. P. (1995). Training and supervision in family therapy: Current issues and future directions. *Family Relations, 44*(4), 489–533.

Anderson, S. A., Schlossberg, M., & Rigazio-DiGilio, S. (2000). Family therapy trainees' evaluations of their best and worst supervision experiences. *Journal of Marital and Family Therapy, 26*(1), 79–91.

Bernard, J., & Goodyear, R. (1992). *Fundamentals of clinical supervision.* Needham Heights, MA: Allyn & Bacon.

Biggs, D. A. (1988). The case presentation approach in clinical supervision. *Counselor Education and Supervision, 27,* 240–248.

Boyd-Franklin, N. (1989). *Black families in therapy: A multisystems approach.* New York: Guilford Press.

Boyd-Franklin, N., & Bry, B. H. (2000). *Reaching out in family therapy: Home-based, school and community interventions.* New York: Guilford Press.

Breunlin, D., Karrer, B., McGuire, D., & Cimmarusti, R. (1989). Cybernetics of videotape supervision. In H. A. Liddle, D. C. Breunlin, & R. C. Schwartz (Eds.), *Handbook of family therapy training and supervision* (pp. 194–206). New York: Guilford Press.

Comas-Diaz, L., & Griffith, E. E. H. (Eds.). (1988). *Clinical guidelines in cross cultural mental health.* New York: John Wiley & Sons.

Deering, C. G. (1994). Parallel process in the supervision of child psychotherapy. *American Journal of Psychotherapy, 48*(1), 102–111.

Doehrman, M. J. G. (1976). Parallel process in supervision and psychotherapy. *Bulletin of the Menninger Clinic, 40*(1), 9–83.

Framo, J. L. (1979). A personal viewpoint on training in marital and family therapy. *Professional Psychology, 10,* 868–879.

Frawley, R. (1986). *Preventive services evaluation report: Parsons Child and Family Center prevention program.* Albany, NY: New York State Council on Families.

Gibbs, J. T., & Huang, L. N. (Eds.). (1998). *Children of color: Psychological interventions with culturally diverse youth.* San Francisco: Jossey-Bass.

Helms, J. E., & Cook, D. A. (1999). *Using race and culture in counseling and psychotherapy: Theory and process.* Needham Heights, MA: Allyn & Bacon.

Holloway, E. L. (1995). *Clinical supervision: A systems approach.* Newbury Park, CA: Sage Publications.

Hunt, P. (1987). Black clients: Implications for supervision of trainees. *Psychotherapy, 24,* 114–119.

Kaplan, L. (1986). *Working with multiproblem families.* Lexington, MA: D. C. Heath.

Koocher, G. P., & Keith Spiegel, P. (1998). *Ethics is psychology: Professional standards and cases* (2nd ed.). New York: Oxford University Press.

Liddle, H. A. (1988). Systemic supervision: Conceptual overlays and pragmatic guidelines. In H. A. Liddle, D. C. Breunlin, & R. C. Schwartz (Eds.), *Handbook of family therapy training and supervision* (pp. 153–171). New York: Guilford Press.

Liddle, H. A., Davidson, G., & Barnett, M. (1988). Outcome of live supervision: Trainee perspectives. In H. A. Liddle, D. C. Breunlin, & R. D. Schwartz (Eds.), *Handbook of family therapy and supervision* (pp. 386–398). New York: Guilford Press.

Lindblad-Goldberg, M., Dore, M. M., & Stern, L. (1998). *Creating competence from chaos: A comprehensive guide to home-based services.* New York: W. W. Norton.

Loganbill, C., Hardy, E., & Delworth, U. (1982). Supervision: A conceptual model. *Counseling Psychologist, 10,* 3–40.

Maluccio, A. N., Fein, E., & Olmstead, K. A. (1986). *Permanency planning for children.* New York: Tavistock Publications.

McGoldrick, M. (1982). Through the looking glass: Supervision of a trainee's "trigger" family. In R. Whiffen & J. Byng-Hall (Eds.), *Family therapy supervision: Recent developments in practice* (pp. 17–37). London: Grune & Strafton.

McGoldrick, M., Almeida, R., Preto, N. G., & Bibb, A. (1999). Efforts to incorporate social justice perspectives into a family training program. *Journal of Marital and Family Therapy, 25*(2) 191–209.

McGoldrick, M., Giordano, J., & Pearce, J. K. (Eds.). (1996). *Ethnicity and family therapy* (2nd ed.). New York: Guilford Press.

Norman, A. (1985). *Keeping families together: The case for family preservation.* New York: The Edna McConnell Clark Foundation.

Oppenheimer, M. (1998). Zen and the art of supervision. *Family Journal, 6*(1), 61–63.

Pope, K. S., & Vasquez, M. J. T. (1991). *Ethics in psychotherapy and counseling.* San Francisco: Josey-Bass.

Pope, K. S., & Vasquez, M. J. T. (1998). *Ethics in psychotherapy and counseling (2nd ed.): A practical guide.* San Francisco: Josey-Bass.

Prichard, K. K. (1988). Reactions to the case presentation approach in supervision. *Counselor Education and Supervision, 27,* 243–251.

Reid, W. J., Kagan, R. M., & Schlosberg, S. B. (1988). Prevention of placement: Critical factors in program success. *Child Welfare, 67,* 25–36.

Sigman, S. (1989). Parallel process at case conferences. *Bulletin of the Menninger Clinic, 53,* 340–349.

Stoltenberg, C. D., & Delworth, U. (1987). *Supervising counselors and therapists.* San Francisco: Josey-Bass.

Whiffen, R. (1982). The use of videotape in supervision. In R. Whiffen & Byng-Hall (Eds.), *Family therapy supervision: Recent developments in practice* (pp. 39–56). London: Academic Press.

Zarski, J. J., Sand-Pringle, C., Greenbank, M., & Cibik, P. (1991). The invisible mirror: In-home family therapy and supervision. *Journal of Marital and Family Therapy, 17*(2), 133–143.

SECTION III

Serious Emotional Disturbance Disorders

Chapter 9

AUTISM SPECTRUM DISORDER

TRISTRAM SMITH, CAROLINE MAGYAR, AND ANGELA ARNOLD-SARITEPE

Since Leo Kanner first introduced autism to the modern literature in 1943, it has become one of the most researched of all childhood behavior disorders. Despite modifications in Kanner's (1943) original description, autism continues to be defined based on the three main characteristics that Kanner originally described: (a) qualitative impairment in reciprocal social interaction, (b) qualitative impairment in verbal and nonverbal communication and in imaginative activity, and (c) markedly restricted repertoire of activities and interests (American Psychiatric Association [APA], 2000; World Health Organization [WHO], 1994).

The severity of these difficulties varies markedly across affected children. For example, some children with autism are so socially impaired that they appear almost completely unaware of others. However, others display attachments to caregivers and a desire to interact with peers, although they may have poor eye contact, lack conversational skills, and have little social reciprocity (e.g., interacting with others to make requests but not sharing experiences or showing empathy for others). Similarly, some children with autism have essentially no verbal or nonverbal language. Yet others echo what people say, and some have communicative speech, although the speech may be limited to stating requests or delivering monologues on topics that preoccupy them. The restricted activities of children with autism may be comprised of motor stereotypies such as flapping their hands in front of their eyes or rocking their bodies back and forth. Alternatively, they may involve actions with objects, such as arranging toys into neat rows, making wheels spin, turning light switches on and off, or pouring water over and over again. In contrast, some children with autism display more complex patterns of restricted behaviors such as insisting on following a specific routine or developing a fascination with a highly specific topic (e.g., memorizing Thomas the Tank Engine books).

In addition to the core features of autism, many other characteristics are common but not universal (APA, 2000). Developmental delays, with discrepancies across domains such that visual motor skills are more advanced than language and social skills, occur in approximately 75% of children with autism. About 10% show splinter skills (i.e., skills that are far more advanced than their overall developmental level) such as precocious reading, rapid mathematical calculation, or strong memory for particular facts. Behavioral difficulties are frequent, with more than 90% having tantrums of some form and perhaps 10% to 20% engaging in either self-injurious or aggressive behaviors. Many children with autism also display unusually picky eating habits, problems initiating and maintaining sleep, and sensory anomalies such as apparent unresponsivity to sounds or pain stimuli.

OTHER PERVASIVE DEVELOPMENTAL DISORDERS AND THE AUTISM SPECTRUM

In the *Diagnostic and Statistical Manual of Mental Disorders, Fourth Edition, Text Revision* (*DSM-IV-TR;* APA, 2000), autistic disorder is classified as one of five pervasive developmental disorders (PDDs). The other four are Rett's disorder, childhood disintegrative disorder, Asperger's disorder, and pervasive developmental disorder—not otherwise specified (PDD-NOS). Rett's disorder has a distinct etiology, presentation, course, and response to treatment (Lambroso, 2000), and therefore should be classified separately in future editions of the *DSM,* as it already is in the *International Classification of Diseases, 10th Revision* (ICD-10; WHO, 1994). Childhood disintegrative disorder is rare and poorly understood. Consequently, it is not considered further here (Volkmar, Klin, Marans, & Cohen, 1997).

Current criteria for Asperger's disorder (AsD) emphasize impairments in social interaction and nonverbal communication similar to those found in autism but without delays in development of cognitive or language skills (Klin, Volkmar, Sparrow, Cicchetti, & Rourke, 1995). Children with AsD have pedantic and poorly modulated speech, poor use of pragmatics, literal use of language, and intense preoccupation with circumscribed topics, such as train timetables or power pylons. They are usually unable to form friends because of their naive, inappropriate, and one-sided social interactions. However, many adults with AsD reportedly desire successful interpersonal relationships and are puzzled when they do not achieve them. According to some accounts (APA, 2000), individuals with AsD commonly have deficits in motor skills and may appear clumsy.

PDD-NOS refers to impairments in social interaction, imaginative activity, verbal and nonverbal communication, and restricted or repetitive activities without meeting criteria for any other PDD. Thus, criteria for this diagnosis substantially overlap those for autistic disorder and AsD. Table 9.1 summarizes similarities and differences among these diagnostic categories, as identified in current classification systems such as the *DSM-IV-TR.* Because of the large number of similarities, there has been much debate over whether autistic disorder, AsD, and PDD-NOS are really separate disorders or are simply variations of the same disorder. In support of the latter view, Wing (1988) introduced the concept of a spectrum or continuum to capture the idea that the same disorder may vary in severity of presentation. From this perspective, the social and communication problems seen in autism, AsD, and PDD-NOS are viewed as different degrees of impaired social understanding, with the mildest impairments "shad[ing] into the eccentric end of the wide range of normal behavior" (Wing, 1992, p. 138). Proponents of the continuum perspective commonly refer to autistic disorder, AsD, and PDD-NOS collectively as *autism spectrum disorder* (ASD). However, other investigators have favored the current *DSM* classification scheme. For example, investigators have argued that AsD is distinct from autism because children with AsD tend to have higher verbal

Table 9.1   Autism Spectrum Disorder: Similarities and Differences in Current Diagnostic Criteria

Clinical Feature	Autistic Disorder	Asperger's Disorder	PDD-NOS
Social impairment			
Poor nonverbal communication	Yes	Yes	Often
Failure to develop friendship	Yes	Yes	Often
Lack of social/emotional reciprocity	Yes	Yes	Often
Language/communication			
Delay/lack of spoken language	Yes	No	Often
Poor prosody and pragmatics	Yes	Sometimes	Often
Idiosyncratic language	Yes	Sometimes	Often
Impoverished imaginative play	Yes	No	Often
Behavior			
All absorbing interests	Yes	Often	Often
Rituals	Yes	Often	Often
Stereotypies	Yes	Often	Often
Developmental delays			
Speech or language	Yes	No	Often
Cognition	Often	No	Unspecified
Motor skills	Seldom	Sometimes	Unspecified
Adaptive behavior (other than social)	Often	No	Unspecified

Sources: APA (2000), Klin et al. (1995).

than visual-motor skills, whereas the reverse tends to be true for children with autistic disorder (e.g., Klin et al., 1995; Ramberg, Ehlers, Nydén, Gillberg, & Johansson, 1996). Also, children with AsD are described as making awkward social approaches and having intellectual preoccupations, whereas children with autistic disorder may tend to avoid all social contact and be preoccupied with repetitive motor activities (Szatmari, Archer, Fisman, Streiner, & Wilson, 1995). Nevertheless, some studies have failed to detect two distinct groups (e.g., Manjiviona & Prior, 1999; Miller & Ozonoff, 2000). Therefore, it remains unclear whether the spectrum or discrete disorder view is more accurate. Because no clear demarcation between diagnostic categories exists at present, this chapter uses the term *autism spectrum disorder (ASD)*.

PREVALENCE

In the past, autism was considered rare, but reported prevalence rates have risen in recent years. The current estimate is that autism occurs in 1 of every 750 to 1,000 children (Bryson & Smith, 1998). For all ASD, the prevalence may be as high as 1 in 200 to 300 (Bryson & Smith, 1998). It is currently unclear whether the rise reflects an actual increase in prevalence, improved detection, relaxed diagnostic criteria, or some combination of these factors. Agencies such as the Centers for Disease Control and

Prevention (CDC; 2000) are currently investigating this issue. ASD occurs more often in males than females, with estimates of the male–female ratio ranging from 2:1 to 5:1. However, as with overall prevalence estimates, there is a need for additional data.

ETIOLOGY

Elucidating the etiology of ASD poses a formidable challenge, given the complexity of the syndrome, the heterogeneity of children with ASD, and the controversies surrounding classification. Nevertheless, some replicable findings about etiology have emerged. These findings indicate that autism is a neurobiological disorder with a strong genetic basis.

In a few cases, children with autism have a known genetic disorder. Smalley, Tanguay, Smith, and Gutierrez (1992) estimated that tuberous sclerosis is present in 1% to 3% of children with autism. An association may also exist between autism and fragile-X syndrome, although some studies have failed to confirm this association (Einfeld, Malony, & Hall, 1989). In addition, behavioral genetics studies have yielded clear evidence of familial aggregation. For example, subsequent siblings born in families with one child with autism have a recurrence risk of 3% to 7% (Simonoff, 1998), and the concordance rate for autism is approximately 60% for monozygotic twins (perhaps rising as high as 93% if all ASD is included; Pickles et al., 1995). However, the nonlinear increase in risk with increased genetic relatedness suggests that the genetic factors responsible for autism are multifaceted, involving perhaps 3–10 genes (Folstein, Bisson, Santangelo, & Piven, 1998; Pickles et al., 1995).

One such gene appears to be the *HOXA1* gene. Ingram et al. (2000) reported that a variant of *HOXA1* was present in approximately 40% of cases of autism in their study. While the variant of this gene is also seen in non-ASD populations, Ingram et al.'s (2000) results suggest that the presence of this allele may increase susceptibility for ASD when allelic variants for other genes are also present. Research has indicated that the *HOXA1* gene is involved in the development of areas of the brain stem (facial nucleus, abducens nucleus, and superior olive), as well as subtle craniofacial features, such as internal and external ear formation (Stodgell, Ingram, & Hyman, 2000).

In addition to genetics, prenatal and perinatal exposure appears to have an etiologic role in some cases of autism. For example, the notorious teratogen thalidomide, a sedative given to reduce nausea in pregnant women during the 1950s and 1960s, has been associated with autism. Approximately one quarter of fetuses exposed to thalidomide during days 20 to 24 of gestation were subsequently diagnosed with autism, whereas no child exposed to thalidomide during other periods of gestation developed the disorder (Rodier, 2000). Thus, these data not only point to the potential importance of prenatal exposure but also suggest a possible critical period during which such exposure may lead to autism. Preliminary evidence indicates that prenatal exposure to valproate may be another risk factor for the disorder (Stodgell et al., 2000). Interestingly, prenatal exposure to either thalidomide or valproate may produce brain stem and craniofacial anomalies similar to those associated with *HOXA1* activity (Stodgell et al., 2000). Perinatal exposure to rubella may be an additional risk factor (Chess, 1977). However, only a small minority of children with autism have had identifiable prenatal or perinatal exposures linked to autism.

A few investigators have proposed that the rising prevalence estimates for autism reflect an actual increase in autism and that this increase is due to postnatal exposure to environmental toxins. Proposed agents include certain foods in children's diets (Reichelt, Knivsberg, Lind, & Nodland, 1991), vaccines (Wakefield et al., 1998), and pollutants (Agency for Toxic Substances and Disease Registry [ATSDR], 1999). As noted previously, however, it remains unclear whether there really has been an increase in the prevalence of autism. In addition, most studies have failed to identify a reliable connection between autism and exposure to these agents or to generate medically plausible explanations for why such associations would exist (ATSDR, 1999; CDC, 2000). Consequently, efforts to prevent or treat autism by modifying children's diets, vaccination schedules, or lifestyle are currently unsupported by research.

Structural and functional brain-imaging studies have indicated that autism may be associated with enlarged overall brain size (Bauman & Kemper, 1994) but decreased size and activity in specific areas of the brain. One of these areas may be the mid-sagittal area of vermal lobules VI and VII in the cerebellum (Courschesne, Yeung-Courschesne, Press, Hesselink, & Jernigan, 1988), a region thought to be involved in sequencing activities. Another is the posterior hippocampus (Saitoh, Courschesne, Egaas, Lincoln, & Schreibman, 1995), which has been associated with complex (non-rote) learning. A third is the amygdala (Baron-Cohen et al., 2000), which is believed to contribute to recognizing faces and decoding emotional expressions. A final area is the brain stem (Rodier, 2000), associated with attention. These findings suggest that children with autism may have an overgrowth of neurons, coupled with underdeveloped organization of neurons into specialized neural systems in some areas of the brain. However, the findings have not been consistently replicated across studies and therefore must be viewed with caution (Minshew, Sweeney, & Bauman, 1997). Research has also indicated that children with autism may have high levels of the neurotransmitter serotonin (Hoshino et al., 1994), but again this finding has not been consistently replicated across studies. Thus, despite some important advances, the etiology of autism and ASD remains incompletely understood.

DIAGNOSIS AND ASSESSMENT

Although most parents report concerns about their child's development during the first 2 years of the child's life, studies have indicated that the average age of diagnosis is 4 to 6 years (Howlin & Moore, 1997; Siegel, Pliner, Eschler, & Elliott, 1988). This delay in diagnosis is likely to be highly stressful to families. Moreover, it often deprives children of the opportunity to receive early intervention services, which likely afford the best chance to improve children's functioning (Smith, 1999).

In response to this problem, the American Academy of Neurology and the American Academy of Pediatrics have recently adopted practice guidelines that call for pediatricians to check for signs of autism in all infants and young children (Filipek et al., 1999). According to the guidelines, which are presented in Figure 9.1, health care providers should provide routine developmental surveillance for every child they see. This surveillance should consist of observing whether children exhibit delays in the development of communicative language during the second year of life or loss of language at any age. As shown in Figure 9.1, if a child displays either of these problems, a hearing evaluation should be performed. If the child also displays pica, an evaluation for lead toxicity should be conducted. If these evaluations are negative, a pediatrician, other health care worker, or mental health practitioner should administer a screening test for autism. A positive finding on an autism screening test warrants referral to early intervention or public school services, as well as formal diagnosis and evaluation by an interdisciplinary team of specialists in developmental disabilities. This evaluation should be comprised of diagnostic interviews with caregivers, behavior observations, developmental testing, and (if the child's history suggests the possibility of medical problems in addition to autism) further medical testing (see Figure 9.1).

The most extensively validated screening test is the CHecklist for Autism in Toddlers (CHAT; Baron-Cohen, Allen, & Gillberg, 1992). The CHAT is a 10-minute test that was designed to detect early signs of autism in 18-month-old children. Such signs may include an absence of joint attention (e.g., looking at a toy, then looking at another person to see whether that person is also looking at the toy, and then looking back at the toy), nonverbal communication (e.g., pointing at objects or following the direction of another person's pointing), and pretend play. The CHAT consists of a brief parent interview and interaction with the child. In a longitudinal study of 16,235 children ages 18 months to 7 years in general pediatric practices, the CHAT was found to have a specificity of 98% and a sensitivity of 38% (Baird et al., 2000). Because of its high specificity, a positive finding on the CHAT indicates an immediate need for further evaluation and intervention. However, because of its relatively low sensitivity, a negative finding on the CHAT does not rule out the possibility that a child may meet criteria for autism or another developmental disorder. Consequently, after a negative

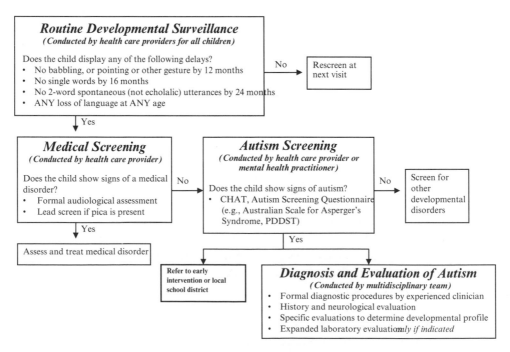

Figure 9.1   Guidelines for Screening and Diagnosing Autism
Source: Adapted with permission from Filipek et al. (1999).

finding, continued monitoring of the child is necessary, and referral for developmental testing may be appropriate.

Investigators have developed several screening tests for children older than 18 months, such as the Autism Screening Questionnaire (Berument et al., 1999), the Pervasive Developmental Disorders Screening Test (Siegel, 1998) and the Australian Scale for Asperger's Syndrome (Garnett & Attwood, 1998). Clinical experience suggests that these tests may be useful (Filipek et al., 1999), but, with the notable exception of a study by Berument et al. (1999), little research exists to confirm this impression. Thus, additional development of screening instruments is an important area for further investigation.

The best-established diagnostic interview and behavior observation instruments are the Autism Diagnostic Interview—Revised (ADI-R; Lord, 1995) and the Autism Diagnostic Observation Scale—Generic (ADOS-G; Lord et al., 2000), respectively. However, these instruments require specialized training and are time consuming to implement (approximately 1.5 to 2 hours for the ADI-R and 30 to 45 minutes for the ADOS-G). Hence, they are more often used in research than in clinical settings, where professionals usually rely on clinical interviews and informal observations or on relatively brief measures such as the Childhood Autism Rating Scale (Schopler, Reichler, DeVellis, & Daly, 1988). At present, no instruments exist that reliably differentiate between autism and Asperger's disorder or PDD-NOS.

Standardized tests of developmental level (e.g., IQ tests) generally yield valid results with children with ASD if two modifications are made. First, tests should be selected based on an estimate of the child's functioning rather than the child's chronological age. For example, a 5-year-old child who is nonverbal should receive an infant test (e.g., the Bayley Scales of Infant Development—2; Bayley, 1993) rather than a test for older children (e.g., the Wechsler Preschool and Primary Scale of Intelligence—Revised [WPPSI-R]; Wechsler, 1989). Also, the examiner should reinforce the child for on-task behavior (Koegel, Koegel, & Smith, 1998). Developmental testing for children with ASD should include measures of cognitive functioning (e.g., Bayley or Wechsler test), adaptive behavior (e.g., Vineland Adaptive Behavior Scales; Sparrow, Balla, & Cicchetti, 1984), and language (e.g., Preschool Language Scale—3; Zimmerman, Steiner, & Pond, 1992). If the child is suspected of having a motor delay, a test of motor skills, such as the Bayley Motor Development Index, may also be appropriate.

Medical evaluation to rule out additional conditions may be warranted by a child's history. For example, hand-wringing while glancing to the side is a behavioral marker for fragile-X syndrome and thus may warrant genetic testing. Episodes of extreme unresponsivity to environmental events may reflect seizure activity and therefore may indicate a need for an electroencephalogram. However, in the absence of specific indications for further medical evaluation, such evaluation is unlikely to be helpful and hence is not recommended.

After the initial diagnosis, professionals commonly perform follow-up developmental testing on a yearly basis during the preschool years and less frequently thereafter (perhaps every 3 years) to assist in monitoring children's progress over time (e.g., Harris & Handleman, 2000). In addition, behavioral assessments are conducted to plan and evaluate interventions. The focus of behavioral assessment is on directly observing an individual in order to obtain precise information on the activities that the individual performs. The main goals are as follows: (a) identify behaviors to address in treatment (target behaviors); (b) examine how events in the environment influence these behaviors (functional analysis); (c) determine what skills an individual needs to acquire in order to perform new behaviors (task analysis); and (d) determine whether interventions have been effective. Detailed descriptions of behavioral assessment procedures are presented by Haynes, O'Brien, and Hayes (2000).

TREATMENT

Behavioral treatment is currently the primary empirically supported intervention for ASD (cf. Green, 1996). Although many other psychological and educational interventions exist, none have been evaluated in controlled studies. Also, no currently available biological interventions effectively treat the core problems in ASD, although some medications may assist in managing disruptive or ritualistic behaviors (McDougle, 1997). In contrast, many hundreds of studies have been conducted on behavioral treatment, and these studies have shown that this treatment significantly improves skill areas such as receptive and expressive language (e.g., Howlin, 1981), social and play activities (e.g., Strain & Kohler, 1999; Matson, Benavidez, Compton, Paclawskyj, & Baglio, 1996), and self-help (e.g., McClannahan & Krantz, 1999; Pierce & Schreibman, 1994). Many children also acquire functional academics such as basic reading and mathematics skills, and most learn vocational skills such as assembling objects and filing documents (e.g., Etzel, Leblanc, Schillmoeller, & Steller, 1981). However, further research is necessary on the ecological validity of the findings (i.e., the efficacy of behavioral treatment in community settings such as public schools, where most children with ASD are served; Magyar, 2000).

In behavioral treatment, techniques derived from research on learning are used to increase adaptive and functional behavioral repertoires in children with ASD (Newsom, 1998). Treatment planning is guided by developmental sequences and educational models for typically developing children. Training in multiple settings, across various instructors, and in collaboration with parents and peers is emphasized. The model is comprehensive, using a variety of techniques to teach skills across all developmental domains.

Procedures for Increasing Skills

Intervention methods are designed to create multiple learning opportunities and enable high rates of success for individuals with autism. The following are the four main instructional formats used for increasing skills:

- *Discrete trial teaching (DTT)* is a highly structured teaching procedure characterized by (a) one-to-one interaction between the practitioner and the child in a distraction-free environment, (b) clear and concise instructions from the practitioner, (c) highly specific procedures for prompting and fading, and (d) immediate reinforcement for responding correctly. DTT allows for fast-paced (up to 12 teaching trials per minute), carefully individualized, and simplified instruction.

Consequently, it is especially appropriate for children with ASD who are beginning treatment or have limited learning-readiness skills (e.g., attending to the teaching situation, learning from a model, and comprehending instructions). However, it can be effective for children with ASD at any stage of treatment or level of functioning. DTT is useful for teaching new forms of behavior, including speech sounds (Lovaas, Berberich, Perloff, & Schaeffer, 1966; Young, Krantz, McClannahan, & Poulson, 1994) and motor movements (Lovaas et al., 1981). It is also very effective for teaching new discriminations (e.g., receptive and expressive language) and the formation of concepts such as categories (Bryant & Budd, 1984).

- *Direct-instruction strategies* (also called *skills training*) have a more flexible format than DTT yet allow for systematic instruction. These strategies have two phases: skill acquisition and skill application. Skill acquisition training consists of (a) the practitioner giving the child an instruction, (b) modeling of the correct response by a practitioner or peer, (c) rehearsal of the skill by the child with ASD, and (d) feedback and reinforcement from the practitioner. For example, to teach a child how to join a play activity, the practitioner first describes the steps involved in this skill (approaching the children engaged in the activity, asking to join, waiting for an answer, and then sitting down to play). The practitioner or a peer then models these steps. Subsequently, the practitioner helps the child rehearse the skill and gives feedback and reinforcement based on the child's performance.

  The application phase targets the generalization of skills to the natural environment. Techniques may include prompting and reinforcing the skill in different situations (Romanczyk, Diament, Goren, Trunell, & Harris, 1975), teaching the child to self-monitor the skill (Koegel & Koegel, 1986), giving the child a script or picture schedule to follow for using the skill (Krantz & McClannahan, 1993), and teaching peers to facilitate the child's application of the skill (Strain & Kohler, 1999).

- *Incidental teaching* is characterized by (a) instructional situations that utilize the child's motivation to access preferred objects, people, or activities, (b) encouragement for the child to initiate teaching trials, and (c) intermittent instruction throughout the day during naturally occurring activities. For example, during play, a puzzle piece may be deliberately withheld so that the child must ask for it in order to complete the puzzle. One commonly used incidental teaching procedure is mand modeling (Rogers-Warren & Warren, 1980), in which directive prompts are used to encourage the child to initiate a request rather than waiting for spontaneous initiations. For example, if a child wants to obtain a crayon in order to color, the practitioner prompts an appropriate response by saying "Tell me what you want" or asking, "What do you want?" In another commonly used procedure, time delay (Halle, Marshall, & Spradlin, 1979), the practitioner focuses his or her attention on the child while withholding a desired object, in order to cue the child to initiate a request. If the child does not initiate within a specified period of time (generally a few seconds), the practitioner may use a mand model or state the correct response for the child to imitate.

- *Free operant instruction* involves the use of differential reinforcement to strengthen appropriate behaviors and reduce or eliminate disruptive behaviors when they occur. The practitioner does not systematically arrange the environment or prompt the behaviors, but rather reinforces the child when the child exhibits a desirable behavior (Smith & Magyar, in press). This approach is implemented throughout the child's day.

In general, DTT promotes more rapid skill acquisition than do the direct instruction, incidental teaching, or free operant approaches. However, these other formats tend to be more effective than DTT for encouraging children with ASD to initiate the use of their skills and to apply the skills in everyday situations (Smith, 2001). Because of their respective strengths and weaknesses, these instructional formats often complement one another. For example, the Picture Exchange Communication System (PECS; Bondy & Frost, 1994) is an alternative and augmentative communication system in which children select pictures to indicate what they want. As a prerequisite for learning such systems, children need to be able to match pictures with the objects that correspond to them, instead of placing them with different objects that are present (Romski & Sevcik, 1996). Children with autism may require DTT in order to learn to match (Lovaas, Koegel, & Schreibman, 1979), but incidental teaching is often used to teach them to go beyond matching to selecting pictures for desired objects or activities (Bondy & Frost, 1994).

In all four formats, practitioners often use shaping and chaining. *Shaping* involves the development of a new behavior through the repeated reinforcement of minor steps toward the target behavior (Panyan, 1980). For example, a practitioner might teach the sound *aah* by first reinforcing any vocalization, then any vowel, then any *a* sound, and then *aah* (Lovaas et al., 1981). *Chaining* involves linking individual skills to form a complex skill. For example, tooth brushing consists of several steps (putting toothpaste on the toothbrush, turning on the water, putting the toothbrush under the water, etc.). Thus, chaining is commonly used to teach this skill.

Across formats, practitioners employ a variety of prompting procedures, including physical guidance to perform the activity, models for correct performance of the activity, positional cues (e.g., placing materials that the child should use near the child), and pictorial symbols (e.g., pictures of each step in a complex activity). In addition, a variety of procedures are used to reduce reliance on prompts, including graduated guidance (progressively reducing physical assistance), most-to-least prompt fading (beginning with physical assistance, moving to a gestural or modeling prompt, and then to verbal instruction), least-to-most prompting (giving the child an opportunity to respond independently and then offering increased assistance as needed), and time delay (gradually increasing the interval between the instruction and the prompt).

Procedures for Managing Behavior Problems

Behavioral practitioners use reductive procedures to decrease the frequency, duration, and intensity of stereotypies, self-injury, aggression, or other behavior problems. The choice of procedure depends on the function or functions the behavior serves for the child, as determined by systematic observations of the child (Reichle & Wacker, 1993). These observations focus on identifying antecedent events that may trigger the behavior and consequences that may maintain the target behavior.

Perhaps the most common reductive procedures are the differential reinforcement strategies, which consist of reinforcing adaptive replacement behaviors for the target behaviors. For example, in *differential reinforcement for alternative behavior* (DRA), a child could be reinforced for raising a hand and asking for help but ignored for yelling out "Help me!" while waving both arms wildly in the air. In *differential reinforcement of incompatible behavior* (DRI), behavior that is topographically incompatible with the target behavior is reinforced. For example, to reduce out-of-seat behavior, in-seat behavior would be reinforced. *Differential reinforcement for other behavior* (DRO) consists of giving reinforcement when the behavior problem has not occurred during an interval of time, and *differential reinforcement for low rates* (DRL) involves giving reinforcement when a behavior occurs infrequently.

An additional reinforcement procedure involves employing the *Premack principle,* whereby an individual is encouraged to complete a less preferred task by following it with an opportunity to engage in a preferred activity. This strategy is often appropriate for classroom settings, where work assignments can be scheduled to follow a pattern of less preferred–preferred task completion. Token economies, in which children accumulate tokens, stickers, or pennies that can be exchanged for other reinforcers, such as the opportunity to play on the computer, are often an effective way to administer reinforcement.

Extinction (withholding reinforcement for previously reinforced behavior) is another common reductive procedure. Extinction can be used for minor behavior problems (e.g., disruptive classroom behavior, excessive noise) but not for behaviors that inflict harm to self or others (e.g., self-injury, aggression, or severe property destruction). Extinction is often implemented in conjunction with reinforcement for alternative behaviors (particularly in the areas of communication and play or leisure skills). For example, the practitioner may seek to eliminate delayed echolalia by directly teaching the child to initiate conversation and comment on others' activities, ignoring the echolalic speech and reinforcing the child for commenting appropriately. An additional reductive procedure, *response cost,* uses a combination of reinforcement and reductive procedures. With response cost, the child loses a previously acquired reinforcer when he or she displays the target behavior. Response cost is often used as part of a token economy. For example, the child may receive a sticker for each task completed but lose a sticker if he or she exhibits out-of-seat behavior. Token systems with response cost can be used effectively in classrooms to manage a variety of interfering behaviors, including time off task and problems with task initiation and completion.

Another reductive procedure, overcorrection, consists of restitution, positive practice, or both. In *restitutional overcorrection,* the child is required to correct his or her misbehavior by restoring the environment to a better state than it was in before the negative behavior. For example, if a child flips over a chair, he or she may be required not only to pick up the chair but also to arrange the rest of the chairs around the table and in the room. In *positive practice overcorrection,* the child repeatedly engages in an appropriate behavior that is similar in form to the target behavior. For example, if a child runs through the classroom while transitioning, he or she would be required to practice walking in the classroom by repeatedly walking from point A to point B. These reductive procedures should be implemented as part of a multicomponent treatment plan that includes methods for increasing alternative, appropriate behaviors.

Models of Treatment

There are two main models for the delivery of behavioral treatment. *Early intensive behavioral intervention* (EIBI) is designed for children who are diagnosed with autism or PDD-NOS and begin treatment prior to age 5. This model consists of 2 to 3 years of intensive behavioral intervention (20 or more hours per week) followed by the continued application of behaviorally based educational approaches and more traditional special or regular education techniques if still needed when the child reaches school age. Studies have indicated that EIBI may enable many children with autism to make major developmental gains such as increases in IQ scores and other standardized test scores, enhanced socioemotional functioning, and mainstream school placements (Smith, 1999). There are large individual differences in response to EIBI; some children make very large improvements, while others derive relatively little benefit. However, a trial of this treatment may be appropriate for most children with autism or PDD-NOS who are under 5 years of age (New York State Department of Health, 1999).

Behavioral treatment remains effective for children older than 5 years, but there is no evidence that intensive implementation of this treatment (>20 hours per week) is more effective than less intensive implementation (e.g., 10 hours per week). Hence, less intensive behavioral treatment focusing on enhancing individual skills is indicated for children older than 5 years. This *specific skills model* is also indicated for children with AsD or children with autism who have age-appropriate cognitive and language skills. These children may not require intensive intervention, because they are able to learn many skills from the natural environment. However, they are likely to benefit from systematic development of skills in one or more developmental areas, such as peer interaction.

EIBI

The beginning phase of EIBI has two interdependent goals: teaching behaviors that promote learning (e.g., sitting in a chair, attending to the practitioner, and looking at the teaching materials) and reducing behaviors that interfere with learning (e.g., aggression, noncompliance, or self-injury). DTT is used to teach learning readiness, along with reductive procedures (usually differential reinforcement and extinction) for interfering behaviors. This phase of treatment establishes basic rules of social interaction and helps the child to distinguish adults as consistent sources of positive and negative consequences. It also introduces the child to the basic teaching framework (stimulus–response–consequence) that will characterize many subsequent teaching interactions (Newsom, 1998).

Once the child has mastered some basic skills and the interfering behaviors are under better control, the next phase of EIBI emphasizes the development of more complex skill repertoires. In this phase, treatment targets the expansion of the child's receptive and expressive language skills, play and social interaction skills, and daily living skills. For example, a child in this phase would learn to follow instruction, express his or her needs, ask questions, match objects and pictures, identify numbers and letters, count, play with toys functionally and interact with peers, draw and write, eat independently, and assist with dressing and bathing. Various teaching techniques are used to expand skill repertoires, including DTT, incidental teaching, and direct instruction.

In the final phase of EIBI, treatment focuses on promoting the child's skill development and application to include observational learning, problem solving, coping, understanding and following social rules, and participating in classroom activities. The main objective of this phase is to prepare the child for placement into the public school setting (Smith & Magyar, in press). EIBI generally takes place in the child's home, and active parent participation is encouraged. Some children may participate in a preschool program in addition to home programming. Treatment is usually delivered by a team that includes a psychologist or behavior analyst, special educator, speech and language pathologist, and paraprofessional skill instructor.

Many children discontinue behavioral treatment when they enter the public school. However, others require additional intervention. Therefore, the next stage of treatment focuses on applying behaviorally based teaching techniques in the education setting in order to help the child with ASD learn in the least restrictive educational environment. This stage emphasizes the further development of the child's social communication skills, academic skills, and classroom participation skills. During this stage it becomes increasingly important for all children involved in the child's education to work collaboratively to meet the child's educational goals. Moreover, the inclusion of peers is important because it enhances social and academic outcomes (e.g., Wang & Birch, 1984). Intervention goals focus on a wide range of functional skills, not just academic development. For example, children are taught how to complete household chores, shop at the mall, go to the movies, and the like.

Specific Skills Model

This model emphasizes the provision of an appropriate educational infrastructure to support the child with ASD. This includes teaching school personnel about ASD; arranging for ongoing collaboration and teamwork among behavioral practitioners, the family, and school personnel; emphasizing the integration of specific skill training into the general education curriculum; and making support available to the child with ASD on an ongoing basis (e.g., having a school psychologist available for in-school counseling with a child or problem solving with a teacher; Klin & Volkmar, 2000). Direct instruction and incidental teaching are used to teach students particular skills in areas such as peer interaction, anger management, self-care, and self-instruction. Curriculum content and requirements are adapted in order to provide opportunities for success (e.g., instructions are presented visually instead of orally, and the child is allowed extra time to complete assignments).

For the child with AsD, instruction on specific skills usually focuses on teaching awareness of pragmatic social or conversational rules, social skills training (Minskoff, 1987, 1994), and social perspective taking (i.e., theory of mind; Howlin, Baron-Cohen, & Hadwin, 1999). As the child with AsD approaches adulthood, he or she should receive training in the social skills required for vocational success, such as interviewing for a job and maintaining proper grooming and hygiene (Klin & Volkmar, 2000). Also, the child should be encouraged to select a job for which he or she demonstrates interest and capability and for which training and transition planning are available.

CONCLUSION AND FUTURE DIRECTIONS

As reviewed in the preceding sections, validated procedures now exist for diagnosing, assessing, and treating children with ASD, and progress is being made toward identifying etiological factors. These are important developments that may substantially improve services for children with ASD. However, a number of questions remain unanswered: Are autism, AsD, and PDD-NOS separate disorders or variants of the same disorder? Is the prevalence of ASD increasing, or is it simply being detected more often? How can practitioners conduct sensitive screening assessments? Are interventions other than behavioral treatment efficacious?

In addition to research on these questions, there is also a need for integrative research. To date, studies on etiology, assessment, and treatment have been largely independent of one another. However, several avenues for integration are currently open. For example, research might address whether the subtle craniofacial anomalies associated with some cases of ASD are associated with the sensory anomalies that many children with ASD display. Also, nonresponders to treatment may constitute a more homogeneous sample for studying associated biomedical problems than would a general group of individuals with autism. For example, individuals who remain nonverbal after treatment, who cannot give up routines for more appropriate leisure activities, or who do not learn to understand others' mental states may be especially informative about the neural basis of each of these deficits. Moreover, the neural functioning of individuals who largely overcome such deficits with treatment may differ from untreated individuals, as has been observed in other clinical populations (Schwartz, Stoessel, Baxter, Martin, & Phelps, 1996). Thus, the exploration of such differences may yield important information about brain-behavior relationships.

REFERENCES

American Psychiatric Association. (2000). *Diagnostic and statistical manual of mental disorders* (4th ed., Text Revision). Washington, DC: Author.

Agency for Toxic Substances and Disease Registry (1999). *Public health assessment: Brick Township assessment.* Available online at www.atsdr.cdc.gov/HAC/PHA/bri/bri_toc.html

Baird, G., Charman, T., Baron-Cohen, S., Cox, A., Swettenham, J., Wheelwright, S., & Drew, A. (2000). A screening instrument for autism at 18 months of age: A 6-year follow-up. *Journal of the American Academy of Child and Adolescent Psychiatry, 39,* 694–702.

Baron-Cohen, S., Allen, J., & Gillberg, C. (1992). Can autism be detected at 18 months? The needle, the haystack, and the CHAT. *British Journal of Psychiatry, 161,* 839–843.

Baron-Cohen, S., Ring, H. A., Bullmore, E. T., Wheelwright, S., Ashwin, C., & Williams, S. C. (2000). The amygdala theory of autism. *Neuroscience and Biobehavioral Reviews, 24,* 355–364.

Bauman, M. L., & Kemper, T. L. (1994). Neuroanatomic observations of the brain in autism. In M. L. Bauman & T. L. Kemper (Eds.), *The neurobiology of autism* (pp. 119–145). Baltimore: Johns Hopkins University Press.

Bayley, N. (1993). *Bayley Scales of Infant Development* (2nd ed). San Antonio: The Psychological Corporation.

Berument, S. K., Rutter, M., Lord, C., Pickles, A., Tomlins, M., & Bailey, A. (1999). Autism screening questionnaire: Diagnostic validity. *British Journal of Psychiatry, 175,* 444–451.

Bondy, A., & Frost, L. (1994). *The picture exchange communication system: Training manual.* Cherry Hill, NJ: Pyramid Educational Consultants.

Bryant, L. E., & Budd, K. S. (1984). Teaching behaviorally handicapped preschool children to share. *Journal of Applied Behavior Analysis, 17,* 45–56.

Bryson, S., & Smith, I. (1998). Epidemiology of autism: Prevalence, associated characteristics, and implications for research and service delivery. *Mental Retardation and Developmental Disabilities Research Reviews, 4,* 97–103.

Centers for Disease Control and Prevention (2000). *Vaccines and autism.* Available online at www.cdc.gov/nip/vacsafe/vsd/research.htm

Chess, S. (1977). Follow-up report on autism in congenital rubella. *Journal of Autism and Childhood Schizophrenia, 7,* 69–81.

Courschesne, E., Yeung-Courschesne, R., Press, G. A., Hesselink, J. R., & Jernigan, T. L. (1988). Hypoplasia of cerebellar vermal lobules VI and VII in autism. *New England Journal of Medicine, 318,* 1349–1354.

Einfeld, S., Malony, H., & Hall, W. (1989). Autism is not associated with the fragile X syndrome. *American Journal of Psychiatry, 136,* 1310–1312.

Etzel, B. C., Leblanc, J. M., Schillmoeller, K. J., & Stella, M. E. (1981). Behavior modification contributions to education. In S. W. Bijou & R. Ruiz (Eds), *Stimulus control procedures in the education of young children* (pp. 3–37). Hillsdale, NJ: Lawrence Erlbaum.

Filipek, P. A., Accardo, P. J., Baranek, G. T., Cook, E. H., Dawson, G., Gordon, B., Gravel, J. S., Johnson, C. P., Kallen, R. J., Levy, S. E., Minshew, N. J., Prizant, B. M., Rapin, I., Rogers, S. J., Stone, W. L., Teplin, S., Tuchman, R. F., & Volkmar, F. R. (1999). The screening and diagnosis of autism spectrum disorders. *Journal of Autism and Developmental Disorders, 29,* 438–484.

Folstein, S. E., Bisson, E., Santangelo, S. L., & Piven, J. (1998). Finding specific genes that cause autism: A combination of approaches will be needed to maximize power. *Journal of Autism and Developmental Disorders, 28,* 439–445.

Garnett, M. S., & Attwood, A. J. (1998). The Australian Scale for Asperger's Syndrome. In T. Attwood (Ed.), *Asperger's syndrome: A guide for parents and professionals* (pp. 17–19). London: Kingsley.

Green, G. (1996). Early behavioral intervention for autism: What does the research tell us? In C. Maurice (Ed.), *Behavioral intervention for young children with autism* (pp 29–44). Austin, TX: Pro-Ed.

Halle, J. W., Marshall, A., & Spradlin, J. E. (1979). Time delay: A technique to increase language use and facilitate generalization in retarded children. *Journal of Applied Behavior Analysis, 12,* 431–439.

Harris, S. L., & Handleman, J. S. (Eds.). (2000). *Preschool education programs for children with autism* (2nd ed.). Austin, TX: Pro-Ed.

Haynes, S. N., O'Brien, W. H., & Hayes, W. (2000). *Principles and practice of behavioral assessment.* New York: Plenum Press.

Hoshino, Y., Yamamoto, T., Kaneko, M., Tachibana, R., Watanabe, M., Ono., Y., & Kumashiro, H. (1994). Blood serotonin and free tryptophan concentration in autistic children. *Neuropsychobiology, 11,* 22–27.

Howlin, P. A. (1981). The effectiveness of operant language training with autistic children. *Journal of Autism and Developmental Disabilities, 21,* 281–290.

Howlin, P., & Moore, A. (1997). Diagnosis in autism: A survey of over 1200 patients in the UK. *Autism, 1,* 135–162.

Howlin, P., Baron-Cohen, S., & Hadwin, J. (1999). *Teaching children with autism to mind-read: A practical guide for teachers and parents.* New York: John Wiley & Sons.

Ingram, J. L., Stodgell, C. J., Hyman, S. L., Figlewicz, D. A., Weitkamp, L. R., & Rodier, P. M. (2000). Discovery of allelic variants of *HOXA1* and *HOXB1:* Genetic susceptibility to autism spectrum disorders. *Teratology, 62,* 393–405.

Kanner, L. (1943). Autistic disturbances of affective contact. *Nervous Child, 2,* 217–250.

Klin, A., & Volkmar, F. R. (2000). Treatment and intervention guidelines for individuals with Asperger syndrome. In A. Klin, F. R. Volkmar, & S. S. Sparrow (Eds.), *Asperger syndrome* (pp 340–366). New York: Guilford Press.

Klin, A., Volkmar, F. R., Sparrow, S. S., Cicchetti, D. V., & Rourke, B. P. (1995). Validity and neuropsychological characterization of Asperger syndrome: Convergence with nonverbal learning disabilities syndrome. *Journal of Child Psychology and Psychiatry, 36,* 1127–1140.

Koegel, R. L., & Koegel, L. K. (1986). Promoting generalized treatment gains through direct instruction of self-monitoring skills. *Direct Instruction News, 5,* 13–15.

Koegel, L. K., Koegel, R. L., & Smith, A. (1997). Variables related to differences in standardized test outcomes for children with autism. *Journal of Autism and Developmental Disorders, 27,* 233–243.

Krantz, P. J., & McClannahan, L. E. (1993). Teaching children with autism to initiate to peers: Effects of a script-fading procedure. *Journal of Applied Behavior Analysis, 26,* 121–132.

Lambroso, P. J. (2000). Genetics of childhood disorders: XIV. A gene for Rett syndrome: News flash. *Journal of the American Academy of Child and Adolescent Psychiatry, 39,* 671–674.

Lord, C. (1995). Follow-up of two-year-olds referred for possible autism. *Journal of Child Psychology and Psychiatry, 36,* 1365–1382.

Lord, C., Risi, S., Lambrecht, L., Cook, E. H., Leventhal, B. L., DiLavore, P. C., Pickles, A., & Rutter, M. (2000). The Autism Diagnostic Observation Schedule—Generic: A standard measure of social and communication deficits associated with the spectrum of autism. *Journal of Autism and Developmental Disorders, 30,* 205–224.

Lovaas, O. I., Ackerman, A., Alexander, D., Firestone, P., Perkins, M., & Young, D. B. (1981). *Teaching developmentally disabled children: The ME Book.* Austin, TX: Pro-Ed.

Lovaas, O. I., Berberich, J. P., Perloff, B. F., & Schaeffer, B. (1966). Acquisition of imitative speech by schizophrenic children. *Science, 151,* 705–707.

Lovaas, O. I., Koegel, R. L., & Schreibman, L. (1979). Stimulus overselectivity in autism: A review of research. *Psychological Bulletin, 86,* 1236–1254.

Magyar, C. I. (2000). *Strong Center for Developmental Disabilities Research action plan: Center for the Diagnosis and Treatment of Autism Spectrum Disorders.* Rochester, NY: University of Rochester Medical Center.

Manjiviona, J., & Prior, M. (1999). Neuropsychological profiles of children with Asperger syndrome and autism. *Autism, 3,* 327–356.

Matson, J., Benavidez, D., Compton, L., Paclawskyj, T., & Baglio, C. (1996). Behavioral treatment of autistic persons: A review of research from 1980 to the present. *Research in Developmental Disabilities, 17,* 433–465.

McClannahan, L. E., & Krantz, P. J. (1999). *Activity schedules for children with autism: Teaching independent behavior.* Bethesda, MD: Woodbine House.

McDougle, C. J., (1997). Psychopharmacology. In D. J. Cohen & F. R. Volkmar (Eds.), *Handbook of autism and pervasive developmental disorders* (2nd ed., pp. 707–729). New York: John Wiley & Sons.

Miller, J., & Ozonoff, S. (2000). The external validity of Asperger disorder: Lack of evidence from the domain of neuropsychology. *Journal of Abnormal Psychology, 109,* 227–238.

Minshew, N. J., Sweeney, J. A., & Bauman, M. L. (1997). Neurological aspects of autism. In D. J. Cohen & F. R. Volkmar (Eds.), *Handbook of autism and pervasive developmental disorders* (2nd ed., pp. 344–369). New York: John Wiley & Sons.

Minskoff, E. H. (1987). *Pass program: Programming appropriate social skills.* Fishersville, VA: Woodrow Wilson Rehabilitation Center.

Minskoff, E. H. (1994). *TRACC workplace social skills program.* Fishersville, VA: Woodrow Wilson Rehabilitation Center.

New York State Department of Health. (1999) *Clinical practice guideline, report of recommendations—Early intervention program: Autism and pervasive developmental disorders.* Available online at www.health.state.ny.us/nysdoh/eip/autism/index.htm

Newsom, C. B. (1998). Autistic disorder. In E. J. Mash & R. A. Barkley (Eds.), *Treatment of childhood disorders* (2nd ed., pp 416–467). New York: Guilford Press.

Ozonoff, S., & Miller, J. N. (1995). Teaching theory of mind: A new approach to social skills training for individuals with autism. *Journal of Autism and Developmental Disorders, 25,* 415–433.

Panyan, M. (1980). *How to use shaping.* Austin, TX: Pro-Ed.

Pickles, A., Bolton, P., MacDonald, H., Bailey, A., LeCouteur, A., Sim, C. H., & Rutter, M. (1995). Latent-class means analysis of recurrence risks for complex phenotypes with selection and measurement error: A twin and family history study of autism. *American Journal of Human Genetics, 57,* 717–726.

Pierce, K. L., & Schreibman, L. (1994). Teaching daily living skills to children with autism in unsupervised settings through pictorial self-management. *Journal of Applied Behavior Analysis, 27,* 471–481.

Ramberg, C., Ehlers, S., Nydén, A., Gillberg, C., & Johansson, M. (1996). Language and pragmatic functions in school-age children on the autism spectrum. *European Journal of Disorders of Communication, 31,* 387–414.

Reichelt, K. L., Knivsberg, A. M., Lind, G., & Nodland, M. (1991). Probable etiology and possible treatment of childhood autism. *Brain Dysfunction, 4,* 308–319.

Reichle, J., & Wacker, D. P. (1993). *Communicative alternatives to challenging behavior: Integrating functional assessment and intervention strategies.* Baltimore: Paul H. Brookes.

Rodier, P. M. (2000). The early origins of autism. *Scientific American, 282*(2), 56–63.

Rogers-Warren, A., & Warren, S. F. (1980). Mands for verbalization: Facilitating the display of newly trained language in children. *Behavior Modification, 4,* 361–382.

Romanczyk, R. G., Diament, C., Goren, E. R., Trunell, G., & Harris, S. L. (1975). Increasing isolate and social play in severely disturbed children: Intervention and post intervention effectiveness. *Journal of Autism and Childhood Schizophrenia, 5,* 57–70.

Romski, M. A., & Sevcik, R. A. (1996). *Breaking the sound barrier: Language development through augmented means.* Baltimore: Paul H. Brookes.

Saitoh, O., Courschesne, E., Egaas, B., Lincoln, A. J., & Schreibman, L. (1995). Cross-sectional area of the posterior hippocampus in autistic patients with cerebellar and corpus collosum abnormalities. *Neurology, 45,* 317–345.

Schopler, E., Reichler, R. J., DeVellis, R. F., & Daly, K. (1988). *The Childhood Autism Rating Scale (CARS).* Los Angeles: Western Psychological Service.

Schwartz, J. M., Stoessel, P. W., Baxter, L. R., Martin, K. M., & Phelps, M. E. (1996). Systemic changes in cerebral glucose metabolic rate after successful behavior modification treatment of obsessive-compulsive disorder. *Archives of General Psychiatry, 53,* 109–113.

Siegel, B. (1998, June). *Early screening and diagnosis in autism spectrum disorders: The Pervasive Developmental Disorders Screening Test (PDDST).* Invited address presented at the NIH State of the Science in Autism Screening and Diagnosis Working Conference, Bethesda, MD.

Siegel, B., Pliner, C., Eschler, J., & Elliott, G. R. (1988). How children with autism are diagnosed: Difficulties in identification of children with multiple developmental delays. *Journal of Developmental and Behavioral Pediatrics, 9,* 199–204.

Simonoff, E. (1998). Genetic counseling in autism and pervasive developmental disorders. *Journal of Autism and Developmental Disorders, 28,* 447–456.

Smalley, S. L., Tanguay, P. E., Smith, M., & Gutierrez, G. (1992). Autism and tuberous sclerosis. *Journal of Autism and Developmental Disorders, 22,* 339–355.

Smith, T. (1999). Outcome of early intervention for children with autism. *Clinical Psychology: Research and Practice, 6,* 33–49.

Smith, T. (2001). Discrete trial training in the treatment of autism. *Focus on Autism and Related Disorders, 16,* 86–92.

Smith, T., & Magyar, C. I. (in press). Behavioral assessment and treatment. In E. Hollander & K. Delaney (Eds.), *Autism spectrum disorders: Practical management.* New York: Marcel Dekker.

Sparrow, S. S., Balla, D. A., & Cicchetti, D. V. (1984). *Vineland Adaptive Behavior Scales.* Circle Pines, MN: American Guidance Service.

Stodgell, C. J., Ingram, J. L., & Hyman, S. L. (2000). The role of candidate genes in unraveling the genetics of autism. *International Review of Research in Mental Retardation, 23,* 57–81.

Strain, P. S., & Kohler, F. (1999). Peer-mediated intervention for young children with autism: A 20 year retrospective. In P. M. Ghezzi, W. L. Williams, & J. E. Carr (Eds.), *Behavior analytic perspectives* (pp. 189–211). Reno, NV: Context Press.

Szatmari, P., Archer, L., Fisman, S., Streiner, D. L., & Wilson, F. (1995). Asperger's syndrome and autism: Differences in behavior, cognition and adaptive functioning. *Journal of the American Academy of Child and Adolescent Psychiatry, 34,* 1662–1671.

Volkmar, F. R., Klin, A., Marans, W., & Cohen, D. J. (1997). Childhood disintegrative disorder. In D. J. Cohen & F. R. Volkmar (Eds.), *Handbook of autism and pervasive developmental disorders* (2nd ed., pp. 47–59). New York: John Wiley & Sons.

Wakefield, A. J., Murch, S. H., Anthony, A., Linnell, J., Casson, D. M., Malik, M., Berelowitz, M., Dhillon, A. P., Thomson, M. A., Harvey, P., Valentine, A., Davies, S. E., & Walker-Smith, J. A. (1998). Ileal-lymphoid-nodular hyperplasia, non-specific colitis, and pervasive developmental disorder in children. *Lancet, 351,* 637–641.

Wang, M. C., & Birch, J. W. (1984). Comparison of a full-time mainstreaming program and a resource room approach. *Exceptional Children, 51,* 33–40.

Wechsler, D. (1989). *Wechsler Preschool and Primary Scale of Intelligence—Revised.* New York: The Psychological Corporation.

Wing, L. (1988). The continuum of autistic characteristics. In E. Schopler & G. Mesibov (Eds.), *Diagnosis and assessment in autism* (pp. 191–110). New York: Plenum Press.

Wing, L. (1992). Manifestations of social problems in high-functioning autistic people. In E. Schopler & G. B. Mesibov (Eds.), *High-functioning individuals with autism* (pp. 129–142). New York: Plenum Press.

World Health Organization. (1994). *International Classification of Diseases* (10th rev.). Geneva, Switzerland: Author.

Young, L. M., Krantz, P. J., McClannahan, L. E., & Poulson, C. L. (1994). Generalized imitation and response-class formation in children with autism. *Journal of Applied Behavior Analysis, 27,* 685–698.

Zimmerman, I. L., Steiner, V. G., & Pond, R. E. (1992). *Preschool Language Scale—3.* San Antonio: The Psychological Corporation.

Chapter 10

COMPREHENSIVE TREATMENT FOR ATTENTION-DEFICIT/ HYPERACTIVITY DISORDER

GREGORY A. FABIANO AND WILLIAM E. PELHAM JR.

Attention-deficit/hyperactivity disorder (ADHD) is a chronic disorder affecting approximately 3% to 5% of children. The disorder is characterized by developmentally inappropriate levels of impulsivity, inattention, and overactivity and is disproportionately represented in boys. Children with ADHD experience severe impairment in multiple domains, including their social relationships, academic progress, and self-esteem. The behaviors characteristic of ADHD also disrupt classroom and family functioning. Given the sustained and substantial impairment associated with ADHD, sustained and substantial treatments must be implemented.

Children with ADHD classified with serious emotional disturbance (SED) are likely to be the combined type of ADHD, highly comorbid, and at the severe end of the continuum of impairment. Children with this profile are conceptualized as the most at-risk for negative outcomes in adolescence and adulthood (Lynam, 1996). This high level of dysfunction and significant risk of negative long-term outcomes justifies a comprehensive, intensive treatment plan that includes home- and school-based behavioral interventions, interventions to improve and sustain appropriate peer relationships, and stimulant medication.

Perhaps reflecting its chronicity and refractoriness to treatment, numerous interventions have been proposed and implemented for treating ADHD. These include, but are not limited to, dietary modifications, perceptual stimulation, exercise, laser acupuncture, meditation, antifungal treatment, EEG biofeedback, and relaxation training. However, convincing evidence for the effectiveness of these treatments is nonexistent (Arnold, 1999; Pelham, Wheeler, & Chronis, 1998). Other ineffective treatments for ADHD include traditional one-to-one therapy, social skills training employed alone, play therapy, and cognitive therapy. In fact, only behavior modification (Pelham et al., 1998) and stimulant medication (Spencer et al., 1996; Swanson, McBurnett, Christian, & Wigal, 1995) are effective treatments in the short term. Combining these two interventions typically results in greater effects than either treatment implemented alone (Pelham & Murphy, 1986; Pelham & Waschbusch, 1999). Given these two effective treatments for ADHD and their combination, how can they be implemented to improve functioning and reduce impairment in ADHD children with serious emotional disturbance?

First, treatment for ADHD must be sustained. Clearly, brief interventions, such as the aforementioned non-evidence-based therapies, or even a few sessions of evidence-based practice, result in no meaningful improvement. For example, in studies where the behavioral intervention is faded long before the endpoint assessment (Klein & Abikoff, 1997; MTA Cooperative Group, 1999), treatment efficacy is less than when it is actively implemented (Klein & Abikoff, 1997; Pelham, Gnagy, Greiner, Hoza et al., 2000), suggesting that although some of the behavioral treatment effects generalize over time and to settings where the treatment is not employed, this generalization is not equal to treatment effects during active intervention. In addition, acute, single-subject studies demonstrate that both pharmacological or behavioral treatment gains are minimized after the treatment is withdrawn (e.g., Atkins, Pelham, & White, 1989; Chronis et al., 2001; Rapport, Murphy, & Bailey, 1982). These results suggest that clinicians can expect deterioration when therapeutic contact is faded unless programs for maintenance and relapse prevention are systematically implemented. Furthermore, treatment must be sustained for sufficient time to appropriately address developmental changes. For example, though following classroom rules (e.g., stay seated, raise your hand) may be problematic areas for younger children, as a child with ADHD matures, treatment may evolve to improve the organization skills required for accurate note taking or long-term homework assignments (e.g., book reports). Practitioners of behavior modification have long known that treatment must be sustained and not time-limited, and therefore they conduct interventions on the order of years and not weeks (Atkins et al., 1989; Chronis et al., 2001; Lovaas, 1987; Lovaas, Koegel, Simmons, & Long, 1973).

Second, effective treatment for children with ADHD must also be comprehensive, improving the functioning of the child within the larger social context. The impairment associated with ADHD is typically severe and pervasive, resulting in problems in multiple settings and domains. A typical child with ADHD is likely to be impaired in social relationships with peers and adults, exhibit delayed academic progress, have low self-esteem, and require treatment and special services for these difficulties (Fabiano et al., 1999). In addition, parental psychological problems, such as depression, substance abuse, or ADHD are overrepresented in families of children with ADHD (Biederman et al., 1992; Pauls, 1991), and therefore these problems often require concurrent treatment focused on these difficulties, particularly as these problems may interfere with effective parenting (Chronis, Gamble, Roberts, & Pelham, 2000; Evans, Vallano, & Pelham, 1994; Pelham, Lang, et al., 1998).

Furthermore, because treatment must be sustained and intensive, it must be sufficiently flexible to be implemented directly in settings where the child evidences problems. Office-based therapies, such as social skills training or cognitive therapy, have resulted in meager outcomes (Abikoff, 1991; Kavale, Forness, & Walker, 1999), perhaps because they are not directly implemented within the settings where the child is most impaired. The poor outcomes associated with office-based therapy may be explained by the nature of the impairment associated with ADHD, in that problem behaviors do not indicate a lack of knowledge regarding appropriate behavior. Rather, the child fails to apply what he or she knows in the appropriate situation (Pelham &

Bender, 1982). Obviously, treatments implemented outside the child's natural environment will fail to intervene with the behavior problems directly. Moreover, because children often do not exhibit behavior problems in an office setting (Copeland, Wolraich, Lindgren, Milich, & Woolson, 1987; Sleator, 1982), the clinician may not be aware of, and therefore fail to treat, important target behaviors (e.g., situation- or task-specific behaviors, covert behaviors) or factors that maintain negative behaviors in the natural environment (e.g., peer attention for negative behavior, ineffective parenting practices).

Behavioral interventions, stimulant medication, and combined treatments are effective because they are consistent with these important parameters of treatment for ADHD. The benefits of stimulant medication have been widely reviewed, and the reader is referred to other sources for information on the stimulants (Pelham, 1993; Swanson et al., Wigal, 1995; Spencer et al., 1996). In this chapter, we will focus on implementing sustained and comprehensive behavioral and combined interventions for severe ADHD.

ASSESSMENT

Before detailing effective treatments for ADHD, a few words on the assessment of ADHD are appropriate. With the advent of the *Diagnostic and Statistical Manual of Mental Disorders* (4th ed.), or *DSM-IV* (American Psychiatric Association, 1994), clinicians were afforded detailed diagnostic criteria for ADHD, and numerous scales have been developed to assist clinicians with making a diagnosis consistent with *DSM-IV* criteria (i.e., Atkins, Pelham, & Licht, 1984; DuPaul, Power, McGoey, Ikeda, & Anastopoulous, 1998; Goyette, Conners, & Ulrich, 1978; Pelham, Gnagy, Greenslade, & Milich, 1992). These scales typically measure whether a *DSM-IV* symptom is present and the degree to which that symptom is exhibited. However, these scales generally provide no information on the degree to which a symptomatic behavior results in problems in daily life functioning and the impact of this dysfunction, codified in *DSM-IV* as *impairment*. This is an unfortunate omission, because treatment is usually sought owing to *impairment* and not *symptoms*.

As Angold, Costello, Farmer, Burns, and Erkanli (1999) reported, families that received mental health services almost always had a child who evidenced impairment. In contrast, families that had a child that met criteria for a *DSM-IV* disorder but did not exhibit impairment were unlikely to be involved in clinical treatment, suggesting that impairment in daily life functioning precipitates service use. Our routine clinical work with families supports this finding. Rarely do presenting problems reported by parents include the *DSM-IV* symptoms of ADHD (e.g., "fidgeting" or "often does not seem to listen when spoken to directly"). Parents and teachers are much more concerned with their child's academic progress, peer and adult relationships, and self-esteem, and in fact spontaneously write in these concerns on standardized symptom rating scales if they are not provided the opportunity to report impairment elsewhere. Therefore, an assessment with an emphasis on diagnosis, without any evaluation of a child's impaired functioning, is missing the very reason most families are seeking services.

Therefore, to adequately address the child's impaired areas and to identify areas of appropriate functioning, clinicians must conduct a comprehensive assessment of the child's behavior. A comprehensive assessment for a child with ADHD involves a systematic evaluation of presenting problem areas with the intent of operationalizing these areas into target behaviors (Mash & Terdal, 1997). In fact, once the target behaviors are operationalized, these become the explicit behavioral rules and daily goals in behavioral interventions and assessments of medication efficacy as well as the goals and indices of treatment outcome (Kratochwill & McGivern, 1996; Scotti, Morris, McNeil, & Hawkins, 1996). To achieve these goals, the clinician obtains information from parents, teachers, and other sources (e.g., day care workers, coaches) about the child's functioning in multiple domains (e.g., academic, peer, family) and contexts (home, school, and recreational settings). Antecedents and consequences of problem behaviors must be clearly documented, as the modification of these factors will be a core treatment component. In addition to assessing for impaired areas, it is useful to obtain information on areas in which the child is not impaired and interventions that have been successful in the past, as this may also be informative during interventions with the family. This type of assessment strategy is ideally suited for the highly individualized treatment that will follow. By using assessment strategies consistent with these applied behavior analytic techniques, assessment is truly integrated with treatment. Construction of the behavioral treatment starts immediately during the initial assessment, and treatment is continually informed by the ongoing assessment that continues during the intervention.

TREATMENT

It is our philosophy that all interventions for ADHD begin with a behavioral intervention. In the context of treatment for ADHD, behavior modification is the application of the principles of social learning theory to modify the behavior of children by training parents and teachers to manipulate environmental antecedents (e.g., commands), consequences (e.g., rewards, punishments), and contingencies (the relationship between target behaviors, antecedent events, and consequences; Jacob & Pelham, 1999). There are theoretical and practical reasons for this position. Theoretically, behavioral treatments have been shown to be highly effective for reducing problematic behaviors in children with ADHD, and to the extent that behavioral interventions are effective, the addition of stimulant medication may not be necessary. Given that the stimulants result in deleterious side effects in the short term, and the long-term risks of steadily medicating children with stimulant medication are at this time unknown, avoiding it entirely is a desirable outcome for many parents and clinicians. Practically, behavioral interventions, as outlined subsequently, explicitly target the child's areas of impaired functioning in the form of behavioral goals and targets. Because these programs target the outcomes parents and teachers desire, they may double as a highly sensitive measure of medication efficacy (Pelham et al., 2001; Pelham et al., in press), as meeting a high proportion of target behavior goals indicates improved functioning in the most clinically meaningful domains. Furthermore, combining medication with an existing behavioral treatment may increase the effectiveness of lower doses of stimulant medication (Carlson, et al., 1992; Pelham, et al., 1993), making high doses of medication unnecessary.

Behavior Modification

Behavioral interventions are well-validated, highly effective treatments for reducing behavior problems and functional impairment in children with ADHD. They have been used in homes and schools for children specifically diagnosed with ADHD for more than 30 years (e.g., O'Leary, Pelham, Rosenbaum, & Price, 1976) and have long been used to treat children with behavior problems (O'Leary & Becker, 1967). DuPaul and Eckert (1997) conducted a meta-analysis of classroom-based behavioral interventions for ADHD. Based on their results, mean effect sizes of between-group (0.45), within-group (0.64), and single-subject (1.16) designs indicated that interventions for ADHD in the classroom are effective. In a review of recently published review articles, Jadad, Booker, et al. (1999) echoed these findings that school-based behavior modification programs lead to improved school-based functioning. Complementing the school-based intervention reviews, Pelham, Wheeler, and Chronis (1998) reviewed the entire behavioral treatment literature on ADHD and included parent-training treatment outcome studies in addition to school interventions. Based on this extensive review of the evidence, the authors concluded that behavioral parent training and classroom contingency management procedures were well-validated, empirically supported treatments. Additional evidence for behavioral parent training is offered by Brestan and Eyberg (1998), who reported on the efficacy of behavioral interventions in a population of conduct-disordered children, many of whom had comorbid ADHD. In total, over 70 studies that include more than 2,000 participants attest to the efficacy of behavioral interventions for ADHD.

Some recent reviews have stated that behavioral interventions add no benefit to stimulant medication treatment and therefore that intervening with stimulant medication alone is preferable (Jadad, Boyle, Cunningham, Kim, & Schachar, 1999; Klassen, Miller, Raina, Lee, & Olsen, 1999; Miller, et al., 1998). However, these reviews are limited by a number of factors. First, the three reviews omitted approximately two thirds of the treatment literature for ADHD by including only studies that used a between-group design. Numerous studies that have employed single-subject methodology (Kazdin, 1998) demonstrated the large effects typically obtained with behavioral treatments. In addition, even within the between-groups designs, all of the behavioral treatment studies available were not included in these reviews, and this prevents any firm conclusions based on the computed effect sizes. Further, the studies included in the reviews were heterogeneous in terms of the type of psychosocial treatment employed. Although DuPaul and Eckert (1997) and Pelham, Wheeler, and Chronis (1998) excluded or separately analyzed cognitive behavioral treatments, studies that used this intervention (e.g., Brown, Borden, Wynne, Schleser, & Clingerman, 1986) were included in the overall effect size computations of the other reviews (Jadad, Boyle, et al., 1999; Klassen et al., 1999; Miller et al., 1998), thus lowering the overall effect size for behavioral and combined treatments. When a distinction has been made between behavior therapy and cognitive therapy in the literature, it is clear that cognitive therapy or cognitive behavioral therapy used alone is ineffective for ADHD (e.g., Abikoff et al., 1988). In reviews in which behavior therapy and cognitive behavior therapy are analyzed separately, behavioral therapy is clearly more effective (DuPaul & Eckert, 1997). For these reasons, it is inappropriate to draw the conclusion that behavior modification is not supported by the research literature for treating ADHD. Even Klassen et al. (1999) and Miller et al. (1998) tempered their findings by echoing this limitation in the interpretation of their results that behavioral and combined treatments are not effective interventions for ADHD.

Taking into account these considerations, we recently conducted a systematic meta-analysis of the behavioral treatment literature that included the computation of effect size estimates and included treatment studies published up to the year 2000. This meta-analysis represented an up-to-date, comprehensive review that included the evidence-based psychosocial treatments for ADHD, parent training, and school interventions, combined treatments, and the effect sizes produced for each modality. It is an improvement over previous meta-analytic work due to its comprehensiveness (e.g., not only are between-group studies included, but also within-subject and single-subject designs). It also improved on the Pelham, Wheeler, and Chronis (1998) review by quantifying their already comprehensive review. The results of this meta-analytic review aligned with and extended DuPaul and Eckert's (1997) review in that behavior modification was certainly an effective treatment for ADHD both in school *and* the home. The review included 70 studies. Results indicated that behavior modification, medication, and combined treatments all resulted in moderate to substantial effect sizes depending on the study design and measure employed (Fabiano, Pelham, Gnagy, Coles, & Wheeler-Cox, 2000).

In agreement with the conclusions of Pelham, Wheeler, and Chronis (1998), Fabiano et al. (2000), and DuPaul and Eckert (1997), numerous professional societies endorse the use of behavioral interventions in state-of-the-art treatment for ADHD. These organizations include the American Academy of Child and Adolescent Psychiatry (1997), the American Medical Association (Goldman, Genel, Bezman, & Slanetz, 1998), the American Psychological Association (Pelham, Wheeler, & Chronis, 1998), the U.S. Department of Education (2000), the American Academy of Pediatrics (2001), and the National Institutes of Health Consensus Conference Statement (1998). As these groups have already recognized, behavior modification is an essential component for any intervention used for treating ADHD.

Behavior modification may be divided into three general components, depending on the individual most involved in the treatment. Parents traditionally participate in parent-training programs in which they receive instruction in behavior management strategies. The goal of these parent programs is to improve and enhance parenting skills and to teach parents how to implement effective behavior modification programs in the home setting. Teachers are taught to concurrently implement behavior modification programs in the classroom to improve classroom functioning and academic productivity. Finally, a comprehensive intervention also incorporates a child-based component, which aims to build skills and foster competencies in school-related skills and friendships. For children with the serious emotional disturbance that characterizes severe ADHD, all three intensive components will be necessary.

Parent Intervention

Parent-training programs typically employ well-manualized approaches that teach the fundamentals of behavior change through rewards, punishments, and modeling, as well as provide basic information about ADHD. Parents are given assigned readings and are taught standard behavioral techniques such as those shown in Table 10.1 (Barkley, 1987; Barkley, 1995; Cunningham, Bremner, & Secord-Gilbert, 1994; Eyberg & Boggs, 1998; Forehand & Long, 1996; Patterson, 1975; Webster-Stratton, 1992). Typical clinical parent-training programs include a series of 8 to 16 weekly sessions for the initial training. Intervention is continued as long as necessary, with built-in programs for maintenance. Parent training is usually accomplished in groups (although additional individual sessions to supplement the group sessions will almost always be necessary), with weekly assignments given to parents to track behavior and practice techniques with their children between sessions.

The behavioral parent-training topics listed in Table 10.1 can best be thought of as a good start, as there are numerous additional topics that may be covered either in the group or individually. The content of additional topics is limited only by the areas of impairment in the treated families. For example, additional sessions might focus on scheduling structured play dates to foster friendships and to reduce the child and mother's social isolation (Wells et al., 2000). Other sessions may seek to directly intervene in marital conflict, as many marital conflicts might already center around parenting (Wilson & Gottman, 1995). Moreover, within the context of parent training, other evidence-based treatments might be employed. One example is the Coping with Depression Course (CWDC; Lewinsohn, Antonuccio, Steinmetz, & Teri, 1984). The CWDC is a 12-week, manualized, psychoeducational group treatment based on a social learning approach to depression. The CWDC emphasizes the relationship among thoughts, feelings, and behaviors to reduce negative affect and mood. Initial data indicate this is a useful adjunct to, and perhaps enhances, standard behavioral parent training (Chronis et al., 2000; Sanders & McFarland, 2000). These are just a few examples of topics that might be included in a clinical parent-training program if impairment is observed at any time during treatment. Evidence suggests that even traditional parent-training programs, in which sessions focus only on parenting skills, have beneficial effects on marital satisfaction and maternal psychopathology, even though these domains are not targeted directly (Anastopoulous, Shelton, DuPaul, & Guevremont, 1993; Pisterman, et al., 1992). Thus, it would be expected that directly intervening in these problem areas in conjunction with parent training would result in even greater improvement.

School Intervention

Those using behavior modification techniques with parents work simultaneously with teachers in a consultation model to teach the same kinds of behavioral strategies that are taught to parents (see Tables 10.1 and 10.2; DuPaul & Stoner, 1994; Pelham, in preparation; Walker & Eaton-Walker, 1991). Behavioral strategies taught to teachers include (a) daily report cards (DRCs; see Figure 10.1) that target individualized impaired areas or problem behaviors, establish procedures for the teacher to monitor and give feedback to the child for these target behaviors, and provide daily feedback to

Table 10.1   Typical Sequence of Sessions for Parent Training and Teacher Consultation in a Clinical Behavioral Intervention

Parent Training*
1. Overview of social learning and behavior management principles
2. Establishing a home and school daily report card; rewarding the daily report card
3. Attending, rewarding appropriate behavior and ignoring minor, inappropriate behaviors (e.g., whining)
4. Giving effective commands and reprimands
5. Using time-out procedures
6. Establishing and enforcing rules and when . . . then contingencies
7. Using home point system—reward and response cost
8. Enforcing contingencies outside of the home
9. Arranging structured play dates
10. Planning for maintenance after weekly therapist contact ends

Teacher Consultation*
1. Introducing rationale for and overview of treatment for ADHD; obtaining teacher/school commitment to implement intervention; introducing social learning theory and behavioral classroom management procedures; assessing teacher knowledge and use of behavioral procedures; designing content of subsequent sessions accordingly
2. Establishing and posting operationalized classroom rules
3. Presenting home/school daily report card (always done)
4. Instituting structure/instructional modifications for an individual child
5. Teaching attending, praising, and rewarding skills
6. Giving effective commands and reprimands; enforcing rules and when . . . then contingencies
7. Offering classwide interventions/group contingencies
8. Using response cost/reward point or token system for the target child
9. Incorporating time-out (classroom, office, systematic exclusion) procedures
10. Maintaining program after weekly therapist contact ends

*Every consultation contact includes a functional assessment of child's current progress toward treatment goals. These goals and treatment strategies are continually added, deleted, and modified based on the effectiveness of current treatment and the child's current functional impairment.

parents on the child's school performance, for which parents provide a positive home-based consequence (Kelley & McCain, 1995; O'Leary et al., 1976); and (b) other classroom management strategies that can be implemented by the teacher with the target child, such as classwide group contingencies, point or token reward systems, and time-outs (DuPaul & Eckert, 1997; Pelham, Wheeler, & Chronis, 1998).

Many children with ADHD receive school-based services under the Individuals with Disabilities Education Act (IDEA). Beginning in 1991, children with severe ADHD whose behavior and learning problems impaired academic progress became eligible for federally mandated, special education services under the modified law.

Table 10.2 Components of Effective, Intensive, Sustained Behavior Modification Treatment for ADHD

Parent Training

Behavioral approach: Therapist teaches parents contingency management techniques to use with the child, and the parent implements the treatment directly in the home setting.

Focus on specific target behaviors that reflect impairment in multiple domains of functioning (e.g., peer and adult relationships, sibling relationships, academic progress, classroom and family functioning, self-esteem).

Typical model is group-based, with individual sessions to supplement group. Weekly sessions with therapist initially, then contact continued over the phone, e-mail, and further booster sessions.

Adherence to treatment components is regularly checked, and treatment goals are continually modified based on an ongoing functional analysis of behavior.

Continue support and contact as long as necessary (e.g., 2 or 3 years after the initial sessions).

Develop program for maintenance and relapse prevention (e.g., develop plans for dealing with backsliding and concurrent parental problems such as maternal depression, parental substance abuse, and parental relationship problems).

Reestablish contact for major developmental transitions (e.g., adolescence).

School Intervention

Behavioral approach: Therapist teaches teacher contingency management techniques to use with the child, and the teacher implements the treatment.

Focus on specific target behaviors that reflect impairment in multiple domains of functioning (e.g., peer and adult relationships, academic progress, classroom functioning, self-esteem).

Consultant works with teacher—initial weekly face-to-face or phone sessions, then contact continued over the phone, e-mail, and further school visits.

Adherence to treatment components is regularly checked (e.g., the teacher faxes in copies of the child's DRC each week), and treatment goals are continually modified based on an ongoing functional analysis of behavior and response to treatment.

Continue support and contact for multiple years after initial consultation (as long as necessary and at the beginning of each new school year).

Program for maintenance and relapse prevention (e.g., schoolwide programs, in-service training all school staff, including administrators; eventually train parent to work with the teacher and monitor or modify).

Reestablish contact for major developmental transitions (e.g., move from elementary school to middle school).

Child Intervention

Use behavioral and developmental approach involving direct work in natural or analog settings—*not* clinic settings.

Focus on specific target behaviors that reflect impairment in multiple domains of functioning and building competencies and skills in functional domains (e.g., friendships, adult relationships, sibling relationships, academic progress, classroom and family functioning, self-esteem, vocational skills).

Provide paraprofessional implementation of procedures

Ensure intensive treatments such as summer treatment programs (9 hours daily for 8 weeks or longer), or school-year, after-school, and Saturday (6-hour) sessions.

Table 10.2   (Continued).

Adherence to treatment components is regularly checked, and treatment goals are
   continually modified based on a current functional analysis of behavior.
Provide treatment as long as necessary (e.g., 2 or 3 years after initial contact).
Develop program for generalization and relapse prevention (e.g., integrate with
   school and parent treatments).
Reestablish contact for major developmental transitions (e.g., move from elementary
   to middle school; adolescence).

John's Daily Report Card   Morning

	Yes	No
Has **4** or fewer reminders for teasing others	🙂	😐
Completes **2** seat-work papers accurately	🙂	😐
Follows directions with **2** or fewer reminders	🙂	😐
Receives a good report from the cafeteria monitor	🙂	😐

Afternoon

	Yes	No
Follows directions with 3 or fewer reminders during specials (gym, art, music)	🙂	😐
Has **6** or fewer reminders for teasing others	🙂	😐
Has **3** or fewer reminders to work quietly during silent reading period	🙂	😐
Has all needed books and folders in backpack by 2:30 dismissal	🙂	😐

Comments: _____

*** *5 minutes of home computer time for each smiley face!!!* ***

100% = ice cream bar for dessert!!!

Figure 10.1   Sample Daily Report Card (DRC)

These special education services might include behavioral and learning interventions to assist with academic progress. Parents have the right to request these special education services (it is often helpful for teachers, physicians, and mental health professionals to inform parents of this right) based on the child's educational impairment. If the schools concur that a learning problem is present, they must then create, implement, and evaluate an Individual Education Plan (IEP) for the student, which may include contingency management strategies, parent training, academic interventions, or some combination (U.S. Department of Education, 2000). Even children in regular education classrooms should have behavioral programs (e.g., preferential seating) under section 504 of the 1973 Rehabilitation Act.

In addition to mandated behavioral interventions implemented under the auspices of IDEA, it is informative to know the vast majority of teachers routinely report the use of behavioral interventions in the classroom (Reid, Maag, Vasa, & Wright, 1994; Rosen, Taylor, O'Leary, & Sanderson, 1990). The initial behavioral assessment should inform the clinician regarding the programs the teacher has implemented and with what degree of success. Therefore, the clinician's task often is to assist the teacher in improving his or her existing classroom management system by modifying its structure (e.g., increasing the frequency of rewards or setting specific operationalized targets, such as those listed in Figure 10.1). Teachers who do not use behavioral interventions will require more extensive initial education in the principles of behavioral modification.

Just as parent training programs are highly individualized, consultations with schoolteachers are likely to be highly idiographic, depending on the teacher's experience, familiarity with behavioral programs, current practices, attitudes toward treatment, and the severity of the child's referring problems. For example, though the DRC represents the backbone of any school/home behavior modification program, this intervention, although effective alone, is typically not sufficient to normalize the impairment evident in a classroom setting (e.g., Atkins et al., 1989), particularly children with a severe variant of ADHD.

In addition to a DRC, which is a reward system, clinicians might suggest a response-cost program, in which children lose points or privileges based on negative behavior. This procedure may be especially appropriate and necessary for children with ADHD/SED and comorbid problems as it is considerably more intense than a reward program alone. Numerous studies demonstrate response-cost programs to be highly effective in the classroom (e.g., Atkins et al., 1989; DuPaul, Guevremont, & Barkley, 1992; Rapport et al., 1980, 1982; Walker, Hops, & Johnson, 1975). For example, Atkins et al., (1989) reported on a response-cost procedure implemented in a regular classroom initially by a paraprofessional and eventually the teacher. In the program, the target child lost a minute of recess time for each occurrence of a target behavior. In this study, the combination of the response-cost procedure and a DRC was equivalent to the combination of medication and the DRC, suggesting this may be an effective classroom-based treatment alternative for families wishing to avoid medication. Manualized procedures for systematically implementing a response-cost procedure in the regular classroom are available (Hops & Walker, 1988).

An alternative to response-cost procedures is a whole-class contingency (Anhalt, McNeil, & Bahl, 1998; Kubany, Weiss, & Sloggett, 1971; Robinson, Newby, & Ganzell,

1981; Rosenbaum, O'Leary, & Jacob, 1975; Witt & Elliott, 1982). In this type of intervention the behavior of an entire group is targeted, especially if it is determined during a functional assessment that peer attention is maintaining the negative behavior of a child with ADHD. To implement a group contingency, children may work individually or collectively to earn highly potent rewards (e.g., a group game) that are contingent on meeting target behaviors. Alternatively, the appropriate behavior of a disruptive child might earn rewards for the entire group, not only decreasing disruptive behavior, but perhaps improving peer status and reducing peer attention for inappropriate behaviors (Kubany et al., 1971). Teachers find this intervention to be very amenable to their classroom situation, and they are generally highly satisfied with its results (Anhalt et al., 1998).

Child Intervention

Since no treatment employed directly in a clinic setting with a child is effective for treating ADHD, treatment must be delivered directly in natural settings. Behavioral interventions with the parent and teacher already target areas of impairment, but it is likely that a child with ADHD will continue to experience dysfunction in other domains, such as friendships or academic competency (Evans, Pelham, & Grudberg, 1995; Pelham & Bender, 1982). Summer treatment programs, after-school groups, and Saturday programs provide one type of venue for this instruction and practice in a naturalistic setting (see Table 10.2). The summer treatment program (STP) for children with ADHD is an example of such a program (Pelham, Greiner, & Gnagy, 1997; Pelham & Hoza, 1996). The STP is a 9-hour-per-day, 8-week program that is a therapeutic summer camp. It includes the aforementioned parent training and school interventions, as well as a complement of other interventions designed to build competencies in key domains. Children engage in highly structured activities such as sports skills training and games, an academic classroom, and group discussions. Interwoven into every activity is a token economy in which children receive immediate feedback for appropriate and inappropriate behavior, and the points earned may be exchanged for daily and weekly reinforcers. Other behavior modification procedures are employed, including time-out, a daily report card, liberal feedback and praise, and rewards for appropriate behavior. Staff members discuss and, more important, model appropriate social interactions and skills in the naturalistic setting, and increased competencies in the academic and peer relationship domains are intensely targeted (e.g., in organized sports activities, reading, and cooperation through peer tutoring).

The intensive intervention with peers warrants discussion. The peer relationships of children with severe ADHD are typically abysmal, resulting in pervasive rejection and isolation (Erhardt & Hinshaw, 1994; Pelham & Bender, 1982). This is highly concerning, given the negative outcomes in adulthood predicted by poor peer relationships in childhood (Coie & Dodge, 1998; Parker & Asher, 1987). The STP is notable in that it was created for the explicit purpose of improving peer relationships, and it employs numerous techniques to achieve this end.

Knowledge of sports rules and developmentally appropriate sports skills are often deficient in children with ADHD (Pelham, et al., 1990), and these problems can negatively impact peer relationships (Pelham & Bender, 1982; Weiss & Duncan, 1992).

Therefore, in the STP, children spend 3 hours per day engaged in structured recreational activities (soccer, baseball, basketball). A portion of these recreational activities is devoted to intensive instruction and drills, and the rest of the time is spent in game play. The goal of these recreational activities is to teach the children sports rules and basic fundamental game skills so that they are proficient in these activities when they return to their community schools and playgrounds. Concurrently, appropriate sportsmanship and game-related behaviors are also targeted (Hupp & Reitman, 1999; Pelham et al., 1997). The importance of sports skills training is highlighted by epidemiological studies that report very little community involvement on the part of the children with ADHD (Achenbach & Edelbrock, 1981; Szmatari, Offord, & Boyle, 1989). To the extent that these activities with peers are necessary for attaining developmentally appropriate social skills and meeting potential friends, not to mention the potential benefits to a child's self-concept and self-esteem, fostering sports proficiency is an essential component of intensive treatment.

Peer relationships are further targeted by daily social skills training. Though office-based social skills training interventions have not been effective for treating ADHD, this intervention has shown promise as an adjunct to behavioral interventions (Pfiffner & McBurnett, 1997). In the STP, after a brief (i.e., 15-minute) morning discussion that focuses on a specific social skill originally outlined by Oden and Asher (1977), social skills training is interwoven into daily activities. For example, counselors are trained to observe and reinforce instances of cooperation, appropriate communication, and active participation in activities through praise, social honors, and the point system. The point system and other behavioral interventions directly target situations where poor social skills are exhibited, such as when a child directs a negative communication at another individual or does not actively participate in group activities. Complementing the adjunctive social skills training is training in group problem solving adapted from the works of Spivak, Platt, and Shure (1976) and Rickard and Dinoff (1965). In this treatment component, children are taught to create solutions to problems that affect group functioning. In response to the problem, group goals are instituted, and the children experience positive consequences for meeting the group goal or negative consequences if the group does not meet the goal. In addition to teaching the children the steps to appropriate problem solving, working toward the group goal is another means of increasing group cohesion and appropriate peer negotiations in the STP.

In the STP classroom, academic achievement and behaviors necessary for school success are also intensively targeted. Academic achievement is targeted through desk work and computer-based assignments individualized to the target child's specific needs. Classroom behavior and academic achievement is targeted by the classroom point system, in which children earn points for assignment completion and accuracy and lose points for behaviors incompatible with school success (e.g., out-of-seat behavior). A DRC, time-outs, and liberal praise are also employed in the classroom setting to maximize academic and behavioral gains. An example of this multifocused approach is illustrated by the classroom peer tutoring program, in which academic achievement *and* friendships are targeted through a manualized peer-tutoring program (Fuchs, Mathes, & Fuchs, 1993; Mathes, Fuchs, Fuchs, Henley, & Sanders, 1994). In this program, a weak reader is paired with a strong reader, and the two must cooperate to complete a reading-comprehension task. This program is manualized and well validated. It improves reading performance in children who are underachieving as well as those achieving as expected. In addition, the peer-tutoring sessions provide a forum for peer negotiation, cooperation, and appropriate role taking (e.g., reader or listener), all areas typically impaired and in need of intervention for children with ADHD (Whalen, Henker, Collins, McAuliffe, & Vaux, 1979; Landau & Milich, 1988).

The disruptive classroom behavior and poor academic progress, lack of skills in important functional domains (e.g., sports), and inappropriate and annoying behaviors exhibited in social interactions contribute to the poor peer relationships characteristic of children with ADHD. Because all of the aforementioned interventions to remediate these difficulties require the presence of a peer group and an intensive concurrent behavior modification system, none of these procedures could be implemented in a traditional mental health setting. In contrast, the STP provides an engaging and highly naturalistic context within which to observe and treat poor peer relationships. Similar programs have been developed to achieve improvement directly in school settings or after-school programs, recognizing the benefits of intervening directly in settings where impairment is evident (Bierman, Greenberg, & the Conduct Problems Prevention Research Group, 1998; Walker, Colvin, & Ramsey, 1995).

Parents and teachers receive the home- and school-based services described here in conjunction with the STP. Parent training is held concurrently with the STP, and booster sessions are provided in the fall to facilitate maintenance of treatment gains. Teacher consultation visits are held at the beginning of the school year and continue until an appropriate and effective classroom behavior management system is implemented. Table 10.2 details the comprehensive treatment aggregated within the context of the STP and clinical follow-up programs. Notably, the vast majority of parents report that they are highly satisfied with the treatment their child received in the STP, and the program results in reductions in impaired areas of functioning and increases in self-esteem (Pelham & Hoza, 1996). It is also notable that the STP, including eight parent-training sessions conducted during the program, two school-based behavioral consultation visits, and two booster parent-training sessions in the fall, can be provided for approximately $2,500 per family (based on year 2000 costs). In sum, families receive 386 hours of direct clinical contact provided at a cost of $6.50 per hour.

Combined Treatment

Children with the serious emotional disturbance characteristic of severe ADHD are likely to need combined pharmacological and behavioral treatment. Combining behavioral treatments and stimulant medication may present a number of advantages over either behavioral treatment or medication alone (Pelham & Murphy, 1986). First, it is clear from numerous studies that unimodal treatments do not routinely result in improvement to normative levels (Conners et al., 2001; Klein & Abikoff, 1997; Swanson et al., 2001) in important functional domains (e.g., peer relationships, academic achievement, disruptive behavior). For this reason, comprehensive, combined treatments are often implemented, and the incremental benefit of combined treatments may be observed in a number of ways. Combining treatments sometimes results in complementary effects. For instance, complementary effects may be observed across settings: Medication may be used to increase on-task behavior in the classroom, and a time-out system may be implemented during recess to reduce instances of aggression. Combined treatments also have additive effects. Several within-subject studies and laboratory studies have shown that low (e.g., 0.3 mg/kg) doses of MPH and behavioral treatments have roughly additive effects, yielding a larger treatment effect than either medication or behavioral intervention alone (e.g., Abramowitz, Eckstrand, O'Leary, & Dulcan, 1992; Atkins et al., 1989; Northup et al., 1999). Combined treatments also have interactive effects: The addition of a low dose of stimulant medication enables relatively greater effects to be achieved with less restrictive and more natural behavioral programs (e.g., Abramowitz et al., 1992; Hoza, Pelham, Sams, & Carlson, 1992). Because combining treatments results in the effective use of less complicated behavioral interventions, the intervention has an increased probability of successful implementation and, therefore, maintenance after therapist contact has faded.

One question of import regarding combined interventions concerns whether they are incrementally better than the unimodal implementation of behavior modification or stimulant medication. Many authors have recently concluded that combined treatments offer incremental benefit over behavior modification alone but that there is no benefit to combining behavior modification with medication (Jadad & Boyle et al., 1999; Jensen & Payne, 1998; Klein & Abikoff, 1997; MTA Cooperative Group, 1999). We beg to differ with this conclusion. We can cite numerous reports that support the incremental benefits of combined treatments (Abramowitz et al., 1992; Carlson, Pelham, Milich, & Dixon, 1992; Kolko, Bukstein, & Barron, 1999; Northup et al., 1999; Pelham et al., 1993; Pelham & Murphy, 1986). Perhaps one reason for controversy in the field concerns a methodological artifact of large clinical trials conducted to determine the efficacy of combined treatment. The large clinical trials conducted to date have actively medicated children at the endpoint assessment while fading the behavioral intervention before the endpoint assessment (Klein & Abikoff, 1997; MTA Cooperative Group, 1999). This results in an unequal comparison between treatment groups: A medication group with treatment implemented in its most intensive form is compared to a combined treatment group composed of medication in its most intensive form combined with a faded behavioral intervention and a behavioral treatment group composed of a faded intervention.

The MTA study, the largest clinical trial for the treatment of a childhood disorder to date, was composed of treatment groups similar to those just described. The treatment groups at the endpoint assessment were (a) a combined treatment group composed of continued medication management and faded behavior modification; (b) a medication management group composed of continued medication management; (c) a behavioral treatment group composed of faded behavioral treatment; and (d) a community comparison group, two thirds of whom were medicated with a central nervous system stimulant, primarily methylphenidate (MTA Cooperative Group, 1999; Pelham, 1999). Information on the effect of the behavioral and combined treatment in their most intensive phases is also available (Pelham, Gnagy, Greiner, Hoza, et al., 2000). Depending on the time in the study when measures were obtained, the results of the respective treatment groups are very different.

Consider, for example, the Pelham, Gnagy, Greiner, Hoza, et al. (2000) study conducted within the context of the STP. In this investigation, the highly intensive, comprehensive STP described earlier was employed. Two groups of children participated in the STP. One was steadily medicated throughout the duration of the STP and one was unmedicated. These two groups did not differ in response to treatment on 82 of 87 dependent measures, indicating that within the context of a highly intensive behavioral treatment, there was little incremental benefit of stimulant medication. The opposite pattern of results occurred in the MTA 14-month treatment outcome report (MTA Cooperative Group, 1999). In this report, because medication treatment was ongoing and behavioral treatment was faded, behavioral treatment added little to the intensive, ongoing treatment, which was medication. However, the behavior modification treatment group (faded and therefore of considerably less intensity) was equivalent to the medicated children in the community comparison group (Pelham, 1999). Based on these results, treatment intensity is an essential parameter to consider when evaluating treatment outcomes. It appears to be the case that combined treatments are not incrementally better than unimodal treatments when the unimodal treatment compared to the combined treatment is highly intensive (i.e., a very high dose of medication and intensive behavioral treatment programs). However, in school and home settings, where highly intensive unimodal treatments are not always feasible, the combination of behavioral interventions and medication of moderate intensity appears to be better than either treatment singly. For children with ADHD classified as SED, it may often be the case that intensive combinations of both unimodal treatments are required to result in meaningful behavior change.

Combined treatments also appear to be incrementally better when the social validity of an intervention is considered. *Social validity* is a term that refers to the clinical meaningfulness and relevance of treatment outcome. As Foster and Mash (1999) reviewed, the social validity of an intervention may be assessed through normative comparisons, subjective consumer satisfaction ratings, or objective indicators of functional impairment. Social validity is an important concept when considering the effectiveness of treatment. That is, interventions that improve functioning to normative levels, that are favorably received by treatment consumers, and that result in clinically meaningful outcomes may be likely to be maintained. Given that a sustained treatment model is necessary for ADHD, treatments that can be maintained are desired. The evidence to date suggests combined treatments are superior to unimodal treatments on all of these indices of social validity.

In studies that have included normative comparisons, combined treatments are nearly always necessary to result in a normative level of posttreatment functioning. In the Klein and Abikoff study (1997) and Multimodal Treatment Study for ADHD (MTA Cooperative Group, 1999; Conners et al., 2001; Swanson et al., 2001), children who received the combined treatment were considerably more likely to be normalized or rated as improved than those in either unimodal treatment group. One caveat to these findings is necessary, however. As mentioned previously, when the intensity of a unimodal treatment is increased substantially, there appears to be little difference between the normalization rates of behavioral and combined treatments (Atkins et al., 1989; Pelham, Gnagy, Greiner, Hoza, et al., 2000).

Studies that have assessed treatment acceptability/satisfaction also support the high social validity of combined treatments. In the MTA study, parents overwhelmingly rated the combined treatments favorably (Pelham Gnagy, Greiner, & the MTA Cooperative Group, 2000). For example, 70% of parents reported they were strongly satisfied with the combined treatment, 64% with the behavioral treatment, and 34% with the medication management treatment.

The third index of social validity concerns improvement in impaired functional domains. To return to the MTA study (MTA Cooperative Group, 1999), the combined treatment was superior to standard community care on parent ratings of oppositional and internalizing symptoms and academic achievement, areas frequently reported as highly impaired. Secondary analyses indicated that the combined treatment was the most likely to result in an "excellent" response to treatment (Swanson et al., 2001). Pelham et al. (1993) also demonstrated the superiority of combined treatments for addressing impaired functioning. In this study, analyses were individualized for each subject by weighting the child's response to treatment in terms of impairment reported in the initial assessment. Results of these analyses, which were conducted to determine the effect of unimodal and combined treatment on individualized areas of impairment, favored combined treatment. In this study, 41% of children performed incrementally better in the classroom in their most impaired areas with a combined treatment versus medication alone, and 78% performed better with a combined treatment versus behavior modification alone, thus providing further support for the benefit of combined treatment versus unimodal treatment for reducing impairment.

CONCLUSION AND FUTURE DIRECTIONS

We have outlined evidence-based treatment for ADHD, a severely impairing disorder. Perhaps the most frustrating aspect of ADHD is that it is a disorder that not only impairs the individual child, but also those in the child's environment. In fact, much of the impairment associated with ADHD is a result of the disruption and annoyance caused to others. Eventually, this chronic disruption results in peer rejection, academic underachievement, low self-esteem, and family problems. Children with ADHD are clearly at risk for poor adolescent and adult outcomes, which significantly tax societal resources (Barkley, Fischer, Edelbrock, & Smallish, 1990; Lynam, 1996; Weiss & Hechtman, 1993). Thus, effectively ameliorating impairment caused by ADHD is an important goal not only for the children with ADHD, but for society at large.

The good news is that effective treatments for ADHD, as outlined in this chapter, are familiar to those in the community and routinely employed. In our clinical work, many parents readily acknowledge using time-outs with their children. In addition, many teachers endorse the use of behavioral techniques in their classroom (Reid et al., 1994; Rosen et al., 1990). Many children with ADHD, particularly those who are the inattentive type or on the mild to moderate end of the severity dimension may respond well to relatively less complicated behavioral treatment, low doses of stimulant medication, or their combination.

Children with ADHD classified as SED, in contrast, need the comprehensive, intensive interventions we have outlined. Unfortunately, these treatments in their most intensive form are not always readily accessible in the community (only 12 communities offer the summer treatment program described). Components of the STP can be found in the community, however. The STP classroom is modeled after 12:1:1 special education classrooms (i.e., 12 students, 1 special education teacher, 1 aide), which is typical of most public school settings. Children with ADHD who are SED may benefit significantly from the increased structure, feedback, and individualized attention afforded by these classrooms. Even greater gains might be obtained with highly individualized academic and behavioral interventions implemented within the context of ongoing class- or schoolwide behavioral interventions. Focus must shift to increasing the prevalence and effectiveness of such school-based interventions and expanding similar interventions into the homes, communities, and playgrounds where children with ADHD exhibit impairment.

This shift in focus is easier said than done. Many barriers exist to implementing evidence-based treatments in the community. Foremost is the fact that millions of dollars and countless training and clinical hours are *wasted* on non-evidence-based treatments for ADHD such as individual counseling, play therapy, and cognitive therapy. Moreover, by far the most common intervention for ADHD is medication prescribed by a community physician. However, most children do not take medication for life or, in fact, for more than a few months (Sherman & Hertzig, 1991), so the treatment is seriously limited in its effectiveness for remitting the pervasive impairment associated with ADHD. Based on these factors, current practice is seriously underserving children with ADHD.

The solution to this problem requires a number of conceptual shifts by caregivers and significant modifications in current practice, the foremost of which is that ADHD must be conceptualized as a chronic disorder. The expectation that problems will remit after eight parent-training sessions, a few school consultation visits, or a few months of medication should be discarded. Because ADHD is a developmental disorder characterized by developmentally inappropriate levels of inattention, overactivity, and impulsivity, the specific areas of impairment will change over time as the child matures, and interventions appropriate for a child at one point may not necessarily improve functioning at another point. Parents and clinicians must be sensitive to this fact and anticipate the need for intervention during important developmental transitions (e.g., the move from elementary to middle school), and mental health and school systems must be structured to adapt to these changes. Developmental changes in impairment also highlight the importance of ongoing applied behavioral assessments throughout treatment.

Furthermore, the intensity of interventions must be increased substantially. Children with severe ADHD and their families experience considerable problems in daily life functioning, so it should not be surprising that they require substantial treatment. Programs such as this already exist, such as the previously mentioned STP, but at present are not universally available. Should high-intensity approaches be impractical or too costly, combining relatively lower intensity behavioral programs with low doses of stimulant medication often approximates high-intensity approaches. This combination is a viable alternative treatment in settings where intensive behavioral treatment programs are not currently employed.

In addition to increasing the intensity and availability of intensive behavioral and combined treatments in the community, applied research on procedures that will increase the maintenance of treatment gains over time is sorely needed. It is clear that compliance with stimulant medication (Sherman & Hertzig; Sleator, Ullmann, & von Neumann, 1982) and behavioral interventions (Barkley et al., 2000; Fuchs & Fuchs, 1989) is less than optimal. Focus must shift to studying ways in which treatment adherence might be increased initially and maintained for a protracted period of time. For example, there have been practically no studies that investigated the relative impact of order effects on combined treatments. In the instance where behavior modification is attempted initially, parents and teachers are reinforced by the improved behavior exhibited by the child and may be likely to maintain behavioral interventions even after medication is added. In contrast, when medication is titrated up to the highest dose tolerated by a child without the emergence of side effects, there is little room for behavioral interventions to further improve behavior. A third-order effect might involve an initial low dose of stimulant medication to reduce deviant levels of problem behaviors and allow the introduction of less complicated and more manageable behavioral interventions (e.g., Atkins et al., 1989). After behavioral interventions are stabilized, assessment of the incremental efficacy of additional medication might be conducted. These possibilities remain empirical questions because no systematic data exist on these order effects.

A second area of research, one that has been grossly understudied, especially for behavioral and combined treatments, is the effect of individual differences on treatment response. Clearly, there are individual differences in response to stimulants (Pelham & Smith, 2000; Swanson et al., 1995), but at this point, differences in response cannot be predicted a priori. The same is the case for behavioral and combined treatments (Pelham et al., 1993). Differences in environmental characteristics (e.g., parenting practices, family or school resources, parental psychopathology, or the availability of treatments in the community) and in characteristics of the child (e.g., age, the presence of comorbidities, and the severity of ADHD symptomatology) may all impact individual responses to treatment. Little is currently known regarding the potential effects of all these factors, and many more, on treatment response.

Little is also currently known about the potential interactive effects of combined treatments. Medication dosage increases must be stopped at the point where side effects become so impairing that discontinuation of that particular medication dose is necessary. Similarly, the time and monetary resources available often limit the intensity of behavioral interventions. The potential interactive effects between varying intensities of medication and behavioral treatments might provide lesser intensities of both treatment modalities to approximate the effects of the unimodal treatments in their most intensive form. In addition, there may be interactive effects whereby each treatment in isolation is ineffective, but the combination of the two treatments results in dramatic gains. These, too, are empirical questions and remain good candidates for future study.

Long-term treatment outcome studies and the efficacy and effectiveness of behavior modification, stimulant medication, and their combination are also needed to elucidate the effects of sustained, intensive treatment on adolescent and adult outcome. At this point, no one knows what impact intensively implemented treatments in childhood have on important long-term outcomes. Clearly, these three treatments are effective in the short term. Whether any of these three interventions results in incremental improvement in long-term outcomes is at this point unknown. Intuitively, because the combined intervention results in incrementally greater effects in the short term, there are reasons to believe it would maximize the chances of optimal long-term outcomes.

In conclusion, severe ADHD is a disorder that results in sustained and substantial impairment. This means that treatment for ADHD must also be sustained and substantial if meaningful behavioral changes are to be obtained. Behavioral treatments are an effective means of reducing impairment, but children who are severely impaired will likely require a combined behavioral and pharmacological approach. In these cases, behavioral treatments should be a first-line treatment for ADHD, with medication administered as needed. Finally, any intervention must be conducted with the expectation that the treated child will require long-term, chronic follow-up and continued maintenance of treatment gains.

REFERENCES

Abikoff, H. (1991). Cognitive training for ADHD children: Less to it than meets the eye. *Journal of Learning Disabilities, 24,* 205–209.

Abikoff, H., Ganeles, D., Reiter, G., Blum, C., Foley, C., & Klein, R. G. (1988). Cognitive training in academically deficient ADDH boys receiving stimulant medication. *Journal of Abnormal Child Psychology, 16,* 411–432.

Abramowitz, A. J., Eckstrand, D., O'Leary, S. G., & Dulcan, M. K. (1992). ADHD children's responses to stimulant medication and two intensities of a behavioral intervention. *Behavior Modification, 16,* 193–203.

Achenbach, T. M., & Edelbrock, C. S. (1981). Behavioral problems and competencies reported by parents of normal and disturbed children aged four through sixteen. *Monographs of the Society for Research in Child Development, 46*(1, Serial No. 1).

American Academy of Child and Adolescent Psychiatry: Practice parameters for the assessment and treatment of children, adolescents, and adults with attention deficit/hyperactivity disorder. (1997). *Journal of the American Academy of Child and Adolescent Psychiatry 36*(Suppl. 10), 85S–121S.

American Academy of Pediatrics, Committee on Quality Improvement, Subcommittee on Attention-Deficit/Hyperactivity Disorder. (2001). Treatment of the school-aged child with attention-deficit/hyperactivity disorder. *Pediatrics, 108,* 1033–1044.

American Psychiatric Association. (1994). *Diagnostic and statistical manual of mental disorders* (4th ed.). Washington, DC: Author

Anastopoulous, A. D., Shelton, T. L., DuPaul, G. J., & Guevremont, D. C. (1993). Parent training for attention-deficit/hyperactivity disorder: Its impact on parent functioning. *Journal of Abnormal Child Psychology, 21,* 581–596.

Angold, A., Costello, E. J., Farmer, E. M. Z., Burns, B. J., & Erkanli, A. (1999). Impaired but undiagnosed. *Journal of the American Academy of Child and Adolescent Psychiatry, 38,* 129–137.

Anhalt, K., McNeil, C. B., & Bahl, A. B. (1998). The ADHD classroom kit: A whole-classroom approach for managing disruptive behavior. *Psychology in the Schools, 35,* 67–79.

Arnold, L. E. (1999). Treatment alternatives for attention-deficit/hyperactivity disorder. *NIH Consensus Development Conference: Diagnosis and Treatment for Attention-Deficit/Hyperactivity Disorder, Programs and Abstracts* (pp. 127–141).

Atkins, M. S., Pelham W. E., & Licht, M. H. (1984). *Behavioral correlates of teacher ratings of attention-deficit disorder.* Paper presented at the annual meeting of the Association for the Advancement of Behavior Therapy, Philadelphia.

Atkins, M. S., Pelham, W. E., & White, K. J. (1989). Hyperactivity and attention deficit disorders. In M. Hersen (Ed.), *Psychological aspects of developments and physical disabilities: A casebook.* Newbury Park, CA: Sage Publications.

Barkley, R. A. (1995). *Taking charge of ADHD: The complete, authoritative guide for parents.* New York: Guilford Press.

Barkley, R. A. (1987). *Defiant children: A clinician's manual for assessment and parent training.* New York: Guilford Press.

Barkley, R. A., Fischer, M., Edelbrock, C. S., & Smallish, L. (1990). The adolescent outcome of hyperactive children diagnosed by research criteria: I. An 8-year prospective follow-up study. *Journal of the American Academy of Child and Adolescent Psychiatry, 29,* 546–557.

Barkley, R. A., Shelton, T. L., Crosswait, C., Moorehouse, M., Fletcher, K., Barrett, S., Jenkins, L., & Metevia, L. (2000). Multi-method psycho-educational intervention for preschool children with disruptive behavior: Preliminary results at post-treatment. *Journal of Child Psychology and Psychiatry and Allied Disciplines, 41,* 319–332.

Biederman, J., Faraone, S. V., Mick, E., Spencer, T., Wilens, T., Kiely, K., Guite, J., Ablon, J. S., Reed, E., & Warburton, R. (1992). High risk for attention deficit hyperactivity disorder among children of parents with childhood onset of the disorder: A pilot study. *American Journal of Psychiatry, 152,* 431–435.

Bierman, K. L., Greenberg, M. T., & Conduct Problems Prevention Research Group. (1996). Social skills training in the Fast Track Program. In R. D. Peters & R. J. McMahon (Eds.), *Preventing childhood disorders, substance abuse, and delinquency.* Thousand Oaks, CA: Sage.

Brestan, E. V., & Eyberg, S. M. (1998). Effective psychosocial treatments of conduct-disordered children and adolescents: 29 years, 82 studies, and 5272 kids. *Journal of Clinical Child Psychology, 27,* 180–189.

Brown, R. T., Borden, K. A., Wynne, M. E., Schleser, R., & Clingerman, S. R. (1986). Methylphenidate and cognitive therapy with ADD children: A methodological reconsideration. *Journal of Abnormal Child Psychology, 14,* 481–497.

Carlson, C. L., Pelham W. E., Milich R., & Dixon, J. (1992). Single and combined effects of methylphenidate and behavior therapy on the classroom performance of children with ADHD. *Journal of Abnormal Child Psychology, 20,* 213–232.

Chronis, A. M., Fabiano, G. A., Gnagy, E. M., Wymbs, B. T., Burrows-MacLean, L., & Pelham, W. E. (2001). Comprehensive sustained behavioral and pharmacological treatment for ADHD: A case study. *Cognitive and Behavioral Practice, 18,* 346–359.

Chronis, A. M., Gamble, S. A., Roberts, J. E., & Pelham, W. E. (2000, November). *Cognitive-behavioral therapy for mothers of children with ADHD: Changing distorted maternal cognitions about child behavior.* Paper presented at the annual meeting of the Association for the Advancement of Behavior Therapy, New Orleans, Louisiana.

Coie, J. D., & Dodge, K. A. (1998). Aggression and antisocial behavior. In W. Damon (Series Ed.) & N. Eisenberg (Vol. Ed.), *Handbook of child psychology: Vol. 3. Social, emotional, and personality development* (5th ed., pp. 779–862). New York: John Wiley & Sons.

Conners, C. K., Epstein, J. N., March, J. S., Angold, A., Wells, K. C., Klaric, J., Swanson, J. M., Arnold, L. E., Abikoff, H. B., Elliott, G. R., Greenhill, L. L., Hechtman, L., Hinshaw, S. P., Hoza, B., Jensen, P. S., Kraemer, H. C., Newcorn, J. H., Pelham, W. E., Severe, J. B., Vitiello, B., & Wigal, T. (2001). Multimodal treatment of ADHD in the MTA: An alternative outcome analysis. *Journal of the American Academy of Child and Adolescent Psychiatry, 40,* 159–167.

Copeland, L., Wolraich, M., Lindgren, S., Milich, R., & Woolson, R. (1987). Pediatricians' reported practices in the assessment and treatment of attention deficit disorders. *Developmental and Behavioral Pediatrics, 8,* 191–197.

Cunningham, C. E., Bremner, R., & Secord-Gilbert, M. (1994). *The community parent education (COPE) program: A school based family systems oriented course for parents of children with disruptive behavior disorders.* Unpublished manual.

DuPaul, G. J., & Eckert, T. L. (1997). The effects of school-based interventions for attention deficit hyperactivity disorder: A meta-analysis. *School Psychology Review, 26,* 5–27.

DuPaul, G. J., Guevremont, D. C., & Barkley, R. A. (1992). Behavioral treatment of attention-deficit hyperactivity disorder in the classroom. *Behavior Modification, 16,* 204–225.

DuPaul, G. J., Power, T. J., McGoey, K. E., Ikeda, M. J., & Anastopoulos, A. D. (1998). Reliability and validity of parent and teacher ratings of attention-deficit/hyperactivity disorder symptoms. *Journal of Psychoeducational Assessment, 16,* 55–68.

DuPaul, G. J., & Stoner, G. (1994). *ADHD in the schools: Assessment and intervention strategies.* New York: Guilford Press.

Erhardt, D., & Hinshaw, S. P. (1994). Initial sociometric impressions of attention-deficit/hyperactivity disorder and comparison boys: Predictions from social behaviors and from nonbehavioral variables. *Journal of Consulting and Clinical Psychology, 62,* 833–842.

Evans, S. W., Pelham, W., & Grudberg, M. V. (1995). The efficacy of notetaking to improve behavior and comprehension of adolescents with attention deficit hyperactivity disorder. *Exceptionality, 5,* 1–17.

Evans, S. W., Vallano, G., & Pelham, W. (1994). Treatment of parenting behavior with a psychostimulant: A case study of an adult with attention-deficit hyperactivity disorder. *Journal of Child and Adolescent Psychopharmacology, 4,* 63–69.

Eyberg, S. M., & Boggs, S. R. (1998). Parent-child interaction therapy: A psychosocial intervention for the treatment of young conduct-disordered children. In J. M. Briesmeister and C. E. Schaefer (Eds.), *Handbook of parent training: Parents as co-therapists for children's behavior problems* (pp. 61–97). New York: John Wiley & Sons.

Fabiano, G. A., Pelham, W. E., Gnagy, E. M., Coles, E. K., & Wheeler-Cox, T. (2000, August). *A meta-analysis of behavioral and combined treatments for ADHD.* Paper presented at the annual meeting of the American Psychological Association, Washington, DC.

Fabiano, G. A., Pelham, W. E., Gnagy, E. M., Kipp, H., Lahey, B. B., Burrows-MacLean, L., Chronis, A. M., Onyango, A. N., & Morrisey, S. (1999, November). *The reliability and validity of the children's impairment rating scale: A practical measure of impairment in children with ADHD.* Paper presented at the annual meeting of the Association for the Advancement of Behavior Therapy, Toronto, Ontario.

Forehand, R., & Long, N. (1996). *Parenting the strong-willed child: The clinically proven five-week program for parents of two- to six-year-olds.* Lincolnwood, IL: Contemporary Books.

Foster, S. L., & Mash, E. J. (1999). Assessing social validity in clinical treatment research: Issues and procedures. *Journal of Consulting and Clinical Psychology, 67,* 308–319.

Fuchs, D., & Fuchs, L. S. (1989). Exploring effective and efficient prereferral interventions: A component analysis of behavioral consultation. *School Psychology Review, 18,* 260–279.

Fuchs, D., Mathes, P. G., & Fuchs, L. S. (1993). *Peabody classwide peer tutoring reading methods.* Unpublished teacher's manual.

Goldman, L. S., Genel, M., Bezman, R. J., & Slanetz, P. J. (1998). Diagnosis and treatment of attention-deficit/hyperactivity disorder in children and adolescents. *JAMA, 279,* 1100–1107.

Goyette, C., Conners, C., & Ulrich, R. (1978). Normative data on revised Conners parent and teacher rating scale. *Journal of Abnormal Child Psychology, 6,* 221–236.

Hops, H., & Walker, H. M. (1988). *CLASS: Contingencies for learning academic and social skills.* Seattle, WA: Educational Achievement Systems.

Hoza, B., Pelham, W. E., Sams, S. E., & Carlson, C. (1992). An examination of the "dosage" effects of both behavior therapy and methylphenidate on the classroom performance of two ADHD children. *Behavior Modification, 16,* 164–192.

Hupp, S. D. A., & Reitman, D. (1999). Improving sports skills and sportsmanship in children diagnosed with attention-deficit/hyperactivity disorder. *Child and Family Behavior Therapy, 21,* 35–51.

Jacob, R., & Pelham, W. E. (1999). Behavior therapy. In H. Kaplan & B. Sadock (Eds.), *Comprehensive textbook of psychiatry/VII* (7th ed., pp. 2080–2127). New York: Williams & Wilkins.

Jadad, A. R., Booker, L., Gauld, M., Kakuma, R., Boyle, M., Cunningham, C. E., Kim, M., & Schachar, R. (1999). The treatment of attention-deficit hyperactivity disorder. An annotated bibliography and critical appraisal of published systematic reviews and meta-analyses. *The Canadian Journal of Psychiatry, 44,* 1025–1035.

Jadad, A. R., Boyle, M., Cunningham, C., Kim, M., & Schachar, R. (1999). *Treatment of attention-deficit hyperactivity disorder* (Evidence Report/Technology Assessment No. 11). Rockville, MD: Agency for Healthcare Research and Quality.

Jensen, P. S., & Payne, P. D. (1998). Behavioral and medication treatments for attention deficit hyperactivity disorder: Comparisons and combinations. *NIH Consensus Development Conference: Diagnosis and Treatment of Attention Deficit Hyperactivity Disorder, Programs and Abstracts.* Rockville, MD: National Institutes of Health, Continuing Medical Education.

Kavale, K. A., Forness, S. R., & Walker, H. M. (1999). Interventions for oppositional defiant disorder and conduct disorder in the schools. In H. C. Quay and A. E. Hogan (Eds.), *Handbook of disruptive behavior disorders* (pp. 441–454). New York: Kluwer Academic Publishers.

Kazdin, A. E. (1998). *Research designs in clinical psychology* (3rd ed.). Boston: Allyn & Bacon.

Kelley, M. L., & McCain, A. P. (1995). Promoting academic performance in inattentive children. *Behavior Modification, 19,* 357–375.

Klassen, A., Miller, A., Raina, P., Lee, S. K., & Olsen, L. (1999). Attention-deficit hyperactivity disorder in children and youth: A quantitative systematic review of the efficacy of different management strategies. *The Canadian Journal of Psychiatry, 44,* 1007–1016.

Klein, R. G., & Abikoff, H. (1997). Behavior therapy and methylphenidate in the treatment of children with ADHD. *Journal of Attention Disorders, 2,* 89–114.

Kolko, D. J., Bukstein, O. G., & Barron, J. (1999). Methylphenidate and behavior modification in children with ADHD and comorbid ODD and CD: Main and incremental effects across settings. *Journal of the American Academy of Child and Adolescent Psychiatry, 38,* 578–586.

Kratochwill, T. R., & McGivern, J. E. (1996). Clinical diagnosis, behavioral assessment, and functional analysis: Examining the connection between assessment and intervention. *School Psychology Review, 25,* 342–355.

Kubany, E. S., Weiss, L. E., & Sloggett, B. B. (1971). The good behavior clock: A reinforcement/time out procedure for reducing disruptive classroom behavior. *Journal of Behavior Therapy and Experimental Psychiatry, 2,* 173–179.

Landau, S., & Milich, R. (1988). Social communication patterns of attention-deficit-disordered boys. *Journal of Abnormal Child Psychology, 16,* 69–81.

Lewinsohn, P. M., Antonuccio, D., Steinmetz, J., & Teri, L. (1984). *The coping with depression course: A psychoeducational intervention for unipolar depression.* Eugene, OR: Castalia.

Lovaas, O. I. (1987). Behavioral treatment and normal educational and intellectual functioning in young autistic children. *Journal of Consulting and Clinical Psychology, 55,* 3–9.

Lovaas, O .I., Koegel, R., Simmons, J. Q., & Long, J. S. (1973). Some generalization and follow-up measures on autistic children in behavior therapy. *Journal of Applied Behavior Analysis, 6,* 131–166.

Lynam, D. R. (1996). Early identification of chronic offenders: Who is the fledgling psychopath? *Psychological Bulletin, 120,* 209–234.

Mash, E. J., & Terdal, L. G. (1997). Assessment of child and family disturbance: A behavioral-systems approach. In E. J. Mash and L. G. Terdal (Eds.), *Assessment of childhood disorders* (3rd ed., pp. 3–68). New York: Guilford Press.

Mathes, P. G., Fuchs, D., Fuchs, L. S., Henley, A. M., & Sanders, A. (1994). Increasing strategic reading practice with Peabody Classwide Peer Tutoring. *Learning Disabilities Research and Practice, 9,* 44–48.

MTA Cooperative Group. (1999). 14-month randomized clinical trial of treatment strategies for attention deficit hyperactivity disorder. *Archives of General Psychiatry, 56,* 1073–1086.

Miller, A., Lee, S., Raina, P., Klassen, A., Zupancic, J., & Olsen, L. (1998). *A review of therapies for attention-deficit/hyperactivity disorder.* Ottawa: Canadian Coordinating Office for Health Technology Assessment (CCOHTA).

NIH Consensus Conference Statement (1998). *Diagnosis and treatment of attention deficit hyperactivity disorder (ADHD), 16,* Washington, DC: National Institutes of Health.

Northup, J., Fusilier, I., Swanson, V., Huete, J., Bruce, T., Freeland, J., Gulley, V., & Edwards, S. (1999). Further analysis of the separate and interactive effects of methylphenidate and common classroom contingencies. *Journal of Applied Behavior Analysis, 32,* 35–50.

Oden, S., & Asher, S. R. (1977). Coaching children in social skills for friendship making. *Child Development, 48,* 495–506.

O'Leary, K. D., & Becker, W. C. (1967). Behavior modification of an adjustment class: A token reinforcement program. *Exceptional Children, 37,* 145–155.

O'Leary, K. D., Pelham, W. E., Rosenbaum, A., & Price, G. H. (1976). Behavioral treatment of hyperkinetic children. *Clinical Pediatrics, 15,* 510–515.

Parker, J. G., & Asher, S. R. (1987). Peer relations and later personal adjustment: Are low-accepted children at risk? *Psychological Bulletin, 102,* 357–389.

Patterson, G. R. (1975). *Living with children: New methods for parents and teachers.* Champaign, IL: Research Press.

Pauls, D. L. (1991). Genetic factors in the expression of attention-deficit hyperactivity disorder. *Journal of Child and Adolescent Psychopharmacology, 1,* 353–360.

Pelham, W. E. (in preparation). *Comprehensive treatment for ADHD: Interventions for schools.*

Pelham, W. E. (1999). The NIMH multimodal treatment study for attention deficit hyperactivity disorder: Just say yes to drugs alone? *The Canadian Journal of Psychiatry, 44,* 981–990.

Pelham, W. E. (1993). Pharmacotherapy for children with attention-deficit hyperactivity disorder. *School Psychology Review, 22,* 199–227.

Pelham, W. E., & Bender M. E. (1982). Peer relationships in hyperactive children. In K. Gadow, & I. Bailer (Eds.), *Advances in learning and behavioral disabilities* (Vol. 1, pp. 366–436). Greenwich, CT: JAI Press.

Pelham, W. E., Carlson C., Sams S. E., Vallano, G., Dixon, J., & Hoza, B. (1993). Separate and combined effects of methylphenidate and behavior modification on boys with ADHD in the classroom. *Journal of Consulting and Clinical Psychology, 61,* 506–515.

Pelham, W. E., Gnagy, E. M., Burrows-Maclean, L., Williams, A., Fabiano, G. A., Morrisey, S. M., Chronis, A. M., Forehand, G. L., Nguyen, C. A., Hoffman, M. T., Lock, T. M., Fielbelkorn, K., Coles, E. K., Panahon, C. J., Steiner, R. L., Meichenbaum, D. L., Onyango, A. N., & Morse, E. (2001). Once-a-day Concerta™ methylphenidate versus t.i.d. methylphenidate in laboratory and natural settings. *Pediatrics, 107,* www.pediatrics.org/cgi/content/full/107/6/e105

Pelham, W. E., Gnagy, E. M., Greenslade, K. E., & Milich, R. (1992). Teacher ratings of *DSM-III-R* symptoms of the disruptive behavior disorders. *Journal of the American Academy of Child and Adolescent Psychiatry, 31,* 210–218.

Pelham, W. E., Gnagy, E. M., Greiner, A. R., & the MTA Cooperative Group (2000). Parent and teacher satisfaction with treatment and evaluation of effectiveness. Poster presented at the annual meeting of the Association for the Advancement of Behavior Therapy, New Orleans, LA.

Pelham, W. E., Gnagy, E. M., Greiner, A. R., Hoza, B., Hinshaw, S. P., Swanson, J. M., Simpson, S., Shapiro, C., Bukstien, O., & Baron-Myak, C. (2000). Behavioral vs. behavioral and pharmacological treatment in ADHD children attending a summer treatment program. *Journal of Abnormal Child Psychology, 28,* 507–526.

Pelham, W. E., Greiner, A. R., & Gnagy, E. M. (1997). *Children's summer treatment program manual.* Buffalo, NY: CTADD.

Pelham, W. E., & Hoza, B. (1996). Intensive treatment: A summer treatment program for children with ADHD. In E. Hibbs & P. Jensen (Eds.), *Psychosocial treatments for child and adolescent disorders: Empirically based strategies for clinical practice* (pp. 311–340). New York: APA Press.

Pelham, W. E., Hoza, B., Pillow, D. R., Gnagy, E. M., Kipp, H. L., Greiner, A. G., Waschbusch, D. A., Trane, S. T., Greenhouse, J., Wolfson, L., & Fitzpatrick, E. (in press). Effects of methylphenidate and expectancy on children with attention-deficit hyperactivity disorder: Behavior, academic performance, and attributions in a summer treatment program and regular classroom settings. *Journal of Consulting and Clinical Psychology.*

Pelham, W. E., Lang, A. R., Atkeson, B., Murphy, D. A., Gnagy, E. M., Greiner, A. R., Vodde-Hamilton, M., Greenslade, K. E. (1998). Effects of deviant child behavior and parental alcohol consumption: Stress induced drinking in parents of ADHD children. *The American Journal on Addictions, 7,* 103–114.

Pelham, W. E., McBurnett, K., Harper, G. W., Milich, R., Murphy, D. A., Clinton, J., & Thiele, C. (1990). Methylphenidate and baseball playing in ADHD children: Who's on first? *Journal of Consulting and Clinical Psychology, 58,* 130–133.

Pelham, W. E., & Murphy, H. A. (1986). Attention deficit and conduct disorder. In M. Hersen (Ed.), *Pharmacological and behavioral treatment: An integrative approach* (pp. 108–148). New York: John Wiley & Sons.

Pelham, W. E., & Smith, B. H. (2000). Prediction and measurement of individual responses to Ritalin by children and adolescents with attention deficit hyperactivity disorder. In L. L. Greenhill & B. B. Osman (Eds.), *Ritalin: Theory and practice* (2nd ed., pp. 193–218). Larchmont, NY: Mary Ann Liebert.

Pelham, W. E., & Waschbusch, D. A. (1999). Behavioral intervention in attention-deficit/hyperactivity disorder. In H. C. Quay & A. E. Hogan (Eds.), *Handbook of disruptive behavior disorders* (pp. 255–278). New York: Kluwer Academic/Plenum Publishers.

Pelham, W. E., Wheeler, T., & Chronis, A. (1998). Empirically supported psychosocial treatments for attention deficit hyperactivity disorder. *Journal of Clinical Child Psychology, 27(2)*, 190–205.

Pfiffner, L. J., & McBurnett, K. (1997). Social skills training with parent generalization: Treatment effects for children with attention deficit disorder. *Journal of Consulting and Clinical Psychology, 65*, 749–757.

Pisterman, S., Firestone, P., McGrath, P., Goodman, J. T., Webster, I., Mallory, R., & Goffin, B. (1992). The effects of parent training on parenting stress and sense of competence. *Canadian Journal of Behavioral Science, 24*, 41–58.

Rapport, M. D., Murphy, H. A., & Bailey, J. S. (1982). Ritalin vs. response cost in the control of hyperactive children: A within subject comparison. *Journal of Applied Behavior Analysis, 15*, 205–216.

Rapport, M. D., Murphy, H. A., & Bailey, J. S. (1980). The effects of a response cost treatment tactic on hyperactive children. *Journal of School Psychology, 18*, 98–111.

Reid, R., Maag, J. W., Vasa, S. F., & Wright, G. (1994). Who are the children with attention deficit-hyperactivity disorder? A school-based survey. *Journal of Special Education, 28*, 117–137.

Rickard, H. C., & Dinoff, M. (1965). Shaping adaptive behavior in a therapeutic summer camp. In L. P. Ullman and L. Krasner (Eds.), *Case studies in behavior modification* (pp. 325–328). New York: Holt, Reinhart, and Winston.

Robinson, P. W., Newby, T. J., & Ganzell, S. L. (1981). A token system for a class of underachieving hyperactive children. *Journal of Applied Behavior Analysis, 14*, 307–315.

Rosen, L. A., Taylor, S. A., O'Leary, S. G., & Sanderson, W. (1990). A survey of classroom management practices. *Journal of School Psychology, 28*, 257–269.

Rosenbaum, A., O'Leary, K. D., & Jacob, R. G. (1975). Behavioral intervention with hyperactive children: Group consequences as a supplement to individual contingencies. *Behavior Therapy, 6*, 315–323.

Sanders, M. R., & McFarland, M. (2000). Treatment of depressed mothers with disruptive children: A controlled evaluation of cognitive behavioral family intervention. *Behavior Therapy, 31*, 89–112.

Scotti, J. R., Morris, T. L., McNeil, C. B., & Hawkins, R. P. (1996). *DSM-IV* and disorders of childhood and adolescence: Can structural criteria be functional? *Journal of Consulting and Clinical Psychology, 64*, 1177–1191.

Sherman, M., & Hertzig, M. E. (1991). Prescribing practices of Ritalin: The Suffolk County, New York study. In L. L. Greenhill and B. B. Osman (Eds.), *Ritalin: Theory and patient management* (pp. 187–193). Larchmont, NY: Mary Ann Liebert.

Sleator, E. K. (1982). Office diagnosis of hyperactivity by the physician. *Advances in Learning & Behavioral Disabilities 1*, 341–364.

Sleator, E. K., Ullmann, R. K., & von Neumann, A. (1982). How do hyperactive children feel about taking stimulants and will they tell the doctor? *Clinical Pediatrics, 21*, 474–479.

Spencer, R., Biederman, J., Wilens, T., Harding, M., O'Donnell, D., & Griffen, S. (1996). Pharmacotherapy of attention-deficit hyperactivity disorder across the life cycle. *Journal of the American Academy of Child and Adolescent Psychiatry, 35*, 409–432.

Spivak, G., Platt, J. J., & Shure, M. B. (1976). *The problem solving approach to adjustment.* San Francisco: Jossey-Bass.

Swanson, J. M., Kraemer, H. C., Hinshaw, S. P., Arnold, L. E., Conners, C. K., Abikoff, H. B., Clevenger, W., Davies, M., Elliott, G. R., Greenhill, L. L., Hechtman, L., Hoza, B., Jensen, P. S., March, J. S., Newcorn, J. H., Owens, E. B., Pelham, W. E., Schiller, E., Severe, J. B., Simpson, S., Vitiello, B., Wells, K., Wigal, T., & Wu, M. (2001). Clinical relevance of the primary findings of the MTA: Success rates based on severity of ADHD and ODD symptoms at the end of treatment. *Journal of the American Academy of Child and Adolescent Psychiatry, 40,* 168–179.

Swanson, J. M., McBurnett, K., Christian, D. L., Wigal, T. (1995). Stimulant medication and treatment of children with ADHD. In T. H. Ollendick & R. J. Prinz (Eds.), *Advances in clinical child psychology* (Vol. 17, pp. 265–322). New York: Plenum Press.

Szatmari, P., Offord, D. R., & Boyle, M. H. (1989). Correlates, associated impairments and patterns of service utilization of children with attention deficit disorder: Findings from the Ontario Child Health Study. *Journal of Child Psychology and Psychiatry, 30,* 205–217.

U.S. Department of Education. (2000). *A guide to the individualized education program.* Jessup, MD: Author.

Walker, H. M., Colvin, G., & Ramsey, E. (1995). *Antisocial behavior in school: Strategies and best practices.* Albany, NY: Brooks/Cole.

Walker, H. M., & Eaton-Walker, J. E. (1991). *Coping with noncompliance in the classroom: A positive approach for teachers.* Austin, TX: Pro-Ed.

Walker, H. M., Hops, H., & Johnson, S. M. (1975). Generalization and maintenance of classroom treatment effects. *Behavior Therapy, 6,* 188–200.

Webster-Stratton, C. (1992). *The incredible years: A trouble-shooting guide for parents of children aged 3–8.* Toronto: Umbrella Press.

Weiss, M. R., & Duncan, S. C. (1992). The relationship between physical competence and peer acceptance in the context of children's sports participation. *Journal of Sport and Exercise Psychology, 14,* 177–191.

Weiss, G., & Hechtman, L. T. (1993). *Hyperactive children grown up: ADHD in children, adolescents and adults* (2nd ed.). New York: Guilford Press.

Wells, K. C., Pelham, W. E., Kotkin, R. A., Hoza, B., Abikoff, H. B., Abramowitz, A., Arnold, L. E., Cantwell, D. P., Conners, C. K., Del Carmen, R., Elliott, G., Greenhill, L. L., Hechtman, L., Hibbs, E., Hinshaw, S. P., Jensen, P. S., March, J. S., Swanson, J. M., & Schiller, E. (2000). Psychosocial treatment strategies in the MTA study: Rationale, methods, and critical issues in design and implementation. *Journal of Abnormal Child Psychology, 28,* 483–505.

Whalen, C. K., Henker, B., Collins, B. E., McAuliffe, S., & Vaux, A. (1979). Peer interaction in a structured communication task: Comparisons of normal and hyperactive boys and of methylphenidate (Ritalin) and placebo effects. *Child Development, 50,* 388–401.

Wilson, B. J., & Gottman, J. M. (1995). Marital interaction and parenting. In M. Bornstein (Ed.), *Handbook of parenting: Vol. 4. Applied and practical parenting.* Mahwah, NJ: Lawrence Erlbaum Associates.

Witt, J. C., & Elliott, S. N. (1982). The response cost lottery: A time efficient and effective classroom intervention. *Journal of School Psychology, 20,* 155–161.

Chapter 11

CHILDHOOD OBSESSIVE-COMPULSIVE AND TIC DISORDERS

SUSANNA CHANG AND JOHN PIACENTINI

Obsessive-compulsive disorder (OCD) and tic disorders, most notably Tourette's disorder (TD), have received increasing research and clinical attention over the past decade. Once thought to be exceedingly rare, recent epidemiologic studies have led to significant upward revisions in the prevalence of both conditions (Apter et al., 1993; Zohar, 1999). Studies examining clinical correlates of OCD and TD have documented the fact that these disorders share many characteristics. Both have a juvenile or young adult onset, a chronic waxing and waning course, and a familial occurrence. In addition, both involve involuntary, repetitive behaviors and aggressive, sexual, or scatological themes in the content of thoughts and behaviors, both can be exacerbated by stress or anxiety, and both share overlapping neuroanatomical sites of dysfunction in the basal ganglia and related structures such as the cortico-striato-thalamo-cortical (CSTC) tracts and frontal lobes (Petter, Richter, & Sandor, 1998). Comorbid emotional and behavioral disturbance are commonly seen in youngsters with these disorders and often serve to complicate both course of illness and treatment outcome (Albano, March, & Piacentini, 1999; Leckman, King, & Cohen, 1999).

This chapter reviews the epidemiology, clinical phenomenology, etiology, and clinical management of childhood OCD and tic disorders, with a particular focus on the current status of evidence-based treatments for each condition. The body of treatment literature for each disorder has grown considerably in the past two decades, from research based on single-case studies and small case series to studies using manualized CBT protocols and large, controlled, multisite medication trials (Carpenter, Leckman, Scahill, & McDougle, 1999; Grados, Scahill, & Riddle, 1999; Piacentini, 1999; Piacentini & Chang, 2001). As a result of recent advances in both psychosocial and psychopharmacological treatment approaches for OCD and TD, clinicians are better able than ever to provide the majority of affected youngsters with acute symptom relief as well as enhanced long-term prospects for satisfying and productive lives.

OBSESSIVE-COMPULSIVE DISORDER

Clinical Features

According to the *Diagnostic and Statistical Manual,* fourth edition, text revision (*DSM-IV-TR*), OCD is defined as the presence of either obsessions or compulsions that "cause marked distress, are time consuming, or significantly interfere with the person's normal routine . . . or functioning" (American Psychiatric Association, 2000). *DSM-IV-TR* defines obsessions as "recurrent or persistent thoughts, impulses, or images" that are experienced as intrusive or inappropriate, that are not simply excess worries about real-life problems, and that cause marked anxiety or distress. Compulsions are repetitive behaviors or mental acts that are performed in response to an obsession or according to some other rigidly applied rules. Compulsions, though meant to reduce anxiety or distress or prevent some dreaded event, are clearly excessive or are not realistically connected with the triggering stimulus. To differentiate OCD from psychosis, a child must recognize the obsessions as being products of his or her own mind as opposed to coming from an external source. Unlike adults, *DSM-IV-TR* does not require that children recognize their OCD symptoms as senseless or unrealistic for the diagnosis to be made.

Although children may be somewhat more likely than adults to engage in compulsive reassurance seeking and involve family members in their rituals (Piacentini & Bergman, 2000), OCD symptomatology appears to be quite consistent across the age span. The most common obsessions in childhood focus on germs or contamination, followed by fears of harm to self or others and excessive moralization or religiosity (Swedo, Rapoport, Leonard, Lenane, & Cheslow, 1989). The most common compulsions include excessive washing, repeating, checking, touching, counting, and ordering (Swedo, Rapoport, et al., 1989). The vast majority of youngsters with OCD experience both obsessions and compulsions. However, not all obsessions are anxiety-related, with some children describing intrusive thoughts or feelings related to disgust, discomfort, or an otherwise vague sensation that something is not right (the so-called just-right phenomenon). Although clinical lore suggests that the just-right phenomenon is more characteristic of individuals with comorbid OCD and tic disorder (King, Leckman, Scahill, & Cohen, 1999), this relationship remains to be empirically demonstrated in children. Similar to adult-onset OCD, the pattern and type of OCD symptoms in childhood typically shift over time, although the absolute number of symptoms generally remains constant (Hanna, 1995; Rettew, Swedo, Leonard, Lenane, & Rapoport, 1992). Childhood OCD is reactive to stress, and many children experience acute symptom exacerbations during times of psychosocial challenge, which may include such events as start of school year, moving to a new home, death of or separation from a family member (Rapoport, Swedo, & Leonard, 1993; Swedo, Rapoport, et al., 1989). Many youngsters with OCD are able to inhibit or control symptoms for short periods of time and with substantial effort—for example, while at school or in social situations (Rapoport et al., 1993). In some cases, parents, teachers, and others close to the child may remain unaware of the child's problem for significant periods of time, learning of it only after the child is no longer able to control his or her symptoms or becomes too overwhelmed to cope.

Childhood OCD is associated with significant impairments in functioning. Dressing and washing rituals may result in chronic lateness to school, and contamination fears often preclude the child from going to parties, movies, restaurants or other social events. Counting and checking rituals and intrusive thoughts can impair focus and concentration and interfere with reading and writing, adversely impacting school and job performance. In more severe cases, symptoms may also interfere with the child's ability to initiate and maintain friendships and adversely impact the adolescent's attempts to develop romantic and sexual relationships. Piacentini et al. (1999) systematically assessed OCD-related impairment in 162 youngsters (mean age 11.9 years) with the disorder and found the most commonly reported areas of interference to be doing assigned chores at home (reported by 78% of parents and 61% of children), getting ready for bed at night (73% of parents, 56% of children), concentrating on schoolwork (71% of parents, 62% of children), getting along with parents (70% of parents, 56% of children), and getting along with siblings (65% of parents, 53% of children). Over 85% of informants reported problems in all three functional areas assessed (school, social, and home/family), thus providing support for the pervasive impact of OCD across multiple psychosocial domains.

Obsessive-compulsive disorder is a highly comorbid disorder in childhood, with up to 80% of affected youngsters meeting diagnostic criteria for an additional *DSM-IV* disorder and up to 50% displaying multiple comorbidities (Zohar, 1999). Although methodologic differences have led to considerable variation in reported comorbidity rates across studies, other anxiety disorders (26% to 75%), depressive disorders (25% to 62%), tic disorders (20% to 30%), and behavioral disorders (18% to 33%) are most commonly observed (Piacentini & Graae, 1997; Rapoport et al., 2000; Zohar, 1999). There is some evidence to suggest that depressive symptoms are more likely to occur in adolescents as opposed to younger children and to appear after OCD onset, suggesting that co-occurring mood disturbance may be reactive (Valleni-Basile et al., 1994).

Follow-up studies of clinical samples provide relatively consistent evidence for the chronicity of childhood-onset OCD, with 43% to 68% of youngsters with OCD continuing to meet diagnostic criteria for the disorder 2 to 14 years after initial identification (Bolton, Luckie, & Steinberg, 1995; Leonard et al., 1993). It is likely, however, that the relatively negative outcomes associated with childhood OCD in the past have been at least partially due to the lack of effective interventions for this condition. As effective treatments, especially cognitive behavior therapy, become more widely available, it is reasonable to expect that the long-term outcome for children with OCD will improve. Leonard and colleagues (1993) found that a poor initial treatment response (to clomipramine), a lifetime history of tic disorder, and the presence of a parental Axis I psychiatric disorder were associated with poor outcome at follow-up of 2 to 7 years.

Epidemiology

Once thought to be rare in children, epidemiological data currently suggest OCD to be nearly as common in children as in adults, with a lifetime prevalence between 1% and 3%, and a 6-month prevalence of 0.5% to 1% (Flament et al., 1989; Shaffer et al.,

1996). Rapoport and colleagues (2000) reported an age-corrected 6-month prevalence rate of 1.72% using the NIMH MECA study sample of 1,285 community youngsters ages 9 to 17. However, the authors caution the interpretation of this rate due to the fact that the diagnostic interviews were conducted by lay interviewers and the study sample was not representative of the United States in general. Of the 35 total positive OCD cases in the MECA sample, 32 were identified by child report only, 4 by parent report only, and only 1 by both informants.

Subclinical OCD, defined as obsessions and compulsions occurring in the absence of significant distress or impairment, is significantly more common, with a reported prevalence of 19% in one school-based adolescent sample (Valleni-Basile et al., 1994). Both clinic (Hanna, 1995) and community-based (Rapoport et al., 2000) studies suggest a mean age of from 6 to 11 years for the onset of childhood OCD, with some suggestion that boys may experience an earlier onset of symptoms than girls (Rapoport et al., 2000). Clinic-based studies of primarily younger patients suggest the disorder to be more common in males than females; however, this finding has not been replicated in epidemiologic surveys. Although data from representative community samples do not exist to rule out referral bias, minorities and youngsters from lower socioeconomic strata appear to be underrepresented in clinical OCD samples (Piacentini & Graae, 1997).

Etiology

Neuropsychiatric

Multiple etiologic theories have been proposed for OCD, with neuropsychiatric explanations receiving the most recent attention. Interest in neuropsychiatric factors was initially spurred by the efficacy of serotonin reuptake inhibitors (SRIs) for treating OCD, which led to the development of the serotonin hypothesis of OCD. More recently, a growing body of evidence from both adult and pediatric samples and using a variety of neuroimaging techniques has implicated dysfunctions in CSTC neural circuitry as a primary locus of pathology in OCD (Fitzgerald, MacMaster, Paulson, & Rosenberg, 1999; Rosenberg & Hanna, 2000; Saxena, Brody, Schwartz, & Baxter, 1998). Although structural neuroimaging studies with adults have yielded inconsistent results, clearer findings have emerged from pediatric research employing similar methodology, including increased localized anterior cingulate volumes (Rosenberg & Keshavan, 1998), reduced striatal volumes (Rosenberg et al., 1997; Luxenberg et al., 1988), and increased thalamic volumes in pediatric OCD patients compared to healthy controls (Gilbert et al., 2000). Positron emission tomography (PET) studies have revealed increased glucose metabolism in orbital frontal and prefrontal cortex, right caudate nucleus, and anterior cingulate gyrus in adults with OCD (Baxter et al., 1988; Schwartz, Stoessel, Baxter, Martin & Phelps, 1996) and children (Swedo, Schapiro, et al., 1989).

Among adults with OCD, successful treatment with either behavior therapy or selective serotonin reuptake inhibitor (SSRI) medication has led to normalization of frontal and basal ganglia glucose metabolisms as well as attenuation of the correlation of activity between these regions (Baxter, Schwartz, & Bergman, 1992; Schwartz et al., 1996). An accumulating body of evidence suggests that dysfunctions in both dopaminergic and glutamatergic systems may also be of etiological importance (Fitzgerald et al., 1999). Rosenberg and colleagues (2000) used magnetic resonance spectroscopy (MRS) to determine that left caudate glutamatergic concentrations (Glx) were significantly greater in treatment-naive youngsters with OCD than in controls, but this difference disappeared following treatment with paroxetine (an SSRI). Moreover, the decrease in caudate Glx concentration was significantly correlated ($r = .80$) with decreased symptom severity.

Immunologic

Researchers at the National Institute of Mental Health (NIMH) have described a subgroup of youngsters whose OCD symptoms appear to be triggered or exacerbated by Group A beta-hemolytic streptococcal infection, or GABHS (Swedo et al., 1998). The obsessions and compulsions in these individuals appear to stem from caudate swelling caused by an autoimmune reaction between caudate tissue and antineuronal antibodies formed against GABHS in a process similar to the development of Sydenham's chorea (Swedo, Leonard, & Kiessling, 1994). This subtype of OCD, called pediatric autoimmune neuropsychiatric disorders associated with streptococcal infection (PANDAS), is characterized by sudden and dramatic onset or exacerbation of OCD or tic symptoms, associated neurological findings, and a recent streptococcal infection (Swedo et al., 1998). Although the proportion of childhood OCD cases with an immunological etiology remains unknown, one recent controlled trial found two forms of antibiotic treatment (plasma exchange and intravenous immunoglobulin, IVIG), both superior to placebo for reducing symptoms of infection-triggered OCD and tic disorders (Perlmutter et al., 1999).

Genetic

Evidence from family aggregation and twin studies support the notion of OCD as a heritable disorder; as many as 50% of childhood OCD cases may be familial in nature (Pauls & Alsobrook, 1999). Nestadt et al. (2000) found a nearly 5-fold higher lifetime prevalence of OCD in the first-degree relatives of probands diagnosed with OCD compared to controls, with obsessions being more specific to the familial aspect of the disorder than compulsions. Evidence also exists suggesting that familial transmission may be more characteristic of early-onset, as opposed to late-onset, OCD (Nestadt et al., 2001; Pauls, Alsobrook, Goodman, Rasmussen, & Leckman, 1995). The heterogeneity of OCD complicates the identification of possible transmission models. However, analyses confined to families with multiple affected members suggest a mixed transmission model for OCD (i.e., a gene of major effect superimposed on a combination of multiple minor genes; Pauls & Alsobrook, 1999).

Psychological

Early conceptualizations of OCD based on psychodynamic models have not held up in light of the poor response to psychoanalytic and similar forms of treatment (Steketee, 1993). The primary behavioral conceptualizations of OCD are based on Mowrer's two-factor conditioning theory (Steketee, 1993), whereby a neutral event or object becomes aversive to the individual as a result of being associated with an unrelated fear-eliciting event (i.e., classical conditioning). According to Mowrer's theory, compulsions become strengthened as a result of their anxiety-reducing properties (i.e., negative reinforcement). Because most individuals cannot recall specific fear-eliciting events associated with the onset of their OCD symptoms, more recent behavioral conceptualizations have incorporated other acquisition mechanisms, including modeling, observation, and informational learning, as necessary precursors to the development of the disorder (Steketee, 1993). Regardless of etiologic explanatory power, operant conditioning principles provide a useful theoretical basis for understanding the maintenance of many OCD symptoms. Cognitive theories of OCD posit that the illness results from the propensity of certain individuals to interpret the occurrence of intrusive thoughts, images, impulses, and doubts in a manner indicating increased self-responsibility for harm to themselves or others (Salkovkis, 1999).

Differential Diagnosis

Repetitive behaviors, habits, and perseverative thinking (e.g., bedtime or mealtime rituals and rigid "rules" for games and other play activities) are characteristic of normal childhood development and serve to enhance the young child's sense of mastery and control. Clinically, OCD can be differentiated from these normal developmental phenomena by the presence of functional impairment and associated distress. OCD is classified as an anxiety disorder in *DSM-IV* due to significant phenomenological similarity with other disorders in this section. The primary distinction between OCD and other *DSM-IV* anxiety disorders is the presence of associated compulsions in the former disorder. Generalized anxiety disorder (GAD) is the anxiety disorder most phenomenologically similar to OCD; and, similar to OCD-related obsessions, the worries that accompany GAD are often experienced as recurrent and intrusive. However, in OCD, obsessions are more likely to involve content of a bizarre or seemingly magical nature, whereas the worries in GAD typically focus on everyday matters, such as school, work, friendships, and future events.

Youngsters with Tourette's disorder may manifest motor and vocal tics that appear virtually identical to compulsive behaviors, and differentiating complex motor tics from OCD compulsions can be extremely difficult. Although tics are characterized by the absence of a triggering obsessional thought, some youngsters report that their tics are preceded by a premonitory sensory urge (Miguel et al., 2000). OCD-related rituals are almost always described as volitional, even though the child may have only limited control over the expression of these behaviors. In contrast, although some individuals report experiencing their tics as volitional in certain instances, this is typically not the case (Miguel et al., 1995). When intrusive obsessive thoughts lead to inattentiveness, and ritualistic or avoidant behaviors cause the child to appear overactive or impulsive, OCD may be misdiagnosed as attention-deficit/hyperactivity disorder (ADHD). OCD can be distinguished from true motor hyperactivity by the more purposeful nature of associated behaviors and the presence of distressing cognitions or triggering sensations. Children with pervasive developmental disorders (PDD) such as autism and Asperger's syndrome often engage in perseverative and stereotypic behaviors (Klin &

Volkmar, 1999). These behaviors can usually be differentiated from compulsions by the fact that the former behaviors are often enjoyable to the child and are not performed in response to a distressing thought or sensation. As with OCD, however, youngsters with PDD may become upset or distressed when interrupted while engaging in ritualistic behaviors. OCD can also be differentiated from PDD by the absence of the particular social and language deficits characteristic of the latter disorder. In extreme cases, the bizarre or unusual content of obsessional beliefs may appear delusional in nature and thus resemble a psychotic disorder. In such situations, OCD may be distinguished from a psychotic disorder by the ability to engage in reality testing and by the absence of other psychotic symptoms (e.g., hallucinations, formal thought disorder). Several neurological disorders should be considered in the differential diagnosis of OCD, including temporal lobe epilepsy and complications secondary to central nervous system insults or tumors (Albano et al., 1999).

Assessment

A thorough diagnostic evaluation is necessary to accurately establish a diagnosis of OCD, to rule out phenomenologically similar conditions, and to identify comorbid conditions that could influence treatment planning. The assessment of baseline symptom severity and impairment helps to establish an accurate diagnostic profile and allows for the systematic and serial evaluation of treatment response, which can be used to identify difficult treatment areas and guide any changes to the treatment plan (Albano et al., 1999). Measures of baseline severity can also provide essential information to develop exposure and response prevention exercises for cognitive behavioral treatment. Data regarding the impact of OCD symptomatology on daily functioning are helpful for challenging patient denial and for enhancing motivation and compliance (Piacentini et al., 1992). Although several diagnostic interviews are available for use, each varying in regard to structure and practicality (Greenhill & Malcolm, 2000), a thorough review of this topic is beyond the scope of this chapter. The following measures are among the most commonly used in the assessment of childhood OCD. *The Anxiety Disorders Interview for DSM-IV: Parent and Child Versions,* designated ADIS-P and ADIS-C (Silverman & Albano, 1997) is a structured diagnostic interview for children that uses an interviewer-observer format to generate *DSM-IV* diagnoses. In addition to directly covering a broad range of anxiety and depressive symptomatology, the ADIS also addresses history, age of onset, impairment, and avoidance. Each diagnosis is assigned a Clinician Severity Rating (CSR) ranging from 0 to 8, with higher ratings indicating increasing levels of disability and distress. The CSR provides a quantitative measure of diagnostic severity, which is useful for treatment planning and monitoring treatment outcome. Earlier versions of the ADIS demonstrated good psychometric properties, and studies of the current version are presently under way (Silverman & Eisen, 1992).

The *Children's Yale-Brown Obsessive Compulsive Scale* (CYBOCS) is a clinician-administered measure adapted from the adult YBOCS (Goodman et al., 1989). It is considered the "gold standard" for rating OCD severity and treatment response in children. The measure demonstrates adequate psychometric performance (Scahill et al., 1997). The initial section of the CYBOCS consists of a comprehensive symptom checklist covering the full array of obsessions and compulsions, which are then collectively rated in terms of time consumption, interference, distress, resistance, and control. Separate scores, ranging from 0 to 20, are obtained for obsessions and compulsions, which when combined yield a total severity score ranging from 0 to 40. A CYBOCS score of 16 or higher indicates clinically significant OCD. The *Child OCD Impact Scale (COIS)* is a self-report questionnaire designed to assess the impact of OCD symptoms on the psychosocial functioning of children and adolescents with OCD (Piacentini, Jaffer, Bergman, McCracken, and Keller, 2001). Initially consisting of 53 items derived from parent and child interviews and clinical chart reviews, a final 21-item version was recently developed based on factor and item analyses. Three subscales assessing OCD-related impairment in the school, social, and family/home domains are summed to yield a total score. Although psychometric study continues, the parent-report version (COIS-P) demonstrates excellent internal consistency, a sound factor structure, and good construct validity (Piacentini et al., 2001). The COIS has also been shown to be a sensitive indicator of response to psychopharmacologic intervention (Geller et al., 2001).

Treatment

Psychodynamic and other insight-oriented or family therapies have not been shown effective for the reduction of OCD symptomatology in either adults or children (March, Leonard, & Swedo, 1995; Rapoport & Mikkelson, 1980). In contrast, current evidence supports the efficacy of exposure-based cognitive behavior therapy and pharmacotherapy with SSRIs for the treatment of this illness across the age span (Abramowitz, 1997; Albano et al., 1999).

Cognitive-Behavior Therapy

Cognitive-behavioral interventions for OCD are based on the behavioral conceptualization of obsessions as intrusive and unwanted thoughts, images or, behaviors that trigger a significant and rapid increase in anxiety or distress and compulsions as overt behaviors or cognitions (covert behaviors) designed to reduce these negative feelings (Albano et al., 1999). The most effective form of behavior therapy consists of systematic in vivo exposure to feared situations and objects paired with supervised response prevention of the relevant ritualistic behavior—that is, exposure plus response prevention, or ERP (Foa & Kozac, 1986; Meyer, 1966). In ERP, treatment progresses in gradual fashion according to a symptom hierarchy, with milder symptoms exposed first followed by more difficult exposures as treatment progresses. Although exposures are typically developed and initially practiced in session, most treatment gains accrue from repeated practice in the natural environment. The most commonly proposed mechanism for ERP effectiveness is that over repeated exposures, associated anxiety dissipates through the process of autonomic habituation. In addition, successful completion of exposure facilitates the development and storage of corrective cognitive information pertaining to the feared situation. Controlled trials using this treatment have yielded response rates of 75% to 90% for adult OCD with impressive maintenance of gains over follow-up periods lasting several months to several years (see Abramowitz, 1997, and Steketee, 1993, for reviews).

The development of appropriate exposures can be complicated by the difficulty many young children have in describing specific obsessions or recognizing the role that obsessions play in triggering rituals. Young children are also more present-oriented than adults and may be less willing to engage in difficult (i.e., anxiety-provoking) therapeutic exercises regardless of the potential for future symptom relief. Children with OCD may also be less likely than adults to describe their symptoms as excessive or unrealistic, which can similarly impair motivation for treatment. High levels of co-morbid behavioral disorders, poorer frustration tolerance and coping abilities, and increased rates of parental involvement in symptoms all serve to complicate treatment in certain instances. Recent CBT protocols for childhood OCD have included elements to address these developmental characteristics, including an increased emphasis on psychoeducation and the use of age-appropriate metaphors to facilitate cognitive restructuring, behavioral reward systems for treatment compliance, and greater family involvement in treatment (Albano et al., 1999; March, 1995; Piacentini, 1999).

Although the family context of OCD has not been well studied, available evidence characterizes the families of children with OCD as exhibiting increased levels of expressed emotion, parent-child conflict, and parental OCD (Hibbs, Hamburger, & Lenane, 1991; Riddle et al., 1990). As with other childhood disorders, family functioning is likely an important predictor of outcome (Hibbs, 1995; Kazdin, 1991; Kendall & Panichelli-Mindel, 1995; Kovacs & Lohr, 1995). Clinical experience and research findings highlight the importance of family involvement in the treatment of childhood OCD and suggest critical targets to be addressed, including reducing parental involvement in the child's OCD symptoms and enhancing family communication and problem-solving strategies (Albano et al., 1999; Knox, Albano, & Barlow, 1996; Piacentini, 1999). In the only study to date systematically examining parental involvement in treatment for children with OCD, Knox and colleagues (1996) studied four youngsters using a multiple baseline design and reported that training parents to be adjunct ERP therapists enhanced child response to treatment. Although intriguing, these results require replication in larger samples and under controlled conditions.

Prior to the mid-1990s, the behavioral treatment literature for childhood OCD consisted primarily of single case reports and small case series, most of which employed some form of exposure-based treatment (see Knox et al., 1996, and March, 1995, for reviews). Although characterized by numerous methodological weaknesses, these early studies were fairly consistent in their support of exposure-based treatment as a useful intervention for obsessive and compulsive symptomatology. More recently, a succession of methodologically more sophisticated studies incorporating the use of treatment manuals, standardized assessment batteries, and the aforementioned developmental considerations have been completed. These small case series and larger open trials (ranging from 3 to 42 subjects, mostly older children and adolescents with OCD, many on concurrent medication) have yielded impressive and durable results for CBT, with response rates ranging from 60% to 100%, mean symptom-reduction rates ranging from 50% to 67%, and gains maintained up to 18 months (Franklin et al., 1998; Knox et al., 1996; March, Mulle, & Herbel, 1994; Piacentini, Bergman, Jacobs, McCracken, &

Kretchman, in press; Piacentini, Gitow, Jaffer, Graae, & Whitaker, 1994; Scahill, Vitulano, Brenner, Lynch, & King, 1996). In one of the earliest of these studies, March and colleagues (1994) treated 15 youngsters, 14 of whom were on concurrent SSRI medication, and found that 12 (80%) evidenced a 30% or greater drop in CYBOCS score posttreatment, with no relapse over an 18-month follow-up period (although several children required booster sessions for "minor setbacks" over that time). Six patients were able to discontinue medication without relapse after being without symptoms for at least 6 months during the follow-up period. Piacentini and colleagues (in press) reported a 79% response rate for their manualized CBT protocol in 42 youngsters (mean age 11.8, range 5 to 17, with 52% on concurrent medication). Of interest, these authors found that youngsters with a poorer degree of symptom reduction over the treatment interval had significantly more severe obsessions, but not compulsions, and more impaired school functioning at baseline. In contrast, no relationship was found between treatment outcome and child age, gender, presence of comorbid tics, or baseline medication status.

Psychopharmacology

Several controlled multisite trials with children and adolescents have demonstrated the efficacy and tolerability of antiserotonergic agents for OCD in this age range. Large, multicenter trials of the tricyclic antidepressant and SRI, clomipramine (Anafranil; DeVeaugh-Geiss et al., 1992), and the SSRIs sertraline (Zoloft; March et al., 1998), fluvoxamine (Luvox; Riddle, et al., 2001), and fluoxetine (Prozac; Geller et al., 2001) have established the efficacy of these medications for childhood OCD, with the first three compounds currently approved by the FDA for use in children and adolescents with the disorder. Paroxetine (Paxil) has demonstrated similar benefit in a recent open trial (Rosenberg, Stewart, Fitzgerald, Tawile, & Carroll, 1999), and a multicenter trial for this compound is nearing completion. Citalopram (Celexa), the most recently introduced medication in this class, has yielded promising results in an open study of 23 youngsters (Thomsen, 1997). Similar to adult studies, response rates from the controlled medication trials average from 40% to 55%, although typical symptom reduction averages only 20% to 50%, and a significant proportion of responders remain mild to moderately ill after the completion of treatment (Grados et al., 1999). The most common adverse effects for the SSRIs include nausea, insomnia, hyperstimulation, agitation, headache, and sexual side effects. These effects are typically transient in nature, and most youngsters are able to tolerate these medications well. In contrast, the SRI clomipramine possesses a side effect profile typical of tricyclic antidepressants, including dry mouth, somnolence, dizziness, fatigue, tremor, and over the long term, the potential development of tachycardia and electrocardiogram abnormalities (Leonard et al., 1995). Given the preferable safety profile and generally similar efficacy of the newer SSRI medications, clomipramine is currently considered a second-line treatment option to be considered only after at least two failed SSRI trials (Albano et al., 1999; Grados et al., 1999).

Approximately one third of patients fail to respond to their initial SRI trial, and the likelihood of any positive response to this form of treatment drops considerably after three failed trials (DeVeaugh-Geiss et al., 1992). Given the variability in response latency across different individuals, medication trials should last at least 8 to 10 weeks before considering a switch to a different agent. Unfortunately, an evidence base for guiding medication combination and augmentation strategies in children with OCD does not yet exist. However, given the observed efficacy of CBT in medication-nonresponsive young-sters (March et al., 1994; Franklin et al., 1998; Piacentini et al., in press), combined medication plus high-quality CBT should be offered to patients prior to attempting complex medication strategies (Albano et al., 1999).

In the only direct comparison of CBT and medication to date (and the only controlled CBT trial in children), de Haan, Hoogduin, Buitelaar, and Keisjer (1998) randomly assigned 22 children to 12 weeks of either clomipramine (mean dose = 2.5 mg/kg) or ERP. Although both treatments led to improvement, ERP was significantly more effective than clomipramine in terms of both response rate (66.7% versus 50%) and reduction in symptom severity (59.9% versus 33.4%). These findings, along with results from medication discontinuation trials (e.g., Leonard et al., 1991) suggesting that symptom return is highly likely upon medication withdrawal, have led to the consensus treatment recommendation that CBT is the first-line treatment of choice for children with OCD (Leonard, Swedo, Allen, & Rapoport, 1994; March, Frances, Carpenter, & Kahn, 1997).

TIC DISORDERS

George Gilles de la Tourette, a 19th-century French neurologist training in Jean-Martin Charcot's clinic, published in 1885 a small case series of patients suffering from a disorder characterized by rapid involuntary motor movements, echolalia, hyperexcitability, echopraxia, and copralalia (Lajonchere, Nortz, & Finger, 1996). The clinical features and associated characteristics described by de la Tourette, including the probable hereditary nature of the condition, childhood onset, lack of associated cognitive disability, and his distinction between rapid tic movements and other abnormal movements, were remarkably accurate and form the basis of the syndrome that today bears his name. Throughout most of the past century, Tourette's disorder (TD) was deemed a rare and exotic condition, based on the fact that only the most severe patients presented for treatment or study. In the past few decades, however, with the surge of neurobiological and psychiatric research into the syndrome, TD has become recognized as a disorder that is less rare and more easily diagnosed, has milder variants, and is more amenable to a growing range of evidence-based treatment options.

Clinical Features

Tics are defined as sudden, repetitive, and stereotyped movements or vocalizations involving one or more muscle groups that are usually experienced as outside voluntary control and often may mimic the appearance of normal movement or behavior (Leckman et al., 1999). Tics are classified as simple or complex tics and as motor or vocal/phonic tics. Simple motor tics occur in isolated muscle group(s) or in one anatomical location and are characterized by fast, darting, meaningless muscle movements (e.g., eye blinking, nose twitching, shoulder shrugging). Complex motor tics, which involve the coordination of multiple muscle groups, are slower and longer in duration, appear more purposeful, and include movements such as touching objects or self, squatting, jumping and facial and hand gestures. Simple vocal tics are typically inarticulate single sounds, including sounds such as throat clearing, coughing, and sniffing/grunting. Complex vocal tics include intelligible syllables, words, or phrases, including echolalia (repetition of others' words), palilalia (repetition of own words), and coprolalia (swearing). Unlike simple tics, complex tics can often be mistaken for volitional behaviors and utterances (Coffey et al., 2000).

According to the *DSM-IV-TR* (APA, 2000), tic disorders can be classified into four distinct categories: transient tic disorder, chronic motor or vocal tic disorder, Tourette's disorder, and tic disorder not otherwise specified. Transient tic disorder is usually characterized by mild tics that are present for at least 4 weeks but not longer than 12 months. Chronic motor or vocal tics and TD are conditions in which frequent tics persist in duration for at least 12 months. Chronic motor tics are by far more common than pure vocal tic disorder. For the diagnosis of TD to be given, multiple motor and at least one vocal tic must be present at some time during the illness, although not necessarily concurrently. Although tic location, number, frequency, and complexity may fluctuate over time, the onset of the tics must be before age 18 to meet criteria for chronic motor and vocal tics and TD. The tic occurrence cannot be attributable to substance intoxication, to a general medical condition, or to a known central nervous system disease such as Huntington's chorea for these diagnoses to be given. TD is the most severe form of tic disorder, and can range from infrequent movements and sounds that are not easily discernable to explosive and disabling tic symptoms. Within an afflicted individual, tic frequency and severity can also wax and wane over time (Sallee & Spratt, 1999). Although symptom exacerbations may be associated with common psychosocial stressors (e.g., peer and family conflicts, school difficulties, significant change in normal routines) as well as other variables such as illnesses, fatigue, and excitement, a certain level of random symptom fluctuation can be expected (Coffey et al., 2000).

The clinical course of TD is commonly marked at onset by simple tics such as eye blinking, facial or head/neck tics at approximately 6 or 7 years of age, followed by a rostral-caudal progression of increasingly complex motor tics over several years. Typically, vocal tics appear at age 8 or 9 and complex tics and obsessive-compulsive symptoms (when they do co-occur) later, at age 11 or 12. Although vocal tics generally emerge years after the initial motor tics, exceptions do exist where a full complement of multiple motor and vocal tics will rapidly emerge over a brief period of a few weeks or more (McCracken, 2000). Children may present initially with signs of disruptive behavioral symptoms such as motoric hyperactivity and inattention in early childhood prior to the onset of tics in as many as 50% of cases (Bruun, 1988). Although tics typically follow a fluctuating course, a greater degree of stabilization is usually reached with increasing age, and it is not unusual for adolescent and young adult patients to report extended periods during which symptoms diminish or remit altogether. The modal age of onset of TD coincides with the onset of puberty. Studies following youngsters with chronic tic disorder longitudinally have found that, for most individuals, tic severity reaches maximum levels in early adolescence, followed by a consistent decrease in symptoms across adolescence. Longitudinal studies indicate that only about 25% of youngsters diagnosed with TD will continue to experience moderate to severe tics into young adulthood (Leckman, Zhang, & Vitale, 1998).

In describing the clinical phenomenology of TD, one seemingly contradictory aspect to the involuntary nature of tics is the ability of some patients to suppress tics for significant periods of time ranging from minutes to hours. This temporary suppressibility makes the assessment process more challenging. Some patients also report voluntarily performing their tics in response to premonitory sensory urges (Sallee & Spratt, 1999). In such instances, tic performance is usually associated with a feeling of tension release or pleasure. Sensory tics such as these are defined as focal, localized, or general uncomfortable sensations relieved by movement of the affected body region. Several studies have reported a high frequency of sensory phenomena immediately preceding tics (Bruun, 1988; Leckman et al., 1998; Miguel et al., 2000). It has been suggested that the relationship between these sensory phenomenon and tics in TD may be analogous to the relationship between obsessions and compulsions in OCD (Shapiro & Shapiro, 1992). Miguel and colleagues (1995) studied the intentional repetitive behaviors in OCD and TD. They found that sensory phenomena (generalized and localized uncontrollable sensations) preceded intentional repetitive behaviors in TD but not in OCD patients, and cognitive phenomena (ideas, thoughts, images) and physiologic symptoms of anxiety preceded such behaviors in OCD but not in TD. Developmental age influences descriptions and reports of tic behavior, with younger children less likely to describe sensory or volitional aspects associated with their tic experience.

Epidemiology

When considering the entire spectrum of tic disorders, epidemiologic studies indicate that between 5% and 15% of school-age children may develop transient tics during childhood (Zohar et al., 1992). Because the incidence of transient tics is fairly common, the challenge is to determine when transient tics are likely to lead to the more serious and debilitating syndrome of TD. The point prevalence estimates of TD in school-age children range from 3.1 to 4.9 per 10,000 in teens (male and female, 16- to 17-year-old Israeli inductees; Apter et al., 1993) and from 10.5 to 13 per 10,000 in children (grades kindergarten to 8, male and female; Caine, McBride, & Chiverton, 1988; Comings, Himes, & Comings, 1990). Although studies vary in sampling strategies and diagnostic procedures, the rate of 5 to 10 in 10,000 derived from population samples is at least two orders of magnitude higher than estimates from clinical samples (Zohar et al., 1999). This difference suggests that a sizable proportion of individuals who meet criteria for TD do not come to professional attention. Tic disorders are found much more commonly in males than in females (5:1) and more frequently in Caucasians than in African Americans or Hispanics (Zohar et al., 1999).

Comorbidity

Tics rarely exist in isolation in individuals with TD, but tend to be accompanied by other cognitive and behavioral difficulties. Chronic tic disorders in childhood have been related to a variety of problems, including aggressivity, impulsivity, mood and anxiety disorders, poor social skills, increased rates of family conflict, and obsessive-compulsive behaviors (Leckman et al., 1999). The predominant psychiatric comorbidities complicating TD are OCD and ADHD, with OCD comorbidity generally noted to be greater in TD than ADHD (Zohar et al., 1999). The comorbidity of TD and OCD is bidirectional, with approximately 23% of TD patients meeting criteria for OCD and up to 46% evidencing subclinical OCD symptoms. Conversely, 7% to 37% of OCD patients also meet criteria for TD (Miguel, Rosário-Campos, Shavitt, Hounie, Mercadante, 2001). There are data to support a distinction between individuals comorbid for OCD and TD versus those with only OCD or only TD (Miguel et al., 2001). Coffey et al. (1998) found that individuals with both OCD and TD have higher rates of affective, anxiety, and substance-use disorders compared to those with either diagnosis only. Patients with comorbid TD and OCD report more aggressive obsessions, whereas OCD alone is characterized by more contamination fears and cleaning compulsions (Sheppard, Bradshaw, Purcell, & Pantelis, 1999). As with OCD, many patients with TD report repetitive behaviors that are preceded by a sensory-perceptual awareness that something is not "just right" (Miguel et al., 1995, 2000, 2001). In cases where OCD and TD are comorbid, it can be difficult to distinguish whether a symptom such as repetitive touching or tapping should be considered a complex tic or a simple compulsion.

In clinical samples, 40% to 60% of children with TD meet criteria for ADHD, possibly suggesting shared neural circuitry deficits in response inhibition and impulse control (Sheppard et al., 1999). Even in mild cases of TD, the incidence of ADHD is 7 to 8 times that of the general population (Walkup et al., 1999). Similar to comorbid OCD and TD, clinical distinctions have been made between TD comorbid with ADHD and TD alone. Compared to children with TD only, children with TD plus ADHD and those with ADHD alone share a similar profile of comorbid conditions, including depression, anxiety, and disruptive behavior. This suggests that the presence of multiple comorbidities in TD is perhaps a function of the comorbid ADHD and not specific to TD itself (Spencer et al., 1998). Based on family genetic studies (Pauls, Leckman, & Cohen, 1993), it has also been proposed that two types of ADHD, based on onset relative to tics, may exist in persons with TD. Studies have attempted to distinguish between ADHD symptoms that appear before tic emergence and those that follow such an event. It has been proposed that TD and ADHD symptoms are genetically related when ADHD symptoms follow tic emergence but not when ADHD symptoms precedes tic onset (Pauls et al., 1993).

Other common comorbidities include depression, non-OCD anxiety disorders, and learning difficulties, primarily in the area of mathematical skills and reading comprehension (Dykens et al., 1990; King, Scahill, Findley, & Cohen, 1999). However, ascertainment of comorbid learning difficulties is often complicated by the distracting effects of the tics themselves on attention, other comorbid psychopathology, and potential demoralization of the child as a result of his or her tic disorder. Pitman, Green, Jenike, and Mesulam (1987) found lifetime prevalences of 44% for both generalized anxiety and unipolar depression in patients with TD, which was significantly higher than normal controls. One common explanation for the increased rates of comorbid affective disturbance and anxiety is the chronic debilitating burden of a disruptive and potentially socially stigmatizing tic disorder. Others have provided a biological explanation for this phenomenon—namely, that TD may be associated with increased stress-induced reactivity of the hypothalamic-pituitary-adrenal axis and increased central and peripheral noradrenergic sympathetic activity (Leckman, Walker, Goodman, Pauls, & Cohen, 1994; Lombroso, Scahill, Chappell, et al., 1995).

Etiology

The etiology and pathophysiology of TD and other tic disorders remains to be fully delineated, but converging evidence supports the idea that tic disorders are genetically transmitted and related to the disruption of the dopaminergic pathways involving the frontal cortex, basal ganglia, and the thalamus. Data supporting genetic transmission have accumulated through both family pedigree and twin studies. Twin studies of TD have yielded a 53% concordance rate for monozygotic twin pairs compared to 8% concordance for dyzygotic (DZ) twin pairs (Walkup et al., 1996). Pauls, Raymond, Leckman, and Stevenson (1991) found first-degree relatives of TD patients to have a higher prevalence of TD (10%), chronic motor tics (18%), and OCD (30%) than controls. Although the genetic basis for TD is not conclusive, segregation analyses from twin and family genetic studies indicate an autosomal dominant inheritance pattern with incomplete penetrance (Pauls, Alsobrook, Gelernter, & Leckman, 1999).

Nongenetic risk factors that have been considered include prenatal exposure to androgenic hormones, lower birth weight, and a history of A beta-hemolytic streptococcal infection (Cohen & Leckman, 1994; Hyde, Aaronson, Randolph, Rickler, & Weinberger, 1992; Kiessling, Marcotte, & Culpepper, 1993). The role of environmental and hormonal factors is currently viewed not as causative, but as modifying either phenotypic expression or severity. Cases in which new onset of tics and OCD symptoms follows a streptococcal illness provide some support for the involvement of immune responses in tic disorders. One early study of TS patients found high concentrations of a lymphocyte antigen, the D8/17 protein, which earlier research associated with risk for development of rheumatic fever in response to streptococcal exposure (Allen, Leonard, & Swedo, 1995). However, such studies await conclusive replication and demonstration of autoimmune abnormalities in patients with TD and related disorders.

Data from the neuroimaging, lesion, and neurochemical literature suggest that tic disorders such as TD may result from aberrant functioning of specific basal ganglia–thalamocortical (BGTC) pathways. Volumetric magnetic resonance imaging (MRI) studies have repeatedly implicated basal ganglia regions in the pathophysiology of TD, including reduced volumes and abnormal asymmetries of the caudate, putamen, lenticular, and globus pallidus nuclei (Sheppard et al., 1999). Functional imaging studies of TD have shown abnormal activity (primarily decreased, some increased) in primary and associated sensorimotor cortex as well as the lenticulate and paralimbic regions. Such studies suggest that the sensorimotor and limbic BGTC circuits have the greatest implications for TD (Eidelberg et al., 1997; Hall et al., 1990). A dopaminergic theory of TD is supported by multiple lines of research, including the apparent efficacy of dopaminergic antagonists in the treatment of tics, the exacerbating effects of functional dopamine agonists such as amphetamines, and postmortem findings of increased dopamine presynaptic carrier sites in the striatum of TD patients (Golden, 1990; Shapiro et al., 1989; Singer et al., 1992).

Differential Diagnosis

A careful clinical history and examination is necessary to differentiate tics from other abnormal-movement disorders. Tic disorders are generally characterized by a combination of simple and complex tics, and vocal tics are uncommon in other non-tic-movement disorders. In addition, premonitory sensations described by tic disorder patients are not frequently reported by those with other movement disorders like Huntington's chorea, nor is there a consequent feeling of tension relief when the tic is performed. The temporary suppressibility of most tics and the intentional performance in response to an irresistible urge are also unique aspects of tic disorders (Towbin, Peterson, Cohen, & Leckman, 1999). However, complex repetitive tics that are performed until a "just right" feeling is achieved or that are preceded at times by complicated mental phenomena are difficult to distinguish from the compulsions of OCD (Miguel et al., 1995). Complex tics may also be difficult to distinguish from the repetitive stereotypical movements associated with mental retardation, psychosis, akathisia, and restless leg syndrome. However, tic disorders are not frequently associated with mental retardation or a dementing process (Sallee & Spratt, 1999). Differential diagnosis should include movement disorders of childhood such as chorea, athetosis, dystonia, tremor, Huntington's disease, tardive dyskinesia, and focal seizures (McCracken, 2000).

Assessment

At present, no conclusive diagnostic tests for tic disorders exist. Rather, diagnosis is made based on clinical interview, neurologic examination, and assessment instruments such as parental self-report inventories. Brain imaging techniques, electroencephalography (EEG), and neuropsychological testing are not routinely used in evaluation, but may be indicated in specific cases to rule out complicating conditions. Although tic disorders are not associated with localized findings on neurological exams, minor motor asymmetries or unilateral impairment of rapid alternating movements have been found in about half of patients, along with nonspecific slowing on EEG in about 12% to 38% of patients (Bergen, Tanner, & Wilson, 1982; Schuerholz, Cutting, Mazzocco, Singer, & Denckla, 1997).

Because of their heterogeneous presentation and tendency to fluctuate over even brief periods of time, tics can be difficult to accurately quantify during a single clinical interview. The child's ability to temporarily suppress tics can also create a misleading presentation during an interview. A brief videotaped recording of the child without the presence of the examiner is often helpful to address this issue. Clinical assessment should document tics by their anatomic location, number, frequency, duration, and complexity. Self-report data from parent and child are also useful and often provide tic information sampled across multiple settings without the potential for observer bias. Two commonly used self-report measures include the Tourette's Syndrome Questionnaire (TSQ) and the Tourette's Syndrome Symptoms List (TSSL;

Cohen, Leckman, & Shaywitz, 1984). Clinician report ratings are often helpful to track tic symptoms across sessions and to assess progress in treatment. The most current and widely used scale is the Yale Global Tic Severity Scale (YGTSS; Leckman et al., 1989), which provides assessment of the number, frequency, intensity, complexity, and interference of motor and vocal tics. The YGTSS is relatively simple and fast to administer and is very useful as a clinical tool. A functional analysis should also be conducted to assess the fluctuating nature of the disorder and the factors associated with tic exacerbation or improvement. A medical and developmental history should review risk factors for tics such as preperinatal trauma, developmental delay, medication exposures, head injury, and genetic history. It is also important to assess past and current life stressors, level of family functioning, coping skills, and social support with respect to optimal treatment planning.

Treatment

Given their complex etiology and variable clinical manifestations, TD and other tic disorders have provided a significant treatment challenge to health care professionals. It is not surprising, therefore, that contemporary therapies for TD and other tic disorders rest on a long tradition of multiple treatment approaches including both psychosocial and psychopharmacological interventions.

Pharmacotherapy

Traditionally, pharmacotherapy has been the cornerstone of treatment for tic disorders. Although potentially effective, the most commonly used medications are associated with significant side effects and rarely eliminate tics entirely. Thus, the decision to use medication for tic control and the risks and benefits of available agents need to be carefully reviewed. High-potency D2 receptor antagonists such as haloperidol (Haldol) and pimozide (Orap) have demonstrated significant tic suppression in 70% to 80% of patients in daily dosages of 1 to 8 mg (Chappell, Leckman, & Riddle, 1995; Sallee, Nesbitt, Jackson, Sine, & Sethuraman, 1997). However, long-term risk for tardive dyskinesia, other extrapyramidal side effects, dysphoria, and cognitive dulling must be weighed against the potential efficacy for tics (Sallee et al., 1997). Significant side effects occur in up to 80% of individuals receiving neuroleptic medication, and as a result only 20% to 30% are able to stay on this treatment for as long as one year (Cohen, Friedhoff, Leckman, & Chase, 1992). Risperidone (Risperdal) and olanzapine (Zyprexa), newer atypical neuroleptics, have been found to reduce tics with less risk for the development of tardive dsykinesia, cognitive dulling, and dysphoria than the typical neuroleptics (Bruun & Budman, 1996). Lombroso, Scahill, King, and colleagues (1995) studied the effects of risperidone on youngsters with tic disorders and reported changes in tic severity from baseline to end of treatment ranging from 26% to 66%. Clonidine (Catapres) and guanfacine (Tenex), both alpha-adrenergic receptor agonists, are frequently preferred over neuroleptics because of their better tolerability and beneficial effect on reducing tics and the associated symptoms of disinhibition, impulsivity, and hyperarousal that are often seen in patients with TD. However, the effectiveness of these medications is limited, with typical improvements in tic severity ranging only from 30%

to 40% (Carpenter et al., 1999). One recent controlled trial of guanfacine for childhood tic disorders reported a 31% decrease in tic severity (Scahill et al., 2001). Common side effects for the alpha-adrenergic agonists include sedation, headaches, stomachaches, and some dysphoria (Leckman et al., 1991). Although there is some concern that stimulant use for children with comorbid ADHD and TD will exacerbate tic symptoms, the benefits of stimulants for ADHD symptoms often outweigh the potential risks for tic increase (Gadow, Sverd, & Nolan, 1992; Gadow, Nolan, Sprafkin, & Sverd, 1995). Unfortunately, there is no complete cure for tic disorders, and although neuroleptic agents are currently the most effective for symptom reduction, their problematic side effect profiles are cause for concern, which is the reason alternative behavior treatments for tic disorders are currently under active investigation.

Behavior Therapy

When behavioral interventions are employed for tic disorders, they are typically done either in conjunction with a psychopharmacological agent or following an unsuccessful, or partially successful, medication trial. Given that not all patients respond to drug therapy, and those who do often experience significant side effects, psychosocial treatments deserve careful consideration as a treatment option, either alone or in combination with medication.

Until recently, however, the collective body of behavioral treatment research for tics, which consists primarily of single-subject experimental designs and small case series, has been a generally confusing collection of results with no clear indication of differential treatment efficacy (Turpin, 1983; Piacentini & Chang, 2001). More recently, a somewhat clearer picture regarding the efficacy of behavioral treatments for tic disorders has begun to emerge, thanks in part to a handful of better-controlled studies (King, Scahill, et al., 1999). The most well studied behavioral interventions to date include massed (negative) practice, operant techniques/contingency management, anxiety management techniques (e.g., relaxation training), awareness training (i.e., self-monitoring), and the multicomponent package of habit-reversal training (Piacentini & Chang, 2001). Only habit reversal appears to have empirical support of efficacy for the treatment of tics. However, the database for this interpretation remains inadequate.

Massed (negative) practice has been until recently the most frequently used behavioral treatment for TD (Azrin & Peterson, 1988). This technique involves the repeated, rapid, voluntary, and effortful performance of an identified tic for a specific time period interspersed with brief periods of rest, with the goal of extinguishing the tic through a buildup of a state of "reactive inhibition." Unfortunately, a relatively extensive body of literature has failed to find any empirical support for the theorized mechanism behind massed practice (Turpin, 1983). Most studies reported no decrease in tic frequency over the study interval, and a substantial number of subjects experienced an actual increase in tics as a result of treatment (Azrin, Nunn, & Frantz, 1980; Peterson, Campise, & Azrin, 1994). Overall, the evidence suggests that massed practice is of limited therapeutic and theoretical importance.

Operant conditioning in the form of contingency management has been the second most frequently employed behavioral treatment approach for tics (Peterson et al.,

1994; Turpin, 1983). This technique is based on the theory that the consequences of a behavior influence the recurrence of that behavior. The treatment for tics, according to operant theory, consists of the manipulation of environmental contingencies so that tic-free intervals are positively reinforced and tic behaviors are punished. As tic behaviors become less reinforcing over time, they gradually diminish. Overall, studies using operant conditioning treatment protocols have not demonstrated the generalizability and durability of this approach for tics (Doleys & Kurtz, 1974; King, Scahill, et al., 1999; Miller, 1970; Turpin, 1983). Although positive reinforcement by itself is not expected to significantly and reliably reduce the frequency or intensity of tics, it can boost patient compliance with other specific treatment techniques for tic control (King, Scahill, et al., 1999).

As the name implies, anxiety management techniques include a variety of methods to control and reduce anxiety. The rationale for this form of intervention is based on the observation that increases in stress and anxiety lead to concomitant increases in tic frequency, intensity, and duration (Cohen et al., 1992). Relaxation-training approaches, including deep breathing, progressive muscle relaxation, and imagery, are the most frequently used anxiety management techniques for tic disorders (Peterson et al., 1994; Turpin, 1983). Studies using anxiety management techniques generally report modest but short-lived improvement in tic behavior with in-session gains failing to generalize outside of the training period (Peterson & Azrin, 1992; Turpin, 1983). In a recent randomized controlled trial, Bergin, Waranch, Brown, Carson, & Singer (1998) found no difference in tic severity between a group of youngsters with TD who received 6 weeks of relaxation training and a minimal-treatment control group. Although the data do not support the use of anxiety management techniques as a frontline treatment for tic disorders, these techniques may have some utility as part of multicomponent treatment interventions, especially for youngsters with increased levels of anxiety and stress.

Several behavioral techniques emphasize developing the youngster's awareness of his or her tic behavior to facilitate better self-control. Awareness training is typically accomplished through a variety of methods, including direct visual feedback using videotapes and mirrors, the use of wrist counters, small notebooks or other devices to record each tic occurrence, or the performance of a conscious response. Despite the fact that many participants in awareness-training protocols are not able to reliably discriminate tic occurrence in session (Wright & Miltenberger, 1987), there is some empirical support from multiple case studies and one analogue study suggesting short-term efficacy of awareness training as a primary treatment intervention (Billings, 1978; Ollendick, 1981; Peterson & Azrin, 1992). However, as with many other behavioral interventions for tic disorders, the generalizability and durability of treatment gains derived from awareness training, along with the potential mechanism of action underlying this approach, remain unclear.

The behavioral technique currently receiving the most attention for the treatment of tic disorders is habit-reversal training (HRT; Azrin and Nunn, 1973). As originally specified by these authors, HRT consisted of eight primary intervention components aimed at increasing tic awareness, developing competing responses to tics, and building and sustaining motivation and compliance. The most distinctive component of habit reversal is competing response (CR) practice. Competing response practice consists of teaching individuals to produce incompatible physical response contingent on the urge to perform a tic. The use of HRT for tic suppression has received some limited empirical support, and one review concluded that the full habit-reversal procedure can lead to reductions in tic frequency of up to 90% at home and up to 80% in clinic settings (Peterson et al., 1994). However, these findings should be interpreted cautiously due to characteristically small sample sizes, analogue settings, and the lack of controlled treatment-outcome designs with adequate follow-up (Azrin et al., 1980; Peterson et al., 1994). In contrast, more recent results from two small controlled trials examining the efficacy of HRT in adults (Wilhelm, Deckersbach, & Coffey, 2001) and children (Piacentini & Chang, 2001) suggest that this treatment may lead to significant yet modest results in both tic behavior and associated impairments. Although of interest, these findings should be considered preliminary; they require replication in larger samples and across multiple settings.

More recent HRT approaches have begun to place less emphasis on the use of physically forceful and antagonistic competing responses and greater emphasis on shaping strategies to reduce tic intensity and intrusiveness (Piacentini & Chang, 2001). In addition, cognitive strategies designed to enhance the early recognition of tic urges and accurate labeling of these urges to facilitate greater control over tic behaviors have also been introduced (e.g., Schwartz, 1998). Such modifications are aimed at enhancing the acceptability and utility of habit-reversal training for many youngsters and their families. In spite of advances in individual treatment modalities, successful outcomes for children and families coping with tic disorders almost certainly depends on a multimodal approach that considers factors such as psychoeducation, school consultation, family social support, and coping skills, in addition to medication or behavior therapy (Peterson & Cohen, 1998).

SUMMARY

This is an exciting and important time in treatment research for OCD and TD. A new generation of better-controlled studies, spurred on in part by advances in assessment technology, is yielding promising, and occasionally provocative, data regarding the kinds of treatment approaches that are (and aren't) effective for children suffering from these impairing and often comorbid disorders. Significant gains have been made in the identification and refinement of effective psychosocial and psychopharmacological interventions for both OCD and tic disorders in childhood. Given that multidisciplinary intervention is often necessary to address the heterogeneity of OCD and tic symptoms as well as their typically complex behavioral, emotional, and psychosocial sequelae, additional study is needed to develop evidence-based practice algorithms to guide the sequencing and combination of different individual intervention strategies. In addition, and of perhaps greater scientific interest, further cross-disciplinary efforts are also required to identify the psychiatric, neurobiological, and familial correlates of treatment outcome to elucidate the mechanisms by which these treatments operate. It will be through these collective efforts that subsequent generations of more carefully targeted and more effective and durable treatment approaches for OCD and TS are developed and refined.

REFERENCES

Abramowitz, J. (1997). Effectiveness of psychological and pharmacological treatments for obsessive-compulsive: A quantitative review. *Journal of Consulting and Clinical Psychology, 65,* 44–52.

Albano, A., March, J., & Piacentini, J. (1999). Cognitive behavioral treatment of obsessive-compulsive disorder. In R. Ammerman, M. Hersen, & C. Last (Eds.), *Handbook of prescriptive treatments for children and adolescents* (pp. 193–215). Boston: Allyn & Bacon.

Allen, A. J., Leonard, H., & Swedo, S. (1995). Case study: New infection-triggered, autoimmune subtype of pediatric OCD and Tourette's syndrome. *Journal of the American Academy of Child and Adolescent Psychiatry, 34,* 307–311.

American Psychiatric Association. (2000). *Diagnostic and statistical manual of mental disorders* (4th ed., text revision). Washington DC: Author.

Apter, A., Pauls, D. L., Bleich, A., Zohar, A. H., Kron, S., Ratzoni, G., Dycian, A., Kotler, M., Weizman, A., Gadot, N., & Cohen, D. (1993). An epidemiologic study of Gilles de la Tourette's syndrome in Israel. *Archives of General Psychiatry, 50,* 734–738.

Azrin N. H., & Nunn, R. G. (1973). Habit reversal: A method of eliminating nervous habits and tics. *Behavior Research & Therapy, 11,* 619–628.

Azrin, N. H., Nunn, R. G., & Frantz S. E. (1980). Habit reversal vs. negative practice treatment of nervous tics. *Behavior Therapy, 11,* 169–178.

Azrin N. H., & Peterson, A. L. (1988). Behavior therapy for Tourette's syndrome and tic disorders. In D. J. Cohen, J. F. Leckman, & R. D. Bruun (Eds.), *Tourette syndrome and tic disorders: Clinical understanding and treatment* (pp. 237–255). New York: Wiley.

Baxter, L., Phelps, M., Mazziotta, J., Guze, B. H., Schwartz, J. M., & Selin, S. E. (1988). Local cerebral glucose metabolic rates in obsessive-compulsive disorder: A comparison with rates in unipolar depression and in normal controls. *Archives of General Psychiatry, 44,* 211–218.

Baxter, L., Schwartz, J., & Bergman, K. (1992). Caudate glucose metabolic rate changes with both drug and behavior therapy for obsessive-compulsive disorder. *Archives of General Psychiatry, 49,* 681–689.

Bergen, D., Tanner, C. M., & Wilson, R. (1982). The electroencephalogram in Tourette syndrome. *Annals of Neurology, 11,* 638–641.

Bergin, A., Waranch, H. R., Brown, J., Carson, K., & Singer, H. S. (1998). Relaxation therapy in Tourette syndrome: A pilot study. *Pediatric Neurology, 18*(2), 136–141.

Billings, A. (1978). Self-monitoring in the treatment of tics: A single-subject analysis. *Journal of Behavior Therapy and Experimental Psychiatry, 9,* 339–342.

Bolton, D., Luckie, M., & Steinberg, D. (1995). Long-term course of obsessive-compulsive disorder treated in adolescence. *Journal of American Academy of Child and Adolescent Psychiatry, 34,* 1441–1450.

Bruun, R. D. (1988). The natural history of Tourette's syndrome. In D. J. Cohen, R. D. Bruun, & J. F. Leckman (Eds.), *Tourette's syndrome and tic disorders: Clinical understanding and treatment* (pp. 21–39). New York: Wiley.

Bruun, R. D., & Budman, C. L. (1996). Risperidone as a treatment for Tourette's syndrome. *Journal of Clinical Psychiatry, 57,* 29–31.

Caine, E. D., McBride, M. C., & Chiverton, P. (1988). Tourette's syndrome in Monroe County school children. *Neurology, 38,* 472–475.

Carpenter, L. L., Leckman, J. F., Scahill, L., & McDougle, C. J. (1999). Pharmacological and other somatic approaches to treatment. In J. F. Leckman & D. J. Cohen (Eds.), *Tourette's syndrome, tics, obsessions, compulsions: Developmental psychopathology and clinical care* (pp. 370–398). New York: Wiley.

Chappell, P., Leckman, J., & Riddle, M. (1995). The pharmacologic treatment of tic disorders. *Child and Adolescent Psychiatry Clinic of North America, 4,* 197–216.

Coffey, B., Biederman, J., Geller, D. A., Spencer, T., Park, K. S., Shapiro, S. J., & Garfield, S. B. (2000). The course of Tourette's disorder: A literature review. *Harvard Review of Psychiatry, 8,* 192–198.

Coffey, B., Miguel, E., Biederman, J., Baer, L., Rauch, S., O'Sullivan, R., Savage, C., Phillips, K., Borgman, A., Green-Leibovitz, M., Moore, E., Park, K., & Jenike, M. (1998). Tourette's Disorder with and without obsessive-compulsive disorder in adults: Are they different? *Journal of Mental Disorders, 186,* 201–206.

Cohen, D. J., Friedhoff, A. J., Leckman, J. F., & Chase, T. N. (1992). Tourette syndrome: Extending basic research to clinical care. In T. N. Chase, A. J. Friedhoff, & D. J. Cohen (Eds.), *Advances in neurology: Vol. 58. Tourette syndrome: Genetics, neurobiology and treatment* (pp. 341–362). New York: Raven Press.

Cohen, D. J., & Leckman, J. F. (1994). Developmental psychopathology and neurobiology of Tourette's syndrome. *Journal of the American Academy of Child and Adolescent Psychiatry, 33,* 2–15.

Cohen, D. J., Leckman, J. F., & Shaywitz, B. A. (1984). The Tourette syndrome and other tics. In D. Shaffer, A. A. Ehrhardt, & L. Greenhill (Eds.), *The clinical guide to child psychiatry* (pp. 3–28). New York: Free Press.

Comings, D. E., Himes, J. A., & Comings, B. G. (1990). An epidemiologic study of Tourette's syndrome in a single school district. *Journal of Clinical Psychiatry, 51,* 463–469.

de Haan, E., Hoogduin, K. A., Buitelaar, J., & Keijser, S. (1998). Behavior therapy versus clomipramine for the treatment of obsessive-compulsive disorder. *Journal of the American Academy of Child and Adolescent Psychiatry, 37,* 1022–1029.

DeVeaugh-Geiss, J., Moroz, G., Biederman, J., Cantwell, D., Fontaine, R., Greist, J. H., Reichler, R., Katz, R., & Landau, P. (1992). Clomipramine hydrochloride in childhood and adolescent obsessive-compulsive disorder—A multicenter trial. *Journal of American Academy of Child and Adolescent Psychiatry, 31,* 45–49.

Doleys, D. M., & Kurtz, P. S. (1974). A behavioral treatment program for the Gilles de la Tourette syndrome. *Psychological Reports, 35,* 43–48.

Dykens, E., Leckman, J. F., Riddle M. A., Hardin, M. T., Schwartz, S., & Cohen, D. (1990). Intellectual, academic, and adaptive functioning of Tourette syndrome children with and without attention deficit disorder. *Journal of Abnormal Child Psychology, 18,* 607–165.

Eidelberg, D., Moeller, J. R., Antonini, A., Kazumata, K., Dhawan, V., Budman, C., & Feigen, A. (1997). The metabolic anatomy of Tourette's syndrome. *Neurology, 48,* 927–934.

Fitzgerald, K., MacMaster, F., Paulson, L., & Rosenberg, D. (1999). Neurobiology of childhood obsessive-compulsive disorder. *Child and Adolescent Psychiatric Clinics of North America, 8,* 533–575.

Flament, M. F., Rapoport, J. L., Berg, C. Z., Sceery, W., Whitaker, A., Davies, M., Kalikow, K., & Shaffer, D. (1989). Obsessive-compulsive disorder in adolescence: An epidemiological study. In S. Chess & M. E. Hertzig (Eds.), *Annual progress in child psychiatry and child development* (pp. 499–515). Philadelphia: Brunner/Mazel, Inc.

Foa, E., & Kozac, M. (1986). Emotional processing of fear: Exposure to corrective information. *Psychological Bulletin, 99,* 450–472.

Franklin, M., Kozak, M., Cashman, L., Coles, M., Rheingold, A., & Foa, E. (1998). Cognitive-behavioral treatment of pediatric obsessive-compulsive disorder: An open clinical trial. *Journal of the American Academy of Child and Adolescent Psychiatry, 37,* 412–419.

Gadow, K. D., Sverd, J., & Nolan, E. E. (1992). Methylphenidate in hyperactive boys with comorbid tic disorder: II. Short-term behavioral effects in school settings. *Journal of the American Academy of Child and Adolescent Psychiatry, 31,* 462–471.

Gadow, K. D., Nolan, E., Sprafkin, J., & Sverd, J. (1995). School observations of children with attention-deficit hyperactivity disorder and comorbid tic disorder: Effects of methylphenidate treatment. *Developmental Behavioural Pediatrics, 16,* 167–176.

Geller, D. A., Hoog, S. L., Heiligenstein, J. H., Ricardi, R. K., Tamura, R., Kluszynski, S., Jacobson, J. G., and the Fluoxetine Pediatric OCD Study Team (2001). The fluoxetine pediatric OCD study team, US fluoxetine treatment for obsessive-compulsive disorder in children and adolescents: A placebo-controlled clinical trial. *Journal of the American Academy of Child and Adolescent Psychiatry, 40,* 773–779.

Gilbert, A. R., Moore, G. J., Keshavan, M. S., Paulson, L. A., Narula, V., MacMaster, F. P.,

Stewart, C. M., & Rosenberg, D. R. (2000). Decrease in thalamic volumes of pediatric patients with obsessive-compulsive disorder who are taking paroxetine. *Archives of General Psychiatry, 57,* 449–56.

Golden, G. S. (1990). Tourette syndrome: Recent advances. *Neurologic Clinics, 8,* 3.

Goodman, W. K., Price, L. H., Rasmussen, S. A., Mazure, C., Fleischman, R., Hill, C., Heninger, G., & Charney, D. (1989). The Yale-Brown Obsessive Compulsive Scale. *Archives of General Psychiatry, 46,* 1006–1011.

Grados, M., Scahill, L., & Riddle, M. (1999). Pharmacotherapy in children and adolescents with obsessive-compulsive disorder. *Child and Adolescent Psychiatric Clinics of North America, 8,* 617–634.

Greenhill, L., & Malcolm, J. (2000). Child and adolescent measures for diagnosis and screening. In American Psychiatric Association (Ed.), *Handbook of Psychiatric Measures* (pp. 277–324). Washington, DC: American Psychiatric Association.

Hall, M., Costa, D. C., Shields, J., Heavens, J., Robertson, M., & Ell, P. J. (1990). Brain perfusion patterns with Tc-99mHMPAO/SPECT in patient with Gilles de la Tourette's syndrome. *European Journal of Nuclear Medicine, 16,* 56.

Hanna, G. (1995). Demographic and clinical features of obsessive-compulsive disorder in children and adolescents. *Journal of the American Academy of Child and Adolescent Psychiatry, 34,* 19–27.

Hibbs, E. (1995). Child and adolescent disorders: Issues for psychosocial treatment research [Special issue]. Psychosocial treatment research. *Journal of Abnormal Child Psychology, 23,* 1–10.

Hibbs, E., Hamburger, S., & Lenane, M. (1991). Determinants of expressed emotion in families of disturbed and normal children. *Journal of Child Psychology and Psychiatry, 32,* 757–770.

Hyde, T. M. Aaronson, B. A., Randolph, C., Rickler, K. C., & Weinberger, D. R. (1992). Relationship of birth weight to the phenotypic expression of Gilles de la Tourette's syndrome in monozygotic twins. *Neurology, 42,* 652–658.

Kazdin, A. (1991). Effectiveness of psychotherapy with children and adolescents. *Journal of Consulting and Clinical Psychology, 59,* 785–798.

Kendall, P., & Panichelli-Mindel, S. (1995). Cognitive-behavioral treatments. *Journal of Abnormal Child Psychology, 23,* 107–124.

Kiessling, L. S., Marcotte, A. C., & Culpepper, L. (1993). Antineuronal antibodies in movement disorders. *Pediatrics, 92,* 39–43.

King, R. A., Leckman, J. F., Scahill, L., & Cohen, D. J. (1999). Obsessive-compulsive disorder, anxiety, and depression. In J. F. Leckman & D. J. Cohen (Eds.), *Tourette's syndrome, tics, obsessions, compulsions: Developmental psychopathology and clinical care* (pp. 43–62). New York: Wiley.

King, R. A., Scahill, L., Findley, D., & Cohen, D. J. (1999). Psychosocial and behavioral treatments. In J. F. Leckman & D. J. Cohen (Eds.), *Tourette's syndrome, tics, obsessions, compulsions: Developmental psychopathology and clinical care* (pp. 338–359). New York: Wiley.

Klin, A., & Volkmar, F. R. (1999). Autism and other pervasive developmental disorders. In S. Goldstein & C. Reynolds (Eds.), *Handbook of neurodevelopmental and genetic disorders in children* (pp. 247–274). New York: Guilford Press.

Knox, L., Albano, A., & Barlow, D. (1996). Parental involvement in the treatment of childhood OCD: A multiple-baseline examination involving parents. *Behavior Therapy, 27,* 93–114.

Kovacs, M., & Lohr, D. (1995). Research on psychotherapy with children and adolescents: An overview of evolving trends and current issues. *Journal of Abnormal Child Psychology, 23,* 11–30.

Lajonchere, C., Nortz, M., & Finger, S. (1996). Gilles de la Tourette and the discovery of Tourette syndrome. *Archives of Neurology, 53,* 567.

Leckman, J. F., Hardin, M. T., Riddle, M. A., Stevenson, J., Ort, S. I., & Cohen, D. J. (1991). Clonidine treatment of Gilles de la Tourette syndrome. *Archives of General Psychiatry, 48,* 324–328.

Leckman, J. F., King, R. A., & Cohen, D. J. (1999). Tics and tic disorders. In J. F. Leckman &

D. J. Cohen (Eds.), *Tourette's syndrome, tics, obsessions, compulsions: Developmental psychopathology and clinical care* (pp. 23–42). New York: Wiley.

Leckman, J., Riddle, M. A., Hardin, M. T., Ort, S., Swartz, K. L., Stevenson, J., & Cohen, D. J. (1989). The Yale Global Tic Severity Scale (YGTSS): Initial testing of a clinical-rated scale of tic severity. *Journal of the American Academy of Child and Adolescent Psychiatry, 28,* 566–573.

Leckman, J. F., Walker, D. E., Goodman, W. K., Pauls, D. L., & Cohen, D. J. (1994). "Just right" perceptions associated with compulsive behaviors in Tourette's syndrome. *American Journal of Psychiatry, 151,* 675–680.

Leckman, J., Zhang, H., & Vitale, A. (1998). Course of tic severity in Tourette's syndrome: The first two decades. *Pediatrics, 102,* 234–245.

Leonard, H., Meyer, M., Swedo, S., Richter, D., Hamburger, S. D., Allen, A. J., Rapoport, J. L., & Tucker, E. (1995). Electrocardiographic changes during desipramine and clomipramine treatment in children and adolescents. *Journal of the American Academy of Child and Adolescent Psychiatry, 34,* 1460–1468.

Leonard, H. L., Swedo, S. E., Allen, A. J., & Rapoport, J. L. (1994). Obsessive-compulsive disorder. In T. H. Ollendick & J. K. Neville (Eds.), *International handbook of phobic and anxiety disorders in children and adolescents* (pp. 207–221). New York: Plenum Press.

Leonard, H. L., Swedo, S. E., Lenane, M. C., Rettew, D. C., Cheslow, D. L., Hamburger, S. D., & Rapoport, J. L. (1991). A double-blind desipramine substitution during long-term clomipramine treatment in children and adolescents with obsessive-compulsive disorder. *Archives of General Psychiatry, 48,* 922–927.

Leonard, H., Swedo, S., Lenane, M., Rettew, D. C., Hamburger, S. D., Bartko, J. J., & Rapoport, J. L. (1993). A two- to seven-year follow-up study of 54 obsessive compulsive children and adolescents. *Archives of General Psychiatry, 50,* 429–439.

Lombroso, P. J., Scahill, L. D., Chappell, P. B., Pauls, D. L., Cohen, D. J., & Leckman, J. F. (1995). Tourette's syndrome. A multigenerational, neuropsychiatric disorder. In W. J. Weiner & A. E. Lang (Eds.), *Advances in neurology: Vol. 65. Behavioral neurology of movement disorders* (pp. 305–318). New York: Raven Press.

Lombroso, P. J., Scahill, L. D., King, R. A., Lunch, K. A., Chappell, P. B., Peterson, B. S., McDougle, C. J., & Leckman, J. F. (1995). Risperidone treatment for children and adolescents with chronic tic disorders: A preliminary report. *Journal of the American Academy of Child and Adolescent Psychiatry, 34,* 1147–1152.

Luxenberg, J. S., Swedo, S. E., Flament, M. F., Friedland, R. P., Rapoport, J., & Rapoport, S. I. (1988). Neuroanatomical abnormalities in obsessive-compulsive disorder detected with quantitative X-ray computed tomography. *American Journal of Psychiatry, 145,* 1089–1093.

March, J., Biederman, J., Wolkow, R., Safferman, A., Mardekian, J., Cook, E. H., Cutler, N., Dominguez, R., Ferguson, J., Muller, B., Riesenberg, R., Rosenthal, M., Sallee, F. R., & Wagner, K. (1998). Sertraline in children and adolescents with obsessive-compulsive disorder: A multicenter randomized controlled trial. *Journal of the American Medical Association, 280,* 1752–1756.

March, J., Frances, A., Carpenter, D., & Kahn, D. (1997). Expert consensus guidelines: Treatment of obsessive-compulsive disorder. *Journal of Clinical Psychology, 58,* 1.

March, J. S., Leonard, H. L., & Swedo, S. E. (1995). Obsessive-compulsive disorder. In J. S. March (Ed.), *Anxiety disorders in children and adolescents* (pp. 251–275). Guilford Press: New York.

March, J., Mulle, K., & Herbel, B. (1994). Behavioral psychotherapy for children and adolescents with OCD. *Journal of the American Academy of Child and Adolescent Psychiatry, 33,* 333–341.

March, J. (1995). Cognitive-behavioral psychotherapy for children and adolescents with OCD: A review and recommendations for treatment. *Journal of the American Academy of Child and Adolescent Psychiatry, 34,* 7–18.

McCracken, J. (2000). Tic Disorders. In H. Kaplan & B. Sadock (Eds.), *Comprehensive Textbook of Psychiatry* (7th ed., pp. 2711–2719). Philadelphia: Lippincott, Williams & Wilkins.

Meyer, V. (1966). Modification of expectations in cases with obsessive rituals. *Behavioral Research Therapy, 4,* 270–280.

Miguel, E. C., Coffey, B. J., Baer, L., Savage, C. R., Rauch, S. L., & Jenike, M. A. (1995). Phenomenology of intentional repetitive behaviors in obsessive-compulsive disorder and Tourette's syndrome. *Journal of Clinical Psychiatry, 56,* 246–255.

Miguel, E. C., Rosário-Campos, M. C., Prado, H. S., Valle, R., Rauch, S. L., Coffey, B. J., Baer, L., Savage, C. R., O'Sullivan, R. L., Jenike, M. A., & Leckman, J. F. (2000). Sensory phenomena in obsessive-compulsive disorder and Tourette's disorder, *Journal of Clinical Psychiatry, 61,* 150–156.

Miguel, E. C., Rosário-Campos, M. C., Shavitt, R., Hounie, A., & Mercadente, M. (2001). The tic-related obsessive-compulsive disorder phenotyoe and treatment implications. In D. J. Cohen, J. Jankovic, & C. Goetz (Eds.), *Advances in Neurology: Tourette syndrome* (Vol. 85, pp. 43–55). Philadelphia: Lippincott, William, & Wilkins.

Miller, A. L. (1970). Treatment of a child with Gilles de la Tourette's syndrome using behaviour modification techniques. *Journal of Behavior Therapy and Experimental Psychiatry, 1,* 319–321.

Nestadt, G., Lan, T., Samuels, J., Riddle, M., Bienvenu, O. J., 3rd, Liang, K. Y., Hoehn-Saric, R., Cullen, B., Grados, M., Beaty, T. H., & Shugart, Y. Y. (2000). Complex segregation analysis provides compelling evidence for a major gene underlying obsessive-compulsive disorder and for heterogeneity by sex. *American Journal of Human Genetics, 67,* 1611–1616.

Nestadt, G., Samuels, J., Riddle, M. A., Liang, K. Y., Bienvenu, O. J., Hoehn-Saric, R., Grados, M., & Cullen, B. (2001). The relationship between obsessive-compulsive disorder and anxiety and affective disorders: Results from the Johns Hopkins OCD Family Study. *Psychological Medicine, 31*(3), 481–487.

Ollendick, T. H. (1981). Self-monitoring and self-administered overcorrection: The modification of nervous tics in children. *Behavior Modification, 5,* 75–84.

Pauls, D., & Alsobrook, J. (1999). The inheritance of obsessive-compulsive disorder. *Child and Adolescent Psychiatric Clinics of North America, 8,* 481–496.

Pauls, D. L., Alsobrook II, J. P., Gelernter, J., & Leckman, J. F. (1999). Genetic Vulnerability. In J. F. Leckman, D. J. Cohen (Eds.), *Tourette's syndrome, tics, obsessions, compulsions: Developmental pathology and clinical care* (pp. 194–212). New York: Wiley.

Pauls, D., Alsobrook, J., Goodman, W., Rasmussen, S., & Leckman, J. F. (1995). A family study of obsessive-compulsive disorder. *American Journal of Psychiatry, 152,* 76–84.

Pauls, D. L., Leckman, J. F., & Cohen, D. J. (1993). Familial relationship between Gilles de la Tourette syndrome, attention deficit disorder, learning disabilities, speech disorders, and stuttering. *Journal of the American Academy of Child Psychiatry, 32,* 1044–1050.

Pauls, D. L., Raymond, C. L., Leckman, J. F., & Stevenson, J. M. (1991). A family study of Tourette's syndrome. *American Journal of Human Genetics, 48,* 154–163.

Perlmutter, S., Leitman, S., Garvey, M., Hamburger, S., Feldman, E., Leonard, H. L., & Swedo, S. (1999). Therapeutic plasma exchange and intravenous immunoglobulin for obsessive-compulsive disorder and tic disorders in childhood. *Lancet, 354,* 1153.

Peterson A. L., & Azrin N. H. (1992). An evaluation of behavioral treatments for Tourette syndrome. *Behavior Research & Therapy, 30,* 167–174.

Peterson, A. L., Campise, R. L., & Azrin, N. H. (1994). Behavioral and pharmacological treatments for tic and habit disorders: A review. *Journal of Developmental & Behavioral Pediatrics, 15,* 430–441.

Peterson, B. S., & Cohen, D. J. (1998). The treatment of Tourette's syndrome: Multimodal, developmental intervention. *Journal of Clinical Psychiatry, 59,* 62–72.

Petter, T., Richter, M. A., & Sandor, P. (1998). Clinical features distinguishing patients with Tourette's syndrome and obsessive-compulsive disorder from patients with obsessive-compulsive disorder without tics *Journal of Clinical Psychiatry, 59,* 456–459.

Piacentini, J. (1999). Cognitive behavioral therapy of childhood OCD. *Child and Adolescent Psychiatric Clinics of North America, 8,* 599–616.

Piacentini, J., & Bergman, R. L. (2000). Obsessive-compulsive disorder in children. *Psychiatric Clinics of North America, 23,* 519–533.

Piacentini, J., Bergman, R. L., Jacobs, C., McCracken, J., & Kretchman, J. (in press). Open trial of cognitive behavior therapy for childhood obsessive-compulsive disorder. *Journal of Anxiety Disorders.*

Piacentini, J., Bergman, L., McCracken, J., Rosenberg, D., Busner, J., Jaffer, M., & Kretchman, J. (1999). Functional impairment in childhood OCD. *Program and Abstracts of the Anxiety Disorders Association of America Annual Meeting, 22,* 69.

Piacentini, J., & Chang, S. (2001). Behavioral treatments for Tourette syndrome: State of the Art. In D. J. Cohen, J. Jankovic, & C. Goetz (Eds.), *Advances in neurology: Tourette syndrome* (Vol. 85, pp. 319–331). Philadelphia: Lippincott, Williams & Wilkins.

Piacentini, J., Gitow, A., Jaffer, M., Graae, F., & Whitaker, A. (1994). Outpatient behavioral treatment of child and adolescent OCD. *Journal of Anxiety Disorders, 8,* 277–289.

Piacentini, J., & Graae, F. (1997). Childhood obsessive-compulsive disorder. In E. Hollander & D. J. Stein (Eds.), *Obsessive-compulsive disorders: Etiology, diagnosis, and treatment* (p. 46). New York: Marcel Dekker.

Piacentini, J., Jaffer, M., Bergman, R. L., McCracken, J., & Keller, M. (2001). Measuring impairment in childhood OCD: Psychometric properties of the COIS [Abstract]. *Scientific Proceedings of the American Academy of Child and Adolescent Psychiatry, 48,* 146.

Piacentini, J., Jaffer, M., Gitow, A., Graae, F., Davis, S. O., Del Bene, D., & Liebowitz, M. (1992). Psychopharmacologic treatment of child and adolescent obsessive compulsive disorder. *Psychiatric Clinics of North America, 15,* 87–107.

Pitman, R. K., Green, R. C., Jenike, M. A., & Mesulam, M. M. (1987). Clinical comparison of Tourette's disorder and obsessive-compulsive disorder. *American Journal of Psychiatry, 144,* 1166–1171.

Rapoport, J., Inoff-Germain, G., Weissman, M. M., Greenwald, S., Narrow, W. E., Jensen, P. S., Lahey, B. B., & Canino, G. (2000). Childhood obsessive-compulsive disorder in the NIMH MECA Study: Parent versus child identification of cases. *Journal of Anxiety Disorders, 14,* 535–548.

Rapoport, J., & Mikkelson, E. (1980). Clinical controlled trial of chlormipramine in adolescents with obsessive compulsive disorder. *Psychopharmacology Bulletin, 16,* 61–63.

Rapoport, J., Swedo, S., & Leonard, H. (1993). Obsessive compulsive disorder. *Child and Adolescent Psychiatry, 3,* 441.

Rettew, D., Swedo, S., Leonard, H., Lenane, M. C., & Rapoport, J. L. (1992). Obsessions and compulsions across time in 79 children and adolescents with obsessive-compulsive disorder. *Journal of the American Academy of Child Adolescent Psychiatry, 31,* 1050–1056.

Riddle, M. A., Reeve, E. A., Yaryura-Tobias, J. A., Yang, H. M., Claghorn, J. L., Gaffney, G., Greist, J. H., Holland, D., McConville, B. J., Pigott, T., & Walkup, J. T. (2001). Fluvoxamine for children and adolescents with obsessive-compulsive disorder: A randomized, controlled, multicenter trial. *Journal of the American Academy of Child & Adolescent Psychiatry, 40,* 222–229.

Riddle, M., Scahill, L., King, R., Hardin, M., Towbin, K. E., Ort, S. I., Leckman, J. F., & Cohen, D. J. (1990). Obsessive compulsive disorder in children and adolescents: Phenomenology and family history. *Journal of the American Academy of Child Adolescent Psychiatry, 29,* 766–772.

Rosenberg, D. R., & Hanna, G. L. (2000). Genetic and imaging strategies in obsessive-compulsive disorder: Potential implications for treatment development. *Biological Psychiatry, 48,* 1210–1222.

Rosenberg, D. R., & Keshavan, M. S. (1998). A. E. Bennett Research Award. Toward neurodevelopmental model of obsessive-compulsive disorder. *Biological Psychiatry, 43,* 623–640.

Rosenberg, D. R., Keshavan, M. S., O'Hearn, K. M., Dick, E. L., Bagwell, W. W., Seymour,

A. B., Montrose, D. M., Pierri, J. N., & Birmaher, B. (1997). Frontostriatal measurement in treatment-naive children with obsessive-compulsive disorder. *Archives of General Psychiatry, 54,* 824–830.

Rosenberg, D. R., MacMaster, F. P., Keshavan, M. S., Fitzgerald, K. D., Stewart, C. M., & Moore, G. J. (2000). Decrease in caudate glutamatergic concentrations in pediatric obsessive-compulsive disorder patients taking paroxetine. *Journal of the American Academy of Child and Adolescent Psychiatry, 39,* 1096–1103.

Rosenberg, D., Stewart, C., Fitzgerald, K., Tawile, V., & Carroll, E. (1999). Paroxetine open-label treatment of pediatric outpatients with obsessive-compulsive disorder. *Journal of the American Academy of Child and Adolescent Psychiatry, 38,* 1180.

Salkovkis, P. (1999). Understanding and treating obsessive-compulsive disorder. *Behavior Research and Therapy, 37,* S29–S52.

Sallee, F. R., Nesbitt, L., Jackson, C., Sine, L., Sethuraman, G. (1997). Relative efficacy of haloperidol and pimozide in children and adolescents with Tourette's disorder. *American Journal of Psychiatry, 154,* 1057–1062.

Sallee, F. R., & Spratt, E. G. (1999). Tic disorders. In R. T. Ammerman, M. Hersen, & C. G. Last (Eds.), *Prescriptive treatments for children and adolescents* (2nd ed., pp. 261–276). New York: Wiley.

Saxena, S., Brody, A. L., Schwartz, J. M., & Baxter, L. R. (1998). Neuroimaging and frontal-subcortical circuitry in obsessive-compulsive disorder. *British Journal of Psychiatry* Supplement, *35,* 26–37.

Scahill, L., Chappell, P. B., Kim, Y. S., Schultz, R. T., Katsovich, L., Shepherd, E., Arnsten, A. F., Cohen, D. J., & Leckman, J. F. (2001). A placebo-controlled study of guanfacine in the treatment of children with tic disorders and attention deficit hyperactivity disorder. *American Journal of Psychiatry, 158,* 1067–1074.

Scahill, L., Riddle, M., McSwiggin-Hardin, M., Ort, S., King, R. A., Goodman, W. K., Cicchetti, D., & Leckman, J. F. (1997). Children's Yale-Brown Obsessive Compulsive Scale: Reliability and validity. *Journal of the American Academy of Child and Adolescent Psychiatry, 36,* 844–853.

Scahill, L., Vitulano, L. A., Brenner, E. M., Lynch, K. A., & King, R. A. (1996). Behavioral therapy in children and adolescents with obsessive-compulsive disorder: A pilot study. *Journal of Child and Adolescent Psychopharmacology, 6,* 191–202.

Schuerholz, L. J., Cutting, L., Mazzocco, M. M., Singer, H. S., & Denckla, M. B. (1997). Neuromotor functioning in children with Tourette syndrome with and without attention deficit hyperactivity disorder. *Journal of Child Neurology, 12,* 438.

Schwartz J. M. (1998). Neuroanatomical aspects of cognitive-behavioral therapy response in obsessive-compulsive disorder: An evolving perspective on brain and behavior. *British Journal of Psychiatry, 173,* 38–44.

Schwartz, J., Stoessel, P., Baxter, L., Martin, K., & Phelps, M. (1996). Systematic cerebral glucose metabolic rate changes after successful behavior modification treatment of obsessive compulsive disorder. *Archives of General Psychiatry, 53,* 109–113.

Shaffer, D., Fisher, P., Dulcan, M., Davies, M., Piacentini, J., Schwab-Stone, M., Lahey, B., Bourdon, K., Jensen, P., Bird, H., Canino, G., & Regier, D. (1996). The NIMH Diagnostic Interview Schedule for Children (DISC-2): Description, acceptability, prevalences, and performance in the MECA Study. *Journal of the American Academy of Child and Adolescent Psychiatry, 35,* 865–877.

Shapiro, A. K., & Shapiro, E. (1992). Evaluation of the reported association of obsessive-compulsive symptoms or disorder with Tourette's disorder. *Comprehensive Psychiatry, 33*(3), 152–165.

Shapiro, E., Shapiro A. K., Fulop, G., Hubbard, M., Mandeli, J., Nordlie, J., & Phillips, R. A. (1989). Controlled study of haloperidol, pimozide, and placebo for the treatment of Gilles de la Tourette's syndrome. *Archives of General Psychiatry, 46,* 722–730.

Sheppard, D. M., Bradshaw, J. L., Purcell, R., & Pantelis, C. (1999). Tourette's and comorbid syndromes: Obsessive compulsive and attention deficit hyperactivity disorder. A common etiology? *Clinical Psychology Review, 19,* 531–552.

Silverman, W., & Albano, A. (1997). *Anxiety disorders interview schedule for DSM-IV: Parent & child version (ADIS-P & C).* Albany, NY: Graywind Publications.

Silverman, W., & Eisen, A. (1992). Age differences in the reliability of parent and child reports of child anxious symptomatology using a structured interview. *Journal of the American Academy of Child and Adolescent Psychiatry, 31,* 117–124.

Singer, H. S., Wong, D. F., Brown, J. E., Brandt, J., Klafft, L., Shaya, E., Dannals, R. F., & Wagner, H., Jr. (1992). Positron emission tomography evaluation of dopamine D-2 receptors in adults with Tourette syndrome. In T. N. Chase, A. J. Friedhoff, & D. J. Cohen (Eds.), *Advances in neurology: Tourette syndrome: Genetics, neurobiology and treatment* (pp. 233–239). New York: Raven Press.

Spencer, T., Biederman, J., Harding, M., O'Donnell, D., Wilens, T., Faraone, S., Coffey, B., Geller, D. (1998). Disentangling the overlap between Tourette's disorder and ADHD. *Journal of Child Psychology and Psychiatry and Allied Disciplines, 39,* 1037–1044.

Steketee, G. (1993). *Treatment of obsessive compulsive disorder.* New York: Guilford Press.

Swedo, S., Leonard, H., Garvey, M., Mittleman, B., Allen, A., Perlmutter, S., Dow, S., Zankoff, J., Dubbert, B., & Lougee, L. (1998). Pediatric autoimmune neuropsychiatric disorders associated with streptococcal infections: Clinical description of the first 50 cases. *American Journal of Psychiatry, 155,* 264–271.

Swedo, S. E., Leonard, H. L., & Kiessling, L. S. (1994). Speculations on antineuronal antibody-mediated neuropsychiatric disorders of childhood. *Pediatrics, 93,* 323–326.

Swedo, S., Rapoport, J., Leonard, H., Lenane, M., & Cheslow, D. (1989). Obsessive-compulsive disorder in children and adolescents: Clinical phenomenology of 70 consecutive cases. *Archives of General Psychiatry, 46,* 335–341.

Swedo, S., Schapiro, M., Grady, C. L., Cheslow, D. L., Leonard, H. L., Kumar, A., Friedland, R., Rapoport, S. I., & Rapoport, J. L. (1989). Cerebral glucose metabolism in childhood-onset obsessive-compulsive disorder. *Archives of General Psychiatry, 46,* 518–523.

Thomsen, P. (1997). Child and adolescent obsessive-compulsive disorder treated with citalopram: Findings from an open trial of 23 cases. *Journal of Child and Adolescent Psychopharmacology, 7,* 157–166.

Towbin, K. E., Peterson, B. S., Cohen, D. J., & Leckman, J. F. (1999). Differential diagnosis. In J. F. Leckman, D. J. Cohen (Eds.), *Tourette's syndrome, tics, obsessions, compulsions: Developmental pathology and clinical care* (pp. 118–139). New York: Wiley.

Turpin, G. (1983). The behavioural management of tic disorders: A critical review. *Advances in Behavioral Research & Therapy, 5,* 203–245.

Valleni-Basile, L., Garrison, C., Jackson, K., Waller, J., McKeown, R., Addy, C., & Cuffe, S. (1994). Frequency of obsessive-compulsive disorder in a community sample of young adolescents. *Journal of the American Academy of Child and Adolescent Psychiatry, 33,* 782–791.

Walkup, J. T., Khan, S., Schuerholz, L., Paik, Y., Leckman, J. F., & Schultz, R. (1999). Phenomenology and natural history of tic-related ADHD and learning disabilities. In J. F. Leckman & D. J. Cohen (Eds.), *Tourette's syndrome, tics, obsessions, compulsions: Developmental pathology and clinical care* (pp. 63–79). New York: Wiley.

Walkup, J. T., LaBuda, M. C., Singer, H. S., Brown, J., Riddle, M. A., & Hurdo, O. (1996). Family study and segregation analysis of Tourette syndrome: Evidence for a mixed model of inheritance. *American Journal of Human Genetics, 59,* 684–693.

Wilhelm, S., Deckersbach, T., & Coffey, B. (2001). Habit reversal for Tourette's disorder. Presentation at World Congress of Behavioral and Cognitive Therapies, Vancouver, Canada.

Wright, K. M., & Miltenberger, R. G. (1987). Awareness training in the treatment of head and facial tics. *Journal of Behavior Therapy and Experimental Psychiatry, 18,* 269–274.

Zohar, A. (1999). The epidemiology of obsessive compulsive disorder in children and adolescents. *Psychiatric Clinics of North America, 8,* 445–460.

Zohar, A. H., Apter, A., King, R. A., Pauls, D. L., Jeckman, J. F., & Cohen, D. J. (1999). Epidemiological Studies. In J. F. Leckman & D. J. Cohen (Eds.), *Tourette's syndrome, tics, obsessions, compulsions: Developmental pathology and clinical care* (pp. 177–193). New York: Wiley.

Zohar, A. H., Ratzoni, G., Pauls, D. L., Apter, A., Bleich, A., Kron, S., Rappaport, M., Weizman, A., & Cohen D. J. (1992). An epidemiological study of obsessive-compulsive disorder and related disorders in Israeli adolescents. *Journal of the American Academy of Child & Adolescent Psychiatry, 31,* 1057–1061.

Chapter 12

ANXIETY DISORDERS

OLIVIA N. VELTING, NICOLE J. SETZER, AND ANNE MARIE ALBANO

Prior to the introduction of a separate section of childhood anxiety disorders in the *Diagnostic and Statistical Manual of Mental Disorders, Third Edition* (*DSM-III;* American Psychiatric Association [APA], 1980), little attention was paid by clinical researchers to understanding anxiety and its sequelae in youth. *DSM-III* introduced the clinical research community to three anxiety disorders unique to children and adolescents: separation anxiety disorder, avoidant disorder of childhood and adolescence, and overanxious disorder. Each disorder was proposed to have its onset in childhood and to be expressed through symptoms unique to childhood or adolescence. Consequently, since the publication of *DSM-III* and the *DSM*'s fourth edition, in 1994 (*DSM-IV;* APA, 1994), epidemiological and clinic-based studies have confirmed that anxiety disorders are among the most common conditions affecting children and adolescents (Costello & Angold, 1995). Of note, only separation anxiety disorder survived in *DSM-IV,* as the other childhood anxiety disorders were subsumed into the adult categories with developmentally sensitive symptom criteria. To date, four large epidemiological studies have estimated the prevalence of impairing anxiety disorders to be 12% to 20% among youth in the United States (Achenbach, Howell, McConaughy, & Stanger, 1995; Gurley, Cohen, Pine, & Brook, 1996; Shaffer et al. 1996). These estimates are staggering, given the paucity of controlled research addressing manifestations of anxiety in youth as clinical disorders prior to 1980. The failure of the clinical research community to move more quickly to address anxiety disorders in children is even more sobering given that, in addition to their high prevalence, anxiety disorders in youth are also associated with significant impairment in functioning across a variety of domains, including school performance and family, social, and peer functioning (Ialongo, Edelsohn, Werthamer-Larsson, Crockett, & Kellam, 1994, 1995). Such distress and impairment may result from a single anxiety disorder of sufficient intensity, but more often these disorders co-occur with each other and with conditions such as depression, school refusal, and externalizing disorders. In fact, children with anxiety disorders are as impaired as children with disruptive behavior disorders on many measures including teachers' global perceptions of competence (Benjamin, Costello, & Warren, 1990). Moreover, childhood anxiety has been implicated as a direct pathway to substance abuse in adolescence (Kessler et al., 1994), is associated with impairment extending into adulthood, and is predictive of adult anxiety disorders, major depression, suicide attempts, and psychiatric hospitalization (Achenbach et al. 1995; Ferdinand & Verhulst 1995; Klein 1995; Pine, Cohen, Gurley, Brook, & Ma, 1998). More than half of adults with anxiety or mood disorders had a history of childhood anxiety disorders. In addition, recently completed prospective studies confirm that anxiety disorders have an early onset in childhood and run a chronic and fluctuating course into adulthood (Costello & Angold 1995; Ferdinand & Verhulst 1995; Pine et al. 1998). In summary, until recently the study and treatment of childhood anxiety disorders had been virtually ignored, and affected youth in the community were unlikely to receive adequate assessment and treatment (Beidel, et al., 1999).

This chapter describes anxiety disorders according to the current psychiatric classification system, focusing on separation anxiety disorder, social phobia, generalized anxiety disorder, panic disorder and phobic disorders. Although it is an anxiety disorder, this chapter does not cover posttraumatic stress disorder (PTSD) because of its relatively low base rate in anxiety specialty clinic settings. PTSD is often found in children and adolescents who have histories of sexual and physical abuse; have been victims of child neglect; have been victims of or witnesses to violence (including domestic violence, assault, robbery); or have been survivors of torture, war, accidents (e.g., motor vehicle collisions), or natural or human-made disasters. Because the diagnosis of PTSD requires an extraordinary precipitating event (a known or identifiable etiology), clinical investigators view this specific anxiety disorder as being distinct from those covered in this review. In addition, this chapter does not cover obsessive-compulsive disorder (OCD), which is covered in chapter 11 of this handbook. Thus, following a brief description of the disorders, this chapter presents an overview of the cognitive behavioral model of anxiety, which leads into the discussion of the current status of empirically supported assessment methods and treatments for anxiety disorders in youth.

DESCRIPTIONS OF ANXIETY DISORDERS DIAGNOSED IN YOUTH

Separation Anxiety Disorder

Originally introduced in *DSM-III* (APA, 1980), separation anxiety disorder (SAD) is the sole anxiety disorder of childhood retained in *DSM-IV* (APA, 1994). The defining feature of SAD, as outlined in *DSM-IV,* is excessive anxiety regarding separation from the home or from primary caretakers to whom the child is attached. To meet diagnostic criteria for SAD, a child's anxiety must exceed that which is expected for the child's age and developmental level, and onset must occur before age 18. Moreover, because mild and transient separation anxiety is expected at various stages of childhood, the symptoms of this disorder must be present and fairly stable for at least 4 weeks and result in clinically significant distress or impairment in social, academic, or other important areas of functioning.

Typically, when children with SAD are or anticipate being separated from home, they manifest preoccupation with fears that accidents, illness, or death will befall their attachment figures or themselves, and they will frequently express fear of being lost and being unable to be reunited with their parents. Children with SAD often are hesitant or refuse to attend school, go to camp, or visit or sleep at friends' homes, and they may be unable to stay in a room by themselves. Most children with this disorder regularly have difficulty at bedtime; that is, they may insist that someone stay with them until they fall asleep or insist on sleeping in an attachment figure's bed during the night. The child may complain of physical symptoms (e.g., stomachaches, headaches, nausea, and vomiting) when separation occurs or is anticipated, in addition to displays of anger or occasional physical aggression. Children diagnosed with SAD frequently are described as demanding, intrusive, and requiring constant attention; parental frustration and family conflict are a characteristic result. Comorbid diagnoses of major depressive disorder and dysthymic disorder are common, and SAD may precede the development of panic disorder with agoraphobia (Gittelman & Klein, 1984). The prevalence estimates of SAD in children and young adolescents average approximately 4%. In clinical samples the disorder is apparently equally common in males and females, but in epidemiological studies SAD is more prevalent in females (APA, 1994).

Social Phobia (Social Anxiety Disorder)

DSM-IV defines the essential feature of social phobia (SoP) as "a marked and persistent fear of social or performance situations in which embarrassment may occur" (APA, 1994, p. 411). In addition, a diagnosis of social phobia requires that, when exposed to the feared social situation, an individual must invariably experience anxiety, possibly in the form of a situationally bound or situationally predisposed panic attack. Children and adolescents with social phobia experience intense distress while in (or else avoid) their feared social situations, which significantly interferes with normal routines, social activities, or academic functioning.

In children, several additional considerations are necessary when diagnosing social phobia. First, a child with social phobia must show the capacity for age-appropriate social relationships with familiar people, and his or her anxiety must occur in peer contexts, not just with adults. Second, the anxiety brought on by social situations may be evidenced in children by crying, tantrums, freezing, or shrinking from social situations with unfamiliar people. This reaction of shrinking away from unfamiliar persons encompasses the essential component of the former *DSM-III* diagnosis of avoidant disorder of childhood. Third, in contrast to adults with the disorder, due to limitations of cognitive and perceptual skills in young children, youth with social phobia need not recognize that their fear in social situations is excessive or unreasonable. Fourth, in order to account for normal, expected rises in social anxiety that occur as part of various developmental stages, in youth under the age of 18 years there must be evidence that the social fears have existed for a minimum of 6 months.

Because avoidant disorder of childhood was frequently diagnosed instead of social phobia under *DSM-III* and *DSM-III-R* (APA, 1984), data regarding the prevalence of social phobia in children and adolescents (according to *DSM-IV* criteria) is just starting to be reported. For example, Essau, Conradt, and Petermann (2000a) found a *DSM-IV* lifetime rate of social phobia of 1.6% in their community sample of 12- to 17-year-olds, while Wittchen, Stein, and Kessler (1999) found lifetime prevalence rates of 9.5% and 4.9% in a community sample of 14- to 24-year-old females and males, respectively. Prevalence rates in preadolescents have not yet been published.

Generalized Anxiety Disorder

A diagnosis of generalized anxiety disorder (GAD) requires excessive worry about several events or activities. These worries must be difficult to control and occur more days than not for at least 6 months. In children, the anxiety is associated with at least one additional symptom such as restlessness, fatigue, difficulty concentrating, irritability, muscle tension, or disturbed sleep. To warrant a diagnosis, the anxiety or physical symptoms associated with the worry must cause clinically significant distress or impairment in social, academic, or other important areas of functioning. In children, GAD frequently takes the form of uncontrollable worries about competence or quality of performance in academic tasks or other performance-based activities (e.g., music or sports). Consequently, children with GAD often seek approval and reassurance about their performance. Unfortunately, this type of GAD worry may result in diagnostic confusion with the essential features of social phobia. Thus, to make a more clean differential diagnosis, the child with GAD is typically focused on a fear of an inability to meet some internal or inappropriate standard for performance, rather than the opinion of others, per se, as noted in social phobia. Other common worries of children with GAD may involve matters of family finances, the parents' marital relationship, things going on in the world or community (e.g., worries about crime or war), punctuality, and health matters.

In *DSM-IV*, GAD subsumes the former category of overanxious disorder (OAD). While epidemiological studies examining the prevalence of OAD have revealed rates of 3% in children and 6% to 10% in 12- to 18-year-olds (see Bell-Dolan & Brazeal, 1993), prevalence rates of GAD in youth using *DSM-IV* criteria have not yet been ascertained. In the results of the Bremer Adolescent Study (the Bremer Jugendstudie), a longitudinal community-based epidemiological study of *DSM-IV* psychiatric disorders in 12- to 17-year-olds, Essau et al. (2000a) recently reported a GAD lifetime prevalence rate of 0.4%.

Panic Disorder With and Without Agoraphobia

The essential features of panic disorder are "the presence of recurrent, unexpected panic attacks followed by at least one month of persistent concern about having another panic attack, worry about the possible implications or consequences of the panic attacks, or a significant behavioral change related to the attacks" (APA, 1994). A *panic attack* involves a sudden onset of distressing physical and cognitive symptoms that typically culminate in intensity within several minutes before slowly subsiding. An *unexpected panic attack* is defined as uncued or not associated with a situational trigger, as it seemingly occurs "out of the blue." However, panic attacks may eventually come to be associated with particular stimuli (either internal physical or cognitive symptoms or external cues), fostering avoidance behavior or agoraphobia (see Barlow, 1988). As defined by *DSM-IV, agoraphobia* is "anxiety about being in places or situations from which escape might be difficult (or embarrassing) or in which help may not be available in the event of having a panic attack or panic like symptoms" and, consequently, this results in certain situations being avoided or endured with significant distress (APA, 1994).

Although significantly more research exists related to panic disorder in adults, investigators have recently begun to study this disorder in youth (e.g., Kearney, Albano, Eisen, Allan, & Barlow, 1997; Hayward et al., 1992). While the existence of panic disorder in youngsters had originally been debated (e.g., Nelles & Barlow, 1988), questions have lately shifted to the phenomenology of the disorder in this age group. For example, Kearney et al. (1997) found that the most frequent and severe symptoms reported by youth diagnosed with panic disorder included accelerated heart rate, nausea, hot and cold flashes, shaking, and shortness of breath. Moreover, relative to children and adolescents diagnosed with nonpanic anxiety disorders, youth with panic disorder demonstrate significantly elevated anxiety sensitivity (Kearney et al., 1997). *Anxiety sensitivity* is defined as a dispositional variable involving the tendency to interpret anxiety symptoms as dangerous and to react fearfully to anxiety-related bodily sensations (Reiss & McNally, 1985). Youth with panic disorder also report higher rates of clinical depression and to some extent greater trait anxiety (Kearney et al., 1997). Nonetheless, reviews of research regarding the prevalence and nature of panic attacks and panic disorder in children and adolescents suggest that panic attacks are common among adolescents, but both panic attacks and panic disorder are less frequent in children (Hayward et al., 1992; also see Ollendick, Mattis, & King, 1994). The general consensus regarding prevalence of panic disorder in adolescents is approximately 1% (Lewinsohn, Hops, Roberts, Seeley, & Andrews, 1993), with the modal age of onset in midadolescence and higher rates in females than males (Thyer, Parrish, Curtis, Nesse, & Cameron, 1985).

Specific Phobia

Exposure to circumscribed situations or objects that almost invariably results in intense, persistent fear is a primary indicator of a specific phobia (SP; formerly known as *simple phobias* in *DSM-III*). While they typically avoid phobic stimuli, children with SP may express their anxiety in the form of tantrums, crying, clinging, or freezing when confronted with phobic stimuli. Specific phobias are classified by type, including animal type (e.g., dogs, spiders, snakes), natural environment type (e.g., storms, water, or heights), blood–injection–injury type (e.g., shots, having blood drawn, or cuts), situational type (e.g., forms of transportation, enclosed places, or elevators), and other type (e.g., vomiting, choking, costumed characters, or loud sounds). Although adults with SP recognize that their fears are excessive or unreasonable, children with the disorder frequently do not recognize this or the fact that the phobia is distressing and causes difficulties for themselves and others.

Because of the normative nature of fears in childhood, two guidelines are particularly important in the diagnosis of SP in children. First, a stable duration of 6 months is required for fears to be considered true specific phobias in individuals under the age of 18 years. Also, the fears must compromise the child's functioning to a clinically significant degree (i.e., they keep the child from doing things he or she is expected to do or would like to do). In making a diagnosis of SP, appropriate differential diagnoses should also be considered, based on the primary content of the youth's fears (e.g., if focused on social situations, consider social phobia; situations that involve separation from caretakers may reflect SAD; if symptoms are related to a traumatic event, consider PTSD; or if fear of contamination is the primary concern, rule out OCD).

While the overall prevalence rate of SP in epidemiological samples of children and adolescents has been estimated around 6% (for a review of studies using *DSM-III* and *DSM-III-R* criteria see Emmelkamp & Scholing, 1997), differences in the rates of SP according to type have been found. For example, in their large sample of German adolescents, Essau, Conradt, and Peterman (2000b) found the animal and natural environment types of SP to be most common (1.1%). Similarly, in a smaller sample of children ages 4 to 12 years, Muris and Merckelbach (2000) found animal phobias (10%) to be most prevalent, followed by environmental phobias (6.3%). The difference in the rates reported in these two studies (e.g., the rates for adolescents being markedly lower than those for the younger children) is noteworthy as it reflects the tendency of SP rates to peak between ages 10 and 13, with an average age of onset between 7.8 to 8.4 years (Last, Perrin, Hersen, & Kazdin, 1992; Strauss & Last, 1993).

THE COGNITIVE-BEHAVIORAL MODEL OF ANXIETY

The cognitive-behavioral approach to the conceptualization and treatment of childhood anxiety disorders has its roots in the basic behavioral principles and models of learning (e.g., operant conditioning, classical conditioning, and social learning theory). For example, the case of "Little Albert," a young boy whose fear of a rat was acquired through pairing of the rat with a loud noise (Watson & Rayner, 1920), provided early support for the classical conditioning paradigm of fear acquisition. Later, Mowrer (1947, 1960) proposed a two-factor learning theory for the development and maintenance of phobic behavior. This two-factor theory proposes that both classical and operant conditioning are involved in the development of anxiety disorders. That is, following an initial classical conditioning event (either direct exposure or via observation), the subsequent avoidance of the fear-eliciting stimulus (or similar stimuli) results in an immediate fear reduction (operant conditioning through negative reinforcement). This two-factor model is offered to account for both the etiological mechanism and the maintaining factors involved in phobic avoidance, and although criticized for not accounting for all instances of fear acquisition, it remains a mainstay in learning theory (for a critique and review, see Albano & Morris, 1998). In addition to avoidance behavior, anxiety may be maintained through certain parental rearing styles (e.g., overprotection and overcontrol; see Albano, Chorpita, & Barlow, 1996) and other environmental conditioning and shaping experiences. Thus, behavioral models of anxiety acquisition and maintenance stress that the anxiety response is learned and reinforced through experience or observation, and maintained primarily through avoidance and further conditioning experiences.

Partly in response to the inadequacy of behavioral models in explaining internalizing reactions (e.g., Davey, 1992), cognitive models were developed that emphasize the role of maladaptive thoughts in individuals suffering from anxiety disorders. Cognitive models of anxiety propose that individuals perceive events in the environment through schemas or "mental templates of the world" (Kendall, 1992). Through experience or observational learning with specific stimuli, individuals with anxiety disorders have developed "threat schemas," which cause them to interpret ostensibly ambiguous stimuli as threatening—that is, they automatically engage in maladaptive (e.g., negative, irrational, or catastrophic) thinking when presented with certain stimuli (Beck &

Emery, 1985; Kendall, 1992, 1993). In support of this cognitive model, change in levels of this maladaptive thinking or "self-talk" in children with anxiety disorders has been found to mediate change in their anxiety levels during treatment (Treadwell & Kendall, 1996). However, whether these thoughts result in or are the product of anxiety has been widely debated and has yet to be determined (Silverman & Ginsburg, 1995).

The integrated cognitive-behavioral conceptualization of anxiety disorders focuses on the role of anxious thoughts, physical sensations, and behaviors in the development and maintenance of anxiety disorders. It proposes that an individual's biological and psychological vulnerabilities to anxiety interact with his or her direct or observational learning in experiences with stressful or ambiguous cues. Together, these create a vicious cycle of anxious thoughts (e.g., "I look stupid," "I'm going to die," "It's going to hurt me"), a focus on physiological sensations (e.g., rapid heart rate, perspiration, fast breathing), and noncoping behaviors (e.g., avoidance, escape, relying on a safe person). This model, which was originally developed to explain adult negative affect, has been found to adequately apply to anxiety disorders in children and adolescents and is the basis for the only empirically supported efficacious interventions for anxious youth (see Labellarte, Ginsburg, Walkup, & Riddle, 1999), including the exemplary program described in the treatment section later in this chapter.

ASSESSMENT OF ANXIETY DISORDERS IN YOUTH

In accord with the cognitive-behavioral model, a thorough assessment of the youth's thoughts, feelings (physical and affective), and behaviors is necessary before treatment can occur. In other words, the psychiatric diagnosis alone is inadequate for guiding treatment. A fuller diagnostic picture consisting of the individual's strengths and weaknesses in managing anxiety across a variety of settings and contexts will ensure that treatment addresses his or her unique clinical presentation. In addition, a thorough assessment provides quantifiable data with which treatment progress and outcomes can be monitored. Thus, a functional analysis of the child or adolescent's anxiety problems must be conducted in order to adequately assess the scope of the problem and define the best course of treatment.

A multimethod assessment approach is commonly used in evaluating anxiety disorders in youth and formulating the functional analysis (March & Albano, 1996). Such an approach allows the clinician to gain information about the child across contexts and from a variety of sources (e.g., child, parents, teachers, and peers). Brief descriptions of the three basic methods commonly used for assessing anxiety in children and adolescents follow.

Clinical Interviews

The clinical interview remains one of the most important sources of information gathering (Stallings & March, 1995). The most reliable diagnoses are made using structured or semistructured interviews, with the semistructured format allowing the clinician the flexibility to pursue specific questions in greater detail when deemed necessary. In addition to permitting diagnoses to be made in a reliable manner, structured and semistructured clinical interviews allow clinical observation of the child, the parents, and their interactions.

One semistructured interview, designed specifically to assess anxiety in youth ages 6 to 17 years, is the Anxiety Disorders Interview Schedule for *DSM-IV* (ADIS-IV); there is an accompanying parent version (Silverman & Albano, 1996a, 1996b). These are separate interviews that evaluate the presence and severity of anxiety, mood, and externalizing disorders, as well as screen for learning and developmental disorders, substance abuse, eating disorders, psychotic symptoms, and somatoform disorders. Information from the parent and child interviews is synthesized into a composite profile of diagnoses and severity ratings. A major benefit of the ADIS-IV over other available semistructured interviews is its clear and detailed sections for evaluating each of the anxiety disorders individually. The original version of the ADIS, which corresponded to earlier versions of *DSM,* possessed the best psychometric profile for the diagnostic assessment of childhood anxiety disorders of available diagnostic measures (e.g., Silverman & Nelles, 1988; Silverman & Eisen, 1992) and demonstrated sensitivity to treatment effects in studies of youth with anxiety disorders (e.g., Kendall et al., 1997; Dadds, Spence, Holland, Barrett, & Laurens, 1997). Silverman, Saavadera, and Pina (2001) report excellent psychometric data for the *DSM-IV* version of the ADIS. Kappa coefficients for the composite diagnoses (combined parent and child report) of SAD, SoP, SP, and GAD were all in the excellent range, spanning from 0.80 to 0.92. Test-retest reliability was reported as excellent, in addition to good to excellent reliability for symptom scores. Finally, Silverman and colleagues report no significant age differences in the reliability of symptom scales scores.

Other structured and semistructured psychiatric interviews for children and adolescents include the Schedule for Affective Disorders and Schizophrenia in School-Aged Children (K-SADS; Puig-Antich & Chambers, 1978), the Child Assessment Schedule (CAS; Hodges, McKnew, Cytryn, Stern, & Kline, 1982), the NIMH Diagnostic Interview Schedule for Children, Version 2.3 (DISC 2.3; Shaffer, et al., 1996), the Interview Schedule for Children (ISC; Kovacs, 1985), the Diagnostic Interview for Children and Adolescents (DICA; Herjanic & Reich, 1982); and the Children's Interview for Psychiatric Syndromes—Child and Parent Versions (ChIPS and P-ChIPS; Weller, Weller, Rooney & Fristad, 1999a, 1999b).

Self-Reports and Self-Rating Scales

Self-administered reports and rating scales for assessing child and adolescent anxiety are numerous and widely used. Popular standardized self-report measures include the Revised Children's Manifest Anxiety Scale (RCMAS; Reynolds & Richmond, 1978) and the State-Trait Anxiety Inventory for Children (STAIC; Spielberger, 1973). However, the RCMAS has been found to be nonspecific with regard to identifying youth with anxiety disorders (Dierker et al., 2001) and to consistently correlate with measures of depression. Thus, the RCMAS may best be viewed as a measure of general negative affectivity. The STAIC is most often used to identify levels of anxiety in the moment (the state form) or in general (the trait form) in research studies, but it is similarly less specific in identifying children with anxiety disorders (see March & Albano, 1996). In response to the nonspecific nature of these self-report scales, two relatively new scales have been developed to correspond with symptoms found in the *DSM* diagnoses. The Multidimensional Anxiety Scale for Children (MASC; March, Parker, Sullivan, Stallings, & Conners, 1997) is a 39-item 4-point Likert self-report rating scale which includes four factors: physical symptoms (tension or restlessness and somatic or autonomic subfactors), social anxiety (humiliation or rejection and public performance subfactors), harm avoidance (anxious coping and perfectionism subfactors) and separation or panic anxiety. Three-week test-retest reliability for the MASC is .79 in clinical samples (March et al., 1997) and .88 in school-based samples (March & Sullivan, 1999). In addition to excellent psychometric properties (March et al., 1997), Dierker et al. (2001) found the MASC to be sensitive and specific in identifying youth with anxiety disorders. The Screen for Child Anxiety Related Emotional Disorders (SCARED; Birmaher et al., 1997, 1999) is a 41-item child and parent self-report instrument that assesses *DSM-IV* symptoms of panic, separation anxiety, social phobia, general anxiety disorders, and symptoms of school refusal. The SCARED has shown very good psychometric properties in two different large clinical samples (Birmaher et al., 1997, 1999) and in a community sample (Muris et al., 1998).

Other self-report scales have been developed to address specific forms of anxiety and related constructs. For example, the Child Anxiety Sensitivity Index (CASI; Silverman, Fleisig, Rabian, & Peterson, 1991) assesses the fear of the physical sensations of anxiety in youth. The Fear Survey Schedule for Children—Revised (FSSC-R; Ollendick, 1983) is perhaps the most widely studied measure of subclinical fears in children and adolescents, and has proven useful in studying the developmental psychopathology of anxiety and cross-cultural examinations of fear. Two self-report measures have been developed specifically for assessing social anxiety in children and adolescents, the Social Phobia and Anxiety Inventory for Children (SPAI-C; Beidel, Turner, & Morris, 1995) and the Social Anxiety Scale for Children—Revised, Child and Adolescent Versions (SASC-R; LaGreca, 1998; LaGreca & Stone, 1993). Each of these scales has demonstrated predictive validity and sensitivity to treatment effects (see Beidel, Turner, & Morris, 2000).

While youth self-report measures are important because of the private and subjective nature of anxiety, parent and teacher report forms are useful in completing the diagnostic picture with their ability to capture aspects that the child fails to report because of social desirability, embarrassment, or obstinacy. Beyond the popular parent and teacher rating scales used to assess a broader range of childhood problems including anxiety, such as the Child Behavior Checklist (CBCL; Achenbach & Edelbrock, 1983) and the Teacher Report Form (TRF; Achenbach, 1991), parent versions exist for the FSSC-R and SASC-R. Although the information from different sources may sometimes be conflicting, gathering youth, parent, and teacher reports regarding a youth's anxiety provides important information about the child's appearance and behavior across settings, as well as about how each person in the youth's environment perceives him or her.

Nonstandardized self-report measures can also be clinically useful, especially in terms of assessing an individual's progress in treatment (e.g., Beidel & Turner, 1998). Children and adolescents can be assigned self-monitoring in the form of a daily diary in which to record anxiety-provoking situations as they occur in their everyday lives. Although the format will vary according to the problem and the youth's developmental level, the youth is typically instructed to record a brief description of the situation and his or her accompanying thoughts, physical sensations, behaviors, and an anxiety rating (on a scale of 0 to 100, for example). Daily diaries have been shown to be useful in providing access to youth's anxiety intensity levels, antecedents to and consequences of anxious behaviors, and anxious thoughts (e.g., Beidel, Neal, & Lederer, 1991), and thus are crucial in identifying the functional relationships between stimuli, anxiety, and behavioral reactions. Another ideographic self-monitoring format that is particularly useful in a cognitive-behavioral assessment is the Fear and Avoidance Hierarchy (FAH). During the initial assessment, a hierarchical list of the youth's "top 10" anxiety-provoking situations is constructed. On a weekly basis thereafter, the youth fills in his or her current anxiety and avoidance ratings on a scale of 0 (not at all) to 8 (extreme). Parents can also complete a weekly FAH for their child. Thus, levels of fear and avoidance in the situations that are most ecologically valid to the individual youth are monitored through treatment. The FAH is particularly useful in determining the specific targets for exposures in the treatment of phobias (Eisen, Kearney, & Schaefer, 1995; Silverman & Kurtines, 1997).

Behavioral Observation

Behavioral observation of anxious children and adolescents can be done in structured or unstructured situations and can involve just the individual youth or include family members. Unstructured behavioral observation typically occurs during the interview process (e.g., the clinician takes note of the youth's body posture, facial expressions, and verbal abilities) but can also be done through visits to the youth's environment (e.g., school, home, and extracurricular activities). In these situations, the clinician is an objective observer, and the information regarding the youth in these naturalistic situations can be compared to that reported by the youth, parents, and teachers.

The Behavioral Approach Test (BAT) provides the opportunity for more structured behavioral observations. A BAT involves purposely exposing the youth to a feared object or situation while the clinician or a trained rater concurrently assesses the youth's subjective level of anxiety, physiological reactions, and motoric or other behavioral responses. Targets of the BAT can be items from the youth's FAH (e.g., "Being in a room with people I don't know") or standardized situations (e.g., giving a brief oral presentation to three strangers on a topic chosen at random; see Albano, 1995). During the exposure to the feared stimuli, the youth's subjective level of anxiety on a scale of 0 to 100 is reported, with the clinician soliciting and recording the ratings each minute. Physiological reactions can be monitored through use of cardiovascular and electrodermal monitoring equipment, although normative data for children from such instruments has yet to be established (Kendall, Chu, Pimentel, & Choudhury, 2000). Prior to informing the child of the task and then again also immediately before beginning it, baseline ratings of the child's anxiety level and physiological data should be obtained in order to have some points of comparison for the data obtained during the BAT. Depending on the developmental level of the youth, additional data obtained from a BAT can include a list of thoughts that the youth recalls having during the task, which he or she is asked to write down immediately following its completion. Thus, the BAT can provide data on all three aspects of anxiety as conceptualized within a cognitive-behavioral framework: thoughts, physiological feelings, and behaviors. Posttreatment BATs are useful in research contexts to fully capture the effectiveness of the treatment (e.g., Albano, Marten, Holt, Heimberg, & Barlow, 1995).

COGNITIVE-BEHAVIORAL TREATMENT OF ANXIETY DISORDERS IN YOUTH

In recent reviews examining the empirical literature for various treatments for children and adolescents with anxiety disorders (Kazdin & Weisz, 1998; Ollendick & King, 1998; Turner & Heiser, 1999), behavioral and cognitive-behavioral protocols received the only endorsement for having empirical support as being efficacious therapeutic interventions. Stated more specifically and unequivocally, traditional therapies such as psychodynamic and play-therapy approaches should not be used in the treatment of anxiety disorders in youth, as only the cognitive-behavioral approach has demonstrated efficacy. The cognitive-behavioral approach to the treatment of childhood anxiety disorders integrates several forms of developmentally sensitive behavioral and cognitive procedures. Cognitive-behavioral treatment (CBT) protocols typically feature components involving education about the nature of anxiety and emotions, somatic management skills, identification and modification of anxious thoughts (cognitive restructuring), reinforcement approaches (self- or parent-administered), exposure to anxiety-provoking situations, and techniques focused on generalization of gains and relapse prevention (e.g., Kendall, 1992).

A Model CBT Protocol for Anxiety Disorders in Youth: The Coping Cat

Kendall's (1990, 2000) Coping Cat protocol is designed as a short-term treatment (16 sessions) for children and young adolescents, consisting of 8 educational sessions followed by 8 practice sessions. The treatment is meant to be delivered flexibly, which means that the therapist should add or delete sessions and treatment components as appropriate for the individual child (see Kendall, Chu, Gifford, Hayes, & Nauta, 1998). Moreover, flexible application of this manual, and CBT in general, assumes that the therapist brings to treatment all the necessary nonspecific factors for enhancing treatment effects (e.g., positive regard, warmth, active listening, and a collaborative relationship). In addition, the therapist must attend to the day-to-day (or extraordinary) issues that could arise and steer a treatment plan off course for a period of time (e.g., a crisis situation). The remainder of this section presents the essential elements and process of the Coping Cat protocol, in addition to empirical support for this program and related CBT interventions.

During the initial eight educational sessions of the Coping Cat program, children learn skills that enable them to recognize and distinguish different emotions and also to identify and modify anxious cognitions and somatic responses to anxiety-provoking situations. In addition, children learn the steps of a problem-solving approach to later apply these steps to imaginal and in vivo anxiety-provoking situations. This preparation lays the foundation for the subsequent practice portion of treatment (exposures), in which children use the strategies learned in the first eight sessions to cope with specific situations identified as particularly anxiety provoking for them. The therapist assesses the child's anxiety-provoking cognitions and works with the child to design learning experiences that may remediate maladaptive cognitions and associated dysfunctional behavioral and affective patterns. In addition, the therapist may meet with the child's parents in order to identify and modify patterns associated with parental modeling of anxious behavior or reinforcement of the child's anxiety-provoking thoughts and behaviors (Kendall, 1992).

Kendall's (1990, 2000) program primarily seeks to teach children to recognize their individual signs of anxious arousal and use these signs as cues for using anxiety management strategies. The program progresses from basic to more complex concepts and skills as children learn a specific four-step coping plan to manage their distress (the FEAR plan). Affective education is the first step, in which children are taught to discriminate between various feelings and the associated facial expressions, nonverbal cues, and postures. Next, children learn an awareness of somatic reactions to different feelings and learn how to detect those reactions that are specific to anxious arousal (e.g., increased heart rate, shaking, "butterflies," and sweating). Children are subsequently trained to use these physical reactions as early warning signs of or cues to the presence of their own anxiety as they learn that the first indication of the need for coping skills is to ask themselves: "Feeling frightened?" Relaxation training is next taught as a means to further develop the children's awareness of their anxious arousal and to provide a sense of control as they learn to reduce physiological and muscular reactions to anxiety. The therapist is encouraged to make audiotapes of these exercises and relaxing imagery for the children to listen to at home so that they can learn both progressive and cue-controlled relaxation techniques (Kendall, 1992).

The next coping skill that is presented targets *self-talk* through teaching children how to recognize and challenge distorted or unrealistic anxious cognitions. The Coping Cat protocol introduces the concept of anxious cognitions using cartoon sequences with blank thought bubbles that the child completes. Children are then taught the second step in the problem-solving model, which is to identify their anxious thoughts or beliefs by asking: "Expecting bad things to happen?" In order to modify anxious self-talk into coping self-talk and develop plans for managing anxiety more effectively in different situations, an accurate assessment and conceptualization of each child's dysfunctional thought composition are crucial. Each child's expectations and fears about what will happen and the role seen for him or herself in the situation are both significant. The therapist discusses any distorted cognitions by focusing on catastrophic expectations and probability overestimations and encourages children to discover and question the likelihood of alternative possibilities. In addition, throughout the training program it is important that the therapist function as a coping model as all new skills are introduced. For instance, a therapist might provide a personal example of an anxiety-provoking situation, identify anxious arousal and cognitions, and explain how he or she effectively managed his or her distress with appropriate coping strategies (Kendall, 1992).

The third skill encourages children to inhibit initial impulses (e.g., avoidance) and create a behavioral strategy of "actions and attitudes that will help." This plan is based on D'Zurilla and Goldfried's (1971) five-stage problem solving sequence that trains the child to ask:

1. What is the problem?
2. What are all the things I could do about it?
3. What will probably happen if I do those things?
4. Which solution do I think will work best?
5. After I have tried it, how did I do?

The objectives of teaching problem solving skills are to develop children's ability to proficiently generate alternatives to situations that initially seemed overwhelming and hopeless and to refrain from engaging in maladaptive or avoidance behavior (Kendall et al., 2000).

The final step of the Coping Cat program emphasizes the importance of rewarding oneself for effort and for successes. The concept of "rate and reward" introduces children to the idea that *perfect* performance is not required. The therapist focuses children on their efforts and aspects of their performance that went well and encourages them to reward themselves. This strategy fosters a relapse-prevention framework in which partial successes and mistakes are interpreted constructively—that is as a necessary and expected part of the learning process rather than as evidence of failure (Kendall & Treadwell, 1996).

In sum, the Coping Cat program's four-step plan for coping with anxiety is symbolized by the word *FEAR,* which reflects the acronym created by the first letter of each step:

Feeling frightened?

Expecting bad things to happen?

Actions and **a**ttitudes that will help?

Rate and **r**ewards?

The second segment of the Coping Cat program is devoted to the application and practice of the newly acquired skills (i.e., applying the FEAR plan) in increasingly anxiety provoking situations. The same educational strategies are to be employed in this training portion, including coping modeling, role playing, and homework assignment tasks labeled "Show That I Can" (STIC) to help reinforce what has been addressed during the session. The specific situations that are presented to children are individually designed for them, based on their particular fears and worries, as identified during the initial assessment and again following the sixth session (cf., FAH). The therapist monitors the level of anticipated and actual anxiety that each child reports experiencing in order to ensure that the anxiety resulting from initial exposure experiences is low level (i.e., situations that do not create too much distress) and that the later exposure experiences result in higher levels of anxiety (i.e., situations that are particularly troublesome for the child). The sequence begins with imaginal, in-office exposure to nonstressful situations, followed by imaginal, in-office exposure to situations designed to induce low levels of anxiety, and then actual, in vivo experiences in low-stress situations. The subsequent sessions involve exposure to situations that cause higher levels of stress in the child, again first in imaginal settings and then, once these are mastered, in actual in vivo situations. This process is then repeated in situations that are even more stressful for children. Exposure to a number of different anxiety-provoking situations, accompanied by processing the postexposure experience to promote future coping behavior, helps children master these coping skills and problem-solving strategies. Finally, the last session includes videotaping a commercial about learning to cope with anxiety (developed by the child with the support of the therapist)—giving the child an opportunity to share what he or she has learned with others (parents and siblings) and a tool to use at home for relapse prevention (Kendall, 1992).

Kendall (1992) maintains that when children decrease their discomfort while more successfully engaging in anxiety-provoking situations, they acquire a sense of competence that they can generalize to other areas. However, although the effectiveness of the treatment protocol has been supported, the cognitive component's impact on treatment gains remains unclear. While the educational and practice portions of the protocol differ, research has not elucidated whether the beneficial effects result from the sequencing of educational segments and then practice segments or from either of these segments alone. Thus, future research needs to specify the contribution of the cognitive versus the behavioral treatment components of the Coping Cat treatment protocol (Kendall & Treadwell, 1996).

Evidence to Support the Efficacy of the Coping Cat Protocol and CBT

Unquestionably, the first protocol to meet the standards of empirically supported (evidence-based) treatment for children and adolescents with anxiety disorders, and the exemplary model for the development of subsequent protocols, is Kendall's Coping Cat program (Kendall, 1990, 2000). Initial support for this protocol comes from two randomized clinical trials (Kendall, 1994; Kendall et al., 1997). Initially, Kendall (1994) tested the 16-session manual-based CBT protocol (*The Coping Cat Workbook*) with children afraid of separation from significant attachment figures (SAD), interaction with peers (SoP), or nonspecific worry situations (OAD and GAD). The sample consisted of 47 youth (ages 9 to 13 years; 60% males), who were randomly assigned to one of two conditions: cognitive-behavioral therapy or a wait-list control. At posttreatment, children in the CBT group evidenced significant treatment gains across multiple methods of assessment (i.e., self-report, direct behavioral observation, and parent and teacher reports). The results also revealed that 64% of the children in the CBT group had remitted from their principal diagnosis at posttreatment, as evidenced by the ADIS interview. The data further documented that treatment gains had generalized to other difficulties (e.g., depression) and that improvement was maintained at a 1-year follow-up. Kendall and Southam-Gerow (1996) additionally demonstrated that treatment gains for all children (the wait-list youth were offered CBT after the waiting period) were maintained over a longer time period, ranging from 2 to 5 years. In a second randomized trial (Kendall et al., 1997), the efficacy of this manual-based CBT protocol was replicated with 94 youth (ages 9 to 13 years) who all had a principal diagnosis of an anxiety disorder. Again the children were randomly assigned to CBT or a wait-list control, and the results revealed that at posttreatment and 1-year follow-up, positive treatment gains of the CBT group were evident and maintained on a variety of measures (Kendall et al., 1997). Further evaluations of the protocol have demonstrated its efficacy in group format (Flannery-Schroeder & Kendall, 2000), in addition to being transportable to independent settings and different cultures (e.g., Barrett, Dadds, & Rapee, 1996; Kendall et al., 1998).

Extensions of the Coping Cat protocol to examine issues such as efficacy with broader age groups and in small peer groups, comorbidity, and family involvement still need to be investigated (Kendall & Treadwell, 1996). For example, researchers have demonstrated the importance of parental and family involvement in the treatment of childhood anxiety disorders (e.g., Barrett et al., 1996; Last, Hansen, & Franco, 1998; Silverman et al., 1999). Barrett et al. (1996) compared their Australian adaptation of the Coping Cat program to an intervention that included this CBT intervention plus family intervention (FAM). In the FAM intervention, the parents were trained in contingency management strategies and communication and problem-solving skills, and taught to recognize and address their own emotional and anxious responses to stimuli. Seventy-nine 7- to 14-year-old children with a primary diagnosis of OAD, SAD, or SoP were randomly assigned to a CBT group, combined CBT and FAM, or a wait-list control for 12 weeks. The results revealed that 60% of the children in both treatment conditions no longer received their principal diagnosis at posttreatment assessment, compared to less than 30% of the wait-list control children. And at the 12 month follow-up, there were considerable significant positive results of the combined CBT and FAM condition, as 95% maintained their treatment gains, compared to 70% of the children in the CBT alone condition (Barrett et al., 1996). However, this effect held up best for younger children, especially girls. Other investigators have suggested that parental involvement may not contribute to or add to the efficacy of CBT in treating anxiety (e.g., Cobham, Dadds, & Spence, 1998; Spence, Donovan, & Brechman-Toussaint, 2000); however, this issue warrants further evaluation. Thus, parenting and family components of cognitive-behavioral therapy in the treatment of childhood anxiety warrant additional research. Fortunately, in recent years researchers have witnessed a literal explosion of clinical trials examining the efficacy of a variety of CBT protocols for treating children and adolescents with anxiety disorders. These trials have targeted anxiety related to school refusal behavior (King et al., 1998; Last et al., 1998), specific phobias (Silverman et al., 1999), and treatment for social phobia in children (Beidel et al., 2000; Spence et al., 2000) and adolescents (Albano et al., 1995; Hayward et al., 2000).

PHARMACOLOGICAL TREATMENT OF ANXIETY DISORDERS IN YOUTH

Recent open and controlled trials of the selective serotonin reuptake inhibitors (SSRIs) in childhood anxiety disorders support the short-term safety and efficacy of these medications for youth. Open-label and similar uncontrolled trials of SSRIs for childhood anxiety are based on data suggesting the continuity of childhood anxiety disorders with anxiety and depressive disorders in adulthood and the responsiveness of anxiety disorders in adults to various medications, including SSRIs. The treatment of choice for anxiety and mood disorders in adults is the SSRIs because of their broad spectrum of clinical activity, ease of use, and low side-effect profile. There is evidence for the use of tricyclic antidepressants (TCAs) and monoamine oxidase inhibitors in the treatment of adult anxiety disorders; however, side-effect issues and potential adverse effects limit the appeal of these medications. Similar to results reported in the adult literature, SSRIs have demonstrated efficacy in treating childhood OCD (March et al., 1998, Riddle et al., 2001).

However, in contrast to the adult literature, there are few well-controlled pharmacological studies on treatment of childhood anxiety disorders (GAD, SAD, and SoP) and for those that are published, results have been equivocal (March, 1999). Specifically, although there is mixed evidence of efficacy for the TCAs (Bernstein et al., 2000; Klein, Koplewicz, & Kanner, 1992), concerns regarding cardiotoxicity limit their use in children (Wilens et al., 1996). Three small trials of high-potency benzodiazepines (Bernstein, Garfinkel, & Borchardt, 1990; Graae, Milner, Rizzotto, & Klein, 1994; Simeon et al. 1992) did not demonstrate efficacy. A single-site comparison of the SSRI fluoxetine and placebo in selective mutism showed benefit (Black & Uhde, 1994). More recently, open studies of SSRIs suggest these medications are likely efficacious in treating the range of anxiety disorders in youth, with perhaps the exception of specific phobia (Labellarte et al., 1999). For example, youth with social anxiety disorder (ages 10 to 14, $n = 14$) demonstrated significant improvement on clinician ratings, self-reports, and behavioral test measures following an open trial of sertraline (Compton et al., 2001).

The RUPP Fluvoxamine Anxiety Study

Based on the efficacy of the SSRIs in treating childhood OCD and adult anxiety disorders, a five-center multisite study examining the efficacy of the SSRI fluvoxamine (FLV) was initiated in 1997 as part of the NIMH Research Units of Pediatric Psychopharmacology (RUPP; RUPP Anxiety Study Group, 2001). Children and adolescents ages 6 to 17 years meeting criteria for SAD, SoP, or GAD participated in the trial. Children were excluded if they had another psychiatric disorder that either required medication treatment (e.g., ADHD) or was more severe than the presenting anxiety disorder. Prior to randomization, 134 children underwent an extensive assessment battery and were treated openly with "supportive, psychoeducation therapy" for the initial 3 weeks, then continued "supportive psychotherapy" during the study. This supportive psychotherapy did not include elements of exposure or formal cognitive restructuring. Subjects who did not improve during the first 3 weeks ($N = 128$) were randomly assigned to receive FLV or placebo for 8 weeks of double-blind treatment. Assessments involved self-, parent-, and clinician ratings on anxiety symptom rating scales and measures of global improvement. At outcome, children on FLV were significantly more improved on multiple measures of anxiety and impairment than were children receiving placebo. The primary outcome measures, the Pediatric Anxiety Rating Scale and the eight-item Clinician Global Impression-Improvement (CGI-I) scale, both demonstrated the efficacy of FLV for the short-term treatment of anxiety disorders in youth. More specifically, using the 8-point CGI-I scale, 48/63 (76%) of children on FLV were considered improved or better (CGI-I 1, 2, or 3) compared to 18/65 (29%) of children on placebo. Parent reports and child self-reports also demonstrated the superiority of FLV over placebo but the results were less robust than those based on clinician's ratings. A total of 16% (10/63) of subjects discontinued from the FLV group and 22% (14/65) discontinued from the placebo group.

The results of the RUPP study were quite encouraging and suggest that children and adolescents who are compromised by anxiety disorders may benefit from medication treatment in the short term. However, the impact of medication treatment beyond an acute 8-week period remains unknown. Thus, future research is needed to examine the stability of these results over the longer term, along with addressing questions of which children should receive medication treatment in the first place. Moreover, questions of medication discontinuation need to be addressed; that is, do the symptoms and disorders return when the SSRI is stopped?

CONCLUSION AND FUTURE DIRECTIONS

Advances in our understanding and treatment of anxiety disorders in children and adolescents have burgeoned over the past 20 years. It is now accepted by the mental health community that these disorders are real, have deleterious effects on the development and functioning of youth, and do not simply dissipate with time. Fortunately, sensitive and specific methods of diagnosis and assessment exist to identify youth who suffer with these conditions and to elucidate the symptom picture and associated impairment in functioning for appropriate treatment planning. On the assessment front, advances are occurring which will assist in identifying those youth who may be at risk for these disorders, or those who may be symptomatic but not yet recognized as functionally impaired. School-based screening techniques using standardized self-reporting measures have already proven promising in this regard, and efforts to evaluate the utility of these techniques in primary care and pediatric settings are underway.

Anxiety disorders are known to run a chronic and fluctuating course throughout the life span (Albano, Chorpita, & Barlow, 1996); however, effective treatments are available for adults and for children ages 7 to 18 years. This chapter describes a model psychosocial treatment program, the Coping Cat protocol, which has demonstrated efficacy and maintenance of effects over the long term. This cognitive-behavioral program, and others like it, offer children and adolescents specific ways to understand the nature of anxiety and their specific vulnerabilities for anxious responding; most important, such programs provide the skills necessary to master the anxiety response and return to a full and complete level of functioning. CBT has wide appeal to and acceptability among youth and parents, is able to be delivered in individual, family, or group format, and has been demonstrated to be transportable to other cultures. It is incumbent upon clinical researchers in this area to advance the field in several ways.

First, young children (below age 7) with anxiety disorders have been neglected by clinical researchers. Effective treatments for this age range are sorely needed to stop the advancement of anxiety in young children, and consequently to allow for a more normal developmental trajectory and improved quality of life.

Second, anxiety rarely comes in a single package, with the possible exception of a circumscribed specific phobia. More often, anxiety occurs with high rates of comorbidity, including other anxiety disorders, mood disorders, substance abuse, and externalizing disorders. Treatment protocols such as the Coping Cat program must be subjected to effectiveness trials whereby "real" clinic patients (not those meeting set inclusion and exclusion criteria) are treated. Information gleaned from effectiveness studies can guide the development of modules or modifications to existing protocols to address these comorbid conditions. Without such studies, it remains unclear to what degree comorbidity may render a youth susceptible to relapse over the long term.

Next, CBT protocols are being adapted for use in nonclinic settings such as schools (Masia, Klein, Storch, & Corda, 2001; Olivares et al., submitted). The transportability of these protocols into nontraditional settings can afford those youth who might otherwise not be referred for treatment, or may be delayed in referral until significantly impaired, the opportunity to recover fully from an otherwise insidious condition. However, a critical issue that must also be addressed in studies of both efficacy and effectiveness involving CBT is the issue of *therapist* effectiveness. To date, the empirical literature utilizes highly skilled and trained therapists who adhere to the CBT model and identify themselves as "cognitive-behaviorists." Whether CBT is equally effective when delivered by eclectic therapists or those espousing a divergent theoretical orientation and training history (e.g., psychodynamic therapists) needs to be examined.

Finally, advances in the pharmacological treatment of anxiety disorders in youth are occurring at a rapid pace. If the efficacy of medication treatments in youth follows the results of studies conducted in adults, we may expect certain patterns of response as compared with CBT. Medication will likely result in symptom relief more quickly than CBT, but will be equivocal or have a slight advantage at immediate posttreatment after a 12-week trial. However, youth treated with CBT should continue to evidence gains over the long term and should maintain these gains following the discontinuation of therapy. Of course, only empirical testing of CBT and medication in the same population of youth, using the same methods of assessing outcome, and subjecting clinicians to the rigors of treatment fidelity for both modalities will address these hypothetical statements. Moreover, issues of treatment acceptability (e.g., determining which modality is preferred) and satisfaction must be examined. The relative efficacy of each monotherapy as compared with youth receiving both treatments simultaneously is also necessary to advance our understanding of what works best for youth in need. Until these studies are conducted, we anxiously await their results.

REFERENCES

Achenbach, T. M. (1991). Manual for the Child Behavior Checklist 4-18 and 1991 Profile. Burlington: University of Vermont, Department of Psychiatry.

Achenbach, T. M., & Edelbrock, C. (1983). Manual for the Child Behavior Checklist and Revised Child Behavior Profile. Burlington: University of Vermont, Department of Psychiatry.

Achenbach T. M., Howell, C. T., McConaughy, S. H., Stanger C. (1995). Six-year predictors of problems in a national sample of children and youth: I. Cross-informant syndromes. *Journal of the American Academy of Child and Adolescent Psychiatry, 34,* 336–347.

Albano, A. M. (1995). Treatment of social anxiety in adolescents. *Cognitive and Behavioral Practice, 2,* 271–298.

Albano, A. M., Chorpita, B. F., & Barlow, D. H. (1996). Anxiety disorders. In E. J. Mash & R. A. Barkley (Eds.), *Child psychopathology* (pp. 196–241). New York: Guilford Press.

Albano, A. M., Marten, P. A., Holt, C. S., Heimberg, R. G., & Barlow, D. H. (1995). Cognitive-behavioral group treatment for adolescent social phobia: A preliminary study. *Journal of Nervous and Mental Disease, 183,* 649–656.

Albano, A. M., & Morris, T. L. (1998). Childhood anxiety, obsessive-compulsive disorder, and depression. In J. J. Plaud & E. H. Eifert (Eds.), *From behavior theory to behavior therapy* (pp. 203–222). Boston: Allyn & Bacon.

American Psychiatric Association. (1980). *Diagnostic and statistical manual of mental disorders* (3rd ed.). Washington, DC: Author.

American Psychiatric Association. (1984). *Diagnostic and statistical manual of mental disorders* (3rd ed., revised). Washington, DC: Author.

American Psychiatric Association. (1994). *Diagnostic and statistical manual of mental disorders* (4th ed.). Washington, DC: Author.

Barlow, D. H. (1988). *Anxiety and its disorders.* New York: Guilford Press.

Barrett, P. M., Dadds, M. R., & Rapee, R. M. (1996). Family treatment of childhood anxiety: A controlled trial. *Journal of Consulting and Clinical Psychology, 64,* 333–342.

Beck, A. T., & Emery, G. (1985). *Anxiety disorders and phobias: A cognitive perspective.* New York: Basic Books.

Beidel, D. C., Albano, A. M., Cooley-Quille, M., Hibbs, E. D., March, J. S., Masia, C., Morris, T. L., Rabian, B., & Warren, S. L. (1999a). Anxiety Disorders Association of America/National Institutes of Mental Health Monograph. In *Conference on Treating Anxiety Disorders in Youth: Current Problems and Future Solutions.* Bethesda, MD: Anxiety Disorders Association of America.

Beidel, D., Neal, A. M., & Lederer, A. S. (1991). The feasibility and validity of a daily diary for the assessment of anxiety in children. *Behavior Therapy, 22,* 505–517.

Beidel, D., & Turner, S. (1998). *Shy children, phobic adults: Nature and treatment of social phobia.* Washington, DC: American Psychological Association.

Beidel, D., Turner, S., & Morris, T. (1995). A new inventory to assess childhood social anxiety and phobia: The Social Phobia and Anxiety Inventory for Children. *Psychological Assessment, 7,* 70–79.

Beidel, D. C., Turner, S. M., & Morris, T. L. (2000). Behavioral treatment of childhood social phobia. *Journal of Consulting and Clinical Psychology, 68,* 1072–1080.

Bell-Dolan, D. & Brazeal, T. J. (1993). Separation anxiety disorder, overanxious disorder, and school refusal. *Child and Adolescent Psychiatric Clinics of North America, 2,* 563–580.

Benjamin, R. S., Costello, E. J., & Warren, M. (1990). Anxiety disorders in a pediatric sample. *Journal of Anxiety Disorders, 4,* 293–316.

Bernstein, G. A., Borchardt, C. M., Perwien, A. R., Crosby, R. D., Kushner, M. G., Thuras, P. D., & Last, C. G. (2000). Imipramine plus cognitive-behavioral therapy in the treatment of school refusal. *Journal of the American Academy of Child and Adolescent Psychiatry, 39,* 276–283.

Bernstein, G. A., Garfinkel, B., & Borchardt, C. (1990). Comparative studies of pharmacotherapy for school refusal. *Journal of the American Academy of Child and Adolescent Psychiatry, 29,* 773–781.

Birmaher, B., Brent, D. A., Chiappetta, L., Bridge, J., Monga, S., & Baugher, M. (1999). Psychometric properties of the screen for child anxiety related emotional disorders scale (SCARED): A replication study. *Journal of the American Academy of Child and Adolescent Psychiatry, 38,* 1230–1236.

Birmaher, B., Khetarpal, S., Brent, D. A., Cully, M., Balach, L., Kaufman, J., & McKenzie-Neer, S. (1997). The Screen for Child Anxiety Related Emotional Disorders (SCARED): Scale construction and psychometric characteristics. *Journal of the American Academy of Child and Adolescent Psychiatry, 36,* 545–553.

Black, B., & Uhde, T. W. (1994). Treatment of elective mutism with fluoxetine: a double-blind, placebo-controlled study. *Journal of the American Academy of Child and Adolescent Psychiatry, 33,* 1000–1006.

Cobham, V. E., Dadds, M. R., & Spence, S. H. (1998). The role of parental anxiety in the treatment of childhood anxiety. *Journal of Consulting and Clinical Psychology, 66,* 893–905.

Compton, S. N., Grant, P. J., Chrisman, A. K., Gammon, P. J., Brown, V. L., & March, J. S. (2001). Sertraline in children and adolescents with social anxiety disorder: An open trial. *Journal of the American Academy of Child and Adolescent Psychiatry, 40,* 564–571.

Costello, E. J., & Angold, A. (1995). Epidemiology in anxiety disorders in children and adolescents. In J. S. March (Ed.), *Anxiety disorders in children and adolescents.* (pp. 109–124). New York: Guilford Press.

Dadds, M. R., Spence, S. H., Holland, D. E., Barrett, P. M., & Laurens, K. R. (1997). Prevention and early intervention for anxiety disorders: A controlled trial. *Journal of Consulting & Clinical Psychology, 65,* 627–635.

Davey, G. C. (1992). Classical conditioning and the acquisition of human fears and phobias: A review and synthesis of the literature. *Cognitive Therapy and Research, 2,* 389–396.

Dierker, L., Albano, A. M., Clarke, G. N., Heimberg, R. G., Kendall, P. C., Merikangas, K. R., Lewinsohn, P. M., Offord, D. R., Kessler, R., & Kupfer, D. J. (2001). Screening for anxiety and depression in early adolescence. *Journal of the American Academy of Child and Adolescent Psychiatry, 40,* 929–936.

D'Zurilla, T. J., & Goldfried, M. R. (1971). Problem-solving and behavior modification. *Journal of Abnormal Psychology, 78,* 107–126.

Eisen, A. R., Kearney, C. A., & Schaefer, C. E. (Eds.). (1995). *Clinical handbook of anxiety disorders in children and adolescents* (p. xvi). Northvale, NJ: Jason Aronson.

Emmelkamp, P. M., & Scholing, A. (1997). Anxiety disorders. In C. A. Essau & F. Petermann (Eds.), *Developmental psychopathology: Epidemiology, diagnostics and treatment* (pp. 219–263). London: Harwood Academic Publishers.

Essau, C., Conradt, J., and Peterman, F. (2000a). Frequency, comorbidity, and psychosocial impairment of anxiety disorders in German adolescents. *Journal of Anxiety Disorders, 14,* 263–279.

Essau, C., Conradt, J., and Peterman, F. (2000b). Frequency, comorbidity, and psychosocial impairment of specific phobia in adolescents. *Journal of Clinical Child Psychology, 29,* 221–231.

Ferdinand, R. F., & Verhulst, F. C. (1995). Psychopathology from adolescence into young adulthood: An 8-year follow-up study. *American Journal of Psychiatry, 152,* 586–594.

Flannery-Schroeder, E., & Kendall, P. C. (2000). Group and individual cognitive-behavioral treatments for youth with anxiety disorders: A randomized clinical trial. *Cognitive Therapy and Research, 24,* 251–278.

Gittelman, R., & Klein, D. F. (1984) Relationship between separation anxiety and panic and agoraphobic disorders. *Psychopathology, 17*[Suppl. 1], 56–65.

Graae, F., Milner, J., Rizzotto, L., & Klein, R. G. (1994). Clonazepam in childhood anxiety disorders. *Journal of the American Academy of Child and Adolescent Psychiatry, 33,* 372–376.

Gurley, D., Cohen, P., Pine, D. S. & Brook, J. (1996). Discriminating anxiety and depression in youth: A role for diagnostic criteria. *Journal of Affective Disorders, 39*(3), 191–200.

Hayward, C., Killen, J. D., Hammer, L. D., Litt, I. F., Wilson, D. M., Simmonds, B., & Taylor, C. B. (1992). Pubertal stage and panic attack history in sixth- and seventh-grade girls. *American Journal of Psychiatry, 149*(9), 1239–1243.

Hayward, C., Varady, S., Albano, A. M., Thieneman, M., Henderson, L., & Schatzberg, A. F. (2000). Cognitive behavioral group therapy for female socially phobic adolescents: Results of a pilot study. *Journal of the American Academy of Child and Adolescent Psychiatry, 39,* 721–726.

Herjanic, B., & Reich, W. (1982). Development of a structured psychiatric interview for children: Agreement between child and parent on individual symptoms. *Journal of Abnormal Child Psychology, 10,* 307–324.

Hodges, K., McKnew, D., Cytryn, L., Stern, L., & Kline, J. (1982). The Child Assessment Schedule (CAS) diagnostic interview: A report on the reliability and validity. *Journal of the American Academy of Child Psychiatry, 21,* 486–473.

Ialongo, N., Edelsohn, G., Werthamer-Larsson, L., Crockett, L., & Kellam, S. (1994). The significance of self-reported anxious symptoms in first-grade children. *Journal of Abnormal Child Psychology, 22,* 441–455.

Ialongo, N., Edelsohn, G., Werthamer-Larsson, L., Crockett, L., & Kellam, S. (1995). The significance of self-reported anxious symptoms in first grade children: Prediction to anxious symptoms and adaptive functioning in fifth grade. *Journal of Child Psychology and Psychiatry and Allied Disciplines, 36,* 427–437.

Kazdin, A. E. & Weisz, J. R. (1998). Identifying and developing empirically supported child and adolescent treatments. *Journal of Consulting and Clinical Psychology, 66,* 19–36.

Kearney, C. A., Albano, A. M., Eisen, A. R., Allan, W. D., & Barlow, D. (1997). The phenomenology of panic disorder in youngsters: An empirical study of a clinical sample. *Journal of Anxiety Disorders, 11,* 49–62.

Kendall, P. C. (1990). *The coping cat workbook.* Ardmore, PA: Workbook Publishers.

Kendall, P. C. (1992). Childhood coping: Avoiding a lifetime of anxiety. *Behavioural Change, 9,* 1–8.

Kendall, P. C. (1993). Cognitive-behavioral therapies with youth: Guiding theory, current status, and emerging developments. *Journal of Consulting and Clinical Psychology, 61,* 235–247.

Kendall, P. C. (1994). Treating anxiety disorders in children: Results of a randomized clinical trial. *Journal of Consulting and Clinical Psychology, 62,* 100–110.

Kendall, P. C. (2000). *The coping cat workbook (2nd ed.).* Ardmore, PA: Workbook Publishers.

Kendall, P. C., Chu, B., Gifford, A., Hayes, C., & Nauta, M. (1998). Breathing life into a manual. *Cognitive and Behavioral Practice, 5,* 177–198.

Kendall, P. C., Chu, B. C., Pimentel, S. S., & Choudhury, M. (2000). Treating anxiety disorders in youth. In P. C. Kendall (Ed.), *Child & adolescent therapy: Cognitive-behavioral procedures* (2nd ed., pp. 235–287). New York: Guilford Press.

Kendall, P. C., Flannery-Schroeder, E., Panicelli-Mindel, S. M., Southam-Gerow, M. A., Henin, A., & Warman, M. (1997). Therapy for youths with anxiety disorders: A second randomized clinical trial. *Journal of Consulting and Clinical Psychology, 65,* 366–380.

Kendall, P. C. & Southam-Gerow, M. (1996). Long-term follow-up of treatment for anxiety disordered youth. *Journal of Consulting and Clinical Psychology, 67,* 285–299.

Kendall, P. C. & Treadwell, K. R. H. (1996). Cognitive-behavioral treatment for childhood anxiety disorders. In E. D. Hibbs & P. S. Jensen (Eds.), *Psychosocial treatments for child and adolescent disorders, emprically based strategies for clinical practice* (pp. 23–41). Washington, DC: American Psychological Association.

Kessler, R. C., McGonagle, K., Zhao, S., Nelson, C. B., Hughes, M., Eshleman, S., Wittchen, H.-U., & Kendler, K. S. (1994). Lifetime and 12-month prevalence of *DSM-III-R* psychiatric disorders in the United States. *Archives of General Psychiatry, 51,* 8–19.

King, N. J., Tonge, B. J., Heyne, D., Pritchard, M., Rollings, S., Young, D., Myerson, N., & Ollendick, T. H. (1998). Cognitive-behavioral treatment of school refusing children: A controlled evaluation. *Journal of the American Academy of Child and Adolescent Psychiatry, 37,* 395–403.

Klein, R. G. (1995). Anxiety disorders. In M. Rutter, E. Taylor, & L. Hersov (Eds.), *Child and adolescent psychiatry: Modern approaches* (3rd ed., pp. 351–374). London: Blackwell Scientific Publications.

Klein, R. G., Koplewicz, H. S., & Kanner, A. (1992). Imipramine treatment of children with separation anxiety disorder. *Journal of the American Academy of Child and Adolescent Psychiatry, 31,* 21–28.

Kovacs, M. (1985). The Interview Schedule for Children (ISC). *Psychopharmacology Bulletin, 21,* 991–994.

Labellarte, M., Ginsburg, G., Walkup, J., & Riddle, M. (1999). The treatment of anxiety disorders in children and adolescents. *Biological Psychiatry, 46,* 1567–1578.

LaGreca, A. M. (1998). *Social anxiety scales for children and adolescents: Manual and instructions for the SASC, SASC-R, SAS-A and parent versions of the scales.* Unpublished manuscript available from author. University of Miami, Coral Gables, FL.

LaGreca, A. M., & Stone, W. L. (1993). Social Anxiety Scale for Children—Revised: Factor structure and concurrent validity. *Journal of Clinical Child Psychology, 22,* 17–27.

Last, C., Hansen, C., & Franco, N. (1998). Cognitive-behavioral treatment of school phobia. *Journal of the American Academy of Child and Adolescent Psychiatry, 37,* 404–411.

Last, C. G., Perrin, S., Hersen, M., & Kazdin, A. E. (1992). DSM-III-R anxiety disorders in children: Sociodemographic and clinical characteristics. *Journal of the American Academy of Child & Adolescent Psychiatry, 31,* 1070–1076.

Lewinsohn, P., Hops, H., Roberts, R., Seeley, J., & Andrews, J. (1993). Adolescent psychopathology: I. Prevalence and incidence of depression and other DSM-III-R disorders in high school students. *Journal of Abnormal Psychology, 102,* 133–144.

March, J. (1999). Pharmacotherapy of pediatric anxiety disorders: A critical review. In D. Beidel (Ed.), *Treating anxiety disorders in youth: Current problems and future solutions* (pp. 42–62). Washington, DC: Anxiety Disorders Association of America.

March, J. S., & Albano, A. M. (1996). Assessment of anxiety disorders in children and adolescents. In M. Riddle (Section Ed.), *Annual Review of Psychiatry* (pp. 405–427). Washington, DC: American Psychiatric Association Press.

March, J. S., Biederman, J., Wolkow, R., Safferman, A., Mardekian, J., Cook, E. H., Cutler, N. R., Dominguez, R., Ferguson, J., Muller, B., Riesenberg, R., Rosenthal, M., Sallee, F. R., Wagner, K. D., & Steiner, H. (1998) Sertraline in children and adolescents with obsessive-compulsive disorder: A multicenter randomized controlled trial [See comments; published erratum appears in *JAMA 283*(10), 1293]. *Journal of the American Medical Association, 280,* 1752–1756.

March, J., Parker, J., Sullivan, K., Stallings, P., & Conners, C. (1997). The Multidimensional Anxiety Scale for Children (MASC): Factor structure, reliability, and validity. *Journal of the American Academy of Child and Adolescent Psychiatry, 36,* 554–565.

March, J. S., & Sullivan, K. (1999). Test-retest reliability of the Multidimensional Anxiety Scale for Children. *Journal of Anxiety Disorders, 13*(4), 349–358.

Masia, C. L., Klein, R. G., Storch, E. A., & Corda, B. (2001). School-based behavioral treatment for social anxiety disorder in adolescents: Results of a pilot study. *Journal of the American Academy of Child and Adolescent Psychiatry, 40*(7), 780–786.

Mowrer, O. H. (1947). On the dual nature of learning: A reinterpretation of "conditioning" and "problem solving." *Harvard Educational Review, 17,* 102–148.

Mowrer, O. H. (1960). *Learning theory and the symbolic processes.* New York: John Wiley & Sons.

Muris, P., & Merckelbach, H. (2000). How serious are common childhood fears? II. The parent's point of view. *Behaviour Research and Therapy, 38,* 813–818.

Muris, P., Merckelbach, H., Mayer, B., van Brakel, A., Thissen, S., Moulaert, V., & Gadet, B. (1998). The Screen for Child Anxiety Related Emotional Disorders (SCARED) and traditional childhood anxiety measures. *Journal of Behavior Therapy and Experimental Psychiatry. 29,* 327–339.

Nelles, W. B., & Barlow, D. H. (1988). Do children panic? *Clinical Psychology Review, 8,* 359–372.

Olivares, J., García-López, L. J., Hidalgo, M. D., Beidel, D. C., Albano, A. M., & Turner, S. M. (Submitted). *Results at long-term among three psychological treatments delivered in the high-school setting for adolescents with generalized social phobia.*

Ollendick, T. H. (1983). Reliability and validity of the Revised Fear Survey Schedule for Children (FSSC-R). *Behaviour Research and Therapy, 21,* 685–692.

Ollendick, T. H., & King, N. J. (1998). Empirically supported treatments for children with phobic and anxiety disorders: Current status. *Journal of Clinical Child Psychology, 27,* 156–167.

Ollendick, T. H., Mattis, S. G., & King, N. J. (1994). Panic in children and adolescents: A review. *Journal of Child Psychology and Psychiatry, 35,* 113–134.

Pine, D. S., Cohen, P., Gurley, D., Brook, J., & Ma, Y. (1998). The risk for early-adulthood anxiety and depressive disorders in adolescents with anxiety and depressive disorders. *Archives of General Psychiatry, 55,* 56–64.

Puig-Antich, J., & Chambers, W. (1978). *The Schedule for Affective Disorders and Schizophrenia in School-Aged Children* (Kiddie-SADS). New York: New York State Psychiatric Institute.

Reiss, S., & McNally, R. J. (1985). Expectancy model of fear. In S. Reiss & R. R. Bootzin (Eds.), *Theoretical issues in behavior therapy* (pp. 107–121). San Diego, CA: Academic Press.

Reynolds, C. R., & Richmond, B. O. (1978). What I think and feel: A revised measure of children's manifest anxiety. *Journal of Abnormal Child Psychology, 6,* 271–280.

Riddle, M. A., Reeve, E. A., Yaryura-Tobias, J. A., Yang, H. M., Claghorn, J. L., Gaffney, G., Greist, J. H., Holland, D., McConville, B. J., Pigott, T., & Walkup, J. T. (2001). Fluvoxamine for children and adolescents with obsessive-compulsive disorder: a randomized, controlled, multicenter trial. *Journal of the American Academy of Child and Adolescent Psychiatry, 40,* 222–229.

RUPP Anxiety Study Group (2001). Fluvoxamine for the treatment of anxiety disorders in children and adolescents. *New England Journal of Medicine, 344,* 1279–1285.

Shaffer, D., Fisher, P., Dulcan, M., Davis, D., Piacentini, J., Schwab-Stone, M., Lahey, B., Bourdon, K., Jensen, P., Bird, H., Canino, G., & Regier, D. (1996). The NIMH Diagnostic Interview Schedule for Children, Version 2.3 (DISC 2.3): Description, acceptability, prevalence rates, and performance in the MECA study. *Journal of the American Academy of Child and Adolescent Psychiatry, 49,* 865–877.

Silverman, W. K., & Albano, A. M. (1996a). *The Anxiety Disorders Interview Schedule for DSM-IV: Parent Interview Schedule.* San Antonio, TX: The Psychological Corporation.

Silverman, W. K., & Albano, A. M. (1996b). *The Anxiety Disorders Interview Schedule for DSM-IV: Child Interview Schedule.* San Antonio, TX: The Psychological Corporation.

Silverman, W. K., & Eisen, A. R. (1992). Age differences in the reliability of parent and child reports of child anxious symptomatology using a structured interview. *Journal of the American Academy of Child and Adolescent Psychiatry, 31,* 117–124.

Silverman, W. K., Fleisig, W., Rabian, B., & Peterson, R. A. (1991). The Child Anxiety Sensitivity Index. *Journal of Clinical Child Psychology, 20,* 162–168.

Silverman, W. K., & Ginsburg, G. (1995). Specific phobia and generalized anxiety disorder. In J. S. March (Ed.), *Anxiety disorders in children and adolescents* (pp. 151–180). New York: Guilford Press.

Silverman, W. K., & Kurtines, W. M. (1997). Theory in child psychosocial treatment research: Have it or had it? A pragmatic alternative. *Journal of Abnormal Child Psychology, 25*(5), 359–366.

Silverman, W. K., Kurtines, W., Ginsburg, G., Weems, C., Lumpkin, P., & Carmichael, D. (1999). Treating anxiety disorders in children with group cognitive-behavioral therapy: A randomized clinical trial. *Journal of Consulting and Clinical Psychology, 67,* 995–1003.

Silverman, W. K., & Nelles, W. B. (1988). The Anxiety Disorders Interview Schedule for Children. *Journal of the American Academy of Child and Adolescent Psychiatry, 27,* 772–778.

Silverman, W. K., Saavadera, L. M., & Pina, A. A. (2001). Test-retest reliability of anxiety symptoms and diagnoses with the Anxiety Disorders Interview Schedule for DSM-IV: Child and Parent Versions. *Journal of the American Academy of Child and Adolescent Psychiatry, 40,* 937–944.

Simeon, J. G., Ferguson, H. B., Knott, V., Roberts, N., Gauthier, B., Dubois, C., & Wiggins, D. (1992). Clinical, cognitive, and neurophysiological effects of alprazolam in children and adolescents with overanxious and avoidant disorders. *Journal of the American Academy of Child and Adolescent Psychiatry, 31,* 29–33.

Spence, S. H., Donovan, C., & Brechman-Toussaint, M. (2000). The treatment of childhood social phobia: The effectiveness of a social skills training-based, cognitive-behavioural intervention, with and without parental involvement. *Journal of Child Psychology and Psychiatry and Allied Disciplines, 41*(6), 713–726.

Spielberger, C. (1973). *Preliminary manual for the State-Trait Anxiety Inventory for Children ("How I Feel Questionnaire").* Palo Alto, CA: Consulting Psychologists Press.

Stallings, P., & March, J. S. (1995). Assessment. In J. S. March (Ed.), *Anxiety disorders in children and adolescents* (pp. 125–147). New York: Guilford Press.

Strauss, C. C., & Last, C. G. (1993). Social and simple phobias in children. *Journal of Anxiety Disorders, 7,* 141–152.

Thyer, B. A., Parrish, R. T., Curtis, G. C., Nesse, R. M., & Cameron, O. G. (1985). Ages of onset of DSM-III anxiety disorders. *Comprehensive Psychiatry, 26,* 113–122.

Treadwell, K. R. H., & Kendall, P. C. (1996). Self-talk in anxiety-disordered youth: States of mind, content specificity, and treatment outcome. *Journal of Consulting and Clinical Psychology, 64,* 941–950.

Turner, S., & Heiser, N. (1999). Current status of psychological interventions for childhood anxiety disorders. In D. Beidel (Ed.), *Treating anxiety disorders in youth: Current problems and future solutions* (pp. 63–76). Washington, DC: Anxiety Disorders Association of America.

Watson, J. B., & Rayner, R. (1920). Conditioned emotional reactions. *Journal of Experimental Psychology, 3,* 1–14.

Weller, E. B., Weller, R. A., Rooney, M., & Fristad, M. A. (1999a). *Children's Interview for Psychiatric Syndromes (ChIPS).* Washington, DC: American Psychiatric Press.

Weller, E. B., Weller, R. A., Rooney, M., & Fristad, M. A. (1999b). *Parent Version—Children's Interview for Psychiatric Syndromes (P-ChIPS).* Washington, DC: American Psychiatric Press.

Wilens, T. E., Biederman, J., Baldessarini, R. J., Geller, B., Schleifer, D., Spencer, T. J., Birmaher, B., & Goldblatt, A. (1996). Cardiovascular effects of therapeutic doses of tricyclic antidepressants in children and adolescents. *Journal of the American Academy of Child and Adolescent Psychiatry, 35,* 1491–1501.

Wittchen, H., Stein, M., and Kessler, R. (1999). Social fears and social phobia in a community sample of adolescents and young adults: Prevalence, risk factors and co-morbidity. *Psychological Medicine, 29,* 309–323.

Chapter 13 ——————————————————————————

MOOD DISORDERS IN CHILDHOOD AND ADOLESCENCE

MARY A. FRISTAD, AMY E. SHAVER, AND KRISTEN E. HOLDERLE

Knowledge about childhood-onset mood disorders has increased dramatically over the past 10 to 20 years. Scientific inquiry initially focused on depressive disorders, then later turned to manic-depressive, or bipolar, disorders. In this chapter, we first review the phenomenology of depressive spectrum and bipolar spectrum disorders—their epidemiology, demographic differences, course, comorbidity, and risk factors. Next, we review psychosocial and biological treatments for preschoolers, school-age children, and adolescents with depression and bipolar disorders. Finally, we make recommendations for future developments in the assessment and comprehensive treatment of childhood-onset mood disorders. The literature search for this chapter was conducted using both PsycINFO and MEDLINE databases, using various combinations of keywords, including *depression, mood disorder, bipolar, children, adolescents, intervention,* and *treatment.* Additional sources were obtained from the references of reviewed articles and book chapters.

PHENOMENOLOGY OF DEPRESSION

Epidemiology

Early-onset mood disorders are now acknowledged as a serious concern. Rates of mild to moderate mood disorders among children and adolescents have been rising since the end of World War II, and symptoms are manifesting at younger ages (Lewinsohn, Rohde, Seeley, & Fischer, 1993; Ryan et al., 1992). Estimates suggest that approximately 1% of preschool age children in the general population meet diagnostic criteria for depression, with rates of 1% to 4% reported in clinically referred preschoolers (Kashani & Carlson, 1987; Kashani, Holcomb, & Orvaschel, 1986; Kashani, Ray, & Carlson, 1984). Clinically significant episodes of major depression are experienced by 0.4% to 2.5% of children and 0.4% to 8.3% of adolescents in the general population (Fleming & Offord, 1990). Among clinical samples, rates of depression range from 13% to 57% of children and 18% to 27% of adolescents (Kashani, Cantwell, Shekim, & Reid, 1982; Petersen et al., 1993; Poznanski & Mokros, 1994). Dysthymic disorder is also prevalent, with rates ranging from 0.6% to 1.7% for children and 1.6% to 8.0% among adolescents (Birmaher et al., 1996; Kashani et al., 1987; Lewinsohn, Clarke, Seeley, & Rohde, 1994; Lewinsohn, Hops, Roberts, Seeley, & Andrews, 1993).

Demographic Differences

Although depression can be found among children of all ages, it is more prevalent among adolescents. Rates of depressed mood tend to increase during early adolescence (ages 13 to 15), peaking at age 17 or 18 before declining to adult levels (Petersen et al., 1993; Poznanski & Mokros, 1994). Although rates of major depressive disorder are equal for boys and girls during childhood, gender differences emerge during adolescence, with rates among girls doubling that of boys, similar to the female–male ratio found in adults (Nolen-Hoeksema & Girgus, 1994). It is unclear whether racial differences exist in early-onset depression, but studies suggest gay and lesbian youth and adolescents living in rural areas may experience higher rates of depression (Petersen et al., 1993).

Course

The average length of a major depressive episode is 7 to 9 months, with 90% of episodes lasting less than 2 years. Rates of recurrence are high, similar to those in adults. Within 2 years of remission, 40% of children and adolescents will have another episode; 70% will experience a recurrence of the disorder within 5 years (Birmaher et al., 1996; Kovacs, Feinberg, Crouse-Novak, Paulauskas, & Finkelstein, 1984; Kovacs, Feinberg, Crouse-Novak, Paulauskas, Pollock, et al., 1984; Lewinsohn, Clarke, Seeley, & Rohde, 1994; Strober, Lampart, Schmidt, & Morrell, 1993). The average duration of dysthymic disorder is 4 years. Children and adolescents with dysthymic disorder have a 69% risk of developing major depressive disorder, with their first depressive episode usually occurring 2 to 3 years after the onset of dysthymic disorder. In addition, 13% of adolescents with dysthymic disorder and 20% to 30% of adolescents with major depressive disorder will develop bipolar disorder within 5 years after the onset of depression (Kovacs, Akiskal, Gatsonis, & Parrone, 1994; Kovacs, Feinberg, Crouse-Novak, Paulauskas, Pollock, et al., 1984; Rao et al., 1995; Strober et al., 1993). Childhood depression is a significant risk factor for depression and other disorders during adulthood. Earlier age of onset is associated with more frequent recurrence of depressive episodes and greater likelihood of conversion to bipolar disorder (Kovacs, 1996; Rao et al., 1995).

Comorbidity

Comorbid conditions are present more frequently in depressed youth than in depressed adults. Overall, 40% to 80% of depressed children and adolescents have one or more comorbid conditions. Anxiety disorders, conduct disorders, and substance use are common (Birmaher et al., 1996; Kovacs, Feinberg, Crouse-Novak, Paulauskas, & Finkelstein, 1984; Rohde, Lewinsohn, & Seeley, 1991). The presence of comorbidity predicts increased duration, severity, and recurrence of depressive episodes and is associated with decreased treatment response, poorer functional outcome, and less utilization of mental health services (Birmaher et al., 1996; Lewinsohn, Rohde, & Seeley, 1995; Rohde et al., 1991). Impairment in school performance and interpersonal relationships is common and may persist even after recovery, particularly among adolescents with recurrent depressive episodes (Birmaher et al., 1996; Rao et al., 1995; Strober et al., 1993).

Risk Factors

Genetic factors are associated with 50% of the variance in the transmission of mood disorders. In addition to parental psychopathology and familial loading for mood disorders, other factors associated with the onset of childhood and adolescent depression include family environment (e.g., high levels of conflict, rejection, communication problems), stressful life events (e.g., bereavement, parental divorce), and cognitive factors (e.g., low self-esteem, negative attributional style, cognitive distortions). The search for biological markers in depressed children and adolescents has focused on growth hormone secretion, serotonergic functioning, hypothalamic-pituitary-adrenal axis dysregulation, and sleep changes (see Birmaher et al. [1996] for a review).

PSYCHOSOCIAL TREATMENTS FOR DEPRESSION

Several forms of psychosocial treatments have been implemented with children and adolescents. Most frequently, these are adaptations of treatments proven successful in adult populations. The literature is still quite preliminary in terms of the numbers and types of treatments currently demonstrated to be empirically supported. According to the criteria presented by Lonigan and colleagues, for a psychosocial intervention to be classified as "well-established," there must be (a) at least two well-conducted group-design studies by different research teams demonstrating that the treatment is either superior to pill or psychological placebo or superior or equivalent to established treatments in studies with adequate statistical power, or (b) a series of more than nine single-case design studies that use good experimental design and compare the intervention to another treatment. In addition, treatment manuals must be used to guide the preferred intervention and the sample characteristics must be clearly specified.

Treatments that do not meet these criteria may be classified as "probably efficacious" if there are (a) two studies demonstrating that the treatment is more effective than a no-treatment control group (e.g., wait-list comparison), (b) two group-design studies meeting "well established" criteria conducted by the same investigator, or (c) more than three single-case design experiments that use good experimental design and compare the intervention to another treatment. Again, treatment manuals must be used for the preferred intervention and sample characteristics must be clearly specified (Lonigan, Elbert, & Bennett Johnson, 1998).

The vast majority of the published literature pertains to treatment of depressed adolescents. A limited number of studies have examined the treatment of depression in mixed-age groups (i.e., studies in which children and adolescents are grouped together or studies focusing on middle school students, commonly referred to as "tweens"). Few studies are available for the treatment of childhood depressive disorders, although some investigators have conducted intervention studies with elementary school students who have depressive symptoms. No data are available for the treatment of depression in preschool-age children.

Preschool-Age Children

Despite evidence that depressive symptoms can occur in early childhood, frequently among the children of depressed parents (Beardslee, Versage, & Gladstone, 1998; Kaslow, Deering, & Racusin, 1994), no published controlled studies address the treatment of depression in young children. Several interventions have been proposed to enhance attachment relationships between young children and their parents. Examples include infant–parent psychotherapy, toddler–parent psychotherapy, and parent–child interaction therapy. Although not directly targeting childhood depression, these therapies have been shown to foster secure attachment, increase positive interactions between parent and child, and promote development. In this way, they may act to lower risk for depression, particularly among children of depressed parents and children with attachment disorders (Sexson, Glanville, & Kaslow, 2001). Additionally, dynamic psychotherapeutic techniques such as play therapy may be recommended for depressed children to allow them to act out worries and concerns that they are unable to express verbally (Shafii & Shafii, 1992). There are, however, no data regarding the efficacy of dynamic therapy in relieving depression in children or adolescents.

School-Age Children

A limited number of controlled studies have tested the efficacy of interventions for depression in children. Cognitive-behavioral therapy (CBT) is the most thoroughly evaluated intervention, although some work has been done in the areas of family therapy and psychoeducation.

Cognitive-Behavioral Therapy

Cognitive-behavioral strategies for depressed students have been tested by several investigators. Stark, Reynolds, and Kaslow (1987) studied the effects of group therapy in a sample of twenty-nine 9- to 12-year-old elementary school students. The children were selected based on elevated Child Depression Inventory (CDI) scores indicating moderate to severe depressive symptoms. Participants were randomly assigned to attend 12 sessions of self-control therapy, behavioral problem-solving therapy, or a waiting-list control group. Structured treatment manuals were used, and procedures to ensure treatment adherence were implemented. Participants in both active treatment conditions showed significant improvement (both self-report and clinician-rated) at posttest, and the effects were maintained at an 8-week follow-up assessment (Stark et al., 1987). No significant differences were found between the two treatments, but the therapies were similar in many ways, including the use of activity-scheduling log sheets, reinforcement for the completion of homework assignments, and instruction in self-monitoring and increasing pleasant activities. The behavioral problem-solving therapy emphasized social relationships and group problem-solving discussions, including education about feelings and social skills. The self-control therapy used a more structured approach, including education about attributional style, setting realistic standards and goals, and increasing self-reinforcement while decreasing self-punishment. Limitations of the study include the short duration of the therapy (the 12 sessions were completed within a 5-week time period), the small sample size, and the lack of a family component. Additionally, the follow-up assessment occurred 7 weeks after the start of summer vacation, and the lack of a comparison group (because those on the wait list had received treatment) limits the interpretation of the results (Stark et al., 1987).

Weisz and associates (1997) evaluated an eight-session group cognitive-behavioral therapy program in a sample of 48 children in the third through sixth grade (mean age 9.6). Again, the children were not clinically depressed but were selected based on elevated scores on the CDI and the Child Depression Rating Scale—Revised (CDRS-R). The Primary and Secondary Control Enhancement Training (PASCET) program consisted of 50-minute small group sessions and focused on primary control (increasing rewards by changing objective conditions, such as engaging in pleasurable activities and building skills) and secondary control (adjusting one's beliefs or interpretations of conditions, such as reducing depressogenic thoughts, relaxation, positive imagery) coping techniques. Self-reported and clinician ratings of depressive symptoms, both immediately after treatment and at a 9-month follow-up assessment, decreased compared to a no-treatment control group. Limitations of this study include the small sample size and the lack of a placebo treatment condition (Weisz, Thurber, Sweeney, Proffitt, & LeGagnoux, 1997).

Kahn, Kehle, Jenson, and Clark (1990) evaluated the efficacy of three treatments for depressive symptoms in a sample of 68 middle school children ages 10 to 14. The children were selected from the entire school population based on elevated scores on the CDI and Reynolds Adolescent Depression Scale (RADS), as well as the Beck Depression Inventory (BDI). Following stratification for grade and sex, participants were randomly assigned to treatment groups and therapists. The cognitive-behavioral treatment was based on an adaptation of Lewinsohn's Coping With Depression course and included psychoeducation, skills training, and self-control strategies. Activities included goal setting, problem solving, and pleasant-event scheduling. Small groups of 2 to 5 students met for twelve 50-minute sessions over a 6- to 8-week time period. Participants assigned to the relaxation training (RT) condition also met in small groups for twelve 50-minute sessions over 6 to 8 weeks. They learned progressive relaxation techniques, mental imagery, and skills generalization. The self-modeling condition used 3-minute videotapes of the participants, edited to show them displaying nondepressed target behaviors (e.g., smiling, making positive comments, good eye contact). Participants participated in 12 individual 10- to 12-minute sessions during which they watched the videotapes of their own behavior. The remaining participants were assigned to a waiting list. Structured treatment manuals, workbooks, and handouts were used, and sessions were observed for treatment reliability. Compared to the wait-list controls, participants in all three treatment conditions improved significantly on measures of depressive symptoms and self-concept. No significant differences were found between the active treatments. Additionally, the majority of all participants in the active treatments moved into the nonclinical range on measures of depression, and those in the CBT and RT groups maintained this improvement at the 1-month follow-up assessment. Limitations of this study include the lack of an attention-placebo condition, small sample size, and short follow-up period.

Family Therapy

When working with children, it is essential that the child's developmental level and dependence on family members be taken into consideration. Stark and colleagues (Stark, Rouse, & Kurowski, 1994; Stark, Swearer, Kurowski, Sommer, & Bowen, 1996) have proposed a multidimensional treatment program for depressed children that incorporates parent training, family therapy, and teacher consultation, as well as interventions for the child. Games and developmentally appropriate homework assignments are used to make the individual and group therapy sessions engaging and to encourage generalization. Program goals include educating children about emotions, activity scheduling, progressive relaxation, anger management, problem solving, social skills training, cognitive restructuring, and self-monitoring. The parent-training component of the intervention is designed to enhance parenting skills and involve the parent as a collaborator in the child's treatment plan. The parent is taught to facilitate the child's use of newly acquired skills and completion of homework assignments. Parents are provided with a notebook and written materials describing the child's treatment sessions. Additionally, they are taught positive behavior management techniques, including noncoercive methods of discipline, anger management skills, empathic listening, positive reinforcement, and pleasant-activity scheduling. The family therapy component focuses on communication, problem solving, and conflict resolution skills (Stark et al., 1994; Stark et al., 1996). The procedures described address the multidimensional nature of childhood depression, targeting deficits in the cognitive, affective, and behavioral domains as well as addressing issues in the family context. Although controlled studies of this intervention have been published, the results of pilot studies appear promising (Stark et al., 1996).

Kaslow and Racusin (1994) describe the use of Interpersonal Family Therapy (IFT) with the families of depressed children and adolescents. This model combines elements from various theories, including family systems, cognitive-behavioral, attachment, and developmental psychopathology (Kaslow & Racusin, 1994). Family therapy approaches the child's depression as an interaction between the child's symptoms and family functioning. The family works together with the therapist to identify dysfunctional patterns of interaction that influence the child's depression and to recognize the effects of depression on the entire family. Therapy targets include understanding the child's symptoms and stressors, identifying and modifying maladaptive beliefs and negative messages within the family, developing strategies for affect regulation, supporting interpersonal and social functioning, building adaptive skills, and identifying and modifying dysfunctional interaction patterns within the family system (Kaslow & Racusin, 1994). Again, although no controlled studies are available, pilot research is described as promising.

Psychoeducational Programs

An alternative method for involving families in the treatment of depressed children is through psychoeducational programs. Brief family psychoeducational interventions are generally well received by participants (Asarnow, Jaycox, & Tompson, 2001) and often provide cost-effective means to distribute information about depression and involve parents in their child's treatment. Asarnow et al. (2001) described an intervention for fourth to sixth graders with depressive symptoms. Following nine sessions of group cognitive-behavioral therapy for the children, parents were invited to participate in a family education session designed to promote generalization. Parents were encouraged to help their children feel positively about their new skills and apply them in new situations, then participated in games with their children to learn CBT skills. A ceremony rewarding the children for their accomplishments was also held. Both parents and children rated the intervention as enjoyable and useful, and the majority of parents felt the single session was sufficient (Asarnow et al., 2001). The group is extending its work by developing family-focused intervention for children ages 8 to 14 (Asarnow et al., 2001). This program combines family psychoeducation about depression with family therapy to improve communication and build problem-solving skills. Techniques are drawn from cognitive-behavioral therapy and family systems theory.

Fristad and colleagues have developed a psychoeducational intervention for families of children with mood disorders. This program is designed to increase knowledge about mood disorders and lower expressed emotion within the family by improving communication and problem-solving skills and is presented as an adjunct to other child and family treatments (Fristad, Gavazzi, Centolella, & Soldano, 1996). A brief version of this intervention, a 90-minute multifamily psychoeducational workshop, was found to increase knowledge about mood disorders and decrease expressed emotion among 25 parents of 20 children and adolescents receiving inpatient treatment for mood disorders, with fathers showing most improvement (Fristad, Arnett, & Gavazzi, 1998). A longer, manual-driven program was developed for use in outpatient settings (Fristad, Gavazzi, & Soldano, 1998). The multiple-session multifamily psychoeducation group (MFPG) includes family segments as well as separate parent and child group activities. Slide presentations and workbooks are used to structure discussions. The content of parent sessions includes factual information about mood disorders (e.g., symptoms, comorbid conditions, risk factors for suicidal behavior, common myths) and treatment (e.g., medication management, side effects, working with treatment providers). The effects of mood disorders on family life are discussed, useful parenting techniques are presented (e.g., recognizing multiple realities, distinguishing between the child and the disorder, being supportive and patient without "analyzing" the child), and basic principles of healthy communication and stress management are reviewed. In addition, the parent groups also provide an important opportunity for social support, as parents are encouraged to share personal experiences (both positive and negative) and offer support to one another. The children's sessions provide opportunities for the children to interact with others who have similar problems and for presenting information about symptoms and symptom management. Skill-building activities (e.g., role plays, games) are an important component of the children's groups, as they focus on social skills, anger management, and conflict resolution techniques. Adolescent groups emphasize group discussion of the current and future impact of their mood symptoms. Common themes include peer issues, substance use, identity issues, suicidal ideation, and school performance. An uncontrolled pilot study of the six-session MFPG program demonstrated participant satisfaction with the program and improvements in family climate both immediately and 4 months after the intervention (Fristad, Gavazzi, et al., 1998). In a more recent controlled study, 35 children ages 8 to 11 and 47 parents were randomly assigned to either immediate MFPG plus treatment as usual (i.e., any ongoing treatment; MFPG + TAU, $n = 18$) or a 6-month wait-list condition plus treatment as usual (WLC + TAU, $n = 17$). At the 6-month follow-up, families who participated in MFPG + TAU reported (a) greater knowledge of mood symptoms in parents, (b) increased positive family interactions as reported by the parent, (c) increased perceptions of parental support in the children, and (d) increased access to appropriate services by families. Results support the need to further investigate the adjunctive role of psychoeducation in the treatment of childhood mood disorders (Fristad, Goldberg-Arnold, & Gavazzi, in submission).

Prevention

In addition to treatments for depression, several research teams have investigated the efficacy of interventions in preventing depression in children and adolescents. These interventions have included both *universal,* or primary, prevention strategies given to a large number of youth regardless of their risk for depression and *selective,* or targeted, strategies administered specifically to children and adolescents judged to be at higher risk for developing later clinical depression due to the presence of mild depressive symptoms or to parental mood disorders.

One prospective study (Jaycox, Reivich, Gillham, & Seligman, 1994) evaluated the effects of a manual-driven, cognitive-behavioral, targeted preventive intervention for fifth- and sixth-grade children judged to be at risk for depression based on mildly elevated levels (0.5 standard deviations above the mean) of self-reported depressive symptoms and perceived marital conflict at home. A total of 143 children (ages 10 to 13, mean 11.4 ± 0.7) participated in the study. Sixty-nine (69) children received one of three versions of the intervention (cognitive, social problem solving, or combined), 24 children were assigned to a wait-list condition, and 50 children completed assessments only, serving as a no-participation control group. Conditions were randomly assigned to schools rather than to individual children. Groups of 10 to 12 children met weekly for twelve 1½-hour sessions. The cognitive component of the intervention is based on traditional cognitive theory and focuses on modifying negative beliefs and challenging inaccurate, pessimistic causal attributions. The social problem-solving component incorporates elements of goal setting, problem solving, and coping techniques such as relaxation training. Both components are included in the combined condition. No differences were found between the three active treatment groups at posttest. Children who received treatment reported fewer depressive symptoms than the control group following the intervention and at a 6-month follow-up assessment. This effect was most evident among children with greater baseline symptomatology and may have been mediated by a reduction in the tendency to attribute negative events to stable, enduring causes (Jaycox et al., 1994). Treatment effects were maintained throughout the 2-year follow-up period, with children in the prevention group reporting lower levels of depressive symptoms than those in the control group. The intervention also produced lasting positive changes in explanatory style, which again served as a mediator for reduction in depressive symptoms (Gillham, Reivich, Jaycox, & Seligman, 1995). A planned 5-year follow-up assessment will provide even more information about the long-term ability of CBT to prevent depression in children (Jaycox et al., 1994).

Mixed-Age Studies

Two controlled treatment studies have examined the effects of cognitive-behavioral strategies in samples that included both children and adolescents. Unfortunately, the number of children versus adolescents was not specified in either study, and results were not examined for age differences. Therefore, it is somewhat unclear whether the results are equally applicable to children and adolescents. A third study, targeted to middle school students, spans the child/adolescent age divide.

Cognitive-Behavioral Treatment

Wood, Herrington, and Moore (1996) studied a clinical sample of 48 mild to moderately depressed outpatients ages 9 to 17 (mean age = 14.2). Participants completed from five to eight individual sessions of either cognitive-behavioral therapy or relaxation training. Treatment manuals were used and procedures were in place to check for treatment adherence. Participants in the CBT condition showed significant improvement on measures of depressive symptoms, self-esteem, and overall functioning at posttreatment compared to those in the relaxation training condition. These differences disappeared at the 3- and 6-month follow-up assessments, as participants in the relaxation therapy condition continued to improve and those in the CBT group relapsed. This development may be due to the more frequent use of additional treatments by those in the relaxation condition during the follow-up period or to the brevity of the CBT intervention (only five to eight sessions). Alternatively, the authors suggested the possible existence of three subgroups within those who received CBT: those who improved and recovered, those who improved, then relapsed, and those who never responded to treatment.

Vostanis, Feehan, Grattan, and Bickerton (1996) compared cognitive-behavioral therapy (CBT) to nonfocused intervention (NFI) in a clinical outpatient sample of 57 children ages 8 to 17 (mean 12.7). The CBT intervention included self-monitoring, social problem solving, and cognitive restructuring, and the NFI consisted of semi-structured interviews reviewing symptoms and social activities. A CBT treatment manual was used, and sessions were checked for treatment reliability. Children participated in nine individual sessions within a 6-month time period. The average number of sessions attended was six (range two to nine), completed on average in 3.5 months (range 1 to 5). Participants in both groups improved statistically and clinically on measures of depression, anxiety, self-esteem, and social functioning, with a majority no longer meeting diagnostic criteria at posttreatment assessment. These improvements were maintained at 9-month and 2-year follow-up assessments. No significant differences were found between groups. Individual self-esteem was the best predictor of outcome. The results may be partially due to the fact that only 50% of the CBT group completed the full intervention, including cognitive restructuring sessions.

Sommers-Flanagan and colleagues (2000) described a new school-based cognitive-behavioral psychoeducational intervention for depressed middle school students. The 12-week structured group sessions incorporate group discussion, role-playing activities, and homework assignments. Treatment targets include understanding the relationship between thoughts, emotions, and behaviors, pleasant-event scheduling, using relaxation techniques, learning basic problem-solving skills, social skills, communication skills, and goal setting (Sommers-Flanagan, Barrett-Hakanson, Clarke, & Sommers-Flanagan, 2000). Although no parent component is involved, the authors recommend facilitating parent awareness through the use of detailed consent forms and written descriptions of the topics to be covered in the group sessions. No treatment outcome studies have yet been conducted to evaluate the efficacy of this intervention.

Prevention

Beardslee et al. (1993) are conducting a longitudinal investigation of a targeted preventive family psychoeducation intervention for children of parents with mood disorders. The intervention is designed to promote resiliency among the children and prevent the onset of depression by enhancing parent and family functioning and reducing the impact of risk factors for depression (Gladstone & Beardslee, 2000). The manual-based psychoeducational intervention provides information about mood disorders and the potential risks to children of parents with mood disorders. Two formats have been evaluated. The clinician-based intervention consists of 6 to 10 sessions (including individual parent sessions, individual child sessions, and family meetings), with telephone contacts or refresher sessions available at 6- to 9-month intervals, and includes assessment of all family members. In addition to presenting the psychoeducational material, the clinician takes an active role in linking information to the family's experiences, discussing future difficulties the child might experience and ways to cope with them and enhance the child's adaptive capacities. The lecture intervention consists of two 1-hour lectures during which the psychoeducational material is presented, followed by question-and-answer periods. Children are not directly involved in this intervention (Beardslee et al., 1993). A total of 100 families with at least one parent with a mood disorder and a nondepressed 8- to 15-year-old child have participated in this program, and results based on subsets of this sample show positive results for both treatment groups (Gladstone & Beardslee, 2000). Both forms of the intervention promote increased parental knowledge about depression as well as about risk and resiliency factors in children. Both forms of intervention were perceived to be helpful. Parents in the clinician-led condition reported greater satisfaction with the intervention and more changes in their attitudes and behavior, including improved family communication (Beardslee et al., 1993). These changes were sustained over time, and additional improvements were often reported at 1- and 3-year follow-up assessments (Beardslee, Wright, Rothberg, Salt, & Versage, 1996). Children in the clinician-led condition reported greater understanding of their parent's disorder and also displayed higher levels of functioning and improved communication skills. Child functioning was correlated with parent behavior and attitude change (Beardslee et al., 1997). Although this research incorporates no control group, long-term follow-up assessments should reveal whether the intervention has an enduring effect on the prevention of depression in children of parents with mood disorder.

Adolescents

Cognitive-behavioral therapies are the only well-established psychosocial intervention for depression in adolescence at present. A variety of cognitive-behavioral techniques have been found to reduce depressive symptoms compared to no-treatment control conditions. Meta-analytic studies suggest that CBT is effective in treating adolescent depression and dysthymia, with effect sizes ranging from 0.41 to 1.70 immediately after treatment and from 0.60 to 1.69 at follow-up assessments ranging from 1 to 9 months (Marcotte, 1997; Reinecke, Ryan, & DuBois, 1998). Results further indicate that CBT may be more effective with older than younger adolescents and that adolescents may benefit more if a parent component is included in the treatment. Finally, results suggest that differences between CBT and other treatments such as relaxation training and self-modeling therapy may be small in the short term, but that youth who receive CBT maintain gains longer than other groups (Marcotte, 1997).

Cognitive-Behavioral Therapy

Several studies have investigated the efficacy of cognitive-behavioral treatment of depressive symptoms among high school student populations. Reynolds and Coats (1986) studied the relative effects of cognitive-behavioral therapy (CBT) and relaxation training (RT) in a sample of 30 moderately depressed high school students (mean age 15.6). The students, selected based on elevated scores on the BDI and RADS, attended 10 small-group sessions over a 5-week time period. Adolescents in both the CBT and RT groups showed statistically and clinically significant reductions in depressive symptoms at posttreatment and at a 5-week follow-up assessment compared to those on a wait list. Relaxation training was more effective at reducing anxiety symptoms, and CBT had more impact on raising academic self-concept (Reynolds & Coats, 1986). Limitations of this study included small sample size and the use of a single therapist for all treatment groups and assessments.

Lewinsohn, Clarke, Hops, and Andrews (1990) developed the cognitive-behavioral Adolescent Coping With Depression Course (CWD-A). Treatment manuals and participant workbooks are included, and a parent course parallels the adolescent curriculum. Several studies have been published evaluating the relative efficacy of CWD-A with and without the parent involvement. The first trial included 59 high school students (ages 14 to 18), who met *DSM-III* or research diagnostic criteria (RDC) for a diagnosis of depression based on the Epidemiologic version of the Schedule for Affective Disorders and Schizophrenia for School-Aged Children (K-SADS-E) diagnostic interview. They were randomly assigned to either wait-list control, the CWD-A with parent intervention, or CWD-A alone. Adolescents in the active treatments attended fourteen 2-hour group sessions over a 7-week time period. The adolescent intervention included sessions focused on relaxation training, pleasant-event scheduling, identifying and modifying negative and irrational thoughts, social skills, communication, and problem solving. The parent group consisted of seven 2-hour group sessions and provided an overview of the skills the adolescents learned. Both treatment groups showed clinically and statistically significant improvements in depressed symptoms and related behaviors, and they maintained these improvements up to a 24-month follow-up assessment, with low rates of relapse (Lewinsohn et al., 1990). The only differences found between the active treatments were in parent perception of adolescent problems, as reported on the Child Behavior Checklist (CBCL). Parents who participated in the intervention perceived their children as better functioning immediately posttreatment.

This difference disappeared at the 24-month follow-up assessment, as the scores of the adolescents in the CWD-A-only group improved to match the level of those with parent involvement. This suggests that although parent involvement may not provide greater relief in symptomatology, it may facilitate earlier improvements in parent perceptions of the child's recovery (Lewinsohn et al., 1990). Adolescents with milder forms of depression were more likely to recover after treatment (Clarke et al., 1992), but those with severe depression showed equal or greater average reductions in depressed symptomatology (Lewinsohn, Rohde, & Seeley, 1998). The second clinical trial tested a revised version of CWD-A, with adolescents attending sixteen 2-hour sessions over 8 weeks, and parent involvement increased to nine 2-hour sessions in that time period (Lewinsohn, Clarke, & Rohde, 1994; Lewinsohn, Clarke, Rohde, Hops, & Seeley, 1996). Booster sessions (up to two 2-hour sessions) were added to the protocol and offered every 4 months for a period of 2 years following the intervention (Lewinsohn et al., 1996). Ninety-six adolescents (ages 14 to 18) meeting *DSM-III-R* criteria for depression or dysthymia were randomly assigned to treatment for adolescents only, treatment for adolescents with parent involvement, or wait-list control. As in the first trial, adolescents in both active treatments had significantly better outcomes than those on the waiting list, but parent involvement offered no additional benefit. Among adolescents who participated in the CWD-A course, 67% did not meet diagnostic criteria at posttreatment compared to 48% of those on the wait list, and 98% had recovered by 24-month follow-up (Clarke, Rohde, Lewinsohn, Hops, & Seeley, 1999; Lewinsohn et al., 1996; Lewinsohn et al., 1998). Adolescents who completed treatment were randomly assigned to three conditions for the follow-up period: booster sessions every 4 months, assessments-only sessions every 4 months, and assessments every 12 months. No significant differences in rates of recurrence of depressive episode were found between the groups at 12- or 24-month follow-up assessments. However, among those adolescents who had not recovered at posttreatment, those who received booster sessions recovered much more quickly (mean time 23.5 weeks) than those who received assessments only (mean time 67.0 weeks; (Clarke et al., 1999). This contrasts with the finding that participation in continuation sessions of adolescent cognitive behavioral therapy for 6 months after remission from major depressive episode lowers the risk of relapse compared to routine aftercare (Kroll, Harrington, Jayson, Fraser, & Gowers, 1996). These data were based on a comparison to a historical control group, however, and need replication.

Brent et al. (1996) conducted a large clinical trial to evaluate the relative efficacy of individual cognitive-behavioral therapy (CBT), systemic behavior family therapy (SBFT), and nondirective supportive treatment (NST) in a clinical population. Each treatment condition consisted of 12 to 16 weekly 1-hour sessions, followed by 2 to 4 monthly booster sessions. Additionally, all adolescents in the study received three sessions of family psychoeducation. Through an outpatient mood and anxiety disorders clinic, 107 adolescents (ages 13 to 18) meeting *DSM-III-R* criteria for major depression were recruited. Following the active-treatment stage, more adolescents in the CBT group had achieved remission than those in SBFT or NST, and CBT produced relief of depressive symptoms faster than the other two treatments, although no differences were found in suicidality or levels of functioning (Brent et al., 1997). However, a 2-year follow-up assessment, no differences were found between groups in rates of remission, recovery, recurrence, or functioning level. Instead, baseline severity of depression and the presence of parent-child conflict were the best predictors of long-term outcome (Birmaher et al., 2000). Poor initial treatment response was predicted by greater severity of initial depression, clinical referral (versus self-referral in response to advertisement), comorbid anxiety disorders, and higher levels of hopelessness and cognitive distortions (Brent et al., 1998). Rapid positive response to treatment, defined as a 50% reduction in BDI score by the second treatment session, predicted better outcome at posttreatment, as well as at 1- and 2-year follow-up assessments (Renaud et al., 1998).

Fine, Forth, Gilbert, and Haley (1991) evaluated the relative efficacy of group social skills training (SST) and therapeutic support groups (TSGs) in a sample of 66 adolescents (ages 13 to 17) meeting *DSM-III-R* criteria for major depression or dysthymia. The social skills training intervention was based on a treatment manual and included sessions focused on recognizing emotions, assertiveness, conversational skills, giving feedback, and social problem solving. The therapeutic support groups emphasized sharing common concerns, expressing mutual support, and improving self-concept through reinforcement of personal strengths. Immediately following treatment, adolescents in the therapeutic support groups showed greater reduction of depressed symptoms and more gains in self-concept. At the 9-month follow-up assessment, the groups were equal, suggesting that while those in the therapeutic support groups maintained their gains, those in the social skills group continued to improve (Fine et al., 1991). The authors suggest a possible latency period before depressed adolescents can use newly learned cognitive skills and perceive an impact on their mood. Perhaps the adolescent's symptoms must improve to some extent before they can be truly successful in using cognitive techniques. This study has some significant limitations, including the omission of an attention-placebo or a waiting-list control group and the lack of true random assignment to treatment conditions. Additionally, a significant proportion of participants in both groups were also receiving concurrent psychotherapy, medications, or both.

Cognitive-behavioral therapy appears to be effective in treating adolescent depression even when not delivered in traditional individual or group therapy formats. Ackerson, Sogin, McKendree-Smith, and Lyman (1998) tested the efficacy of cognitive bibliotherapy in a group of 22 adolescents (ages 14 to 18) with elevated scores on the CDI and Hamilton Rating Scale for Depression (HRSD). Adolescents were randomly assigned to an immediate-treatment or delayed-treatment control condition. Those in the immediate-treatment condition were given a self-help book (based on cognitive therapy) to read, and weekly phone calls were made to collect information about the number of pages read and exercises completed. Adolescents in the delayed-treatment condition received weekly phone calls (Ackerson et al., 1998). Adolescents in the treatment condition experienced improvements in depressive symptoms and number of dysfunctional thoughts. They demonstrated good comprehension and retention of the information at posttreatment and at a 1-month follow-up assessment. The adolescents in the delayed-treatment condition experienced similar results at posttreatment, with the majority moving into the nonclinical range on self-report measures of depression (Ackerson et al., 1998).

Interpersonal Therapy (IPT)

Next to cognitive-behavioral therapy, interpersonal therapy (IPT) is the best supported psychosocial treatment for adolescent depression. Two groups of investigators are currently studying the efficacy of IPT in depressed adolescents, and initial results have been very promising. Further controlled studies are needed to replicate the findings and to allow generalization to non-Hispanic populations.

Mufson and colleagues developed a modified version of interpersonal therapy for adolescents (IPT-A) ages 12 to 18 (Moreau, Mufson, Weissman, & Klerman, 1991; Mufson, Moreau, & Weissman, 1996). The intervention consists of 12 weekly 45-minute individual psychotherapy sessions, with telephone contacts as necessary when sessions are missed. The primary treatment goals are to decrease depressive symptomatology and improve interpersonal functioning by enhancing communication skills in significant relationships. The treatment manual addresses problems dealing with grief, role transitions, interpersonal role disputes, interpersonal deficits, and single-parent families. Parents are involved in all phases of therapy. Results from an open clinical trial involving 14 clinically depressed adolescents (ages 12 to 18, mean age 15.4, primarily Hispanic females) were promising. At posttreatment, fewer symptoms of depression were reported, 90% were no longer depressed according to self-report and clinician ratings, and no adolescents met *DSM-III* or *DSM-III-R* criteria for depressive disorder. Improvements in overall functioning level were also noted (Mufson et al., 1996; Mufson et al., 1994). The majority of participants maintained improvements at 1-year follow-up assessment. Only 1 of 9 (11%) adolescents met criteria for mood disorder at the follow-up assessment, and she had completed only three sessions of therapy (Mufson & Fairbanks, 1996). This open trial was followed by a controlled clinical trial comparing IPT-A to a clinical monitoring condition (Mufson, Weissman, Moreau, & Garfinkel, 1999). Forty-eight adolescents (ages 12 to 18, mean 15.8, 73% female, 71% Hispanic) who met *DSM-III-R* criteria for major depressive disorder were randomly assigned to treatment and control groups. The IPT-A intervention met for 12 weekly 45-minute sessions, with additional weekly telephone contacts during the first month of treatment. The clinical monitoring condition required one 30-minute session per month, during which the clinician listened supportively to the adolescent and asked about depressive symptoms, school attendance, and suicidality. Therapists in both conditions were available for contact between sessions if necessary. After 12 weeks, adolescents who participated in IPT-A group showed fewer symptoms of depression and greater improvement in social functioning and problem solving (Mufson et al., 1999). However, the strength of these findings is limited by the small sample size, the high attrition rate in the control condition, and the exclusive use of self-report measures of social functioning. Of note, the control condition did not provide less therapist contact than the treatment condition. Although these results are promising, future research is needed to evaluate the relative efficacy of IPT-A compared to other treatments of depression, particularly CBT and antidepressant medications, and to evaluate the efficacy in populations other than late-adolescent Hispanic females.

Rossello and Bernal (1996) developed another adaptation of interpersonal therapy and compared it to an adaptation of cognitive-behavioral therapy in a sample of depressed Puerto Rican adolescents. Treatment manuals for both CBT and IPT were translated into Spanish and adapted to be more culturally sensitive to Puerto Rican values such as importance of family and personal contacts (Rossello & Bernal, 1996). Their version of IPT focuses on interpersonal relationships in four problem areas: grief, interpersonal disputes, role transitions, and interpersonal deficits. The primary goals are to improve interpersonal relationships, reduce symptoms, and enhance emotional well-being. Expression of feelings, communication skills, and problem-solving skills may be included in the therapy. Their CBT focuses on the relationships between thoughts, daily activities, interactions with other people, and mood. The primary goals are to alleviate symptoms of depression, shorten depressive episodes, teach techniques for preventing future depression, and develop a greater sense of control over one's life. Activities include self-monitoring, identifying and modifying thinking errors, pleasant-activity scheduling, developing a social support system, and communication and social skills training (Rossello & Bernal, 1996). A clinical trial compared the relative efficacy of CBT and IPT in a sample of 71 depressed Puerto Rican adolescents (ages 13 to 18, mean = 14.7) meeting *DSM-III-R* criteria for depression. Adolescents were randomly assigned to 12 weekly 1-hour sessions of either IPT or CBT or to a waiting list. Following treatment, adolescents in both CBT and IPT groups were less depressed than those on the wait list. Clinically significant improvement was observed, with 82% of those in the IPT group and 59% of those in CBT reporting scores in the nonclinical range (17 or below) on the CDI. Adolescents in IPT also showed improvements in self-esteem and social adjustment (Rossello & Bernal, 1999). No significant differences were found between CBT and IPT at posttreatment or a 3-month follow up assessment, although a nonsignificant trend toward further improvement in depressive symptomatology was noted in the CBT group. Limitations of the study include the small sample size, exclusive use of self-report outcome measures, failure to assess for comorbid conditions, and lack of a control condition at the follow-up assessment (Rossello & Bernal, 1999).

Family Therapy

Diamond and Siqueland (1995) designed a family therapy model for use with depressed adolescents. The model is based primarily on attachment theory and builds on concepts from structural family therapy and multidimensional family therapy. The therapy focuses on dysfunctional cycles of family interaction that occur in response to the adolescent's depressive symptoms and that act to perpetuate the depression. The therapist works to identify and disrupt these cycles and engage family members in new healthy ways of relating to one another within the therapy session. In this way, the family can begin to restore parent-child attachment relationships, improving family functioning and perhaps reducing the risk of future relapse (Diamond & Siqueland, 1995). In addition to family sessions, individual sessions with parents may focus on parenting practices, marital distress, and parent psychopathology and stress. Individual sessions with adolescents address issues of trust, as well as building skills in problem solving, conflict resolution, and emotion management. Other goals of treatment include strengthening the family's social support system and beginning to negotiate normative developmental issues of adolescence such as autonomy and parental authority (Diamond & Sique-land, 1995). Although no treatment outcome studies have yet been published, the results of a randomized pilot study are promising. Among a sample of 32 adolescents, teens who completed a 12-week intervention reported greater reductions in depressive symptomatology than those on a wait list (Diamond & Siqueland, 2001).

As previously described, Brent et al. (1996) compared the relative efficacy of systemic behavior family therapy (SBFT), cognitive behavior therapy (CBT), and nondirective supportive therapy (NST) in a clinical sample of adolescents. Immediately after treatment, CBT appeared more effective than SBFT and NST in relieving symptoms of depression (Brent et al., 1997). At the 2-year follow-up assessment, no differences in the rates of recovery, recurrence of depressive episodes, or overall level of functioning were found (Birmaher et al., 2000). The results of the follow-up assessment also suggest that SBFT may reduce family conflict and parent-child relationship problems more than does CBT (Kolko, Brent, Baugher, Bridge, & Birmaher, 2000).

Lewinsohn and colleagues also included a parent component in their Coping With Depression course. Parents attended eight 2-hour sessions, in which they learned the same communication and problem-solving skills taught to the adolescents. Goals of this component were to reduce parent-child conflict and increase the amount of support and positive reinforcement adolescents received for using their new skills (Lewinsohn et al., 1996). Results of two studies indicated that parent participation provided no additional improvement in adolescent depressive symptoms (Clarke et al., 1999; Lewinsohn et al., 1990). One possible explanation for this lack of efficacy is that parents may not have been fully involved in the intervention, as it was designed to be a supplement to the adolescent course. The authors report inconsistent attendance at parent sessions, especially for fathers (Clarke et al., 1999). A more integrated approach might prove more successful. Also, the effects of parallel parent sessions might be more potent with a younger age group.

Psychoeducational Programs

Brent, Poling, McKain, and Baugher (1993) studied the effects of a single 2-hour manual-based psychoeducation session. Sixty-two parents of 34 adolescents seen in an outpatient program for suicidal adolescents with mood disorders (mean age 15.4) participated in the program. They received information about the symptoms and course of depression (emphasizing its recurrent and chronic nature), medications and their side effects, and signs of recurrence of depressive episodes and suicidality. Additionally, the genetic components of depression were emphasized, and referrals were provided for parents with untreated mood disorders as necessary. Results indicated improvements in parent knowledge of adolescent depression and positive evaluations of the program by the participants (Brent et al., 1993).

Prevention

Clarke, Hawkins, Murphy, and Sheeber (1993) evaluated two short-term school-based interventions administered as part of mandatory high school health classes. As primary prevention strategies, the adolescents were included regardless of their risk for depression and were randomly assigned by class to receive the intervention or a control condition (curriculum as usual). The first intervention was a three-session educational intervention providing information about the symptoms, causes, and treatments of depression, delivered in three structured lectures and two 20-minute videotapes. The sample consisted of 672 ninth and tenth graders (mean age 15 years). The second intervention consisted of a five-session skill-training program, with one introductory educational lecture and 20-minute videotape followed by four sessions of a behavioral intervention emphasizing pleasant-activity scheduling. The sample for the second intervention consisted of 380 ninth and tenth graders (mean age 15 years). Results showed no lasting effects of intervention on depressive symptoms, on knowledge about depression, on attitudes toward treatment, or on the likelihood of seeking treatment (Clarke et al., 1993).

Hains and Ellmann (1994) also examined a school-based primary prevention program. A self-selected sample of 21 high school students (grades 9 to 12) was randomly assigned to a stress-inoculation training group or a waiting-list control group. The active intervention used a number of cognitive-behavioral strategies, including self-monitoring, cognitive restructuring, problem solving, and progressive muscle relaxation. Results indicated positive effects on levels of depression, anxiety, and anger, particularly for those adolescents with higher levels of baseline symptoms. These effects were maintained at a 2-month follow-up assessment (Hains & Ellmann, 1994).

Clarke et al. (1995) evaluated a cognitive-behavioral targeted prevention program for adolescents with elevated depressive symptomatology but no current depressive disorder. A sample of 172 ninth- and tenth-grade adolescents (mean age 15.3 years) was identified as potentially at risk for developing depression following a two-stage schoolwide screening procedure. The adolescents were randomly assigned to a "usual care" control condition or 15 sessions of group cognitive-behavioral therapy (the Coping with Stress Course) over 5 weeks. The intervention produced short-term reductions in self-reported depressive symptoms, increases in overall functioning level, and lower rates of diagnosable major depression and dysthymia up to 12 months after the end of the intervention.

Summary

There is a significant need to evaluate individual and family therapies in clinical populations of depressed preschoolers, school-age children, and adolescents. To date, a variety of cognitive-behavioral approaches appear to be effective in the treatment of depression in adolescence. Studies of interpersonal therapy and family psychoeducation are promising. Well-designed studies of other interventions are needed to clarify which components of active treatments are most effective for which age groups of children and adolescents. Additionally, to move from efficacy to effectiveness studies, it will be important to measure the impact of treatment on youth with varying comorbid disorders and in varying clinical settings.

BIOLOGICAL TREATMENTS FOR DEPRESSION

Biological treatments for depression include antidepressants, herbal (over-the-counter) remedies, phototherapy, and electroconvulsive therapy (ECT). Most studies assessing the safety and efficacy of these treatments have been done with adults; therefore, evidence of their clinical utility in children is sparse. Clinicians who work with children must be careful not to directly extrapolate from adult treatment studies. It is important for treatment providers to take developmental considerations into account when making treatment decisions for children and adolescents (American Academy of Child and Adolescent Psychiatry, 1998). The following section will review the safety and efficacy literature on biological treatments for depression in children and adolescents.

Preschool-Age Children

Between 1991 and 1995, the prevalence of psychotropic medication treatment for preschool-age children increased dramatically (Zito, Safer, dosReis, & Gardner, 2000). Next to stimulants, antidepressants were the second most commonly prescribed medication for this population. Of the antidepressants prescribed for this age group, tricyclics accounted for the majority, followed by SSRIs. Although the use of psychotropic medications is rapidly increasing in this population, no outcome studies have been done to evaluate the dosage, efficacy, or safety of such agents with this population. Randomized, double-blind controlled studies are needed to determine the safety and efficacy of psychotropic medications for preschool-age children.

School-Age Children

Antidepressants

At best, antidepressant treatment for depressed youth is only moderately effective (Wagner & Ambrosini, 2001). Older drugs include tricyclic antidepressants (TCAs) and monoamine oxidase inhibitors (MAOIs); newer antidepressants are selective serotonin uptake inhibitors (SSRIs) and serotonin-norepinephrine reuptake inhibitors (SNRIs). Currently, there have been no significant results indicating the superiority of either TCAs or MAOIs. SSRIs are considered the treatment of choice for children and adolescents with depression, as they have received the most positive outcomes in treatment studies (American Academy of Child and Adolescent Psychiatry, 1998; Ryan & Varma, 1998; Wagner & Ambrosini, 2001). More detailed information about the various medications follows.

Tricyclic antidepressants (TCAs) were the first antidepressants studied in children (Weller & Weller, 2000). The persistent finding in the literature has been that TCAs are not superior to placebo in children (Wagner & Ambrosini, 2001). In addition, they have potentially severe side effects (i.e., cardiac problems and sudden death) and overdose lethality. Recent consensus among researchers and practitioners is that TCAs should not be a first-line treatment for children with depression (American Academy of Child and Adolescent Psychiatry, 1998; Wagner & Ambrosini, 2001).

Data regarding the efficacy of MAOIs are lacking for depressed children. MAOIs have severe side effects, including drug–diet and drug–drug interactions, making them dangerous for this population. According to a treatment algorithm proposed by Hughes et al. (1999), MAOIs should be used only in patients who fail to respond to earlier stages of treatment and in situations where the benefits outweigh the risks. Even then, they should be used with extreme caution (Hughes et al., 1999).

SSRIs (fluoxetine, sertraline, paroxetine, fluvoxamine) experienced a 4-fold increase in use with children between the years 1989 and 1994 (Emslie et al., 1997). Although data supporting their efficacy are limited, multiple studies are currently under way. The promising potential of these antidepressants, combined with a low incidence of side effects, has earned them designation as the first-line treatment for children and adolescent with MDD (American Academy of Child and Adolescent Psychiatry, 1998; Hughes et al., 1999; Wagner & Ambrosini, 2001; Weller & Weller, 2000). The most common side effects associated with SSRI use include dry mouth, somnolescence, headache, and constipation (Weller & Weller, 2000).

SNRIs (i.e., venlafaxine) are novel antidepressants that inhibit the reuptake of serotonin, norepinephrine, and, to a lesser extent, dopamine (Mandoki, Tapia, Tapia, & Sumner, 1997). Its efficacy for adults has been investigated in several short- and long-term studies, and it appears to be well tolerated. Venlafaxine is rapidly absorbed by the body and has a low side effect profile, making it an ideal drug to test on the child and adolescent population (Mandoki et al., 1997). Further studies are needed to test the safety and efficacy of this drug for child and adolescent populations.

Herbal Remedies

Medical herbalism is the treatment of illness with plants, parts of plants, or plant extracts (Ernst, Rand, & Stevinson, 1998). Anecdotally, a number of plants have been named as having antidepressant properties (e.g., wild oats, lemon balm, ginseng, wood betony, basil), yet Saint-John's-wort (*Hypericum perforatum*) is the only herbal treatment with empirical support. In a meta-analysis of 23 randomized controlled trials (RCTs) including a total of 1,757 adult outpatients with mild to moderate depression, Linde et al., (1996) found Saint-John's-wort was significantly more effective than placebo and appeared to have an efficacy similar to that of standard antidepressants. Compared to traditional antidepressant therapies, Saint-John's-wort has a lower incidence of side effects, causing some to speculate that it may be a safe and effective alternative in the treatment of mild or moderate depression (White, 2000).

There are currently no studies that examine the use of herbal remedies in children or adolescents with depression. Although many herbal products are marketed toward children and adolescents, little is known about their safety and efficacy in this age group (Jurgens, 1999). Doses are usually determined as fractions of adult doses with no clearly defined criteria. In addition, clinical trials are difficult because the content of herbal products is variable. Recent evidence suggests herbal remedies affect the rate of metabolism and extent of absorption of other psychiatric medication; therefore, care should be taken when combining herbal and standard treatments. Saint-John's-wort in particular should not be combined with SSRIs, TCAs, or MAOIs. Such combination may lead to a hypertensive crisis or serotonin syndrome (Jurgens, 1999). Additionally, there is evidence that Saint-John's-wort interferes with birth control pills, a very relevant complication for adolescent females on birth control. Before herbal remedies can be considered a first-line treatment for psychiatric disorders, they must be more strictly regulated; they must demonstrate efficacy in the same rigorous clinical trials as other pharmaceutical agents; and quality and safety issues must be addressed (Jurgens, 1999).

Phototherapy

Light therapy is most often used as a treatment for seasonal affective disorder (SAD). In SAD, mood changes and neurovegetative symptoms regularly occur during winter months and disappear completely during spring and summer (Swedo et al., 1997). The most widely used protocol for light therapy is a light box with 10,000 lux at a distance of 1 foot from the patient's face for 30 minutes a day. In resistant cases, treatment can be extended up to 1 hour. Patients may respond better to treatment in the morning hours (American Academy of Child and Adolescent Psychiatry, 1998).

Electroconvulsive Therapy (ECT)

Information about electroconvulsive therapy (ECT) in children and adolescents is limited (Walter & Rey, 1997). In a treatment algorithm proposed by Hughes et al. (1999), ECT was designated as a last-resort therapy for patients who had not improved clinically in any of six preceding stages or who had intolerable side effects and were continuing to experience severe and disabling depression. Of note, some states have statues limiting the ability to perform ECT. In Texas, for example, it is illegal to perform ECT on patients younger than 16 years (Hughes et al., 1999).

Mixed-Age Studies

Antidepressants

Evidence concerning the efficacy of tricyclic antidepressants in child and adolescent depression is mixed, and studies comparing active treatment to placebo have often been small and variable in quality. In a meta-analysis, Hazell, O'Connell, Heathcote, Robertson, and Henry (1995) pooled the results of 12 randomized controlled trials comparing tricyclic antidepressants with placebo. Overall, they found no significant differences in levels of improvement between the actively treated group and the placebo group. In some studies, the placebo response rate was 50% or higher. Although a high placebo effect is not uncommon in drug studies, a 50% response rate is higher than usual. This may indicate that children and adolescents with major depression can be expected to respond to other treatment strategies, including removal from stressors, the development of a treatment alliance, and treatment planning (Hazell et al., 1995).

One mixed-age study provided promising results for the efficacy of fluoxetine in children and adolescents. In an 8-week, double-blind study of children and adolescent outpatients (ages 7 to 17 years) with nonpsychotic MDD, Emslie et al. (1997) found greater improvement of depressive symptoms in the active-treatment group compared to placebo. Overall, participant responses to this medication were similar to those found in adult studies. There were no differences between patient responses to fluoxetine or placebo based on age or sex. Although the depressive symptoms of children in the fluoxetine group did improve over the length of the trial, complete remission of depressive symptoms was uncommon (Emslie et al., 1997).

In a double-blind, placebo-controlled, 6-week study, Mandoki et al. (1997) tested the efficacy of venlafaxine in 40 outpatient children and adolescents (8 to 18 years of age). Three important issues related to the use of venlafaxine in children and adolescents were addressed in this study. First, venlafaxine treatment plus psychotherapy was compared to placebo plus psychotherapy. Patient scores on the Hamilton Depression Rating Scale (HAM-D), Child Depression Rating Scale (CDRS), and Child Behavior Checklist (CBCL) indicated a significant improvement in depressive symptoms over time, but this improvement could not be attributed uniquely to medication treatment.

The study also examined whether venlafaxine treatment is associated with a more rapid improvement of symptoms compared to placebo. Findings indicated that the pattern of improvement was the same for both groups. Last, the side effect pattern of venlafaxine was examined. The most common side effect among children and adolescents was nausea (43%). Adolescents also reported increased appetite (50%). No side effects were severe enough to warrant discontinuing medication, and in general venlafaxine was well tolerated (Mandoki et al., 1997). Data from this study provide initial support for venlafaxine's safety and efficacy in children and adolescents. Future study is warranted to determine its efficacy with this population.

Phototherapy

To date, there has been one double-blind, placebo-controlled study of phototherapy with children and adolescents (7 to 17 years old) with pediatric SAD (Swedo et al., 1997). The study consisted of a 1-week baseline period during which children wore dark glasses for 1 hour between 4 and 8 P.M. After baseline, children were randomly assigned to receive either active or placebo treatment. Active treatment consisted of 2 hours of dawn stimulation and 1 hour of bright-light therapy. Placebo treatment consisted of 5 minutes of low-intensity dawn stimulation and 1 hour of wearing clear glasses while doing sedentary activities. After a week of either active or placebo treatment, subjects entered a washout phase (1 to 2 weeks) where they wore dark glasses. After the washout phase, children received the alternate treatment.

When compared to baseline scores, there were significant decreases in depressive symptoms during light therapy compared with placebo. No differences were found between placebo and control phases. Phototherapy appeared to be well tolerated by participant children: There were no significant differences in side effect frequency between active and placebo phases of treatment. At the end of the study, 78% of the parents and 80% of children rated light therapy as the phase during which the child "felt best." All parents reported that their children were able to fully comply with wearing the special glasses and sitting in front of the light box as directed. As a result of this study, it appears that adhering to a phototherapy regimen (consisting of bright-light therapy and dawn stimulation) is not difficult for children and their families and that phototherapy is a safe and effective treatment for children and adolescents with SAD.

Adolescents

Antidepressants

Two recent studies examined the effects of TCAs on adolescents with MDD and found no significant advantages of active treatment over placebo (Birmaher et al., 1998; Kutcher et al., 1994). Kutcher et al. (1994) performed a fixed-dose, placebo-controlled trial of the tricyclic antidepressant desipramine (DMI) on 60 adolescents with MDD.

Forty percent of participants who completed the study had improved Hamilton Depression Rating Scale (HDRS) and Beck Depression Inventory (BDI) scores. There were no significant differences in symptom improvement between active and placebo groups. Participants in the DMI group did have a significantly greater number of side effects, including difficulty sleeping and changes in heart rate compared to placebo. Major adverse side effects led to study discontinuation in 10 participants (17%) in the DMI group. These included allergic-type reactions and cardiovascular and gastrointestinal side effects.

In a randomized, controlled trial of amitriptyline (AMI) versus placebo, Birmaher et al. (1998) assessed the response of 27 adolescent inpatients with treatment-resistant MDD. Both treatment groups showed significant improvement (70% to 80%) in clinical outcome measures, and 65% to 70% showed functional improvement. There were no differences in improvement between active and placebo groups. At the end of treatment, 30% of patients still fulfilled criteria for MDD and had impaired functioning, and 60% of patients continued to have subsyndromal symptoms of MDD. The only significant side effects in the AMI group were dry mouth and mild, nonclinically significant resting and orthostatic tachycardia. The only cardiovascular side effect was a mild increase in heart rate (Birmaher et al., 1998; Keller et al., 2001). Data from these studies support the conclusion that TCAs are not efficacious for adolescents and should not be a first-line option for treating depression in this population.

In the first double-blind, placebo-controlled comparison of an SSRI (paroxetine) and a tricyclic antidepressant (imipramine), Keller et al. (2001) concluded that paroxetine is a generally well tolerated and effective treatment for major depression in adolescents. Paroxetine was significantly more effective than placebo in reducing depressive symptoms as measured by HAM-D and CGI scores. The response to imipramine was not significantly different from placebo on any of the depression-related variables used in the study (Keller et al., 2001).

Paroxetine was generally well tolerated in this adolescent population. The most common side effects were headache, nausea, dizziness, dry mouth, and somnolence. Dizziness, dry mouth, headache, nausea, and tachycardia were most commonly reported in the imipramine group. Neither paroxetine nor placebo was associated with changes in heart rate, whereas nearly one third of patients who stopped therapy in the imipramine group experienced cardiovascular effects. This study provides evidence for the safety and efficacy of paroxetine in depressed adolescents.

Phototherapy

No phototherapy treatment studies have been reported for adolescent-only samples.

Electroconvulsive Therapy (ECT)

Recent data suggest ECT is a useful treatment for depressed adolescents who have not responded to other treatments (Ghaziuddin et al., 1996; Strober et al., 1998). Ghaziuddin et al. (1996) studied the safety and efficacy of ECT in 11 hospitalized adolescents with mood disorders who had failed to respond to three or more adequate trials of antidepressants. ECT was administered three times weekly, with patients receiving a mean number of 11.2 treatments. There were significant changes in the Children Depression Rating Scale—Revised (CDRS-R) and the Global Assessment of Functioning Scale (GAF) from pre- to post-ECT. Seven patients (64%) achieved euthymia (signified by a score of 40 or less on the CDRS-R). Side effects experienced by this group were mild to moderate in severity. The most common were headache, experienced by 80% of patients, and nausea or vomiting (64%). No clinical signs of cognitive impairment were noted in any patients following ECT treatment. Additionally, there were no significant changes in cognitive functioning as measured by the Mini-Mental Status Examination (MMSE).

Strober et al. (1998) found dramatic improvements as the result of ECT therapy in 10 treatment-resistant adolescents with primary, endogenous, psychotic depression. Change in symptom severity from baseline was assessed weekly with Hamilton Depression Rating Scale (HDRS) ratings, and outcome was measured at 1 month and 1 year post-ECT. The mean number of treatments received by patients over a 4 to 6 week period was 12.1. By Week 3 of treatment, 9 of 10 patients had attained a 50% or greater reduction in HDRS scores. By the end of the treatment, 6 of 10 patients achieved full remission and 3 were in partial remission. Only 1 patient continued to meet full syndromal criteria for major depression. By the 1-month follow-up, 8 of the 10 patients had been restarted on the antidepressant treatment they had been prescribed at the time of ECT. All 9 patients who had achieved remission or partial remission retained their treatment gains. At the 1-year follow-up, 6 of the 9 patients remained free of any significant affective symptomatology, and no patients had received ECT during the follow-up period (Strober et al., 1998). ECT treatment appeared to be well tolerated by participants, with the most common side effect being headaches (reported by 5 of the participants).

Summary

Much research is still needed on the efficacy of biological treatments for children and adolescents with depression. In terms of antidepressant medication, past research has found no clear evidence for the efficacy of TCAs or MAOIs. Currently, SSRIs are considered the first-line treatment. There have also been promising results for the efficacy of novel antidepressants such as venlafaxine. Although studies have demonstrated the safety and efficacy of phototherapy and ECT in this population, further research is needed to establish the efficacy of these treatments. Adult studies have demonstrated that herbal remedies such as Saint-John's-wort may have antidepressant effects, but their mechanism of action is unknown, and caution should be exercised when using them in children and adolescents. Future studies are needed to examine the safety and efficacy of herbal remedies under the same rigorous conditions as other psychopharmacological agents.

PHENOMENOLOGY OF BIPOLAR DISORDER

Epidemiology

The lifetime prevalence of bipolar disorders (bipolar I, bipolar II, and cyclothymia) in a community sample of 1,709 older adolescents is approximately 1% (i.e., 0.94% to

0.99%), with a point prevalence of 0.53% to 0.64%. Additionally, 5.7% of adolescents in this sample reported core symptoms of mania that did not meet full diagnostic criteria (Lewinsohn, Klein, & Seeley, 1995).

Bipolar disorder is uncommon before adolescence, although a number of case reports indicate the existence of prepubertal bipolar disorder, and 16% of a sample of 262 children referred to a psychiatric clinic met *DSM-III-R* diagnostic criteria for mania (Wozniak et al., 1995). Misdiagnosis may be common in this age group, given the overlap with symptoms of externalizing disorders and the reluctance of some clinicians to diagnose early-onset bipolar disorder (Carlson, 1996; Weller, Weller, & Fristad, 1995). Additionally, the disorder may be underdiagnosed because the child's parents may have undiagnosed bipolar disorder themselves and may not be aware of the seriousness of their child's symptoms (Geller & Luby, 1997).

Demographic Differences

Prepubertal-onset of bipolar disorder is associated with continuous, rapid cycling, mixed episodes of mania and depression, and irritability. Children with bipolar disorder often cycle numerous times daily. In a sample of manic and hypomanic children and early adolescents, 77.4% reported ultradian rapid cycling, compared to rates of less than 20% in adults (Geller et al., 2000). Compared to adults, these children also reported higher rates of mixed mania, longer episodes, and more comorbid ADHD (Geller et al., 2000). In general, prepubertal-onset bipolar disorder is considered to be severe and more similar to treatment-resistant adult bipolar disorder (Geller & Luby, 1997). This contrasts with the onset of bipolar disorder in late adolescence, which resembles the adult pattern, in which there is a sudden onset of discrete manic or depressive episodes, with improved functioning interepisodically and high likelihood for relapse (Strober et al., 1995).

In a large community sample of adolescents, Lewinsohn, Klein, et al. (1995) found that although major depression is more common in female adolescents, the prevalence, age of onset, and course of bipolar disorder appears to be similar in males and females. No studies have been done on differences in prevalence rates of bipolar disorder according to racial group or sexual orientation.

Course

It appears that early-onset bipolar disorder (EOBPD) may not present in the same form as it does in adults (Geller & Luby, 1997). Adults with bipolar disorder often experience an acute onset and experience improved functioning between episodes. In contrast, children with EOBPD often experience brief episodes of rapid-cycling mixed mania (simultaneous experience of depressive and manic symptoms). According to Geller and Luby (1997), parents frequently report children who rapidly cycle numerous times in one day. The mean age of onset of the first episode reported by adolescents with bipolar disorder (11.8 ± 3.0 years) is significantly earlier than that reported by adolescents with major depression only (15.0 ± 2.8). The median duration of illness was 48.3 months, with a median total time spent in episodes of 28.0 months. The duration of the most recent episode ranged from 0.2 to 96.0 months, with a median of 10.8 months (Lewinsohn, Klein, et al., 1995). A majority of adolescents with bipolar disorder (61.1%) report having an initial episode of depression, with 5.5% reporting an initial manic or hypomanic episode, and the polarity of initial episode is indeterminate for 33.3% (Lewinsohn, Klein, et al., 1995). This is consistent with data from studies of adults with bipolar disorder, as 20% to 40% report that the onset of symptoms occurred during childhood or adolescence, often with an initial depressive episode (Lish, Dime-Meenan, Whybrow, Price, & Hirschfeld, 1994). Adolescents with depression are at increased risk of "switching" to bipolar disorder. Studies suggest that 13% to 28% of depressed children and adolescents will experience a manic episode within 5 to 12 years (Strober, 1996).

Comorbidity

Comorbid diagnoses of ADHD and conduct disorder are frequent among children and adolescents with bipolar disorder (Carlson, 1996). It is unclear how often this may be due to early symptoms of mania (hyperactivity, irritability, poor judgment, grandiosity) and how many children truly have both disorders. In a clinical sample of children age 12 or younger, 16% met criteria for mania. Of these, 98% also met criteria for ADHD. The overlap was asymmetrical, with only 20% of children with ADHD meeting criteria for mania (Wozniak et al., 1995). In addition to disruptive behavior disorders, high rates of anxiety disorders, substance abuse, and suicidality are frequently found in children and adolescents with bipolar disorder (Geller & Luby, 1997; Lewinsohn, Klein, et al., 1995).

Bipolar disorder in children and adolescents is associated with impaired functioning in social, family, and school domains (Geller et al., 2000; Lewinsohn, Klein, et al., 1995). Adolescents with bipolar disorder are more functionally impaired than youth with major depressive disorder. They also report more suicide attempts and experience longer episodes and longer duration of illness than depressed adolescents (Lewinsohn, Klein, et al., 1995). Even adolescents who have never met diagnostic criteria for bipolar disorder but who have experienced core symptoms of mania show greater impairment and have higher rates of comorbidity than adolescents who are not mentally ill. This suggests that even subthreshold levels of bipolar symptoms may have a significant effect on adolescent functioning (Lewinsohn, Klein, et al., 1995).

Risk Factors

Risk factors for the development of bipolar disorder include earlier onset of depression, the presence of psychomotor retardation or psychotic features, family history of bipolar disorder, and hypomanic response to antidepressants (Birmaher et al., 1996).

PSYCHOSOCIAL ADJUNCTIVE TREATMENTS FOR BIPOLAR DISORDER

Little research has been conducted regarding the use of adjunctive psychosocial therapy in the comprehensive treatment of bipolar disorder in children and adolescents. In treatment of adult bipolar disorder, psychosocial treatments are commonly recommended as an adjunct to pharmacological treatments. Psychoeducational family interventions, interpersonal and social rhythm therapy, and cognitive-behavioral therapy are empirically supported in adult populations and can help to improve medication adherence and overall functioning and reduce relapse rates (Miklowitz & Craighead, 2001). Research is needed to determine whether adaptations of these therapies are effective in children and adolescents with bipolar disorder.

Preschool-Age Children

No descriptive or empirical data are available on psychosocial interventions for bipolar disorder in preschool-age children. This is not surprising, as controversy exists regarding the diagnosis of bipolar disorder in this age group.

School-Age Children

Fristad and colleagues' multifamily psychoeducation group (MFPG) provides psychoeducation for children with mood disorders and their families. Information relevant to both depression and bipolar disorder is presented to parents and children. Fristad, Goldberg-Arnold, and Gavazzi (in press) compared the baseline functioning and treatment response to MFPG in their randomized trial of families of children with bipolar spectrum versus depressive spectrum disorders. They found at baseline, parents in BPD families ($n = 16$) were more knowledgeable than parents in MDD/DD families ($n = 19$) about mood symptoms ($p < .04$). Additionally at baseline, children with BPD evidenced greater mood severity, both currently ($p < .007$) and historically ($p < .001$), and had experienced more hospitalizations, day treatment, outpatient treatment, medication trials, and placement in severely behavior-handicapped classrooms than children with MDD/DD. Immediately following and 4 months posttreatment, both BPD and MDD/DD families reported having benefited from the knowledge, skills, support, and attitudinal shift gained during treatment. MDD/DD families increased their knowledge to the same level as BPD families. MFPG group leaders' impressions, confirmed by independently reviewed audiotapes, suggested no particular difficulties with combined group membership. These results suggest that even though BPD families enter treatment with more severely impaired children and a more extensive treatment history, both BPD and MDD/DD families benefit from intervention. Further, they reported that grouping BPD and MDD/DD families together is clinically feasible as long as a buddy system is used (i.e., no group has only one member from the bipolar spectrum or the depressive spectrum category).

Adolescents

No published studies have evaluated the efficacy of adjunctive psychosocial interventions for adolescents with bipolar disorder. Axelson, Schlonski, and Wassick (2001) at the Child and Adolescent Bipolar Services Clinic of the Western Psychiatric Institute and Clinic in Pittsburgh have been providing assessment and outpatient treatment for children and adolescents with bipolar disorder, and psychoeducation, supportive psychotherapy, individual cognitive-behavioral therapy, family therapy, and parent support groups are offered as adjuncts to medication management. Although no treatment outcome data are yet available, one of the goals of the clinic is to conduct research about pediatric bipolar disorder.

BIOLOGICAL TREATMENTS

The medical management of a child or adolescent during a manic episode often requires treatment with both antipsychotics and mood-stabilizing agents; however, the efficacy of these medications has not been adequately studied (Emslie, Kennard, & Kowatch, 1994). To date, there has been one placebo-controlled trial of lithium for bipolar disorder in children and adolescents and none for carbamazepine (CBZ) or divalproex (Kowatch, 2001). Some open clinical trial research data indicate these medications may be effective mood stabilizers for this population. Other novel anticonvulsants have been suggested to have mood-stabilizing uses in adult bipolar disorder, including lamotrigine and gabapentin, but no data exist on their potential efficacy as mood stabilizers in children and adolescents (Hagino et al., 1995; Hughes et al., 1999; Ryan, Bhatara, & Perel, 1999). Neuroleptics have also been used as an adjunct to mood-stabilizer therapy. To date, there are no controlled studies that assess their utility in child bipolar disorder (Ryan et al., 1999). In the following section, we will review existing literature on the safety and efficacy of biological treatments for children and adolescents with bipolar disorder.

Preschool Children

Data on the safety and efficacy of pharmacologic interventions for preschoolers with bipolar disorder are rare. Hagino et al. (1995) studied the adverse side effects of lithium treatment on 20 hospitalized aggressive or mood-disordered children ages 4 to 6. The results of their study suggest that adverse effects may be common during initiation of lithium treatment in preschool and kindergarten-age children; however, the majority of these effects are not serious. Eight children (40%), experienced nuisance side effects (e.g., tremor, nausea), and four (20%) had serious side effects (ataxia, slurred speech, confusion). In general, the appearance of side effects was associated with higher lithium levels. Children were also more likely to experience side effects early in treatment. Children with concurrent medical illness appeared to be at greater risk for developing potentially serious side effects from lithium. Another important finding was that children taking lithium with imiprimine, methylphenidate, or haloperidol were not at higher risk for side effects than children treated with lithium alone (Hagino et al., 1995).

School-Age Children

Lithium

Lithium has been well documented for use in children with extreme, impulsive aggression (Alessi, Naylor, Ghaziuddin, & Zubieta, 1994). Studies of lithium for pediatric bipolar disorder are limited to 15 case reports, four crossover trials, and one double-blind placebo-controlled trial (Kowatch, 2001). In an open study of 10 children, lithium alone appeared efficacious in reducing the symptoms of prepubertal children with psychotic bipolar disorder (Varanka, Weller, Weller, & Fristad, 1988). In a double-blind, placebo-controlled study, Campbell et al. (1995) found lithium treatment superior to placebo for aggressive children with conduct disorder. There were also no differences in adverse effects experienced by children in the active versus the placebo treatment groups (Campbell et al., 1995). These studies suggest lithium treatment may be safe and efficacious for childhood bipolar disorder. Future studies are needed to provide additional support for its use in this population.

Anticonvulsants

Carbamazepine (CBZ) and valproic acid are often used as alternatives or adjuncts to lithium treatment for children with bipolar disorder (Kafantaris, 1995). The research data on children with bipolar disorder treated with CBZ consists of a total of six open trials and case reports (Kowatch, 2001). The most common side effects experienced by children taking CBZ are drowsiness, loss of coordination, and vertigo (Ryan et al., 1999). Although CBZ has been used to treat children with a variety of psychiatric disorders, it is not labeled by the FDA for psychiatric indications in any age group (Ryan et al., 1999). Additionally, although CBZ is often used as an adjunct to lithium therapy, there are currently no controlled studies on the safety and efficacy of this medication in children with bipolar disorder. Controlled studies on the use of CBZ for children with behavioral problems have indicated a high response rate for active treatment compared to control (Ryan et al., 1999). Further studies are needed to test the safety and efficacy of this medication in children with bipolar disorder.

Another anticonvulsant, valproic acid, has been widely used in the treatment of children with seizures. The research data on valproic acid treatment for children with bipolar disorder is limited to six open trials and three case reports (Kowatch, 2001). The most common side effects experienced by children and adolescents taking valproate include sedation, nausea, vomiting, increased appetite and weight gain, tremor, possible sterility in females, and hepatic toxicity. Isojarvi, Laatikainen, Pakarinen, Juntunen, and Myllyla (1993) found that 80% of women treated with valproate before the age of 20 developed polycystic ovaries or hyperandrogenism. Hepatic toxicity, which may lead to death, appears to occur almost exclusively in young children (Ryan et al., 1999). The existence of such a severe side effect may be one reason for the lack of controlled data on the effects of valproic acid on children with behavioral disorders (Kafantaris, 1995).

Atypical Antipsychotics

Medications in this class include risperidone (Risperdol), olanzapine (Zyprexa), quetiapine (Seroquel), and ziprasidone (Geodon). Concerns about using atypical antipsychotics with the pediatric population include the potential side effects of sedation and weight gain. Currently, there are no data on their efficacy in school-age children alone. Efficacy data for mixed-age samples are presented in the next section.

Benzodiazepines

Benzodiazepines are sometimes used as adjuncts to lithium or anticonvulsants because they are helpful for relieving the psychomotor agitation, irritability, and insomnia experienced by acutely manic patients. Currently, there are no controlled studies examining their use in children and adolescents with bipolar disorder. Given the lack of supporting research and the high potential for dependency, their long-term use in children and adolescents with bipolar disorder is discouraged (American Academy of Child and Adolescent Psychiatry, 1997).

Herbal Remedies

Studies on adults with bipolar disorder have shown promising results for the use of omega-3 fatty acids in mood stabilization. Essential fatty acids (of which omega-3 is one family) are crucial for growth and development but cannot be manufactured in the body (Papolos & Papolos, 2001). Omega-3 fatty acids are found in the tissues of oily fish (e.g., mackerel, anchovies, herring, salmon), and in green leafy vegetables, canola oil, flaxseed, and walnuts. Researchers have suggested omega-3 fatty acids have a mechanism of action similar to lithium and valproate. In a 4-month double-blind placebo-controlled study, Stoll et al. (1999) compared omega-3 fatty acids to placebo, in addition to usual treatment, in 30 adult patients with bipolar disorder. They found significant differences between active and placebo groups, suggesting that omega-3 fatty acids may act as a mood stabilizer.

Although anecdotal stories from parents who give their bipolar children fish oil supplements suggests it may influence behavior change in such children, to date no randomized controlled studies have examined the use of omega-3 in children and adolescents with bipolar disorder (Papolos & Papolos, 2001). Research is needed to determine whether children and adolescents with bipolar disorder do, in fact, have a deficiency in essential fatty acids or perhaps are not metabolizing them correctly and, if so, whether supplementation will correct such imbalances.

Electroconvulsive Therapy

Though data are sparse, case reports indicate that ECT is beneficial for children and adolescents with bipolar disorder (Bertagnoli & Borchardt, 1990). Despite its potential efficacy, ECT is rarely used for patients with EOBPD. The AACAP suggests that ECT may be the most appropriate treatment for some patients and should not be denied because of concern for social stigma (American Academy of Child and Adolescent Psychiatry, 1997).

Mixed-Age Studies

In a recent study, Kowatch et al. (2000) examined the effect size of three mood stabilizers for the treatment of bipolar disorder in children and adolescents (ages 8 to 18 years). Forty-two outpatients were randomly assigned to 6 weeks of open treatment with either lithium, divalproex sodium, or CBZ. Treatment efficacy was examined using Clinical Global Impression Improvement scores and the Young Mania Rating Scale (Y-MRS). All three mood stabilizers showed a large effect size and were well tolerated by participants. Response rates were 46% to 50% for divalproex sodium, 42% to 45% for lithium, and 34% to 44% for CBZ. There were no significant differences between the three treatment groups. Data from this study suggest that at least 8 weeks are necessary for lithium treatment to be effective, whereas 6 weeks appear adequate for divalproex and CBZ. Limitations of this study include that psychiatrists were not blind to treatment status and there was no placebo control. Importantly, more than half of the patients did not respond to monotherapy with any of these mood stabilizers. Research is currently under way to determine which combination of mood stabilizer, antipsychotic agents, and stimulants works best for children and adolescents with bipolar disorder (Kowatch et al., 2000).

Atypical Antipsychotics

Frazier et al. (1999) used a retrospective chart-review method to evaluate the efficacy and tolerability of risperidone for 28 children and adolescents (ages 4 to 17) with bipolar disorder. Risperidone treatment was associated with a rapid, robust, and sustained response in controlling manic, psychotic, and aggressive symptoms in the majority of participants. No children experienced serious adverse side effects. The most common side effects were weight gain and sedation. This study provides initial encouraging results for the use of risperidone in children and adolescents. Future controlled studies are needed.

Adolescents

Lithium

Several studies have demonstrated the safety and efficacy of lithium for bipolar adolescents (Geller, Cooper, & Sun, 1998; Strober, Morrell, Lampert, & Burroughs, 1990). Strober et al. (1990) reported that lithium is effective in preventing or decreasing relapses in adolescents with bipolar disorder. This 18-month prospective study of 37 adolescents treated with lithium found that participants who did not complete the medication trial relapsed nearly 3 times more often than completers. In the only well controlled prospective study to date, Geller et al. (1998) found that adolescents who had BPD and a secondary substance abuse disorder treated with lithium showed a significant improvement in global assessment of functioning. This study provides preliminary evidence for the efficacy of lithium in the treatment of bipolar adolescents with comorbid substance abuse.

Anticonvulsants

There have been few studies on the efficacy and safety of anticonvulsant medication for adolescents with bipolar disorder. CBZ has been found to be effective as a second-line treatment of acute mania in adults, but no controlled studies exist on its efficacy in bipolar adolescents. Papatheodorou and Kutcher (1993) reported the first results of a clinical trial with divalproex sodium in adolescents with acute mania. Of the 6 patients enrolled in the open trial, 5 (83%) showed marked improvement, 1 (17%) showed some improvement, and none failed to improve. The patients also reported few side effects, suggesting that divalproex sodium may be well tolerated in adolescents.

Summary

The lack of controlled trials on medications for children and adolescents with bipolar disorder makes it difficult to draw conclusions on safety and efficacy of these treatments. Kowatch (2001) outlined a number of areas in which future research is needed. Controlled monotherapy studies are needed for lithium, divalproex sodium, all atypical medications, toiprimate, CBZ, and lamotrigine, as well as for herbal remedies such as omega-3 fatty acids. Studies are also needed on combination treatments, on how to treat bipolar depression, and on treating bipolar disorder with comorbid conduct, anxiety, and oppositional defiant disorders.

CONCLUSION

Considerable advancements have been made in the development of empirically based assessments and treatments for children and adolescents with depressive spectrum and bipolar spectrum disorders. However, much additional work is needed. Developmentally appropriate, empirically validated assessment techniques and treatment strategies for preschoolers and young school-age children with affective disturbances and disorders are sorely lacking. Similarly, clinical guidelines to ensure the accurate diagnosis of bipolar spectrum disorders in children and early adolescents and effective biological and psychosocial treatments for depressive spectrum and bipolar spectrum conditions in children and adolescents require further investigation and development. Because depressive spectrum and bipolar spectrum disorders are associated with significant morbidity and mortality (see chapter 15 in this book for a discussion of suicidality), child and adolescent psychopathology researchers need to maintain a sense of urgency in their development of safe and efficacious assessment and treatment modalities.

REFERENCES

Ackerson, J., Scogin, F., McKendree-Smith, N., & Lyman, R. D. (1998). Cognitive bibliotherapy for mild and moderate adolescent depressive symptomatology. *Journal of Consulting and Clinical Psychology, 66*(4), 685–690.

Alessi, N., Naylor, M. W., Ghaziuddin, M., & Zubieta, J. K. (1994). Update on lithium carbonate therapy in children and adolescents. *Journal of the American Academy of Child and Adolescent Psychiatry, 33,* 291–304.

American Academy of Child and Adolescent Psychiatry. (1997). Practice parameters for the assessment and treatment of children and adolescents with bipolar disorder. *Journal of the American Academy of Child and Adolescent Psychiatry, 36*(1), 138–157.

American Academy of Child and Adolescent Psychiatry. (1998). Summary of the practice parameters for the assessment and treatment of children and adolescents with depressive disorders. *Journal of the American Academy of Child and Adolescent Psychiatry, 37*(11), 1234–1238.

Asarnow, J. R., Jaycox, L. H., & Tompson, M. C. (2001). Depression in youth: Psychosocial interventions. *Journal of Clinical Child Psychology, 30*(1), 33–47.

Axelson, D., Schlonski, A., & Wassick, S. (2001, June 16). *Establishing a specialty clinic for children and adolescents.* Paper presented at the Fourth International Conference on Bipolar Disorder, Pittsburgh, PA.

Beardslee, W. R., Salt, P., Porterfield, K., Rothberg, P. C., van de Velde, P., Swatling, S., Hoke, L., Moilanen, D. L., & Wheelock, I. (1993). Comparison of preventive intervention strategies for families with parental affective disorder. *Journal of the American Academy of Child and Adolescent Psychiatry, 32*(2), 254–263.

Beardslee, W. R., Versage, E. M., & Gladstone, T. R. G. (1998). Children of affectively ill parents: A review of the past 10 years. *Journal of the American Academy of Child and Adolescent Psychiatry, 37,* 1134–1141.

Beardslee, W. R., Wright, E., Rothberg, P. C., Salt, P., & Versage, E. (1996). Response of families to two preventive intervention strategies: Long-term differences in behavior and attitude change. *Journal of the American Academy of Child and Adolescent Psychiatry, 35*(6), 774–782.

Beardslee, W. R., Wright, E. J., Salt, P., Drezner, K., Gladstone, T. R. G., Versage, E. M., & Rothberg, P. C. (1997). Examination of children's responses to two preventive intervention strategies over time. *Journal of the American Academy of Child and Adolescent Psychiatry, 36*(2), 196–204.

Bertagnoli, M. W., & Borchardt, C. M. (1990). A review of ECT for children and adolescents. *Journal of the American Academy of Child and Adolescent Psychiatry, 29*(2), 302–307.

Birmaher, B., Brent, D. A., Kolko, D., Baugher, M., Bridge, J., Holder, D., Iyengar, S., & Ulloa, R. E. (2000). Clinical outcome after short-term psychotherapy for adolescents with major depressive disorder. *Archives of General Psychiatry, 57*(1), 29–36.

Birmaher, B., Ryan, N. D., Williamson, D. E., Brent, D. A., Kaufman, J., Dahl, R. E., Perel, J., & Nelson, B. (1996). Childhood and adolescent depression: A review of the past 10 years, Part I. *Journal of the American Academy of Child and Adolescent Psychiatry, 35*(11), 1427–1439.

Birmaher, B., Waterman, G. S., Ryan, N. D., Perel, J. M., McNabb, J., Balach, L., Beaudry, M. B., Nasr, F. N., Karambelkar, J., Elterich, G., Quintana, H., Williamson, D. E., & Rao, U. (1998). Randomized, controlled trial of amitriphtyline versus placebo for adolescents with "treatment resistant" major depression. *Journal of the American Academy of Child and Adolescent Psychiatry, 37*(11), 527–535.

Brent, D. A., Poling, K., McKain, B., & Baugher, M. (1993). A psychoeducational program for families of affectively ill children and adolescents. *Journal of the American Academy for Child and Adolescent Psychiatry, 32*(4), 770–774.

Brent, D. A., Holder, D., Kolko, D., Birmaher, B., Baugher, M., Roth, C., Iyengar, S., & Johnson, B. A. (1997). A clinical psychotherapy trial for adolescent depression comparing cognitive, family, and supportive therapy. *Archives of General Psychiatry, 54*(9), 877–885.

Brent, D. A., Kolko, D. J., Birmaher, B., Baugher, M., Bridge, J., Roth, C., & Holder, D. (1998). Predictors of treatment efficacy in a clinical trial of three psychosocial treatments for adolescent depression. *Journal of the American Academy of Child and Adolescent Psychiatry, 37*(9), 906–914.

Brent, D. A., Roth, C. M., Holder, D. P., Kolko, D. J., Birmaher, B., Johnson, B. A., & Schweers, J. A. (1996). Psychosocial interventions for treating adolescent suicidal depression: A comparison of three psychosocial interventions. In E. D. Hibbs & P. S. Jensen (Eds.), *Psychosocial treatments for child and adolescent disorders: Empirically based strategies for clinical practice* (pp. 187–206). Washington, DC: American Psychological Association.

Campbell, M., Adams, P. B., Small, A. M., Kafantaris, V., Silva, R. R., Shell, J., Perry, R., & Overall, J. E. (1995). Lithium in hospitalized aggressive children with conduct disorder: A double-blind and placebo-controlled study. *Journal of the American Academy of Child and Adolescent Psychiatry, 34,* 445–453.

Carlson, G. A. (1996). Clinical features and pathogenesis of child and adolescent mania. In K. I. Shulman, M. Tohen & S. P. Kutcher (Eds.), *Mood disorders across the life span* (pp. 127–147). New York: Wiley-Liss.

Clarke, G. N., Hawkins, W., Murphy, M., & Sheeber, L. B. (1993). School-based primary prevention of depressive symptomatology in adolescents: Findings from two studies. *Journal of Adolescent Research, 8*(2), 183–204.

Clarke, G. N., Hawkins, W., Murphy, M., Sheeber, L. B., Lewinsohn, P. M., & Seeley, J. R. (1995). Targeted prevention of unipolar depressive disorder in an at-risk sample of high school adolescents: A randomized trial of group cognitive intervention. *Journal of the American Academy of Child and Adolescent Psychiatry, 34*(3), 312–321.

Clarke, G. N., Hops, H., Lewinsohn, P. M., Andrews, J., Seeley, J., & Williams, J. (1992). Cognitive-behavioral group treatment of adolescent depression: Prediction of outcome. *Behavior Therapy, 23*(3), 341–354.

Clarke, G. N., Rohde, P., Lewinsohn, P. M., Hops, H., & Seeley, J. R. (1999). Cognitive-behavioral treatment of adolescent depression: Efficacy of acute group treatment and booster sessions. *Journal of the American Academy of Child and Adolescent Psychiatry, 38*(3), 272–279.

Diamond, G., & Siqueland, L. (1995). Family therapy for the treatment of depressed adolescents. *Psychotherapy: Theory, Research, Practice, Training, 32*(1), 77–90.

Diamond, G., & Siqueland, L. (2001). Current status of family intervention science. *Child and Adolescent Psychiatric Clinics of North America, 10*(3), 641–661.

Emslie, G. J., Kennard, B. D., & Kowatch, R. A. (1994). Affective disorders in children: Diagnosis and management. *Journal of Affective Disorders,* S42–S49.

Emslie, G. J., Rush, J. A., Weinberg, W. A., Kowatch, R. A., Hughes, C. W., Carmody, T. J., & Rintelmann, J. (1997). Double-blind, randomized, placebo-controlled trial of fluoxetine in children and adolescents with depression. *Archives of General Psychiatry, 54,* 1031–1037.

Ernst, E., Rand, J. I., & Stevinson, C. (1998). Complementary therapies for depression. *Archives of General Psychiatry, 55,* 1026–1032.

Fine, S., Forth, A., Gilbert, M., & Haley, G. (1991). Group therapy for adolescent depressive disorder: A comparison of social skills and therapeutic support. *Journal of the American Academy of Child and Adolescent Psychiatry, 30*(1), 79–85.

Fleming, J. E., & Offord, D. R. (1990). Epidemiology of childhood depressive disorders: A critical review. *Journal of the American Academy of Child and Adolescent Psychology, 29*(4), 571–580.

Frazier, J. A., Meyer, M. C., Biederman, J., Wozniak, J., Wilens, T. E., Spencer, T. J., Kim, G. S., & Shapiro, S. (1999). Risperidone treatment for juvenile bipolar disorder: A retrospective chart review. *Journal of the American Academy of Child and Adolescent Psychiatry, 38*(8), 960–965.

Fristad, M. A., Arnett, M. M., & Gavazzi, S. M. (1998). The impact of psychoeducation workshops on families of mood disordered children. *Family Therapy, 25*(3), 151–159.

Fristad, M. A., Gavazzi, S. M., Centolella, D., & Soldano, K. (1996). Psychoeducation: A promising intervention strategy for families of children and adolescents with mood disorders. *Contemporary Family Therapy, 18*(3), 371–383.

Fristad, M. A., Gavazzi, S. M., & Soldano, K. W. (1998). Multi-family psychoeducation groups for childhood mood disorders: A program description and preliminary efficacy data. *Contemporary Family Therapy, 20*(3), 385–402.

Fristad, M. A., Goldberg-Arnold, J. S., & Gavazzi, S. M. (in press). Multifamily psychoeducation groups (MFPG) for families of children with bipolar disorder. *Bipolar Disorders.*

Fristad, M. A., Goldberg-Arnold, J. S., & Gavazzi, S. M. (in submission). The efficacy of multifamily psychoeducation as an adjunctive intervention for families of children with mood disorders. *Journal of Marital and Family Therapy.*

Geller, B., Bolhofner, K., Craney, J. L., Williams, M., DelBello, M. P., & Gundersen, K. (2000). Psychosocial functioning in a prepubertal and early adolescent bipolar disorder phenotype. *Journal of the American Academy of Child and Adolescent Psychiatry, 39*(12), 1543–1548.

Geller, B., Cooper, T. B., & Sun, K. (1998). Double-blind and placebo-controlled study of lithium for adolescent bipolar disorders with secondary substance abuse. *Journal of the American Academy of Child and Adolescent Psychiatry, 37,* 171–178.

Geller, B., & Luby, J. (1997). Child and adolescent bipolar disorder: A review of the past 10 years. *Journal of the American Academy of Child and Adolescent Psychiatry, 36*(9), 1168–1176.

Ghaziuddin, N., King, C. A., Naylor, M. W., Ghaziuddin, M., Chaudhary, N., Giordani, B., DeQuardo, J. R., Tandon, R., & Greden, J. (1996). Electroconvulsive treatment in adolescents with pharmacotherapy-refractory depression. *Journal of Child and Adolescent Psychopharmacology, 6,* 259–271.

Gillham, J. E., Reivich, K. J., Jaycox, L. H., & Seligman, M. E. P. (1995). Prevention of depressive symptoms in schoolchildren: Two-year follow-up. *Psychological Science, 6*(6), 343–351.

Gladstone, T. R. G., & Beardslee, W. R. (2000). The prevention of depression in at-risk adolescents: Current and future directions. *Journal of Cognitive Psychotherapy, 14*(1), 9–23.

Hagino, O. R., Weller, E. B., Weller, R. A., Washing, D., Fristad, M. A., & Kontras, S. B. (1995). Untoward effects of lithium treatments in children aged four through six years. *Journal of the American Academy of Child and Adolescent Psychiatry, 34,* 1584–1590.

Hains, A. A., & Ellmann, S. W. (1994). Stress inoculation training as a preventative intervention for high school youths. *Journal of Cognitive Psychotherapy, 8*(3), 219–232.

Hazell, P., O'Connell, D., Heathcote, D., Robertson, J., & Henry, D. (1995). Efficacy of tricyclic drugs in treating child and adolescent depression: A meta-analysis. *BMJ, 310*(6984), 897–901.

Hughes, C. W., Emslie, G. J., Crismon, M. L., Wagner, K. D., Birmaher, B., Geller, B., Pliszka, S. R., Ryan, N. D., Strober, M., Trivedi, M. H., Toprac, M. G., Sedillo, A., Llana, M. E., Lopez, M., & Rush, A. J. (1999). The Texas Children's Medication Algorithm Project: Report of the Texas Consensus Conference Panel on medication treatment of children with major depressive disorder. *Journal of the American Academy of Child and Adolescent Psychiatry, 38*(11), 1442–1454.

Isojarvi, J., Laatikainen, T. J., Pakarinen, A. J., Juntunen, K., & Myllyla, V. V. (1993). Polycystic ovaries and hyperandrogenism in women taking valproate for epilepsy. *The New England Journal of Medicine, 329*(19), 1383–1388.

Jaycox, L. H., Reivich, K. J., Gillham, J., & Seligman, M. E. P. (1994). Prevention of depressive symptoms in school children. *Behaviour Research and Therapy, 32*(8), 801–816.

Jurgens, T. M. (1999). The use of herbal medicines in younger psychiatric patients. *Child and Adolescent Psychopharmacology News, 4,* 2–4.

Kafantaris, V. (1995). Treatment of bipolar disorder in children and adolescents. *Journal of the American Academy of Child and Adolescent Psychiatry, 34*(6), 732–741.

Kahn, J. S., Kehle, T. J., Jenson, W. R., & Clark, E. (1990). Comparison of cognitive-behavioral, relaxation, and self-modeling interventions for depression among middle-school students. *School Psychology Review, 19*(2), 196–211.

Kashani, J. H., Cantwell, D. P., Shekim, W. O., & Reid, J. C. (1982). Major depressive disorder in children admitted to an inpatient community mental health center. *American Journal of Psychiatry, 139,* 671–672.

Kashani, J. H., & Carlson, G. A. (1987). Seriously depressed preschoolers. *American Journal of Psychiatry, 144,* 348–350.

Kashani, J. H., Carlson, G. A., Beck, M. C., Hoeper, E. W., Corcoran, C. M., McAllister, J. A., Fallahi, C., Rosenberg, T. K., & Reid, J. C. (1987). Depression, depression symptoms, and depressed mood among a community sample of adolescents. *American Journal of Psychiatry, 144,* 931–934.

Kashani, J. H., Holcomb, W. R., & Orvaschel, H. (1986). Depression and depressive symptoms in preschool children from the general population. *American Journal of Psychiatry, 143,* 1138–1143.

Kashani, J. H., Ray, J. S., & Carlson, G. A. (1984). Depression and depressive-like states in preschool-age children in a child development unit. *American Journal of Psychiatry, 141,* 1397–1402.

Kaslow, N. J., Deering, C. G., & Racusin, G. R. (1994). Depressed children and their families. *Clinical Psychology Review, 14*(1), 39–59.

Kaslow, N. J., & Racusin, G. R. (1994). Family therapy for depression in young people. In W. M. Reynolds & H. F. Johnston (Eds.), *Handbook of depression in children and adolescents* (pp. 345–363). New York, NY: Plenum Press.

Keller, M. B., Ryan, N. D., Strober, M., Klein, R. G., Kutcher, S. P., Birmaher, B., Hagino, O. R., Koplewicz, H., Carlson, G. A., Clarke, G. N., Kusumakar, V., Papatheodorou, G., Sack, W. H., Sweeny, M., Wagner, K. D., Weller, E. B., Winters, N. C., Oakes, R., & McCafferty, J. P. (2001). Efficacy of paroxetine in the treatment of adolescent major depression: A randomized, controlled, trial. *Journal of the American Academy of Child and Adolescent Psychiatry, 40,* 762–772.

Kolko, D. J., Brent, D. A., Baugher, M., Bridge, J., & Birmaher, B. (2000). Cognitive and family therapies for adolescent depression: Treatment specificity, mediation, and moderation. *Journal of Consulting and Clinical Psychology, 68*(4), 603–614.

Kovacs, M. (1996). Presentation and course of major depressive disorder during childhood and later years of the life span. *Journal of the American Academy of Child and Adolescent Psychiatry, 35,* 705–715.

Kovacs, M., Akiskal, H. S., Gatsonis, C., & Parrone, P. L. (1994). Childhood-onset dysthymic disorder. Clinical features and prospective naturalistic outcome. *Archives of General Psychiatry, 51,* 365–374.

Kovacs, M., Feinberg, T. L., Crouse-Novak, M. A., Paulauskas, S. L., & Finkelstein, R. (1984). Depressive disorders in childhood: I. A longitudinal prospective study of characteristics and recovery. *Archives of General Psychiatry, 41,* 229–237.

Kovacs, M., Feinberg, T. L., Crouse-Novak, M. A., Paulauskas, S. L., Pollock, M., & Finkelstein, R. (1984). Depressive disorders in childhood: II. A longitudinal study of the risk for a subsequent major depression. *Archives of General Psychiatry, 41,* 643–649.

Kowatch, R. A. (2001, June 14–16). *Pharmacological treatments of children and adolescents with bipolar disorders.* Paper presented at the Fourth International Conference on Bipolar Disorder, Pittsburgh, PA.

Kowatch, R. A., Suppes, T., Carmody, T. J., Bucci, J. P., Hume, J. H., Kromelis, M., Emslie, G. J., Weinberg, W. A., & Rush, A. J. (2000). Effect size of lithium, divalproex sodium, and carbamazepine in children and adolescents with bipolar disorder. *Journal of the American Academy of Child and Adolescent Psychiatry, 39*(6), 713–720.

Kroll, L., Harrington, R., Jayson, D., Fraser, J., & Gowers, S. (1996). Pilot study of continuation cognitive-behavioral therapy for major depression in adolescent psychiatric patients. *Journal of the American Academy of Child and Adolescent Psychiatry, 35*(9), 1156–1161.

Kutcher, S. P., Boulous, C., Ward, B., Marton, P., Simeon, J., Ferguson, H. B., Szalai, J., Katic, M., Roberts, N., Dubois, C., & Reed, K. (1994). Response to desipramine treatment in adolescent depression: A fixed dose, placebo-controlled trial. *Journal of the American Academy of Child and Adolescent Psychiatry, 33,* 686–693.

Lewinsohn, P. M., Clarke, G. N., Hops, H., & Andrews, J. A. (1990). Cognitive-behavioral treatment for depressed adolescents. *Behavior Therapy, 21*(4), 385–401.

Lewinsohn, P. M., Clarke, G. N., & Rohde, P. (1994). Psychological approaches to the treatment of depression in adolescents. In W. M. Reynolds & H. F. Johnston (Eds.), *Handbook of depression in children and adolescents* (pp. 309–344). New York: Plenum Press.

Lewinsohn, P. M., Clarke, G. N., Rohde, P., Hops, H., & Seeley, J. R. (1996). A course in coping: A cognitive-behavioral approach to the treatment of adolescent depression. In E. D. Hibbs & P. S. Jensen (Eds.), *Psychosocial treatments for child and adolescent disorders: Empirically based strategies for clinical practice* (pp. 109–135). Washington, DC. American Psychological Association.

Lewinsohn, P. M., Clarke, G. N., Seeley, J. R., & Rohde, P. (1994). Major depression in community adolescents: age at onset, episode duration, and time to recurrence. *Journal of the American Academy of Child and Adolescent Psychiatry, 33,* 809–818.

Lewinsohn, P. M., Hops, H., Roberts, R. E., Seeley, J. R., & Andrews, J. A. (1993). Adolescent psychopathology: I. Prevalence and incidence of depression and other *DSM-III-R* disorders in high school students. *Journal of Abnormal Psychology, 102,* 133–144.

Lewinsohn, P. M., Klein, D. N., & Seeley, J. R. (1995). Bipolar disorders in a community sample of older adolescents: Prevalence, phenomenology, comorbidity, and course. *Journal of the American Academy of Child and Adolescent Psychiatry, 34*(4), 454–463.

Lewinsohn, P. M., Rohde, P., & Seeley, J. R. (1995). Adolescent psychopathology: III. The clinical consequences of comorbidity. *Journal of the American Academy of Child and Adolescent Psychiatry, 34,* 510–519.

Lewinsohn, P. M., Rohde, P., & Seeley, J. R. (1998). Major depressive disorder in older adolescents: Prevalence, risk factors, and clinical implications. *Clinical Psychology Review, 18*(7), 765–794.

Lewinsohn, P. M., Rohde, P., Seeley, J. R., & Fischer, S. A. (1993). Age-cohort changes in the lifetime occurrence of depression and other mental disorders. *Journal of Abnormal Psychology, 102,* 110–120.

Linde, K., Ramierz, G., Mulrow, C. D., Pauls, A., Weidenhammer, W., & Melchart, D. (1996). St. John's wort for depression—An overview and meta-analysis of randomised clinical trails. *British Medical Journal, 313,* 253–258.

Lish, J. D., Dime-Meenan, S., Whybrow, P. C., Price, R. A., & Hirschfeld, R. M. (1994). The National Depressive and Manic-Depressive Association (DMDA) survey of bipolar members. *Journal of Affective Disorders, 31,* 281–294.

Lonigan, C. J., Elbert, J. C., & Bennett Johnson, S. (1998). Empirically supported psychosocial interventions for children: An overview. *Journal of Clinical Child Psychology, 27*(2), 138–145.

Mandoki, M. W., Tapia, M. R., Tapia, M. A., & Sumner, G. S. (1997). Venlafaxine in the treatment of children and adolescents with major depression. *Psychopharmacology Bulletin, 33*(1), 149–154.

Marcotte, D. (1997). Treating depression in adolescence: A review of the effectiveness of cognitive-behavioral treatments. *Journal of Youth and Adolescence, 26*(3), 273–283.

Miklowitz, D. J., & Craighead, W. E. (2001). Bipolar affective disorder: Does psychosocial treatment add to the efficacy of drug therapy? *TEN, 3*(1), 58–64.

Moreau, D., Mufson, L., Weissman, M. M., & Klerman, G. L. (1991). Interpersonal psychotherapy for adolescent depression: Description of modification and preliminary application. *Journal of the American Academy of Child and Adolescent Psychiatry, 30*(4), 642–651.

Mufson, L., & Fairbanks, J. (1996). Interpersonal psychotherapy for depressed adolescents: A one-year naturalistic follow-up study. *Journal of the American Academy of Child & Adolescent Psychiatry, 35*(9), 1145–1155.

Mufson, L., Moreau, D., & Weissman, M. M. (1996). Focus on relationships: Interpersonal psychotherapy for adolescent depression. In E. D. Hibbs & P. S. Jensen (Eds.), *Psychosocial treatments for child and adolescent disorders: Empirically based strategies for clinical practice* (pp. 137–155). Washington, DC: American Psychological Association.

Mufson, L., Moreau, D., Weissman, M. M., Wickramaratne, P., Martin, J., & Samoilov, A. (1994). Modification of interpersonal psychotherapy with depressed adolescents (IPT-A): Phase I and II studies. *Journal of the American Academy of Child and Adolescent Psychiatry, 33*(5), 695–705.

Mufson, L., Weissman, M. M., Moreau, D., & Garfinkel, R. (1999). Efficacy of interpersonal psychotherapy for depressed adolescents. *Archives of General Psychiatry, 56,* 573–579.

Nolen-Hoeksema, S., & Girgus, J. S. (1994). The emergence of gender differences in depression during adolescence. *Psychological Bulletin, 115*(3), 424–443.

Papatheodorou, G., & Kutcher, S. P. (1993). Divalproex sodium treatment in late adolescent and young adult acute mania. *Psychopharmacology Bulletin, 29,* 213–219.

Papolos, D., & Papolos, J. (2001). Topic: The A–Zs of omega-3's. *The Bipolar Child Newsletter, 7,* 1–7.

Petersen, A. C., Compas, B. E., Brooks-Gunn, J., Stemmler, M., Ey, S., & Grant, K. E. (1993). Depression in adolescence. *American Psychologist, 48*(2), 155–168.

Poznanski, E. O., & Mokros, H. B. (1994). Phenomenology and epidemiology of mood disorders in children and adolescents. In W. M. Reynolds & H. F. Johnston (Eds.), *Handbook of depression in children and adolescents* (pp. 19–39). New York: Plenum Press.

Rao, U., Ryan, N. D., Birmaher, B., Dahl, R. E., Williamson, D. E., Kaufman, J., Radhika, R., & Nelson, B. (1995). Unipolar depression in adolescents: Clinical outcome in adulthood. *Journal of the American Academy of Child and Adolescent Psychiatry, 34*(5), 566–578.

Reinecke, M. A., Ryan, N. E., & DuBois, D. L. (1998). Cognitive-behavioral therapy of depression and depressive symptoms during adolescence: A review and meta-analysis. *Journal of the American Academy of Child and Adolescent Psychiatry, 37*(1), 26–34.

Renaud, J., Brent, D. A., Baugher, M., Birmaher, B., Kolko, D. J., & Bridge, J. (1998). Rapid response to psychosocial treatment for adolescent depression: A two-year follow-up. *Journal of the American Academy of Child and Adolescent Psychiatry, 37*(11), 1184–1190.

Reynolds, W. M., & Coats, K. I. (1986). A comparison of cognitive-behavioral therapy and relaxation training for the treatment of depression in adolescents. *Journal of Consulting and Clinical Psychology, 54*(5), 653–660.

Rohde, P., Lewinsohn, P. M., & Seeley, J. R. (1991). Comorbidity of unipolar depression: II. Comorbidity with other mental disorders in adolescents and adults. *Journal of Abnormal Psychology, 100*(2), 214–222.

Rossello, J., & Bernal, G. (1996). Adapting cognitive-behavioral and interpersonal treatments for depressed Puerto Rican adolescents. In E. D. Hibbs & P. S. Jensen (Eds.), *Psychosocial treatments for child and adolescent disorders: Empirically based strategies for clinical practice* (pp. 157–185). Washington, DC: American Psychological Association.

Rossello, J., & Bernal, G. (1999). The efficacy of cognitive-behavioral and interpersonal treatments for depression in Puerto Rican adolescents. *Journal of Consulting and Clinical Psychology, 67*(5), 734–745.

Ryan, N. D., Bhatara, V. S., & Perel, J. M. (1999). Mood stabilizers in children and adolescents. *Journal of the American Academy of Child and Adolescent Psychiatry, 38*(5), 529–536.

Ryan, N. D., & Varma, D. (1998). Child and adolescent mood disorders with Serotonin-based therapies. *Biological Psychiatry, 44,* 336–340.

Ryan, N. D., Williamson, D. E., Iyengar, S., Orvaschel, H., Reich, T., Dahl, R. E., & Puig-Antich, J. A. (1992). A secular increase in child and adolescent onset affective disorder. *Journal of the American Academy of Child and Adolescent Psychiatry, 31,* 600–605.

Sexson, S. B., Glanville, D. N., & Kaslow, N. J. (2001). Attachment and depression: Implications for family therapy. *Child and Adolescent Psychiatric Clinics of North America, 10*(3), 465–486.

Shafii, M., & Shafii, S. L. (1992). Dyamic psychotherapy of depression. In M. Shafii & S. L. Shafii (Eds.), *Clinical guide to depression in children and adolescents.* Washington, DC: American Psychiatric Press.

Sommers-Flanagan, R., Barrett-Hakanson, T., Clarke, C., & Sommers-Flanagan, J. (2000). A psychoeducational school-based coping and social skills group for depressed students. *Journal for Specialists in Group Work, 25*(2), 170–190.

Stark, K. D., Reynolds, W. M., & Kaslow, N. J. (1987). A comparison of the relative efficacy of self-control therapy and a behavioral problem-solving therapy for depression in children. *Journal of Abnormal Child Psychology, 15*(1), 91–113.

Stark, K. D., Rouse, L. W., & Kurowski, C. (1994). Psychological treatment approaches for depression in children. In W. M. Reynolds & H. F. Johnston (Eds.), *Handbook of depression in children and adolescents* (pp. 275–307). New York, NY: Plenum Press.

Stark, K. D., Swearer, S., Kurowski, C., Sommer, D., & Bowen, B. (1996). Targeting the child and the family: A holistic approach to treating child and adolescent depressive disorders. In E. D. Hibbs & P. S. Jensen (Eds.), *Psychosocial treatments for child and adolescent disorders: Empirically based strategies for clinical practice* (pp. 207–238.). Washington, DC: American Psychological Association.

Stoll, A. L., Severus, E., Freeman, M., Reueter, S., Zboyan, H. A., Diamond, E., Cress, K. K., & Marangell, L. B. (1999). Omega 3 fatty acids in bipolar disorders. *Archives of General Psychiatry, 56,* 407–412.

Strober, M. (1996). Outcome studies of mania in children and adolescents. In K. I. Shulman, M. Tohen, & S. P. Kutcher (Eds.), *Mood disorders across the life span* (pp. 149–158). New York: Wiley-Liss.

Strober, M., Lampart, C., Schmidt, S., & Morrell, W. (1993). The course of major depressive disorder in adolescents: I. Recovery and risk of manic switching in a follow-up of psychotic and non-psychotic types. *Journal of the American Academy of Child and Adolescent Psychiatry, 32*(1), 34–42.

Strober, M., Morrell, W., Lampert, C., & Burroughs, J. (1990). Relapse following discontinuation of lithium maintenance therapy in adolescents with bipolar illness: A naturalistic study. *American Journal of Psychiatry, 147,* 457–461.

Strober, M., Rao, U., DeAntonio, M., Liston, E., State, M., Amaya-Jackson, L., & Latz, S. (1998). Effects of electroconvulsive therapy in adolescents with severe endogenous depression resistant to pharmacotherapy. *Biological Psychiatry, 43,* 335–338.

Strober, M., Schmidt-Lackner, S., Freeman, R., Bower, S., Lampert, C., & DeAntonio, M. (1995). Recovery and relapse in adolescents with bipolar affective illness: A five-year naturalistic, prospective follow-up. *Journal of the American Academy of Child and Adolescent Psychiatry, 34*(6), 724–731.

Swedo, S. E., Allen, J. A., Glod, C. A., Clark, C. H., Teicher, M. H., Richter, D., Hoffman, C., Hamburger, S. D., Dow, S., Brown, C., & Rosenthal, N. E. (1997). A controlled trial of light therapy for the treatment of pediatric seasonal affective disorder. *Journal of the American Academy of Child and Adolescent Psychiatry, 36*(6), 816–821.

Varanka, T. M., Weller, R. A., Weller, E. B., & Fristad, M. A. (1988). Lithium treatment of manic episodes with psychotic features in prepubertal children. *American Journal of Psychiatry, 145,* 1557–1559.

Vostanis, P., Feehan, C., Grattan, E., & Bickerton, W. L. (1996). Treatment for children and adolescents with depression: Lessons from a controlled trial. *Clinical Child Psychology & Psychiatry, 1*(2), 199–212.

Wagner, K. D., & Ambrosini, P. J. (2001). Childhood depression: Pharmacological therapy/treatment (pharmacotherapy of child depression). *Journal of Clinical Child Psychology, 30*(1), 88–97.

Walter, G., & Rey, J. M. (1997). An epidemilogical study of the use of ECT in adolescents. *Journal of the American Academy of Child and Adolescent Psychiatry, 36*(6), 809–815.

Weisz, J. R., Thurber, C. A., Sweeney, L., Proffitt, V. D., & LeGagnoux, G. L. (1997). Brief treatment of mild-to-moderate child depression using primary and secondary control enhancement training. *Journal of Consulting and Clinical Psychology, 65*(4), 703–707.

Weller, E. B., & Weller, R. A. (2000). Treatment options in the management of adolescent depression. *Journal of Affective Disorders, 61,* S23–S28.

Weller, E. B., Weller, R. A., & Fristad, M. A. (1995). Bipolar disorder in children: Misdiagnosis, underdiagnosis, and future directions. *Journal of the American Academy of Child and Adolescent Psychiatry, 34*(6), 709–714.

White, K. (2000). Focus on herbals: St. John's wort. *Child and Adolescent Psychopharmacology News, 5,* 4–6.

Wood, A., Harrington, R., & Moore, A. (1996). Controlled trial of a brief cognitive-behavioural intervention in adolescent patients with depressive disorders. *Journal of Child Psychology and Psychiatry and Allied Disciplines, 37*(6), 737–746.

Wozniak, J., Biederman, J., Kiely, K., Ablon, J. S., Faraone, S. V., Mundy, E., & Mennin, D. (1995). Mania-like symptoms suggestive of childhood-onset bipolar disorder in clinically referred children. *Journal of the American Academy of Child and Adolescent Psychiatry, 34*(7), 867–876.

Zito, J. M., Safer, D. J., dosReis, S., & Gardner, J. F. (2000). Trends in the prescribing of psychotropic medications to preschoolers. *The Journal of the American Medical Association, 283*(3), 1025–1030.

Chapter 14

PSYCHOSIS AND PSYCHOTIC CONDITIONS IN CHILDHOOD AND ADOLESCENCE

FRED R. VOLKMAR AND KATHERINE TSATSANIS

Although often used somewhat imprecisely, the term *psychosis* generally implies a serious disturbance in reality testing as reflected by hallucinations, delusions, or disturbance in thinking. Various conditions are characterized by psychosis or some degree of psychotic phenomena (American Psychiatric Association [APA], 1994). These are among the most serious disorders clinically encountered. Historically, the notion of psychosis was used rather broadly (Volkmar, 1996), but it is now used much more specifically; a recurrent tension has been the degree to which concepts derived from work with adults can simply be extended to children, whose conceptualizations of reality undergo major changes over the course of development (Volkmar, Becker, King, & McLashen, 1994).

Early attempts to understand psychotic phenomena in adults—for example, by Freud and his colleagues—often postulated a regression to earlier levels of functioning (Freud, 1911/1957). In contrast, studies of normative developmental processes, such as Piaget's work on the development of reality concepts (e.g., Piaget, 1955), pointed toward major developmental issues in the understanding of children's notions of reality.

This chapter reviews aspects of psychotic phenomena relative to hallucinations, delusions, and thought disorder. It then turns to the major psychotic conditions, notably childhood schizophrenia. Aspects of differential diagnosis are discussed, and the current state of research on these conditions is briefly summarized.

PSYCHOTIC PHENOMENA

Hallucinations

Hallucinations have similarities to normative phenomena, such as dreaming, illusions, and hypnopompic and hypnogogic imagery (Bentall & Slade, 1985). Bleuler (1911/1951) defined *hallucinations* as "perceptions without corresponding stimuli from without." Asaad (1990) has noted that hallucinations can be categorized along various dimensions, such as complexity, modality (e.g., auditory or visual), affective tone, and so forth. Hallucinations related to sensory experiences are relatively common in the normative population, occurring in about 4% of adults each year (Tien, 1991). Hallucinations can also be induced in nonclinical subjects, for example, through severe stress or administration of certain drugs. Although hallucinations are characteristically seen in schizophrenia, they are not, of themselves, diagnostic of a particular disorder, and indeed are observed in various clinical syndromes, including bipolar disorder and unipolar depression. Despite earlier impressions to the contrary, hallucinations are not characteristic of autism. Transient hallucinations may be seen in various conditions, such as in posttraumatic stress disorders (Waldfogel & Mueser, 1988). Hallucinations may be associated with various medical conditions and are occasional side effects of many drugs.

Before a child has at least some language and capacity for reporting internal experiences, hallucinations are difficult to document. Hallucinations are sometimes seen in preschool children, particularly in relation to sleep (King & Noshpitz, 1991). Vivid dreams or the occasional imaginary companions are sometimes incorrectly assumed to suggest hallucinations, but young children have limited capacities to reflect on reality/nonreality distinctions (Piaget, 1955).

Transient hallucinations also occur in preschool children, especially in reaction to acute anxiety or stresses (Rothstein, 1981). These tend to be visual or tactile in otherwise normally developing children and often seem to be related to sleep, although they sometimes persist into the daytime. In older children and adolescents, hallucinations tend to be more persistent and may be indicative of serious psychopathology (Volkmar, 1996)

In children, hallucinations are typically more fluid and less complicated than those in adults. They often are characterized by child-related content, with animals, monsters, and so forth (Russell, Bott, & Sammons, 1989). Hallucinations are frequently observed in childhood schizophrenia (which is discussed subsequently). They can also be occasional side effects of stimulants and other agents.

Delusions

Delusions are false beliefs, which remain solidly held in the face of considerable evidence to the contrary (Yager, 1989). Delusions can be classified in many ways—as simple or more complex, as systematized or fragmented, and so forth. Kendler, Glazer, and Morganstern (1983) have proposed a classification system for delusions along five dimensions:

- *Conviction*—the degree to which the delusion is experienced as real
- *Extension*—the degree to which the delusion involves multiple aspects of the individual's life
- *Bizarreness*—the extent to which the delusion departs from culturally sanctioned reality
- *Disorganization*—the extent to which the delusion is systematized
- *Pressure*—the degree to which the delusion preoccupies the person

In considering delusional thinking in childhood, it is important to understand children's developmental progression in logical thinking (Piaget, 1955). Children have greater difficulty than adults in drawing firm distinctions between reality and fantasy, and culturally bound beliefs in fantasy figures are common (e.g., Santa Claus).

In clinical disorders of childhood, delusions are rather less common, compared to adult disorders. When present, they also tend to be simpler and less well systematized. Delusions may center around concerns relative to the body. Persecutory and grandiose delusions are also observed (Garralda, 1985; Kydd & Werry, 1982; Russell, et al., 1989; Volkmar, Cohen, Hoshino, Rende, & Paul, 1988).

Thought Disorder

Thought process disorder refers to diverse difficulties in the form, rather than content, of thought. Conceptualizations of thought disorder have varied historically (Andreasen & Grove, 1986; Butler & Braff, 1991), so that at one time thought disorder was thought to be specific to schizophrenia, but more recently it has been viewed as a more general and less specific collection of clinical signs (Holzman, 1986). Most recently, the trend has been to focus on the patently observable, that is, describing disorganized speech rather than disorganized thought. This tendency is exemplified in the *Diagnostic and Statistical Manual of Mental Disorders, Fourth Edition* (*DSM-IV;* APA, 1994). Features typical of this area include loosening of associations, flight of ideas, derailment, illogicality, and incoherence. Neologisms, words with idiosyncratic meaning, are also observed. Evaluation of thought disorder, particularly in children, requires careful consideration of the individual's developmental and communicative level and cultural background. Disturbances in the organization of speech are noted in a range of psychotic conditions.

Most work on thought disorder has focused on adults, particularly those with schizophrenia. Disturbances of thought are particularly difficult to diagnose in preschool children (Green et al., 1984; Russell et al., 1989; Volkmar et al., 1988). As children enter middle childhood, thought disorders do appear in much the same form as in adults (Bettes & Walker, 1987; Garralda, 1984). Caplan and colleagues (Caplan, Guthrie, Fish, Tanguay, & David-Lando, 1989; Caplan, Perdue, Tanguay, & Fish, 1990) have developed a rating scale for assessment of thought disorder in children; this scale employs operational definitions of illogical thinking, incoherence, loosening of association, and poverty of speech content.

Summary

Psychotic phenomena are manifest in a variety of childhood disorders. The remainder of this chapter is devoted to a consideration of the diagnoses that are most common in children who present with hallucinations, delusions, and/or a disturbance in thinking. The following section presents an overview of childhood schizophrenia. In addition to diagnostic issues, a description of its course, neurobiologic features, and outcome are presented, based on current research findings. Assessment and treatment are also considered. Subsequent sections focus, more briefly, on bipolar disorder and depression with psychosis in children.

CHILDHOOD SCHIZOPHRENIA

Diagnostic Issues

Until the late 1970s there was much confusion about the nature of childhood "psy choses," so that autism and schizophrenia of childhood were inappropriately lumped together. The seminal work of Kolvin (1971) and others (Rutter, 1972) suggested that differentiations could be made within the broad group of "psychotic" children on the basis of various features, such as age of onset, clinical characteristics, family history, and evidence of central nervous system (CNS) dysfunction (Green et al., 1984; Kolvin, 1971; Russell et al., 1989; Volkmar et al., 1988). The group of children with earlier onset exhibited difficulties in the first years of life more consistent with Kanner's description of autism, whereas the group with later onset exhibited the delusions, hallucinations, and clinical features more commonly associated with schizophrenia and also were more likely to have positive family histories for schizophrenia (Kolvin, 1971). The recognition of childhood schizophrenia as a more narrowly defined clinical entity helped to clarify what appears to be its general continuity with adult forms of the disorder (e.g., Frazier et al., 1997; Jacobsen, Hong, et al., 1996; Zahn et al., 1997).

A diagnosis of schizophrenia in children requires features represented in the current diagnostic criteria for schizophrenia, which include characteristic positive psychotic symptoms such as delusions, hallucinations, disorganized speech, and grossly disorganized or catatonic behavior, and negative symptoms such as flattened affect. These symptoms are associated with deficits in adaptive functioning and duration of at least 6 months (with at least 1 month during which active symptoms are present). Some relatively minor modifications are made for children, such as an emphasis on deterioration in academic functioning, and the text clarifies some important considerations in making the diagnosis in children. This is particularly critical, as problems may arise both in applying concepts like psychosis to children and in the specification of criteria applicable to children with the disorder.

In this regard, certain symptoms, such as disorganized speech and behavior, are relatively common in *nonpsychotic* children and may tend to produce overdiagnosis (see Werry, 1996, for a discussion). Conversely, the rigorous application of exclusionary rules relative to substance abuse in adults, for example, may tend to underdiagnose the condition. Interpretation of symptoms also can be more complicated in children. For children under 10 years of age or for children with developmental disabilities, difficulties in communication, changes in conceptions of reality, and the nature of symptom expression may complicate the diagnostic picture. Children's conceptions of reality change, and beliefs in fantasy figures are a common aspect of development (Piaget, 1955). In addition, it is clear that children become more organized in their thinking and communication of ideas over time. Conversely, sometimes children with hallucinations may not share the experience, delaying recognition of their difficulties (Russell, 1994). In such circumstances, difficulties in conduct and attention may suggest incorrect diagnoses.

A final problem relates to that of comorbidity. It has long been recognized that in some cases the overt or frank psychotic symptoms are preceded by a long period, sometimes years, of relatively nonspecific learning or conduct problems. Schizophrenia can also be observed in association with various other psychiatric and developmental problems, for example, conduct disorder, learning disabilities, mental retardation, and even autism (Russell et al., 1989). Issues of the definition of psychosis or thought disorder become extremely complex for children who do not talk and are likely never to do so (Caplan, 1994). These observations suggest the significance of incorporating a truly developmental point of view in conceptualizing the nature of psychosis in childhood.

In addition to a careful history, it becomes important to follow the child over time. Schizophrenia cannot be diagnosed in the presence of schizoaffective disorder or mood disorder with psychotic features, nor can it be due to the direct effects of substance abuse or a general medical condition (e.g., seizure disorder). The differentiation of schizophrenia from affective disorders can be difficult because, to some degree, mood disturbance can be observed in schizophrenia. Prominent mood disturbance, particularly if prolonged, suggests the need to consider the various affective disorders and schizoaffective disorder. Rarely, children with an obsessive-compulsive disorder may exhibit ideas that are difficult to distinguish from delusions, although the individual usually recognizes the irrational nature of such ideas.

Epidemiology, Onset, Course, and Clinical Features

Epidemiology

Various factors limit our knowledge regarding the prevalence and epidemiology of childhood-onset schizophrenia. As noted previously, the diagnostic concept has changed markedly over the years, and few studies conducted prior to 1980 are readily interpretable. It does appear that childhood schizophrenia is less common than autism (Burd & Kerbeshian, 1987) and is quite rare before 12 years of age, with rates of onset increasing dramatically during adolescence to yield adult rates of approximately 0.1% incidence (new cases) per year (McClellan & Werry, 1997). Studies employing stringent criteria suggest that the disorder is very rarely observed before age 5. Distinctions between *early onset* (before 18 years of age) and *very early onset* (before 13 years of age) in childhood and adolescence have been suggested (see Werry, 1996).

Onset

The onset of disturbance is generally described to follow at least three patterns: (a) acute onset, without apparent premorbid signs of incipient disturbance; (b) insidious onset, with a gradual deterioration in functioning; and (c) insidious onset, with an acute exacerbation of disturbance (Green et al., 1984; Kolvin, 1971). The most common pattern appears to be insidious onset of illness (Alaghband-Rad et al., 1995; Asarnow, Brown, and Strandburg, 1995; Eggers, Bunk, & Krause, 2000; Russell, 1994). The course is characterized by early emergence of various developmental, behavioral, and psychiatric problems, followed by gradual onset of psychotic symptoms (about 2 to 3 years later), and then eventual diagnosis of the full clinical syndrome, which unfortunately tends to be chronic. There is also evidence to suggest that the pattern of developmental disturbances varies with age of onset; impairments of language, but not social or motor functioning, are more common for childhood-onset schizophrenia relative to adolescent- or adult-onset schizophrenia (Hollis, 1995).

Clinical Features

Reported sex ratios of the disorder have varied. Both a slight male predominance, on the order of 2 males to 1 female (Kolvin, 1971; Russell et al., 1989; Volkmar et al., 1988), and essentially equal sex ratios (Eggers, 1978; Jacobsen & Rapoport, 1998) have been found. For both children and adults, there is some suggestion that males have an earlier onset of the disorder (Green et al., 1984). In addition, boys have been reported to be more likely to show early signs of abnormal development and more likely to have had an insidious onset relative to girls with the disorder (Alaghband-Rad et al., 1995; Asarnow et al., 1995; Hollis, 1995).

Alaghband-Rad et al. (1995) reported that one half of the children with schizophrenia in their sample had repeated at least one grade before the onset of psychotic symptoms, 65% had been placed in special education classes, and a specific learning disability was diagnosed in 30%. When compared to children with major depression, children with early onset schizophrenia showed poorer levels of overall premorbid adjustment and greater premorbid impairment with regard to peer relationships, school performance, school adaptation, and interests (Asarnow et al., 1995).

Rigorous studies of the phenomenology of thought disturbance in childhood schizophrenia, although limited in number, have been surprisingly consistent (Green et al., 1984; Kolvin, 1971; Russell et al., 1989; Volkmar et al., 1988). Auditory hallucinations are consistently the most frequently reported symptoms, usually exhibited in about 80% of cases; they may include persecutory or command hallucinations, voices conversing, voices commenting about the child, and the like (Russell et al., 1989). Although delusional beliefs can be difficult to assess, available studies suggest that these are exhibited in at least 50% of cases; they may take the form of ideas that involve persecution, somatic concerns, ideas of reference, or grandiose or religious notions (Russell et al., 1989). The content of hallucinations and delusions appears to vary with age; younger children typically express less complicated hallucinations or delusional beliefs, and the content of the delusions or hallucinations may center around parents, fantasy figures, and animals (Arboleda & Holzman, 1985; Russell et al., 1989). The presence of formal thought disorder was reported with greater variability (40% to 100% of the samples), reflecting the nature of specific definitions used. In addition, it is sometimes the case that children may not clearly exhibit a degree of thought disturbance sufficient to satisfy strict diagnostic criteria, particularly in the early phases of the illness (McClellan & Werry, 1994).

Outcome

The outcome for childhood-onset schizophrenia tends to be poor, with the majority of individuals experiencing chronic impairment. Eggers and colleagues (Eggers, 1978; Eggers & Bunk, 1997; Eggers et al., 2000) have conducted the longest follow-up study on childhood-onset schizophrenia (with the first follow-up examination between 1965 and 1967). They reported that about 20% of patients had experienced remission, about 30% showed improvement, and the remaining 50% had had moderate or poor outcomes. The worst prognostic feature was an early onset (before age 10) in children with premorbid personality difficulties; all such cases had a poor outcome at follow-up. In the more recent report on a small subgroup of patients ($n = 11$), Eggers et al. (2000) also noted that the individuals in their sample showed a change in diagnostic subtype at different points in the total course of their disorder, indicating marked variability in the production of psychotic symptoms in the course of childhood-onset schizophrenia. The early origins of this longitudinal study may raise questions about the accuracy of the initial diagnoses and clinical information in these cases. However, other more recent studies have also found that at least half of children originally diagnosed with schizophrenia continued to meet criteria upon follow-up and continued to exhibit chronic difficulties and relatively severe impairment (Asarnow, Tompson, & Goldstein, 1994; Kydd & Werry, 1982). The remaining children showed more substantial improvement, with about one third being in remission. In general, acute onset, older age at onset, premorbid adjustment, and well-differentiated symptomatology were associated with better outcome.

PATHOGENESIS

Neurobiological Factors

Although various lines of evidence suggest the involvement of biological processes in syndrome pathogenesis, no specific biological marker for the disorder has been identified. Investigations of neurotransmitter systems have been uncommon and have not produced consistent results (Werry, 1996). Cerebrospinal fluid monoamine metabolites were studied in relation to treatment response and revealed no significant changes in monoamine ratios and concentration, despite improved clinical symptomatology (Jacobsen, Frazier, et al., 1997). Immune processes similarly have not been found to mediate clinical response to antipsychotic medications, but a relative failure of cellular immunity was observed in children with schizophrenia compared to children with attention-deficit/hyperactivity disorder (ADHD) and children with obsessive-compulsive disorder (Mittleman et al., 1997).

Other areas have been the subject of more focused study, corresponding to emphases within the adult literature. For example, there have been numerous studies of smooth-pursuit eye movements in adults with schizophrenia, with consistent findings of abnormalities. In studies of childhood-onset schizophrenia, the results have been similar to those of previous studies of adults. Compared to age-matched controls and children with ADHD, children with schizophrenia showed significantly greater smooth-pursuit impairments, a lower amount of time overall spent engaged in tracking the target, and a higher rate of anticipatory saccades (Jacobsen, Hong, et al., 1996). Anticipatory saccades during smooth-pursuit eye movements and elevated P50 auditory evoked response to repeated stimuli are of particular interest, as they may represent physiologic markers of some aspect of genetic risk (Ross et al., 1999).

Genetic and family studies provide what is probably the most convincing evidence of some biological basis for schizophrenia. Rates of schizophrenia and related disorders among the first-degree relatives of schizophrenic children are substantially elevated in comparison to those observed in the normal population, as is the case in relatives of adult schizophrenic patients (Kallman & Prugh, 1971; Kolvin, 1971; Nicolson et al., 2000). Additional abnormalities other than schizophrenia may represent a risk factor relevant to the early onset of the disorder Alaghband-Rad et al. (1998) report a preliminary finding of an increased rate of mental retardation in the siblings of children with schizophrenia, which may also be associated with sex chromosome abnormalities. Cytogenetic abnormalities have been examined in children with schizophrenia and also show an increased rate (Kumra, Wiggs, et al., 1998; Nicolson, Giedd, et al., 1999; Usiskin et al., 1999). In particular, there is support for an association between deletions of chromosome 22q11 (velocardiofacial syndrome) and schizophrenia. In these cases, the loss of gene product balance may represent another factor predisposing the child to greater risk or susceptibility to additional genetic and environmental events. To date, there have been negative findings for a role for apolipoprotein E alleles, trinucleotide repeats, and human leukocyte antigen in childhood-onset schizophrenia (Fernandez et al., 1999; Jacobsen, Mittleman, et al., 1998; Sidransky, Burgess, & Ikeuchi, 1998).

The nature of the underlying mechanisms that might account for the early onset of schizophrenia in some individuals remains uncertain. General considerations include a higher genetic loading; structural differences in the brain have also been examined in childhood schizophrenia using magnetic resonance imaging. Current findings represent the systematic investigation of researchers at the National Institute of Mental Health (NIMH), which have been detailed in a series of reports and reflect preliminary data that will need to be independently replicated (Giedd et al., 1999; Jacobsen, Giedd, et al., 1996; Jacobsen, Giedd, Rajapakse, et al., 1997; Jacobsen, Giedd, Tanrikut, et al., 1997; Nicolson et al., 2000; Rapoport et al., 1997). Smaller total cerebral volume, increased ventricular volume, and reduced area of the thalamus were obtained in the group of children with schizophrenia compared to healthy controls, which is consistent with findings in adult-onset schizophrenia. Increased size of the corpus callosum and reduced cerebellar volume were also shown (Jacobsen, Giedd, Berquin, et al., 1997; Jacobsen, Giedd, Rajapakse, et al., 1997). Differences in the volume of the prefrontal lobes were not found (Nicolson et al., 2000), although there is some evidence from functional imaging studies that is suggestive of abnormalities in this region (Bertolino et al., 1998; Jacobsen, Hamburger, et al., 1997). Lateral temporal lobe structures, particularly the superior temporal gyrus, were significantly enlarged in the group of children with schizophrenia compared to controls. The volumes of medial temporal lobe structures, such as the amygdala and hippocampus, were not significantly different in the two groups, although there were discrepancies in symmetry patterns (Jacobsen, Giedd, et al., 1996). Area measurements of the planum temporale also did not reveal significant differences (Jacobsen, Giedd, Tanrikut, et al., 1997), consistent with a pattern of relative sparing of some temporal lobe structures. The results of prospective longitudinal studies revealed a differential decrease in thalamic and temporal lobe structures and a differential increase in ventricular volume over time (Rapoport et al., 1997; Jacobsen, Giedd, et al., 1998). This evidence was interpreted to suggest progressive changes in the brain in childhood-onset schizophrenia that are present during adolescence and may taper off in adulthood (Giedd et al., 1999).

In a similar vein, a pattern of intellectual decline in children with schizophrenia was interpreted as further evidence of an ongoing or progressive pathologic process in this disorder (Bedwell et al., 1999). In this report, a significant decline in Full Scale IQ scores in children with schizophrenia was found, when measured prior to and following onset of psychosis. This did not represent a deterioration of performance but rather a failure to make age-appropriate gains, as indicated by a comparison of raw scores on this test (Bedwell et al., 1999).

On measures of intelligence, children with schizophrenia are generally found to perform in the low average range. When groups of children with childhood-onset schizophrenia and high-functioning autism were compared, they did not differ in their Full Scale IQ score or performance on the Perceptual Organization and Verbal Comprehension factors of the Wechsler Intelligence Scale for Children—Revised (WISC-R; (Asarnow, Asamen, & Granholm, 1994). The group with childhood-onset schizophrenia did show a significantly lower score on the distractibility factor. Neuropsychological studies have also revealed deficits in attentional capacities and the processing of information. Current findings chiefly represent the report of a series of investigations conducted by Asarnow and colleagues (Asarnow, Asamen, & Granholm, 1994; Asarnow et al., 1995; Karatekin & Asarnow, 1998a; 1998b; 1999). Rote language skills and simple perceptual functions were not impaired in children with schizophrenia, but a significantly reduced performance on measures of fine motor speed and tasks that place demands on attention and short term memory was shown. Kumra et al. (2000) report a similar pattern of neuropsychological deficits in the areas of auditory attention, verbal memory, and mental flexibility. Deficits in some areas of spatial organization were also observed. In addition, fairly detailed studies of performance on visual search tasks have been conducted, which are thought to tap into the presumed core attentional deficit in schizophrenia. Taken together, the findings indicate inadequate representation of context and use of self-guided hypothesis testing for control of action in children with schizophrenia (Karatekin & Asarnow, 1998b, 1999; Zahn et al., 1998).

Environmental Events

In addition to neurobiologic factors, a role for environmental events has been considered in the pathogenesis of schizophrenia. Studies of adults with schizophrenia suggest that complications in pregnancy, labor, and delivery may be more frequent and related to an earlier age of onset, but this has not been the finding in childhood-onset schizophrenia (Nicolson, Malaspina, et al., 1999). In addition, there does not appear to be a relationship between age at onset of puberty and onset of symptoms of psychosis (Frazier et al., 1997). There is evidence that stressful life events may play a role in precipitating episodes of psychosis in children (Birley & Brown, 1970). However, there is no evidence at present to suggest that unusual psychological trauma accounts for the earlier age of onset in this group. In addition, no single personality pattern or pattern of premorbid adjustment appears to uniformly characterize children in this group prior to onset of schizophrenia. Although patterns of family interaction in the families of individuals with schizophrenia have been examined, the role of family dynamics in syndrome pathogenesis remains to be established. Some data suggest that children with schizophrenia are more likely to come from lower socioeconomic status families (Green, Padron-Gayol, Hardesty, & Bassiri, 1992; Kolvin, 1971). However, it is not clear to what extent socioeconomic status (SES) suggests a role for the environment in pathogenesis, because lower SES might also be the result of parental psychopathology leading to a downward drift in occupational status. In addition, this finding may represent a selection bias of samples obtained from inpatient or clinic settings.

ASSESSMENT

Diagnostic Evaluation

As noted, to date, no single biological marker for schizophrenia in childhood has been found. Because overt psychosis can be observed in association with organic mental disorders, it is important to conduct a careful medical history and examination, particularly if there are unusual or atypical features. Generally, multiple informants must be interviewed to obtain an adequate history, and several sessions with the child will usually be required to obtain an adequate mental status examination. It has also been observed that diagnostic accuracy is improved when structured instruments are used (McClellan & McCurry, 1999). Such instruments include the Structured Clinical Interview for *DSM-IV* (SCID; First, Gibbon, Spitzer, Williams, & Pincus, 1996) and the Schedule for Affective Disorders and Schizophrenia for School-Age Children (K-SADS; Puig-Antich and Chambers, 1983); the applicability of specific instruments varies depending on the age and verbal ability of the individual. Given the infrequency of the condition, a complete neurological examination including an electroencephalogram (EEG) is indicated. Genetic testing may also be advised in some cases, given the findings of a higher rate of cytogenetic abnormalities in children with schizophrenia, which, notably, had been previously undetected. If substance abuse, particularly of stimulants or phencyclidine, is suggested by history or physical signs are manifest, appropriate toxicological screening should be obtained.

Psychological Testing

Schizophrenic disorders in childhood are infrequently associated with mental retardation, but various developmental and learning problems may be present. Psychological testing is helpful both in documenting current levels of intellectual and adaptive functioning and in determining areas of specific strength or weakness important for educational programming. In addition to information provided by formal intellectual assessment, projective tests should be administered. Many children with schizophrenia may not exhibit disorganized thinking at interview (Russell, 1994). Thus, projective tests may provide important information about the severity of thought disorder and psychotic thinking, supplementing information obtained from other sources. Several assessment instruments have been developed explicitly for the assessment of psychosis or thought disorder in childhood (Caplan, 1994; Caplan et al., 1989). Although these do not replace the need for careful psychological testing, including projectives, they do help quantitate the nature of thought difficulties present—derailment, tangentiality, and so forth. Speech and language assessments should also be obtained, particularly in cases where communication problems are prominent.

TREATMENT

As with other aspects of the disorder, studies of treatment in childhood schizophrenia are few in number and limited in various respects. Practice parameters for assessment and treatment have recently been published (McClellan & Werry, 1997). To a considerable extent, treatment programs should be developed with the child's specific profile of functioning in mind (i.e., specific patterns of strength and weakness); treatment modalities will also depend on the stage of illness (i.e., the presence of active psychotic symptomatology). Typically, multiple treatment modalities will be needed, including medication, educational and family interventions, and supportive psychotherapy; depending on the clinical situation, inpatient treatment may be indicated.

Medication

There is good evidence to suggest the efficacy of antipsychotic (neuroleptic) medications in the treatment of schizophrenia in adults. The few available reports suggest that they also have a role in treatment in children (Kydd & Werry, 1982). As with adults, the use of psychotropic medications appears to be of particular benefit in relation to the positive symptoms of the disorder, although the dearth of studies in this area makes this observation only tentative at best (McKenna et al., 1994). Concerns about the possible long-term side effects of these medications (such as extrapyramidal symptoms and tardive dyskinesia) suggest the need for informed consent, careful monitoring, and periodic reevaluation (McClellan & Werry, 1997). In general, no specific major tranquilizer is clearly superior, and the choice of medication should be guided by the particular constellation of problems exhibited. Particularly for children and adolescents whose disturbance does not respond to more usual agents, the atypical antipsychotic clozapine may be considered (Frazier, Gordon, McKenna, Jih, & Rapoport, 1994; Jacobsen et al., 1994; McClellan & Werry, 1997). Reports of trials of clozapine (Kumra et al., 1996) and olanzapine (Kumra, Jacobsen, et al., 1998) in children with schizophrenia suggest that these medications can be effective in decreasing psychosis in at least some of the neuroleptic-nonresponsive children (also see Kumra et al., 2000). However, clinical experience reflecting the use of these agents in the pediatric population is limited. In all cases, recommendation is made for using the minimum effective dosage of antipsychotic medication and monitoring for both efficacy and side effects. Evidence regarding the use of other classes of medications is even more restricted. Given the potential for stimulant medications to induce a psychotic illness, their use is probably contraindicated.

Psychosocial Interventions

In addition to medication, family interventions should involve several aspects: education about the nature of the illness, enhancement of the child and family's understanding of the child's experience of the child, and development of a treatment plan. It will also be important to identify pertinent issues related to family functioning and to support effective communication among family members. Many children with schizophrenia exhibit associated problems in development and learning, which must be addressed through the provision of a comprehensive educational program. The disorder can have a deleterious impact on the acquisition of basic developmental and adaptive skills. Special education should be provided to address associated learning and developmental problems. Behavior-modification procedures may be useful in reducing levels of maladaptive behaviors and increasing the availability of the child for educational and other interventions. Generally speaking, it is important that the treatment program provided be integrated and that all of the various professionals involved be aware of the need for close communication and a consistent treatment approach.

OTHER PSYCHOTIC CONDITIONS

Various conditions may present with psychotic features. These most commonly include the various mood disorders (see chapter 13) as well as other conditions. The mood disorders, particularly bipolar disorders, are frequently confused with schizophrenia (Strober & Carlson, 1982). Furthermore, a small group of individuals who initially present with major depressive disorder will go on to exhibit more typical bipolar I disorder, and psychotic depression can be observed in children (Chambers, Puig-Antich, Tabrizi, & Davies, 1982). Symptoms of mood disorder also vary with the age of the child (Carlson, 1983; Tumuluru et al., 1995).

A number of other conditions may be confused with schizophrenia. These include brief reactive psychosis, substance-induced psychosis, or mood disorder related to the effects of a general medical condition. Usually, history and examination clarify the diagnosis of these conditions. Occasionally, the unusual behaviors and preoccupations associated with obsessive-compulsive disorder may be suggestive of schizophrenia; in such cases, careful mental status examination typically clarifies that thought processes are preserved even in the face of unusual rituals and preoccupations, as it becomes clear that the individual recognizes the irrational nature of the compulsive actions. At times the differential diagnosis can be difficult, particularly when preoccupations are highly bizarre. Although diagnoses of autism and schizophrenia can be jointly made, this combination of conditions appears rather uncommon (Volkmar, 1996). There has been some speculation that individuals with other pervasive developmental disorders, notably Asperger's disorder, may be at increased risk for schizophrenia. However, the combination of the tendency of patients with this condition to be highly verbose and socially insensitive complicates the task of diagnosis, and it remains unclear whether they are at increased risk for schizophrenia (see Klin, Sparrow, & Volkmar, 2000 for a discussion).

Children with schizophrenia have an increased risk of exhibiting other problems, including conduct disorder, learning disabilities, and mental retardation (Russell et al., 1989). In individuals with mental retardation or specific language disorders, particular care should be exercised in making a diagnosis of schizophrenia (Volkmar, 1996). Similarly, for children under 10 years of age careful evaluation is required, and it should be clear that the symptoms do not reflect the presence of an organic process. At times, the onset of schizophrenia can be highly insidious, and patients may receive a number of other diagnoses before the diagnosis of schizophrenia is made; in such cases, often the diagnosis is clarified with certainty only over time. As Kumra et al. (2000) have reported, there are large numbers of children who have psychotic disorders but whose difficulties do not, at least initially, fit classic syndrome pictures.

CONCLUSION AND FUTURE DIRECTIONS

Research on psychotic disorders in children has increased markedly during the past decade, but much work is still needed. A great deal of the information on these disorders still derives from work with adults, and although important points of phenomenological similarity are apparent, there are major differences, as well. Studies of the natural history, epidemiology, neurobiology, and treatment of these disorders are needed. Although some modifications of diagnostic criteria are made for children, additional work is warranted because it is clear that the difficulties of some children with psychotic disorders fall outside currently recognized syndrome boundaries (McKenna, et al., 1994).

REFERENCES

Alaghband-Rad, J., Kumra, S., Lenane, M. C., Jacobsen, L. K., Brown, A. S., Susser, E., Rapoport, J. L. (1998). Early-onset schizophrenia: Mental retardation in siblings. *Journal of the American Academy of Child and Adolescent Psychiatry, 37,* 137–138.

Alaghband-Rad, J., McKenna, K., Gordon, C. T., Albus, K. E., Hamburger, S. D., Rumsey, J. M., Frazier, J. A., Lenane, M. C., & Rapoport, J. L. (1995). Childhood-onset schizophrenia: The severity of premorbid course. *Journal of the American Academy of Child and Adolescent Psychiatry, 34,* 1273–1283.

American Psychiatric Association (1994). *Diagnostic and statistical manual of mental disorders* (4th ed.). Washington, DC: Author.

Andreasen, N. C., & Grove, W. M. (1986). Thought, language, and communication in schizophrenia: Diagnosis and prognosis. *Schizophrenia Bulletin, 12,* 346–359.

Arboleda, C., & Holzman, P. S. (1985). Thought disorder in children at risk for psychosis. *Archives of General Psychiatry, 42,* 1004–1013.

Asaad, G. (1990). *Hallucinations in clinical psychiatry: A guide for mental health professionals.* New York: Brunner/Mazel.

Asarnow, R. F., Asamen, J., & Granholm, E., (1994). Cognitive/neuropsychological studies of children with a schizophrenic disorder. *Schizophrenia Bulletin, 20,* 647–669.

Asarnow, R. F., Brown, W., & Strandburg, R. (1995). Children with a schizophrenic disorder: neurobehavioral studies. *European Archives of Psychiatry and Clinical Neuroscience, 245,* 70–79.

Asarnow, J. R., Tompson, M. C., & Goldstein, M. J. (1994). Childhood-onset schizophrenia: A follow-up study. *Schizophrenia Bulletin, 20,* 599–617.

Bedwell, J. S., Keller, B., Smith, A. K., Hamburger, S., Kumra, S., & Rapoport, J. L. (1999). Why does postpsychotic IQ decline in childhood-onset schizophrenia? *American Journal of Psychiatry, 156,* 1996–1997.

Bentall, R. P., & Slade, P. D. (1985). Reliability of a measure of disposition towards hallucination. *Personality and Individual Differences, 6*, 527–529.

Bertolino, A., Kumra, S., Callicott, J. H., Mattay, V. S., Lestz, R. M., Jacobsen, L., Barnett, I. S., Duyn, J. H., Frank, J. A., Rapoport, J. L., & Weinberger, D. R. (1998). Common pattern of cortical pathology in childhood-onset and adult-onset schizophrenia as identified by proton magnetic resonance spectroscopic imaging. *American Journal of Psychiatry, 155*, 1376–1383.

Bettes, B. A., & Walker, E. (1987). Positive and negative symptoms in psychotic and other psychiatrically disturbed children. *Journal of Child Psychology and Psychiatry, 28*, 555–568.

Birley, J. L., Brown, G. W. (1970). Crisis and life changes preceding the onset or relapse of acute schizophrenia: Clinical aspects. *British Journal of Psychiatry, 116*, 327–333.

Bleuler, E. (1911/1951). *Dementia praecox, or the group of schizophrenia* (J. Zinkin, Trans.) New York: International Universities Press.

Burd, L., & Kerbeshian, I. (1987). A North Dakota prevalence study of schizophrenia presenting in childhood. *Journal of American Academy of Child and Adolescent Psychiatry, 26*, 347–350.

Butler, R. W., & Braff, D. L. (1991). Delusions: A review and integration. *Schizophrenia Bulletin, 17*, 633–647.

Caplan, R. (1994). Thought disorder in childhood. *Journal of the American Academy of Child and Adolescent Psychiatry, 33*, 605–615.

Caplan, R., Guthrie, D., Fish, B., Tanguay, P. E., & David-Lando, G. (1989). The Kiddie Formal Thought Disorder Rating Scale (K-FTDS). Clinical assessment, reliability, and validity. *Journal of the American Academy of Child and Adolescent Psychiatry, 28*, 208–216.

Caplan, R., Perdue, S., Tanguay, P. E., & Fish, B. (1990). Formal thought disorder in childhood onset schizophenia and schizotypal personality disorder. *Journal of Child Psycholology and Psychiatry, 31*, 1103–1114.

Carlson, G. A. (1983). Bipolar affective disorders in childhood and adolescence. In D. P. Cantwell & G. A. Carlson (Eds.), *Affective disorders in childhood and adolescence: An update.* New York: Spectrum Publications.

Chambers, W. J., Puig-Antich, J., Tabrizi, M. A., & Davies, M. (1982). Psychotic symptoms in prepubertal major depressive disorder. *Archives of General Psychiatry, 39*, 921–927.

Eggers, C. (1978). Course and prognosis of childhood schizophrenia. *Journal of Autism and Childhood Schizophrenia, 8*, 21–36.

Eggers, C., & Bunk, D. (1997). The long-term course of childhood onset schizophrenia. *Schizophrenia Bulletin, 23*, 83–92.

Eggers, C., Bunk, D., & Krause, D. (2000). Schizophrenia with onset before the age of eleven: Clinical characteristics of onset and course. *Journal of Autism and Developmental Disorders, 30*, 29–38.

Fernandez, T., Yan, W. L., Hamburger, S., Rapoport, J. L., Saunders, A. M., Schapiro, M., Ginns, E. I., & Sidransky, E. (1999). Apolipoprotein E alleles in childhood-onset schizophrenia. *American Journal of Medical Genetics, 88*, 211–213.

First, M. B., Gibbon, M., Spitzer, R. L., Williams, J., & Pincus H. (1996). *User's guide for the Structured Clinical Interview for DSM-IV Axis I Disorders—Research Version.* Washington, DC: American Psychiatric Press.

Frazier, J. A., Alaghband-Rad, J., Jacobsen, L., Lenane, M. C., Hamburger, S., Albus, K., Smith, A., McKenna, K., & Rapoport, J. L. (1997). Pubertal development and onset of psychosis in childhood onset schizophrenia. *Psychiatry Resource, 70*, 1–7.

Frazier, J. A., Gordon, C. T., McKenna, K., Jih, D., & Rapoport, J. L. (1994). An open trial of clozapine in 11 adolescents with childhood-onset schizophrenia. *Journal of the American Academy of Child and Adolescent Psychiatry, 33*, 658–663.

Freud, S. (1911/1957). Psychoanalytic notes on an autobiographical account of a case of paranoia. *The standard edition of the complete works of Sigmund Freud* (Vol. 12). London: Hogarth Press.

Garralda, M. E. (1984). Hallucinations in children with conduct and emotional disorders: I. The clinical phenomena. *Psychological Medicine, 14,* 589–596.

Garralda, M. E. (1985). Characteristics of the psychoses of late onset in children and adolescents: A comparative study of hallucinating children. *Journal of Adolescence, 8,* 195–207.

Giedd, J. N., Jeffries, N. O., Blumenthal, J., Castellanos, F. X., Vaituzis, A. C., Fernandez, T., Hamburger, S. D., Liu, H., Nelson, J., Bedwell, J., Tran, L., Lenane, M., Nicolson, R., & Rapoport, J. L. (1999). Childhood-onset schizophrenia: Progressive brain changes during adolescence. *Biological Psychiatry, 46,* 892–898.

Green, W. H., Campbell, M., Hardesty, A. S., Grega, D. M., Padron-Gayol, M., Shell, J., & Erlenmeyer-Kimling, L. (1984). A comparison of schizophrenic and autistic children. *Journal of the American Academy of Child and Adolescent Psychiatry, 4,* 399–409.

Green, W. H., Padron-Gayol, M., Hardesty, A., & Bassiri, M. (1992). Schizophrenia with childhood onset: A phenomenological study of 38 cases. *Journal of the American Academy of Child and Adolescent Psychiatry, 31,* 968–976.

Hollis, C. (1995). Child and adolescent (juvenile onset) schizophrenia: A case control study of premorbid developmental impairments. *British Journal of Psychiatry, 166,* 489–495.

Holzman, P. S. (1986). Thought disorder in schizophrenia: Editor's introduction. *Schizophrenia Bulletin, 12,* 342–345.

Jacobsen, L. K., Frazier, J. A., Malhotra, A. K., Jacobsen, L. K., Karoum, F., McKenna, K., Gordon, C. T., Hamburger, S. D., Lenane, M. C., Pickar, D., Potter, W. Z., Rapoport, J. L. (1997). Cerebrospinal fluid monoamine metabolites in childhood-onset schizophrenia. *American Journal of Child Psychiatry, 154,* 69–74.

Jacobsen, L. K., Giedd, J. N., Berquin, P. C., Krain, A. L., Hamburger, S. D. Kumra, S., & Rapoport, J. L. (1997). Quantitative morphology of the cerebellum and fourth ventricle in childhood-onset schizophrenia. *American Journal of Psychiatry, 154,* 1663–1669.

Jacobsen, L. K., Giedd, J. N., Castellanos, F. X., Vaituzis, A. C., Hamburger, S. D., Kumra, S., Lenane, M. C., & Rapoport, J. L. (1998). Progressive reduction of temporal lobe structures in childhood-onset schizophrenia. *American Journal of Psychiatry, 155,* 678–685.

Jacobsen, L. K., Giedd, J. N., Rajapakse, J. C., Hamburger, S. D., Vaituzis, C., Frazier, J. A., Lenane, M. C., & Rapoport, J. L. (1997). Quantitative magnetic resonance imaging of the corpus callosum in childhood onset schizophrenia. *Psychiatry Resource, 68,* 77–86.

Jacobsen, L. K., Giedd, J. N., Tanrikut, C., Brady, D. R., Donohue, B. C., Hamburger, S. D., Kumra, S., Alaghband-Rad, J., Rumsey, J. M., & Rapoport, J. L. (1997). Three-dimensional cortical morphometry of the planum temporale in childhood-onset schizophrenia. *American Journal of Psychiatry, 154,* 685–687.

Jacobsen, L. K., Giedd, J. N., Vaituzis, C., Hamburger, S. D., Rajapakse, J. C., Frazier, J. A., Kaysen, D., Lenane, M. C., McKenna, K., Gordon, C. T., & Rapoport, J. L. (1996). Temporal lobe morphology in childhood-onset schizophrenia. *American Journal of Psychiatry, 153,* 355–361.

Jacobsen, L. K., Hamburger, S. D., Van Horn, J. D., Vaituzis, A. C., McKenna, K., Frazier, J. A., Gordon, C. T., Lenane, M. C., Rapoport, J. L., & Zametkin, A. J. (1997). Cerebral glucose metabolism in childhood onset schizophrenia. *Psychiatry Resource, 75,* 131–144.

Jacobsen, L. K., Hong, W. L., Hommer, D. W., Hamburger, S. D., Castellanos, F. X., Frazier, J. A., Giedd, J. N., Gordon, C. T., Karp, B. I., McKenna, K., & Rapoport, J. L. (1996). Smooth pursuit eye movements in childhood-onset schizophrenia: Comparison with attention-deficit hyperactivity disorder and normal controls. *Biological Psychiatry, 40,* 1144–1154.

Jacobsen, L. K., Mittleman, B. B., Kumra, S., Frazier, J. A., Malhotra, A. K., Karoum, F., McKenna, K., Gordon, C. T., Hamburger, S. D., Lenane, M. C., Pickar, D., Potter, W. Z., & Rapoport, J. L. (1998). HLA antigens in childhood onset schizophrenia. *Psychiatry Resource, 78,* 123–132.

Jacobsen, L. K., & Rapoport, J. L. (1998). Research update: Childhood-onset schizophrenia: Implications of clinical and neurobiological research. *Journal of Child Psychology and Psychiatry, 39,* 101–113.

Jacobsen, L. K., Walker, M. C., Edwards, J. E., Chappell P. B., & Woolston J. L. (1994). Clozapine in the treatment of a young adolescent with schizophrenia. *Journal of the American Academy of Child and Adolescent Psychiatry, 33,* 645–650.

Kallman, F. J., & Prugh, D. G. (1971). Genetic aspects of pre-adolescent schizophrenia. *American Journal of Psychiatry, 112,* 599–606.

Karatekin, C., & Asarnow, R. F. (1998a). Working memory in childhood-onset schizophrenia and attention-deficit/hyperactivity disorder. *Psychiatry Resource, 80,* 165–176.

Karatekin, C., & Asarnow, R. F. (1998b). Components of visual search in childhood-onset schizophrenia and attention-deficit/hyperactivity disorder. *Journal of Abnormal Child Psychology, 26,* 367–380.

Karatekin, C., & Asarnow, R. F. (1999). Exploratory eye movements to pictures in childhood-onset schizophrenia and attention-deficit/hyperactivity disorder. *Journal of Abnormal Child Psychology, 27,* 35–49.

Kendler, K. S., Glazer, W. M., & Morgenstern, H. (1983). Dimensions of delusional experience. *American Journal of Psychiatry, 140,* 466–469.

King, R. A., & Noshpitz, J. (1991). *Pathways of growth: Essentials of child psychiatry, Volume 2: Psychopathology.* New York: John Wiley & Sons.

Klin, A., Sparrow, S., & Volkmar, F. R. (Eds.). (2000). *Aspeger's syndrome.* New York: Guilford Press.

Kolvin, I. (1971). Studies in the childhood psychoses: I. Diagnostic criteria and classification. *British Journal of Psychiatry, 118,* 381–384.

Kumra, S., Frazier, J., Jacobsen, L. K., McKenna, K., Gordon, C. T., Lenane, M. C., Hamburger, S. D., Smith A. K., Albus, K. E., Alaghband-Rad, J., & Rapoport, J. L. (1996). Childhood-onset schizophrenia: A double-blind clozapine-haloperidol comparison. *Archives of General Psychiatry, 53,* 1090–1097.

Kumra, S., Jacobsen, L. K., Lenane, M., Karp, B. I., Frazier, J. A., Smith, A. K., Bedwell, J., Lee, P., Malanga, C. J., Hamburger, S., & Rapoport, J. L. (1998). Childhood-onset schizophrenia: An open-label study of olanzapine in adolescents. *Journal of the American Academy of Child and Adolescent Psychiatry, 37,* 377–385.

Kumra, S., Wiggs, E., Bedwell, J., Smith, A. K., Arling, E., Albus, K., Hamburger, S. D., McKenna, K., Jacobsen, L. K., Rapoport, J. L., & Asarnow, R. F. (2000). Neuropsychological deficits in pediatric patients with childhood-onset schizophrenia and psychotic disorder not otherwise specified. *Schizophrenia Resource, 42,* 135–144.

Kumra, S., Wiggs, E., Krasnewich, D., Meck, J., Smith, A. C., Bedwell, J., Fernandez, T., Jacobsen, L. K., Lenane, M., & Rapoport, J. (1998). Brief report: Association of sex chromosome anomalies with childhood-onset psychotic disorders. *Journal of the American Academy of Child Adolescent and Psychiatry, 37,* 292–296.

Kydd, R. R., & Werry, J. S. (1982). Schizophrenia in children under 16 years. *Journal of Autism and Developmental Disorders, 12,* 343–357.

McClellan, J., & McCurry, C. (1999). Early onset psychotic disorders: Diagnostic stability and clinical characteristics. *European Child and Adolescent Psychiatry, 8*(Suppl. 1), I/13–I/19.

McClellan, J., & Werry, J. (1994). Practice parameters for the assessment and treatment of children and adolescents with schizophrenia. *Journal of the American Academy of Child and Adolescent Psychiatry, 33,* 616–635.

McClellan, J., & Werry, J. (1997). Practice parameters for the assessment and treatment of children and adolescents with schizophrenia. *Journal of the American Academy of Child and Adolescent Psychiatry, 36*(Suppl. 10), 177S–193S.

McKenna, K. M., Gordon, C. T., Lenane, M., Kaysen, D., Fahey K., & Rapoport, J. L. (1994). Looking for childhood onset schizophrenia: The first 71 cases screened. *Journal of the American Academy of Child and Adolescent Psychiatry, 33,* 636–644.

Mittleman, B. B., Castellanos, F. X., Jacobsen, L. K., Rapoport J. L., Swedo, S. E., Shearer, G. M. (1997). Cerebrospinal fluid cytokines in pediatric neuropsychiatric disease. *Journal of Immunology, 159,* 2294–2299.

Nicolson, R., Giedd, J. N., Lenane, M., Hamburger, S., Singarachariu, S., Bedwell, J., Fernandez, T., Thaker, G. K., Malaspina, D., & Rapoport, J. L. (1999). Clinical and neurobiological correlates of cytogenetic abnormalities in childhood-onset schizophrenia. *American Journal of Psychiatry, 156,* 1575–1579.

Nicolson, R., Lenane, M., Hamburger, S. D., Fernandez, T., Bedwell, J., & Rapoport, J. L. (2000). Lessons from childhood-onset schizophrenia. *Brain Research Reviews, 31,* 147–156, 2000.

Nicolson, R., Malaspina, D., Giedd, J. N., Hamburger, S., Lenane, M., Bedwell, J., Fernandez, T., Berman, A., Susser, E., & Rapoport, J. L. (1999). Obstetrical complications in childhood-onset schizophrenia. *American Journal of Psychiatry, 156,* 1650–1652.

Piaget, J. (1955). *The child's construction of reality.* London: Routledge and Kegan Paul.

Puig-Antich, J., & Chambers, W. (1983). *The Schedule for Affective Disorders and Schizophrenia for School-Age Children (Kiddie-SADS).* New York: New York State Psychiatric Institute.

Rapoport, J. L., Giedd, J., Kumra, S., Jacobsen, L., Smith, A., Lee, P., Nelson, J., & Hamburger, S. (1997). Childhood-onset schizophrenia: Progressive ventricular change during adolescence. *Archives of General Psychiatry, 54,* 897–903.

Ross, R. G., Olincy, A., Harris, J. G., Radant A., Hawkins M., Adler L. E., & Freedman, R. (1999). Evidence for bilineal inheritance of physiological indicators of risk in childhood-onset schizophrenia. *American Journal of Medical Genetics, 88,* 188–199.

Rothstein, A. (1981). Hallucinatory phenomena in childhood: A critique of the literature. *Journal of the American Academy of Child Psychiatry, 20,* 623–635.

Russell, A. T. (1994). The clinical presentation of childhood-onset schizophrenia. *Schizophrenia Bulletin, 20,* 631–646.

Russell, A. T., Bott, L., & Sammons, C. (1989). The phenomenology of schizophrenia occurring in childhood. *Journal of the American Academy of Child and Adolescent Psychiatry, 28,* 399–407.

Rutter, M. (1972). Childhood schizophrenia reconsidered. *Journal of Autism and Childhood Schizophrenia, 2,* 315–337.

Sidransky, E., Burgess, C., & Ikeuchi, T. (1998). A triplet repeat on 17q accounts for most expansions detected by the repeat-expansion-detection technique. *American Journal of Human Genetics, 62,* 1548–1551.

Strober, M., & Carlson, G. (1982). Bipolar illness in adolescents with major depression. *Archives of General Psychiatry, 39,* 549–555.

Tien, A. Y. (1991). Distributions of hallucinations in the population. *Social Psychiatry and Psychiatric Epidemiology, 26,* 287–292.

Tumuluru, S., Vaylayan, R. V., Weller, E. B., & Weller, R. A. (1996). Affective psychoses in children and adolescents: Major depression with psychosis. In F. Volkmar (Ed.), *Psychoses and pervasive developmental disorders in childhood and adolescence* (pp. 57–80). Washington, DC: American Psychiatric Press.

Usiskin, S. I., Nicolson, R., Krasnewich, D. M., Yan, W., Lenane, M., Wudarsky, M., Hamburger, S. D., & Rapoport, J. L. (1999). Velocardiofacial syndrome in childhood-onset schizophrenia. *Journal of the American Academy of Child and Adolescent Psychiatry, 38,* 1536–1543.

Volkmar, F. R. (1996). Childhood and adolescent psychosis: A review of the past 10 years. *Journal of the American Academy of Child and Adolescent Psychiatry, 35,* 843–851.

Volkmar, F. R., Becker, D. F., King, R. A., & McLashen, T. (1994). Psychotic processes. In D. Cicchetti & D. Cohen (Eds.), *Handbook of developmental psychopathology,* (vol. 1, pp. 512–534). New York: John Wiley & Sons.

Volkmar, F. R., Cohen, D. J., Hoshino, Y., Rende, R., & Paul, R. (1988). Phenomenology and classification of the childhood psychoses. *Psychological Medicine, 18,* 191–201.

Waldfogel, S., & Mueser, K. T. (1988). Another case of chronic PTSD with auditory hallucinations [letter]. *American Journal of Psychiatry, 145,* 1314.

Werry, J. (1996). Childhood schizophrenia. In F. Volkmar (Ed.), *Psychoses and pervasive developmental disorders in childhood and adolescence.* Washington, DC: American Psychiatric Press.

Yager, J. (1989). Clinical manifestations of psychiatric disorders. In H. I. Kaplan & B. J. Sadock (Eds.), *Comprehensive textbook of psychiatry* (5th ed., pp. 553–582). Baltimore: Williams & Wilkins.

Zahn, T. P., Jacobsen, L. K., Gordon, C. T., McKenna, K., Frazier, J. A., & Rapoport, J. L. (1997). Autonomic nervous system markers of psychopathology in childhood-onset schizophrenia. *Archives of General Psychiatry, 54,* 904–912.

Zahn, T. P., Jacobsen, L. K., Gordon, C. T., McKenna, K., Frazier, J. A., & Rapoport, J. L. (1998). Attention deficits in childhood-onset schizophrenia: Reaction time studies. *Journal of Abnormal Psychology, 107,* 97–108.

Chapter 15

THE SPECTRUM OF SUICIDAL BEHAVIOR

JOSEPH D. HOVEY AND CHERYL A. KING

Suicides among youth are a continuing tragedy. Between 1956 and 1996, the suicide rate in the United States increased from 0.4 to 1.6 for the 10- to 14-year age group, and from 2.3 to 9.7 for the 15- to 19-year age group (McIntosh, 2000). According to a National Vital Statistics Report (Centers for Disease Control [CDC], 2000), suicide is the third leading cause of death for these age groups, accounting for 13.4% of all deaths. Furthermore, severe suicidal ideation and suicide attempts among youth are associated with substantial psychopathology and adaptive impairment (Fergusson & Lynskey, 1995; Lewinsohn, Rohde, & Seeley, 1995; Reinherz et al., 1995), extreme distress for suicidal youth and their families, and innumerable psychiatric hospitalizations.

This chapter begins with a review of recent findings on the prevalence of suicidal thoughts and behaviors among youth. Research pertinent to the continuum of youth suicidality is then presented, with an emphasis on the links among suicidal thought, attempts, and completed suicide. This information is followed by a review of known risk factors, including a discussion of the psychiatric disorders that increase risk for suicidal behaviors. Our knowledge of these risk factors has increased rapidly during the past 20 years. Findings from epidemiologic and clinic-based studies have converged to form a consensus of primary risk factors. Finally, the latter part of the chapter outlines treatment interventions that may be effective in reducing suicidal ideation and, perhaps, suicide attempts among youth.

DEFINITION OF SUICIDAL BEHAVIOR

For the purposes of this discussion, *suicidal behavior* refers to the full spectrum of suicidality, which includes the traditional categories of suicidal ideation, suicide attempts, and completed suicide. *Suicidal ideation* represents thoughts or wishes to be dead or to kill oneself. *Suicide attempts* are self-injurious behaviors with some degree of suicidal intent. *Completed suicides* are self-inflicted and intended deaths. These three categories have often been conceptualized (e.g., Brent et al., 1988; King, 1997; Lewinsohn, Rohde, & Seeley, 1996) as distinct yet overlapping aspects of the spectrum of suicidal behavior.

It should be noted that there is much variability within each component of this spectrum. For example, suicidal ideation may range from the adolescent thinking that other individuals (such as friends or family members) would be better off if he or she were dead, to thinking through and planning a specific suicide attempt method. Similarly, a suicide attempt may range from an attempt of relatively low medical lethality and ambivalent or impulsive intent to one of much greater lethality in which the adolescent carefully develops and carries out a suicidal plan.

PREVALENCE OF SUICIDAL BEHAVIORS

Suicidal Ideation

It is not uncommon for adolescents to think about suicide. For example, the 1999 Youth Risk Behavior Surveillance (YRBS; Kann et al., 2000) found that, in the previous year, 19.3% of high school students nationwide had seriously considered attempting suicide, and 14.5% had made a specific plan to attempt suicide. In an epidemiologic longitudinal study of high school students (Oregon Adolescent Depression Project [OADP]), Lewinsohn et al. (1996) found that 12.9% of youths had considered hurting or killing themselves at some point in their lives, and 8.3% had made a suicide plan.

Prevalence rates indicate that adolescent females are 1.5 to 2 times more likely to report suicidal ideation than are adolescent males (King, 1997). For example, according to the 1999 YRBS (Kann et al., 2000), 24.9% of female students versus 13.7% of male students had seriously considered suicide, and 18.3% of females versus 10.9% of males had made a plan. Lewinsohn et al. (1996) found that 23.7% of OADP females and 14.8% of OADP males reported lifetime experiences of suicidal ideation.

Recent data suggest that rates of suicidal ideation in adolescence may peak at about the age of 16 years. Among OADP adolescents (Lewinsohn et al., 1996), lifetime suicidal ideation rates increased through the age of 16 (age 14 = 14.6%; 15 = 16.8%; 16 = 22.5%), then stabilized (17 = 20.1%; 18 = 21.0%). The 1999 YRBS data (Kann et al., 2000) showed a similar pattern as suicidal thoughts tended to peak in 10th grade. Twenty-two percent of 10th graders had seriously considered suicide in the previous 12 months (9th grade = 18.1%; 11th = 18.3%; 12th = 18.4%) and 17.7% had made suicide plans (9th = 14.6%; 11th = 13.6%; 12th = 11.4%).

As alluded to, the notion of suicidal ideation comprises suicidal thoughts that vary in their level of specificity and severity of intent. Within some studies (e.g., Andrews & Lewinsohn, 1992; Kienhorst, DeWilde, Van den Bout, Diekstra, & Wolters, 1990), researchers have captured this variability by operationalizing and measuring different aspects of suicidal ideation. Findings suggest that suicidal thoughts fall on a single continuum, with increasing levels of severity. For example, in the OADP (Andrews & Lewinsohn, 1992), the lifetime prevalence of each type of suicidal thought declined as the severity of intent of each thought increased: 16.3% of adolescents reported thoughts of death, 13.3% wished they were dead, 12.9% thought about killing themselves, and 8.3% made a plan.

Suicide Attempts

Although suicide attempts among youth occur less often than the experience of suicidal ideation, they are not infrequent. In fact, the rates of nonlethal attempts among adolescents are striking. General population studies have consistently shown that the percentage of adolescents reporting suicide attempts varies between 7% and 16% (King, 1997). Findings from the OADP (Andrews & Lewinsohn, 1992; Lewinsohn et al., 1996) indicated that 7.1% of individuals (females = 10.9%; males = 3.8%) reported having made one or more suicide attempts at some point in their lives. The 1999 YRBS (Kann et al., 2000) revealed that 8.3% of high school students nationwide (females = 10.9%; males = 5.7%) had made one or more attempts during the past year. Adcock, Nagy, and Simpson (1991) examined suicide attempt rates in 8th- and 10th-grade students in Alabama (N = 3,803) and found that 16% (females = 19%; males = 12%) reported at least one lifetime incident of attempted suicide.

As the preceding statistics suggest, similar to the gender difference for suicidal ideation, researchers have consistently found that a greater percentage of adolescent females report having attempted suicide. Moreover, also similar to the findings for suicidal ideation, some researchers have found that age is linked to prevalence rates. For example, according to the 1999 YRBS data (Kann et al., 2000), 10.6% of 10th graders reported at least one suicide attempt during the previous year. In contrast, 6.1% of 11th graders and 5.6% of 12th graders reported having made an attempt during the previous year. Utilizing a longitudinal design, Kovacs, Goldston, and Gatsonis (1993) examined ongoing rates of suicide attempts among outpatient adolescents with depressive disorders. They found that ages 13 to 15 years were peak periods for suicide attempts. At age 12, 3% of the adolescents made an attempt during the previous year; at age 13, 12% attempted suicide; at 14, 13% attempted suicide; and at 15, 11% made an attempt. Suicide attempt rates declined in later adolescence: 9% at 16; 6% at 17; and 2% at 18. According to Kovacs et al. (1993), younger adolescents may have a limited ability to regulate or tolerate intense negative affect or emotional distress. As they mature, they may develop better tolerance for dysphoric mood states and diverse coping resources and may therefore be less likely to resort to attempted suicide when they are despondent.

Any discussion of suicide attempts among adolescents would be incomplete without mention of the varying levels of lethality and intent involved in these attempts. Although the rates of suicide attempts among adolescents are relatively high, most attempts are low in medical lethality (i.e., the likelihood that the behavior will result in death). OADP findings (Lewinsohn et al., 1996) indicated that the most common suicide attempt methods for females were ingestion (55% of attempts) and cutting (31%). Males more often used methods of higher lethality. In addition to ingestion (20%) and cutting (25%), their methods included gun use (15%), hanging (11%), and other methods (22%), such as acts of injecting air into the veins or running into traffic. Other researchers have also documented that adolescent males use more lethal means when attempting suicide. For example, in a study of 3,437 adolescent students (469 of whom attempted suicide), Reynolds and Mazza (1994) found that female attempters were more likely to ingest pills (45.2% vs. 22.5%) and cut their wrists (30.4% vs. 18.6%) than were male attempters. In contrast, males were more likely to report the use of guns (12.4% vs. 0.4%), hanging or drowning (7.8% vs. 3.3%), and stabbing (7.0% vs. 6.6%).

Medical lethality can also be inferred through findings that detail the percentage of adolescents who receive medical attention following their suicide attempts. The 1999 YRBS data (Kann et al., 2000) revealed that, of those students who had attempted suicide during the previous 12 months, 31.3% had made an attempt that required medical attention. In corroboration of the preceding findings on suicide methods, the YRBS findings support the notion that suicide attempts by male adolescents are of higher lethality: 36.8% of male attempters required medical attention, compared to 28.4% percent of female attempters.

Suicidal intent can be defined as the extent to which an individual wishes to die. Findings from several clinical and community-based studies have indicated that suicidal intent and medical lethality are highly associated. For example, Robbins and Alessi (1985) found a high correlation ($r = .90$) between the seriousness of intent and the lethality of adolescent inpatients' most recent suicidal behavior. Andrews and Lewinsohn (1992) found a high positive correlation ($r = .67$) between intent and lethality among the OADP students. Despite the documented association between intent and lethality, it would be a mistake to assume that the medical lethality of a suicide attempt by an adolescent automatically matches the adolescent's intent to die. An adolescent may choose a method such as acetaminophen ingestion without having much knowledge about its actual toxicity. Because of the possible discrepancy between level of intent and lethality, it is extremely important to assess suicidal intent *and* medical lethality when determining the severity of the attempt.

Completed Suicides

According to National Center for Health Statistics data for 1998 (CDC, 2000), the suicide rate for individuals age 15 to 24 years in the United States is 11.1 per 100,000 individuals. There is a gender difference in completed suicides, although it is the reverse of what is seen with ideation and attempts (Figure 15.1). For female youth, the rate is 3.3. For males, it is 18.5. In contrast to the diminishing rate of nonlethal attempts that occurs during late adolescence and early adulthood, the rate for completed suicides increases with adulthood. The rate for children age 5 to 14 is 0.8. This is much lower than the rate of 11.1 found for individuals age 15 to 24, which is lower than the rate of 14.6 found for adults age 25 to 44.

As already noted, adolescent males more often use lethal methods when attempting suicide. This has commonly been used to explain the gender difference in adolescent suicide rates. Firearms are the most common method of suicide completion among adolescents (McIntosh, 2000). In the year 1996, firearms were used by 66.4% of male suicide victims and by 48.3% of female victims (age 15 to 19). After firearms, the most common methods for adolescent males were hanging (including instances of strangulation and suffocation, 22.7%), gas poisoning (3.4%), and poisoning that involved solid or liquid substances (2.3%). Methods of suicides for female victims included hanging (29.3%), solid or liquid poisoning (12.1%), jumping from heights (3.1%), and gas poisoning (2.5%).

One strategy for reducing the number of adolescent suicides in the United States may be to restrict the access of adolescents to firearms. In a case-control study, Brent et al. (1988) compared the characteristics of adolescent suicide victims to those of suicidal psychiatric inpatients and found that availability of firearms in the home was one

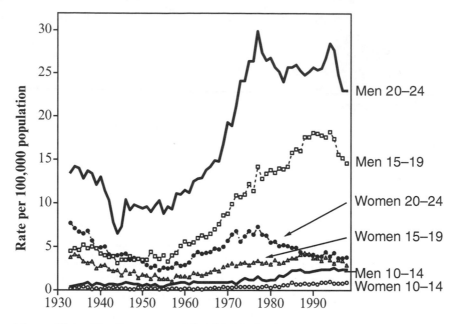

Figure 15.1   The Spectrum of Suicidal Behavior
Source: Data from the National Center for Health Statistics for 1998
(CDC, 2000).

differentiating factor. Firearms had been present in the homes of 74.1% of the suicide victims, compared to 33.9% of the homes of psychiatric inpatients. More recent studies have also found an association between completed suicide and the availability of firearms (Brent, Kolko, et al., 1993; Kellermann et al., 1992).

CONTINUUM OF SUICIDAL BEHAVIOR

Findings from a number of studies (e.g., Andrews & Lewinsohn, 1992; Brent et al., 1988; Kienhorst et al., 1990) suggest that suicidal ideation, suicide attempts, and completed suicides fall on a continuum of severity. These components of the spectrum of suicidality are each somewhat distinct, yet clearly overlapping. Among adolescents who think about suicide, a certain percentage will make a suicide attempt. And among those adolescents who make attempts, a smaller number will complete suicides. Information concerning this continuum derives from studies that have explored the relationship between the intensity of suicidal ideation and suicide attempts, as well as from retrospective and prospective studies that document continuity between history of attempts and completed suicides.

Kienhorst et al. (1990) explored numerous psychosocial predictors of suicidality in a sample of 9,393 students (age 14 to 20) from the Netherlands. They found that the best predictor of suicide attempts was frequent thoughts of suicide. According to the OADP findings (Andrews & Lewinsohn, 1992; Lewinsohn et al., 1996), 87.8% of females and 87.1% of males who attempted suicide at some point in their lives also reported suicidal ideation. Of the nonattempters, 1.7% of females and 0.6% of males reported suicidal ideation. The OADP findings further indicated that the level of severity of suicidal ideation increased the likelihood for suicide attempts. Specifically, 16.7% of adolescents who reported high baseline ideation attempted suicide over the course of the next year. This contrasts to suicide attempt rates of 6.7% for adolescents with moderate baseline ideation, 2.8% for mild levels of baseline ideation, and 0.3% for those with no baseline ideation.

Brent et al. (1988) found that adolescent suicide completers were similar to suicidal psychiatric inpatients over a broad range of domains, including their history of suicide attempts and most psychiatric disorders. They stated that this overlap suggests a continuum between suicidal attempts and completed suicide. Forty-four percent of suicide completers had made previous suicide attempts. Marttunen, Aro, and Lonnqvist (1992), in a retrospective psychological autopsy study of 53 suicides (age 13 to 19) in Finland, found that 34% of suicide completers had a history of suicide attempts.

Several longitudinal studies (e.g., Kotila, 1992; Motto, 1984; Otto, 1972) have tracked the outcome of adolescent patients who had been hospitalized for suicide attempts. In an early study in Sweden, Otto (1972) followed 321 male youth over the course of 10 to 15 years and found that 11.3% committed suicide. Kotila (1992), in a shorter time frame of 5 years, tracked the welfare of 120 male adolescents and 302 females adolescents, age 15 to 19. Within 5 years, 1.2% of females died from suicide and 8.7% of males died from suicide or possible suicide (e.g., drowning). Thirty-nine percent of these deaths occurred within 6 months after hospitalization. Although a history of suicide attempt is a predictor of a future suicide attempt and completed suicide in males and females, it is clearly a stronger predictor among males.

RISK FACTORS

Study Methodologies

Researchers have used various study methodologies to form an integrated understanding of risk factors for suicidal behavior. Knowledge about risk factors for completed suicide derive primarily from national mortality statistics, psychological autopsy studies, and longitudinal studies of suicidal individuals. In the United States, data concerning deaths by suicide are compiled by the National Center for Health Statistics (NCHS) within the Centers for Disease Control (CDC). This information is primarily demographic. Individual states submit data from death certificates that have been completed by coroners and medical examiners. Complementing this information are data from population-based psychological autopsy studies, which involve a detailed examination of consecutive deaths by suicide within a defined geographic area. The psychological autopsy study methodology is considered to be a powerful tool for identifying risk factors for completed suicide (Moscicki, 1999). It involves obtaining retrospective information from people who knew the deceased and from medical, school, and other records. Information typically gathered include the victim's state of health, history of treatment, level of functioning, psychosocial symptoms, and environmental circumstances in the victim's life preceding the suicide. In contrast to these two population-based methodologies, clinic- and hospital-based studies generally sample individuals who have expressed significant suicidal ideation or engaged in suicidal behaviors. Researchers may examine predictors of future suicidal behaviors in the context of a longitudinal design.

Information concerning risk factors for suicidal ideation and suicide attempts has been obtained from large-scale community-based studies as well as from clinic- and hospital-based studies. Prospective studies have been used to track the developmental course of psychopathology in adolescents from general community samples (e.g., Lewinsohn, Rohde, & Seeley, 1994) and to study the outcome of hospitalized adolescent suicide attempters (e.g., Brent, Kolko, et al., 1993; Goldston et al., 1999; King et al., 1995; King, Hovey, Brand, Wilson, & Ghaziuddin, 1997). Numerous descriptive and correlational studies have also enriched our understanding of the factors associated with suicidal ideation and suicide attempts among youth.

Psychopathology

Shneidman (e.g., 1993, 1996) has written in detail about precipitants of suicide. He believes that most suicides are associated with "psychache," which he defines as intolerable psychological pain. Suicidal behavior usually occurs when an individual has surpassed her or his threshold for psychological pain. In that sense, as Shneidman would argue, each suicidal act is an intensely personal act. Research has, however, substantiated the existence of commonalities or common pathways involving psychopathology or psychiatric disorders that are predictive of suicide risk (King, 1998). These include depression, alcohol and substance abuse, and a pattern of conduct disorder or aggressive and impulsive behavior. Although not discussed here, several other forms of psychopathology (e.g., anxiety disorders and schizophrenia) have also been associated with suicidal behavior in youth.

Depression

Rates of depression rise sharply during adolescence (e.g., Petersen et al., 1993), and studies of depressive disorders across the lifespan indicate that the risk of developing a depressive disorder is particularly high among older adolescents (Burke, Burke, Rae, & Reiger, 1991). Point prevalence and lifetime prevalence rates of major depressive disorder (MDD) among adolescents are approximately 2% to 4% (e.g., Garrison et al., 1997) and 20% (Lewinsohn, Hops, Roberts, Seeley, & Andrews, 1993), respectively. A disorder of substantial public health significance, MDD in adolescents is associated with a wide range of psychiatric comorbidity (e.g., Kovacs, 1996), substantial psychosocial impairment (e.g., Puig-Antich et al., 1993), and increased risk of suicide (Marttunen, Aro, Henriksson, & Lonnqvist, 1991; Rao, Weissman, Martin, & Hammond, 1993; Shaffer, Garland, Gould, Fisher, & Trautman, 1988).

Suicidal behaviors are common and often unrelenting among adolescents with depression. Lewinsohn et al. (1996) found that 41% of OADP students with MDD had considered suicide, compared to 6.5% of adolescents without MDD. In a prospective study of childhood-onset depression, Kovacs et al. (1993) identified a four- to five-fold increase in suicidal ideation and behavior among youth with MDD or dysthymic disorder, compared to youth with other psychiatric disorders. By late adolescence, 85% of those with depression had experienced significant suicidal ideation and 32% had attempted suicide. During a 6-month follow-up of adolescent inpatients, Brent, Perper, et al. (1993) found that 100% of adolescents who attempted suicide reported major depressive disorder, compared to 59% of adolescents who did not attempt suicide. Finally, in the nationwide retrospective study in Finland (Marttunen et al., 1991), half of the male suicide fatalities and two-thirds of the females suffered from a depressive disorder. As noted by Lewinsohn et al. (1996), community-based studies indicate that the strongest predictors of future suicide attempts are a past suicide attempt and a current episode of major depression.

Alcohol and Substance Abuse and Dependence

Alcohol abuse and dependence appear to be primary risk factors for adolescent suicidal behavior. They have been associated with suicidal behavior in numerous studies of adolescent suicide risk (e.g., Andrews & Lewinsohn, 1992; Kienhorst et al., 1990; King, Hill, Naylor, Evans, & Shain, 1993; Pfeffer, Newcorn, Kaplan, Mizruchi, & Plutchik, 1988). Pfeffer et al. (1988) analyzed the hospital charts of 200 consecutively admitted adolescent psychiatric inpatients and found significant positive associations among alcohol abuse, MDD, and the severity of recent suicidal behavior. During the baseline period of the OADP (Andrews & Lewinsohn, 1992), adolescents with alcohol abuse or dependence were nearly 7 times more likely to have attempted suicide than were adolescents without alcohol abuse or dependence. Moreover, compared to adolescents without alcohol abuse or dependence, those with alcohol abuse or dependence were 22 times more likely to attempt suicide during the first year of the study. In Kotila's (1992) 5-year follow-up of hospitalized adolescent suicide attempters in Finland, alcohol abuse was a significant predictor of eventual completed suicide.

Findings from retrospective studies also suggest that alcohol abuse and dependence are significant risk factors for suicide. For example, in an early matched control study, Garfinkel, Froese, and Hood (1982) reviewed the hospital records of 505 adolescent suicide attempters and found that substance abuse was a significant factor in differentiating attempters from matched controls. Hoberman and Garfinkel (1988) reviewed the medical examiner records of 229 adolescent suicide victims and found that 28% had detectable blood alcohol levels following death, and nearly half had abused alcohol at the time of their death. Finally, Marttunen et al.'s (1991) study found evidence of alcohol abuse or dependence for 23% of the male suicide victims and 44% of the female victims. In 51% of the suicides, the adolescent had drunk alcohol in the time period immediately preceding the suicide. Marttunen et al. (1991) conjectured that, given the retrospective nature of their findings, their estimates and those from similar studies might actually underestimate the prevalence of alcohol use among adolescent suicide victims.

The studies indicate that a significant proportion of adolescent suicides occur among individuals with histories of alcohol problems. Alcohol abuse increases impulsive behavior, impaired judgment, and mood changes, thus increasing the likelihood of a suicide attempt. Moreover, alcohol that is consumed preceding the suicide act may add to the risk of a medically serious attempt (Robbins & Alessi, 1985). Not surprisingly, comorbid depression and alcohol abuse appears to enhance the risk for suicidal behavior (Kovacs et al., 1993; Shafii, Steltz-Lenarsky, Derrick, Beckner, & Whittinghill, 1988). For example, Shafii et al.'s (1988) retrospective study of adolescent suicides (age 11 to 19) found that 76% of victims suffered from major depression or dysthymia, 62% experienced alcohol or substance abuse, and 38% (vs. 5% of matched controls) had comorbid depression and alcohol or substance abuse.

Antisocial Behavior, Aggression, and Impulsivity

In their prospective study of OADP adolescents, Lewinsohn et al. (1996) reported that the baseline presence of disruptive behavior disorder was a significant predictor of future suicide attempts, but only when it was comorbid with major depression. Similarly, Kovacs et al. (1993) found that conduct disorder behavior increased the likelihood for suicide attempts when linked with depression. They found that 57.5% of suicide attempts made during follow-up occurred during episodes of major depression or dysthymia, 16.1% occurred during episodes of depression that were comorbid with conduct or substance use disorder, and only 8% were made during episodes of conduct or substance use disorder without depressive features. Pfeffer et al. (1988), in their evaluation of the hospital charts of adolescent psychiatric inpatients, found that aggressive behavior was linked to suicidal behavior. Finally, in regard to psychological autopsy studies, Marttunen et al. (1992) reported that 43.4% of adolescents who had killed themselves had displayed antisocial behavior during the last year of their lives; and Shafii, Carrigan, Whittinghill, and Derrick (1985) reported that 70% of adolescent suicide victims in the Louisville area had a history of antisocial behavior.

Studies such as those previously mentioned (see also Brent et al., 1988; Rich, Young, & Fowler, 1986) suggest that patterns of impulsivity, aggression, and violent behavior are connected to suicidal behavior in adolescents. Moreover, these personality features—which are characteristic of conduct disorder and adult antisocial personality disorder—further increase the risk for suicidal behavior when they are comorbid with depression and substance abuse. As noted by King (1997), because these aggressive, antisocial patterns of behavior tend to emerge relatively early in life and are associated with a variety of negative outcomes, they have important predictive validity and represent an important developmental pathway in our understanding of depression comorbidity and suicidal behavior.

Summary

Significant psychopathology and continued, severe psychosocial impairment seem to be the rule, rather than the exception, for suicidal adolescents. In fact, authors such as Marttunen et al. (1991, 1992) have argued that suicide among adolescents is most often the endpoint of a long course of severe pathology and distress.

Family and Interpersonal Stress

A growing number of empirical studies (e.g., Brent et al., 1994; Lewinsohn et al., 1996; Marttunen, Aro, & Lonnqvist, 1993; Pfeffer et al., 1988; Shaffer et al., 1996) indicate that family and interpersonal difficulties are associated with suicidal behavior. In a psychological autopsy study of completed suicides, Shaffer et al. (1988) documented a strong relationship between suicide and instances of being rejected, ridiculed, or teased by others. Moreover, among OADP youth, Lewinsohn et al. (1996) found that low social self-competence, along with low social support from friends, significantly predicted future suicide attempts.

In a nationwide retrospective study of adolescent suicides in Finland, Marttunen et al. (1993) conducted a more thorough examination of interpersonal precipitants. They examined the incidence of precipitant stressors that occurred during the last month of the victims' lives. Interpersonal conflicts and separation were the most common precipitants. Eleven percent of victims experienced conflict with parents, 21% with a girlfriend or boyfriend, and 9% with someone other than a parent, girlfriend, or boyfriend. Fifteen percent underwent separation from a girlfriend or boyfriend, 6% from parents, and 6% from someone else. Twenty-six percent endured interpersonal problems other than separation and conflict. Forty-eight percent of the interpersonal stressors occurred during the last 24 hours of the adolescents' lives; 76% took place during the last week.

Brent et al. (1988) assessed the frequency of precipitants that took place during the 6 weeks before the suicidal episodes of adolescent suicide attempters and suicide victims. Very high rates of overall interpersonal conflict were found for both the suicidal inpatients (SI; 87.5%) and victims of completed suicide (CS; 70.4%). Interpersonal conflicts were highest with parents (SI 69.6%; CS 22.2%), peers (SI 43%; CS 11.1%), and girlfriend or boyfriend (SI 35.7%; CS 25.9%). High frequencies were also found in both groups for overall interpersonal loss (SI 44.6%; CS 18.5%) and losses tied to peers (SI 8.9%; CS 11.1%) and girlfriend or boyfriend (SI 12.5%; CS 3.7%). Pfeffer et al. (1988) found that loss of boyfriend, recent change in school, and parental discord were associated with suicidal behavior among female adolescent psychiatric inpatients. According to Pfeffer et al., each of these variables can be conceptualized as an expression of loss of social attachments.

As reviewed by Wagner (1997), several familial stressors have been linked to suicide attempts and completions. Previous research suggests that a history of physical or sexual abuse, the loss of or separation from family members, and poor communication and problem solving within the family are risk factors for suicide attempts. Furthermore, research suggests that a history of physical or emotional abuse or neglect, the loss of or separation from family members, poor communication and problem solving within the family, and psychopathology in the family—namely depression, alcohol or substance abuse, and history of suicide attempts of immediate family members—may be risk factors for completed suicide. Individual studies may help in bringing these generalizations to light.

King, Segal, Naylor, and Evans (1993) identified family characteristics connected to suicidal behavior in depressed adolescents by comparing groups of depressed suicidal inpatients, depressed nonsuicidal inpatients, and normal comparison adolescents. They discovered that suicidal adolescents more often had fathers who reported significant depressive symptoms, and that the suicidal adolescents appeared to have more distant relationships with their fathers. Brent et al. (1994) used a retrospective case-control study to identify familial risk factors for completed suicide. They found that, in contrast to the community controls, suicide victims were less likely to have lived in a two-parent home; were exposed more often to parent–child discord, physical abuse, and residential instability; and more often lived in families with a history of depression and substance abuse.

Suicide Risk Among Gay, Lesbian, and Bisexual Youth

A recent body of literature (e.g., Faulkner & Cranston, 1998; Fergusson, Horwood, & Beautrais, 1999; Garofalo, Wolf, Wissow, Woods, & Goodman, 1999; Remafedi, French, Story, Resnick, & Blum, 1998) has established that gay, lesbian, and bisexual (GLB) adolescents are at substantial risk for suicidal behavior. General population surveys found (Garofalo, Wolf, Kessel, Palfrey, & DuRant, 1998; Remafedi et al., 1998), for example, that 42% of GLB youth experienced suicidal ideation during the past year, and 28% of GLB youth made at least one suicide attempt during the year.

GLB youth face some of the same risk factors for suicide attempts that affect heterosexual youth, although factors such as comorbid depression, substance abuse, and conduct disorder have been found to be amplified in GLB youth (Fergusson et al., 1999). However, there are some risk factors that appear to be particular to GLB youth. For example, stigmatization and discrimination against GLB individuals are still commonplace in society. The negative, hostile attitudes from society are especially heightened because discrimination and intolerance are openly supported by many societal institutions such as churches, schools, and youth programs who may not accept or support GLB adolescents (McDaniel, Purcell, & D'Agelli, 2001; McFarland, 1998). Living in a homophobic environment may lead GLB youth to internalize negative self-images of shame and self-hatred that are based on societal myths and stereotypes of homosexuality (McDaniel et al., 2001; McFarland, 1998).

GLB adolescents may be caught in a double-bind situation. GLB youth who disclose their sexuality suffer increased levels of social isolation, rejection, frequent harassment, and violence from both peers and family members (Bagley & Tremblay, 2000; Faulkner & Cranston, 1998; Garofalo et al., 1999; McDaniel et al., 2001; McFarland, 1998). However, GLB youth who have not disclosed their sexuality may experience intense anxiety from the fear of being persecuted if their sexuality were brought into the open.

Developmentally, GLB youth may not experience intimate relationships until a later age than other adolescents. They may thus be relatively less skilled in maintaining intimate relations, and they may perceive the breaking up of relationships as confirming negative self-evaluations (McFarland, 1998). GLB youth are more likely than heterosexual youth to be pressured to leave home and live self-sufficiently (McFarland, 1998). This may be developmentally premature. Some GLB youth who leave home may not be prepared to live independently.

Finally, issues surrounding HIV and AIDS are possible linkages to suicide risk (McDaniel et al., 2001; McFarland, 1998). For individuals who are just becoming aware of their sexual orientation, intense anxiety may be experienced over the possibility of contracting HIV and AIDS. Such anxiety may lead to other psychiatric symptoms and, for some, to an increased risk for suicide. Second, individuals who have contracted HIV or AIDS may engage in self-destructive actions that include suicidal behavior.

Theoretical Considerations

Because, on quick perusal, the literature on youth suicide risk may appear to consist of static categories of predictors, it is worth noting that theoretical attempts have been made to understand relationships among these risk factors and their influences on suicidal behavior (e.g., Linehan, 1993). King (1997) argues that because adolescence is characterized by certain developmental tasks, role requirements, and social contexts, models are needed that specifically address risk for suicidal behavior *during* adolescence. She notes that it is possible to move beyond a catalogue of risk factors by conceptualizing youth suicidal behavior and associated pathologies (e.g., increased prevalence levels of depression and alcohol abuse) as conditions that unfold over time within a context of multiple developmental changes. Transactional models of development (e.g., Sameroff & Chandler, 1975) provide these types of conceptualizations. A transactional model is a useful tool in our efforts to understand and prevent adolescent suicidal behavior because of its emphasis on the continuous interplay among risk variables (and thus an ability to detail specific windows of preventive opportunity) for specific profiles of at risk youth.

TREATMENT OF SUICIDAL YOUTH

The American Academy of Child and Adolescent Psychiatry (AACAP, 2001) recently published practice parameters for the assessment and treatment of children and adolescents with suicidal behavior. These parameters provide detailed suggestions for clinicians on the assessment, crisis management, and treatment of suicidal youth. They are complemented by other recent efforts to provide clinicians with practical guidelines (e.g., Brent, 1997; Rudd, Joiner, Jobes, & King, 1999). Although empirically based knowledge concerning the effective treatment of suicidal behavior is limited, these sets of recommendations integrate empirical knowledge with clinically derived expertise. As Rudd et al. (1999) state in their guidelines for outpatient treatment, this is consistent with the goal of integrating science and practice, while acknowledging the current empirical limitations in our understanding of effective interventions. The following discussion emphasizes studies that are part of a developing empirical foundation for the effective treatment of suicidal individuals.

Efficacy of Treatment Strategies for Suicidal Youth

The effort to prevent suicide attempts and completed suicide in youth is challenged by the near-complete absence of empirically validated, effective treatments for suicidal behavior in youth (King & Knox, 2000). The meager state of our knowledge has been highlighted in several recent reviews, including practitioner guidelines for the aftercare of suicidal adolescents (Brent, 1997), randomized clinical trials of interventions designed to reduce suicidal behavior (Linehan, 1997), and guidelines for the outpatient treatment of suicidality (Rudd et al., 1999). The current scientific basis provides only tentative answers to some of the most fundamental questions concerning interventions, their effectiveness, and their potential associated harm.

No randomized controlled study targeting suicidality in youth has clearly demonstrated efficacy in terms of reduced adolescent suicide attempts, and few controlled studies have demonstrated reductions in suicidal ideation (Rudd et al., 1999). In addition, to the authors' knowledge, no controlled study specifically targeting suicidal behavior in preadolescents has ever been conducted.

Rudd et al. (1996) evaluated the efficacy of a brief cognitive-behavioral outpatient treatment intervention and demonstrated reductions (over the course of 1 to 12 months) in suicidal ideation among older adolescents and young adults. Their cognitive-behavioral intervention incorporated a strong emphasis on problem solving, which is consistent with other interventions demonstrating reductions in suicidal ideation, depression, and hopelessness (as reviewed in Rudd et al., 1999).

In a randomized trial of youth (age 16 and younger) who had deliberately poisoned themselves, Harrington et al. (1998) examined the outcome differences (at 2 and 6 months) between "routine care" and a home-based family intervention. The family intervention consisted of an assessment session and four home visits by social workers who conducted sessions on family problem solving. No significant group differences were found in suicidal ideation, hopelessness, or adolescent perceptions of family functioning. Harrington et al. found, however, that the family intervention was associated with a reduction in suicidal ideation among youth without major depression. In addition, parents in the intervention group were more satisfied with treatment than were parents in the routine-care group.

Cotgrove, Zirinsky, Balck, and Weston (1995) randomized hospitalized adolescent suicide attempters to either a treatment group ($n = 58$) that received "standard care," or an experimental group ($n = 47$) that received a token that allowed for immediate rehospitalization—without question—if the adolescent felt suicidal and felt the need to be hospitalized. Of the adolescents in the token group, 11% used their tokens and 6% attempted suicide during the next year. In contrast, 12% of adolescents in the control group attempted suicide. Although the group differences were not statistically significant, a 1-year reduction in suicide attempts was evident for adolescents who received tokens, even among those who chose not to use them. Even though the findings from this study are limited, this approach appears promising.

Other treatment studies targeting suicidal adults include a study of young adult females with borderline personality disorder. Linehan, Armstrong, Suarez, Allmon, and Heard (1991) compared a cognitive-behavioral treatment (i.e., dialectical behavior therapy [DBT]) intervention with "treatment as usual" (treatment of choice in the community) and found that—at 4-month intervals during the course of treatment—those females who received the cognitive-behavioral treatment had fewer suicide attempts, attempts of less lethality, and better treatment adherence. At 1-year follow-up (Linehan, 1993), the DBT group reported fewer suicidal attempts, less anger, and better social adjustment for the 6-month period directly following treatment, and better social adjustment and fewer psychiatric inpatient days for the following year. In a randomized controlled study of an outreach intervention program for adult suicide attempters evaluated in an emergency room, Welu (1977) found a significant reduction (at 1-month and 4-month follow-up) in suicide reattempts and alcohol use among individuals assigned to the outreach program, compared to individuals who were assigned to normal treatment. Outreach efforts consisted of home visits and telephone contacts.

Treatments targeting the family unit are often considered to be a key component of interventions with youth with depression and suicidal behavior because of the connections between suicidal behavior and family conflict, parent–adolescent communication problems, parental psychopathology, and family history of suicidal behavior (Keitner et al., 1987; King, Segal, et al., 1993; Shafii et al., 1985, Wagner, 1997). In a clinical trial comparing three psychosocial treatments for adolescent depression, Brent et al. (1998) found that the efficacy of cognitive behavioral treatment for these adolescents "plummeted" in the presence of self-reported maternal depression, suggesting the need to assess and treat maternal psychopathology. A family therapy program called Successful Negotiation/Acting Positively (SNAP; Rotheram-Borus, Piacentini, Miller, Graae, & Castro-Blanco, 1994) was developed to target family functioning in families of youth suicide attempters. The program's primary goal is to increase positive family communication skills and improve the family's ability to use effective problem-solving strategies during conflict. This is a promising approach that suggests the possibility of positively impacting treatment adherence among female adolescent suicide attempters presenting to an emergency room (Rotheram-Borus et al., 1999).

Summary

Taken together, the preceding findings from controlled studies of adolescents and adults suggest that individual cognitive-behavioral treatments that focus on problem solving and depressive cognitions may be helpful for depressed and suicidal persons (e.g., Brent et al., 1997; Linehan, 1993; Linehan et al., 1991; Rudd et al., 1996). Moreover, follow-up outreach that includes home visits or telephone contact may help reduce suicidal behavior after individual treatment. Cognitive-behavioral family therapy programs may be helpful for adolescent suicidal behaviors that appear to be linked to familial stressors and pathology.

In closing this section, it should be noted that it is essential to treat the identifiable psychopathology in adolescents who present with suicidal behaviors (Brent, 1997). As previously discussed, the large majority of these youth have severe emotional and behavioral disturbances—treatable psychiatric or mental disorders—that are risk factors for suicidal ideation, suicide attempts, and completed suicide. The reader is advised to refer to other chapters in this book concerning the effective treatment of these disorders.

GAPS IN OUR KNOWLEDGE

Although our understanding of youth suicide risk factors has grown rapidly during the last 2 decades, substantial gaps in our knowledge remain. The most visible or glaring gap concerns information about effective treatments that target suicidality in youth. As highlighted in *The Surgeon General's Call to Action to Prevent Suicide* (U.S. Public Health Service, 1999), effective suicide prevention and intervention strategies are sorely needed. Few randomized controlled intervention trials have been conducted with youth (Rudd et al., 1999), evaluated interventions have shown limited impact on suicidal ideation and behavior, and suicidal adolescents' follow-through with treatment recommendations has generally been poor (Spirito, Boergers, & Donaldson, 2000).

Additional questions concerning risk factors for the spectrum of suicidal behaviors also remain. Further empirical studies of psychobiologic and genetic risk factors are essential, as are detailed prospective examinations of the roles of social anxiety, hopelessness, and personality traits. There has been a relative absence of research that details culturally specific factors that may contribute to adolescent suicidal behavior (Hovey & King, 1997). Difficulties encountered during the process of acculturation may be linked to suicidal behavior in different immigrant ethnic (e.g., Chinese Americans, Shiang, 2000; Mexican immigrants, Hovey, 2000) and Native American groups (Range et al., 1999). As an example, in a study of immigrant and second-generation Mexican adolescents in southern California, Hovey and King (1996) found that youth suffering from acculturative stress were more likely to experience high levels of depression and suicidal ideation. As another example, close examination of the nationwide YRBS data (Kann et al., 2000) reveals that 12.8% of Hispanic students (females 18.9%) attempted suicide during the previous 12 months, compared to 8.3% of all YRBS students. Although these findings do not address specific Latin subgroups, generational status, or levels of acculturative stress, they do expose the need for a detailed exploration of cultural factors that may contribute to elevated rates of suicidal behavior.

CONCLUSION AND FUTURE DIRECTIONS

Suicide is the third leading cause of death for adolescents in the United States. The continuum of adolescent suicidal behavior includes suicidal ideation of varying intensity and specificity, suicide attempts of varying intent and lethality, and completed suicide. According to general population surveys, approximately 7% to 20% of adolescents experience suicidal ideation on a yearly basis, and 7% to 16% make a suicide attempt at some point in their lives. Rates of suicidal ideation and suicide attempts tend to decrease by late adolescence. Although female youth report higher rates of suicidal ideation and suicide attempts, male youth show a higher rate of suicide completion. Suicide attempts by male youth more often involve lethal means.

Findings from population-based and clinical studies during the past 20 years have resulted in a consensus regarding primary risk factors for suicide attempts and completed suicide among youth. Predictors of suicide attempts include suicidal ideation, a previous suicide attempt, identifiable psychopathology, family and interpersonal difficulties, and stressors such as those that are often present in the lives of gay, lesbian, and bisexual youth. In addition to these factors, availability of firearms is a known risk factor for completed suicide.

There is a paucity of knowledge concerning evidence-based interventions or treatments that target and reduce suicidal behaviors in youth. Nevertheless, the limited data available suggest that cognitive-behavioral interventions with some type of followup outreach and contact may be beneficial. In addition, a family intervention and supplemental efforts to improve treatment adherence are often warranted.

The Surgeon General's Call to Action to Prevent Suicide (U.S. Public Health Service, 1999), the efforts of national organizations and advocacy groups, and recent initiatives of the National Institute of Mental Health (e.g., spearheading reviews of suicide risk assessment instruments and publishing a document addressing ethical issues in research with suicidal individuals) have combined to create a sense of urgency and commitment for research related to suicide prevention. During the past 20 years, researchers have accumulated a rich knowledge base concerning prevalence rates and primary risk factors for suicidal behaviors among youth. It is hoped that over the next 20 years, this will be supplemented by information concerning risk factors among specific racial and ethnic minority groups in addition to information about the nuances and mediators of risk among all youth. Finally, it is anticipated that by the year 2020, a chapter such as this will necessitate review of an entire body of evidence-based intervention strategies targeting the spectrum of suicidal behaviors in youth.

REFERENCES

Adcock, A., Nagy, S., & Simpson, J. A. (1991). Selected risk factors in adolescent suicide attempts. *Adolescence, 26,* 817–828.

American Academy of Child and Adolescent Psychiatry (2001). Practice parameter for the assessment and treatment of children and adolescents with suicidal behavior. *Journal of the American Academy of Child and Adolescent Psychiatry, 40* (Suppl.), 24S–51S.

Andrews, J. A., & Lewinsohn, P. M. (1992). Suicidal attempts among older adolescents: Prevalence and co-occurrence with psychiatric disorders. *Journal of the American Academy of Child and Adolescent Psychiatry, 31,* 655–662.

Bagley, C., & Tremblay, P. (2000). Elevated rates of suicidal behavior in gay, lesbian, and bisexual youth. *Crisis, 21,* 111–117.

Brent, D. A. (1997). Practitioner review: The aftercare of adolescents with deliberate self-harm. *Journal of the American Academy of Child and Adolescent Psychiatry, 38,* 277–286.

Brent, D. A., Holder, D., Kolko, D., Birmaher, B., Baugher, M., Roth, C., Iyengar, S., & Johnson, B. A. (1997). A clinical psychotherapy trial for adolescent depression comparing cognitive, family, and supportive therapy. *Archives of General Psychiatry, 54,* 877–885.

Brent, D. A., Kolko, D. J., Birmaher, B., Baugher, M., Bridge, J., Roth, C., & Holder, D. (1998). Predictors of treatment efficacy in a clinical trial of three psychosocial treatments for adolescent depression. *Journal of the American Academy of Child and Adolescent Psychiatry, 37,* 906–914.

Brent, D. A., Kolko, D. J., Wartella, M. E., Boylan, M. B., Moritz, G., Baugher, M., & Zelenak, J. P. (1993). Adolescent psychiatric inpatients' risk of suicide attempt on six-month follow-up. *Journal of the American Academy of Child and Adolescent Psychiatry, 32,* 95–105.

Brent, D. A., Perper, J. A., Goldstein, C. E., Kolko, D. J., Allan, M. J., Allman, C. J., & Zelenak, J. P. (1988). Risk factors for adolescent suicide. A comparison of adolescent suicide victims with suicidal inpatients. *Archives of General Psychiatry, 45,* 581–588.

Brent, D. A., Perper, J. A., Moritz, G., Baugher, M., Schweers, J., & Roth, C. (1993). Firearms and adolescent suicide: A community case-control study. *American Journal of Diseases of Children, 147,* 1066–1071.

Brent, D. A., Perper, J. A., Moritz, G., Liotus, L., Schweers, J., Balach, L., & Roth, C. (1994). Familial risk factors for adolescent suicide: A case-control study. *Acta Psychiatrica Scandinavica, 89,* 52–58.

Burke, K. C., Burke, J. D., Rae, D. S., & Reiger, D. A. (1991). Comparing age at onset of major depression and other psychiatric disorders by birth cohorts in five U.S. community populations. *Archives of General Psychiatry, 48,* 789–795.

Centers for Disease Control. (2000). *National Vital Statistics Report* (Vol. 48, No. 11). Washington, DC: Author.

Cotgrove, A., Zirinsky, L., Balck, D., & Weston, D. (1995). Secondary prevention of attempted suicide in adolescence. *Journal of Adolescence, 18,* 569–577.

Faulkner, A. H., & Cranston, K. (1998). Correlates of same-sex sexual behavior in a random sample of Massachusetts high school students. *American Journal of Public Health, 88,* 262–266.

Fergusson, D. M., Horwood, J., & Beautrais, A. L. (1999). Is sexual orientation related to mental health problems and suicidality in young people? *Archives of General Psychiatry, 56,* 876–880.

Fergusson, D. M. & Lynskey, M. T. (1995). Suicide attempts and suicidal ideation in a birth cohort of 16-year-old New Zealanders. *Journal of the American Academy of Child and Adolescent Psychiatry, 34,* 1308–1317.

Garfinkel, B. D., Froese, A., & Hood, J. (1982). Suicide attempts in children and adolescents. *American Journal of Psychiatry, 139,* 1257–1261.

Garofalo, R., Wolf, C., Kessel, S., Palfrey, J., & DuRant, R. H. (1998). The association between health risk behaviors and sexual orientation among a school-based sample of adolescents. *Pediatrics, 101,* 895–902.

Garofalo, R., Wolf, C., Wissow, L. S., Woods, E. R., & Goodman, E. (1999). Sexual orientation and risk of suicide attempts among a representative sample of youth. *Archives of Pediatrics and Adolescent Medicine, 153,* 487–493.

Garrison, C. Z., Waller, J. L., Cuffe, S. P., McKeown, R. E., Addy, C. L., Jackson, K. L. (1997). Incidence of major depressive disorder and dysthymia in young adolescents. *Journal of the American Academy of Child and Adolescent Psychiatry, 36,* 458–465.

Goldston, D. B., Daniel S. S., Reboussin, D. M., Reboussin, B. A., Frazier, P. H., & Kelley, A. E. (1999). Suicide attempts among formerly hospitalized adolescents: A prospective naturalistic study of risk during the first 5 years after discharge. *Journal of the American Academy of Child and Adolescent Psychiatry, 38,* 660–671.

Harrington, R., Kerfoot, M., Dyer, E., McNiven, F., Gill, J., Harrington, V., Woodham, A., & Byford, S. (1998). Randomized trial of a home-based family intervention of children who have deliberately poisoned themselves. *Journal of the American Academy of Child and Adolescent Psychiatry, 37,* 512–518.

Hoberman, H. M., & Garfinkel, B. D. (1988). Completed suicide in children and adolescents. *Journal of the American Academy of Child and Adolescent Psychiatry, 27,* 689–695.

Hovey, J. D. (2000). Acculturative stress, depression, and suicidal ideation in Mexican immigrants. *Cultural Diversity and Ethnic Minority Psychology, 6,* 134–151.

Hovey, J. D., & King, C. A. (1996). Acculturative stress, depression, and suicidal ideation among immigrant and second generation Latino adolescents. *Journal of the American Academy of Child and Adolescent Psychiatry, 35,* 1183–1192.

Hovey, J. D., & King, C. A. (1997). Suicidality among acculturating Mexican-Americans: Current knowledge and directions for research. *Suicide and Life-Threatening Behavior, 27,* 92–103.

Kann, L., Kinchen, S. A., Williams, B. I., Ross, J. G., Lowry, R., Grunbaum, J., Kolbe, L. J. (2000). *Youth Risk Behavior Surveillance—United States, 1999.* (CDC Surveillance Summaries MMWR 2000: 49 No. SS-5, pp. 1–96). Washington, DC: Author.

Keitner, G. I., Miller, I. W., Fruzzetti, A. E., Epstein, N. B., Bishop, D. S. & Norman, W. H. (1987). Family functioning and suicidal behavior in psychiatric inpatients with major depression. *Psychiatry, 50,* 242–255.

Kellermann, A. L., Rivara, F. P., Somes, G., Reay, D. T., Francisco, J., Banton, J. G., Prodzinski, J., Fligner, C., & Hackman, B. B. (1992). Suicide in the home in relation to gun ownership. *New England Journal of Medicine, 327,* 467–472.

Kienhorst, C. W. M., DeWilde, E. J., Van den Bout, J., Diekstra, R. F. W., & Wolters, W. H. G. (1990). Characteristics of suicide attempters in a population-based sample of Dutch adolescents. *British Journal of Psychiatry, 156,* 243–248.

King, C. A. (1997). Suicidal behavior in adolescence. In R. Maris, M. Silverman, & S. Canetto (Eds.), *Review of Suicidology, 1997.* New York: Guilford Press.

King, C. A. (1998). Suicide across the life span: Pathways to prevention. *Suicide and Life-Threatening Behavior, 28,* 328–337.

King, C. A., Hill, E. M., Naylor, M. W., Evans, T., & Shain, B. (1993). Alcohol consumption in relation to other predictors of suicidality among adolescent inpatient girls. *Journal of the American Academy of Child and Adolescent Psychiatry, 32,* 82–88.

King, C. A., Hovey, J. D., Brand, E., Wilson, R., & Ghaziuddin, N. (1997). Suicidal adolescents after hospitalization: Parent and family impacts on treatment follow-through. *Journal of the American Academy of Child and Adolescent Psychiatry, 36,* 85–93.

King, C. A., & Knox, M. (2000). Recognition and treatment of suicidal youth: Broadening our research agenda. In T. Joiner & M. D. Rudd (Eds.), *Suicide science expanding the boundaries,* (pp. 251–269). Norwell, MA: Kluwer Academic Publishers.

King, C. A., Segal, H., Kaminski, K., Naylor, M. W., Ghaziuddin, N., & Radpour, L. (1995). A prospective study of adolescent suicidal behavior following hospitalization. *Suicide and Life-Threatening Behavior, 25,* 327–338.

King, C. A., Segal, H.G., Naylor, M., & Evans, T. (1993). Family functioning and suicidal behavior in adolescent inpatients with mood disorders. *Journal of the American Academy of Child and Adolescent Psychiatry, 32,* 1198–1206.

Kotila, L. (1992). The outcome of attempted suicide in adolescence. *Journal of Adolescent Health, 13,* 415–417.

Kovacs, M., (1996). Presentation and course of major depressive disorder during childhood and later years of the lifespan. *Journal of the American Academy of Child and Adolescent Psychiatry, 35,* 705–715.

Kovacs, M., Goldston, D., & Gatsonis, C. (1993). Suicidal behaviors and childhood-onset depressive disorders. A longitudinal investigation. *Journal of the American Academy of Child and Adolescent Psychiatry, 32,* 8–20.

Lewinsohn, P. M., Hops, H., Roberts, R. E., Seeley, J. R., Andrews, J. A., (1993). Adolescent psychopathology: I. Prevalence and incidence of depression and other DSM-III-R disorders in high school students. *Journal of Abnormal Child Psychology, 103,* 133–144

Lewinsohn, P. M., Rohde, P., & Seeley, J. R. (1994). Psychosocial risk factors for future adolescent suicide attempts. *Journal of Consulting and Clinical Psychology, 62,* 297–305.

Lewinsohn, P. M., Rohde, P. & Seeley, J. R. (1995). Adolescent psychopathology: III. The clinical consequences of comorbidity. *Journal of the American Academy of Child and Adolescent Psychiatry, 34,* 510–519.

Lewinsohn, P. M., Rohde, P., & Seeley, J. R. (1996). Adolescent suicide ideation and attempts: Prevalence, risk factors, and clinical implications. *Clinical Psychology Science and Practice, 3,* 25–46.

Linehan, M. M. (1993). *Cognitive-behavioral treatment of borderline personality disorder.* New York: Guilford Press.

Linehan, M. M. (1997). Behavioral treatment of suicidal behaviors: Definitional obfuscation and treatment outcomes. *Annals of the New York Academy of Science, 836,* 302–328.

Linehan, M. M., Armstrong, H. E., Suarez, A., Allmon, D., & Heard, H. L. (1991). Cognitive-behavioral treatment of chronically parasuicidal borderline patients. *Archives of General Psychiatry, 48,* 1060–1064.

Marttunen, M. J., Aro, H. M., Henriksson, M. M., & Lonnqvist, J. K. (1991). Mental disorders in adolescent suicide: DSM-III-R Axes I and II diagnoses in suicides among 13- to 19-year-olds in Finland. *Archives of General Psychiatry, 48,* 834–839.

Marttunen, M. J., Aro, H. M., & Lonnqvist, J. K. (1992). Adolescent suicide: Endpoint of long-term difficulties. *Journal of the American Academy of Child and Adolescent Psychiatry, 31,* 649–654.

Marttunen, M. J., Aro, H. M., & Lonnqvist, J. K. (1993). Precipitant stressors in adolescent suicide. *Journal of the American Academy of Child and Adolescent Psychiatry, 32,* 1178–1183.

McDaniel, J. S., Purcell, D., & D'Augelli, A. R. (2001). The relationship between sexual orientation and risk for suicide: Research findings and future directions for research and prevention. *Suicide and Life-Threatening Behavior, 31*(Suppl.), 84–105.

McFarland, W. P. (1998). Gay, lesbian, and bisexual student suicide. *Professional School Counseling, 1,* 26–29.

McIntosh, J. L. (2000). Epidemiology of adolescent suicide in the United States. In R. W. Maris, S. S. Canetto, J. L. McIntosh, & M. M. Silverman (Eds.), *Review of suicidology.* New York: Guilford Press.

Moscicki, E. K. (1999). Epidemiology of suicide. In D. G. Jacobs (Ed.), *The Harvard Medical School guide to suicide assessment and intervention* (pp. 40–51). San Francisco: Jossey-Bass.

Motto, J. A. (1984). Suicide in male adolescents. In H. S. Sudak, A. B. Ford, & N. B. Rushforth (Eds.), *Suicide in the young,* (pp. 227–244). Boston: John Wright PSG.

Otto, U. (1972). Suicidal acts by children and adolescents: A follow-up study. *Acta Psychiatrica Scandinavica,* (Suppl. 233).

Petersen, A. C., Compas, B.E., Brooks-Gunn, J., Stemmler, M., Ey, S., & Grant, K. E. (1993). Depression during adolescence. *American Psychologist, 48,* 155–168.

Pfeffer, C. R., Newcorn, J., Kaplan, G., Mizruchi, M. S., & Plutchik, R. (1988). Suicidal behavior in adolescent psychiatric inpatients. *Journal of the American Academy of Child and Adolescent Psychiatry, 27,* 357–361.

Puig-Antich, J., Kaufman, J., Ryan, N. D., Williamson, D. E., Dahl, R. E., Lukens, E., Todak, G., Ambrosini, P., Rabinovisch, H., & Nelson, B. (1993). The psychosocial functioning and family environment of depressed adolescents. *Journal of the American Academy of Child and Adolescent Psychiatry, 32,* 244–253.

Range, L. M., Leach, M. M., McIntyre, D., Posey-Deters, P. B., Marion, M. S., Kovac, S. H., Banos, J. H., & Vigil, J. (1999). Multicultural perspectives on suicide. *Aggression and Violent Behavior, 4,* 413–430.

Rao, U., Weissman, M. M., Martin, J. A., & Hammond, R. W. (1993). Childhood depression and risk of suicide: A preliminary report of a longitudinal study. *Journal of the American Academy of Child and Adolescent Psychiatry, 32,* 21–27.

Reinherz, H. Z., Giaconia, R. M., Silverman, A. B., Friedman, A., Pakiz, B., Frost, A. K., & Cohen, E. (1995). Early psychosocial risks for adolescent suicidal ideation and attempts. *Journal of the American Academy of Child and Adolescent Psychiatry, 34,* 599–611.

Remafedi, G., French, S., Story, M., Resnick, M. D., & Blum, R. (1998). The relationship between suicide risk and sexual orientation: Results of a population-based study. *American Journal of Public Health, 88,* 57–60.

Reynolds, W. M., & Mazza, J. J. (1994). Suicide and suicidal behaviors in children and adolescents. In W. M. Reynolds & H. F. Johnston (Eds.), *Handbook of depression in children and adolescents* (pp. 525–580). New York: Plenum Press.

Rich, C. L., Young, D., & Fowler, R. C. (1986). San Diego suicide study: I. Young vs. old subjects. *Archives of General Psychiatry, 43,* 577–582.

Robbins, D. R., & Alessi, N. E. (1985). Depressive symptoms and suicidal behavior in adolescents. *American Journal of Psychiatry, 142,* 588–592.

Rotheram-Borus, M. J., Piacentini, J., Miller, S., Graae, F., & Castro-Blanco, D. (1994). Brief cognitive-behavioral treatment for adolescent suicide attempters and their families. *Journal of the American Academy of Child and Adolescent Psychiatry, 33,* 508–517.

Rotheram-Borus, M. J., Piacentini, J., Van Rossem, R., Graae, F., Cantwell, C., Castro-Blanco, D., & Feldman, J. (1999). Treatment adherence among Latina female adolescent suicide attempters. *Suicide and Life-Threatening Behavior, 29,* 319–331.

Rudd, M. D., Joiner, T. E., Jr., Jobes, D. A., & King, C. A. (1999). The outpatient treatment of suicidality: An integration of science and recognition of its limitations. *Professional Psychology: Research and Practice, 30,* 437–444.

Rudd, M. D., Rajab, M. H., Orman, D. T., Joiner, T., Stulman, D. A., & Dixon, W. (1996). Effectiveness of an outpatient intervention targeting suicidal young adults: Preliminary results. *Journal of Consulting and Clinical Psychology 64,* 179–190.

Sameroff, A., & Chandler, M. (1975). Reproductive risk and the continuum of caretaking casualty. In F. Horowitz (Ed.), *Review of child development research* (Vol. 4, pp. 187–244). Chicago: University of Chicago Press.

Shaffer, D., Garland, A., Gould, M., Fisher, P., & Trautman, P. (1988). Preventing teenage suicide [A critical review]. *Journal of the American Academy of Child and Adolescent Psychiatry, 27,* 675–687.

Shaffer, D., Gould, M. S., Fisher, P., Trautman, P., Moreau, D., Kleinman, M., & Flory, M. (1996). Psychiatric diagnosis in child and adolescent suicide. *Archives of General Psychiatry, 53,* 339–348.

Shafii, M., Carrigan, S., Whittinghill, J. R., & Derrick, A. (1985). Psychological autopsy of completed suicide in children and adolescents. (1985). *American Journal of Psychiatry, 142,* 1061–1064.

Shafii, M., Steltz-Lenarsky, J., Derrick, A. M., Beckner, C., & Whittinghill, J. R. (1988). Comorbidity of mental disorders in the post-mortem diagnosis of completed suicide in children and adolescents. *Journal of Affective Disorders, 15,* 227–233.

Shiang, J. (2000). Considering cultural beliefs and behaviors in the study of suicide. In R. W. Maris, S. S. Canetto, J. L. McIntosh, & M. M. Silverman (Eds.), *Review of suicidology, 2000.* New York: Guilford Press.

Shneidman, E. (1993). *Suicide as psychache: A clinical approach to self-destructive behavior.* New York: Aronson.

Shneidman, E. (1996). *The suicidal mind.* New York: Oxford University Press.

Spirito, A., Boergers, J., & Donaldson, D. (2000). Adolescent suicide attempters: Post-attempt course and implications for treatment. *Clinical Psychology and Psychotherapy, 7,* 161–173.

U.S. Public Health Service (1999). *The surgeon general's call to action to prevent suicide* (pp. 1–23). Washington, DC: Author.

Wagner, B. M. (1997). Family risk factors for child and adolescent suicidal behavior. *Psychological Bulletin, 121,* 246–298.

Welu, T. C. (1977). A follow-up program for suicide attempters: Evaluation of effectiveness. *Suicide and Life-Threatening Behavior, 7,* 17–30.

Chapter 16

ADOLESCENT SUBSTANCE ABUSE AND PSYCHIATRIC COMORBIDITY

RAMON SOLHKHAH AND MARIE ARMENTANO

Despite recent studies that show that adolescent drug and alcohol use has remained essentially stable, adolescent substance abuse remains a concern (Johnston, O'Malley, & Bachman, 2001). With the increase in the use of "club drugs" such as ecstasy (3,4-methylenedioxymethamphetamine [MDMA]), ketamine, and GHB (gamma-hydroxybutyrate) over the past several years, as well as evidence that the age of first use of drugs continues to get younger and younger, it is hard to claim victory in the war on drugs. In fact, the average American youth first experiments with drugs in sixth or seventh grade. Adolescents with substance use disorders (SUDs) exhibit a high prevalence of psychiatric disorders compared to the general population (Brook, Whiteman, Cohen, Shapiro, & Balka, 1995; Bukstein, Brent, & Kaminer, 1989; Chatlos, 1996; Christie et al., 1988; DeMilio, 1989; Hovens, Cantwell, & Kiriakos, 1994; Kaminer, 1991; Kandel et al., 1997; Kellam, Ensminger, & Simon, 1980). Studies of adolescents seeking treatment for SUDs have documented that 50% to 90% also have non-SUD comorbid psychiatric disorders (Clark & Bukstein, 1998; Deykin, Buka, & Zeena, 1992; Hovens et al., 1994; Kashani, Keller, Solomon, Reid, & Mazzola, 1985; King, Naylor, Hill, Shain, & Greden, 1992; King et al., 1996; Milin, Halikas, Meller, & Morse, 1991; Stowell & Estroff, 1992). Not only are specific psychiatric disorders associated with drug abuse, but other problems that affect teenagers, such as suicide, violence, and pregnancy, are also associated with increased risk of substance use. Awareness of the most likely disorders and formulation of an integrated treatment plan are important. This chapter reviews what is known about comorbidity and offers guidelines for management and consultation.

Certain factors put children and adolescents at risk for the development of a SUD. These include the following:

- Genetic factor

  Having one or both parents who have a substance abuse problem
- Constitutional and psychological factors

    Psychiatric comorbidity

    History of physical, sexual, or emotional abuse

    History of attempted suicide

- Sociocultural factors

  Family

  - Parental experiences and attitudes toward drug use
  - History of parental divorce (or separation)
  - Low expectations for the child

  Peers

  - Friends who use drugs
  - Friends' attitudes towards drug use
  - Antisocial or delinquent behavior

  School

  - School failure or dropping out

  Community

  - Attitudes toward drug use
  - Economic and social deprivation
  - Availability of drugs and alcohol (including cigarettes)

Adolescents who manifest other psychiatric diagnoses in addition to substance abuse have elicited increasing concern (American Academy of Pediatrics [AAP], 2000; Armentano, 1995; Bukstein et al., 1989; Bukstein, Glancy, & Kaminer, 1992; Bukstein et al., 1993; Burke, Burke, & Rae, 1994; Crowley & Riggs, 1995; Deykin & Buka, 1997; Fergusson, Horwood, & Lynskey, 1993; Geller et al., 1998; Grilo et al., 1995; Horowitz, Overton, Rosenstein, & Steidl, 1992; Hovens et al., 1994; Kaminer, Tarter, Bukstein, & Kabene, 1992; Stowell & Estroff, 1992; Westermeyer, Specker, Neider, & Lingenfelter, 1994; Wilcox & Yates, 1993; Wilens, Biederman, & Spencer, 1996). In this chapter, the terms *dual diagnosis* and *comorbidity* are used as general terms to refer to patients who meet the criteria for a psychoactive substance use disorder and for another psychiatric diagnosis on Axis I or II using the *Diagnostic and Statistical Manual of Mental Disorders, Fourth Edition (DSM-IV;* American Psychiatric Association [APA], 1994). The term *substance use disorder (SUD)* is used as a generic term that includes substance abuse and dependence. The adolescents who initially seek treatment for SUD may be different from those who seek psychiatric treatment (Caton, Gralnick, Bender, & Simon, 1989; Ries, Mullen, & Cox, 1994); this chapter focuses on adolescents who were diagnosed and treated initially for substance use disorders.

According to Bukstein and Kaminer (1994), issues of nosology in adolescent substance abuse continue to be problematic despite the advent of *DSM-IV* (APA, 1994). The criteria that have been developed have not been validated with adolescents. There may be some discontinuities between adolescent and adult populations (Bukstein & Kaminer, 1994; Clark, Kirisci, & Tarter, 1998). When diagnostic criteria are based on problem behaviors, it is often unclear whether the behaviors are due to substance use or a coexisting or preexisting problem. Although craving and loss of control are included in the criteria, no studies have established whether these criteria are present in adolescents (Bukstein & Kaminer, 1994). Nosology is only the best attempt to make sense of reality; therefore, an imperfect system designed for adults is used to make substance abuse diagnoses in adolescents (Bukstein & Kaminer 1994; Clark et al., 1998; Kaminer, 1994; Weinberg, Rahdert, Colliver, & Glantz, 1998).

Dual diagnosis issues, as well, were studied initially in adults (Miller, 1993; Miller & Fine, 1993; Ries, 1993b; Schuckit, 1985; Schuckit, 1986; Schuckit 1994), leaving the clinician to extrapolate from this research to the adolescent population. More recently (Bukstein et al., 1992; Burke, Burke, Regier, & Rae, 1990; Burke et al., 1994; Crowley & Riggs, 1995; Deykin et al., 1992; Deykin & Buka, 1997; Fergusson et al., 1993; Flory, 1996; Giaconia et al., 1994; Grilo et al., 1995; Horowitz et al., 1992; Hovens et al., 1994; Kaminer et al., 1992; Kandel, Raveis, & Davies, 1991; Kandel et al., 1999; Kessler et al., 1996; Lewisohn, Hops, Roberts, Seeley, & Andrews, 1993; Mason & Siris, 1992; Morrison, Smith, Wilford, Ehrlich, & Seymour, 1993; Stowell & Estroff, 1992; Weiss, Mirin, & Frances, 1992; Westermeyer et al., 1994; Wilcox & Yates, 1993), adolescent clinical and community populations have been studied. For adults and adolescents, some of the methodological questions are the same. The course and treatment of the same two disorders may vary depending on which one is primary—in other words, which disorder preceded the other (Miller & Fine, 1993)—and on their relative severity (American Academy of Child and Adolescent Psychiatry [AACAP], 1998; Caton et al., 1989; King et al., 1996; Ries et al., 1994; Schuckit, 1985; Weiss et al., 1992). It is unhelpful to assume that all patients with dual diagnoses are the same and require the same treatment (Weiss et al., 1992). Although a high prevalence of comorbidity has been reported among adolescent inpatients with drug use disorders (Clark et al., 1995; Clark, Lesnick, & Hegedus, 1997; Grilo et al., 1995; Hovens et al., 1994; Kaminer et al., 1992; Van Hasselt, Ammerman, Glancy, & Bukstein, 1992), it is unclear how many exhibit psychiatric symptoms secondary to the substance abuse disorder and how many have a primary or coexisting psychiatric diagnosis. Miller and Fine (1993) argue that methodological considerations, including the length of abstinence required before the diagnosis is made, the population sampled, and the perspective of the examiner, affect prevalence rates for psychiatric disorders in persons who abuse substances and account for the variability. They see the prevalence rates for psychiatric disorders as artificially elevated by the tendency to make a diagnosis before abatement of some of the psychiatric symptomatology secondary to substance use.

Despite the controversy about the degree of comorbidity, psychologists, psychiatrists and other mental health professionals in practice need to treat the patients they encounter. Some of the patients will have a psychiatric diagnosis, and the treatment provided may need modification. Clinicians will serve these patients well if they take the following measures:

- Conduct a comprehensive evaluation of each patient that includes a mental status examination and an inquiry into other psychiatric symptomatology and obtain information from multiple sources.
- Have a high index of suspicion for comorbidity in adolescents whose conditions do not respond to treatment or who are presenting problems in treatment.
- Individualize treatment to accommodate other psychiatric diagnoses.
- Obtain a comprehensive substance abuse history.
- Know when to consult a psychiatrist or substance abuse specialist.

Clinicians should know the kinds of comorbidity they are likely to encounter in practice. Until recently, large-scale population studies did not focus on adolescents. The National Institute of Mental Health (NIMH) Epidemiological Catchment Area (ECA) Study (Burke et al., 1990) attempted to estimate the true prevalence rates of alcohol use disorders, other drug use disorders, and mental disorders in an adult community and institutional sample of more than 20,000 subjects standardized to the U.S. census. Of the total, 37% of persons with alcohol use disorders had another mental disorder, with the highest prevalence for affective, anxiety, and antisocial personality disorders. More than 50% of those with drug use disorders other than alcohol use had a comorbid mental disorder; 28% had anxiety disorders, 26% had affective disorders, 18% had antisocial personality disorder, and 7% had schizophrenia. This study verified the widely held impression that comorbidity rates are much higher among clinical and institutional populations than in the general population.

Until very recently, studies involving adolescents were smaller and involved clinical populations. Stowell and Estroff (1992) studied 226 adolescents receiving inpatient treatment in private psychiatric hospitals for a primary substance abuse disorder. Psychiatric diagnoses were made 4 weeks into treatment by using a semistructured diagnostic interview. Of the total, 82% of the patients met *DSM-III-R* (APA, 1987) criteria for an Axis I psychiatric disorder; 61% had mood disorders; 54% had conduct disorders; 43% had anxiety disorders; and 16% had substance-induced organic disorders. Three quarters of the patients (74%) had two or more psychiatric disorders. Westermeyer et al. (1994), studied 100 adolescents 12 to 20 years of age who sought care at two university-based outpatient substance abuse treatment programs and found similar high rates of comorbidity and multiple diagnoses. Of the adolescents, 22 had eating disorders, 8 had conduct disorders, 7 had major depressive disorder, 6 had minor depressive disorder, 5 had bipolar disorder, 5 had schizophrenia, and 4 had anxiety disorders. Three had another psychotic disorder, 3 had an organic mental disorder, and 2 had attention-deficit/hyperactivity disorder (ADHD). The distribution of diagnoses as a function of age showed that older adolescents had increased eating disorder diagnoses and depressive symptoms (Westermeyer et al., 1994).

Several recent population studies have included adolescents. Giaconia et al. (1994) also studied the issue of age in a predominantly White, working class community sample of 386 adolescents 18 years of age. They compared adolescents who had met the criteria for one of six psychiatric diagnoses, including substance abuse, before and after they were 14 years of age. Adolescents with early onset of any psychiatric disorder were 6 times as likely to have one and 12 times as likely to have two additional disorders by 18 years of age than those with later onset psychiatric disorder (Giaconia et al., 1994). This would imply that the clinician's index of suspicion for dual diagnosis must be particularly high for younger patients with substance abuse disorders. Burke et al. (1990) studied data from the NIMH ECA Study to determine hazard rates for the development of disorders and concluded that 15 to 19 years were the peak ages for the onset of depressive disorders in females and for the onset of substance use disorders and bipolar disorders in both sexes.

The National Comorbidity Study (NCS) included a large noninstitutional sample of persons 15 to 24 years of age, although adolescents were not studied separately from young adults (Kessler et al., 1996). Compared with older adults, 15- to 24-year-olds had the highest prevalence of three or more disorders occurring together and the highest prevalence of any disorder, including substance use disorders. The Methods for the Epidemiology of Child and Adolescent (MECA) Mental Disorders Study obtained data for 401 subjects 14 to 17 years of age (Kandel et al., 1999). Adolescents with substance use disorders had much higher rates of mood and conduct disorder than did those without substance use disorders.

MAJOR DIAGNOSTIC CATEGORIES

Depressive Disorders

Much has been written about the interplay between depression and substance abuse (Bukstein et al., 1992; Deykin et al., 1992; Flory, 1996; Kandel et al., 1991; Lewisohn et al., 1993; King et al., 1996; Rao et al., 1999; Schuckit, 1985; Schuckit, 1986; Schuckit, 1994; Wilcox & Yates, 1993). The emerging concept is that in adolescents (Bukstein et al., 1992; Bukstein & Kaminer, 1994; Deykin et al., 1992; Hovens et al., 1994; King et al., 1996; Rao et al., 1999) and adults (Schuckit, 1985; Schuckit, 1986; Schuckit, 1994), two groups exhibit significant depressive symptoms: those with a substance-induced mood disorder and those with primary depressive disorders (APA, 1994). The chief symptom of depression consists of a disturbance of mood usually characterized as sadness or feeling "down in the dumps" and a loss of interest or pleasure. Adolescents may report or exhibit irritability instead of sadness. In addition, depression is characterized by guilt, hopelessness, sleep disturbances, appetite disturbances, loss of the ability to concentrate, diminution of energy, and thoughts of death or suicide. To meet the criteria, the patient must exhibit or experience depressed mood most of the day, every day, for 2 weeks (APA, 1994). Patients with a substance-induced mood disorder may exhibit the same depressive symptoms.

Schuckit (1985, 1986, 1994) and Miller (1993) stress the importance of distinguishing between the two disorders. Studies of adults who abused substances showed that the substance-induced mood disorder dissipated with abstinence, but the primary depressive disorder did not and, if left untreated, could interfere with treatment and recovery (Burke et al., 1990; Miller, 1993; Miller & Fine, 1993; Schuckit, 1985). Deykin et al. (1992) interviewed 223 adolescents in residential treatment for substance abuse and found that almost 25% met the *DSM-III-R* (APA, 1987) criteria for depression. Of these, 8% met the criteria for a primary depression; the other 16% had a secondary mood disorder. Bukstein et al. (1992) studied adolescent inpatients on a dual diagnosis unit and reported that almost 31% had a comorbid major depression, with secondary depressive disorder much more common than primary depressive disorder. Unlike findings reported for adults, Bukstein et al. (1992) found that the secondary depression did not remit with abstinence. This finding, if replicated, would argue for more vigorous treatment of depressive syndromes in adolescents.

During the mental status examination, adolescents with depression may seem taciturn and show poor eye contact and a sad-looking face. They may be poorly groomed or drably dressed and may become tearful during the interview. Often they deny feelings of sadness, although their demeanor states it eloquently. Depression interferes with treatment, owing to the lack of concentration, motivation, and hope, as well as the tendency toward isolation. Kempton, Van Hasselt, Bukstein, and Null (1994) found cognitive distortions, including magnification (all-or-nothing thinking) and personalizing, to be particularly prominent among adolescents with the multiple diagnoses of conduct disorder, depressive disorder, and substance abuse. An adolescent with depression may benefit from a specific cognitive intervention for depression (Beck, Rush, Shaw, & Emery, 1979; Kaminer, 1994).

If the adolescent has a depressive disorder that predates the substance abuse, has a family history of depression, and has a mood disorder that interferes with treatment several weeks into abstinence despite cognitive interventions, pharmacotherapy is indicated. Serotoninergic agents, such as fluoxetine, have a relatively safe profile for side effects and may be most appropriate, considering reports that young substance abusers have a preexisting serotonin deficit (Crowley & Riggs, 1995; Horowitz et al., 1992; Riggs, Mikulich, Coffman, & Crowley, 1997). It would be advisable, before prescribing medication, to determine the following:

- Is the patient abstinent from substances; is the patient's abstinence secure; and are supports for abstinence in place, or is the patient in a secure drug-free environment?
- Will the patient adhere to a medication regimen, or does the patient have a family to help with adherence to the medication regimen?

If there are doubts about the diagnosis of depression or about treatment, consultation with a psychiatrist experienced in treating adolescents with addictions is indicated. When the primary clinician is concerned about possible suicidal behavior, a consultation should be sought without delay (Bukstein et al., 1993; Flory, 1996; Kandel et al., 1991).

Bipolar Disorder

The diagnosis of bipolar disorder may be among the hardest to make in children and adolescents, and is even more difficult in substance-abusing teens. Issues such as change in sleeping patterns and mood swings can be symptoms of bipolar disorder, substance abuse, or even normal adolescence. The diagnosis of bipolar disorder should certainly be considered in substance-abusing youth, particularly those with a binge pattern.

In bipolar disorder, which often begins during late adolescence (Burke et al., 1994; Giaconia et al., 1994; Wilens et al., 1999), the initial symptoms of mania include a persistent elevated, expansive, or irritable mood lasting at least 1 week, accompanied by grandiosity or inflated self-esteem, decreased need for sleep, pressured speech, racing thoughts, increased purposeful activity, and excessive involvement in pleasurable activities, such as spending money, sexual indiscretions, or substance abuse (APA, 1994). Wilens et al. (1999) have found an increased risk for substance use disorders in adolescents with bipolar disorder. Children who were diagnosed and treated appropriately at a younger age had a lower risk for substance abuse. Some patients use substances, particularly alcohol, to calm themselves during a manic phase. Clearly, some of these symptoms also are seen with substance intoxication. If a patient exhibits these symptoms after a period of abstinence, the diagnosis of bipolar disorder should be considered. Bipolar disorders are most often treated with mood stabilizers, the most common of which is lithium carbonate (Geller et al., 1998). Valproic acid, carbamazepine, and other anticonvulsants also are used, as are the atypical antipsychotics, such as olanzapine and risperidone (Kaminer, 1995; Wilens, Spencer, Frazier, & Biederman, 1998; Wilens et al., 1999). Before treating for bipolar disorder, a psychiatric consultation should be obtained.

Anxiety Disorders and Posttraumatic Stress Disorder

Anxiety disorders are among the most common psychiatric conditions coexisting in adolescents and adults with substance use disorders. Typically, this includes disorders such as generalized anxiety disorder, panic disorder, social phobia, obsessive-compulsive disorder, and posttraumatic stress disorder (PTSD; APA, 1994). Anxiety disorders often are not detected or treated, especially when present with depression or psychoactive substance use disorders (Burke et al., 1994; Clark et al., 1995). In fact, many adolescents (and adults) believe that drugs and alcohol may contribute to reduction of anxiety and stress, and this may lead to first use or continued abuse. Sometimes a closer examination of patients who resist attending self-help meetings may reveal a social phobia or agoraphobia. Furthermore, to make things more confusing, there are some well-done studies that have shown that teenagers who *never* use drugs or alcohol may be at higher risk to develop problems with anxiety later in life.

Panic attacks are periods of intense discomfort that develop abruptly and reach a peak within 10 minutes. Symptoms include palpitations, sweating, trembling, sensations of shortness of breath or choking, chest discomfort, nausea, dizziness, and fear of losing control or dying. Since some of these symptoms also might be seen in substance intoxication or withdrawal, it is important to establish abstinence before making a diagnosis. Patients with a social phobia may isolate themselves on an inpatient unit or in a group. A careful interview in which anxiety symptoms and family history of anxiety disorders are pursued may be quite revealing. Behavioral treatment, including relaxation training, often is helpful for anxiety disorders (Kaminer, 1994). The issue of pharmacotherapy is controversial. Many argue that the use of benzodiazepines is contraindicated in anyone with a history of substance abuse. Buspirone hydrochloride and serotonin reuptake inhibitors have been recommended as nonaddictive antianxiety agents (Wilens et al., 1998). Clinical experience and anecdotal reports suggest that for many, buspirone is ineffective. Often, when treating patients who insist that only benzodiazepines are effective, it is unclear whether the statement represents drug-seeking behavior or a bona fide observation. If abstinence has been established, adequate trials of behavioral or cognitive therapy (Kaminer, 1994) and alternative medications have failed, and the patient adheres to the treatment and medication regimen, the judicious use of a long-acting benzodiazepine, such as clonazepam, may be justified.

In clinical reports on adolescents, the incidence of severe trauma and symptoms of posttraumatic stress disorder are surprisingly high (Clark et al., 1995; Clark et al., 1997; Deykin & Buka, 1997; Kandel et al., 1999; Van Hasselt et al., 1992). An adolescent who has been acting out and abusing substances may not have dealt with previous trauma, such as physical and sexual abuse or exposure to violence, or with the trauma that may be incurred when abusing substances (Clark et al., 1997). Symptoms and memories of trauma may manifest themselves only during abstinence. Symptoms of posttraumatic stress disorder can be divided into three groups (APA, 1994). The first group involves reexperiencing the trauma through intrusive thoughts, dreams, or flashbacks, which make the person feel as if the event is reoccurring. Second, the patient has a numbing of general responsiveness and avoids thinking about the trauma. Third, there are symptoms of increased arousal, including difficulty sleeping, irritability, hypervigilance, and an exaggerated startle response. Trauma and the symptoms associated with trauma should be considered and inquired about to ensure adequate treatment of adolescents who abuse substances. Care should be taken to acknowledge the trauma without arousing anxiety that will interfere with abstinence and substance abuse treatment. Groups that support self-care and a first-things-first attitude may be the best approach; the patient needs to learn to stay safe, and treatment for substance abuse is a most important aspect of safety. The patient can be counseled that recovery is a process and must be taken in stages and that some of the effects of the trauma can be dealt with later when the patient's abstinence and safety are better established.

Organic Mental Disorders

The abuse of substances, including alcohol, marijuana, cocaine, ecstasy, hallucinogens, and inhalants, is associated in some patients with acute and residual cognitive damage (APA, 1994; Kempton et al., 1994; Stowell & Estroff, 1992). Acute symptoms may include impaired concentration and receptive and expressive language abilities, as well as irritability. Long-term interference with memory and other executive functions occurs. The possibility of a substance-induced dementia should be considered in adolescents who have difficulty coping with the cognitive and organizational demands of a structured and supportive program. Some of these adolescents will be able to use the program if instructions are simplified and if they comprehend information accurately. There may be rapid improvement in cognitive functioning, but the cognitive functioning of some patients continues to improve for as long as a year or more after cessation of the chemical assault to the brain. Some may be left with residual impairment.

Adolescents and their families should be informed about the cognitive consequences of their substance use in a way that does not engender despair but clearly warns against further abuse. The presence of cognitive deficits, if they persist, should be considered in rehabilitation, educational, and vocational planning for the adolescent. These adolescents need neuropsychological evaluation and follow-up.

Schizophrenia

Patients who simultaneously meet the criteria for schizophrenia and a substance abuse diagnosis are less likely to receive treatment on a substance abuse unit than on a psychiatric unit (Caton et al., 1989; Ries et al., 1994). As the late adolescent years are a time when many schizophrenic disorders begin, and the use of substances may precipitate an incipient psychosis, patients with this disorder may seek treatment during the early stages of schizophrenia (Kaminer et al., 1992; Miller & Fine, 1993; Ries 1993b). The characteristic symptoms are hallucinations that are more often auditory, delusions, disorganized speech, grossly disorganized or catatonic behavior, and negative symptoms, including affective flattening, impoverished speech, or avolition and the tendency to interrupt (AAP, 1999; APA, 1994). Therefore, for patients with bizarre manifestations that seem grossly different from those of the rest of the treatment population, the diagnosis of schizophrenia should be considered. Increasingly, younger schizophrenic patients abuse substances (Buckley, 1999; Minkoff, 1989; Ries, 1993b), some in an attempt to manage or deny their symptoms. Their abuse of substances often interferes with treatment for their psychotic disorder. These patients are best managed in special dual diagnosis programs for psychotic patients in which the psychosis and the substance abuse are addressed in integrated mental health and substance abuse treatment (Buckley, 1999; Caton et al., 1989; Costello et al., 1988; Mason & Siris, 1992; Minkoff, 1989; Ries, 1993a; Ries et al., 1994; Van Hasselt et al., 1992).

Attention-Deficit/Hyperactivity Disorder

Many involved in the treatment of adolescents who abuse substances have noted the large numbers of adolescents who also have attention-deficit/hyperactivity disorder (ADHD; AACAP, 1998; AAP, 2000; Bukstein et al., 1989; Crowley & Riggs, 1995; Morrison et al., 1993; Riggs, 1998; Wilcox & Yates, 1993; Wilens et al., 1996). Bukstein et al. (1989) postulate that there is no direct connection, but that both are often comorbid with conduct disorder. Crowley and Riggs (1995) note comorbidity with affective, anxiety, and antisocial disorders in the patients and their families. The symptoms of ADHD include inattention, such as failure to listen, difficulty with organization, the tendency to lose objects, or easy distractibility, and hyperactivity and impulsivity, such as fidgeting, restlessness, and the tendency to interrupt (AAP, 2000; APA, 1994). These symptoms must be present in more than one setting, and it may be helpful to use rating scales to establish the diagnosis and monitor progress. Treatment should include behavioral and educational intervention. Pharmacotherapy for adolescents has been controversial, particularly because some have argued that the use of psychostimulants might predispose adolescents to abuse other substances (Riggs, 1998). Riggs, Mikulich, and Pottle (1998) have reported some success with the use of bupropion. Wilens et al. (1996) suggest that the successful treatment of adolescents with ADHD with stimulants may actually lower the probability of developing a substance use disorder. Because the successful treatment of substance abuse involves teaching patients to plan and to delay impulses, the effective treatment of ADHD is necessary in an integrated plan.

Conduct Disorder and Antisocial Personality Disorder

Conduct disorder and antisocial personality disorder are the most common comorbid diagnoses with substance abuse, particularly in males (AACAP, 1998; Crowley & Riggs, 1995; Kaminer et al., 1992; Kandel et al., 1999; King et al., 1996; Rao et al., 1999; Schuckit, 1985; Stowell & Estroff, 1992; Westermeyer et al., 1994; Wilcox &

Yates, 1993; Wilens et al., 1996). The characteristic symptom of antisocial personality disorder is a pervasive pattern of disregarding and violating the rights of others, and the disorder may include deceitfulness, impulsivity, failure to conform to rules or the law, aggressiveness, and irresponsibility (APA, 1994). Conduct disorder has similar criteria but includes manifestations that are likely to be seen in younger persons, such as cruelty to animals, running away, truancy, and vandalism. Many who have studied adolescent substance abuse have commented that it usually occurs as part of a constellation of problem behaviors (Crowley & Riggs, 1995; Fergusson et al., 1993; Kandel et al., 1999; Morrison et al., 1993; Riggs, 1998). Cloninger (1987) presents an interesting scheme of hereditary factors on three axes that may account for many psychiatric diagnoses and their interrelationships. The three axes are reward dependence, harm avoidance, and novelty seeking. Based on these axes, Cloninger (1987) distinguished Type 1 and Type 2 alcoholic patients. Type 2 alcoholic patients score low on reward dependence and harm avoidance and high on novelty seeking. Younger alcoholic patients with antisocial personality fit the Type 2 classification. The higher prevalence of antisocial personality and conduct disorder among younger alcoholic patients may explain why many clinicians find adolescent substance abusers more difficult to treat. Horowitz et al. (1992) consider many young patients who abuse substances to have a combination of characteristics, including increased hostility, depression, and suicidal ideation, that suggest an underlying, perhaps neurochemically determined, difficulty with self-regulation and aggression. Adolescents with conduct disorders and antisocial personality disorder need a strong behavioral program with clear limits. If there is a comorbid disorder (such as a mood or attention disorder that can be treated successfully), the adolescents are more likely to do well (Crowley & Riggs, 1995; Riggs 1998; Wilens et al., 1996).

Borderline and Narcissistic Personality Disorders

In addition to psychiatric diagnoses on Axis I, the personality disorders described on Axis II of *DSM-IV* are relevant to the treatment of adolescents who abuse substances (APA, 1994; Groves, 1978; Jellinek & Ablon, 1995; Myers, Burket, & Otto, 1993). Personality disorders are enduring patterns of inner experience and behavior that affect cognition, interpersonal behavior, emotional response, and impulse control. It is often personality factors that make an adolescent difficult to treat. Borderline personality disorder is marked by impulsivity and instability of interpersonal relationships that affects self-image. A marked sensitivity and wish to avoid abandonment, chronic feelings of emptiness, inappropriate and intense anger, and suicidal or self-mutilating behavior are characteristic of borderline personality disorder. In a treatment setting, patients with borderline personality disorder can wreak havoc because of the severe regression often manifested and the divisiveness they often cause among staff.

A pervasive pattern of grandiosity, a need for admiration, and a lack of empathy characterize narcissistic personality disorder. The patient feels unique and entitled to special treatment. A patient with narcissistic personality disorder may have difficulty participating in groups or seeing other people in ways other than as need gratifiers.

Both of these personality disorders can present challenges for the clinician and the staff in the treatment setting. Powerful and negative feelings, conscious and unconscious (King et al., 1996), can be aroused easily by patients who are manipulative and full of rage, who feel entitled, and whose behavior saps the emotional strength of the staff and clinicians (Groves, 1978). If the treatment of a patient requires a great amount of emotional energy, personality issues likely are involved. It is essential to be aware of the effect that such patients exert and to take care of the clinicians and the staff in the treatment setting, as well as the patient.

Eating Disorders

As the incidence of eating disorders and substance abuse have increased in our adolescent population (Katz, 1990; Ross & Ivis, 1999; Westermeyer et al., 1994; Westermeyer & Specker, 1999), it is not uncommon to find them together. In fact, one quarter of all patients with an eating disorder have a history of substance abuse or are currently abusing substances (Katz, 1990). Anorexia nervosa, which involves weight restriction and increased activity, a distorted body image, and an intense fear of losing control and becoming fat (APA, 1994), is not as prevalent as bulimia in the general population and among persons who abuse substances (Westermeyer & Specker, 1999). Bulimia involves recurrent episodes of binge eating, sometimes accompanied by compensatory measures such as vomiting or laxative abuse, and a preoccupation with food and weight. Of all eating disorders, 90% to 95% occur in females (Katz, 1990). Although anorexic patients have a characteristic emaciated appearance, bulimic patients can be any weight. Patients who consistently spend time in the bathroom after meals may be purging. Persons with an eating disorder may abuse amphetamines to lose weight. Katz (1990) postulates that the proneness to substance abuse in bulimic patients may be due to borderline personality features.

CONCLUSION

In sum, psychiatric disorders and substance abuse frequently occur together. This leads to difficulty in both assessment and treatment. An awareness of the prevalence and manifestations of psychiatric diagnoses is essential to the quality of treatment of adolescents who abuse substances. An ongoing relationship with a psychiatrist who can be available for consultation as needed is helpful. The clinician should keep up to date on psychopharmacologic interventions (Kaminer, 1995; Solhkhah & Wilens, 1998). Frequently, the use of psychiatric medications such as antidepressants, mood stabilizers, psychostimulants, and others is of benefit. However, care must be taken to avoid potential interactions between the illicit drugs and the prescribed medications (Wilens, Biederman, & Spencer, 1997). In addition, the use of groups such as Alcoholics Anonymous (AA), Narcotics Anonymous (NA), or Double-Trouble groups that deal with mental illness and chemical abuse (MICA) or dual-diagnosis issues can oftentimes be a useful adjunct to treatment with a mental health professional (Brown, 1993; Hohman & LeCroy, 1996; Simkin, 1996). Careful observation, history taking, and appropriate consultation result in better detection and treatment of comorbid disorders and, ultimately, of the initial substance abuse problem.

REFERENCES

American Academy of Child and Adolescent Psychiatry. (1998). Practice parameters for the assessment and treatment of children and adolescents with substance abuse disorders. *Journal of the American Academy of Child and Adolescent Psychiatry, 37,* 122–126.

American Academy of Pediatrics, Committee on Quality Improvement, Subcommittee on Attention-Deficit/Hyperactivity Disorder. (1999). Diagnosis and evaluation of the child with attention-deficit/hyperactivity disorder. *Pediatrics, 105,* 1158–1170.

American Academy of Pediatrics, Committee on Substance Abuse. (2000). Indications for management and referral of patients involved in substance abuse. *Pediatrics, 106,* 143–148.

American Psychiatric Association. (1987). *Diagnostic and statistical manual of mental disorders* (3rd ed., revised). Washington, DC: Author.

American Psychiatric Association. (1994). *Diagnostic and statistical manual of mental disorders* (4th ed.). Washington, DC: Author.

Armentano, M. (1995). Assessment, diagnosis, and treatment of the dually diagnosed adolescent. *Pediatric Clinics of North America, 42,* 479–490.

Beck, A. T., Rush, A. J., Shaw, B. F., & Emery, G. (1979). *Cognitive therapy of depression.* New York: Guilford Press.

Brook, J. S., Whiteman, M., Cohen, P., Shapiro, J., & Balka, E. (1995). Longitudinally predicting late adolescent and young adult drug use: Childhood and adolescent precursors. *Journal of the American Academy of Child and Adolescent Psychiatry, 34,* 1230–1238.

Brown, S. A. (1993). Recovery patterns in adolescent substance abuse. In J. S. Bae, G. A. Marlatt, & R. J. McMahon (Eds.), *Addictive behaviors across the life span: Prevention, treatment, and policy issues* (pp. 161–183). Newbury Park, CA: Sage Publications.

Buckley, P. F. (1999). Substance abuse in schizophrenia: A review. *Journal of Clinical Psychiatry, 59*(Suppl. 3), 26–30.

Bukstein, O. G., Brent, D. A., & Kaminer, Y. (1989). Comorbidity of substance abuse and other psychiatric disorders in adolescents. *American Journal of Psychiatry, 146,* 1131–1141.

Bukstein, O. G., Brent, D. A., Perper, J. A., Moritz, G., Bargher, M., Schweers, J., Roth, C., & Balach, C. (1993). Risk factors for completed suicide among adolescents with a lifetime history of substance abuse: a case-control study. *Acta Psychiatrica Scandinavica, 88,* 403–408.

Bukstein, O. G., Glancy, L. J., & Kaminer, Y. (1992). Patterns of affective comorbidity in a clinical population of dually diagnosed adolescent substance abusers. *Journal of the American Academy of Child and Adolescent Psychiatry, 31,* 1041–1045.

Bukstein, O., & Kaminer, Y. (1994). The nosology of adolescent substance abuse. *American Journal on Addictions, 3,* 1–13.

Burke, J. D., Jr., Burke, K. C., & Rae, D. S. (1994). Increased rates of drug abuse and dependence after onset of mood or anxiety disorders in adolescence. *Hospital and Community Psychiatry, 45,* 451–455.

Burke, K. C., Burke, J. D., Jr., Regier, D. A., & Rae, D. S. (1990). Age at onset of selected mental disorders in five community populations. *Archives of General Psychiatry, 47,* 511–518.

Caton, C. L., Gralnick, A., Bender, S., & Simon, R. (1989). Young chronic patients and substance abuse. *Hospital and Community Psychiatry, 40,* 1037–1040.

Chatlos, J. C. (1996). Recent trends and a developmental approach to substance abuse in adolescents. *Child and Adolescent Psychiatric Clinics of North America, 5,* 1–27.

Christie, K. A., Burke, J. D., Jr., Regier, D. A., Rae, D. S., Boyd, J. H., & Locke, B. Z. (1988). Epidemiologic evidence for early onset of mental disorders and higher risk of drug abuse in young adults. *American Journal of Psychiatry, 145,* 971–975.

Clark, D. B., & Bukstein, O. G. (1998). Psychopathology in adolescent alcohol abuse and dependence. *Alcohol Health and Research World, 22,* 117–126.

Clark, D. B., Bukstein, O., Smith, M. G., Kaczynski, N. A., Mezzich, A. C., & Donovan, J. E. (1995). Identifying anxiety disorders in adolescents hospitalized for alcohol abuse and dependence. *Psychiatric Services, 46,* 618–620.

Clark, D. B., Kirisci, L., & Tarter, R. E. (1998). Adolescent versus adult onset and the development of substance abuse disorders in males. *Drug and Alcohol Dependence, 49,* 115–121.

Clark, D. B., Lesnick, L., & Hegedus, A. M. (1997). Traumas and other adverse life events in adolescents with alcohol use and dependence. *Journal of the American Academy of Child and Adolescent Psychiatry, 36,* 1744–1751.

Cloninger, C. R. (1987). Neurogenetic adaptive mechanisms in alcoholism. *Science, 236,* 410–416.

Costello, E. J., Costello, A. J., Edelbrock, C., Burns, B. J., Dulcan, M. K., Brent, D., & Janiszewski, S. (1988). Psychiatric disorders in pediatric primary care: Prevalence and risk factors. *Archives of General Psychiatry, 45,* 1107–1116.

Crowley, T. J., & Riggs, P. D. (1995). Adolescent substance use disorder with conduct disorder and comorbid conditions. *NIDA Research Monograph, 156,* 49–111.

DeMilio, L. (1989). Psychiatric syndromes in adolescent substance abusers. *American Journal of Psychiatry, 146,* 1212–1214.

Deykin, E. Y., & Buka, S. L. (1997). Prevalence and risk factors for posttraumatic stress disorder among chemically dependent adolescents. *American Journal of Psychiatry 154,* 752–757.

Deykin, E. Y., Buka, S. L., & Zeena, T. H. (1992). Depressive illness among chemically dependent adolescents. *American Journal of Psychiatry, 149,* 1341–1347.

Fergusson, D. M., Horwood, L. J., & Lynskey, M. T. (1993). Prevalence and comorbidity of *DSM-III-R* diagnoses in a birth cohort of 15 year olds. *Journal of the American Academy of Child and Adolescent Psychiatry, 32,* 1127–1134.

Flory, M. (1996). Psychiatric diagnosis in child and adolescent suicide. *Archives of General Psychiatry, 53,* 339–348.

Geller, B., Cooper, T. B., Sun, K., Zimmerman, B., Frazier, J., Williams, M., & Heath, J. (1998). Double-blind and placebo-controlled study of lithium for adolescent bipolar disorders with secondary substance dependency. *Journal of the American Academy of Child and Adolescent Psychiatry, 37,* 171–178.

Giaconia, R. M., Reinherz, H. Z., Silverman, A. B., Pakiz, B., Frost, A. K., & Cohen, E. (1994). Ages of onset of psychiatric disorders in a community population of older adolescents. *Journal of the American Academy of Child and Adolescent Psychiatry, 33,* 706–717.

Grilo, C. M., Becker, D. F., Walker, M. L., Levy, K. N., Edell, W. S., & McGlashan, T. H. (1995). Psychiatric comorbidity in adolescent inpatients with substance use disorders. *Journal of the American Academy of Child and Adolescent Psychiatry, 34,* 1085–1091.

Groves, J. E. (1978). Taking care of the hateful patient. *New England Journal of Medicine, 298,* 883–887.

Hohman, M., and LeCroy, C. W. (1996). Predictors of adolescent A.A. affiliation. *Adolescence, 31,* 339–352.

Horowitz, H. A., Overton, W. F., Rosenstein, D., & Steidl, J. H. (1992). Comorbid adolescent substance abuse: A maladaptive pattern of self-regulation. *Adolescent Psychiatry, 18,* 465–483.

Hovens, J. G., Cantwell, D. P., & Kiriakos, R. (1994). Psychiatric comorbidity in hospitalized adolescent substance abusers. *Journal of the American Academy of Child and Adolescent Psychiatry, 33,* 476–483.

Jellinek, M. S., & Ablon, S. (1995). Character disorders in adolescence. In S. B. Friedman, M. Fisher, S. K. Schonberg, & E. M. Alderman, *Comprehensive adolescent health care* (2nd ed., pp. 911–920). New York: Mosby Year-Book.

Johnston, L. D., O'Malley, P. M., & Bachman, J. G. (2001). *Monitoring the future: National results on adolescent drug use: Overview of key findings, 2000.* Bethesda, MD: National Institute on Drug Abuse.

Kaminer, Y. (1991). The magnitude of concurrent psychiatric disorders in hospitalized substance abusing adolescents. *Journal of Abnormal Child Psychology, 25,* 122–132.

Kaminer, Y. (1994). *Adolescent substance abuse: A comprehensive guide to theory and practice.* New York: Plenum Press.

Kaminer, Y. (1995). Pharmacotherapy for adolescents with psychoactive substance use disorders. *NIDA Research Monograph, 156,* 291–324.

Kaminer, Y., Tarter, R. E., Bukstein, O. G., & Kabene, M. (1992). Comparison between treatment completers and noncompleters among dually diagnosed substance-abusing adolescents. *Journal of the American Academy of Child and Adolescent Psychiatry, 31,* 1046–1049.

Kandel, D. B., Johnson, J. G., Bird, H., Canino, G., Goodman, S. H., Lahey, B. B., Reiger, D. A., & Schwab-Stone, M. (1997). Psychiatric disorders associated with substance use among children and adolescents: Findings from the methods for the epidemiology of child and adolescent mental disorders (MECA) study. *Journal of Abnormal Child Psychology, 25,* 122–132.

Kandel, D. B., Johnson, J. G., Bird, H. R., Weissman, M. M., Goodman, S. H., Lahey, B. B., Regier, D. A., & Schwab-Stone, M. E. (1999). Psychiatric comorbidity among adolescents with substance use disorders: Findings from the MECA study. *Journal of the American Academy of Child and Adolescent Psychiatry, 38,* 693–699.

Kandel, D. B., Raveis, V. H., & Davies, M. (1991). Suicidal ideation in adolescence: Depression, substance use, and other risk factors. *Journal of Youth and Adolescence, 20,* 289–309.

Kashani, J. H., Keller, M. B., Solomon, N., Reid, J. C., & Mazzola, D. (1985). Double depression in adolescent substance abusers. *Journal of Affective Disorders 8,* 153–157.

Katz, J. L. (1990). Eating disorders: A primer for the substance abuse specialist: I. Clinical features. *Journal of Substance Abuse Treatment, 7,* 143–149.

Kellam, S. G., Ensminger, M. E., & Simon, M. B. (1980). Mental health in first grade and teenage drug, alcohol, and cigarette use. *Drug and Alcohol Dependence, 5,* 273–304.

Kempton, T., Van Hasselt, V. B., Bukstein, O. G., & Null, J. A. (1994). Cognitive distortions and psychiatric diagnosis in dually diagnosed adolescents. *Journal of the American Academy of Child and Adolescent Psychiatry, 33,* 217–222.

Kessler, R. C., Nelson, C. B., McGonagle, K. A., Edlund, M. J., Frank, R. G., & Leaf, P. J. (1996). The epidemiology of co-occurring addictive and mental disorders: Implications for prevention and service utilization. *American Journal of Orthopsychiatry, 66,* 17–31.

King, C., Ghaziuddin, N., McGovern, L., Brand, E., Hill, E., & Naylor, M. (1996). Predictors of comorbid alcohol and substance abuse in depressed adolescents. *Journal of the American Academy of Child and Adolescent Psychiatry, 35,* 743–751.

King, C. A., Naylor, M. W., Hill, E. M., Shain, B. N., & Greden, J. F. (1992). Dysthymia characteristic of heavy alcohol use in depressed adolescents. *Biological Psychiatry, 33,* 210–212.

Lewisohn, P. M., Hops, H., Roberts, R. E., Seeley, J. R., & Andrews, J. A. (1993). Adolescent psychopathology: I. Prevalence and incidence of depression and other *DSM-III-R* disorders in high school students. *Journal of Abnormal Psychology, 102,* 133–144.

Mason, S. E., & Siris, S. G. (1992). Dual diagnosis: The case for case management. *American Journal on Addictions, 1,* 77–82.

Milin, R., Halikas, J. A., Meller, J. E., & Morse, C. (1991). Psychopathology among substance abusing juvenile offenders. *Journal of the American Academy of Child and Adolescent Psychiatry, 30,* 569–574.

Miller, N. S. (1993). Comorbidity of psychiatric and alcohol/drug disorders: Interactions and independent status. *Journal of Addictive Diseases, 12,* 5–16.

Miller, N. S., & Fine, J. (1993). Current epidemiology of comorbidity of psychiatric and addictive disorders. *Psychiatric Clinics of North America, 16,* 1–10.

Minkoff, K. (1989). An integrated treatment model for dual diagnosis of psychosis and addiction. *Hospital and Community Psychiatry, 40,* 1031–1036.

Morrison, M. A., Smith, D. E., Wilford, B. B., Ehrlich, P., & Seymour, R. B. (1993). At war in the fields of play: Current perspectives on the nature and treatment of adolescent chemical dependency. *Journal of Psychoactive Drugs, 25,* 321–330.

Myers, W. C., Burket, R. C., & Otto, T. A. (1993). Conduct disorders and personality disorders in hospitalized adolescents. *Journal of Clinical Psychiatry, 54,* 21–26.

Olfson, M., & Klerman, G. L. (1992). The treatment of depression: Prescribing practices of primary care physicians and psychiatrists. *Journal of Family Practice, 35,* 627–635.

Rao, U., Ryan, N. D., Dahl, R. E., Birmaher, B., Rao, R., Williamson, D. E., & Perel, J. M. (1999). Factors associated with the development of substance use disorder in depressed adolescents. *Journal of the American Academy of Child and Adolescent Psychiatry, 38,* 1109–1117.

Ries, R. K. (1993a). Clinical treatment matching models for dually diagnosed patients. *Psychiatric Clinics of North America, 16,* 167–175.

Ries, R. K. (1993b). The dually diagnosed patient with psychotic symptoms. *Journal of Addictive Diseases, 12,* 103–122.

Ries, R., Mullen, M., & Cox, G. (1994). Symptom severity and utilization of treatment resources among dually diagnosed inpatients. *Hospital and Community Psychiatry, 45,* 562–568.

Riggs, P. D. (1998). Clinical approach to treatment of ADHD in adolescents with substance use disorders and conduct disorder. *Journal of the American Academy of Child and Adolescent Psychiatry, 37,* 331–332.

Riggs, P. D., Mikulich, S. C., Coffman, L., & Crowley, T. (1997). Fluoxetine in drug-dependent delinquents with major depression: An open trial. *Journal of Child and Adolescent Psychopharmacology, 7,* 87–95.

Riggs, P. D., Mikulich, S. C., & Pottle, L. C. (1998). An open trial of bupropion for ADHD in adolescents with substance use disorder and conduct disorder. *Journal of the American Academy of Child and Adolescent Psychiatry, 37,* 1271–1278.

Ross, H. E., & Ivis, F. (1999). Binge eating and substance abuse among male and female adolescents. *International Journal of Eating Disorders, 26,* 245–260.

Schuckit, M. A. (1985). The clinical implications of primary diagnostic groups among alcoholics. *Archives of General Psychiatry, 42,* 1043–1049.

Schuckit, M. A. (1986). Genetic and clinical implications of alcoholism and affective disorder. *American Journal of Psychiatry, 143,* 140–147.

Schuckit, M. A. (1994). Alcohol and depression: A clinical perspective. *Acta Psychiatrica Scandinavica, 377*(Suppl.), 28–32.

Simkin, D. R. (1996). Twelve-step treatment from a developmental perspective. *Child and Adolescent Psychiatric Clinics of North America, 5,* 165–175.

Solhkhah, R., & Wilens, T. E. (1998). Pharmacotherapy of adolescent alcohol and other drug use. *Alcohol Health and Research World, 22,* 122–125.

Stowell, J. A., & Estroff, T. W. (1992). Psychiatric disorders in substance-abusing adolescent inpatients: A pilot study. *Journal of the American Academy of Child and Adolescent Psychiatry, 31,* 1036–1040.

Van Hasselt, V. B., Ammerman, R. T., Glancy, L. J., & Bukstein, O. G. (1992). Maltreatment in psychiatrically hospitalized dually diagnosed adolescent substance abusers. *Journal of the American Academy of Child and Adolescent Psychiatry, 31,* 868–874.

Weinberg, N. Z., Rahdert, E., Colliver, J. D., & Glantz, M. D. (1998). Adolescent substance abuse: A review of the past 10 years. *Journal of the American Academy of Child and Adolescent Psychiatry, 37,* 252–261.

Weiss, R. D., Mirin, S. M., & Frances, R. J. (1992). Alcohol and drug abuse: The myth of the typical dual diagnosis patient. *Hospital and Community Psychiatry, 43,* 107–108.

Westermeyer, J., & Specker, S. (1999). Social resources and social function in comorbid eating and substance disorder: A matched-pairs study. *American Journal on Addictions, 8,* 332–336.

Westermeyer, J., Specker, S., Neider, J., & Lingenfelter, M. A. (1994). Substance abuse and associated psychiatric disorder among 100 adolescents. *Journal of Addictive Diseases, 13,* 67–89.

Wilcox, J. A., & Yates, W. R. (1993). Gender and psychiatric comorbidity in substance-abusing individuals. *American Journal on Addictions, 2,* 202–206.

Wilens, T. E., Biederman, J., Millstein, R. B., Wozniak, J., Hahesy, A. L., & Spencer, T. J. (1999). Risk for substance use disorders in youths with child- and adolescent-onset bipolar disorder. *Journal of the American Academy of Child and Adolescent Psychiatry, 38,* 680–685.

Wilens, T. E., Biederman, J., & Spencer, T. J. (1996). Attention deficit hyperactivity disorder and psychoactive substance use disorders. *Child and Adolescent Psychiatric Clinics of North America, 5,* 73–91.

Wilens, T. E., Biederman, J., & Spencer, T. J. (1997). Case study: Adverse effects of smoking marijuana while receiving tricyclic antidepressants. *Journal of the American Academy of Child and Adolescent Psychiatry, 36,* 45–48.

Wilens, T., Spencer, T., Frazier, J., & Biederman, J. (1998). Psychopharmacology in children and adolescents. In T. Ollendick & M. Hersen (Eds.), *Handbook of child psychopathology* (pp. 603–636). New York: Plenum Press.

SECTION IV

Systems of Care

Chapter 17

WRAPAROUND CARE

THOMAS J. GRUNDLE

Childhood is characterized by change and transition and by an extensive range of normal development. Nevertheless, during the course of a year, approximately 1 in 5 children and adolescents experience diagnosable symptoms of emotional disturbance, and about 5% of all youth experience an extreme functional impairment usually labeled *serious emotional disturbance* (Satcher, 2000). Serious emotional disturbance (SED) is associated with various risk factors, including poverty, abuse, neglect, developmental disabilities, medical problems, and family dysfunction. Numerous biopsychosocial interventions have demonstrated a certain degree of effectiveness in meeting the needs of children and adolescents with SED. However, the multiple problems that characterize this population can be better addressed through a systemic approach in which multiple services are organized, integrated, and delivered to these young people and their families (Satcher, 2000).

Unfortunately, because of the fragmentation and disorganization of community services for youth with SED, there is consensus among professionals that services have failed to meet their needs in the past. In response to this community failure, service systems have traditionally relied heavily on the use of institutional care as the primary delivery system.

CHILD AND ADOLESCENT SERVICE SYSTEM PROGRAM

In 1984, Congress responded to these concerns by funding an initiative through the National Institute of Mental Health (NIMH) that established the Child and Adolescent Service System Program (CASSP). Operating at the state level, the program promotes interagency collaboration in the development of services for youth with SED (Stroul & Friedman, 1986). These children and adolescents often require a range of services from the mental health system, as well as services from the educational, social service, health care, and juvenile justice systems. Accordingly, multiple systems of integrated services are required for the delivery of care to these young clients, whose needs cannot be met by a fragmented single-system approach. What is required is a system of care that can address all of the needs of this vulnerable population in the community.

The CASSP initiative specified two core principles that should underlie the development of a system of care. First, the system should be *youth-centered.* That is, as the service plan is developed and implemented, professionals should work as equal partners with these children and adolescents and with their families. Second, services should be *community-based.* When services are delivered at the community level, decision making remains in the community as well (Stroul & Friedman, 1986).

Other CASSP principles also guide the development of systems of care for children and adolescents with SED. These youth should have access to a comprehensive array of services that can meet their needs. Services should be guided by an individualized service plan and delivered within the least restrictive environment appropriate. These young clients should be identified early, and their rights should be protected. Their families should be full participants in the planning and delivery of integrated services designed to meet their needs, and services should be delivered in a culturally competent manner. Interventions are coordinated through the use of an intensive case management system. When necessary, the system should ensure a smooth transition to the adult service system. The system should build on the strengths of the youth and the family, as well as addressing their challenges and needs. Finally, a system of care must be designed by the community in which these children and adolescents reside to reflect the unique characteristics of the setting (Stroul & Friedman, 1986).

As these principles are applied to systems of care for young people with SED throughout the country, the systems will have commonalities along with differences that reflect the unique aspects and values of each community. Similarly, for a given child or adolescent, the individualized service plan may incorporate services from the mental health, educational, social service, health care, and juvenile justice systems, as well as other service systems deemed necessary for the promotion of healthy change and development.

THE WRAPAROUND APPROACH

One example of this multisystem approach to services for children and adolescents with SED is *wraparound,* which was developed through CASSP grants to the states. Elements of the wraparound process include a strength-based approach to youth and families; family involvement in treatment design; needs-based services; individualized, culturally competent service plans; and unconditional care. The services are community-based, outcome-focused, and supported by flexible funding. The critical components emanating from the wraparound approach are (a) an extensive and intensive case management system that provides the glue for developing a child and family team of professionals, natural supports, and family members that can guide service delivery; (b) an extensive array of services and service providers selected by the team to deliver the care; and (c) a competent crisis response component, which supports families in maintaining their child in the community.

Early examples of the wraparound approach were the Kaleidoscope Program developed in Chicago by Karl Dennis (1994) and the Alaska Youth Initiative developed by John Vandenberg (Katz-Leavy, Lourie, Stroul, & Zeigler-Dendy, 1992). Both projects offered individualized care, developed flexible programming and funding, and provided unconditional care to these young people and their families. The wraparound approach has been further expanded by the Children's Mental Health Services Program of Substance Abuse and Mental Health Services Administration (SAMHSA), which has provided grants to help communities design and implement systems of care unique to their locale (Kamradt & Meyers, 1999).

To date, outcome evaluations of systems of care have shown them to be effective in improving access to services, reducing the use of institutional care, and increasing family satisfaction (Satcher, 2000; Stroul, 1993). Some evaluations have demonstrated improvements in functional behavior for the youth both during and after participation in the project (Stroul, 1993). Some projects have also demonstrated a reduction in cost, which frequently results in an expansion of the population served (Meyers, 2000; Stroul, 1993), although cost has not been reduced in all such projects (Bickman, 1996). In fact, Bickman (1997) and Satcher (2000) conclude that services delivered within systems of care do not necessarily result in cost reductions or in better clinical outcomes than services delivered by more traditional systems.

Bickman (1997) maintains that it remains to be determined empirically that our clinical treatments are effective, regardless of whether treatments are delivered within a system of care or by a traditional system. The initial belief that simply reshaping a system of services would lead to improved clinical outcomes has not been supported to date. Furthermore, cost is often a significant driving force in the reshaping or redesigning health care systems within communities. Bickman (1996) suggests that a capitated system might lead to cost savings within an integrated system of care. Such savings would allow providers to maintain the intensity of services needed for children and adolescents with SED while acknowledging fiscal realities.

WRAPAROUND MILWAUKEE

Wraparound Milwaukee is one project that has both demonstrated significant reduction in financial costs and resulted in a dramatic redesign of service delivery in the community. In response to the yearly budgetary crises facing Milwaukee County and the impact of those crises on services for youth with SED, in 1994 the National Center for Mental Health Services awarded a program grant (Comprehensive Community Mental Health Services for Children and Their Families) to the State Bureau of Mental Health and the Milwaukee County Human Services Department. The grant was administered by the Child and Adolescent Services branch of the Milwaukee County Mental Health Division. It was through this grant that the division initiated both Wraparound Milwaukee and the "25 Kid Project," a pilot project designed to demonstrate the use of a wraparound approach for children and adolescents with SED returning to the community from lengthy out-of-home placements.

Background

Historically, as in other communities, there was limited collaboration among the child welfare, juvenile justice, mental health, and educational systems. Consequently, a central mission of the Wraparound Milwaukee program was to develop an integrated and coordinated system of care. It was equally important to provide both individualized and comprehensive care to families in the community and, at all levels of decision making, to establish an equal partnership with families for establishing their child's treatment plan and for designing, developing, and implementing system change. Further, it was Wraparound Milwaukee's mission to promote cultural competency and diversity in the provision of mental health services and to create and provide cost-effective community-based alternatives to categorical out-of-home care. Finally, to monitor the quality of any systems change, it was essential to evaluate outcomes at many levels.

To demonstrate the effectiveness of the wraparound approach to providing comprehensive SED services, a pilot project was designed for 25 youth who were returning to the community from residential treatment centers. These young clients, who were identified by the child welfare or juvenile justice systems, had no immediate discharge plan and had been in out-of-home placement for significant periods of time. The pilot study demonstrated the feasibility of using the wraparound approach to provide integrative care to youth with SED in the community. For example, the program was not only able to return these young people to the community within a relatively short period of time, but also to maintain the vast majority in community placements (Meyers, 2000).

Flowing from the success of this pilot, stakeholders from the mental health, child welfare, juvenile justice, and educational systems came to the table to develop a new system of care in Milwaukee. From 1994 through 1999, Wraparound Milwaukee evolved into its present form and is now a publicly operated managed care system with defined populations. The program operates with pooled funds from Medicaid and the mental health, child welfare, and juvenile justice systems; and it uses an extensive network of public and private providers. Case management services are provided by private agencies that mirror the community culturally and that adhere to a wraparound philosophy. Wraparound Milwaukee uses a comprehensive quality-assurance/quality-improvement plan and has established outcomes to begin to measure program effectiveness.

Population

The defined population is youth with SED who are identified by the child welfare or juvenile justice systems. These young clients are on the verge of out-of-home placement primarily in residential treatment, but also potentially in juvenile corrections. Their families generally have complex needs. Demographically, these service recipients are overwhelmingly male (around 75%), and approximately 85% are ages 12 to 17, with the remainder as young as age 6. Ethnic representation has remained relatively stable: African American (65%), Caucasian (28%), Hispanic (6%), and Native American (1%). Two thirds (68%) of the current population have been adjudicated delinquent and are court-ordered into the program.

Almost 60% of the youth are in the custody of their biological mothers; 17% are in the custody of both biological parents; and over 16% have someone other than biological parents as their guardian. Almost half (49%) come from families that earn less than $15,000 per year. Regarding diagnostic groups, over 70% are diagnosed with a behavior disorder; 33% are diagnosed with attention-deficit/hyperactivity disorder, sometimes in addition to the behavior disorder. In fact, many of these young clients have multiple diagnoses. For example, over 40% arc also diagnosed with depression, and 20% are diagnosed with alcohol and drug-related problems. Other common problems include learning disabilities, developmental disabilities, anxiety disorders, and posttraumatic stress disorder.

This population presents with many behavioral issues, including school and community concerns (70%), severe aggression (over 50%), prior physical and sexual abuse (over 50%), runaway behavior (37%), substance abuse (32%), and suicidal behavior (19%). The primary family issues are family violence (60%), a substance-abusing caretaker (39%), parental incarceration (28%), parental abandonment (over 27%), and parental mental illness (17%). These factors have remained relatively constant over the course of the project.

Program

Financially, Wraparound Milwaukee owes its success to its ability to pool funds. The mental health, child welfare, and juvenile justice systems have contributed significant monies in their respective budgets toward the development of a capitated, carve-out managed care organization. In addition, after a period of time, a Medicaid capitation rate was established, along with a crisis service benefit, and those monies were added to pooled funds. In all, $28 million is available for the delivery of care. These funds include of all child welfare and juvenile justice funds budgeted for institutional care ($17 million). In addition, the capitated Medicaid rate, actuarily based at $1,470 per enrollee, added another $10 million. Finally, estimated crisis service billing, residual block grant funds, and commercial insurance were estimated at another $1 million to arrive at the budgeted amount. Theoretically, this would allow $3,300 per month to be spent if 700 children and their families were in the project at all times. However, some children's needs exceeded the budgeted amount, whereas other children were served for less.

These funds are accessed by the child and family team as they develop a plan of care. The case manager helps the team to identify the strengths and the needs of the youth and family and assists the team to meet the goals specified in the plan of care. With access to an extensive provider network of well over 200 providers that deliver over 70 services, this uniquely individualized plan of care is the vehicle for reaching the goals of each family.

In addition to family members and the case manager, the child and family team includes natural supports, crisis team members, family advocates, and other identified members from the provider network who can bring about the necessary changes. The case manager assesses the needs and strengths of the youth and family, assembles the team, identifies the necessary services, and assumes administrative and some legal functions previously performed by child welfare and juvenile justice workers. The case manager also obtains all data needed for client outcome measures. Federal guidelines specify the credentials of case managers and the size of caseloads (no more than eight families per case manager).

Once the plan of care is developed, services are organized on a fee-for-service basis with prior authorization, as in managed care systems. Units of service are approved and communicated to both the service provider and the child and family. An open panel that is updated at least once a year allows for the addition and deletion of services and providers. Consumer choice of service providers drives the system, rather than artificially imposed limits or mandates.

As noted, case management and the provider network are two integral components of Wraparound Milwaukee. The crisis component is also essential for success; in some ways this component is the most critical. Clearly, youth diagnosed with SED are at risk for going into crisis with some frequency. This risk, of course, has led to a significant use of institutional care, such as hospitalization, residential treatment, group and foster care, and juvenile justice services. Often, lack of flexibility in the delivery of services and in payment for services results in overuse of the most restrictive and most expensive level of care. To make the service delivery system as seamless as possible, Wraparound Milwaukee has depended heavily on the rapid assessment and delivery of crisis services that are designed to avoid unnecessary use of institutionalization and to offer timely delivery of appropriate services.

The Mobile Urgent Treatment Team is a publicly and privately staffed team of child psychologists, psychiatric social workers, and case managers who deliver an array of services to all residents of Milwaukee County, including youth who receive services from Wraparound Milwaukee. Crisis beds, which are maintained in the community at strategic locations, offer brief respite care for families who require such services to maintain their children in their homes or in the community, thus avoiding hospitalization. Short-term case management services are available to support families whose children have less severe problems and are not eligible for Wraparound Milwaukee. The team also serves in a gatekeeping role regarding psychiatric hospitalization. For example, the team director reviews and authorizes all hospital admissions and many of the short-term residential treatment admissions for Milwaukee Wraparound youth.

Outcomes

Results of current outcome studies are consistent with outcomes reported in the general wraparound literature (Stroul, 1993). In the Wraparound Milwaukee project, there was a 65% reduction in the use of residential treatment over time. In May 1996, over 370 youth were in residential treatment on a daily basis; in 2000, an average of 130 were in placement. The average cost per month of wraparound services continues to be lower than the cost of residential treatment. In 1999, the average cost per month for treatment in Wraparound Milwaukee was $3,300, compared to $5,200 for residential treatment. All savings were reinvested in the program. As a result, in contrast to the 370 children and adolescents who were previously served in residential treatment (when services were "rationed"), Wraparound Milwaukee has been able to serve between 600 and 700 young clients and their families for the same amount of money.

Further, as measured by the Child Behavior Checklist (CBCL; Achenbach & Edelbrock, 1993), the Youth Self-Report (YSR; Achenbach, 1991), and the Child and Adolescent Functional Assessment Scale (CAFAS; Hodges, 1990, 1994), caregiver, youth, and case manager reports demonstrated significant reductions in behavior problems from intake to discharge, generally after approximately 1 year in the program. Results of a repeated measures analysis of variance provided evidence of a significant decline ($p < .001$) in raw scores on the CBCL ($n = 223$), the YSR ($n = 153$), and the CAFAS ($n = 430$) from intake to 1 year in the program.

Based on juvenile justice data obtained 1 year prior to enrollment, additional findings point to a reduction in legal offenses and adjudications among these young offenders during their participation in the program. Results of a repeated measures analysis of variance also demonstrated significant reductions ($p < .001$) in legal offenses and adjudications for the year postdischarge from the program (Meyers, 2000; Seybold, 2001). Specifically, 295 youth committed 2.18 offenses during the year prior to their involvement in the program, 1.15 offenses during participation in the program, and 0.64 offenses for the year following disenrollment from the program. Although these are preliminary results, they provide evidence that Wraparound Milwaukee enables young people with SED to remain in their home community with their families and to maintain their gains over time.

Wraparound Milwaukee outcomes on the use of inpatient care are consistent with other outcome data that point to a significant decrease in the use of inpatient care when crisis services are available (Henggeler et al., 1999; Satcher, 2000). For example, in the Milwaukee project, Medicaid use decreased 57%. In 1994, a total of 23,280 Medicaid days were used, compared to fewer than 10,000 Medicaid days in 1999. In contrast to an average length of stay of 14 days for young clients who were not in the wraparound project, the average length of inpatient stay for those in wraparound was approximately 6 days in 1999. In 2000, hospitalization was further reduced to an average length of stay of approximately 2 days. This dramatic decrease is reflected in the cost of inpatient monies paid for inpatient care. In 1993, prior to the development of a crisis team, $10.5 million was paid to Milwaukee County for inpatient care of these youth; in 1999, with a crisis team functioning, only $5.8 million was paid. This downward trend was evident when the program was implemented in 1995, and the trend has increased yearly (Morano, 2000).

Follow-Up Projects

The success of the 5-year demonstration project has led to two different applications within Milwaukee County. First, a special program was developed by Wraparound Milwaukee for a high-risk population of youth who were sexual offenders referred from the juvenile justice system. Their average age is 13.7, and their demographics are consistent with those of the larger group. A majority (70%) of these youth are adjudicated delinquent. In need of special care and planning, they have been sexually abused, are sexually aggressive, and display fire-setting behavior. Case managers for these high-risk youth work with the child and family team to determine specialized treatment needs. They establish a partnership with the youth's bureau worker or probation officer and create a multicontext safety plan based on individualized strengths, protective factors, risks, and needs of the entire family. The team also prioritizes the needs of the victims of sexual abuse. Victims of these young offenders are predominantly females; most (75%) are under 10 years of age; and many are family members or neighbors.

Interventions that have demonstrated effectiveness with delinquent youth include those that promote attachments to significant family members and peers, connections with communities, and prosocial values (Gilbertson, 2000). Frequently-used services for this high-risk population include youth mentoring, in-home family therapy, human sexuality education, parent support groups, and safe out-of-home placement options in the community. Also essential is symptom-specific treatment designed to develop coping and relapse-prevention skills within a strength-based framework.

Continued development of this program has been made possible by the award of an 18-month implementation grant from the Comprehensive Approach to Sex Offender Management Grant Program of the Violence Against Women Office in the Department of Justice. This population is served by a collaborative team that has cross-system representation from the juvenile justice, victim advocacy, mental health, and educational systems and that undertakes joint data collection and analysis from the juvenile justice and mental health systems. A multisystemic offense-specific psychological assessment is undertaken for all adjudicated juveniles, and families and victims assist with treatment planning for the family. This comprehensive approach to sex offender management involves collaboration among team members who provide offender assessment, supervision monitoring, and treatment; those who offer public education and community notification; and those who work with victims.

Parents of youth offenders typically have problems in multiple areas, such as domestic violence, substance abuse, severe mental illness, physical abuse and neglect, and child abandonment. Sexual offense characteristics range from verbal coercion to inappropriate touching and rape. The youth are overwhelmingly male; over 62% of the offenses are committed against children, the remainder against peers. Compared with CBCL profiles of juveniles who are not sex offenders, the profiles of juvenile sex offenders are significantly more delinquent and aggressive.

Current outcome data regarding sexual offenses indicate that 89% of 146 high-risk youth did not recidivate during enrollment in the project; 99% of 79 high-risk youths who had completed the 1-year postprogram follow-up also did not recidivate. With respect to nonsexual offenses, 72% did not recidivate during enrollment; 69% did not recidivate during the 1-year postprogram follow-up. At the same time, more youth between 1998 and 1999 were treated in the community, resulting in fewer days in institutional care. In connection with wraparound clinical outcomes, results of a repeated measures analysis of variance pointed to significant reductions ($p < .05$) in CBCL ($n = 25$) and CAFAS ($n = 38$) intake scores between 6 months and 1 year in the program. Scores on the YSR also demonstrated a trend toward reduction in the intensity and number of symptoms, but these differences were not found to be significant.

In addition, results of a repeated measures analysis of variance provided evidence of significant decreases ($p < .05$) in CBCL ($n = 33$) and CAFAS ($n = 48$) scores among victims of sexual abuse within the family. Again, although scores on the YSR decreased between intake and 1 year, the differences were not significant (Gilbertson, 2000; Seybold, 2001). In light of variations in populations, treatments, and time intervals, it is difficult to compare the current rate of sexual recidivism with those of other investigations. Unfortunately, no local statistics are available for comparison. Preliminary results suggest that a wraparound approach can be used effectively with a high-risk population such as young sexual offenders and that standard treatment techniques from the sexual treatment literature can be used to treat these youth in the community. Moreover, victim and community safety can be maintained while reducing the use of institutional care.

In the second follow-up project, the wraparound approach was used for a demonstration program in a primary care setting. Wraparound Milwaukee was awarded a small grant to use the approach in a population of minority women with an acute life-threatening illness—namely, breast cancer, which is the leading cause of cancer death in women between ages 15 and 54. Although the incidence of breast cancer is higher among Caucasian women than among minority women, the mortality rate for African American women is higher than for Caucasian women. The population served in the project was small, and the results only anecdotal. Nevertheless, the project seemed to positively impact the mother's ability to comply with the rigors of treatment. For instance, anecdotal comments from medical personnel, physicians, and nurses were promising regarding their patient's treatment adherence (maintaining appointments, undertaking chemotherapy, etc.). The program provided case management, respite care, and services for youth in the family who were at risk due to their mother's illness. Although the project will not continue in the absence of a home and stable funding stream, either in mental health or medical health, further work in primary care and chronic illness might be a logical extension for this approach.

CONCLUSION

In conclusion, the 5-year demonstration project known as Wraparound Milwaukee has been a success. There has been a marked reduction in the cost attributed to comprehensive treatment of children and adolescents with SED, as well as increased access and strong family satisfaction. Clinically, preliminary results based on the Child Behavior Checklist, the Child and Adolescent Functional Assessment Scale, and the Youth Self Report suggest improvement between intake and completion of the program. The change was significant on the CBCL and the CAFAS, with a positive trend on the YSR.

In addition, preliminary results look promising for two follow-up projects involving specialized treatment for high-risk youth and for youth whose mothers are medically compromised. In the first project, following participation in a wraparound program, high-risk sexual offenders showed reduced levels of reoffending for both sexual and nonsexual crimes, but a greater reduction in sexual crimes during participation in the program and 1 year following discharge. In the second project, the approach was applied in the medical arena; anecdotal reports on a small number of families suggested greater medical treatment compliance for women who received wraparound services for their children.

Most important, the Wraparound Milwaukee project has not only resulted in system changes but has maintained that change over time. Specifically, almost twice as many children diagnosed with SED are currently receiving comprehensive services compared to the old system. These preliminary results are consistent with findings from other evaluations of systems of care. Because these programs generally use a pre- and post-model of evaluation without a control group, there are some unresolved questions, including the possibility of improvement over time without any intervention. It is also essential to compare the effectiveness of similar clinical interventions delivered in traditional and integrated systems of care. In spite of these limitations, the Milwaukee Wraparound experience strongly supports the effectiveness of this approach as a model for delivering comprehensive services to children and adolescents with SED within the fiscal constraints of the evolving health care and social service systems.

REFERENCES

Achenbach, T. M. (1991). *Youth self-report.* Burlington, VT: University of Vermont, Department of Psychiatry.

Achenbach, T. M., & Edelbrock, C. (1993). *Child Behavior Checklist.* Burlington, VT: University of Vermont, Department of Psychiatry.

Bickman, L. (1996). A continuum of care: More is not always better. *American Psychologist, 51,* 689–701.

Bickman, L. (1997). Resulting issues raised by the Fort Bragg Evaluation: New directions for mental health services research. *American Psychologist, 52,* 562–565.

Clancy, P. (2000, August). *Wraparound services for families coping with maternal breast cancer.* Presentation at the annual convention of the American Psychological Association, Washington, DC.

Dennis, K. (1994, June). *An introduction to the New Child Mental Health Services Initiative.* Presentation at Wraparound Milwaukee, Milwaukee, WI.

Gilbertson, S. (2000, August). *Wraparound Milwaukee. Community safety and resource development for "high-risk" youth and their families.* Presentation at the annual convention of the American Psychological Association, Washington, DC.

Henggeler, S. (1995). *Multi-systemic therapy using home-based services: A clinically effective and cost effective strategy for treating serious clinical problems in youth.* Columbia, SC: Family Services Research Center, Department of Psychiatry and Behavioral Sciences, Medical University of South Carolina.

Henggeler, S., Rowland, M., Randall, J., Ward, D., Pickrel, S., Cunningham, P., Miller, S., Edwards, J., Zealberg, J., Hand, L., & Santos, A. (1999). Home based, multi-systemic therapy as an alternative to the hospitalization of youths in psychiatric crisis: Clinical outcome. *Journal of the American Academy of Child and Adolescent Psychiatry, 938,* 1331–1339.

Hodges, K. (1990, 1994). *Child and Adolescent Functional Assessment Scale.* Ypsilanti, Michigan: Eastern Michigan University, Department of Psychology.

Kamradt, B., & Meyers, M. J. (1999, November). *Curbing violence in juvenile offenders with serious emotional and mental health needs: The effective utilization of wraparound approaches in an urban American setting.* Jerusalem, Israel: Presentation at the International Seminar on Violence in Adolescence.

Katz-Leavy, J., Lourie, I., Stroul, B., & Zeigler-Dendy, C. (1992). *Individualized services in a system of care.* Washington, DC: Georgetown University Child Development Center, CASSP Technical Assistance Center.

Meyers, M. J. (2000, August). *Wraparound Milwaukee. Developing a system of care: What does it take?* Presentation at the annual convention of the American Psychological Association, Washington, DC.

Morano, C. (2000, August). *Wraparound Milwaukee. Mobile crisis intervention for high-risk youth.* Presentation at the annual convention of the American Psychological Association, Washington, DC.

Satcher, D. (2000). Mental health: A report of the surgeon general. Chapter 3: Children and mental health (pp. 124–219). Washington, DC: U.S. Public Health Service.

Seybold, E. (2001, March). *Evaluation study for Wraparound Milwaukee.* Milwaukee, WI: Milwaukee County Mental Health Division, Adolescent Services Branch.

Stroul, B., & Friedman, R. (1986). *A system of care for severely emotionally disturbed children and youth.* Washington DC: Georgetown University Child Development Center, CASSP Technical Assistance Center.

Stroul, B. (1993). *Systems of care for children and adolescents with severe emotional disturbances: What are the results?* Washington DC: Georgetown University Child Development Center, CASSP Technical Assistance Center.

Wraparound Milwaukee. (1998). *Annual report.* Milwaukee, WI: Milwaukee County Mental Health Division, Child and Adolescent Services Branch.

Wraparound Milwaukee. (1999). *Annual report.* Milwaukee, WI: Milwaukee County Mental Health Division, Child and Adolescent Services Branch.

Chapter 18

HOME-BASED TREATMENT FOR CHILDREN WITH SERIOUS EMOTIONAL DISTURBANCE

JEAN ADNOPOZ

Although systems of care for children with serious emotional disturbance (SED) have begun to address the multidimensionality of children's experiences, programs and funding continue to be categorical and systems remain self-contained and isolated. Thus, the barriers established between important domains of children's lives are contrary to our knowledge that children's functioning is conditioned by the interaction between their innate structural capacity, physiology, cognition and developmental status, and the community-based systems that comprise their world.

Arguably, the earliest and most significant influence on children is their family system. Its functional capacity is central to children's ability to adapt to and cope with the vicissitudes of their lives. However, it was not until the latter decades of the 20th century that program planners and policymakers recognized that many families in need of services for their children were unable or unwilling to access traditional treatment programs. Some children failed to receive appropriate care because parents could not advocate effectively across the systems with which they were involved. For these families, it was believed that moving the locus of treatment from traditional outpatient settings to the child's home would ensure care while also creating an important alternative service delivery site. By 1985, the child's home and family had become a focus of interventions designed to prevent negative parent and child behaviors in at-risk populations or to ameliorate problems of serious emotional disturbance, inadequate or abusive parenting, or delinquent behaviors that placed children at risk for placement outside of their homes (Lindblad-Goldberg, Dore, & Stern, 1998). The fact that many families in need of service were unable or unwilling to access traditional treatment programs or advocate for their children across systems of care with which they were involved prevented them from receiving the help they needed.

Although scientifically derived evidence of their efficacy and effectiveness has been slow to accumulate, home-based services have proliferated across America. Such services are based largely on principles first articulated by the Child and Adolescent Service System Program (CASSP) and further codified in Public Law 94-142, the Education for All Handicapped Children Act Public Law 96-272, and the Family Preservation and Support Act (Solnit, Adnopoz, Saxe, Gardner, & Fallon, 1997). Although *home visiting* describes a strategy for the delivery of preventive or interventive services (Olds, Hill, Robinson, Song, & Little, 2000) and does not represent a single treatment modality, the rhetoric of home-based services tends to obliterate the significant differences that exist among programs that use the home as the primary treatment site.

This chapter describes the events leading to the present interest of mental health, physical health, juvenile justice, and child welfare systems in supporting services delivered in the home as an important treatment component in any system of mental health care; reviews home-based programs reported in the literature ranging from preventive, educational, and support models to intensive, focused interventions with delinquent adolescents and dysfunctional families; and describes in detail a model program for children and adolescents with SED.

THE CHILD AND THE FAMILY

Although foster care and other residential treatment facilities may be available in some communities to provide 24-hour care for those children who need it, few resources can replace the family as the most effective, long-term institution for raising children. Adequately functioning families provide safe and secure environments in which the normal developmental processes of childhood and adolescence can unfold. In such environments children are likely to feel nurtured, cherished, protected, and secure. Consistent relationships with their adult caregivers support the positive use of curiosity and imagination, empower children to explore their world, and move them toward eventual independence and self-sufficiency. Solnit (1976) has described the family as "the bridge from the past to the future." The family provides continuity and a sense of being rooted in time, place, history, and culture. Families socialize children, transmit intergenerational values and beliefs, and provide a place of respite from the challenges of the outside world.

Current Realities

Although the majority of children in the United States live in families that are able to offer them adequate care, society remains challenged by the substantial numbers of families that are unable to provide stable, consistent, and caring relationships for their offspring. Currently, many states are facing a serious shortage of children's beds in mental health facilities; in some states this has approached crisis proportions (Governor's Blue Ribbon Commission on Mental Health, 2000). Some of the problems affecting these children may be associated with inconsistent and inadequate family functioning. Studies have demonstrated that risk and protective factors associated with child and adolescent problems are determined primarily by the quality of parenting and family functioning (Harrison, Boyle, & Farley, 1999). Children in unstable families with high levels of conflict demonstrate higher rates of both internalizing and externalizing behaviors; negative family functioning has also been highly correlated with adolescent substance abuse (Harrison et al., 1999).

Although the federal government has made serious attempts to assist states in providing services and community supports to maintain children within their own families (Solnit et al., 1997), foster care and institutional placements remain overused treatment options for needy children and families in communities where there are few less restrictive alternatives. In 1998, approximately 500,000 children in the United States were in out-of-home, nonrelative placements (Nelson, 1996). Another 4.3 million children were living with mothers in the homes of other relatives (Casper & Bryson, 1998). An additional half million children are estimated to live in other kinship care arrangements, the majority being cared for by their grandmothers (Adnopoz & Ezepchick, in press; Scannapieco & Jackson, 1996).

Even though the effects of multiple caregiving disruptions on child development have been well documented (Goldstein, Solnit, Goldstein, & Freud, 1996; Rosenfeld, Wasserman, & Pilowsky, 1998; Solnit, 1980), the incidence of out-of-home placements has more than doubled within the past decade. This marked change in removals and placements may be associated with an increase both in the severity of symptomatology and in the numbers of children being referred for intervention and protection (Child Welfare League of America, 1994). However, moving children in and out of placement in an attempt to address their needs for treatment and safety may, in fact, foster even more serious disturbances. Children who are denied consistent, long-term relationships may become depressed and feel helpless in the face of their life experiences, and they may direct anger at the parents who have abandoned them to the vagaries of the child welfare system. Those children most affected may be developmentally and intellectually compromised and unable to form positive, intimate attachments as adults (Goldstein et al., 1996). Society's zeal to protect and treat children by removing them from their families and placing them in institutions, foster homes, or other caregiving arrangements may, in reality, be putting them in harm's way.

Federal Supports for Families

In the 1970s, the adoption of state and national child abuse and neglect statutes codified child protection policies and practices concerning the removal of abused, neglected, and at-risk children in all 50 states. The passage of the Adoption Assistance and Child Welfare Act of 1980 (Public Law 96-272) was designed to help families improve their parenting capacity (Hegar, 1993). Although the act made permanence a central goal for all children entering the child welfare system (Wells & Tracy, 1996), policies that address the most appropriate means of assuring permanency for vulnerable children continue to evolve. The Adoption Assistance and Safe Families Act of 1997 provided financial incentives to states to discourage multiple placements made without a suitable plan for permanency, to prevent foster care drift, and to ensure stable, safe, and long-term caregiving arrangements for high-risk children.

During the past decade, several pronounced and disturbing trends emerged concerning children involved in the foster care system. These trends raise questions about the efficacy of the foster care system as an effective intervention and treatment option for high-risk children and further underscore the problems associated with out-of-home care. Since the early 1990s, the age of children in out-of-home care has decreased. Recent statistics indicate that 25% of all children entering the foster care system in the five largest states are under the age of 6 (Berrick, Barth, Needell, & Jonson-Reid, 1997).

In addition, children entering foster care are more likely to be victims of trauma and to suffer from chronic medical conditions and mental health disorders, although they often fail to receive the health care necessary to mitigate these problems while they are in foster care (Brereton, 2001).

Children placed in foster care are also likely to experience more than one placement. In Connecticut, for example, the average number of placements for every child who enters the child welfare system is 3.5 (Sharon Martin, former deputy director, Department of Children and Families, State of Connecticut, in private correspondence to the author, 1998). Child welfare data released in 1998 indicated that 66% of children in the child welfare system who were placed outside their homes were eventually reunited with one or more family members. However, during their child's placement, many if not most families receive neither services nor assistance to prepare for the child's return (Adnopoz & Ezepchick, in press). Disturbingly, the available care while the child was out of the home was likely to be fragmented and episodic. As children moved from place to place, their social and medical histories were often left behind. New caregivers were often unprepared, uninformed, and unsure how to cope with behavioral or medical problems as they arose.

Even as children are being placed out of their homes in record numbers, many states face both a shortage of institutional beds and an inadequate supply of licensed foster homes. In addition, traditional outpatient mental health services, such as office- or clinic-based treatment, have not proven to be a good fit for working with chaotic and distrustful families in which children and parents suffer from multiple competing problems, including serious mental disorders, many of which are reactive and cannot be relieved without concurrent changes in the environment. The combined weight of these factors increases the interest in and support of child-centered, family-focused interventions as important alternatives for children for whom out-of-home placement might otherwise be seriously considered.

With the support of advocates such as The Edna McConnell Clark Foundation, a number of states were encouraged and funded to implement programs that could maintain children within their own homes and communities, promote permanency for the child, reduce the probability of placement outside of the home, and prevent the inevitable problems associated with foster care drift (Nelson, 1996).

INTERVENTIONS THAT SERVE THE CHILD AND FAMILY IN THE HOME

Although federal legislation supporting family-focused interventions was not enacted until the last decades of the 20th century, home-based services had their origins in 19th-century social work practice, when "friendly visitors" representing charitable organizations called on families to determine their needs and to work with them to increase their self-sufficiency. Many of these methods were adapted in the early years of the 20th century by social workers who recognized the advantages of entering and observing the family's environment firsthand and assisting families to mobilize natural, community-based networks on their own behalf (Wells, 1995; Woodford, 1999).

Then, as now, when clinicians enter the diagnostically rich, textured, and highly personal environment of the home, they are able to step directly into the family's own ecosystem. Their observations help them to piece together a tapestry of knowledge about the real-world experiences of the child and family that not only may facilitate treatment, but also may be unavailable to those working exclusively in more traditional clinical settings (Adnopoz & Culler, 2000). The process of working in the home enhances the clinician's ability to understand and address the complexity of the dynamic reality that constitutes the everyday world of both children and parents.

Families in which children are at high risk for out-of-home care may be difficult to engage, distrustful of the traditional clinic-based mental health system, and often unable to maintain regular appointment schedules (Adnopoz & Grigsby, 2002). However, clinicians have found many of these same families are more likely to become supportive of and consistently involved in their child's treatment and recovery when providers are willing to enter into their own home and local community environments (Adnopoz & Ezepchick, in press; Woodford, 1999). Evidence supports in-home, family-focused intervention as a necessary component of comprehensive systems of care for children and youth with problems of mental health, substance abuse, and delinquency (Fraser, Hawkins, & Howard, 1988; Harrison et al., 1999; Henggeler, Schoenwald, Borduin, Rowland, & Cunningham, 1998; Kaufman & Kaufman, 1992). Some programs that have been studied offer sustained, relationship-based services that generally address three domains: parent, parent-child, and child functioning (Heinicke & Ponce, 1999). Their success has enabled in-home intervention and treatment to emerge as an effective means of engaging difficult-to-reach families and preparing them to make better use of more traditional treatment modalities.

In-Home Prevention and Early-Intervention Programs

Provence, a pioneer in the use of home visitation as part of a comprehensive intervention for single, poor, inner-city mothers, was among the first researchers to find that mothers and children who received sustained services from a consistent group of providers through the child's first 30 months of life had positive, long-term outcomes in several domains compared with nonintervention controls (Cicchetti & Toth, 1998). At the end of the intervention, children in the experimental group scored higher in language development. By the 5-year follow-up, these children demonstrated higher school achievement, maintained better school attendance, and were more task-oriented. At 5-year follow-up, their mothers had fewer additional pregnancies, were more likely to be employed, had improved their socioeconomic status, and made better use of community support resources. After 7½ years, their mothers had completed more years of education, were more likely to be self-supporting, had more satisfying personal relationships, and had waited longer to have a second child. Mothers who received intervention were more responsive to the needs of their children and reported a more pleasing relationship with them (Provence, Naylor, & Rescarla, 1983).

Olds, Henderson, and colleagues (1999, 2000) have methodically tested a model of nurse-delivered in-home visitation for pregnant, single-parent, poor, primiparous mothers with few social supports. This preventive public health intervention was designed to improve quality of parenting, to prevent abuse, and to improve maternal and infant health. Olds, Henderson, and colleagues conducted their initial randomized study in Elmira, New York. They found that after 2 years of a structured, curriculum-driven home visitation program, mothers had fewer preterm deliveries, smoked less, and had fewer kidney infections compared with community controls. The quality of the mother-child relationship was enhanced in that mothers provided more play materials to their children and used less punishment. Rates of child abuse and neglect were lower than for the community control group. In addition, the experimental-condition mothers were better able to make use of their own partners as well as community supports in managing the problems of everyday living. Children were seen in the emergency room less frequently and had fewer accidents than children in the control group. These positive findings were sustained when families were reevaluated as the children turned 15 years old. Child abuse and neglect rates remained lower at 2 and 15 years. Additionally, the experimental-group children were considerably less likely to have been arrested, used alcohol, smoked cigarettes, or had multiple sex partners (Olds & Kitzman, 1993). When the children were 15 years old, mothers in the intervention group were reported to be less impaired by drugs and alcohol since the birth of the index children (Olds, Henderson, et al., 1999).

This initial study was replicated in Memphis, Tennessee, with a primarily urban, African American population. Many effects reported in the Elmira study were replicated, although the effect size was somewhat smaller. The number of health care encounters for injuries and injections was 23% lower than for the control group, and the number of hospital days required for serious injuries was significantly less. Parental reports of child behavior problems did not differ between the experimental and control groups in either study. Based on an extrapolation of Olds's data at 15 years, an economic analysis conducted by the Rand Corporation found that the savings to the government and society for providing services to families in which the mother was low-income and unmarried at registration exceeded the cost of the program by a factor of 4 over the life of the child. The return on investment was realized by the child's 4th birthday. Cost savings were reflected in reduced welfare and criminal justice expenses and increased tax revenues. These findings did not hold for higher SES families and married women (Olds et al., 2000).

In a careful review of numerous early-intervention studies, Heinicke and Ponce (1999) found considerable evidence to support the effectiveness of home visitors in improving maternal self-concept and satisfaction and in enhancing maternal responsiveness to the needs of her infant (Cichetti & Toth, 1998). In the UCLA Family Development Project, Heinicke et al. (1999) demonstrated that a randomized, home-visiting, relationship-based intervention for third-trimester pregnant women classified at high risk for inadequate parenting was able to increase experienced partner and family support by the infant's 1st birthday compared to controls. In addition to home visiting, the experimental group participated in a weekly mother-infant group; the controls received regular pediatric follow-ups. At 1 year of age, children in the intervention group were more securely attached and more autonomous. The intervention did not affect maternal depression or anxiety, although continued follow-up at Year 2 may reveal statistically significant differences between groups. Heinicke et al. (1999) point out that the ability to achieve positive, sustainable outcomes with inadequately functioning families is dependent on the capacity of the intervention to address the parent's needs as well as those of the child.

The aforementioned studies demonstrate that sustained, relationship-based, in-home visits can be effective in improving maternal competence and enhancing maternal capacity to enter into positive relationships, to use partner and community supports, and to attend to issues of self-development. In addition, preventive in-home services encourage more effective maternal limit setting and the use of appropriate controls; as well as the promotion of the child's autonomy, capacity for exploration, task orientation, and cognition. These studies have also demonstrated the centrality of the sustained relationship between the mother and the intervener in achieving desired outcomes. The development of a trusting, accepting alliance provides the means through which behavioral changes are able to occur. Process variables associated with positive outcomes include the duration of contact between the mother and home visitor, the extent of focus on parenting issues, the mother's attitude, her willingness to work with the visitor, and her view of the visitor as helpful (Korfmacher, Kitzman, & Olds, 1998).

TARGETED IN-HOME INTERVENTIONS FOR HIGH-RISK CHILDREN

Family Preservation

Family preservation and support services for families in which children are at high risk for out-of-home placement due to abuse or neglect have been available for more than a decade. Homebuilders, a model intensive home-based intervention developed in Tacoma, Washington, was endorsed by funders and policymakers because its developers believed that positive outcomes for children at risk could be achieved by addressing the interactions among children, their families, and the environment. Homebuilders programs have demonstrated the ability to reduce out-of-home placements. The belief that children who are maintained within their own homes would represent cost savings to taxpayers has also supported the popularization of family-preservation services.

Homebuilders serves as a well-replicated family-preservation program prototype, although variations on the model have proliferated across the United States (Lindblad-Goldberg et al., 1998). By principle, family-preservation programs are time-limited (approximately 12 to 16 weeks), relationship-based, family-focused, child-centered, flexible services that are available to families 24 hours a day, 7 days a week. Service providers maintain a small caseload to accommodate these principles. Family-preservation programs are designed to prevent unnecessary out-of-home placements and to promote family reunification by assisting parents to address their own needs and those of their children (Adnopoz & Grigsby, 2002). Although most studies have shown that placement is prevented for 75% to 90% of the children receiving such services, attempts to determine the effectiveness of family-preservation programs have been limited by small effect sizes, lack of randomized controlled studies, and inadequate program standardization. These limitations call into question both the adequacy of the programs and the research methodologies used to evaluate them (Burns, Schoenwald, Burchard, Faw, & Santos, 2000).

Multisystemic Therapy (MST)

In the past decade, family-focused, in-home services have been specifically tailored to meet the needs of children and adolescents with problems of mental health, delinquency, or substance abuse (Henggeler & Borduin, 1990; Henggeler et al., 1999; Woolston, Berkowitz, Schaefer, & Adnopoz, 1998). Several randomized clinical trials have tested these models and found them to be effective in decreasing problem behaviors, improving family functioning, promoting the recovery of the index child, and reducing the need for more costly out-of-home placements, either in hospitals or residential programs. Henggeler and his associates have developed a curriculum-driven, home-based therapeutic approach called *multisystemic therapy* (MST). MST has demonstrated effectiveness with chronic juvenile offenders (Henggeler et al., 1999), adolescent sex offenders (Borduin et al., 1995), and substance-abusing delinquents (Henggeler & Borduin, 1990). MST directly addresses the interpersonal and systemic factors associated with adolescent antisocial behavior (Henggeler et al., 1998) and considers the child's view of his or her world as well as the direct and persistent influence of the child's family, peer, and school environments. Sessions frequently are held in the child's home and in the community. Services are time-limited and are designed to empower parents to understand and manage behavioral crises that arise following the intervention.

The Missouri Delinquency Project examined long-term effects of MST on the prevention of criminal activity in a sample of predominantly serious juvenile offenders by comparing MST with individual therapy (Burns et al., 2000). This study demonstrated positive effects on perceived family relations, family interactions, parental symptomatology, interfamilial conflict, and youth behavior problems. The intervention also produced long-term changes in the youths' criminal behaviors.

Central to the success of Henggeler's programs has been an understanding of the familial and social contexts in which children function and by which they are strongly influenced, as well as the willingness to address contextual issues within a structured curriculum. Borduin and colleagues (1995) suggest that improved family functioning, a result of in-home and community services, was the primary influence on the reduction of criminal behavior in the Missouri study.

Henggeler and his colleagues have studied whether MST could be modified effectively for use with children presenting with psychiatric emergencies. Based on hypotheses that the child's family plays a central role in predicting and preventing the need for hospitalization and that behaviors are socially and ecologically influenced, Henggeler designed and tested an intervention for children ages 10 to 17 who were approved for emergency psychiatric hospitalization at the Medical University of South Carolina. These youth were randomly assigned either to an experimental MST condition or to a treatment-as-usual (TAU) group (i.e., hospitalization and aftercare). Services were provided in the homes of family, relatives, or friends and in community shelters, respite beds, or the hospital. Caseloads were reduced from the MST standard of five families per clinician to three. Children in the experimental group had judicious but controlled access to community resources, including hospitalization and therapeutic foster care. Children in the control group received treatment as usual, often using some of the same resources.

Henggeler reports that MST was at least as effective, and in some cases more effective, than emergency psychiatric hospitalization at decreasing child symptomatology. Although rates of decreased internalizing problems were similar across the two conditions, MST was more effective in decreasing rates of externalizing symptoms. Youth in the control condition reported increased self-esteem, whereas families in the experimental condition showed improved cohesion and increased structure. Henggeler and colleagues (1999) note that the treatment of youth with serious psychiatric problems and their families may be even more challenging and require more clinical supervision than intervention with youth in the juvenile justice system. Further study, some of which is already in progress, is needed to address the issues raised by this evaluation.

Wraparound

The wraparound services concept, which places children in the context of their family and broader social ecology, emerged from the Child and Adolescent Service System Program (CASSP), which advocates interagency collaborations; community-based, advocacy-oriented systems of care; and the expansion of parental decision making and involvement to meet the multisystemic needs of children with serious emotional disturbance (Woolston et al., 1998). Theoretically based in environmental ecology, wraparound stresses unconditional care and assumes that changes in the environment will foster changes that persist over time for children, families, and communities (Burns et al., 2000). Wraparound is a strength-based intervention process that values parental empowerment, culturally competent providers, and the use of natural supports to augment professional involvement.

Outcomes are measured against goals established by the family. Wraparound teams are led by a bachelor's-level resource coordinator who does not provide direct clinical care. Thus, the quality of clinical care is dependent on the resources of the local system of care. Wraparound services are designed to have no time limit; to be available 24 hours a day, 7 days a week; and to be offered in home, school, clinic, and community settings. To date, the effectiveness of wraparound services has not been demonstrated clearly in randomized trials (Burns et al., 2000), which is noteworthy given the speed with which they have been replicated nationally. However, randomized effectiveness trials are expected, given the many existing variations of wraparound services, their potential cost savings relative to out-of-home treatment, and the increasing availability of standards and measures of fidelity that would support rigorous study (Burns et al., 2000).

Summary

Although research on the effectiveness of home-based intensive clinical services for children with SED is limited, there is some indication that these services can enhance child and family functioning and prevent crisis-driven hospitalization of children (Lindblad-Goldberg et al., 1998). As a result, programs incorporating elements of family preservation, MST, and wraparound have gained interest as potentially useful alternatives to more restrictive and expensive out-of-home treatment facilities. Many state agencies, managed care companies, and private payers have endorsed home-based psychiatric services as both clinically and fiscally effective and have added them to the existing local continuum of care.

THE YALE IN-HOME CHILD AND ADOLESCENT PSYCHIATRIC SERVICE (YICAPS)

YICAPS is an intensive, in-home, goal-oriented intervention for children with serious emotional disturbance. It represents an integration of theory and clinical practice that is guided by principles of developmental psychopathology, attachment, object relations, cognitive behavioral and family systems theory, and the wraparound process. Children referred to YICAPS may be in the process of discharge from hospitals or residential treatment facilities or may be diverted from admission to such institutions as a result of the intervention. YICAPS is funded both by managed care as a strategy to reduce the need for more costly treatments and by the state agency responsible for children's mental health services. The basic tenets of a medical model are essential to the program's design.

Services are provided by teams consisting of a master's-level therapist and a mental health counselor who work under the direct, weekly supervision of an experienced clinician. A child and adolescent psychiatrist assumes medical responsibility for the care of all patients and presides at weekly rounds. Treatment is focused on specific problems whose amelioration is measurable. The result is a program that integrates a well-defined medical model with an ecologically oriented and family-focused approach to meet the needs of children and adolescents with SED.

Principles of Intervention

The unfolding interaction between the child and his or her psychosocial environment is seen as comparable in importance to any of the child's individual characteristics. As a result, all evaluations and assessments are considered simultaneously at the level of (a) the individual child's and family's functioning; (b) the child's home and community environment; and (c) the child's and family's social networks. Human relationships are viewed as the mediating agents for behavioral and environmental change. Critical relationships exist on multiple levels: between the child and the family; between the team and the child and family; between the family and its physical environment; and between the child, the family, and the community. The ability to understand and address the complexity of interactions between these levels is central to the child's treatment success.

The YICAPS approach is child-centered and home- and family-based. It relies on the development of a therapeutic alliance between family members and the team to assure progress toward established goals. Goals common to all cases include development of a clinical formulation of the child and his or her relationship with the family and the broader environment; stabilization; improved child and family functioning; and preparation for entry into more traditional, less intensive forms of community-based outpatient treatment. Each treatment plan respects the individuality of the child and the family and is developed in partnership with them. The team works with the family to achieve the lowest level of change necessary to improve and sustain the child's more adaptive functioning and to assure his or her ability to remain at home in the community.

With the engagement and support of the managed care coordinator and the state agency staff member, each of whom is enlisted as a collaborator in the work, the program is able to be sufficiently flexible to allow for a titration of intensity from 3 to 20 contacts per week and to maintain involvement with the child and family for as long as is clinically appropriate. In rare instances, contact with the family has continued for 18 months or more. However, the overarching aim of YICAPS is to move the child and family to self-sufficiency with deliberate speed so that their need for intervention is as brief and at the lowest level of intensity as possible (Woolston et al., 1998).

Program Elements

There are six key features to the YICAPS program. These can be augmented by other community-based services as deemed necessary for each child and family's individualized plan of care.

1. Available services include home-based evaluation, individual and family psychotherapy, parent guidance, case management, crisis intervention, and medication management. These services are provided consistently by the aforementioned two-person clinical team, with supervision and support from a child and adolescent psychiatrist.

2. In partnership with the family, the team assesses the strengths and the risk factors present in the home and in the environment to determine variables that may influence treatment.

3. Team tasks include developing collaborations and linkages with the resources and systems in the community with which the child is involved. This may include, but is not limited to, the extended family system, health care and mental health care providers, schools, and faith-based organizations. The team assists the family in advocating for their own interests within these systems and institutions.

4. The team joins with the child and family to develop and implement a treatment plan that meets the approval of the managed care company and state funding agency and that addresses the therapeutic, environmental, and concrete needs identified in the initial assessment.

5. Services are titrated both in intensity and duration to be responsive to the needs of the child and family.

6. The team is available 24 hours, 7 days per week to respond to child and family crises. Response may range from telephone consultation to in-home services.

Who Benefits?

The primary beneficiaries of the YICAPS approach are three distinct groups of children and their families. However, all children appropriate for YICAPS have demonstrated significant problems in more than one functional domain. The first group includes children being discharged from psychiatric hospitalization who may require temporary but intensive services to sustain the behavioral and emotional gains they have made while hospitalized. These children may have successfully negotiated the crisis that necessitated their hospitalization, but they typically return to unaltered environments that may not promote continued recovery. In these cases, a primary goal of the in-home treatment is to continue and expand the treatment begun on the hospital unit and to engage the child's school and other community resources more intensively. The long-term goal is the prevention of rehospitalization or placement in a residential treatment facility.

A second group of children are those whose behavior is so seriously out of control that they become candidates for acute hospitalization. These children may be referred to YICAPS from home, school, clinic settings, or the emergency room. The immediate goal of the home-based team is to join with the family and the referral source to assess the family's capacity to work with the team and to ensure the child's safety in the home. If the family is willing and able to maintain the child at home, the team and family develop a crisis intervention plan that will lead to the establishment of more distal goals as the therapeutic alliance deepens and the underlying psychodynamic and individual issues come into view.

The third group of children is composed of those with serious emotional or behavioral disorders for whom home-based services are a particularly viable option because traditional outpatient treatment or partial hospitalization has been insufficient or unsuccessful. Services delivered in the home to both the child and family are able to augment these services, not to supplant them, and in fact may enhance their use and effectiveness.

Outcomes

Outcome data from a sample of 138 successive cases indicate that the program has been particularly effective for youth who present with diagnostic comorbidity, severe impairment, extensive psychosocial adversity, and who are in greatest need of acute psychiatric stabilization. YICAPS intervention for a mean of 19.25 weeks resulted in the successful diversion from psychiatric hospitalization for 42% of the children served and a reduced length of stay among the 26% of children who required rehospitalization. Clinical improvement over the course of home-based treatment was evident. Statistically significant changes in psychosocial functioning occurred, with children attaining stability during the course of treatment. A small proportion experienced decreased levels of functioning, although a somewhat larger minority experienced functional improvements.

The most common admitting diagnoses among the 108 children served in fiscal year 1999–2000 included disruptive disorders such as attention-deficit/hyperactivity disorder and oppositional defiant disorder, depressive disorders, parent-child relational problems, and posttraumatic stress disorder. Children have also been referred to YICAPS with diagnoses ranging from anxiety to pervasive developmental disorders. Patients most commonly were male, lived in a one-parent family (65%), and were Caucasian (59%). African American children comprised 17% and Latino children 21% of the cases. By comparison, 34% of the children under age 18 in the City of New Haven are Caucasian, 51.6% are African American, and 21.6% are Latino (New Haven Children and Youth, 1998). The obvious disparities suggest that ethnicity may be a factor in determining treatment options for children. Forty-eight percent of the children were between 6 and 11 years of age; 38% were between 12 and 19 years; and 4% ranged from 0 to 5. A majority had a history of abuse (69%) and parents with a history of psychiatric disorder (65%). Parental substance abuse and domestic violence were present in 44% and 37% of the cases, respectively.

Case Illustration

Robert, a 13-year-old Caucasian male, was referred to YICAPS following his discharge from a partial hospitalization program because of concerns about his family's ability to manage his continuing depression and the possibility that his explosive, out-of-control behavior would erupt in a dangerous way. Robert initially had been referred to the hospital following a verbal threat to kill his teacher. He lived in a two-bedroom apartment with his divorced parents, mother's boyfriend, and his four full brothers, ages 19, 17, 15, and 10. The mother was diagnosed with dysthymic disorder and had difficulty attending to her own needs and those of her family. The father, a former accountant, variously diagnosed with schizoaffective and bipolar disorders, had bouts of violent and threatening behavior. Robert's father had made six suicide attempts in the 3 years before his son's YICAPS referral; though on psychotropic medication, he was noncompliant with recommendations for outpatient treatment. At the time of referral, Robert's father was on active probation for an incident that had occurred while he was actively psychotic, during which he destroyed several household items and verbally threatened his ex-wife. The circumstances of his life have prevented Robert's father from returning to work and have forced him to declare bankruptcy, with a subsequent loss of his home.

Although Robert lived with both parents, his primary attachment was to his father, his mother having abandoned her husband and her sons psychologically many years previously. In fact, Robert's mother declined to participate in any aspect of the treatment planning or in the implementation of the plan. Working with Robert and his father, the team identified the following goals: (a) engage Robert in home-based, individual psychotherapy with the psychologist on the team; (b) support Robert's primary attachment to his father and help him to acknowledge and cope with his rage at his mother's inability to value and protect him; (c) assist Robert, his siblings, and his father to find permanent housing away from the chaotic, sexualized environment in which they lived without privacy and support; and (d) work with the local school to enroll Robert in a program able to meet his educational and social needs.

Six weeks after the intervention began, Robert's father raged against his family, gathered his belongings, and sought shelter with his own parents. The YICAPS team assisted Robert's father to find a temporary and then a permanent home in which he was able to establish consistent structure and organization. Once Robert and his family were settled, the team turned their attention to Robert's schooling. Prior to his hospitalization, Robert had been placed on a program of homebound instruction because of his behavioral problems. As his behavior improved, that program was insufficient to meet his educational and social needs. When the team met with the administration of the school at which he was entitled to enroll, the team met considerable resistance. Afraid that he would present problems of management and additional expense to the system, the administrators were slow to respond to the team's representation of Robert's wish to enter the classroom. It took the persistent efforts of the team to persuade the school administrators to enroll him as a classroom student; even then, it was many months before Robert was admitted as an active student.

With YICAPS services, Robert and his family achieved the following: (a) Robert developed a successful therapeutic alliance and was able to articulate and integrate his feelings of rage and abandonment; (b) he responded well to medication and stated that he felt much better; (c) he attended school regularly; (d) his sense of self-adequacy and autonomy improved; and (e) his father attended therapy regularly, was able to create a supportive home for his sons, and became an adequate cook. He began to verbalize his affection for his sons and take pride in his ability to meet their needs. His ability to control his own behavior as well as his home environment exerted a positive influence on Robert and his siblings. On discharge, following 6 months of 5 intervention hours per week, treatment goals were met, and Robert and his father were stabilized with less intensive, traditional mental health services.

Summary

The YICAPS treatment model derives from the conceptualization that the most promising approach to children with SED lies in identifying, understanding, and addressing the complex set of internal, familial, peer, and social interactions that characterize the world of each child and family referred for care. The therapeutic relationship developed among the child, the family, and the team is used to mediate behavioral changes both within the family and between the family and the various systems with which the child and family interact. The team provides support for parents who previously have been unable to advocate effectively for their children while simultaneously modeling appropriate parental responses to the children. By working with and between child protection, juvenile justice, educational, social service, and health care systems, YICAPS has been able to bring about improvement in child and family functioning while encouraging these systems to respond to the child in question more appropriately.

Although YICAPS has begun to demonstrate that good treatment outcomes are associated with the capacity to sustain intervention as long as clinically necessary, randomized studies of interventions such as YICAPS are required if their value to children with serious emotional disturbance is to be understood. There is a developing literature that provides evidence of the benefits of home- and community-based interventions for dealing with high-risk, vulnerable children and that speaks to the importance of providing carefully constructed and standardized programs that are monitored for treatment fidelity. The future support of effective, home-based mental health services such as YICAPS depends on the ability of program planners to develop and test interventions that meet specific, quantifiable standards while allowing for the clinical flexibility that defines the work.

CONCLUSION

Home-based services can be an important component of comprehensive care for children and adolescents struggling with mental disorders. The development and testing of home-based service models is critical. YICAPS represents one such model, and preliminary efforts to assess its efficacy are encouraging. Further work to design, implement, and evaluate other models of home-based services is encouraged.

REFERENCES

Adnopoz, J., & Ezepchick, J. (in press). Family focus: A promising strategy for serving high-risk children. *Abandoned Infants Assistance Best Practices Monograph.*

Adnopoz, J., & Culler, E. (2000). Multiproblem families: An update on intensive family preservation. Unpublished report.

Adnopoz, J., & Grigsby, K. (2002). High-risk children, adolescents and families: Organizing principles for mental health prevention and intervention. *Child and adolescent psychiatry: A comprehensive textbook,* Philadelphia: Lippincott, Williams & Wilkins.

Berrick, J., Barth, R., Needell, B., & Jonson-Reid, M. (1997). Group care and young children. *Social Service Review, 71, 72,* 258–271.

Borduin, C. M., Mann, B. J., Cone, L. T., Henggeler, S. W., Fucci, B. R., Blake, D. M., & Williams, R. A. (1995). Multisystemic treatment of serious juvenile offenders: Long term prevention of criminality and violence. *Journal of Consulting and Clinical Psychology, 63,* 569–578.

Brereton, M. (2001). The Connecticut safe home model: An outcome study to evaluate the effectiveness of this program for children placed in out-of-home care. Unpublished master's essay, University of Connecticut, School of Social Work, West Hartford, CT.

Burns, B. J., Schoenwald, S. K., Burchard, J. D., Faw, L., & Santos, A. (2000). Comprehensive community-based interventions for youth with severe emotional disorders: Multisystemic therapy and the wraparound process. *Journal of Child and Family Studies, 9*(3), 283–313.

Casper, M., & Bryson, K. R. (1998). *Co-resident grandparents and their grandchildren: Grandparent maintained families* (Population Division working paper, No. 26). New Haven, CT: U.S. Bureau of the Census.

Child Welfare League of America. (1994). Kinship care: A natural bridge (pp. 15–21). Washington, DC: Author.

Cicchetti, D., & Toth, S. (Eds.). (1998). Developmental approaches to prevention and intervention, *Rochester Symposium of Developmental Psychopathology, 9,* (153–193).

Fraser, M. W., Hawkins, J. D., & Howard, M. O. (1988). Parenting training for delinquency prevention. *Child and Youth Services, 2*(1), 93–125.

Goldstein, J., Solnit, A. J., Goldstein, S., & Freud, A., (1996) *The best interests of the child.* New York: Free Press.

Governor's Blue Ribbon Commission on Mental Health. (2000. July). Report. New Haven, CT: Governor's Office.

Harrison, R. S., Boyle, S., & Farley, O. W. (1999). Evaluating the outcomes of family-based intervention for troubled children: A pretest-posttest study. *Research on Social Work Practice, 9*(6), 640–655.

Hegar, R. L. (1993). Assessing attachment, permanence and kinship in choosing permanent homes. *Child Welfare 72,* 367–378.

Henggeler, S., Schoenwald, S., Borduin, C., Rowland, M., & Cunningham, P. (1998). Multisystemic treatment of antisocial behavior in children and adolescents: Treatment manuals for practitioners. New York: Guilford Press.

Henggeler, S., Rowland, M., Randall, J., Ward, D., Pickrel, S., Cunningham, P., Miller, S., Edwards, J., Zealberg, J., Hand, L., & Santos, A. (1999). Home based multisystemic therapy as an alternative to the hospitalization of youths in psychiatric crisis. *Journal of the American Academy of Child and Adolescent Psychiatry, 38,* 11.

Henggeler, S. W., & Borduin, C. M. (1990). *Family therapy and beyond: A multisystemic approach to treating the behavior problems of children and adolescents.* Pacific Grove, CA: Brooks/Cole.

Heinicke, C. M., & Ponce, V. A. (1999). Relations based early family intervention. In D. Cichetti & S. L. Toth (Eds), *Rochester Symposium on Developmental Psychopathology:* Vol. 10. *Developmental approaches to prevention and intervention.* Rochester, NY: University of Rochester Press.

Heinicke, C. M., Fineman, N., Ruth, G., Recchia, S., Guthrie, D., Rodning, C. (1999). Relationship based intervention with at risk mothers: Outcome in the first year of life. *Infant Mental Health Journal, 20,* 349–374.

Kaufman, E., & Kaufman, P. N. (1992). Multiple family therapy with drug abusers. In E. Kaufman & P. N. Kaufman (Eds.), *Family therapy of drug and alcohol abuse* (2nd ed., pp. 72–84). New York: Gardner Press.

Korfmacher, J., Kitzman, H., & Olds, D. (1998). Intervention processes as predictors of outcomes in a preventive home visitation program. In D. Cichetti & S. L. Toth (Eds), *Rochester Symposium on Developmental Psychopathology: Vol. 10. Developmental approaches to prevention and intervention.* Rochester, NY: University of Rochester Press.

Lindblad-Goldberg, M., Dore, M., & Stern L. (1998). *Creating competence from chaos.* New York: W.W. Norton & Co.

Nelson H. (1996). What is appropriate care for the children of troubled families? (pp. 1–30). New York: Millbank Memorial Fund.

New Haven Children and Youth. (1998). *Connecticut voices for children.* New Haven, CT: U.S. Bureau of the Census.

Olds, D., Henderson, C., Kitzman, H., Eckenrode, J., Cole, R., & Tatelbaum, R. (1999). Prenatal and infancy home visitation by nurses: Recent findings. *The future of children: Home visiting: Recent program evaluations, 9*(1).

Olds, D., Hill, P., Robinson, J., Song, N., & Little, C. (2000). Update on home visiting for pregnant women and parents of young children. *Current Problems in Pediatrics, 30*(4) 105–148.

Olds, D., Kitzman, H. (1993). Review of research on home visiting for pregnant women and parents of young children. *Future Child, 3,* 53–92.

Provence, S., Naylor, A., & Rescarla, L. A. (1983). The Yale Child Welfare Research Program: description and results. In E. F. Zigler & E. W. Gordon (Eds.), *Day care: Scientific and social policy issues* (pp. 183–199). Boston: Auburn.

Rosenfeld, A., Wasserman, S., & Pilowsky, D. (1998). Psychiatry and children in the child welfare system, in *Child and Adolescent Clinics of North America, 7*(3), 515–536.

Scannapieco, M., & Jackson, S. (1996). Kinship care: The African American response to family preservation. *Social Work, 41,* 190.

Solnit, A. J. (1976). Marriage: changing structure and functions of the family. In V. C. Vaughn, T. B. Brazelton (Eds), *The family—Can it be saved?* (p. 234). Chicago: Year Book Medical Publishers.

Solnit, A. J. (1980). Too much reporting, too little service: Roots and prevention of child abuse. In G. Gerbner, C. Ross, & E. Zigler (Eds.), *Child abuse, An agenda for action.* New York: Oxford University Press.

Solnit, A. J., Adnopoz, J., Saxe, L., Gardner, J., & Fallon, T. (1997). Evaluating systems of care for children: Utility of the clinical case conference, *American Journal of Orthopsychiatry, 67*(4), 554–567.

Wells, K. (1995). Family preservation services in context: Origins, practices and current issues. In I. M. Schwartz & P. AuClaire (Eds.), *Home based services for troubled children* (pp. 1–28). Lincoln: University of Nebraska Press.

Wells, K., & Tracy, E. (1996). Reorienting intensive family preservation services in relation to public child welfare practice. *Child Welfare, 75*(6), 667–692.

Woodford, M. (1999). Home-based family therapy: Theory and process from "friendly visitors" to multisystemic therapy. *The Family Journal: Counseling and Therapy for Couples and Families, 7*(3), 265–269.

Woolston, J., Berkowitz, S., Schaefer, M., & Adnopoz, J. (1998). Intensive, integrated, in-home psychiatric services: The catalyst to enhancing outpatient intervention, *Child and Adolescent Psychiatric Clinics of North America, 7*(2), 615–635.

Chapter 19

MENTAL HEALTH, JUVENILE JUSTICE, AND LAW ENFORCEMENT RESPONSES TO YOUTH PSYCHOPATHOLOGY

ROBERT A. MURPHY

Children and adolescents from backgrounds characterized by familial psychopathology, criminality, community violence, and psychosocial adversity are themselves at high risk for psychiatric disturbance, substance abuse, criminal activity, and aggressive behavior. The documented comorbidity of risk factors in vulnerable families implies a greater likelihood of finding adolescents at risk in nonnormative settings, such as the law enforcement and juvenile justice systems. In many regions, the juvenile justice system has become a default provider of mental health services to youth who have not benefited from traditional outpatient and inpatient psychiatric care. This chapter addresses aspects of mental health, law enforcement, and juvenile justice cooperation from the perspective of collaborative and developmentally informed interventions designed to augment access to and utilization of services, improve clinical outcome, and accentuate effective alliances across systems.

MENTAL HEALTH NEEDS IN JUVENILE JUSTICE AND LAW ENFORCEMENT

Decreases in rates of juvenile crime have not kept pace with widely lauded decreases in adult criminality (Scott, 1999; Snyder & Sickmund, 1999). Although a majority of youth engages in transitory delinquent or illegal activity during adolescence (Moffitt, 1993), most youth commit relatively few offenses and, as they enter adulthood, desist from criminal activity. Of youth who enter the juvenile justice system, 54% of males and 73% of females have a single referral over the course of their adolescence and do not recidivate (Snyder & Sickmund, 1999). A much smaller proportion, perhaps 20% of adolescents who engage in delinquent activity, become chronic offenders involved in repeated, severe, or violent criminal activity (Scott, 1999). Youth continue to be disproportionately represented in statistics on victimization and perpetration of violent offenses, including homicides and armed assaults (Group for the Advancement of Psychiatry Committee on Preventive Psychiatry [GAPCPP], 1999), with the majority of offenses occurring in afternoon and early evening hours when adult supervision is at its lowest level. The relative ubiquity of violent and nonviolent youthful offending, combined with the alarm at the unpredictability of dramatic and isolated offenses (e.g., school shootings) highlight the importance of a proactive stance toward juvenile offending that emphasizes coordinated interventions by multiple service systems early in the trajectory of offending (Borum & Modzeleski, 2000).

The prevalence of psychiatric disorders and functional psychological impairment among youth involved in the adult and juvenile justice systems has been well documented (Cocozza & Skowyra, 2000; Steiner, Garcia, & Matthews, 1997; Teplin, 2000; Thomas & Stubbe, 1996), as has the relative dearth of adequate mental health services for this population (Cocozza & Skowyra, 2000; Fagan, 1991; Flisher et al., 1997). For example, more than 80% of youth involved with the juvenile justice system meet diagnostic criteria for conduct disorder. Comorbid conditions of attention-deficit/ hyperactivity disorder, major depressive disorder, posttraumatic stress disorder, and substance abuse disorders are common (Scott, 1999). Psychosocial disadvantage, individual and family psychopathology, punitive and erratic disciplinary practices, and severity of offense history are among the more robust predictors of criminal recidivism and violence perpetration (Benda & Tollett, 1999; Hawkins et al., 1998; Patterson, Forgatch, Yoerger, & Stoolmiller, 1998; Weisz, Martin, Walter, & Fernandez, 1991; Widom, 1998, 1999). An earlier age of onset of antisocial behavior and of first arrest suggest greater chronicity and severity, as youth become involved in an increasingly deviant developmental trajectory (Huizinga & Jakob-Chien, 1998; Huizinga, Loeber, Thornberry, & Cothern, 2000; Patterson et al., 1998). Although arrest at a young age represents a poor prognostic sign, the initial arrest may also represent a useful point at which the juvenile justice system can exert a deterrent effect and influence a youngster away from antisocial and delinquent behavior.

Practitioners and researchers have increasingly drawn links from traumatization and violence exposure to psychopathology and perpetration of violence (Marans et al., 1995; Marans & Berkman, 1997; Osofsky, 1995). Although estimates vary widely depending on sampling and assessment methodologies, at minimum, millions of children are exposed to violence in their homes and communities each year (Richters & Martinez, 1993; Schwab-Stone et al., 1995; Schwab-Stone et al., 1999; Snyder & Sickmund, 1999). Perhaps one third or more of children in the United States witness domestic violence between their parents or caregivers, and many of these children are themselves victims of abuse or neglect (Edleson, 1999; Widom, 1999). Exposure to violence and related trauma may result in a range of childhood psychopathologies, including posttraumatic and depressive disorders and antisocial and defiant behaviors, with prevalence rates higher among urban youth who are also confronted with social and family adversity (Gorman-Smith & Tolan, 1998; Marans & Adelman, 1997; Mazza & Reynolds, 1999; Miller, Wasserman, Neugebauer, Gorman-Smith, & Kamboukos, 1999). Chronic exposure may lead to enduring maladaptation and impairment across cognitive, emotional, and physiological domains of development as youngsters fail to develop adequate capacities for self-regulation and modulation of distress.

Youth and families who experience the most deleterious effects of violence may also lack access to sufficient mental health care (Cocozza & Skowyra, 2000; Grisso, 2000).

In addition to constraints on overall resources, families who simultaneously contend with the chronic and acute effects of violence, poverty, social disadvantage, and co-morbid individual and family psychopathology may be unable to access traditional clinic- or office-based services when they are available. In essence, those with the greatest need may receive the least care. One result has been a proliferation of community-based services in which mental health care is provided in homes, schools, and community settings, with an emphasis on acute stabilization of individual and family psychopathology and collaboration with other community providers, as an alternative to more costly and restrictive institutional care (Aber, Jones, Brown, Chaudry, & Samples, 1998; Burns, Hoagwood, & Mrazek, 1999; Woolston, Berkowitz, Schaefer, & Adnopoz, 1998).

Youth with comorbid psychiatric and delinquent presentations have been increasingly shunted to a juvenile justice system that lacks necessary and appropriate treatment resources (Cocozza & Skowyra, 2000; Grisso, 2000; Marans & Schaefer, 1998). At first glance, it might appear that the populations of the child psychiatric and juvenile justice systems are similar, yet closer examination reveals that those within the juvenile justice system are more likely to be from minority or economically disadvantaged backgrounds. Even among court-adjudicated youth, those remanded to juvenile facilities tend to be disproportionately older, adolescent males from minority backgrounds and urban locales relative to those remanded by a juvenile court to a psychiatric facility (Thomas & Stubbe, 1996). Within the mental health system, the penetration of stringent utilization management and the application of medical necessity criteria by managed care organizations may have lessened the availability of care to youth with serious externalizing problems, despite the existence of psychiatric symptoms that approach levels of severity seen in inpatient settings (Atkins et al., 1999). In contrast to their marked symptomatology, youth in the juvenile justice system have lower rates of mental health service utilization relative to either inpatient or outpatient mental health samples (Pumariega et al., 1999). The widespread reliance on judicial waiver of serious offenders to adult criminal courts has further altered the face of the juvenile court population. Whereas criminal histories of repeated serious offences once typified the incarcerated or detained juvenile population, youth who present with more modest criminal histories accompanied by comorbid psychiatric diagnoses, family dysfunction, and academic underachievement now predominate. The shift in juvenile sentencing toward an adult model of corrections and its attendant reliance on an adversarial legal system, rather than a rehabilitative approach, continues to be an object of criticism and debate (Grisso, 2000), yet the result has been the creation of a de facto and inadequate mental health system within the juvenile justice system.

Mental health service delivery to complex patient populations similar to those encountered by juvenile justice and law enforcement professionals has increasingly emphasized a system-of-care approach based on a continuum of community-based care, with attention to quality and utilization of services (Bickman, 1997). Although the system-of-care tenets of service integration and coordination have not demonstrated the expected benefits in terms of clinical outcomes that exceed those afforded by traditional models of mental health care, it remains difficult to disentangle null findings that may be attributable to ineffective service coordination, insufficient availability and quality of specific services, or inappropriate combination of the two (Saxe &

Cross, 1997). Not all youth with mental health problems appear to require the comprehensive approach proffered by a system-of-care model; rather, those with more serious forms of psychopathology may benefit from this form of coordinated intervention (Fagan, 1991; Weisz et al., 1991). Most interventions have not involved this level of service and system integration.

MENTAL HEALTH SYSTEM INTERVENTIONS

Despite the existence of empirically supported intervention programs for youth diagnosed with conduct disorder, relatively few of these programs have been extended to the juvenile justice system, where youth tend to present with more serious histories of antisocial and delinquent behavior. Traditional models of individual therapy that emphasize insight and self-inspection have not shown benefits for this population (GAPCPP, 1999), while cognitive-behavioral models that emphasize contingency management, cognitive restructuring, and alterations in interpersonal behavior have showed greater promise (Dodge, 1993; Henggeler, Shoenwald, Borduin, Rowland, & Cunningham, 1998; Kazdin & Wassell, 2000; Patterson et al., 1998). Youth with greater levels of symptom severity and more extensive barriers to treatment participation routinely derive fewer benefits from treatment (Kazdin & Wassell, 2000), and these treatment-refractory youth come into contact with justice and law enforcement personnel in disproportionate numbers.

Community programs have a checkered history of success, with recidivism and increased psychopathology all too frequent across a range of programs involving counseling, diversion, and sanctions, a trend that is especially evident among programs that adopt a single focus and fail to bridge the multiple systems that effect a delinquent trajectory. Peer-based programs may be especially problematic, with evidence for potential iatrogenic effects of increased involvement and group cohesion among antisocial peers (McCord, 1999). Programs that provide specific interventions encompassing individual, parent, family, and community systems have shown greater promise in terms of decreased symptomatology, criminal activity, and recidivism (Henggeler, Melton, & Smith, 1992; Henggeler et al., 1999; Henggeler et al., 1998; McCord, 1999; Tate, Reppucci, & Mulvey, 1995).

In a well-known meta-analysis of delinquency interventions, Lipsey, Wilson, and colleagues (Lipsey & Derzon, 1998; Lipsey & Wilson, 1998; Lipsey, Wilson, & Cothern, 2000) examined overall treatment effects for delinquent youth, as well as those for a subset of youth adjudicated for serious offenses. Compared to youth who were not remanded to treatment, those involved in some form of treatment initiated by the juvenile justice system experienced a 12% decrease in recidivism, a modest yet significant improvement. Among noninstitutionalized youth, treatments of a longer duration proved more beneficial, and youth with more serious criminal histories appeared to derive greater benefit. Programs involving interpersonal skills training, individual counseling, and behavioral intervention proved most effective, while wilderness, early release, deterrence, and vocational programs were least effective. Results were more mixed for programs characterized by an emphasis on service coordination, case management, restitution, academic intervention, and employment. Although these findings are encouraging in that they suggest that community treatment interventions for delinquent youth can reduce recidivism, the authors were careful to note the wide variability in the quality of programmatic design, implementation and outcome assessment that precluded the specification of essential treatment ingredients.

JUVENILE JUSTICE SYSTEM INTERVENTIONS

The past decade has witnessed significant and sometimes contradictory developments within the juvenile justice system, as tensions between punishment and rehabilitation have resulted in polarization and dichotomy. In terms of the former, greater numbers of youth are arrested and prosecuted for their criminal offenses. Prosecution of serious felonies is routinely waived to adult criminal courts, and substantial numbers of youth are incarcerated for extended periods of time in adult correctional settings that are ill equipped for these young inmates (Snyder & Sickmund, 1999; Tate et al., 1995). This apparent rejection of the traditional rehabilitative role of the juvenile justice system, which was originally designed to reflect the different developmental capacities of youth, mirrors wider trends toward longer sentencing of those convicted of serious crimes (Grisso, 2000).

Concurrently, juvenile justice personnel in many districts have responded to the 48% increase in juvenile caseloads over the past decade (Scahill, 2000) by adopting a community-based approach to juvenile diversion, probation, and intervention, particularly for youth who are convicted of relatively minor offenses, including status offenses (e.g., truancy or running away) whose definition as illegal is based on the status of the youth as a minor (Ash & Derdeyn, 1997; Roush, 1996; Sherman et al., 1998). This approach, with its emphasis on diversion and community remediation, is consistent with the original intent of the first juvenile court established in Chicago in 1899: to protect the welfare of children involved in the criminal justice system. To a considerable extent, these developments have occurred independently of system-of-care efforts to integrate community-based mental health services for children and adolescents (Black & Krishnakumar, 1998; GAPCPP, 1999), yet both trends are united in an emphasis on tertiary prevention of criminality and psychopathology through coordinated responses involving individual youth, families, communities, and affiliated social agencies (Coordinating Council of Juvenile Justice and Delinquency Prevention, 1996; Wandersman & Nation, 1998).

As part of a community approach, a system of graduated sanctions has been combined with neighborhood-based services that exist along a continuum of restrictiveness. Youth with relatively modest histories of offense are likely to receive alternative sentences involving mandated probation, community programming, or victim restitution in place of detention (Clear & Karp, 2000; Coolbaugh & Hansel, 2000; Holsinger & Latessa, 1999). Clear and Karp (2000) have described the interplay between offender, victim, and community as one that is ideally directed toward reconciliation and remediation of a breach in the social fabric brought about by the offender's transgressions. Victim restitution and offender acceptance of personal responsibility represent key components in an effort to increase stability among families, neighborhoods, and social institutions. When standards and laws are violated, the juvenile justice system may exert its authority in a reparative fashion, addressing victim and offender needs, attending to issues of risk management, and enforcing legal consequences for an offender's actions. Practitioners of community justice combine their traditional responsibilities involving crime management and punishment with a proactive role oriented toward reducing crime and recidivism.

Probation Officers

As the embodiment of the community juvenile justice model, probation officers serve as the direct interface between youthful offenders and community restitution and response. In contrast to traditional approaches in which youth were required to attend impersonal meetings at a remote probation office, community probation officers may be assigned to various neighborhood locales, including schools and police substations, to facilitate regular contact and relationships with youth on their caseloads. Community probation officers, and their community policing counterparts, become familiar in and with neighborhoods and can exert a direct prosocial effect on individual youth. For delinquent youth, who may present with scant intrinsic motivation to alter their behavior or to comply with recommended treatment, probation officers represent important figures of benevolent authority and containment. They have the potential to reduce delinquent youth's feelings of anonymity and invulnerability in their communities and can complement community-based clinical interventions that would be unlikely to succeed in the absence of probation officers' direct intervention. Clinical and juvenile probation services are more easily integrated when they serve this complementary role in communities and neighborhoods.

Evaluations of the Juvenile Justice System

Research on juvenile justice system efforts to prevent crime has focused on a range of strategies, including detention of offenders in secure facilities, restriction of liberty in the community (e.g., curfews, electronic monitoring), and mandates for community treatment (Sherman et al., 1998). While detention, by its nature, precludes further criminal activity, it unduly restricts the freedom of all but the most serious offenders and represents a costly alternative to community justice responses. Efforts at deterrence through monetary fines or brief incarceration followed by monitoring in the community have not resulted in decreases in criminal activity, perhaps because such approaches rely on offenders' making the rational decision to desist from criminal activity. Increased probation supervision has also yielded disappointing results, with continued high rates of recidivism and increased rates of violations of probationary conditions, although the combination of probation with treatment may be more promising. Results from rehabilitative and treatment programs have shown more potential, as those designed to reduce antisocial and aggressive behavior, substance abuse, and criminal activity have been successful. Although their quality of implementation has been variable at best, effective programs provide for greater treatment intensity according to the severity and chronicity of offenses and emphasize risk as well as protective factors associated with violence and criminality (Catalano, Loeber, & McKinney, 1999).

In recent years, attention has turned to the role of police, probation officers, and other justice personnel in mandating outpatient treatment for individuals with serious psychiatric illness who are unlikely to otherwise comply with voluntary care (Borum, 1999a; Swartz et al., 1999). Studies of mandated treatment, alternatively known as *outpatient commitment,* have been limited to adult populations, although similar procedures have been widely employed with juvenile populations. Outpatient commitment operates from a perspective similar to that of involuntary hospitalization, in which the state orders compliance with a specific treatment program based on the common law doctrine of *parens patrie,* a principle that allows the state to act in its own interest or for its own good. In this instance, *parens patrie* represents a justification for court actions that supersede individual liberty in favor of treatment mandates designed to protect disabled persons and ensure public safety (Fischer & Sorenson, 1996; Marans & Schaefer, 1998; Snyder & Sickmund, 1999). In the two randomized clinical trials of outpatient commitment to date, results have been contradictory. Short-term outpatient commitment showed no appreciable benefit, while in one trial, outpatient commitment in excess of 180 days, when provided in conjunction with outpatient mental health treatment, resulted in decreased inpatient psychiatric hospitalization and criminal arrest.

With their increasing proportion of delinquent youth with serious psychopathology, neither the mental health system nor the juvenile justice system can sustain a stance as a sole provider to disturbed youth. Relatively few youth whose disturbances are marked by the predominance of externalizing symptoms and projection of personal responsibility into the social realm avail themselves of psychotherapy. Yet when psychotherapy is integrated as a condition of probation and is paired with ongoing relationships with a community probation or patrol officer, the sense of anonymity and invulnerability that characterizes many delinquent youth wanes. For youth lacking intrinsic motivation and the ability to sufficiently mediate their actions on an internal basis, external containment through such benevolent authority figures can represent an opportunity for treatment engagement that might be otherwise lacking.

LAW ENFORCEMENT INTERVENTIONS

Beginning in the 1970s and gathering momentum in the latter 1980s, community leaders recognized that the academic, social, and emotional health of youth could not be separated from their feelings of safety and security in their schools and neighborhoods. As youth violence peaked in the late 1980s and early 1990s, leaders in law enforcement recognized the need for a change in traditional policing. Many departments began a critical transition from a crisis-oriented and response-driven system to one reflecting the principles of problem-oriented and community-based policing (Marans et al., 1995). In contrast to a reactive, crime-fighting response, community policing adopts a proactive, solution-based, and community-driven perspective in which the need to arrest offenders is balanced with a preventive approach based on relationships and problem-solving efforts with a range of community constituencies. Despite variation across communities, departments that have embraced community policing emphasize accessibility of police to the citizens they serve, rely on problem solving and preventive approaches, engage in proactive order maintenance designed to diffuse situations prior to an emergency complaint, collaborate with community agencies and resources, encourage neighborhood involvement in policing; and sponsor community crime-prevention initiatives (Goldstein, 1987; Thurman, 1995).

Community policing has expanded dramatically since the 1994 passage of the Violent Crime Control and Law Enforcement Act, designed to increase the ranks of community police officers by 100,000. The resulting Office of Community Oriented Policing Services (COPS) within the U.S. Department of Justice spearheaded efforts to hire and train community police officers nationwide (Roth & Ryan, 2000). Funding has largely benefited communities that have been disproportionately affected by violent crime, through the hiring and assignment of these officers to community policing duties. Results of programmatic evaluation (Roth & Ryan, 2000) suggest that funding of officers and related support positions has been particularly beneficial in advancing moves toward community policing among communities that have already initiated such changes.

Effective collaborations between police and mental health providers are related to and dependent on the reorientation of many police departments to reflect the philosophy of community policing as a means for strengthening social structures that deter crime and facilitate social functioning, detecting high-risk situations likely to lead to criminal activity, and interrupting patterns of criminality at their roots. Community policing integrates officers within the community, where they are known as individuals, rather than only by role, and where they know the people they serve. Community officers come into regular contact with children and families within a given neighborhood, a process that requires specialized training, supervision, and support in order to sustain a proactive and preventive approach. Institutional commitments are realized in the reorientation of law enforcement toward collaborative work that recognizes the contributions of police officers as benign external authorities with valuable perspectives on the developmental context in which children experience adversity. Changes in officers' responses to children can be evidenced by their participation in youth-oriented community activities, recognition of children's involvement during service calls, referrals to mental health system colleagues, and developmentally informed responses in situations involving troubled children. Collaboration with mental health system colleagues may succeed in developing a cadre of better informed and more effective officers; however, extant programs have not yet sufficiently evaluated changes in officers' recognition of and response to the mental health needs of at-risk youth.

School Resource Officers

One of the essential processes of development involves the incorporation of characteristics of adult authority figures into aspects of children's emotional and cognitive worlds in the form of conscience or morality. The most important people in this process are parents, yet other adult authority figures may play an essential role, especially for children whose parents have provided inconsistent and confusing messages about self-esteem, rules, violence, and personal conduct. Police officers, as societal representations of authority, compensation, retribution, and punishment, can have a profound impact on children's development, sense of security, and ability to cope with traumatic events (Berkowitz & Murphy, 2000).

School resource officers (SROs) represent the leading edge of police officers' interactions with children and may serve as a potential antidote to the view of authorities as malevolent, threatening, capricious, or neglectful. Many of the beliefs and theories about police and authority that children hold and maintain will come from their inter-actions with officers in their classrooms and schools. The basic duties of the SRO involve enforcement, education, and consultation with children (Center for the Pre-vention of School Violence, 1998). Awareness of child development principles and their relevance to policing can provide an invaluable context for youth-oriented polic-ing, when officers recognize that assignment to schools provides unique opportunities and challenges that are distinct from their previous patrol assignments (Marans et al., 1995; Marans & Schaefer, 1998). With the school as their regular beat, officers have the opportunity to enhance and intervene in the lives of children, many of whom are at risk for or currently experience significant mental health problems. With a working knowledge of developmental principles, they are able to adapt their responses accord-ing to assessments of specific children (Marans, Berkowitz, & Cohen, 1998).

As children develop, their assumptions about police officers change. During the ele-mentary school years, children may be fascinated by police officers. Once any initial discomfort or shyness is overcome, they will often question officers about their equip-ment, uniforms, badges, guns, and cruisers, reflecting a developmentally appropriate interest in logical inferences about how things work and attention to detail. Adoles-cence represents a time of ambivalence toward most authority figures, police included (Hurst & Frank, 2000), when youth alternately view adults as models for emulation and defiance in the service of identity formation. The simple assignment of an SRO to a school is insufficient for improving relationships between youth and police. Rather, improved perspectives on police are dictated by the frequency of benign contact with officers and the benevolent quality of the relationships that are established (Hopkins, Hewstone, & Hanzi, 1992).

Evaluations of Community Policing

Despite its popularity, evidence for the effectiveness of community policing has been limited. Community policing may be more effective at improving residents' satisfac-tion with police services and subjective feelings of neighborhood safety and security than in directly reducing criminal activity and victimization (Catalano et al., 1999; Zhao & Thurman, 1997). While residents favorably view the involvement of patrol and supervisory officers in community initiatives, concerns for safety may overshadow improved police–community relationships in districts with high rates of criminal activity (Davis & Mateu-Gelabert, 2000). Despite a stated goal of enhancing collabo-rative relationships between police departments and other service agencies, many partnerships with police remain in the planning stage, representing ideological com-mitments to collaboration rather than true working partnerships. Thus, many depart-ments appear to have embraced the concept of collaboration without its enactment (Zhao & Thurman, 1997). A more optimistic interpretation would suggest that a promising minority of departments have engaged with outside agencies to the extent that they can sustain a consistent, collaborative relationship involving mutual decision making and problem solving.

Although police routinely confront the psychological sequelae of trauma, violence, and psychiatric illness, their options traditionally have been limited to an evaluation of an individual's danger to self and others with the possibility of involuntary transportation to a psychiatric emergency room for further evaluation, arrest in instances of criminal activity, or informal efforts to secure psychosocial support (Teplin, 2000). Despite decades of practical experience in responding to psychiatric crises, few police departments provide extensive training in the identification and management of acute mental health problems. Teplin (2000) noted that the likelihood of arrest was 67% greater for criminal suspects who exhibited signs of mental disorder than for suspects whose mental status police did not question. This finding could be taken as an indication of insufficient police training in responding to citizens with psychiatric disturbances, as well as a reflection of diminished access to public sector behavioral health care, with the result that police may become more likely to resort to arrest as means of securing treatment for them.

A survey of procedures among 174 police departments serving urban locales with a population of at least 100,000 residents revealed that more than half (55%, $n = 96$) had no specialized response procedures for mental health crises, despite a large proportion of service calls involving individuals with serious mental illness (Deane, Steadman, Borum, Veysey, & Morrissey, 1999). Within the remaining 45% of departments ($n = 78$), 3% ($n = 6$) relied on specific officers with crisis-intervention training to act as liaisons with mental health providers. Another 12% ($n = 20$) retained civilians as mental health consultants, and the remaining 30% of departments ($n = 52$) relied on mental health professionals who were not directly affiliated with the police department itself. Although most departments, including those lacking any specialized response, perceived their efforts on behalf of citizens with psychological impairments as effective, none were able to point to specific outcomes or benefits that accrued to the individuals in question. Furthermore, none of these programs specifically addressed the mental health concerns of children, suggesting that the relative paucity of organized police responses to psychiatric concerns is amplified in regard to children, whose difficulties may go unrecognized by officers who lack the training and resources to respond to their psychiatric and developmental needs.

Although limited, research to date indicates that programs involving law enforcement or juvenile justice system efforts to reduce crime are most effective when they provide a comprehensive array of community-based therapeutic services over an extended period of time (Borum, 1999b; Catalano et al., 1999; Cocozza & Skowyra, 2000; Tate et al., 1995). The Office of Justice Programs in the U.S. Department of Justice (Sherman et al., 1998) outlined a range of effective crime- and violence-prevention programs, yet few involved joint participation by the justice system and mental health service providers. Despite this caveat, several approaches from the law enforcement and juvenile justice systems have resulted in appreciable decrements in criminal and violent activity by youth. Intensified monitoring of repeat offenders by community police and probation officers, as well as additional police patrols in areas with high rates of youth crime, can ameliorate recidivism. Presumably, these approaches reduce anonymity, increase supervision and security, and promote proactive intervention by police and probation officers. Community policing has been associated with improvements in police–community relationships and in residents' perceptions of security in their neighborhoods and homes. Structured, adult-supervised police programs designed specifically for youth, including after-school programs, athletic and recreational leagues, and mentoring programs, also appear promising, particularly when they include an explicit focus on behavior change (Chaiken, 1998).

Ineffective Strategies

The Drug Abuse Resistance Education (DARE) program was designed as a preventive approach to drug abuse, although multiple evaluations of the program have not yielded significant results (Ringwalt et al., 1994). Negative findings highlight the fact that research may fail to inform public policy, as the program remains popular among law enforcement and school officials and community members, perhaps due to its positive effects on children's views of police. Overall, the report from the Office of Justice Programs highlights the dire need for further evaluation of youth crime- and violence-prevention programs, as well as their extension to system-of-care principles.

Other popular responses to youth violence have been ineffective, and in some instances, they have exacerbated violent activity. Policies based on mandatory waiver of certain serious felony offenses to the adult criminal justice system and increased lengths of sentences have resulted in greater numbers of incarcerated youth with no evidence for either a deterrent effect or a decrease in recidivism (Chaiken, 1998). At the other end of the spectrum, preventive and early-intervention approaches often fail to address the complex nature of violence exposure and perpetration and instead focus on specific and isolated problems. Despite the popularity of mentoring and peer-based after-school programs, few utilize well-trained adults in positions of authority who are prepared for the challenging and complex presentations of traumatized or delinquent youth. Many well-intentioned programs adopt a rather naive approach and implicitly assert that benign activity or adult presence can ameliorate chronic and severe psychopathology. In fact, some peer programs appear to enculturate antisocial norms of behavior, resulting in an increase rather than a decrease in problem, antisocial, and criminal activity (Chaiken, 1998). This has been the case with juvenile boot camps and "scared straight" programs, which appeal to the public's desire for strict consequences for offenders but may enhance recidivism through the encouragement of a harsh culture of criminality.

The utility of police and mental health treatment system collaboration received support from a programmatic evaluation of a joint intervention involving clinical providers and police detectives in an urban European police department (Scholte, 1992). After being trained to recognize risk factors for psychopathology among adolescents, juvenile division detectives participated in daily rounds with clinicians to discuss juvenile cases from the previous day and develop appropriate treatment recommendations. Programmatic analysis revealed a 74% concordance between youth identified as at risk for serious psychopathology by police and those identified by a standardized screening instrument. Although subsequent interventions were not well operationalized, post hoc analyses suggested that a greater number of youth about whom detectives and clinicians consulted engaged in treatment more readily and experienced fewer psychiatric symptoms in the 6 months following referral (Scholte, 1992).

COLLABORATIONS AMONG THE MENTAL HEALTH, JUVENILE JUSTICE, AND LAW ENFORCEMENT SYSTEMS

Traditionally, mental health professionals have played a consultative role to the juvenile justice system, with their primary responsibilities involving the provision of evaluations, treatment recommendations, and assessments of competency. Subsequent interventions, including referral to community programs staffed by paraprofessionals, supervised probation, juvenile detention, or referral to a residential or corrections facility, have operated in a relatively self-contained manner, with little input from mental health providers beyond the point of referral. Among the more promising recent collaborations are those allied with research related to children's mental health systems of care (Bickman et al., 1995; Friedman & Burns, 1996), in which multiple systems converge in an integrated manner to maximize quality and continuity of care. Concepts of mental health care systems that have been focused on psychiatric and community support services can be expanded to encompass law enforcement, juvenile justice, and adult justice system personnel in an effort to correct the historical isolation of mental health care providers from the law enforcement and justice systems (Murphy, 2001). Ideally, these extensions should result in an overall shift in service utilization and cost from a reliance on acute services toward nonacute and community-based responses. The community orientation of law enforcement and juvenile justice system professionals should be reflected through improved relationships with community members and enhanced feelings about the security and responsiveness of legal and law enforcement system professionals.

Challenges to Effective Collaboration

Professionals from divergent disciplines and backgrounds approach children with widely varying assumptions about their development and psychological reactions. Systems that have traditionally operated in relative isolation from one another, including mental health care agencies, school districts, police departments, and juvenile courts, are unaccustomed to the necessity of coordinating their services. Professionals from each of these backgrounds may be uncomfortable and defensive when challenged by the unfamiliar viewpoints of new colleagues. For example, law enforcement officers may expect clinicians to excuse criminal activity and its consequences due to explanations based on prior adversity. Similarly, clinicians may approach law enforcement officials with trepidation due to their own notions about the authority of police and courts, which lead them to feel ill at ease or even guilty when confronted by the bearers of legal and social authority. All too often, the result becomes the status quo of fragmentary and inadequate services for those children with the greatest psychological needs. Few professionals in any field reject the notion of collaboration, yet its actual practice remains fraught with ambivalence. Agencies may readily agree to work together and develop formal procedures for referral. However, in the absence of direct working relationships and knowledge of one another's professional responsibilities, strengths, and limitations, these formal collaborations may be short-lived, as key stakeholders develop scant investment in the results of collaboration.

When legal and care systems interact, concerns about confidentially inevitably move to the forefront, yet solutions are possible. For example, clinicians may become privy to confidential material from legal investigations; probation or police officers may learn detailed clinical information. While there is no inviolable solution for determining the extent of mutual disclosure, professionals on each side must balance the need for effective collaboration and mutual trust with their individual responsibilities to protect the privacy of a clinical encounter or the integrity of an investigation (Marans & Schaefer, 1998). When collaboration is based on actual relationships and mutual contact, these issues will become an ongoing aspect of discussions, with participants less likely to use the issue of confidentiality to displace unacknowledged suspicion or anxiety about partners from a different professional orientation.

Confidentiality and service provision can become further complicated in the context of juvenile court proceedings, where the defendant's right to due process may interfere with the provision of psychological evaluation and treatment. As Marans and Schaefer (1998) have noted, to the extent that juvenile court proceedings mirror those of adult criminal court, attorneys may be reluctant to advise their clients to enter into evaluative or treatment relationships that might reveal findings detrimental to their defense. At other times, parents may be willing to waive strict confidentiality in the service of longer term planning for a youngster's mental health needs. The process of meshing mental health services and juvenile court proceedings can be helped immeasurably by the development of relationships across disciplines so that mental health providers become knowledgeable about law enforcement and juvenile court practices and begin to forge working alliances with prosecutors and defense attorneys.

Home-Based Treatment

The limitations of many peer programs and the recognition of the complex mental health needs of youth and families involved in the juvenile justice system has resulted in a range of home-based treatment initiatives that attempt to reduce delinquent and antisocial activity while keeping youth in their communities (Butts & Barton, 1995) by adapting the systems-of-care model to the juvenile justice system. These programs have a secondary goal of limiting expenditures, as they may provide a cost-effective alternative to institutional care in the justice or mental health care systems. Home-based treatment has earned equivocal support in the research literature (St. Pierre & Layzer, 1998), yet represents a growing and insufficiently understood trend in behavioral health care.

Multisystemic therapy (MST) represents the most widely disseminated and evaluated program for home-based intervention with delinquent and antisocial youth (Borduin et al., 1995; Henggeler et al., 1992; Henggeler et al., 1998; Henggeler et al., 1999). Multisystemic therapists address the broad ecology of childhood psychopathology as manifested in family, peer, school, and other settings. MST clinicians provide home-based parent and family treatment and coordinate access to necessary community supports and entitlements (Henggeler et al., 1998). MST has shown particular promise in reducing antisocial and criminal behavior and substance use among adolescents. Results from randomized clinical trials indicate that providing home-based interventions comprised of ecologically, behaviorally, and family-focused treatment and case management for a relatively brief duration of several months produces treatment gains that are maintained well beyond termination of clinical services (see Henggeler et al., 1992; Henggeler et al., 1998). Results include modest yet significant improvements in symptoms of youth psychopathology and family functioning, accompanied by substantial reductions in severity and frequency of rearrest that have been maintained for as long as 4 years (Borduin et al., 1995; Henggeler et al., 1992; Henggeler et al., 1998).

The Family Support Service of the Yale Child Study Center has implemented another model of home-based treatment that is informed by a synthesis of a medical model, developmental psychopathology, systems theory, and wraparound concepts (Adnopoz, Woolston, Schaefer, & Tebes, 1999; Tebes et al., 1996; Woolston et al., 1998). The program builds on recognition that disturbed familial relationships may serve as a pathogenic context for childhood psychopathology (Allen, Hauser, & Borman-Spurrell, 1996). For children with severe disturbances and their families, the therapeutic relationship that is developed with the home-based treatment team members may serve as the primary vehicle for delivering focused psychosocial and supportive interventions. The core of the intervention consists of the coordinated efforts of a clinician–case manager team who forge a consistent and supportive relationship with the family. A focus on specific risk behaviors and their amelioration occurs in the context of the clinical relationship, which itself serves a catalytic function in promoting family change. Pragmatic and discrete interventions assist the family in supporting changes in the adolescent's behavior—for example, by providing access to affordable health insurance, via Medicaid or programs to cover uninsured and underinsured children, and access to longer term medical and mental health care providers.

Home-based individual and family therapy, case management, and coordination of medical and mental health care services are combined with the efforts of a community probation officer with specialized training in child and adolescent development. From the perspective of the juvenile justice system, the program is based on observations of the prevalence of treatment-refractory youth in the juvenile justice system population, as well as the finding that diversionary programs seldom include a substantial treatment program (Sherman et al., 1998). The collaboration between the clinical staff and personnel from the juvenile probation office is crucial to the success of the intervention, as the probation officer represents an important figure of benevolent authority and containment. Probation officers reduce delinquent youths' feelings of anonymity in their communities and can complement community-based clinical interventions that would be unlikely to succeed in a clinic setting.

THE CHILD DEVELOPMENT COMMUNITY POLICING PROGRAM

The Child Development Community Policing (CDCP) program represents a collaboration between law enforcement and mental health service professionals on behalf of children and families exposed to violence in their communities. Recognizing that no system—police, juvenile justice, or mental health care—possesses the resources and acumen to respond to the gamut of youth psychopathology, traumatization, and criminal activity, professionals from each group can benefit from a common frame of reference by which to guide their actions (Marans et al., 1995; Marans et al., 1998; Marans & Schaefer, 1998). The partnership between clinicians and police officers provides opportunities to understand the relationship between victimization and exposure to violence, traumatic stress reactions, and the perpetration of violent actions, as well as to develop more effective ways for intervening in the lives of traumatized children and families. Long-range goals are to improve the delivery of police and mental health services, particularly acute responses to incidents of violence involving children; increase children's experiences of safety, security, and positive relationships with police; and decrease children's maladaptive responses following exposure to potentially traumatic episodes of violence.

The CDCP program consists of several interrelated training and service components, which aim to share knowledge between police officers and clinicians and respond collaboratively to the needs of children who are victims and witnesses of violence. The program operates from the assumption that an understanding of child development comprises the core of effective clinical and law enforcement responses to children's needs and that mutual knowledge and relationships between professionals form the basis for effective collaboration on behalf of children. Members from each professional group ascribe to a youth-oriented and community-based approach to intervention. Departments that follow a community policing model integrate developmental principles into their work, while their clinical counterparts learn about principles of law enforcement and acquire direct experience in service communities (Marans et al., 1995).

Police Officers

Police officers bring experience and observation skills developed in other law enforcement settings to their work with children and adolescents. Their powers of observation, combined with their knowledge of the community, become an invaluable foundation for understanding and working with children of various ages and levels of development. This simple statement becomes more complex when put into practice, as police officers attempt to connect their direct experiences involving children with their knowledge of key developmental tasks and struggles of childhood and adolescence (Berkowitz & Murphy, 2000).

Training in Child Development and Trauma

Patrol officers, detectives, and supervisory officers receive training in basic principles of child development and their application to child-oriented community policing. At the beginning of their training in the police academy, new recruits participate in seminars in child development and trauma. As officers progress in their careers and acquire further experience, they participate in an intensive 3- to 4-day series of seminars that cover phases of development from infancy to adolescence. A specific concentration on violence, trauma, and the meaning of police to children at various stages of development maintains the overall focus of the seminars. Each seminar series is co-led by a senior mental health clinician and a supervisory police officer, reflecting the collaborative nature of the partnership, in which each discipline contributes unique perspectives on policing and child development. Senior officers who opt for daily involvement in program operations enter a more intensive developmental fellowship in which they observe children in a range of mental health care settings, including outpatient and inpatient psychiatric, juvenile detention, and pediatric emergency settings. They receive intensive consultation regarding their methods of applying child development principles to policing and responding to traumatized children from senior program faculty who are psychologists, psychiatrists, social workers, pediatricians, and attorneys. Over the course of several months, senior officers move into a leadership role within their departments and supervise junior officers in the application of child development principles to community policing. The entire New Haven, Connecticut, police department—more than 450 sworn officers, including academy trainees, line officers, detectives, supervisors, and the chief of police—has received training in applied child development through the Child Development Seminar and Clinical Fellowship components of the CDCP program.

One officer's appreciation of developmental principles is apparent in a response to family violence (adapted from Marans, Murphy, & Berkowitz, 2002).

> Sergeant T responded to the scene of a stabbing in which a 7-year-old girl witnessed a neighbor fatally stab an aunt. Hoping to spare her the sight of the bloody scene within, Sergeant T had the child wait on the porch while officers conducted their investigation. He could not rid himself of the memory of the girl's intense gaze, an admixture of despair and rage that she fixed on him when he finally invited her back into the apartment as the officers were leaving. The next day the sergeant returned to the house and spoke with the girl and her grandmother. He realized that his attempt to spare this girl a gruesome site had been without the benefit of considering her current experience and needs.
>
> He later commented, "In the midst of so much blood and terror, she needed to be close to her grandmother, the most stable figure in her life, not to be stranded alone with images of a violent killing." Both the girl and her grandmother eagerly accepted his offer of a referral for clinical services. It later emerged during treatment that being alone with frightening ideas and fantasies readily evoked previous experiences of an erratic and frequently rejecting drug-addicted mother, as well as worries about the health of her elderly grandmother, the only stable caregiver she had known.

Training in Community Policing Principles

Clinicians participate in a related fellowship designed to familiarize them with community policing and law enforcement strategies. Supervisory officers lead a 3-day series of seminars designed to acquaint clinicians with the basic tenets of community policing. Topics include an overview of departmental command structure, rules governing arrest and evidence gathering, investigative techniques, arrest and incarceration procedures, and regulations governing the application of force. As clinicians learn about policing, they begin a series of regular ride-alongs in which they accompany officers on their patrols, becoming familiar with police perspectives and solidifying relationships with officers, which then become the basis for mutual collaboration on behalf of children.

Acute Consultation Service

A 24-hour consultation service is staffed by a team of mental health clinicians who are available for immediate response to police requests for consultation and intervention with children and families exposed to violence. Clinicians respond in person

to a range of police scenes at any time of the day or night, allowing immediate intervention for children who otherwise might not receive services until much later, when
symptoms have crystallized into enduring psychopathology. Clinicians commonly
meet children in the immediate aftermath of serious incidents of violence and crime,
including homicides, domestic and neighborhood assaults, suicides, threats, physical
altercations, burglaries, accidents, and unexpected deaths. Clinicians' availability
cements their partnership with police officers, who in other instances may recognize
various needs among children but lack the available resources to respond when
crises occur outside of usual business hours.

The interplay of the law enforcement and clinical responses is evident in the following case involving a domestic homicide:

> As officers were collecting evidence following a domestic homicide, they learned that two
> boys had been across the street at the home of neighbor when the shooting occurred.
> Realizing that the 5- and 11-year-old boys would soon learn of the loss of both their par-
> ents—their mother dead and their father incarcerated—they quickly paged the CDCP cli-
> nician through the acute consultation service. Two clinicians responded immediately and
> arranged to meet the boys at the home of their maternal grandmother who lived nearby.
>
> In the midst of a rapidly expanding retinue of grief-stricken adults sat two young boys
> staring blankly ahead with stunned looks on their faces. While they were with loved ones,
> the adults were unable to hold their distress in abeyance and attend to the boys. A clini-
> cian took the boys aside and provided an opportunity to draw or talk. The younger boy
> began to quickly draw a series of hearts with his mother's name in the center, stating that
> he was creating cards that she might use in heaven. The older boy spoke in a monotone
> about previous domestic violence in his home and his feelings of rage and impotence at
> the night's events. In the meantime, the other clinician spoke with the grandmother and
> coordinated with child protective services to ensure that the children would remain with
> family members. The grandmother was helped to consider how the boys would react,
> including the types of symptoms she could expect in the coming days. A plan of follow-
> up care involving home visits by clinicians and neighborhood officers was arranged.
> While these interventions could accomplish relatively little in the face of sudden and
> overwhelming grief, a preliminary sense of predictability was established. The concern of
> police and clinicians fostered a therapeutic relationship that allowed both boys to con-
> sider the loss and anger in a contained manner that facilitated their continuing with age
> appropriate school and social functioning.

The CDCP program has intervened in an average of 450 cases per year, involving
more than 750 children annually since its implementation in 1991. Approximately 50%
of cases involve an immediate intervention in the wake of violence, with the remainder
divided equally between direct clinical response within 24 hours of an event and consultation to police officers on broader issues of responding to children's needs. As a
result of acute consultation, children have been seen both individually and in groups
for both brief and extended treatment, in homes, schools, police stations, hospitals
and clinical offices. In addition, the CDCP program has provided consultation and
direct services to school and child welfare systems at times of communitywide crisis
through a school-based crisis-response program that emphasizes preparation of local
providers to respond to emergent incidents (Newgass & Schonfeld, 2000; Schonfeld,
1989; Schonfeld & Kline, 1994).

Coordinated responses to domestic violence that involve mental health service, social service, police, and judicial personnel have gained popularity (Gamache, Edleson, & Schock, 1988; Groves, 1999), yet only recently have providers recognized the role of law enforcement in promoting the adaptation of children affected by domestic violence. A specialized CDCP response component combines the acute clinical response with coordinated follow-up by clinicians, paraprofessional outreach workers, neighborhood patrol officers, and domestic violence court advocates. Clinicians and outreach workers attend to posttraumatic symptoms among children and family members, facilitate engagement with treatment or other social service providers, and assist in the development of plans designed to reduce subsequent abuse. Neighborhood officers provide specific guidance in safety planning, assist in securing necessary protective orders, and become a resource in case of future emergency. Advocates from a specialized domestic violence court assist families in complex or lengthy legal proceedings and ensure that court rulings are understood. Many women who have been unable to act on their own behalf in the face of serious or chronic domestic violence may be engaged through a child-centered approach that integrates specific and concrete assistance with a developmental focus on the effects of exposure to domestic violence on young children.

Weekly Program Conference for Officers and Clinicians

Clinicians meet with police and probation officers in a weekly program conference to review, evaluate, and develop response plans for specific cases that have been referred to the CDCP program. The program conference fosters consistent and forthright relationships across disciplines and constitutes ongoing recognition that the CDCP program represents a partnership between agencies which have not been able to respond adequately to the needs of traumatized children on their own. The utility of collaboration among familiar partners is exemplified when officers and clinicians depart from their stereotyped responses. For example, officers may raise concerns about family context and trauma history as mediating factors in cases of youth violence. Under the same circumstances, clinicians might address the therapeutic use of arrest as leverage for treatment engagement. Both responses highlight the distance professionals have come in adopting the viewpoints of their colleagues without sacrificing their professional standards and integrity.

Program Dissemination

In addition to providing local training and consultation, the CDCP program has served as a national model for police and mental health service collaboration on behalf of children, particularly children exposed to violence. The dissemination of the CDCP model has culminated in the development of the National Center for Children Exposed to Violence, created to disseminate information about the effects of violence on children's development and to provide training and technical assistance to related programs throughout the country, including the Department of Justice's Safe Start Initiative demonstration sites. Ongoing CDCP evaluation activities include investigation of children's acute trauma responses, officers' applications of training in child development, and changes in police and mental health service utilization.

The CDCP model has been implemented in 13 cities across the nation. Although it has remained largely an urban phenomenon, several suburbs have implemented the model, with an explicit focus on domestic violence. Other sites have adapted the model to focus on younger children or to include additional partners, such as child protective service workers and community leaders. Each program has applied the basic CDCP model of interdisciplinary training and coordinated responses to the needs of children affected by violence, yet their specific implementation has, by necessity, been adapted to local conditions. The majority of sites have opted for gradual implementation, beginning with districts in which children are most affected by violence and crime. This pragmatic approach has substantially reduced the level of resources required to develop a CDCP program.

The basic requirements for launching a CDCP program include identifying senior police and mental health service partners to assume joint responsibility for program development and implementation. The model relies on a community-oriented policing philosophy, so departments with an exclusive reliance on traditional 911-driven police responses are less likely to support the CDCP approach. At a practical level, clinical and law enforcement agencies often have been able to reallocate job responsibilities to allow adequate time for training and attendance at collaborative meetings. The greatest expense has involved instances in which additional support has been necessary to cover the cost of officers who are involved in CDCP training. Clinicians, too, may require salary support or some other form of compensation for time spent on call for the acute consultation service, although this represents one aspect of a salaried position in many agencies. Formal CDCP replication involves a 5-day training series during which clinical and police leaders receive intensive training in the CDCP model and its implementation. As a precursor to formal training, the majority of CDCP sites initiated a process of informal consultation to assess community needs and determine the preparedness of proposed clinical and law enforcement partners.

CONCLUSIONS

Promising new approaches are extending traditional interactions among the mental health care, juvenile justice, and law enforcement systems through mutual training across disciplines and the development of collaborations in which traditionally disparate disciplines collectively accept responsibility for intervening with youth who have severe emotional disturbance. A key challenge involves moving beyond an approach that emphasizes the cataloging of risk factors associated with benign or malignant outcomes to one that facilitates the development, implementation, and study of theoretically driven interventions that are designed to ameliorate specific risk factors and pathological conditions (Burns et al., 1999) and that addresses the mechanisms through which different types of providers can intervene. A combination of efficacy and effectiveness studies will be required, with the former addressing the development of specific theoretical models and accompanying interventions and the latter focusing on transportability to real-world settings. Evaluations of collaborative interventions will need to address training components that allow professionals to coordinate care across disciplines, while attending to desired clinical outcomes in excess of those that could be attained with less intensive services that are already available through traditional treatment centers. The sheer complexity of efforts to integrate child mental health care, juvenile justice, and law enforcement system responses presents a daunting challenge to service providers and evaluators, who must attend to a range of indicators of process and outcome so that interdisciplinary collaboration can be measured at the individual and systems levels with reference to changes in the functioning of children and families, as well as the practices of providers in these three systems.

REFERENCES

Aber, J. L., Jones, S. M., Brown, J. L., Chaudry, N., & Samples, F. (1998). Resolving conflict creatively: Evaluating the developmental effects of a school-based violence prevention program in neighborhood and classroom context. *Development and Psychopathology, 10,* 187–213.

Adnopoz, J., Woolston, J., Schaefer, M., & Tebes, J. (1999). *Husky plus behavioral: An intervention manual.* New Haven, CT: Yale Child Study Center.

Allen, J. P., Hauser, S. T., & Borman-Spurrell, E. (1996). Attachment theory as a framework for understanding sequelae of severe adolescent psychopathology: An 11-year follow-up study. *Journal of Consulting and Clinical Psychology, 64,* 254–263.

Ash, P., & Derdeyn, A. P. (1997). Forensic child and adolescent psychiatry: A review of the past 10 years. *Journal of the American Academy of Child and Adolescent Psychiatry, 36,* 1493–1502.

Atkins, D. L., Pumariega, A. J., Rogers, K., Montgomery, L., Nybro, C., Jerrers, G., & Sease, F. (1999). Mental health and incarcerated youth: I. Prevalence and nature of psychopathology. *Journal of Child & Family Studies, 8,* 193–204.

Benda, B. B., & Tollett, C. L. (1999). A study of recidivism of serious and persistent offenders among adolescents. *Journal of Criminal Justice, 27,* 111–126.

Berkowitz, S. J., & Murphy, R. A. (2000). Child development and education. In National School Safety Center (Ed.), *COPS in schools SRO training curriculum.* Westlake Village, CA: Author.

Bickman, L. (1997). Resolving issues raised by the Fort Bragg evaluation. *American Psychologist, 52,* 562–565.

Bickman, L., Guthrie, P. R., Foster, E. M., Lambert, E. W., Summerfelt, W. T., Breda, C. S., & Helfinger, C. A. (1995). *Evaluating managed mental health services: The Fort Bragg experiment.* New York: Plenum Press.

Black, M. M., & Krishnakumar, A. (1998). Children in low-income, urban settings: Interventions to promote mental health and well-being. *American Psychologist, 53,* 635–646.

Borduin, C. M., Mann, B. J., Cone, L. T., Henggeler, S. W., Fucci, B. R., Blaske, D. M., & Williams, R. A. (1995). Multisystemic treatment of serious juvenile offenders: Long-term prevention of criminality and violence. *Journal of Consulting and Clinical Psychology, 63,* 569–578.

Borum, R. (1999a). *Increasing court jurisdiction & supervision over misdemeanor offenders with mental illness.* Tampa, FL: University of South Florida, Department of Mental Health Law & Policy, Louis de la Parte Florida Mental Health Institute.

Borum, R. (1999b). *Misdemeanor offenders with mental illness in Florida: Examining police response, court jurisdiction, and jail mental health services.* Tampa, FL: University of South Florida. Department of Mental Health Law & Policy, Louis de la Parte Florida Mental Health Institute.

Borum, R., & Modzeleski, W. (2000). *U.S.S.F. Safe School Initiative: An interim report on the prevention of targeted violence in schools.* Washington, DC: U.S. Secret Service, National Threat Assessment Center.

Burns, B. J., Hoagwood, K., & Mrazek, P. J. (1999). Effective treatment for mental disorders in children and adolescents. *Clinical Child and Family Psychology Review, 2,* 199–254.

Butts, J. A., & Barton, W. H. (1995). In-home programs for juvenile delinquents. In I. M. Schwartz & P. AuClaire (Eds.), *Home-based services for troubled children* (pp. 131–157). Lincoln: University of Nebraska Press.

Catalano, R. F., Loeber, R., & McKinney, K. C. (1999, October). School and community interventions to prevent serious and violent offending. *OJJDP Juvenile Justice Bulletin.*

Center for the Prevention of School Violence. (1998). The school as "the beat": Law enforcement officers in schools. *CPSV Research Bulletin, 1,* 1–5.

Chaiken, M. R. (1998). *Kids, cops, and communities.* Washington, DC: National Institute of Justice.

Clear, T. R., & Karp, D. R. (2000, October). Toward the ideal of community justice. *National Institute of Justice Journal,* 20–28.

Cocozza, J. J., & Skowyra, K. R. (2000). Youth with mental disorders: Issues and emerging responses. *Juvenile Justice, 7,* 3–13.

Coolbaugh, K., & Hansel, C. J. (2000, March). The comprehensive strategy: Lessons learned from pilot studies. *OJJDP Juvenile Justice Bulletin,* 1–12.

Coordinating Council of Juvenile Justice and Delinquency Prevention. (1996). *Combating violence and delinquency: The national juvenile justice action plan.* Washington, DC: U.S. Department of Justice, Office of Juvenile Justice and Delinquency Prevention.

Davis, R. C., & Mateu-Gelabert, P. (2000, July). Effective police management affects citizen perceptions. *National Institute of Justice Journal,* 24–25.

Deane, M. W., Steadman, H. J., Borum, R., Veysey, B. M., & Morrissey, J. P. (1999). Emerging partnerships between mental health and law enforcement. *Psychiatric Services, 50,* 99–101.

Dodge, K. A. (1993). Social-cognitive mechanisms in the development of conduct disorder and depression. *Annual Review of Psychology, 44,* 559–584.

Edleson, J. L. (1999). Children's witnessing of adult domestic violence. *Journal of Interpersonal Violence, 14,* 839–871.

Fagan, J. (1991). Community-based treatment for mentally disordered juvenile offenders. *Journal of Clinical Child Psychology, 20,* 42–50.

Fischer, L., & Sorenson, G. P. (1996). *School law for counselors, psychologists, and social workers.* White Plains, NY: Longman.

Flisher, A. J., Kramer, R. A., Grosser, R. C., Alegria, M., Bird, H. R., Bourdon, K. H., Goodman, S. H., Greenwald, S., Horwitz, S. M., Moore, R. E., Narrow, W. E., & Hoven, C. W. (1997). Correlates of unmet need for mental health services by children and adolescents. *Psychological Medicine, 27,* 1145–1154.

Friedman, R. M., & Burns, B. J. (1996). The evaluation of the Fort Bragg Demonstration Project: An alternative interpretation of the findings. *Journal of Mental Health Administration, 23.*

Gamache, D. J., Edleson, J. L., & Schock, M. D. (1988). Coordinated police, judicial, and social service response to women battering: A multiple-baseline evaluation across three communities. In G. Hotaling (Ed.), *Coping with family violence: Research and police perspectives.* Thousand Oaks, CA: Sage Publications.

Goldstein, H. (1987). Toward community-oriented policing: Potential, basic requirements and threshold questions. *Crime & Delinquency, 33,* 6–30.

Gorman-Smith, D., & Tolan, P. (1998). The role of exposure to community violence and developmental problems among inner-city youth. *Development and Psychopathology, 10,* 101–116.

Grisso, T. (2000). The changing face of juvenile justice. *Psychiatric Services, 51,* 425–426, 438.

Group for the Advancement of Psychiatry Committee on Preventive Psychiatry. (1999). Violent behavior in children and youth: Preventive intervention from a psychiatric perspective. *Journal of the American Academy of Child and Adolescent Psychiatry, 38,* 235–241.

Groves, B. M. (1999). Mental health services for children who witness domestic violence. *The Future of Children, 9,* 122–132.

Hawkins, J. D., Herrenkohl, T., Farrington, D. P., Brewer, D., Catalano, R. F., & Harachi, T. W. (1998). A review of predictors of youth violence. In R. Loeber & D. P. Farrington (Eds.), *Serious and violent juvenile offenders: Risk factors and successful interventions.* Thousand Oaks, CA: Sage Publications.

Henggeler, S. W., Melton, G. B., & Smith, L. A. (1992). Family preservation using multisystemic therapy: An effective alternative to incarcerating serious juvenile offenders. *Journal of Consulting and Clinical Psychology, 60,* 953–961.

Henggeler, S. W., Rowland, M. D., Randall, J., Ward, D. M., Pickrel, S. G., Cunningham, P. B., Miller, S. L., Edwards, J., Zealburg, J. J., Hand, L. D., & Santos, A. B. (1999). Home-based multisystemic therapy as an alternative to the hospitalization of youths in psychiatric crisis: Clinical outcomes. *Journal of the American Academy of Child and Adolescent Psychiatry, 38,* 1–9.

Henggeler, S. W., Schoenwald, S. K., Borduin, C. M., Rowland, M. D., & Cunningham, P. B. (1998). *Multisystemic treatment of antisocial behavior in children and adolescents.* New York: Guilford Press.

Holsinger, A. M., & Latessa, E. J. (1999). An empirical evaluation of a sanction continuum: Pathways through the juvenile justice system. *Journal of Criminal Justice, 27,* 155–172.

Hopkins, N., Hewstone, M., & Hanzi, A. (1992). Police-schools liaison and young people's image of the police: An intervention evaluation. *British Journal of Psychology, 83,* 221–231.

Huizinga, D., & Jakob-Chien, C. (1998). The contemporaneous co-occurrence of serious and violent juvenile offending and other problem behaviors. In R. Loeber & D. P. Farrington (Eds.), *Serious and violent juvenile offenders: Risk factors and successful interventions.* Thousand Oaks, CA: Sage Publications.

Huizinga, D., Loeber, R., Thornberry, T. P., & Cothern, L. (2000, November). Co-occurrence of delinquency and other problem behaviors. *OJJDP Juvenile Justice Bulletin.*

Hurst, Y. G., & Frank, J. (2000). How kids view cops: The nature of juvenile attitudes toward the police. *Journal of Criminal Justice, 28,* 189–202.

Kazdin, A. E., & Wassell, G. (2000). Therapeutic changes in children, parents, and families resulting from treatment of children with conduct problems. *Journal of the American Academy of Child and Adolescent Psychiatry, 39,* 414–420.

Lipsey, M. W., & Derzon, J. H. (1998). Predictors of violent or serious delinquency in adolescence and early adulthood. In R. Loeber & D. P. Farrington (Eds.), *Serious and violent juvenile offenders: Risk factors and successful interventions.* Thousand Oaks, CA: Sage Publications.

Lipsey, M. W., & Wilson, D. B. (1998). Effective interventions for serious juvenile offenders. In R. Loeber & D. P. Farrington (Eds.), *Serious and violent juvenile offenders: Risk factors and successful interventions.* Thousand Oaks, CA: Sage Publications.

Lipsey, M. W., Wilson, D. B., & Cothern, L. (2000). *Effective intervention for serious juvenile offenders.* Washington, DC: U.S. Department of Justice, Office of Juvenile Justice and Delinquency Prevention.

Marans, S., & Adelman, A. (1997). Experiencing violence in a developmental context. In J. Osofsky (Ed.), *Children in a violent society.* New York: Guilford Press.

Marans, S., Adnopoz, J., Berkman, M., Esserman, D., MacDonald, D., Nagler, S., Randall, R., Schaefer, M., & Wearing, M. (1995). *The police-mental health partnership: A community-based response to urban violence.* New Haven, CT: Yale University Press.

Marans, S., & Berkman, M. (1997, March). Child development–community policing: Partnership in a climate of violence. *OJJDP Juvenile Justice Bulletin.*

Marans, S., Berkowitz, S. J., & Cohen, D. J. (1998). Police and mental health professionals: Collaborative responses to the impact of violence on children and families. *Child and Adolescent Psychiatric Clinics of North America, 7*(3), 635–651.

Marans, S., Murphy, R. A., & Berkowitz, S. J. (2002). Police-mental health responses to children exposed to violence: The Child Development Community Policing Program. In M. Lewis (Ed.), *Comprehensive textbook of child and adolescent psychiatry.* Baltimore: Williams & Wilkins.

Marans, S., & Schaefer, M. (1998). Community policing, schools, and mental health: The challenge of collaboration. In D. S. Elliott, B. A. Hamburg, & K. R. Williams (Eds.), *Violence in American schools* (pp. 312–347). New York: Cambridge University Press.

Mazza, J. J., & Reynolds, W. M. (1999). Exposure to violence in young inner-city adolescents:

Relationships with suicidal ideation, depression, and PTSD symptomatology. *Journal of Abnormal Child Psychology, 27,* 203–213.

McCord, J. (1999). Interventions: Punishment, diversion, and alternative routes to crime prevention. In A. K. Hess & I. B. Weiner (Eds.), *The handbook of forensic psychology* (pp. 559–579). New York: John Wiley & Sons.

Miller, L. S., Wasserman, G. A., Neugebauer, R., Gorman-Smith, D., & Kamboukos, D. (1999). Witnessed community violence and antisocial behavior in high-risk, urban boys. *Journal of Clinical Child Psychology, 28,* 2–11.

Moffitt, T. E. (1993). Adolescence-limited and life-course-persistent antisocial behavior: A developmental taxonomy. *Psychological Review, 100,* 674–701.

Murphy, R. A. (2001). Community psychiatric collaborations with juvenile justice and law enforcement. In C. Newman, C. Liberton, K. Kutash, & R. M. Friedman (Eds.), *The 13th annual research conference proceedings, a system of care for children's mental health: Expanding the research base* (pp. 256–258). Tampa, FL: University of South Florida, Louis de la Parte Florida Mental Health Institute, Research and Training Center for Children's Mental Health.

Newgass, S., & Schonfeld, D. J. (2000). School crisis intervention, crisis prevention, and crisis response. In A. R. Roberts (Ed.), *Crisis intervention handbook: Assessment, treatment, and research* (pp. 209–228). New York: Oxford University Press.

Osofsky, J. (1995). The effects of exposure to violence on young children. *American Psychologist, 50,* 782–788.

Patterson, G. R., Forgatch, M. S., Yoerger, K. L., & Stoolmiller, M. (1998). Variables that initiate and maintain an early-onset trajectory for juvenile offending. *Development and Psychopathology, 10,* 531–547.

Pumariega, A. J., Atkins, D. L., Rogers, K., Montgomery, L., Nybro, C., Caesar, R., & Millus, D. (1999). Mental health and incarcerated youth: II. Service utilization. *Journal of Child & Family Studies, 8,* 205–215.

Richters, J. E., & Martinez, P. (1993). The NIMH community violence project: I. Children as victims of and witnesses to violence. *Psychiatry, 56,* 7–21.

Ringwalt, C., Greene, J., Ennett, S., Iachan, R., Clayton, R. R., & Leukefeld, C. G. (1994). *Past and future directions for the DARE program: An evaluation review.* Washington, DC: National Institute of Justice.

Roth, J. A., & Ryan, J. F. (2000). *The COPS program after 4 years—National evaluation.* Washington, DC: National Institute of Justice.

Roush, D. W. (1996). *Desktop guide to good juvenile detention practice.* Washington, DC: U.S. Department of Justice, Office of Juvenile Justice and Delinquency Prevention.

Saxe, L., & Cross, T. P. (1997). Interpreting the Fort Bragg Children's Mental Health Demonstration Project: The cup is half full. *American Psychologist, 52,* 553–556.

Scahill, M. C. (2000, November). Juvenile delinquency probation caseload, 1988–1997. *OJJDP Fact Sheet.*

Scholte, E. M. (1992). Identification of children at risk at the police station and the prevention of delinquency. *Psychiatry, 55,* 354–369.

Schonfeld, D. J. (1989). Crisis intervention for bereavement support: A model of intervention in the children's school. *Clinical Pediatrics, 28,* 27–33.

Schonfeld, D. J., & Kline, M. (1994). School-based crisis intervention: A role for pediatricians. *Current Problems in Pediatrics, 24,* 48–54.

Schwab-Stone, M. E., Ayers, T. S., Kaprow, W., Voyce, C., Barone, C., Shriver, T., & Weissberg, R. P. (1995). No safe haven: A study of violence exposure in an urban community. *Journal of the American Academy of Child and Adolescent Psychiatry, 34,* 1343–1352.

Schwab-Stone, M. E., Chen, C., Greenberger, E., Silver, D., Lichtman, J., & Voyce, C. (1999). No safe haven: II. The effects of violence exposure on urban youth. *Journal of the American Academy of Child and Adolescent Psychiatry, 38,* 359–367.

Scott, C. L. (1999). Forensic psychiatry: Juvenile violence. *Psychiatric Clinics of North America, 22,* 72–83.

Sherman, L. W., Gottfredson, D. C., MacKenzie, D. L., Eck, J., Reuter, P., & Bushway, S. D. (1998). *Preventing crime: What works, what doesn't, what's promising.* Washington, D.C.: National Institute of Justice.

Snyder, H. N., & Sickmund, M. (1999). *Juvenile offenders and victims: 1999 national report.* Washington, DC: U.S. Department of Justice, Office of Juvenile Justice and Delinquency Prevention.

Steiner, H., Garcia, I., & Matthews, Z. (1997). Posttraumatic stress disorder in incarcerated juvenile delinquents. *Journal of the American Academy of Child and Adolescent Psychiatry, 36,* 357–365.

St. Pierre, R. G., & Layzer, J. I. (1998). *Improving the life chances of children in poverty: Assumptions and what we have learned.* Ann Arbor, MI: Society for Research in Child Development.

Swartz, M. S., Swanson, J. W., Wagner, H. R., Burns, B. J., Hiday, V. A., & Borum, R. (1999). Can involuntary commitment reduce hospital recidivism?: Findings from a randomized trial with severely mentally ill individuals. *American Journal of Psychiatry, 156,* 1968–1975.

Tate, D. C., Reppucci, N. D., & Mulvey, E. P. (1995). Violent juvenile delinquents: Treatment effectiveness and implications for future action. *American Psychologist, 50,* 777–781.

Tebes, J. K., Adnopoz, J. A., Canning, J. J., Kaufman, J. S., Racusin, G. R., & Nagler, S. (1996). *Family support for children of mentally ill parents: Intervention manual.* New Haven, CT: Yale University School of Medicine.

Teplin, L. A. (2000, July). Keeping the peace: Police discretion and mentally ill persons. *National Institute of Justice Journal, 8–15.*

Thomas, W. J., & Stubbe, D. E. (1996, Fall). A comparison of correctional and mental health referrals in the juvenile court. *The Journal of Psychiatry and Law,* 379–400.

Thurman, Q. C. (1995). Community policing: The police as a community resource. In P. Adams & K. Nelson (Eds.), *Reinventing human services: Community and family centered practice* (pp. 175–187). New York: Aldene de Gruyter.

Wandersman, A., & Nation, M. (1998). Urban neighborhoods and mental health: Psychological contributions to understanding toxicity, resilience, and interventions. *American Psychologist, 53,* 647–656.

Weisz, J. R., Martin, S. L., Walter, B. R., & Fernandez, G. A. (1991). Differential prediction of young adult arrests for property and personal crimes: Findings of a cohort follow-up study of violent boys from North Carolina's Willie M program. *Journal of Child Psychology and Psychiatry and Allied Disciplines, 32,* 783–792.

Widom, C. S. (1999). Posttraumatic stress disorder in abused and neglected children grown up. *American Journal of Psychiatry, 156,* 1223–1229.

Widom, K. S. (1998). Child abuse, neglect, and witnessing violence. In D. M. Stoff, J. Breiling, & J. D. Maser (Eds.), *Handbook of antisocial behavior* (pp. 159–170). New York: John Wiley & Sons.

Woolston, J. L., Berkowitz, S. J., Schaefer, M. C., & Adnopoz, J. A. (1998). Intensive, integrated, in-home psychiatric services: The catalyst to enhancing outpatient intervention. *Child and Adolescent Psychiatric Clinics of North America, 7,* 615–633.

Zhao, J., & Thurman, Q. C. (1997). Community policing: Where are we now? *Crime & Delinquency, 43,* 345–358.

Chapter 20

SERIOUS EMOTIONAL DISTURBANCE: WORKING WITH FAMILIES

MARSALI HANSEN, ANN LITZELMAN, AND BEATRICE R. SALTER

Working with the families of children with serious emotional disturbance (SED) in the context of working with the child is not a new idea. In the early 1900s in the United States, the child guidance movement flourished and social services were often provided in the home (Lourie, 2000). Subsequently, emerging influences of psychotherapy such as psychoanalysis, psychiatry, and individual psychotherapy caused a shift from the focus on the family in both the setting of services and the orientation to children's problems (Woods, 1988). Individuals began to be served in hospitals and outpatient clinics as the person's inner experience became more important than social or environmental factors in understanding emotional problems.

Beginning in the 1960s, family therapy as a modality developed as a number of different ideas converged, including study and interventions with groups, anthropological conceptualizations and observations, and psychodynamic perspectives of parent–child relationships (Goldenberg & Goldenberg, 1996). Within the last 40 years, acceptance of family therapy as a modality has increased dramatically, and working with families has become an accepted component of most child outpatient and inpatient settings. This chapter focuses on new developments in working with families of children with SED, highlights some of the most promising approaches, and suggests several challenges, including culturally competent service delivery, that face individuals committed to the inclusion of evidence-based approaches and new developments in service delivery into their work with children with SED and their families.

Controversy continues to surround the use of family therapy in the treatment of children with SED. Much of the early work, although intended to be systemic, explored parental contributions to and the perceived causes of the child's disturbance, a perspective that was easily practiced when the parent brought the child to treatment and both were present at the start of therapy. Mental health professionals presented themselves as experts to families and presented well-thought-out solutions to parents. These interventions often implied, intentionally or unintentionally, that the parents contributed to or were accountable for their child's problems. In addition, such professionals expressed their opinions to colleagues in other decision-making settings such as courts and schools.

Other similar clinical approaches by therapists have increased the reluctance of parents to participate in their child's treatment as well as their expectation that solutions will be generated by the therapist. For example, when the practitioner specifically seeks to increase parental resourcefulness, the parent may respectfully await the therapist's wisdom. Pejorative terminology (e.g., "dysfunctional families," "resistance," "noncompliant families") has tended to dominate professional and public literature (Hansen, 1998). Cultural factors and lack of cultural competence compound these difficulties and are described in more detail later in this chapter as one of the major challenges facing the field. Family therapy, particularly family therapy that focuses on the disturbance of the child, has evolved from its earlier roots, but these concerns remain.

Therapeutic work with families has expanded to include larger systems such as schools and social and environmental contexts (Broffenbrenner, 1979). In the 1960s, the early work of Auerswald (1968), Aponte (1976), and others addressed the needs of the family within the context of larger systems. This work was somewhat peripheral to the expanding use of family therapy that intensified in the 1970s and 1980s, resulting in the development of major training centers and specific theoretical orientations within the family systems framework. However, Imber-Black's (1988) work built on these early efforts and expanded to focus on the larger systems. Most recently, Mary Pipher's (1996) popular work has intensified the focus of attention on families within the context of their communities and challenged the perpetuation of the family as the cause of the child's problem:

> Families need to be supported, affirmed, protected and validated. . . . The therapist's job becomes connecting people—parents and children, families and extended families, parents and other parents and families to schools and communities. . . . The new millennium will be about restoring community and rebuilding the infrastructure of our families. (p. 32)

Her work is accessible to a popular audience and truly focuses on the needs of families raising children in a complex society. However, both Pipher's and Imber-Black's efforts have targeted the practice of clinicians in the private sector and have not yet incorporated advances in services for the families of children with SED, many of whom must interact with multiple child-serving systems in the public sector and have major environmental concerns.

DEVELOPMENTS IN FAMILY THERAPY

Parent advocacy has promoted a partnership model of family involvement (Simpson, Koroloff, Friesen, & Gac, (1999). Such an approach differs significantly from traditional therapeutic models in that both the family and the therapist contribute expertise to the process. Partnerships with the families of children with SED within service delivery models have followed a parallel course to the practice of family therapy, but until recently have not been integrated into the therapeutic efforts with families (Hansen, Anderson, Marsh, Harbaugh, & Gray, 1999), and the emphasis has been largely on service provision rather than treatment (Osher, deFur, Nava, Spencer, & Toth-Dennis, 1998; Simpson et al., 1999). The expansion of families as partners in service delivery can be traced to the development of the Child and Adolescent Service System Program (CASSP) and, subsequently, systems of care.

In 1982, Jane Knitzer published her well-known monograph, *Unclaimed Children* (reviewed in Chapter 7), which highlighted the multisystemic context of children with SED and their families (Knitzer, 1982). Subsequent literature proposed a significant new role for families within the context of larger systems and described this specific approach as *systems of care* (Stroul & Friedman, 1986). As is noted in Chapter 7, the new approach detailed a partnership between families and service providers that included family representatives at all levels of service delivery. Lourie (2000) has praised these efforts as a return to the early turn-of-the-century child guidance center work on integrated services.

In recent years, partnerships between clinicians and family members and among larger systems and natural supports have flourished. *Wraparound,* an off-site model for partnering with families and coordinating provision of services, exists in most states and communities throughout the country and is becoming an increasingly refined model with specific characteristics and supported by research (Burns & Goldman, 1998). However, specific treatment approaches for working with families within this perspective are only recently being explored, and therapist involvement and therapeutic interventions may or may not be recognized as central components.

One of the more recent advances in family therapy is that of seeing the family in the home, and there appear to be many advantages to seeing a family in an off-site location, principally at the family's own residence. For example, it is usually more convenient for the family; families with lower incomes, single-parent families, or those with high environmental stressors sometimes have difficulty keeping office appointments. These families often have transportation difficulties, experience restraints due to employment, or lack the organizational and financial resources to get all members of the family together and on time for a weekly session in an office that may be on the other side of town (Woods, 1988).

In addition, in-home therapy presents the family in a different light than an office setting. In the office, the family members treat the therapist with deference and lose some of their spontaneity, or they put the best face on the family when coming into a professional office. When the worker goes into the home, there are many clues to help unravel the nature of the family's distress. During therapy in the home, homebound or other extended members of the family who can be influential and might not otherwise attend a session can be seen. The physical characteristics of the home, special items and keepsakes, and who sits where are immediately apparent to the therapist (Speck, 1964; Woods, 1998).

Another advantage is that home-based therapy can be seen as a signal that the therapist truly wants to join the family. This helps to counteract the family's perception, particularly if the therapist is of a different background, that he or she does not really understand their situation (Woods, 1988). Finally, Friedman (1962) states that "The transfer value of therapy conducted 'in vivo' in the real milieu of the family and home is greater than that of psychotherapy done in the socially isolated context of office or hospital" (p. 133).

On the other hand, in-home therapy presents a number of challenges. The therapist going into a home is a reversal of roles—the family is in its natural environment and comfortable, and the therapist is a guest in the home (Speck, 1964). The in-home setting for therapy also delivers the message that the entire family is being assisted and that the visitor (the therapist) is the one who needs to adapt (Speck, 1964). The therapist must remain apart from family patterns, allowing these patterns to unfold and reveal themselves before intervening (Woods, 1988). Maintaining a therapeutic position while immersed in another's environment (which can be chaotic) is difficult. Speck suggests that two therapists go together into a home. His plan would be for one therapist to join with the identified patient and focus the work on the entire family, while the other one either remains neutral or joins with the rest of the family. Another challenge is that the intervention is immediate, so that when an intervention does not work, the therapist is present and has to be accountable for it (Woods, 1988).

Other challenges are more logistical in nature. Often the therapist does not live in the same neighborhood as the family and may feel uncomfortable going into some neighborhoods, either during the day or at night. There are also financial challenges. Outpatient therapists today who are accountable for billable hours have difficulty finding time to venture outside the office, even when they recognize the value of doing so. In addition, there is the cost to the agency of travel time on the part of the therapist, especially in rural areas.

PROMISING APPROACHES

The current in-home service model for working with families and larger systems originated in the child welfare system. According to Nelson and Landsman (1992), these services began in child welfare agencies as early as 1949, but expanded after the Adoption Assistance and Child Welfare Act of 1980. This federal law stated that all child welfare agencies must show that they are making "reasonable efforts" to prevent out-of-home placement in order to continue to receive funds for child welfare services (Nelson & Landsman, 1992). Schoenwald and Henggeler (1997) describe these family preservation services as

> (a) delivered in the home; (b) intense (ranging from 2 to 15 hours per week); (c) flexible (workers are generally available 24 hours per day, 7 days a week); (d) time-limited (4–6 weeks to 4–6 months); and (d) characterized by low caseloads (2 to 10 families per worker). (p. 122)

Such programs in the child welfare arena have been categorized into three models by Nelson, Landsman, and Deutelbaum (1990): the *crisis intervention model,* the *home-based model,* and the *family treatment model.*

The Crisis Intervention Model

Briefly, the crisis intervention model is based on the perspective that families are receptive to change when in a state of crisis. Social learning theory and behavior modification are most frequently the theoretical framework of the interventions with families (Nelson & Landsman, 1992). Providing concrete and daily life assistance (transportation, child care, shopping, cleaning, etc.) is very important to this model. In comparing three studies of these models, Nelson et al. (1990) found that crisis intervention services were the briefest of the three, and crisis intervention therapists also have the lowest caseloads at any given time.

The Home-Based Model

The home-based model is focused on family systems interventions; in addition to therapy, daily life assistance is provided to the parents (Nelson & Landsman, 1992). Schoenwald and Henggeler (1997) state that these programs include behavioral interventions, such as parent training, and daily life services that are provided by the therapist. The home-based Model is most often provided for a longer period of time than the other two models and has the lowest average annual caseload (Nelson et al., 1990).

The Family Treatment Model

The third model, family treatment, emphasizes family systems therapeutic interventions as well, but has a lower involvement in the provision of daily life services (Nelson & Landsman, 1992). Case managers rather than therapists provide these ancillary services (Schoenwald & Henggeler, 1997). The family treatment model appears to be less intensive, has the highest caseload, and some cases are treated in the office (Nelson et al., 1990).

In summarizing the three models, Henggeler et al. (1999) stated:

> The overall objective of crisis intervention and home-based programs is to stabilize critical situations until additional services can be provided. In contrast, intensive family treatment programs are designed to alter family functioning sufficiently to alleviate the need for additional services and such programs tend to emphasize therapeutic intervention over the provision of concrete services. (p. 231)

Evaluation of the effectiveness of these models suggests that there are three generations of studies, each with increasing levels of sophistication in design (Nelson & Landsman 1992). The first-generation studies involved small numbers of cases, did not have control groups or outcome measures related to placement and cost saving, were posttest-only studies, and are described as nonexperimental program evaluations (Nelson & Landsman, 1992; Schoenwald & Henggeler, 1997). The second-generation studies are largely descriptive, using larger numbers of cases and multiple outcomes, and include quasi-experimental designs (Nelson & Landsman, 1992). Some of these studies include equivalent (or matched) comparison groups and some do not (Schoenwald & Henggeler, 1997).

> Essentially, findings of the few quasi-experimental studies that have not been characterized by serious methodological flaws have failed to support the effectiveness of family preservation in preventing placement, regardless of the population (child welfare or combinations of child welfare, juvenile justice, and mental health) targeted for services. (p. 125)

Most of the research done thus far is in these first two groups or generations of studies (Nelson & Landsman, 1992; Schoenwald & Henggeler, 1997). Few of these studies include randomly assigned control groups (which are included in Nelson and Landsman's third-generation studies), indicating there is little irrefutable evidence thus far to suggest that family preservation services are successful (Schoenwald & Henggeler, 1997). Professionals need to continue to be cognizant of the methodological difficulties with this research before drawing conclusions about the effectiveness of family preservation services, particularly when applying the model to families of children with SED.

Additional cautions should be kept in mind when applying the family preservation model to children with SED. First, other promising services might remain unfunded while financial resources are directed into this model, even though its effectiveness in children with SED is yet unproven (Cunningham, Henggeler, Brondino, & Pickrel, 1999). Lambert, Salzer, and Bickman (1998) also warned that customer satisfaction with developing mental health services is not the same as improved clinical outcomes. A second major concern with family preservation models is that of internal validity. While the models may sound plausible, they are not built solidly on a foundation of the causes and correlates of the problems being treated. For example, the family preservation model was developed to prevent placement of children served by child welfare agencies. Schoenwald and Henggeler (1997) note that although the crisis intervention and home-based models acknowledge the multiproblem aspects of the families served, the interventions are not yet based on sufficient empirical research detailing the contributing factors to yield reliable outcomes. They refer to the extensive psychological literature on the causes of delinquency and substance abuse and note that most of the literature acknowledges that serious childhood problems are multidetermined and multidimensional. They argue that the population served must be well defined and the model of treatment developed specific to the many relevant determinants of that population.

Although some treatment approaches have been shown effective in university-based research, a third major concern is the transfer of interventions to the community settings—effective transfer cannot be assumed. Community clinicians serve a more severe clinical population, see more clients, receive less training and supervision, and use more eclectic approaches than are found in university-based studies (Weisz, Donenberg, Han, & Weiss, 1995). Hence, any model found effective in a university setting would need to be evaluated in the community before the theory is adopted by real-life programs and treatment is implemented according to the model.

Moving beyond the family preservation model in the direction of working with families with SED is multisystemic therapy (MST), developed by Henggeler and colleagues. They have worked extensively with youth who are delinquent and have substance abuse problems as well as with adolescents who are sexual offenders (Henggeler, Schoenwald, Pickrel, Rowland, & Santos, 1994; Santos, Henggeler, Burns, Arana, & Meisler, 1995). Henggeler and associates describe MST as a hybrid extension of the earlier home-based model and family treatment model that is based on both broad and specific theoretical concepts (Henggeler et al., 1994; Schoenwald & Henggeler, 1997). The foundation for MST includes Bronfenbrenner's (1979) theory of social ecology—a theory that has been widely applied to systems-of-care interventions. The child develops not only in the context of intrapersonal factors (both biological and cognitive), but also in the context of interpersonal factors, including the family, peer, neighborhood, and school systems within which the child functions (Bronfenbrenner, 1979; Schoenwald & Henggeler, 1997). A second foundation of MST is family systems theory, especially the work of Salvador Minuchin and Jay Haley. This is reflected in the emphasis on targeting factors (either within or between systems) that maintain the identified problems, as well as focusing on problem solving with a current and action orientation. Behavioral parent training and cognitive behavioral therapy are also incorporated as interventions as part of the broad conceptual base (Henggeler et al., 1994).

Research findings on the predictive factors on the development of adolescent antisocial behavior support the use of this theoretically integrated model, and these findings represent some of the specific theoretical base of MST. The predictive factors include family dynamics such as conflict, discipline, and emotional support; associations with peers with deviant behavior; problems at school, whether because of poor family–school relationships or poor performance academically and socially; and neighborhood issues such as mobility and crime (Schoenwald & Henggeler, 1997). Another specific underpinning is the notion that engagement of the youth and the family is the responsibility of the clinician and that the lack of engagement not be perceived as the result of resistance or motivational deficits on the part of the family (Cunningham & Henggeler, 1999).

To ensure the fidelity of the model, there are extensive training and supervision requirements for MST. The model requires a commitment from the program director and a degree of administrative flexibility for things such as flextime, increased clinical supervision, work routines, and so on. Policy and financial support are needed from the state, as is a state-level commitment to interagency collaboration (Santos et al., 1995). Such requirements may be staggering for clinicians and administrators who are used to providing traditional mental health services. Santos et al. (1995) challenge the traditional mental health system for children in two areas. First, they state that the research strongly indicates that serious clinical problems for youth are multidetermined, yet traditional services address only a few of the causes. Second, they note that traditional services are rarely offered in the youth's natural environment. Young people in a residential placement often receive services only at the placement site and not in the home environment to which they will return. Santos et al. (1995) also report that public mental health outpatient settings have high no-show rates, which makes it difficult to deliver effective treatment in the youth's home setting.

Henggeler and associates have conducted extensive research to evaluate the effectiveness of MST, using randomly assigned control groups. They have identified repeat offending as well as the seriousness of the new offense, reports of problem or criminal behaviors by adolescents, parents and teachers, out-of-home placements, and the cost of services as the ultimate outcome variables. They go on to identify instrumental outcome variables as intermediate goals and these include improved family relationships, more monitoring of activities by parents, movement toward involvement with positive peers and away from deviant peers, improved academic performance, and more social support for families (Santos et al., 1995).

Henggeler has dealt primarily with adolescents who are adjudicated. Although these populations are included among youth who experience SED (due to comorbidity), intensive research on youth with SED is still in the formative stages. A pilot study compared the use of MST as an alternative to psychiatric hospitalization for 26 youth

(Henggeler, Rowland, et al., 1997). These initial findings show that many more clinical resources were needed with the SED population than with the juvenile justice population, including increases in the availability of staff and supervision, as well as training time to address the high level of stress on the staff. Burnout of mental health staff was a specific concern. As a result, services for the SED population will be considerably more expensive than programs for juvenile justice populations, but are still judged to be less expensive than inpatient hospitalization. In addition, the availability of quality shelters and respite therapeutic foster homes is a major concern; such services needed to be developed within the communities to make the pilot project work. Hence, extensive collaboration between the program and community agencies is essential to make MST a viable option to youth with SED.

Two years later, a larger study followed 116 youth approved for emergency psychiatric hospitalization who were randomly assigned to either an inpatient unit or MST. Remarkably, 56 of the 57 families assigned to receive MST completed their treatment, with an average of 123 days of service and an average of 97.1 direct contact hours, far more than the 40 to 60 service hours usually found in MST studies (Henggeler et al., 1999; Santos et al., 1995). Even with this intensive and well-developed model, 44% of the youth receiving MST were hospitalized at some point for an average of 3.8 days. The authors concluded that hospitalization remains a critical component of services for treating children with SED, even when quality intensive family-based services are available. "Overall, youths in the MST condition experienced a 72 percent decrease in days hospitalized and a 50 percent decrease in days in other out-of-home placements in comparison with their hospitalized counterparts" (Henggeler et al., 1999, pp. 1334–1335).

Medication was used often in both groups. Those in the MST group demonstrated reduced externalizing symptoms compared to the hospital group. The youth who were hospitalized reported higher self-esteem than did the MST youth by the end of treatment. The authors felt that this resulted from traditional services placing more emphasis on individual change, whereas MST placed more emphasis on caregiver, structure, and social change. Another interpretation is that the study demonstrated that youth need interpersonal connections throughout treatment to make behavioral changes. Youth in the MST group spent significantly more days in school than the other group.

This study of MST as an alternative to hospitalization (Henggeler et al., 1999) is important because it demonstrates that different groups of youth (those with SED versus those who are adjudicated) and their families have different treatment needs. In addition, this study underscores the need for a continuum of care that includes other traditional mental health services (inpatient hospitalization and individual counseling) and cross-systems collaboration.

Another promising approach is the Family-Based Mental Health Services model in Pennsylvania. The national focus on CASSP and systems of care resulted in many statewide efforts, including the development of new service and treatment models in Pennsylvania (Lindblad-Goldberg, Dore, & Stern, 1998). A unique partnership between the state's policy office and Philadelphia Child Guidance Center (PCGC), an internationally recognized family therapy training institute, was established, resulting in the development and delivery of an integrated family treatment approach specific to children with SED. Pennsylvania's Family-Based Mental Health Services (FBMHS) were created based on an expansion of the ecosystemic model of family therapy practiced by PCGC. Marion Lindblad-Goldberg, who was then the director of the Family Therapy Training Center at PCGC, and Lenora Stern, then the statewide CASSP coordinator, collaborated to develop and implement a statewide, theoretically based model of family therapy that would specifically treat children and adolescents at risk for out-of-home placement due to psychiatric disturbances. Martha Dore served as the researcher who assisted in the development of a model that could be validated and replicated. The program has served over 35,000 families in a 10-year period and trained 600 staff persons. Research has followed nearly 2,000 families through a 1-year follow-up period after treatment ended (Lindblad-Goldberg et al., 1998).

Pennsylvania's model has three specific objectives for home-based services: (a) Decrease the numbers of all mental health placements of youth (including hospitalizations); (b) improve the family's ability to support a youth who has SED; and (c) improve the psychosocial functioning of all members of these families (Lindblad-Goldberg et al., 1998). As noted, the model implements ecosystemic structural family therapy and incorporates the previously detailed research on the importance of environmental factors. In this way the model resembles Henggeler's in that it used both specific and broad concepts for its framework. Lindblad-Goldberg et al. recognize the inherent vulnerability of children to SED and believe that these vulnerabilities can be increased by both familial and environmental stressors. Risks and resiliency factors are addressed with children and their families from the perspective of current research literature. In addition, emphasis is placed on natural supports, as families of children with special needs require community supports to continue to care for their children. Finally, assessment and intervention on the families' interactions with external systems is crucial.

The four key program components of FBMHS in Pennsylvania are "family support services, therapeutic intervention, case management/service coordination, and emergency crisis intervention" (Lindblad-Goldberg et al., 1998, p. 59). Family support services are funded by the state and are used in a creative and flexible manner. The case management role is the responsibility of the therapist, but the model aims to build and support the family's own ability to work effectively with other agencies. The model was designed to be implemented by therapeutic teams. Caseloads are small, with a team serving about eight families for up to 32 consecutive weeks; this time period can be lengthened if needed. Usually between 2 and 10 hours of direct service is given each week, although clinicians are available 24 hours a day, 7 days a week (Lindblad-Goldberg et al., 1998).

Extensive training and supervision is provided. Both the program directors and the staff receive a total of 54 days of training over a 3-year period, based on an understanding that therapeutic skill is built over time and with practice and that use of random workshops or conferences will not suffice. The training, given at regional sites, was originally developed by PCGC with input from the state, program directors, and staff and families. (The training is currently provided by the Philadelphia Child and Family Therapy Training Center and by Western Psychiatric Institute and Clinic.) In addition, there is specific training for supervisors. Training is both didactic and experiential, and consultation on specific cases is also provided through the training format.

The training component is a key to this model for home-based services. The authors note:

> Conducting home-based therapy with high-risk families whose children and/or adolescents exhibit severe emotional disturbances is stressful and emotionally demanding. The job requires the practitioner to have an extensive knowledge base, well-developed clinical skills, maturity, and the ability to assume a significant amount of responsibility. Typically, however, the home-based practitioner is a master's or bachelor's level clinician who has had little formal training in family theory, family therapy skills, or home-based family service practice. Often, the practitioner's supervisor lacks formal training in these areas as well. (pp. 243–244)

In the early 1990s, the state Office of Mental Health in Pennsylvania showed that:

> Only about 25 percent of children in families receiving home-based services had experienced a psychiatric inpatient placement in the year following treatment termination, as compared with 80 percent in the year prior to participating in a home-based program. In those placements that did occur, lengths of stay were shorter and placement was more likely to be deliberately planned rather than occurring as a reaction to a crisis. These data were so persuasive to legislators that funding for Pennsylvania's home-based programs was expanded rather than cut that year. (pp. 265–266)

The models of MST and FBMHS provide new approaches to longstanding concerns of families and children with SED and add to the early work of the family preservation movement. They demonstrate effective methods of off-site treatment, adhering to strict therapeutic models while offering services in community (rather than in university) settings. In addition, they specify the variations needed in supervision, training, and caseload size to support this new intervention. These models also integrate the value system begun with the CASSP movement to fully involve parents, reframe resistance as a barrier to be addressed in treatment, and initiate strong cross-system coordination efforts.

CHALLENGES

Identifying a qualified workforce to provide treatment for families of children with SED is a particular challenge (see Chapter 7). Few academic training programs combine training in systems of care with training on SED; even fewer provide training in family therapy from these combined perspectives. A subcommittee of the Children, Youth and Families Task Force of APA sought to identify commendable training programs (Meyers, Kaufman, & Goldman, 1999), but the numbers were so few that they were never published. Both the MST program and the FBMHS program have instituted their own training, not only to ensure fidelity to the model, but also to prepare a workforce in the fundamentals of ecosystemic family work. Pennsylvania's effort specifically focuses on training in fundamental family therapy skills as well as in the unique qualities of the specific model, and the state financially supports this effort because of the urgency of the need. Preparing a knowledgeable and competent workforce is a specific concern identified by both APA and the surgeon general (U.S. Department of Health and Human Services, 2000), particularly a workforce with the skills and values of both the system-of-care perspective and the major advances from the therapeutic community.

As noted earlier in this chapter, much of current family therapy training continues to focus on the interests of the private sector and has yet to stress the multisystemic collaboration needed to work with families of children with SED. With few exceptions, such as the Philadelphia Child Guidance Center and more recently the work of Diane Marsh and Carol Anderson (2000), professionals skilled in the new developments of systems of care have not been welcomed into the training forums of the majority of these family therapists. The exposure to these new approaches is just beginning; skill building and value shifts have yet to be implemented on a substantial scale.

Another challenge that is identified throughout this chapter and recognized throughout this volume is the dissemination of evidence-based practice models that have been formulated in university clinics. Much of the university-based work evaluates interventions with specific diagnoses and specifically programmed interventions. However, two key principles identified as necessary for working with children with SED are an individualized approach and a multisystemic collaborative model. As Knitzer (1982) recognized, these children and their families are involved in multiple systems, and the children have received multiple diagnoses, have had multiple therapists, and have taken multiple medications. One youth aptly stated when asked his diagnosis, "They gave me five million diagnoses," and also said regarding the medications he has taken, "If it's in the [*Physician's Desk Reference*], I've taken it" (Rabasca, 2000). The application of a university-based program that focuses on a specific diagnosis and evaluates one therapeutic intervention is particularly difficult to disseminate outside the highly controlled clinical environment. Combining the new approaches of working with families heightens the challenge. Preparing a workforce of both new practitioners and individuals currently in the field requires substantial efforts from current educators as well as leaders in the professional community. However, current research indicates that without this massive change in how families are viewed, involved, and incorporated into current treatment approaches for children with SED, the effectiveness of all services will be limited (Pires, 1997).

CULTURALLY COMPETENT SERVICE DELIVERY

The greatest challenge, perhaps, to the effective provision of community-based and home-based services, is to ensure that these services are delivered in a culturally competent manner. Demographic trends have changed the face of American society and thrust diversity issues into the forefront of every area of mental health services. In the 1980s, there was growing documentation of deficiencies in the mental health system in the United States, particularly in the service systems for children and adolescents. In 1990, the American Psychological Association issued *Guidelines for Providers of Psychological Services to Ethnic, Linguistic and Culturally Diverse Populations*. Within these guidelines is the directive that "psychologists recognize ethnicity and culture as significant parameters in understanding psychological processes" (American Psychological Association, 1990, p. 2). In 1999, the U.S. surgeon general issued an extensive report on mental health.

> This report presents clear evidence that mental health and mental illness are shaped by age, gender, race and culture as well as additional facets of diversity that can be found within all of these population groups—for example, physical disability or a person's sexual orientation. The consequences of not understanding these influences can be profoundly deleterious. (U.S. Department of Health and Human Services, 1999, p. 456)

Serious emotional disturbance is an additional complex issue that is found in all racial, ethnic, cultural, and socioeconomic groups. As articulated earlier, home-based models of family therapy present many challenges to therapists and service-delivery systems alike on an individual and systemic level. It is important to address not only the educational and experience level of the therapist, but also the person issues that come into play in every therapeutic encounter. These issues can be exacerbated by the inclusion of the therapist or helper into the family's home, where there are more indications and cues of race, culture, ethnicity, and socioeconomic level than exist in a therapist's office. When the therapist is from a different racial, ethnic, cultural, or socioeconomic group, a multitude of variables come into play. Frequently, the competence of therapists and their ability to understand the basic issues that impact the difficulties that the family faces are questioned (Aponte & Johnson, 2000; Sue & Sue, 1999). Therapy services take place within the broader societal context. Therapists and administrators must be mindful that minority group families have to be aware of realistic institutional and interpersonal threats to their personal, educational, and vocational security. It is easy to see how a poor family could assume that a seemingly middle-class therapist from a different culture does not have a basis or the experiences for truly understanding their world. When this occurs, families may be suspicious, close ranks to exclude the therapist, refuse to participate, or sabotage the therapy process in innumerable ways.

A family's responses to familial and environmental stressors are intricately linked to their racial, cultural, or ethnic identity and level of acculturation into the broader American culture (Alarcón, Foulks, & Vakkur, 1998; Aponte & Johnson, 2000). For purposes of this discussion, *race* is "a category of persons who are related by a common heredity or ancestry and who are perceived and responded to in terms of external features or traits" (Wilkinson, 1993, p. 19). *Ethnicity* refers to "shared culture and lifestyle" (Wilkinson, 1993, p. 19) or the customs, language, and social views of a particular ethnic group (Spencer, Swanson, & Cunningham, 1991). Culture as used here refers to those variable systems of meaning that are learned and shared by a group of people and passed down through generations.

Development of the therapeutic relationship is essential to any work with families, regardless of their racial, ethnic, cultural, or socioeconomic group. Sue and Zane (1997) state that recommendations to therapists to be culturally sensitive and know the culture of the client have not been particularly helpful. This admonition to therapists has frequently led to overgeneralized assessments and interventions based on the presumed cultural values of a group, regardless of their appropriateness for a particular client and family. In the 1980s and early 1990s, many believed that assessment and treatment with multicultural groups would be enhanced if racial and ethnic barriers between the client and therapist were minimized. Sue, Fujino, Hu, Takeuchi, and Zane (1991) found that racial "match[ing] failed to be a significant predictor of treatment outcome, except for Mexican Americans" (p. 539). The other groups examined in this study were African Americans, Asian Americans, and White Americans.

These findings suggest that other variables in the therapeutic relationship are at least as important as race, ethnicity, culture, or socioeconomic factors. Sue and Zane (1987) propose that credibility and giving are two factors in effective treatment that have been overlooked in working with culturally and ethnically different populations. *Credibility* is the client's perception of the therapist as an effective and trustworthy helper. *Giving* refers to the client's perception that he or she received something positive from the therapeutic encounter. The authors call this giving the client a "gift" in the form of benefit from treatment. Gifts are tangible and include factors such as symptom reduction, reassurance, skill acquisition, or goal setting. Credibility and giving have particular relevance for ethnic and cultural minority populations as they relate to basic issues of expectancy, trust, and effectiveness in therapeutic interactions. They propose that the goal of treatment is to minimize problems in credibility while maximizing gift giving. Racial, ethnic, and cultural minority clients often leave treatment early, following multiple frustrations, misunderstandings, and disappointments (Sue & Sue, 1999). For families coping with a child who has a serious emotional disturbance, these issues are even more important because their daily interactions typically involve interfacing with multiple social service and health agencies and systems. Potential complications from racial, ethnic, cultural, and socioeconomic values are further exacerbated by the presence of a serious emotional disturbance and the family's and therapist's potentially differing perceptions of the aberrant behavior. *Or* they may be exacerbated by the family's and therapist's differing perception of mental illness. Even though both the family and the therapist may recognize that there is a problem with the behaviors, their interpretations of the etiology and consequences of the behaviors can be drastically different, placing them at odds with one another. Cultural belief systems will influence how problems are conceptualized and what resolutions and treatment goals are possible within the family and community.

It is important that the helping professional entering a family's home not define the family as the problem. Madsen (1999) states that the term *multiproblem families* as typically used promotes identifying the family as the problems they are experiencing. He refers to families as *multistressed* as a means of promoting awareness of the external influences that impact families, thus keeping their identity separate and distinct from the problems. Madsen emphasizes that the way we view clients and what garners our attention in interactions begins with the language and labels that the therapist attaches to the client and the family.

Multisystemic therapy, as articulated earlier, is a family- and community-based treatment model developed by Henggeler and associates (Cunningham & Henggeler, 1999; Henggeler, 1999). Multisystemic therapy has been used and evaluated extensively with youth involved in the juvenile justice system (Henggeler, Brondino, Melton, Scherer, & Hanley, 1997). Multisystemic therapy has also been used with children and families experiencing serious clinical problems (Henggeler, 1999; Henggeler, Rowland, et al.,

1997; Henggeler, Schoenwald, & Munger, 1996; Schoenwald & Henggeler, 1999). Their studies have shown that multisystemic therapy has achieved a high rate of treatment completion with children and families experiencing serious clinical problems (Henggeler et al., 1999).

Henggeler and associates have proposed multisystemic therapy as an alternative to inpatient hospitalization and other out-of-home placements for children with serious emotional disorders. The vast numbers of projects they have undertaken have shown that the tenets of multisystemic therapy are consistent with current trends in mental health toward strength-based, child-centered, family-focused, community-based, and culturally competent services that are performed in the least restrictive environment possible (Brondino et al., 1997; Santos et al., 1995). These areas are the core principles of the Child and Adolescent Service System Program (CASSP) of the National Institute of Mental Health (Stroul & Friedman, 1986).

It is likely that the multisystemic therapy model achieves the goal of culturally relevant services because it emphasizes that building a strong therapeutic alliance with families is essential for positive outcomes. Multisystemic therapy recognizes that family members will not invest the energy necessary to achieve productive outcomes if they are not engaged and active in the treatment process (Cunningham & Henggeler, 1999; Henggeler, 1999). To this end, therapists using multisystemic therapy must earn the family's trust, thereby increasing credibility and gift giving. This model demands that the therapist or helper develop empathy for the family, employ collaborative strategies that supply the family with immediate benefits, be accountable for the outcomes of the strategies employed, and be flexible in designing interventions. For the therapeutic interaction to be successful, racial, ethnic, cultural, and socioeconomic variables must be taken into consideration, increasing the efficacy for individual families. Working within the context of a treatment team helps the therapist to remain personally and professionally grounded within this process.

It is exciting that empirically based treatment approaches are emerging that have relevance to diverse populations of children and families. Consistent with the move toward innovative models of mental health services for children and their families, the work of Henggeler (1999), Marsh (2001), Boyd-Franklin and Bry (2000), and Madsen (1999) emphasizes treatments in the child's and family's natural environment that are family-focused and strength-based. A strength-based approach highlights and honors the racial, ethnic, and cultural factors within a family that mediate the impact of mental illness in a family member. This approach also encourages the helping professional to identify resilience factors within the culture and the environment for the particular child and family in the process of coping with mental illness.

CONCLUSION

Throughout the current chapter, we have attempted to identify specific models that show particular promise for working with families of children with SED. The work of both Henggeler and associates and of Lindblad-Goldberg and associates incorporates the specific needs of the children with the needs and resources of the family and larger community. Although both of these programs are implemented on a large and programmatic scale, much can abstracted and applied by the individual clinician or educator. First and foremost, the needs and characteristics of children with SED are complex, as are the needs and resources of their families and communities. One size does not fit all, and these families require more than traditional office-based interventions. However, characteristics identified from the research on these large-scale efforts are directly applicable to individual interventions and in particular to the preparation of the current and future workforce. These new developments have significant implications for theory, practice, and research in the area of SED, including the importance of true partnerships with families, collaboration with systems both formal and informal, interventions outside the office, application of recognized cultural values, and the integration of these values throughout the assessment and intervention process. Major challenges and rewards await clinicians who explore the offerings of these recent advances in practice with families of children with SED.

REFERENCES

Alarcón, R. D., Foulks, E. F., & Vakkur, M. (1998). *Personality disorders and culture.* New York: John Wiley & Sons.

American Psychological Association. (1990). *Guidelines for providers of psychological services to ethnic, linguistic, and culturally diverse populations.* Washington, DC: Author. (Office of Ethnic Minority Affairs)

Aponte, H. J. (1976). The family-school interview: An ecological structural approach. *Family Process, 15,* 303–311.

Aponte, J. F., & Johnson, L. R. (2000). The impact of culture on the intervention and treatment of ethnic populations. In J. F. Aponte & J. Wohl (Eds.), *Psychological intervention and cultural diversity* (2nd ed., pp. 19–39). Boston: Allyn & Bacon.

Auerswald, E. H. (1968). Interdisciplinary versus ecological approach. *Family Process, 7,* 202–215.

Boyd-Franklin, N., & Bry, B. H. (2000). *Reaching out in family therapy: Home-based, school and community interventions.* New York: Guilford Press.

Brondino, M. J., Henggeler, S. W., Rowland, M. D., Pickrel, S. G., Cunningham, P. B., & Schoenwald, S. K. (1997). Multisystemic therapy and the ethnic minority client: Culturally responsive and clinically effective. In D. K. Wilson, J. R. Rodrique, & W. C. Taylor (Eds.), *Health promoting and health compromising behaviors among minority adolescents* (pp. 229–250). Washington, DC: APA Books.

Bronfenbrenner, U. (1979). *The ecology of human development: Experiences by nature and design.* Cambridge, MA: Harvard University Press.

Burns, B. J., & Goldman, S. K. (1999). Promising practices in wraparound for children with serious emotional disturbance and their families. In *Systems of care: Promising practices in children's mental health* (1998 series, Vol. 4). Washington, DC: Center for Effective Collaboration and Practice, American Institutes for Research.

Cunningham, P. B., & Henggeler, S. W. (1999). Engaging multiproblem families in treatment: Lessons learned throughout the development of multisystemic therapy. *Family Process, 38*(3), 265–281.

Cunningham, P. B., Henggeler, S. W., Brondino, M. J., & Pickrel, S. G. (1999). Testing underlying assumptions of the family empowerment perspective. *Journal of Child and Family Studies, 8*(4), 437–449.

Friedman, A. S. (1962). Family therapy as conducted in the home. *Family Process, 1,* 132–140.

Goldenberg, I., & Goldenberg, H. (1996). *Family therapy: An overview* (4th ed.). Pacific Grove: Brooks/Cole.

Hansen, M. (1998). *Symposium: Family interventions in child and adolescent public mental health.* Paper presented at the annual meeting of the American Psychological Association, San Francisco, CA.

Hansen, M., Anderson, C., Marsh, D. T., Harbaugh, S., & Gray, C. (1999). *Child, family and community core competencies.* Harrisburg, PA: PA CASSP Training and Technical Assistance Institute.

Henggeler, S. W. (1999). Multisystemic therapy: An overview of clinical procedures, outcomes, and policy implications. *Child Psychology and Pyschiatry Review, 4,* 2–10.

Henggeler, S. W., Brondino, M. J., Melton, G. B., Scherer, D. G., & Hanley, J. H. (1997). Multisystemic therapy with violent and chronic juvenile offenders and their families: The role of treatment fidelity in successful dissemination. *Journal of Consulting and Clinical Psychology, 65,* 821–833.

Henggeler, S. W., Rowland, M. D., Pickrel, S. G., Miller, S. L., Cunningham, P. B., Santos, A. B., Schoenwald, S. K., Randall, J., & Edwards, J. E. (1997). Investigating family-based alternatives to institution-based mental health services for youth: Lessons learned from the pilot study of a randomized field trial. *Journal of Clinical Child Psychology, 26*(3), 226–233.

Henggeler, S. W., Rowland, M. D., Randall, J., Ward, D. M., Pickrel, S. G., Cunningham, P. B., Miller, S. L., Edwards, J., Zealberg, J. J., Hand, L. D., & Santos, A. B. (1999). Home-based multisystemic therapy as an alternative to the hospitalization of youths in psychiatric crisis: Clinical outcomes. *Journal of the American Academy of Child and Adolescent Psychiatry, 38*(11), 1331–1339.

Henggeler, S. W., Schoenwald, S. K., & Munger, R. (1996, January/February). Multisystemic therapy proving to be effective treatment model. *Family Matters,* pp. 1–3.

Henggeler, S. W., Schoenwald, S. K., Pickrel, S. G., Rowland, M. D., & Santos, A. B. (1994). The contribution of treatment outcome research to the reform of children's mental health services: Multisystemic therapy as an example. *The Journal of Mental Health Administration, 21*(3), 229–239.

Imber-Black, E. (1988). *Families and larger systems: A family therapist's guide through the labyrinth.* New York: The Guilford Press.

Knitzer, J. (1982). *Unclaimed children: The failure of public responsibility to children and adolescents in need of mental health services.* Washington DC: Children's Defense Fund.

Lambert, W., Salzer, M. S., & Bickman, L. (1998). Clinical outcome, consumer satisfaction, and ad hoc ratings of improvement in children's mental health. *Journal of Consulting and Clinical Psychology, 66*(2), 270–279.

Lindblad-Goldberg, M., Dorc, M. M., & Stern, L. (1998). *Creating competence from chaos.* New York: W.W. Norton & Company.

Lourie, I. S. (2000, September). As the twig is bent. *Readings: A Journal of Reviews and Commentary in Mental Health,* 18–22.

Madsen, W. C. (1999). *Collaborative therapy with multi-stressed families: From old problems to new futures.* New York: Guilford Press.

Marsh, D. T. (2001). *A family-focused approach to serious mental illness: Empirically supported interventions.* Sarasota, FL: Professional Resource Press.

Marsh, D. T., & Anderson, C. A. (2000, November). *The ones we left behind: Family therapy and the treatment of mental illness.* Plenary presentation at the 2000 American Association of Marriage and Family Therapy Annual Conference, Denver, CO.

Meyers, J., Kaufman, M., & Goldman, S. (1999). Promising practices: Training strategies for serving children with serious emotional disturbance and their families in a system of care. In *Systems of care: Promising practices in children's mental health* (1998 series, Vol. 5). Washington, DC: Center for Effective Collaboration and Practice, American Institutes for Research.

Nelson, K. E., & Landsman, M. J. (1992). *Alternative models of family preservation: Family-based services in context.* Springfield, IL: Charles C. Thomas.

Nelson, K. E., Landsman, M. J., & Deutelbaum, W. (1990). Three models of family-centered placement prevention services. *Child Welfare, 69*(1), 3–21.

Osher, T. W., deFur, E., Nava, C., Spencer, S., & Toth-Dennis, D. (1999). New roles for families in systems of care. In *Systems of care: Promising practices in children's mental health* (1998 series, Vol. 1). Washington, DC: Center for Effective Collaboration and Practice, American Institutes for Research.

Pipher, M. (1996). *The shelter of each other: Rebuilding our families.* New York: Ballatine Books.

Pires, S. A. (1997). Human resource development. In B. Stroul (Ed.), *Children's mental health: Creating systems of care in a changing society* (pp. 281–297). Baltimore, MD: Paul H. Brookes Publishing Co.

Rabasca, L. (2000, October). In their own words. *Monitor on Psychology, 39*(9), 58–59.

Santos, A. B., Henggeler, S. W., Burns, F. J., Arana, G. W., & Meisler, N. (1995). Research on field-based services: Models for reform in the delivery of mental health care to populations with complex clinical problems. *The American Journal of Psychiatry, 152*(8), 1111–1123.

Schoenwald, S. K., & Henggeler, S. W. (1997). Combining effective treatment strategies with family preservation models of service delivery. In R. J. Illback, C. T. Cobb, & H. M. Joseph Jr. (Eds.), *Integrated services for children and families: Opportunities for psychological practice* (pp. 121–136). Washington, DC: American Psychological Association.

Schoenwald, S. K., & Henggeler, S. W. (1999). Treatment of oppositional defiant disorder and conduct disorder in home and community settings. In H. C. Quay & A. E. Hogan (Eds.), *Handbook of disruptive behavior disorders* (pp. 475–493). New York: Plenum Press.

Simpson, J. S., Koroloff, N., Friesen, B. J., & Gac, J. (1999). Promising practices in family-provided collaboration. In *Systems of care: Promising practices in children's mental health* (1998 series, Vol. 2). Washington, DC: Center for Effective Collaboration and Practice, American Institutes for Research.

Speck, R. V. (1964, February). Family therapy in the home. *Journal of Marriage and the Family,* 72–76.

Spencer, M. B., Swanson, D. P., & Cunningham, M. (1991). Ethnicity, ethnic identity, and competence formation: Adolescent transition and cultural transformation. *Journal of Negro Education, 60,* 366–387.

Stroul, B. A., & Friedman, R. M. (1986). *A system of care for children and youth with severe emotional disturbances.* Washington, DC: Georgetown University Child Development Center.

Sue, D. W., & Sue, D. (1999). *Counseling the culturally different: 3rd ed. Theory and practice.* New York: John Wiley & Sons.

Sue, S., Fujino, D. C., Hu, L., Takeuchi, D. T., & Zane, N. (1991). Community mental health services for ethnic minority groups: A test of the cultural responsiveness hypothesis. *Journal of Consulting and Clinical Psychology, 59,* 533–540.

Sue, S., & Zane, N. (1987). The role of culture and cultural techniques in pyschotherapy: A critique and reformation. *American Psychologist, 42,* 37–45.

U.S. Department of Health and Human Services. (1999). *Mental health: A report of the surgeon general.* Rockville, MD: Author. (Substance Abuse and Mental Health Services Administration, Center for Mental Health Services, National Institute of Mental Health)

U.S. Department of Health and Human Services. (2000). *Report of the surgeon general's Conference on Children's Mental Health: A national action agenda.* Washington, DC: Author.

Weisz, J. R., Donenberg, G. R., Han, S. S., & Weiss, B. (1995). Bridging the gap between laboratory and clinic in child and adolescent psychotherapy. *Journal of Consulting and Clinical Psychology, 63*(5), 688–701.

Wilkinson, D. (1993). Family ethnicity in America. In H. P. McAdoo (Ed.), *Family ethnicity: Strength in diversity* (pp. 15–59). Newbury Park, CA: Sage.

Woods, L. J. (1988, May–June). Home-based family therapy. *Social Work,* 211–214.

Chapter 21

THE HOME–SCHOOL–AGENCY TRIANGLE

VALERIE J. COOK-MORALES

Approximately one in five children and adolescents experience the signs and symptoms of a diagnosable mental disorder during the course of a year, and about 5 percent of all children experience extreme functional impairment (U.S. Department of Health and Human Services, 1999; note that henceforth in this chapter, the term *children* includes adolescents). Numerically, approximately 8 million children in the United States are in need of some form of mental health services (Day & Roberts, 1991), with over 3 million children estimated to be disabled by serious emotional disturbance (SED). It is unconscionable that only 400,000 of these children receive services in the schools (U.S. Department of Education, 1994). Over 2.5 million children with SED are falling into a canyon-sized gap in our service delivery systems.

Author's Note: I wrote this chapter not only as a professional but also as the parent of a child with SED. I have repeatedly witnessed the failure of the system to meet my son's needs and can attest to the devastating consequences of that failure for our entire family. It was difficult to write this chapter because I was caught in a dysfunctional home–school–agency triangle: No one was coordinating my son's services in the school or community. Like so many other parents, I found myself having two full-time jobs and subsequently needing to hire an advocate to effect appropriate services. The illustrative experiences reported in this chapter come from my family's experiences, my consultation with school personnel about other children with SED, and my collaboration with colleagues and students; and also from professional and consumer listservs and participation in parent support groups. I offer this chapter in the hope that professionals will develop better understanding of our children's needs across ecologies. If this will prevent even one other parent from having to go through struggles with the system like my own, it is well worth the effort.

I want to thank my son, Fernando, for the depth and breadth of his pragmatic teaching and the rekindling of my research and service on behalf of all children with SED. I also thank my colleagues at San Diego State University, Patricia Cegelka, Don Doorlag, Kelli Beard, and Eva Jarosz, with whom I collaborated on a federally funded project (1997–2000) to train SED specialists (i.e., teachers, school psychologists, and school counselors). These colleagues and our graduate students contributed greatly to my experiences and my thinking about services to children with SED. Finally, I thank my editor, Diane Marsh, for her patience, encouragement, and reframing that allowed me to complete this chapter.

The socioemotional needs of children today are greater than at any other point in history. Advocates and Congress have tried to be responsive to these needs by reaching children where they are on a daily basis: the schools. Thus was born the movement toward school-linked or school-based mental health services (Adelman, 1993), full-service schools (Dryfoos, 1994), and wraparound models. But frankly, "the consensus is that most programs that should interface with each other do not do so. Rather than a comprehensive, systematic, and sophisticated attack on problems, the picture that emerges is one of a great deal of nonintegrated, piecemeal activity" (Adelman, 1993, p. 310). This chapter is written from the perspective of *not* having an integrated, comprehensive continuum of services already in place and what can be done to better coordinate services for an *individual* child, because it is each of those individual children, one at a time, who combine to account for the 2.5 million unserved children. As Hill (1984) emphasized:

> A smoothly operating alliance between parents, school and therapist acts as [a] solid framework for the child, and a secure frame itself has a therapeutic effect. . . . which provides a strong sense of security and protection. Over time this experience can aid in the development of unity and solidarity in the child's internal world. (p. 236)

The child with SED is the defining unit of the treatment team and must negotiate the systems of home, school, and agency (see Figure 21.1). These triangles involve

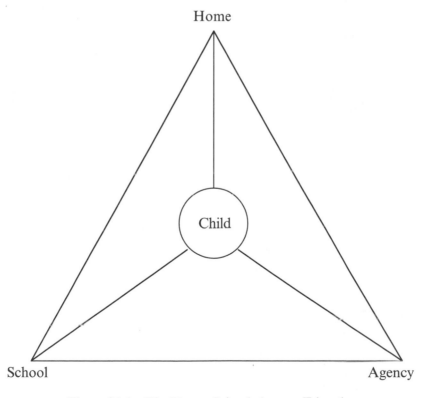

Figure 21.1   The Home–School–Agency Triangle

various combinations of children, parents, teachers, administrators, physicians, and other mental health professionals (Doherty & Peskay, 1992). Bowen's (1978) concept of triangles is an attempt to articulate and operationalize the dynamic shifts of alliance and discordance that continually occur among individuals and systems. Treatment-team triangles can be extremely effective. They can also become dysfunctional when distortions occur in boundaries, responsibility, communication, and coordination; and these distortions result in misattribution and escalating negative interactions. In the context of these dynamic processes, the goal is to relate to each system (home, school, and agency) in a clear, attentive, and respectful manner and to acknowledge—but not become significantly involved in—the emotionality between systems (Tittler & Cook, 1981).

HOME–SCHOOL–AGENCY SYSTEMS

All children are members of at least two main systems: home-family and school. The child with SED has the added complexity of the myriad systems of agencies, whether public or private. These systems interface, and what happens in one system is likely to affect the child's behavior in the other (Fine, 1984). In order to understand a child's behavior in any one system, we must recognize that (a) children's behaviors vary across settings and (b) adults in those settings view the same behavior differently.

Ecological and systemic-thinking psychologists speak to the *unity* of person–setting–behavior. Behavior is inextricably intertwined in the complex network of persons and settings, and, whether adaptive or disturbing, is a function of the reciprocal and cyclic relationship of person and ecology (Cook & Plas, 1984). Classic examples of behavior settings are "when in church, people act church" and "when in elevators, people act elevator." As Corrales and Ro-Track (1984) note, "No longer is the dancer isolated from the dance: The essence of systemic thinking is to look at the *patterns* of the dance of which the dancer is a part" (p. 135).

The term *niche* captures the unique functional role of the individual within the ecology (Cook & Plas, 1984). Given the press of the behavior setting and the individual's niche in the ecology, it is understandable, albeit sometimes surprising, that a child's behavior may well differ at home, in school, and at the therapist's office. Although it is *normal* for a child's behavior to vary across settings, it is intriguing that many children with SED (a) are fine at home but have behavior problems at school; or (b) are fine at school but have behavior problems at home or in the community; or (c) at some point are fine at home with problems at school, then are fine at school with problems at home. The problems and challenges of SED will manifest in both environments, but not necessarily in the same way. Fluctuations in symptom expression are not only common but are a sine qua non of childhood (Garber et al., 1988, cited by Hoagwood, Jensen, Petti, & Burns, 1996).

Darren, for example, had extreme oppositional defiant disorder (ODD) at home (including violent attacks on his mother), yet was frequently awarded "citizen of the month" recognition at school. He was fully compliant with articulated school discipline rules, but absolutely refused to learn to read—after 5 years of special education and remediation he was still "struggling" with consonant-vowel-consonant words (e.g., *cat*).

It took tremendous effort to get school personnel to understand that his reading problems were in part a refusal to learn to read. After Darren's problems with reading were reframed (and subsequent changes in intervention strategies), he made 2 years' gain in less than 6 months. He remained well-behaved at school; however, he began to appear to fall asleep in the classroom—another passive manifestation of his ODD.

Even when behavior across settings is identical, the adults in those settings may have very different perspectives on the behavior—including on what is "normal" and what should be of concern. Marsh, Stoughton, and Williams (1985) found, for example, that "clinical and school psychologists are significantly more likely to attribute psychological significance to many childhood behavior problems than are teachers and especially parents" (p. 176). They also found evidence that parents and teachers underestimate the significance of some behaviors (even hallucinations), given their lack of psychological perspectives. Significance ratings of some behaviors also differed by raters' age, gender, and parental status. These discrepancies are especially important because psychologists, teachers, and parents must be collaboratively involved in identifying children in need of mental health services and in developing treatment plans.

Finally, schools and agencies work from different definitions of emotional disturbance. From a mental health perspective, a child with a psychiatric disorder that substantially interferes with or limits the child's role or functioning in family, school, or community activities is considered to have SED. When that disability has a *demonstrated adverse impact* on the child's *educational performance,* the child has the right to be served and protected in the schools under Section 504 of the Americans with Disabilities Act (referred to as a *504 plan*). When that adverse impact is so significant as to preclude benefit from the general education classroom and require individualized special instruction, the student should be served through an Individual Education Plan (IEP) under the Individuals with Disabilities Education Act (IDEA). Under these federal laws, schools are to provide a continuum of services, and students are to be served in the least restrictive environment as identified by the IEP team for that individual child.

Ideally, potential services would range from consultative support or instruction within the general education classroom (called *full inclusion*) to specialized classrooms or schools. Schools more readily identify as having SED those students who disrupt daily (school or classroom) life and disturb others' emotions (Hobbs, 1979, 1980). The tendency to equate disruption with SED may create problems in proper identification and early intervention for many students with SED who present low-profile behaviors (i.e., those who are overly quiet, withdrawn, or depressed are frequently ignored and unserved; Conoley & Conoley, 1991). Disruption also may explain why students with SED are overwhelmingly represented in the most segregated classes (Cegelka & Cook-Morales, 1996).

KEY PLAYERS IN THE HOME–SCHOOL–AGENCY TRIANGLE

Cross-ecology treatment teams are most effective when key players from each ecology understand each other's perspectives and experiences. This section of the chapter addresses the unique factors and perspectives of those key players. The goal is to provide a glimpse into each ecology so that readers may begin to walk in the shoes of those different from themselves.

Understanding Parents as Team Members

Involving parents as key members of the treatment team is perhaps the single most important element in overall team effectiveness. Given our shared history of "blaming the parents" for their child's SED, or more recently our attempts to "fix the family," it is no small mental task to shift our view of parents from problems to contributors to solutions (Carlson, Hickman, & Horton, 1992; Friesen & Koroloff, 1990; Friesen & Poertner, 1995; Marsh, 1998, 2001; Marsh & Johnson, 1997). Hanson and Carta (1995) contend that team effectiveness

> is likely to be linked to the degree to which [we] are able to listen to children and families as they identify their needs and concerns. Further, effectiveness is enhanced by the educator's or service provider's ability to be sensitive to the range of these issues, to be respectful of children's and families' needs even though they may differ widely from that of the service provider, and to be knowledgeable about the range of options and supports available and valued by individual children and their families. (pp. 208–209)

Eggshells and *roller coasters* are two of the descriptors most frequently used by parents to capture their daily lives with children with SED. "Normal" takes on a whole new dimension. One of my parent peers in a support group commented, "When I say it's going 'well' I mean it's going well—for Terry—for now—it's not *really* going well— it's just Terry, well for him." What is "normal" for our sons or daughters with SED is not normal. We see this in the reactions of unknown adults at the supermarket, in the shaking heads of teachers and principals, in the wagging-finger lectures of neighbors, in the policeman's knock on the front door, and in the startled responses of other children. We feel the blame and experience the shame.

Whether birth parents, foster or adoptive parents, or caretaking grandparents, primary caregivers want to bring normalcy into their child's disturbed life. All parents have hopes and dreams for their children, and when SED emerges, many of those hopes and dreams are shattered and replaced by sorrow and grief. My husband laments:

> Every time Nando talks about being a policeman, FBI, or Secret Service agent, it's like someone is squeezing my heart. I know they won't have a disturbed guard at the White House. He's been set on being a policeman for 10 years now. At least it helps me keep him out of gangs.

Professionals often refer to the family experience of mental illness in terms of family burden (Lefley, 1996; Marsh, 2001). The everyday experience of symptomatic behavior, caregiving, family disruption and stress, stigma, and interface with service-delivery systems (school and agency) combine as objective burdens. The family also experiences subjective burdens: the emotional suffering that comes with a child's SED. For parents, especially, these burdens accumulate to the point where exhaustion and burnout are inevitable (Marsh, 2001).

When parents come to the table as members of the treatment team, they bring their burdens as well as their expertise about their child, their family, their home, and their needs. They also bring their singular focus and advocacy toward effecting interventions on behalf of their child and no other. School and agency professionals need to be able to enter the family ecosystem to understand and appreciate the home perspective on the situation and potential resolutions. Our goal must be to empower parents to become effective members of the team; thus, our services for parents and families must shift. A full discussion of family needs and responsive services is beyond the scope of this chapter; see Marsh's (1998, 2001) comprehensive reviews. In brief, we need to provide parents with the acceptance, knowledge, and support necessary to be strong members of the treatment team (see Table 21.1; Cook-Morales, 1999).

Given the depth and breadth of family needs, it may be challenging to engage parents as full members of the treatment team. These parents may be overwhelmed by the responsibilities of meeting the basic needs of the entire family, not just the educational and psychological needs of their child with SED. Families of children with SED disproportionately have low or poverty-level incomes (68%) and have a single parent as head of household (nearly 40%; Marder & Cox, 1991; U.S. Department of Education, 1994). Still, they are more likely than parents of children with other disabilities to make financial sacrifices to secure services for their children (U.S. Department of Education, 1994).

Table 21.1   Family Experiences With Serious Emotional Disturbance

Needs and Concerns	Effective Interventions
Affirmation and understanding	Build on strengths and resilience Cultural mediation and advocacy

Information
  Diagnosis and prognosis
  Treatment options
	Family education
	Family support groups
	Family consultation
	Liaison services

Education—school Range of programs	Family empowerment (e.g., knowledge of rights) Advocate or legal counsel
Caregiving	Respite care Community support Residential treatment
Social services	Systems broker (e.g., social worker) Legal counsel
Coping	Family psychoeducation Bibliotherapy and videotherapy
Stress and distress	Family therapy Marital therapy Individual therapy
Financial and job stress	Systems broker (e.g., social worker)

Source: Cook-Morales (1999).

Additional challenges may be expected because SED is also associated with a family history of mental or addictive disorders (U.S. Department of Health and Human Services, 1999). Even when these parents recognize that their child is experiencing problems, they may not feel capable of discussing their concerns with professionals or sufficiently safe to do so (Dryfoos, 1994; Hanson & Carta, 1995). When supervising my graduate student's reevaluation of a student receiving special education services due to SED, it became clear in our first meeting that his mother faced her own challenges emotionally (i.e., depression) and financially. She had refused referral for therapeutic services from the local mental health center (at no cost) for years. When listening to her story, we learned that she had had previous negative experiences with the mental health treatment system and that, in her best judgment, she wanted to protect her son from similar experiences. Arrangements were made to provide services at the school so that mother and son would not be behind locked doors. We must pursue parental involvement with the firm belief that parents will do *the best they can* to fulfill their responsibilities in the context of the constraints of their own situation.

Understanding Team Members From the School

Children with SED present the greatest challenge to educators and some of the most difficult cases for school psychologists and counselors. Unlike the singular focus of parents, the highest priority of school personnel is the education of all students in their school. Adelman and Taylor (1998) advise:

> That efforts to address mental health and psychosocial concerns are not a primary item on a school's agenda should surprise no one, as schools are not in the mental health business. Their mandate is to educate. . . . [I]n working with schools, we approach mental health and psychosocial concerns from the broader framework of addressing barriers to development, learning, and teaching. (p. 141)

If one word captures school personnel's perceptions of SED, that word is *fear*. A recent (spring 2001) thread on the listserv of the National Association of School Psychologists (NASP) focused on the need for a new SED classroom at an elementary school and approaches to use to help schoolteachers and staff accept it. Almost universally, teachers rate themselves as underprepared to deal with behavioral issues (Cegelka & Doorlag, 1995; Morvant, Gersten, Gillman, Keating, & Blake, 1995). Where direct knowledge and preparation are lacking, stereotypes, fear, and suspicion take over, influencing teachers' assumptions regarding their students (Dusek & Joseph, 1983). Forness, Kavale, and Lopez (1993) attribute the school's underidentification of SED to the reluctance of school personnel to identify or label students as having SED for a myriad of reasons (e.g., stigmatizing labeling, lack of services, and fear of limited disciplinary options).

For example, I consulted at length with another school psychologist who was reluctant to apply the SED label to a first grader who had just been released from a psychiatric hospital and was on a cocktail of seven medications. To the teacher and school psychologist, Sara appeared happy-go-lucky. After I pointed out that (a) if they were on the same medication regimen, they would be zombies, and (b) they really didn't want to see the impact of taking this little girl off medication just so they could experience her SED behavior, Sara was found eligible for special education and received services.

Teachers as Team Members

Teachers are second only to parents in the amount of time and range of experiences they have with children. As such, they are invaluable resources for understanding both the child's dysfunction and coping strategies that become apparent on a daily basis. The teacher's observations are essential to the understanding and resolution of problems; thus, an effective treatment team embraces teachers as active contributors (Hill, 1984). At the same time, teachers have the responsibility of teaching *all* students in their classrooms, whether that means 7 students in a self-contained class, or more than 30 in a general education class, or more than 200 in the course of the day in middle or high school. General education teachers, especially, often feel overwhelmed in dealing with children who have special needs or problems (Doherty & Peskay, 1992). We must be realistic in our expectations for teacher involvement as team members and for teacher receptiveness to proposed interventions.

The nationwide shortage of qualified teachers is well known. The greatest teacher shortage is in special education, and within special education, the greatest shortage is for qualified teachers of students with SED (Cegelka & Cook-Morales, 1996). This personnel shortage translates to having adults in teaching roles who are neither prepared to teach nor prepared to understand students with SED. Special-education teachers of children with SED are uniformly referred to, in the literature and in the schools, as *SED teachers.* The job of the SED teacher is highly stressful; most teeter on the verge of burnout (Cegelka & Doorlag, 1995), and over half typically leave the profession within 5 years (Morsink, 1987). Although SED teachers report that disruptive students and dealings with parents are among the top 10 stressors, the most stressful aspects of the job are associated with school setting factors (Pullis, 1992): "The most significant factor and the one that appears to be somewhat unique to these teachers is their perception about relationships and interactions with other school professionals and how their program and effort are not adequately supported" (p. 200).

I had a recent discussion with Yolanda, a counselor at an elementary school that houses an SED class. She reported that the SED teacher had been on disability leave the year before, and the class was taught by a series of substitutes, several of whom called the front office to say, "I'm leaving in 5 minutes." As a result, Yolanda had felt "like an ill-equipped SED counselor while the rest of the school was waiting for their counselor to arrive."

When working with teachers as team members, the ideal relationship involves appreciation and respect by the teacher and mental health professionals for their mutual roles, with all oriented toward the welfare of the child and family (Doherty & Peskay, 1992). Whether a general education teacher overwhelmed by numbers of students and insufficient preparation to meet the needs of a child with SED, or a highly stressed SED teacher, the teacher needs the recognition, support, and collaborative consultation of mental health professionals to participate effectively on the team. The team's willingness to focus on teacher-identified problems (even if they seem trivial) frequently promotes the teacher's willingness to work on the student's mental health problems (Conoley & Conoley, 1991).

School Support Personnel as Team Members

Although school-based psychologists, counselors, and social workers are prepared to work with children and teachers, they have an acute lack of preparedness to serve children with SED (Cegelka & Cook-Morales, 1996) or their families (Taylor, 2001). Mental health professionals in the schools are often overwhelmed by demand for their services; for example, the nationwide student:professional ratio is almost double that recommended by professional associations (Carlson, Paavola, & Talley, 1995).

The models of services vary enormously not only from state to state, or district to district, but even between schools in the same district. Some elementary schools, for example, have a full-time school psychologist who provides full service delivery, including responsibility for services offered by school counselors or school social workers in other schools. Some high schools have a full-time school counseling staff with services offered by itinerant school psychologists and school social workers. It would be a rare school to have available all three types of mental health professionals engaged in broad service delivery as defined by professional best practices. It would be fairly common for the school to rely on itinerant services from support personnel. Adelman and Taylor (1998) joke that it can be difficult to coordinate team meetings because "they must come to school on different days because the boiler room to which they are all assigned can only hold one at a time" (p. 138). Overall, this situation often results in an emphasis on indirect interventions, time-limited counseling for individual students, and reliance on community agencies to provide the more intensive therapeutic interventions needed by children with SED and their families.

Understanding Team Members From Community Agencies

Just as the mental health services in schools vary greatly, each community has a different array of mental health services, systems, and private practitioners. For children with SED and their families, community systems are likely to include mental health counseling, consumer support groups (self-help groups), social service agencies, and juvenile justice. Apter (1992) noted:

> The task of finding and accessing these resources seems almost impossible, not only for families but also for the persons who are trying to assist them. The piecemeal delivery and narrow boundaries of each service often make it difficult to decipher just what it is an agency does. . . . Each agency may have something to offer, but each also has its own sets of rules as to who can access it and for what purpose. (p. 487)

This is precisely why wraparound services have been developed. Most families, however, do not have the benefit of wraparound services and must interface with a range of mental health professionals including psychiatrists, psychologists, counselors, family therapists, and social workers—even when the parents cannot discern the differences among the professions. Preparation programs obviously vary widely for these different professions, but it is likely that what these agency team members lack in common is preparation (a) to work with children with SED and (b) to understand and collaborate with the schools. (Note that *agency team members* here refers to all professionals in mental health services and related fields outside of the schools.) A frequent theme on consumer listservs is the failure of agency team members to effect ongoing contact with teachers or support service providers.

Ideally, the agency team member would strive to support home and school with the goal of helping these systems and the child to better accommodate each other (Tittler & Cook, 1981). Agency team members are constrained, however, by (a) their own professional preparation; (b) the boundaries of their agencies; (c) a traditional model of practice (e.g., 50-minute sessions, squeezing in phone contacts between clients; Early & Poertner, 1995); and (d) the waiting list of clients (i.e., time). Few agencies are organized to enable agency members to participate in sorely needed coordination of services and outreach to the schools, to other agencies, or even between professionals in the same agency.

Although my family works with a psychiatrist and therapist within the same agency, I am the conduit of information between the two—neither seems to know what the other is doing. Their services and their interface with the schools are supposedly coordinated by a psychologist at an umbrella agency, whom we have seen twice for assessment and twice for subsequent IEP meetings in the past 6 years. In that same time span, only two of the three therapists (high agency turnover) have attended one IEP meeting each (of more than 25 IEPs), and none of the four psychiatrists has even graced the schools with a phone call. We do understand the constraints under which they work; they even say they would *like* to collaborate, but reality interferes on a regular basis.

Summary: Members of the Treatment Team

When members of the treatment team come to the table together, they all bring their own perspectives, preparedness (or lack thereof), and constrictions of the system—and, perhaps most important, they bring a fairly pervasive theme of stress centered on the child with SED and their own systems. Thus, there is a high potential for triangulation and dysfunction on the team, *unless* one of the professional team members assumes the role of facilitating clear communication and stress reduction.

HOME–SCHOOL–AGENCY RELATIONSHIPS

In addition to understanding these three different perspectives, it is important to consider that as members of the team assemble, each walks into the history of the relationships that exist between the members of the other two ecologies. It would be unfair to ask the parent to be aware of the histories and relationships between the school and the agencies; thus, this section addresses professionals in schools and agencies who need to be cognizant of the impact of these relationships on the effectiveness of the triangle.

Home–School Relationships

> In any given case, there is a particular quality of relationship between school and family. Sometimes this relationship is flexible and able to shift comfortably, allowing for communication when appropriate or necessary. . . . In other instances the school-family relationship takes on a fixed and troubled character, as is often seen around children with school problems. (Tittler & Cook, 1981, p. 186)

These relationships have already been established before the therapist comes on the scene; they may be characterized as positive, neutral, or antagonistic. The agency member needs to know of them *before* attempting a treatment triangle—or triangulation can occur (Hill, 1984). If parents and teacher are "locked in conflict" (p. 235), the therapist will need to mediate and reframe. Often, the child is regarded by the teacher as an extension of the family, and his or her problems are attributed directly to the family—occasionally with a great deal of conviction and a minimum of information (Tittler & Cook, 1981). Conversely, many parents are dissatisfied or disappointed in the school program for their child, but have been unable to effect change.

Christenson, Rounds, and Franklin (1992) report that a very large majority (over 90%) of teachers and parents report positive relationships and responsiveness on the part of the other. But for the child with SED, home–school relationships typically revolve around poor report cards, problematic behaviors and events at school, and the legalistic processes surrounding special education. In short, positive home–school interactions are extremely rare for the child with SED. Although the school may purport that it cannot operate effectively without family involvement, "such involvement is available only from families who have children with no problems" (Conoley & Conoley, 1991, p. 824).

Home–Agency Relationships

Home–agency relationships are *unnatural* extensions of the family ecosystem and must be *created;* thus, responsibility for the quality of this relationship falls on the therapist's shoulders. This unnatural relationship may have been initiated in response to a referral regarding either the child's behavior and needs or parental behavior (e.g., child abuse, neglect, or substance abuse) and needs (e.g., mental illness). In the latter case, the parents may not possess the optimal internal resources to complement the child's emotional growth (Hill, 1984, p. 231). Working with these families is challenging and frustrating, as the lack of parental resources interferes with therapists' efforts to apply their expertise.

As Vernberg, Roberts, and Nyre advise in chapter 22 of this handbook, many parents may come to an agency with extensive experience with the mental health system. When this is the case, the family is probably bringing a *negative* experience to the establishment of a therapist–family relationship. Parents who have been frustrated with one therapist's approach are usually unaware that a variety of approaches are possible and that this new therapist–family relationship may hold promise.

This was problematic for my family, even though we were working within the same agency. Our first therapist concentrated on our son and emphasized verbal approaches with him (which were ineffective given his language disability and age; he wasn't old enough to take another's perspective) and occasionally touched base with us as parents. It was difficult to energize the family to meet with the next assigned therapist. The new therapist decided to alternate between working with Nando and working with us as parents, occasionally creating a family event (e.g., playing a Pokeman game, which everyone in our family felt was pointless). Within the first three sessions with my husband and me, triangulation occurred. The therapist reinforced everything I said, then turned her attention to "fix" my husband, using a psychoanalytic framework. This rapidly deteriorated to affect our marital relationship, and I empathized with my husband, who dropped out of therapy because he felt we were ganging up on him. Following his father's modeling, Nando began to refuse therapy, as well. Precipitously, the therapist left the agency, and we were assigned a new therapist.

After concerted effort, we returned to try again. This time it is working. What accounts for this difference? Our new therapist focuses on empowering my husband and me to be a team in responding to Nando's needs and emotional development. He enlists our participation as equals in the therapeutic process and takes time with us to celebrate our accomplishments as well us focusing on our challenges. Most resistant parents will engage in the ongoing process if they are treated as collaborators and can identify as members of the treatment team, rather than as patients in treatment (Hill, 1984, p. 232).

School–Agency Relationships

The histories of school–agency relationships vary even more than the school and agency resources in any one community. Histories may be characterized by shared collaboration toward provision of school-based or school-linked services (Adelman & Taylor, 1998), thwarted attempts at such collaboration, peaceful coexistence without communication, or occasionally by antagonistic relationships between school and agency or individual team members from schools and agencies. The parent cannot foster these relationships; thus, it is incumbent upon team members from both schools and agencies to effect strong and healthy relationships.

Conoley and Conoley (1991) report that teachers' hopes rise when they learn that a child is to be seen by a psychologist, followed by disappointment surrounding unrealistic or vague recommendations for interventions and insufficient communication (input from teachers is rarely sought, and they receive no or vague communication regarding therapeutic progress). The teacher–therapist relationship may be strained by differences in values: The teacher seeks less disruption in the classroom (a quick fix), whereas the therapist seeks the comfort and emotional growth of the child (Hill, 1984). It is important to reframe these differences into positive forces on behalf of the child with SED:

> The therapist can help the teacher understand what is occurring inside the child emotionally, but the teacher is in a unique position to offer the therapist valuable diagnostic data concerning the quality of the child's object relationships and what types of experiences throughout the day trigger certain responses in the child. (Hill, 1984, p. 234)

The relationship between school-based and agency-based mental health professionals is easily thwarted by endemic professional issues. Adelman and Taylor (1998) caution:

> When outside professionals are brought in, school specialists often view it as a discounting of their skills and a threat to their jobs. The "outsiders" often feel unappreciated and may be rather naïve about the culture of schools (Sarason, 1996). Conflicts arise over "turf," use of space, confidentiality, and liability (p. 141).

Similarly, Conoley and Conoley (1991) warn that clinic-based therapists may hold stereotypes about educators and school-based psychologists or counselors that interfere with collegial efforts. Agency team members typically stereotype and dismiss school psychologists as psychometricians and school counselors as guidance-office paper pushers. Finally, agency personnel may be susceptible to professional arrogance despite the proven effectiveness of teachers and school-based mental health practitioners (Conoley & Conoley, 1991). In short, we need to cross professional boundaries and overcome bureaucratic limitations to serve the child (Hanson & Carta, 1995).

BEST PRACTICES: EFFECTIVE HOME–SCHOOL–AGENCY TRIANGLES

> The complexity of the difficulties in the lives of children [with SED] and their families appears overwhelming. Certainly families are challenged to overcome tremendous obstacles. So too are educators and service providers challenged to develop and implement appropriate and supportive service. Only through an interactive, multilevel, coordinated approach can we address many of these challenges. (Hanson & Carta, 1995, pp. 209–210)

The home–school–agency triangle is ripe for dysfunction: Each adult key player faces multiple challenges and experiences stress, and all three systems have their own constraints and barriers. To create effective triangles requires new collaborative arrangements and redistributed power, "all of which is easy to say and extremely hard to accomplish" (Adelman & Taylor, 1998, p. 148). Mental health clinicians, whether school- or agency-based, must recognize the value of a home–school–agency triangle as well as the possible dangers of failing to create a working alliance (Hill, 1984). It will take at least one mental health professional who understands systems dynamics to rise to leadership on behalf of the child.

Because the problems children with SED, their families, and their teachers face do not come from single causes, single interventions are not likely to be effective (Hanson & Carta, 1995). The goals of the home–school–agency triangle are to design, implement, and evaluate the effectiveness of multifaceted interventions coordinated across the three ecologies. As the treatment team begins to work toward these goals, it is helpful to keep at the forefront five essential components for effectiveness: communication, cooperation, coordination, collaboration, and consultation (see Table 21.2).

Communication

It is common sense that team effectiveness will depend on ongoing clear communication. It is essential that team members be able to share their perspectives openly, which

Table 21.2   Essential Components for Effective Home–School–Agency Triangles

Component	Root Word	Definition
Communication	*Commune*	To share; to participate; to have a connection or passage from one to another
Cooperation	*Cooperate*	To act or operate jointly with another or others, to the same end; to work or labor with mutual efforts to promote the same object
Coordination	*Coordinate*	To place in the same rank; to make of equal value; to bring into proper and relative order; to harmonize; to adjust
Collaboration	*Collaborate*	To labor, especially in . . . scientific pursuits, as an associate of another or others; to cooperate with the enemy
Consultation	*Consult*	To take counsel together; to discuss, decide or plan something

Source: Definitions from *Webster's New Universal Dictionary* (1995), New York: Simon & Schuster.

requires both trust and formal information releases from parents, to enable full communication across school–agency partnerships. Conoley and Conoley (1991) suggest that school–agency partnerships will be more effective when members learn the jargon and acronyms used in the other setting. Although shared professional languages may assist school–agency talk, using jargon in home–school–agency team meetings will only complicate and interfere with the empowerment of parents and teachers as team members. Accordingly, it is important to reduce or eliminate jargon from team meetings.

Communication goes beyond imparting information; the keys to effective communication include active listening, understanding and empathizing with parents and teachers, and seeking others' opinions and contributions. Communication is the act of coming together to create shared connections (see Table 21.2). Failure to connect ultimately results in damage to the child. Leon is one of those children. I was passing through the middle school's office and found a young man sobbing his heart out. He was waiting for the vice principal and impending suspension because he had hit another boy, and this was a zero-tolerance school. Leon explained that he was crying because he knew he had disappointed his parents and his therapist, that just last week he had returned to school from the hospital where he had worked hard on his impulse control. In pulling the child's records, I learned that he had been evaluated for special education at his parents' request within the past year. The school team had concluded that he was not eligible for special education because there was no discrepancy between his intelligence and his achievement level (i.e., he did not have a learning disability). Clearly, the adults in Leon's life had not connected. The team reconvened with Leon's parents and therapist. After full communication was effected, the team agreed that although Leon's SED was a disability at school, he did not need specialized instruction (i.e., special education); but he did need a behavior support plan and system, which were effected under his Section 504 rights.

Cooperation

Once effective communication is established, the team can begin to work on coopera-tion. By definition (see Table 21.2), cooperation requires articulation of shared goals and understanding of the situation. This chapter began with a discussion of behavior—different behaviors across settings and different perspectives on the same behavior. During communication, these differences will be highlighted. Through cooperation, the team will strive to develop consensus (i.e., full agreement).

Some of the concepts used by family systems therapists inform this process. School and agency mental health professionals must *join* with both the family and teacher. Joining family members (or teachers) basically involves entering (at least perceptually) the clients' map or model of the world (Corrales & Ro-Track, 1984). These subjective experiences are viewed or *framed* by each person in a different way. "The art of *refram-ing* involves the process of introducing a more useful view or map of the situation than the one currently used by the individual or family" (p. 146). Reframing can be used to bridge the divergent perspectives of team members, and to unite the team in a shared definition of the problem situation. Changing views of the problem opens the doors to unrecognized possibilities and untried interventions. (Review Darren's problems with reading presented earlier.)

Coordination

Given the team's consensual definition of the problem and articulated goals, it is pos-sible to begin coordination of interventions, services, and efforts across home, school, and agency. Throughout this handbook, the importance of the role of the *case man-ager* is emphasized. Hobbs (1979) criticized that term as "semantically infelicitous. No one wants to be a 'case,' and no one wants to be 'managed' " (p. 30). Furthermore, *case management* suggests a transfer of responsibility from parents and teachers to an expert who takes over (Hobbs, 1980). A variety of role descriptors has emerged to characterize this leadership position: *liaison specialist* (Hobbs, 1979, 1980; Plas, 1981), *systems spanner* (Conoley & Conoley, 1991), and *coordinator for community outreach and program integration* (Adelman, 1993). I prefer the larger paradigm shift embedded in moving from case management to *service coordination,* as proposed by Friesen and Poertner (1995).

The primary function of the services coordinator is to facilitate and coordinate the endeavors of the home–school–agency team. In many ways it makes sense for the school psychologist to serve the team in this role: (a) The school is the second most important ecological system experienced by the child; (b) there may be numerous key players involved with the child at school (e.g., general and special-education teachers, speech-language therapists, and occupational therapists); and (c) there are numerous teams already in place at the school (e.g., student study teams, student assistance teams, and IEP teams) that can serve as a natural point of entry into the system.

For the most complex situations, it is best to have co-coordinators representing each of the major service systems, that is, school and agency. In this instance, the agency-based therapist coordinates with the school psychologist to bridge between these two complex systems. Individually, each is an outsider in one system and an insider in the other. External status reduces effectiveness; internal status facilitates acceptance. Combined, the co-coordinators share the most effective internal status across systems. Finally, if the family is aligned with or in an adversarial relationship with either the school or an agency, the shared voice of co-coordinators can bring harmony to and restore the balance of the home school agency triangle.

Collaboration

Collaboration is the process by which coordinated services are delivered, supported, monitored, and evaluated. Every team member is both a collaborating interventionist and a supporter of other collaborating interventionists. However the team organizes its work, the following points are crucial: (a) Cooperation and collaboration must be at the forefront; (b) each team member should learn from all others; (c) members need to feel comfortable in asking the team for help; and (d) all need to focus on accomplishing therapeutic work on behalf of the child (Conoley & Conoley, 1991).

When I found that the definition of *collaborate* includes a reference to war terminology—"to cooperate with the enemy" (see Table 21.2)—I almost omitted that meaning. Then I recalled Quinn and McDougal's (1998) advice, and cooperating with the enemy made special sense as applied to home–school–agency triangles on behalf of children with SED: "The chore of mobilizing the energy and resources needed . . . on behalf of individuals whose behavior many people find aversive and noxious should not be underestimated" (p. 200).

Consultation

Consultation is the single most powerful ecological intervention tool because it starts with the consultee's repertoire at the time, empowers the consultee to deliver interventions, and is faded out as the consultee develops knowledge or skills and accepts responsibility for ongoing maintenance of the intervention. Too often, mental health professionals assume an expert posture in consultation; such expert consultation is doomed to failure (Conoley & Conoley, 1991, p. 825). The very meaning of consultation (see Table 21.2) is grounded in equal-status relationships and problem solving. Consultation is brainstorming and jointly creating interventions to be carried out by the consultee. The *expertise* of the consultant must be the *process* of consultation, which requires sophisticated skills that often go unaddressed in practitioner-preparation programs.

Teachers and parents are most commonly the consultees when the client is a child with SED. The school-based psychologist or counselor who has direct knowledge of the child in school, skills in behavior interventions, and established relationships with school staff, is likely to be the most effective with teachers. Similarly, the agency-based practitioner who has developed strong rapport with the family is likely to be the most effective consultant for the parents. The agency practitioner is cautioned, however, to make a clear distinction between family or parent consultation and therapy: Consultation is the process of discussing and deliberating various intervention options together, as compared to receiving treatment via therapy (Marsh, 2001). Finally, when these school- and agency-based consultants are also co-coordinators of services, complementary consultative strategies can be effected, thus enhancing the potential power of the interventions across home and school.

CONCLUSION

Because most children with SED are not involved in full-service schools or wraparound programs, it is incumbent on us as mental health professionals to create an effective home–school–agency triangle on a child-by-child basis. In bringing the team to the table, it is important to remember that home–school–agency adults experience different realities of the child, and the child's behavior does indeed vary across settings. The five *C*s are essential components of team work: communication, cooperation, coordination, collaboration, and consultation. DeChillo, Koren, and Mezera (1995) offer pragmatic principles that support the effectiveness of the home–school–agency triangle:

- Everyone has strengths. Recognizing strengths is the key ingredient of coordination and collaboration. Building on these strengths is the key to effective interventions.
- Everyone has constraints. Be pragmatic and realistic. Trust that everyone will do the best they can under their circumstances.
- Roles are permeable but not interchangeable; learn from one another.
- The best goals and interventions are mutually defined and tailor-made.
- Evaluation of effectiveness is everyone's job.
- Support and understanding are foremost.
- Support and understanding are *not* enough.

The teamwork of the home-school-agency triangle is never done. Discontinuity can be disruptive—teachers change annually; school assignments of psychologists, counselors, and social workers may change; community mental health center therapists and psychiatrists move through the system as if there were revolving doors. Each time a member of the team changes, the team needs to return to the basics of communication and continue to attend to all five *C*s. Finally, as Conoley and Conoley (1991) said so well, "Adults, like children, must learn to play together nicely if positive outcomes are expected" (p. 826).

REFERENCES

Adelman, H. S. (1993). School-linked mental health interventions: Toward mechanisms for service coordination and integration. *Journal of Community Psychology, 21,* 309–319.

Adelman, H. S., & Taylor, L. (1998). Reframing and mental health in schools and expanding school reform. *Educational Psychologist, 33,* 135–152.

Apter, D. (1992). Utilization of community resources: An important variable for the home-school interface. In S. L. Christenson & J. C. Conoley (Eds.), *Home-school collaboration: Enhancing children's academic and social competence* (pp. 487–498). Silver Spring, MD: National Association of School Psychologists.

Bowen, M. (1978). *Family therapy and clinical practice.* New York: Jason Aronson.

Carlson, C. I., Hickman, J., & Horton, C. B. (1992). From blame to solutions: Solution-oriented family-school consultation. In S. L. Christenson & J. C. Conoley (Eds.), *Home-school collaboration: Enhancing children's academic and social competence* (pp. 193–214). Silver Spring, MD: National Association of School Psychologists.

Carlson, C., Paavola, J., & Talley, R. (1995). Historical, current, and future models of schools as health care delivery settings. *School Psychology Quarterly, 10,* 184–202.

Cegelka, P. T., & Cook-Morales, V. J. (1996). *Transdisciplinary collaboration for preparation of specialists in serious emotional disturbance: Teachers, school psychologists, and school counselors.* A grant proposal to the U.S. Department of Education, Office of Special Education Programs (84.029G). San Diego, CA: San Diego State University Foundation.

Cegelka, P. T., & Doorlag, D. H. (1995). *A summary of the data on special education teacher shortage in California. 1984–85 to 1994–94.* San Diego, CA: San Diego State University, Department of Special Education.

Christenson, S. L., Rounds, T., & Franklin, M. J. (1992). Home-school collaboration: Effects, issues, and opportunities. In S. L. Christenson & J. C. Conoley (Eds.), *Home-school collaboration: Enhancing children's academic and social competence* (pp. 19–51). Silver Spring, MD: National Association of School Psychologists.

Conoley, J. C., & Conoley, C. W. (1991). Collaboration for child adjustment: Issues for school- and clinic-based child psychologists. *Journal of Consulting and Clinical Psychology, 59,* 821–829.

Cook, V. J., & Plas, J. M. (1984). Intervention with disturbed children: The ecological viewpoint. In M. J. Fine (Ed.), *Systematic intervention with disturbed children* (pp. 157–178). Boston: Spectrum, SP Medical & Scientific Books.

Cook-Morales, V. J. (1999, August). Serious emotional disturbance: Family issues and interventions. In D. Marsh (Chair), *Serious mental illness: Family issues and interventions.* Symposium conducted as part of the Miniconvention on Serious Mental Illness at the annual meeting of the American Psychological Association, Boston.

Corrales, R. G., & Ro-Track, L. G. (1984). Family systems therapy. In M. J. Fine (Ed.), *Systematic intervention with disturbed children* (pp. 133–155). Boston: SP Medical & Scientific Books, Spectrum Publications.

Day, C., & Roberts, M. C. (1991). Activities of the Child and Adolescent Service System Program for improving mental health services for children and families. *Journal of Clinical Child Psychology, 20,* 340–350.

DeChillo, N., Koren, P. E., & Mezera, J. (1995). Families and professionals in partnership. In B. A. Stroul (Ed.), *Children's mental health: Creating systems of care in a changing society* (pp. 389–407). Baltimore: Brookes.

Doherty, W. J., & Peskay, V. E. (1992). Family systems and the school. In S. L. Christenson & J. C. Conoley (Eds.), *Home-school collaboration: Enhancing children's academic and social competence* (pp. 1–18). Silver Spring, MD: National Association of School Psychologists.

Dryfoos, J. G. (1994). *Full-service schools: A revolution in health and social services for children, youth, and families.* San Francisco: Jossey-Bass.

Dusek, J., & Joseph, G. (1983). The bases of teacher expectancies: A meta-analysis. *Journal of Educational Psychology, 75,* 327–346.

Early, T. J., & Poertner, J. (1995). Examining current approaches to case management for families with children who have serious emotional disorders. In B. J. Friesen & J. Poertner (Eds.), *From case management to service coordination for children with emotional, behavioral, or mental disorders: Building on family strengths* (pp. 37–59). Baltimore: Brookes.

Fine, M. J. (1984). The treatment of disturbed children: Introduction. In M. J. Fine (Ed.), *Systematic intervention with disturbed children* (pp. 3–24). Boston: SP Medical & Scientific Books, Spectrum Publications.

Forness, S. R., Kavale, K. A., & Lopez, M. (1993). Conduct disorders in school: Special education eligibility and comorbidity. *Journal of Emotional and Behavioral Disorders, 1,* 101–108.

Friesen, B. J., & Koroloff, N. M. (1990). Family-centered services: Implications for mental health administration and research. *Journal of Mental Health Administration, 17,* 13–25.

Friesen, B. J., & Poertner, J. (Eds.) (1995). *From case management to service coordination for children with emotional, behavioral, or mental disorders: Building on family strengths.* Baltimore: Brookes.

Hanson, M. J., & Carta, J. J. (1995). Addressing the challenges of families with multiple risks. *Exceptional Children, 63,* 201–212.

Hill, N. (1984). The parent-school-therapist alliance in the treatment of emotionally disturbed children. In M. Fine (Ed.), *Systematic intervention with disturbed children,* (pp. 227–243). New York: SP Medical & Scientific Books, Spectrum Publications.

Hoagwood, K., Jensen, P. S., Petti, T., & Burns, B. J. (1996). Outcomes of mental health care for children and adolescents: I. A comprehensive conceptual model. *Journal of the American Academy of Child and Adolescent Psychiatry, 35,* 1055–1063.

Hobbs, N. (1979). *Helping disturbed children: Psychological and ecological strategies, II: Project Re-ED, twenty years later.* Nashville, TN: Vanderbilt University Institute for Public Policy Studies.

Hobbs, N. (1980). An ecologically oriented, service-based system for the classification of handicapped children. In S. Salzinger, J. Antrobus, & J. Glick (Eds.), *The ecosystem of the "sick" child: Implications for classification and intervention for disturbed and mentally retarded children.* New York: Academic Press.

Lefley, H. P. (1996). *Family caregiving in mental illness* (Family Caregiver Applications Series, Vol. 7). Thousand Oaks, CA: Sage.

Marder, C., & Cox, R. (1991). More than a label: Characteristics of youth with disabilities. In M. Wagner, L. Newman, R. D'Amico, E. D. Jay, P. Butler-Nalin, C. Marder, & R. Cox (Eds.), *Youth with disabilities: How are they doing? The first comprehensive report from the National Longitudinal Transition Study of special education students.* Menlo Park, CA: SRI International.

Marsh, D. T. (1998). *The practitioner's guide: Serious mental illness and the family.* New York: John Wiley & Sons.

Marsh, D. T. (2001). *A family-focused approach to serious mental illness: Empirically supported interventions.* Sarasota, FL: Professional Resource Press.

Marsh, D. T., & Johnson, D. L. (1997). The family experience of mental illness: Implications for intervention. *Professional Psychology: Research and Practice, 28,* 229–237.

Marsh, D. T., Stoughton, N. L., & Williams, T. A. (1985). Effects of role, gender, age, and parental status on perception of childhood problems. *Exceptional Children, 52,* 170–177.

Morsink, K. (1987). Competencies for teachers of students with high incidence handicaps. *B. C. Journal of Special Education, 11,* 109–122.

Morvant, M., Gersten R., Gillman, J., Keating, T., & Blake, G. (1995, March). *Attrition/retention of urban special education teachers: Multi-faceted research and strategic action planning* (Final Performance Report: Vol. 1). Eugene, OR: University of Oregon, Eugene Research Institute.

Plas, J. M. (1981). The psychologist in the school community: A liaison role. *School Psychology Review, 10,* 72–81.

Pullis, M. (1992). An analysis of the occupational stress of teachers of the behaviorally disordered: Sources, effects, and strategies for coping. *Behavioral Disorders, 17,* 191–201.

Quinn, K. P., & McDougal, J. L. (1998). A mile wide and a mile deep: Comprehensive interventions for children and youth with emotional and behavioral disorders and their families. *School Psychology Review, 27,* 191–203.

Sarason, S. B. (1996). *Revisiting "The culture of school and the problem of change."* New York: Teachers College Press.

Taylor, B. A. (2001). *The minority families of children with disabilities project: Preparing related services personnel to serve diverse families of children with disabilities.* A grant proposal to the U.S. Department of Education, Office of Special Education Programs (84.325E). San Diego, CA: San Diego State University Foundation.

Tittler, B. I., & Cook, V. J. (1981). Relationships among family, school, and clinic: Toward a systems approach. *Journal of Clinical Child Psychology, 10,* 184–187.

U.S. Department of Education. (1994). *To assure the free appropriate public education of all children with disabilities: Sixteenth annual report to Congress on the implementation of the Individuals with Disabilities Education Act (IDEA).* Washington, DC: U.S. Government Printing Office.

U.S. Department of Health and Human Services. (1999). *Mental health: A report of the surgeon general—executive summary.* Rockville, MD: U.S. Department of Health and Human Services, Substance Abuse and Mental Health Services Administration, Center for Mental Health Services, National Institutes of Health, National Institute of Mental Health.

Chapter 22

SCHOOL-BASED INTENSIVE MENTAL HEALTH TREATMENT

ERIC M. VERNBERG, MICHAEL C. ROBERTS, AND JOSEPH E. NYRE

Educational, social service, and mental health agencies have collectively encountered significant difficulties in attempting to meet the educational and mental health needs of children exhibiting severely debilitating psychiatric disturbance. Within this subset of children and youth, those exhibiting serious emotional disturbance (SED) have arguably received the least effective interventions, consumed the greatest amount of resources, and shown the poorest outcomes. Although the general conclusions in the professional literature have called for more effective and comprehensive programs to educate and treat this population, the agencies charged with this responsibility have largely been unable to collectively and sufficiently affect outcomes (Quinn & McDougal, 1998). School systems have historically used one or more options in attempting to address the educational and mental health needs of children with SED. This chapter reviews the approaches schools have taken to serve these children. It then outlines an intensive program to serve the complex needs and challenges presented by elementary school children with SED.

Options for the treatment and education of children with SED have included inpatient hospitalization, partial-hospitalization (day treatment) programs, and community mental health services. Inpatient hospitalization is costly, averaging over $500 per day, and does not produce good long-term outcomes (Friesen & Koroloff, 1990; Henggeler, 1994; Kiesler, 1993; Weisz, Donenburg, Han, & Weiss, 1995). Health care funding changes have reduced stays at inpatient psychiatric units to only a few days. Community mental health services are less expensive, but also have questionable effectiveness and ecological validity (Friesen & Poertner, 1995; Knitzer, 1993; Koyanagi & Gaines, 1993; Weisz, Weiss, & Donenberg, 1992). They often lack comprehensive services and are uncoordinated in organizing care.

Within the context of schools, self-contained behavioral disorder programs are often the primary intervention option for children with a range of disturbances, including those with SED. These programs are defined to provide an educational setting, typically one classroom, where children with SED spend the entire day, or the majority of it. These programs often include a strong behavioral modification component and additional teacher assistance, but seldom offer psychotherapy or other mental health services. Children and youth receiving services in these programs often do not make the transition to less restrictive settings and have shown significantly lower academic performance, graduation rates, and rates of attendance at postgraduate institutions. Moreover, this population is at significantly greater risk for inpatient psychiatric hospitalization, incarceration, and school failure or expulsion. These traditional school-based programs are limited by a narrow focus on in-school behavior (Conoley & Conoley, 1991); limited knowledge, skills, and confidence on the part of service providers; piecemeal, noncomprehensive practices (Adelman, 1993; Adelman & Taylor, 1998); and a general lack of services (Knitzer, 1993; Marder, 1992).

In response to acknowledged difficulties in treating and educating children with SED, school-based mental health programs have proliferated. Available evidence, however, suggests that such programs continue to be planned and implemented in a narrow, piecemeal fashion, resulting in little coordination, integration, and continuity among staff and community based-programs (Adelman & Taylor, 1998). The absence of these critical collaborative components often results in fragmented and disjointed services, leading to a lack of plan monitoring, failure to address evolving needs, and duplication or omission of services (Quinn, Epstein, & Cumblad, 1995; Stroul & Friedman, 1996). There is also a tendency for schools and communities to rely on narrowly focused, short-term, cost-intensive crisis interventions for a small number of the many students requiring assistance (Adelman & Taylor, 1998).

Many professionals call for increased comprehensiveness of intervention programs to better address the needs of those served, to serve greater numbers, and to increase and enhance accessibility (Adelman & Taylor, 1998). Schools are identified as a logical, efficient context in which to provide a significant portion of the basic interventions that constitute a comprehensive approach to meeting the needs of children with SED (Adelman & Taylor, 1998). In response to these needs, there is a growing movement to create comprehensive school-based centers that incorporate staff and services usually accessed through community mental health and private practice arenas. These may serve youth with a wide range of problem severity.

A related approach to treating children with SED is to integrate mental health services with the schools, using therapeutic classroom settings. Several advantages relative to traditional service delivery may result. This chapter describes a model program developed through a university–public school collaboration to serve children with early-onset, severely debilitating psychiatric disorders. Now in its fourth year of operation, the Intensive Mental Health Program (IMHP) is designed to treat elementary school children (5 to 12 years old) who have such extreme disturbance with emotional regulation and behavioral control that they are unable to function in regular or special education settings. In many communities, children with such severe disturbance receive fragmented, ineffective interventions from overwhelmed social service, educational, and mental health agencies that lack sufficient resources to formulate and carry out comprehensive, empirically based, individualized treatment plans. Children with such impairments often consume many education, health, mental health, and legal resources without notable improvement.

IMHP delivers empirically supported, ecologically sensitive, comprehensive mental health services within a public school setting. Interprofessional collaboration is an important component of the IMHP. The program focuses on developing and implementing a coherent, consistent service plan for each child, using collaboration and consensus building among teaching staff, health providers, social service agencies, parents, and the children themselves. The children attend the IMHP classroom for half of the school day (either morning or afternoon). They continue to attend their regular school (the "home school") throughout the treatment process whenever possible. The ability to function effectively at home and school is a primary objective.

INNOVATIVE CONTRIBUTIONS OF IMHP

IMHP provides a unique and intensive model of intervention for children with SED who have severe impairments in functioning at school and at home. The model innovates through its combination of components:

- The IMHP model provides a highly structured system to manage children's behavior. While the behavior management programs, token economies, and positive reinforcement contingent upon displaying appropriate behavior used are similar to those found in more traditional behavior disorders classrooms, the behavior management system is extended to the home school and the child's home.

- Children continue to attend their home schools for half of the day, and receive IMHP services for the remaining half day. The IMHP staff communicates continuously with each student's home school teachers and special education specialists regarding progress in the IMHP classroom, including effective behavior management strategies. This facilitates the eventual transition to full-time placement back within the home school.

- IMHP creates a treatment setting for children that offers an individually tailored array of empirically supported psychosocial and biomedical interventions, including group and individual therapy, social skills training, relaxation training, targeted behavior management, and carefully evaluated medication trials.

- IMHP therapists continuously consult with parents and child care providers regarding management issues, educational concerns, and therapeutic issues.

- Empirically valid data are gathered for the clinical assessment of individual children and for overall program evaluation. Data are collected from referral sources and consultation partners to formulate a comprehensive conceptualization of factors influencing each child's functioning.

- In addition to working continuously with families and school personnel, the IMHP staff collaborates and coordinates with community agencies, often including case managers, therapists, and psychiatrists at the community mental health center; private psychotherapists; foster care providers and support staff; protective service providers from the state social service agency; health specialists; and family court. This interprofessional collaboration among various treatment providers and community-based professionals facilitates generalization of treatment effects and decreases fragmentation of services between agencies.

This model is intensive and comprehensive in providing therapeutic services for students who have significant emotional and psychological needs not effectively served in traditional special education programs or in traditional mental health settings. The IMHP model focuses on returning children with severe mental disorders to a less restrictive educational environment; increasing the accessibility of mental health services; coordinating separate services into a coherent, consistent whole; utilizing empirically supported treatments, and increasing the probability of positive outcomes. The integrative combination of these intervention modalities and orientations makes IMHP a promising model for mental health services for children with SED.

SERVICE AND TREATMENT FEATURES

It is important to differentiate the service-delivery features (i.e., how treatment is delivered) and the treatment features (i.e., what is delivered) of IMHP. Service-delivery features are the same for each child, whereas treatment features are tailored to individual needs. Both the service-delivery features and the treatment features are designed to be consistent with nine basic principles guiding IMHP:

- *Maintain placement in the child's home and home school.*   This allows children to maintain relationships with family members, teachers, and peers. This has important bidirectional components—relationships are not severed, and the responsibility to care for and educate the child is not diminished.

- *Emphasize an empirical approach to guide interventions.*   Treatment components are selected to be consistent with research on empirically supported psychosocial and pharmacological interventions (e.g., American Academy of Child and Adolescent Psychiatry, 1998; Lonigan, Elbert, & Johnson, 1998).

- *Focus on cognitive and behavioral skill development.*   Professional attention is given to teaching and promoting appropriate behaviors and social-cognitive skills. Cognitive-behavioral and behavioral techniques for specific child problems have thus far achieved the strongest empirical support among psychosocial interventions (Lonigan et al., 1998), and they can be directly applied to improve functioning in home and school settings.

- *Attend to cross-setting linkages and events.*   Point sheets are completed each day in the home school, IMHP, and the child's home. All respondents view the ratings to facilitate communication. These data are aggregated to assist in understanding the interrelationship between settings and events. Service plans are developed to address multiple settings and to offer direct assessment and intervention in multiple settings. By utilizing this data set, individual problem behaviors can be targeted in multiple settings by various providers, therefore maximizing effort and impact.

- *Emphasize generalization and maintenance of treatment outcomes.*   An analog classroom schedule is used in the IMHP to focus on skills needed in the home school and family for successful functioning. In addition, there is frequent communication with the school, home, and community service providers. This enhances active involvement in the child's treatment by every important adult in the child's life. Moreover, collaborating agencies can use the interagency collaboration model established by IMHP when providing follow-up care after the child has been discharged from IMHP.

- *Collaborate with everyone involved with the child.*   Team and individual meetings are used to establish consensus on goals and treatment. This approach is based on the foundations established by the Child and Adolescent Service System Program (CASSP) principles (Day & Roberts, 1991). That is, collaborative services are to be child-centered, family-focused, community-based, culturally competent, and least restrictive or least intrusive.

- *View assessment and diagnosis as ongoing process.*   Children are seen daily by master's-level clinicians, who receive close supervision by doctoral-level, licensed clinical child psychologists. Comprehensive case conceptualizations are formulated based on the child's history and careful, ongoing observations and assessments. Detailed records of school reports and hospitalization summaries are maintained and integrated into the overall treatment and planning process for each child.

- *Maintain a developmental focus.*   The nature of the intervention varies based on the developmental level of each child and his or her family. The child's maturity and ability to reason are always considered in treatment planning. A developmental perspective is integrated with behavioral and cognitive-behavioral approaches.

- *Cultivate an authoritative parenting style for adults involved with the child.*   Each significant adult involved with each IMHP student is taught an interaction style consistent with an authoritative parenting style. Warmth and emotional closeness are cultivated; effective discipline techniques are taught; and age-appropriate expectations, demands, and challenges are nurtured with families, teachers, and other caregivers.

STAFFING REQUIREMENTS FOR IMHP

Each IMHP classroom requires several personnel to work together toward implementation of service plans (see Table 22.1). Allocation of time for the master's-level therapists deserves special mention, because this diverges from typical practice. Specifically, each therapist is allocated 20 hours per week for the IMHP classroom (sessions are 3 hours per day, morning or afternoon). Two therapists are assigned to each classroom, and each therapist is in the classroom every other day. Through this arrangement, each therapist spends an average of 7.5 hours weekly with the six children assigned to each classroom. Each therapist has primary therapeutic responsibility for three of the six children. This arrangement allows for 2.5 hours per week of clinical supervision and 10 hours per week for home visits and for consultations with the home school or community service providers.

Case management and interagency coordination are conducted by the therapists and social workers assigned to each family. Therapists and social workers serve to broker and access other community-based services available for the family outside IMHP. Similarly, therapists and social workers coordinate core team meetings with the student's parents, home school, community agencies, and IMHP staff. IMHP therapists, social workers, and paraprofessionals provide consultation with the home school staff.

Table 22.1   Staffing Requirements for the Intensive Mental Health Program

Title	Primary Roles	Weekly Time Allocation
Special education teacher	Lead teacher	20 hours
Paraprofessional teacher	Assist in behavior management and instruction	20 hours
Masters'-level therapists (2)	Conduct individual and group therapy; coordinate implementation of service plan and home contacts	20 hours each
Doctoral-level psychologist	Supervise mental health component	3 hours
School social work intern	Consult with home school; assist with service plan as needed	10 hours
School social worker	Supervise social work intern; facilitate implementation of service plan	3 hours
School psychologist	Consult regarding service plan design and implementation	2 hours
Treatment, outcome, and process consultant (research staff)	Record and summarize data for clinical decision making and research	20 hours
Child psychiatrist	Consult regarding service plan and medication management	As needed

Note: Classes last 3 hours; maximum of 6 children per classroom.

Therapists and social workers consult at both an administrative and direct-service level by modeling appropriate classroom use of point sheets and a modified token economy (using a "gotcha ticket" system adapted from Jenson, Rhode, & Reavis, 1996). By design, the point sheets utilize response cost or negative punishment. Points are lost for failing or refusing to exhibit specific target behaviors. Losing more than 20% of total points costs the child an opportunity to participate in a weekly special fun activity. The gotcha ticket system operates entirely on positive reinforcement. Gotcha tickets are disbursed liberally for appropriate or desired behavior, and are exchanged for a variety of rewards. In addition, the awarding of a gotcha ticket for appropriate behavior is paired with a positive verbal statement identifying the behavior. Gotcha tickets serve as reinforcements for the children, and also measure the frequency of adults' positive comments to the child. Finally, therapists and social workers also conduct biweekly home visits to provide support to parents and to implement home-based interventions.

SERVICE DELIVERY

Key elements of the IMHP service-delivery model are summarized in Figure 22.1. These include *IMHP classroom features* (e.g., individual and group therapy; behavior

IMHP Classroom Features

Child attends classroom daily, 3 hours/day.
Individual therapy 2 days/week, 30 minutes each.
Group check-in, 15 minutes/day.
Group therapy, 4 days/week, 40 minutes each.
Target behaviors recorded on point sheet, daily.
Psychiatric and behavioral symptoms rated by therapist, daily.
Gotcha ticket coupons awarded, daily.
Gotcha ticket shopping offered, daily.

IMHP Supervision Features

Therapists discuss child with doctoral-level psychologist during clinical supervision, ≥1/week.
Classroom staff meets weekly, ≥40 minutes.
Staff complete comprehensive evaluation form, giving baseline history and assessment of current functioning within 1 month of program entry, with updates ≥1/month thereafter.

IMHP Collaboration Features

Consult with home school staff regarding behavior, ≥1/week.
Meet individually with parents or guardians, ≥1/2 weeks.
Attend core team meeting with home school staff and community service providers, ≥1/month.
Provide summary of target behaviors and psychiatric or behavioral symptoms to medication prescriber (if applicable), ≥1/month.
Distribute collaborative contacts form, which lists all service providers involved with child, to all providers within 1 month of program entry, with updates ≥1/month.
Distribute service plan schematic to service providers within 1 month of program entry, update ≥1/month thereafter (see Figure 22.2 for example).
Observe home school use of behavior management system, ≥1/month.

Home School Service Features

Child attends home school classes daily, 3 hours/day.
Target behaviors recorded on point sheet, daily.
Teaching staff uses gotcha tickets to reward desired behavior, daily.
Gotcha ticket shopping offered, daily.

Home Service Features

Child lives with parents or guardians (whenever possible), daily.
Target behaviors recorded on point sheet, daily.
Parents use gotcha ticket coupons to reward desired behavior, daily.
Parents or guardians allow home visits by IMHP staff, ≥2/month.

Transition Features (Upon Completion of IMHP)

Sign written agreement with home school, family, and other service providers for services to be offered following transition.
Review transition plan implementation with above team 2 and 4 weeks after transition.
Follow-up contact with family and home school 3 and 6 months after transition.

Figure 22.1   Key Elements of Service Delivery Model for the Intensive Mental Health Program

management system); *IMHP supervision features* (e.g., weekly 2-hour supervisory sessions with doctoral-level psychologist); *IMHP collaboration features* (e.g., consultation with home school staff, family, other service providers); and *IMHP transition features* (e.g., written plan for transition and regular monitoring of postdischarge implementation of plan). For each child in IMHP, the provision of each element is recorded on an ongoing basis, providing documentation of treatment fidelity.

TREATMENT FEATURES

The IMHP treatment-planning process determines the "active ingredients" to be delivered to each child through the service-delivery model described in Figure 22.1. Service plans differ depending on each child's symptomatology and life circumstances, and are developed following comprehensive consideration of the potential factors that might cause and maintain the child's problematic behavior (see Figure 22.2). Service plans are distributed to providers and parents to establish treatment congruency and to assign roles and responsibilities. Service plans are modified and refined in consultation with the family and other service providers.

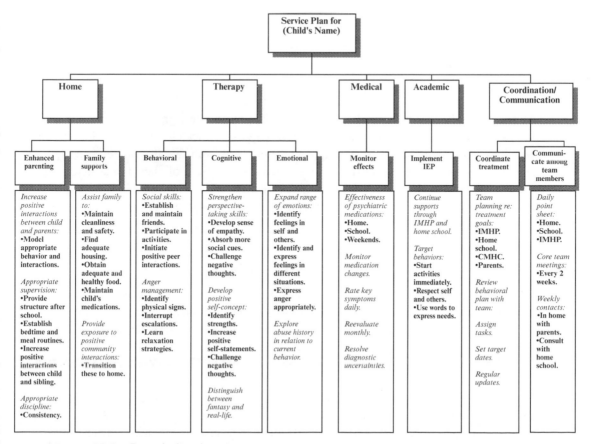

Figure 22.2   Sample Service Plan for Child in the Intensive Mental Health Program

Rigorous ongoing assessment of behavioral, cognitive, and emotional status guides decision making. Daily point sheets are used to track three or four (depending on age) specific target behaviors developed by the treatment team. The students earn points across all settings (i.e., home, home school, and IMHP classroom). The point sheet serves as an indicant of cooperation and involvement in the therapeutic mission of the program. Sometimes the daily sheets are annotated with critical comments, mismarked with points inappropriately removed or added, or not returned at all. In these situations, the therapists and the treatment team must redouble their efforts to engage the home school staff and the parents who misunderstand, misuse, or sabotage the point sheets. When cooperation from home school staff and families is strong, point sheets provide a record of the child's behavior during waking hours. The point sheets also serve as a tool to identify patterns in children's behavior related to medication changes, treatment gains, and environmental factors. Daily ratings of symptoms observed directly in the IMHP classroom are another valuable source of continuous, high-quality clinical data.

The treatment features listed in Figure 22.3 are tracked continuously to gauge fidelity to the principles guiding the IMHP, monitor overall therapeutic progress, and guide treatment decisions. Categories of treatment features include *case conceptualization* (e.g., analyzing presenting problems from multiple conceptual paradigms); *treatment selection* (e.g., utilizing empirically supported treatments for each identified target of change); and *treatment implementation* (e.g., monitoring fidelity to treatment plan).

EVIDENCE FOR EFFECTIVENESS

Since its inception 4 years ago, 43 children have participated in IMHP. Of these, 18 are currently enrolled, with 12 of the current enrollees having been in the program for 8 months or more. Results from ongoing clinical research indicate that 74% of children who have been enrolled in and subsequently discharged from the program eventually achieve full-time placement in the less restrictive environment of their home school. This suggests that therapeutic goals have been met, behavioral manifestations are under control, and the child is better prepared to function in more normalized academic settings.

Symptoms and Diagnoses of Children Receiving Services

All children enrolled in IMHP had a recent history of one or more episodes at school involving an acute threat of harm to self or others, such as attacking teachers or peers, serious threats of self-injurious behavior, or markedly disorganized or bizarre behavior at the time of admission. Nearly all met criteria for one or more Axis I Diagnostic and Statistical Manual of Mental Disorders, Fourth Edition (*DSM-IV;* American Psychiatric Association [APA], 1994) diagnoses on admission. Attention-deficit/hyperactivity disorder (ADHD) or another disruptive behavior disorder was diagnosed in 90% of the children. A majority also had a diagnosed learning disability. Completing the process of differential diagnosis and clarifying contradictory or incomplete histories has been an important task.

Case Conceptualization

Case history and assessment of current functioning conforms to practice parameters for primary presenting problems.

Empirically supported, psychometrically sound, age-normed measures of child functioning are included in evaluation.

Information from multiple sources is considered, including:
   Home school personnel
   Other service providers
   Parents or guardian
   Direct observation using validated observational system
   Child self-report

Case formulation includes consideration of presenting problems from multiple conceptual paradigms, including:
   Biological
   Behavioral
   Cognitive and cognitive-behavioral
   Family systems
   Attachment relationships
   Cultural and socioeconomic

Treatment Selection

Identify measurable targets for change in each of the following areas:
   Biological regulation (e.g., arousal, mood, activity level, and basic cognitive processes)
   Overt behavior
   Social cognition (e.g., social information processing, and knowledge structures)
   Family relations
   Peer relations
   Teaching staff–child relations
   Other environmental factors contributing to dysfunction

Utilize empirically supported interventions to address each identified target for change (i.e., defined as efficacious or probably efficacious using criteria specified by Lonigan et al., 1998).

Treatment Implementation

Review in clinical supervision ≥1/month:
   Progress on implementing selected strategies for each child
   Objective indicators of child functioning (i.e., graphs of point sheets from home, home school, IMHP settings; data from daily ratings of symptoms in IMHP)
   Level of cooperation from home school and family in carrying out service
   Progress in individual therapy for each child
   Progress in group treatment for each child

Clinical supervision provided as needed for:
   Therapists addressing difficulties in individual therapy
   Therapists addressing difficulties in cooperation from family and home school staff
   Therapists addressing difficulties in group therapy
   References to relevant research-based justification for treatment decisions

Figure 22.3 Treatment Features of the Intensive Mental Health Program

Anxiety disorders, especially posttraumatic stress disorder (PTSD), were common. About a third of the children were diagnosed with a mood disorder, and 10% received a diagnosis of pervasive developmental disorder—not otherwise specified. Eighteen percent of the children had chronic health conditions (e.g., cerebral palsy, epilepsy, chronic intestinal pseudoobstruction). About one third of the children exhibited notable psychotic features at some point during treatment. Serious family dysfunction (e.g., history of child maltreatment, psychiatric or behavior disturbance in parent, domestic abuse, or foster care placement) was noted in 70% of cases, with mild to moderate family dysfunction reported for the remainder. Ratings on the Global Assessment of Functioning Scale from *DSM-IV* at the time of enrollment in the IMHP ranged from 50 (i.e., serious symptoms or impairment) to 20 (i.e., frequently violent; manic excitement, danger of hurting self or others).

Functioning During Treatment and at Discharge From the IMHP

Nearly all of the children (41/43, 95%) enrolled in IMHP to date began to attend educational programs in their home school for half of each school day within 1 month of IMHP enrollment. Using detailed records of teacher-reported performance on four key target behaviors, most enrollees met or exceeded their treatment goal (to keep 80% of total possible points from the IMHP classroom and home school for over 50% of the time) within a few weeks of program entry. Considering that all of the children were at imminent risk for school suspension or expulsion or removal from their homes, were psychiatrically hospitalized just prior to enrollment, or both, IMHP has proven very effective in enabling children with SED to function half time in their home schools during the active treatment phase.

Of the first 27 children enrolled and subsequently discharged from IMHP, 20 (74%) were returned to their home schools full time and were living with their biological or adoptive parents at discharge. Of the 7 children not returned to a full-time home school placement, 1 child entered a residential treatment center, 1 was placed in a juvenile detention center, 4 were placed in foster care within another community, and 1 moved with his family out of the region.

Services Outcomes

IMHP has sought to measure a variety of outcome indicators, including families' and schools' experiences and perspectives, burden and stress of care, and satisfaction with treatment. Ratings of families' participation in treatment for the first 17 cases indicated good participation in treatment for 12 cases, and fair participation in 5 cases. No parent to date has requested that his or her child be removed from IMHP.

Subjectively, it has required considerable time and effort to establish a collaborative, cooperative relationship with the majority of families, many of which have had a deep distrust of the schools and social service agencies at the time of enrollment in IMHP. Parents are asked to use the IMHP behavioral rating system at home, and are often asked to modify their own behavior for the benefit of the child. A particular strength of IMHP is the small caseload for each therapist (3 primary cases). This, coupled with the therapist's dogged determination to win the trust and cooperation of parents, leads to increased effective collaboration between the IMHP staff and families.

School personnel vary in their acceptance and expertise in carrying out IMHP behavioral recommendations. The primary request from home schools over the first 3 years of IMHP was for more on-site consultation with IMHP staff. This concern was addressed by including social work interns in IMHP with a primary responsibility for on-site school consultation. These interns have been integrated into the treatment team and utilize plans adopted by the interprofessional team. At present, IMHP appears to be highly valued by most school personnel. The seemingly miraculous improvements shown by a number of children during IMHP treatment has led to frequent praise from home school staff. Behavioral indicators of school system satisfaction with IMHP include expanded funding of the program to serve more children, continued referrals, and decisions by school principals to allocate scarce faculty teaching allocations to fund additional IMHP staff.

Environmental Outcomes

Improved family functioning is one goal of IMHP. Improved functioning by children in IMHP is integrally related to improved conditions at home. The behavioral charting and daily symptom ratings for individual children show a clear and convincing relationship between adverse family events and episodes of acute dysfunction in many children enrolled in the program. The chronic history of family dysfunction for many children in IMHP often requires long-term supports and extended home-based interventions. Family functioning improved notably in the majority of the first 17 cases, albeit this change required months of effort by IMHP staff and other community agencies. Case management, family therapy, or youth specialist support was utilized in 10 of the first 17 cases. Children's psychiatric symptoms also place substantial stress on families. Improved emotional regulation for children resulting from proper medication and psychosocial treatments has seemed to enable some parents to function more adaptively.

IMHP appears to reduce family stress, in part by streamlining and coordinating service delivery. As a case in point, one family currently enrolled in IMHP has 22 professionals involved with their child (6 IMHP staff, 5 home school staff, 4 community mental health center staff, 1 child protective services staff, and 6 health care system staff). The potential for misinformation, duplication of services, and incompatible intervention plans is tremendous. Indeed, months of effort are often required following IMHP admission to reduce the fragmentation and overwhelming demands of various service providers.

Systems Outcomes

Service-related outcomes include the level, type, and duration of service recommended at discharge, as well as changes in service utilization from admission to discharge. For the first 17 cases enrolled, treatment duration ranged from 2 to 18 months (mean = 8.2 months, $SD = 5.6$). IMHP is one of the most intensive treatment services offered by the local public school system, rivaled only by an intensive autism treatment program. IMHP is perceived by school administrators to be worth the cost. Indeed, financial support has been increased each year to allow more children access to the program and to provide additional staff to optimize outcomes.

Organization and cost-related systems outcomes include assessment of relationships between service providers and assessments of costs and services. IMHP has increasingly become known and respected in the community, and new procedures and processes for enhanced collaboration have been developed since its inception. Core team meetings at home schools now include representatives from almost all providers in contact with the child, rather than just school personnel. Team meetings have been held with increasing regularity, averaging once a month per child, with more frequent meetings during crisis periods. The IMHP staff has developed very close ties with the local community mental health center and with child protective services.

Fiscal analyses of IMHP indicate it is a cost-effective program. Annual expenditures are approximately $10,000 per slot. This figure includes dedicated teaching staff, clinical service personnel, doctoral-level clinical supervisors, special equipment, and supplies. Much of this cost is recouped from state or federal funds earmarked for special education or mental health services.

To fully understand the cost-effective nature of the IMHP, it is helpful to compare the cost of alternative programs and future expense of treating and educating youth in other settings. For example, the per child costs exceed $54,750 per year for local juvenile detention programs. Those for local residential programs exceed $120,000 per year. The average daily cost of hospitalization is $500, which translates to $15,000 per month, or $180,000 per year. These alternatives are very expensive and produce questionable outcomes in terms of helping children function outside institutional settings (Burns & Friedman, 1990). Coupling these costs with recidivism rates and multiplying by the average length of intervention, the cost-prohibitive nature of alternative programs in comparison to the IMHP becomes quite clear.

Boundary Conditions Influencing Outcomes

Treatment effectiveness research suggests that several important factors may influence the effects of IMHP services on individual children (Kazdin & Kendall, 1998). These may be categorized along the lines proposed by Hoagwood, Jensen, Petti, and Burns (1996) as characteristics of the child (e.g., severity of psychopathology), characteristics of the family and home environment (e.g., ongoing hostility or neglect), and characteristics of broader systems of school and community (e.g., disorganization or lack of resources).

Child Characteristics

Severity and chronicity of disturbance at the time of admission often influence treatment outcomes. In the present project, detailed descriptions of severity and chronicity are available due to the comprehensive, in-depth review of history and careful attention to conflicting information typically found in case material for children with SED. Key variables include the age of onset of severely disruptive or abnormal behavior; the degree to which impairment has been continuous versus episodic; and the intensity of disturbance in mood, thought qualities, and activity or arousal.

Characteristics of the Family and Home Environment

Parental psychopathology is a frequent barrier to treatment progress, especially when expressed through erratic, antisocial behavior. The extensive, extended contact with families in IMHP presents an excellent opportunity to examine these indicators as prognostic signs. Parents who exhibit psychological problems are referred to practitioners in the community, especially to the community mental health center. Many of the parents have already had extensive experience with the mental health system for their own problems prior to their child's referral to IMHP.

Characteristics of the Schools and the Community

Through extensive contact with home schools and community service providers, it appears that some children served by IMHP receive a notably higher standard of education and mental health service than do others. Operationally defined, children appear to make much less progress if they attend home school settings wherein staff are unwilling or unable to follow the basic IMHP behavior management program. Through daily ratings of child behavior and weekly visits to the home school, the project has access to very robust data pertaining to the quality of service offered to IMHP children.

Similarly, other community service providers vary in their willingness or ability to collaborate in developing and carrying out a consistent, coherent service plan. Once again, data gathered for the project provide an excellent chance to demonstrate how good teamwork in pursuit of a well-developed, empirically based service plan can make a major difference for children with SED. Ongoing ratings by IMHP staff of cooperation and follow-through by other providers is gathered routinely, and should enable an empirical test of this intuitively posited influence on treatment outcomes.

Barriers and Solutions

Experience with IMHP since its inception has led to the development of several useful tools for establishing and maintaining collaboration among the various care providers. These include a collaborative contacts sheet listing names and roles and a contact information form for all adults directly engaged in providing education or services; both these documents are distributed to all parties involved in the service plan. However, barriers to collaboration across settings and agencies remain, and a continuous search for effective solutions to such barriers is an important component of IMHP.

Barriers are conceptualized as arising from four ecologically nested factors: (a) *characteristics of individual providers* (e.g., limitations in knowledge, skill, motivation, or attitudes and beliefs); (b) *within-setting factors* (e.g., conflict among teaching staff or administrators in the home school or among team members in a mental health center); (c) *interagency barriers* (e.g., turf issues and barriers to effective interagency communications); and (d) *policy and larger system issues* (e.g., poor funding and high turnover among child protective service workers or inadequate funding for mental health services).

Ongoing record keeping regarding collaboration among providers offers a naturalistic single-case study of efforts to increase teamwork. Combining these case studies eventually enables a test of two basic assumptions: (a) Solutions must match the factors causing the barriers, and (b) barriers caused by factors at various levels of social ecology likely require action at various levels. Successful collaboration is judged on objective measures, such as rate of accurate completion of behavioral point sheets by the home school or parents, observed improvement in carrying out behavior management practices, and improved adaptive functioning by the child. Methods from single-case designs are used to organize information, identify barriers, and measure progress. Chronologically ordered outcomes are graphed, with notation of specific efforts taken to address collaboration barriers. Through the accretion of cases, it is possible to distinguish between effective and ineffective solution strategies and to build an empirically supported set of guidelines to address difficulties in the collaborative process that is so crucial to IMHP.

CONCLUSION

The development of effective, sustainable interventions for children with SED is a high priority for public schools. Traditional school-based services for these children appear inadequate in many regards. IMHP provides a possible model for school-based interventions for the most disturbed children in the school-age population. Cost analyses suggest that IMHP is significantly less expensive than the alternative placements for students served by IMHP. Ongoing research addresses the key issues of boundary conditions and barriers, which are important qualifiers of any treatment approach. IMHP offers an opportunity to assess the limits of high-quality services from schools and mental health systems to make a meaningful impact on children's functioning when the home environment continues to represent an ongoing source of stress. Building effective, evidence-based interventions for children with SED in school settings offers the possibility of improved school performance *and* better mental health outcomes for children with severe emotional and behavioral disorders.

REFERENCES

Adelman, H. S. (1993). School-linked mental health interventions: Toward mechanisms for service coordination and integration. *Journal of Community Psychology, 21,* 309–319.

Adelman, H. S., & Taylor, L. (1998). Reframing and mental health in schools and expanding school reform. *Educational Psychologist, 33,* 135–152.

American Academy of Child and Adolescent Psychiatry (1998). Practice parameter of the assessment and treatment of children and adolescents with posttraumatic stress disorder. *Journal of the American Academy of Child and Adolescent Psychiatry, 37*(Suppl.), 4S–26S.

American Psychiatric Association. (1994). *Diagnostic and statistical manual of mental disorders* (4th ed.). Washington, DC: Author.

Burns, B. J., & Friedman, R. M. (1990). Examining the research base for child mental health services and policy. *The Journal of Mental Health Administration, 17,* 87–97.

Conoley, J. C., & Conoley, C. W. (1991). Collaboration for child adjustment: Issues for school- and clinic-based child psychologists. *Journal of Consulting and Clinical Psychology, 59,* 821–829.

Day, C., & Roberts, M. C. (1991). Activities of the child and adolescent service system program for improving mental health services for children and families. *Journal of Clinical Child Psychology, 20,* 340–350.

Friesen, B. J., & Koroloff, N. M. (1990). Family-centered services: Implications for mental health administration and research. *Journal of Mental Health Administration, 17,* 13–25.

Friesen, B. J., & Poertner, J. (1995). *From case management to service coordination for children with emotional, behavioral, or mental disorders: Building on family strengths.* Baltimore: Brookes.

Henggeler, S. W. (1994). A consensus: Conclusion of the APA Task Force report on innovative models of mental health services for children, adolescents, and their families. *Journal of Clinical Child Psychology, 23*(Suppl.), 3–6.

Hoagwood, K., Jensen, P. S., Petti, T., & Burns, B. J. (1996). Outcomes of mental health care for children and adolescents: I. A comprehensive conceptual model. *Journal of the American Academy of Child and Adolescent Psychiatry, 35,* 1055–1063.

Jenson, W. R., Rhode, G., & Reavis, H. K. (1996). *The tough kid tool box.* Longmont, CO: Sopris West.

Kazdin, A. E., & Kendall, P. C. (1998). Current progress and future plans for developing effective treatments: Comments and perspectives. *Journal of Clinical Child Psychology, 27,* 217–226.

Kiesler, C. A. (1993). Mental health policy and mental hospitalization. *Current Directions in Psychological Science, 2,* 93–95.

Knitzer, J. (1993). Children's mental health policy: Challenging the future. *Journal of Emotional and Behavioral Disorders, 1,* 8–16.

Koyanagi, C., & Gaines, S. (1993). *All systems failure: An examination of the results of neglecting the needs of children with serious emotional disturbance.* Alexandria, VA: National Mental Health Association.

Lonigan, C. J., Elbert, J. C., & Johnson, S. B. (1998). Empirically supported psychosocial interventions for children: An overview. *Journal of Clinical Child Psychology, 27,* 138–145.

Marder, C. (1992). *Secondary school students classified as serious emotionally disturbed: How are they being served?* Menlo Park, CA: SRI International.

Quinn, K. P., Epstein, M. H., & Cumblad, C. (1995). Developing comprehensive individualized community-based services for children and youth with emotional and behavior disorders: Direct service providers' perspective. *Journal of Child and Family Studies, 4,* 19–42.

Quinn, K. P., & McDougal, J. L. (1998). A mile wide and a mile deep: Comprehensive interventions for children and youth with emotional and behavioral disorders and their families. *School Psychology Review, 27,* 191–203.

Stroul, B. A., & Friedman, R. M. (1996). The system of care philosophy. In B. A. Stroul (Ed.), *Children's mental health: Creating systems of care in a changing society* (pp. 2–22). Baltimore: Brookes.

Weisz, J. R., Weiss, B., & Donenberg, G. R. (1992). The lab versus the clinic: Effects of child and adolescent psychotherapy. *American Psychologist, 47,* 1578–1585.

Weisz, J. R., Donenberg, G. R., Han, S. S., & Weiss, B. (1995). Bridging the gap between lab and clinic in child and adolescent psychotherapy. *Journal of Consulting and Clinical Psychology, 634,* 688–701.

Chapter 23

PRIMARY CARE

RONALD T. BROWN AND WENDY S. FREEMAN

In this chapter, we review the essential issues associated with the prevalence, identification, and management of emotional and behavioral disturbances among pediatric patients seen in primary care settings. For our discussion, *primary care* refers to the provision of pediatric services to children and adolescents in outpatient and ambulatory care clinics, where most children receive their medical care (Stancin, 1999). It is timely to review these issues when the delivery of health care services in this country is changing considerably. The cost of health care in the United States has risen dramatically, paralleling increases in technology that better manage diseases, enhance quality of life, and reduce mortality. A systematic effort by third-party payers (e.g., Medicaid, private health maintenance organizations, third-part insurers) endeavors to limit spending and manage care so that services, including mental health services, are provided in the most cost-effective manner. Health care has become expensive, and these efforts to contain and drive down the costs of medical care are ongoing. In this chapter, we conceptualize the delivery of diagnostic and treatment services to those with mental illness as an important and integral component of the health care system.

One way to contain health care costs is to limit services provided by specialists, including psychologists, psychiatrists, and other mental health professionals. By initiating point of service within the primary care system and by limiting referrals to specialty providers, costs are contained (American Academy of Pediatrics, 2000), but the result has been a decrease in the availability of mental health services for children and adolescents. This decrease is attributed to insurance packages that provide limited mental health services. Before managed care, pediatricians referred their patients with emotional or behavioral disturbances to mental health providers, making it more likely that caregivers and school personnel would have direct access to mental health professionals. Increased evidence regarding the efficacy of specific mental health services (Kazdin, Bass, Ayers, & Rodgers, 1990) and decreased availability of these services has resulted in a burgeoning trend to deliver mental health services within the primary care setting.

Primary care providers can adequately perform some of the basic services of specialists. For example, the most widely used intervention for attention-deficit/ hyperactivity disorder (ADHD) is stimulant medication (Safer, Zito, & Pine, 1996), and in cases where there is no serious comorbidity of other psychiatric disorders, pharmacotherapy may be readily managed in the primary care setting, eliminating the necessity of referrals to a mental health provider (American Academy of Pediatrics, 2000). The rationale is that this will result in more cost-effective symptom management. In fact, for some psychiatric disorders that were previously managed in specialty clinics (e.g., child and adolescent psychiatry, mental health centers), there has been a trend for many insurance companies to advocate for the management of these disorders in primary care settings (e.g., a pediatrician's office). At best, insurance companies require that the primary care physician initiate referrals for mental health services.

It is clear, then, that the primary care provider plays a critical role in accessing and providing mental health services (Stancin, 1999), including coordination of their patients' mental health care. This necessitates clear lines of communication and coordination, particularly for children with severe and comorbid conditions that require coordinated and multiple services (American Academy of Pediatrics, 2000; King, Rosenbaum, & King, 1996).

Currently, efforts to drive down the costs of health care are running parallel with increasing mental health needs of children and adolescents and decreasing access to services (American Academy of Pediatrics, 2000). Over the past two decades the rate of psychosocial problems identified in primary care settings has increased from 7% to 20% (Kelleher, McInerny, Gardner, Childs, & Wasserman, 2000), with estimates suggesting that 13 million children are in need of mental health or substance abuse services (American Psychiatric Association, 1999). More alarming is the Lavigne and associates (1999) finding that the percentage of emotional disorders has increased in recent years, particularly for preschool children.

The pediatrician has an active role in facilitating health care choices for children and adolescents, in promoting optimal development, and in preventing injuries. This puts the pediatrician in a prime position to address mental health needs at a primary, secondary, and tertiary prevention level (Drotar, 1995). Bradbury, Janicke, Riley, and Finney (1999) identified predictors of unintentional injuries to schoolchildren seen in primary care settings. Participants were 295 children who ranged in age from 5 to 11 years and who were receiving primary care in a health maintenance organization. Predictors of increased injury liability included younger age, more children at home, more behavior problems, less social competence, more maternal anxiety, and multiple indices of compromised child health. The findings are important because they underscore the importance of developing programmatic interventions at the level of the primary care setting (e.g., flyers, pamphlets, videos) to alert caregivers of the serious impact of injuries and, hopefully, to prevent child injuries.

Because they screen individual patients for various psychopathologies, pediatricians and family practice physicians serve as gatekeepers for mental health services (Costello et al., 1988; Stancin, 1999). This is a critical role for the primary care provider, given that the costs of failing to identify and treat children with serious emotional disturbance are high. For example, the National Advisory Mental Health Council (1990) reported that costs of treating mental health disorders in children and adolescents exceed $1.5 billion annually. A substantial portion of these costs are associated with long-term care that is required when diagnostic and prevention efforts are not implemented early during the course of the disorder, perhaps at a time when briefer interventions may have significant effect and be less costly (Richardson, Keller,

Selby-Harrington, & Parrish, 1996). Lavigne et al. (1998) also argued that screening at the primary care level is especially important because pediatricians play a central role in caregivers' adherence to recommended mental health services.

Emotional disturbances among children seen by pediatricians are quite high, with estimates of up to 1 in 5 children meeting criteria for an Axis I psychiatric disorder (Costello et al., 1996; Costello et al., 1988). Some serious psychiatric disorders in children are relatively rare (e.g., autism, psychotic disorders), but others are more prevalent and are likely to be encountered in the primary care setting (e.g., ADHD, oppositional defiant disorder, anxiety and depressive disorders). Furthermore, there is evidence that psychiatric disturbances in children are associated with a greater frequency of visits to physicians (Garralda, Bowman, & Mandalia, 1999). Thus, a question arises about whether psychological services in the primary care setting may reduce the levels of pediatric health care use. This issue was addressed by Finney and associates (Finney, Riley, & Cataldo, 1991) when they examined the effect of a psychological consultation service designed to provide brief psychotherapy for children and adolescents with common behavioral and emotional problems. Care was provided within a large health maintenance organization. Caregivers assisted in the intervention program to define specific behaviors and develop treatment focused on changing behaviors. Most caregivers reported their children's behavioral problems were completely resolved, but a second major finding of the investigation is that there were significant decreases in medical encounters relative to a matched comparison group of untreated children from the same health maintenance organization. The reduction in the use of services was attributed to children with behavioral and toileting problems who received mental health treatment. Similar findings were reported by Finney, Lemanek, Cataldo, Katz, and Fuqua (1989), who found improvement in pain symptoms and decreased use of medical services for children with recurrent abdominal pain who received psychological intervention in their primary care setting.

Kinsman, Wildman, and Smucker (1999) asked caregivers about health care use for their children as a means of identifying children at risk for psychosocial problems. Caregivers of children and adolescents who ranged in age from 2 to 16 years completed questionnaires about their own, their child's, and their family's psychosocial functioning and health care use. Consistent with the findings of Finney and colleagues (1989, 1991), children and parents with high health care utilization were more likely to evidence psychosocial problems. Thus, using health care data in combination with other screening measures may alert primary care practitioners to possible child and parent psychosocial problems (Kinsman et al., 1999).

Over the years, evidence of significant psychological consequences of physical illness in children and adolescents has emerged (Cadman, Boyle, Szatmari, & Offord, 1987; Gortmaker, Walker, Weitzman, & Sobol, 1990). Hence, the primary care setting is a highly appropriate environment in which to address emotional disturbances in children and adolescents. With increasing interest in mental health issues, pediatricians are receiving more training in behavior and developmental pediatrics and in addressing psychosocial issues during well-child visits (Coury, Berger, Stancin, & Tanner, 1999; Perrin, 1999).

The training and interests of psychologists allow for excellent partnerships for mental health problems seen in primary care settings (Drotar, 1995). In the field of ambulatory care pediatrics, there is significant emphasis on child development and screening for developmental deviations across numerous spheres of functioning—for example, physical, cognitive, emotional, psychosocial (Perrin, 1999). This supports the argument that mental health issues fall well within the domain of pediatric primary care. An example of advocacy for the inclusion of psychosocial issues in pediatric primary care is the Bright Futures Program (National Center for Education in Maternal and Child Health, 2000), a compendium of health and mental health promotion in the context of the family and community across developmental periods. The source provides primary health care professionals with developmental information and specific data for prevention efforts; it also addresses areas of concern for office practice (e.g., early recognition and management of emotional disorders at various stages of development).

Provision of mental health services within the primary care setting is particularly critical for children in underserved areas. For example, there is a shortage of mental health providers, especially those trained to work in pediatrics, in rural and disadvantaged communities (American Academy of Pediatrics, 2000; Morris, 1996). In some locations, access to mental health care from providers other than primary care physicians or pediatricians is almost nonexistent. Data from the first wave of the Great Smoky Mountains Study of Youth, an epidemiologic investigation of psychopathology and mental health service use among regional children, suggest that the major system providing mental health services to children is the educational system, with 70% to 80% of children receiving services in educational settings (Burns, Costello, Angold, Tweed, & Stangl, 1995). For most of these children, the school system was the only provider of mental health services. In this study, fewer than 15% of children received mental health services in a general medical setting. Although the investigators recommended research to replicate their findings, clearly the pediatric primary care setting and school health clinics represent two critical venues to address children's emotional and behavioral disturbances.

IDENTIFICATION OF EMOTIONAL DISORDERS

Emotional disturbances in children and adolescents are relatively common, but there are data to suggest that primary care providers underidentify these psychiatric disorders in pediatric populations (Chang, Warner, & Weissman, 1988; Costello et al., 1988; Dulcan et al., 1990; Lavigne et al., 1993; Richardson et al., 1996). Primary care providers seem to exhibit good specificity in that the children they identify do meet criteria for psychiatric disorders. However, many more children meet criteria for psychiatric disorders from reports by caregivers on behavior checklists, psychologists' ratings (Lavigne et al., 1993), and standardized psychiatric interviews (Costello et al., 1988). The thoroughness of these measures versus the less formally psychologically trained sensitivity of primary care providers may account for many children who may be underdiagnosed for mental health problems (for review, see Perrin, 1999).

Because pediatricians are gatekeepers for subsequent services and because they may underidentify psychosocial dysfunction (Costello et al., 1988), it is of great concern that many children are likely to go without needed mental health services. This is likely to result in potentially serious long-term negative outcomes, including more frequent use of health care services (Durlak, 1997; Finney et al., 1991; Finney et al., 1989) and the persistence of mental health problems (Graham & Rutter, 1973; Starfield et al., 1984).

A number of factors may contribute to primary care physicians' underidentification of psychosocial problems in pediatric patients. Caregivers may not spontaneously report concerns of a psychological nature. They may be reluctant to disclose such concerns to the primary care provider. In a survey of over 200 mothers, 70% of the mothers had primary concerns regarding emotional and behavioral issues, but fewer than one third of the mothers discussed these concerns with their child's pediatrician (Hickson, Altemeier, & O'Conner, 1983). Parental nondisclosure of emotional and behavioral concerns is also evident in more recent surveys. It has been consistently demonstrated that although 40% to 80% of parents have questions or concerns about their children's behavioral and emotional development, many do not raise these concerns with their pediatricians (Lynch, Wildman, & Smucker, 1997; Richardson et al., 1996; Young, Davis, Schoen, & Parker, 1998).

Perrin (1999) suggests that primary care pediatricians are not cognizant of their patients' developmental and psychosocial problems. Perrin has attributed this in part to the reluctance of pediatricians to inquire about children's behavior, development, or family functioning, despite the fact that ample research is available to indicate that caregivers are eager to discuss psychosocial issues. Perhaps as a result, approximately 50% of caregivers seen for well-child visits report having psychosocial concerns that go unaddressed (Sharpe, Pantell, Murphy, & Lewis, 1992). Thus, given that caregivers have generally endorsed high consumer satisfaction and high efficacy ratings pertaining to psychological services in the primary care setting (Charlop, Parrish, Fenton, & Cataldo, 1987; Kanoy & Schroeder, 1985), it would be prudent for primary providers to solicit concerns that parents may have about their children's psychological adjustment so that intervention efforts may quickly ensue.

Only recently have significant efforts been put forth to improve primary care providers' identification of mental health problems among their patients. The most seminal development in improving the identification of children with emotional and behavioral disturbances was the formulation of the *Diagnostic and Statistical Manual for Primary Care (DSM-PC) Child and Adolescent Version* (American Academy of Pediatrics, 1996). The *DSM-PC* is compatible with the *Diagnostic and Statistical Manual* (4th ed., *DSM-IV;* American Psychiatric Association, 1994) and provides standardized nomenclature to describe a wide spectrum of potential childhood difficulties ranging from developmental variations to overt psychopathology. The *DSM-PC* extends the *DSM-IV* by providing a broader range of symptoms and reflecting problems encountered in primary care settings. The manual is the collaboration of the American Academy of Pediatrics, the American Psychiatric Association, and the Society for Pediatric Psychology of the American Psychological Association.

Rather than confining the content to psychopathology, the nomenclature in the *DSM-PC* considers both developmental and environmental situations in the classification of problems. There are several tenets and assumptions underlying the *DSM-PC* that differentiate it significantly from the *DSM-IV.* As outlined by Wolraich (1997), underlying the construction of the *DSM-PC* system was the assumption that children exhibit symptoms and behaviors along a continuum ranging from developmentally normal variations of behavior to symptoms of a disorder. Another assumption is that children's mental health is affected by the environment and that addressing such environmental factors may prevent the exacerbation or development of more severe psychopathology.

The nomenclature of the *DSM-PC* was prepared such that the system is compatible with the *DSM*, yet also provides a vocabulary to classify psychosocial problems encountered in a typical pediatric practice. Thus, the *DSM-PC* is better applied to general pediatric practice than the *DSM-IV* because it includes subthreshold psychopathology and considers paramount the notion of environmental factors that contribute to psychosocial problems. Furthermore, the *DSM-PC* may encourage primary care providers to consider psychosocial problems by providing a tool to document and code such activity. Most important, the manual legitimizes the role of the primary care setting in addressing comprehensive and developmental psychosocial issues and familiarizes pediatricians with these issues, potentially improving access to needed mental health services.

The development of the *DSM-PC* is the first large-scale collaborative effort to legitimize psychosocial concerns in the primary care setting. To date, there are no data on the effect of the *DSM-PC* on identification of and intervention for psychosocial problems, but we hope that future research will document its utility. The use of the *DSM-PC* also will serve psychologists' abilities to conduct research on the prevalence of behavioral and developmental problems, document collaborative practices in primary care, and train pediatricians to manage these problems (Drotar, 1999).

The identification of mental health problems among pediatric patients also may be facilitated by the use of routine screening for symptoms of emotional and behavioral disturbances. The goal of screening in the primary care setting is to identify children at risk for psychological dysfunction who may benefit from further evaluation. Screening can be accomplished via standardized questionnaires completed by the patient's caregiver. The primary care provider may elect to screen en masse (screening all children) or to selectively screen children considered at risk (e.g., children with poor school performance or a family history of significant psychiatric pathology). As Perrin (1998) observed, psychometrically valid instruments are available for the pediatric primary care provider, but screening is not systematically used in primary care settings.

Several reviews provide guidelines for the selection of appropriate screening instruments and implementing screening procedures in primary care settings (e.g., Simonian, Tarnowski, Stancin, Friman, & Atkins, 1991; Stancin & Palermo, 1997). Perrin (1998) questioned the appropriateness of routine behavior screening for all children in situations where there are inadequate resources to address the emotional and behavioral disturbances that are identified in the screening process.

Although screening procedures are associated with increased identification of emotional disturbances in children and adolescents (e.g., Riekert, Stancin, Palermo, & Drotar, 1999), screening alone does not guarantee that further evaluation and adequate intervention will follow. Riekert and colleagues examined the effects of behavioral screening on primary care providers' management of children's behavioral problems. A behavioral screening program was developed by pediatric psychologists who served as consultants to a large pediatric ambulatory clinic at a county medical center. By reviewing information in children's medical charts, the researchers found that the screening procedure did appear to be used by primary care providers to guide decisions about the prescription of psychotropic medication, with physicians beginning medication after completion of the screening procedure. However, many of the children who were referred to a specialist for mental health services were referred before the physician had received the screening information, suggesting that the physicians used information other than the screening results to make decisions about mental health referrals.

In another study conducted in an inner-city community health clinic, Murphy, Arnett, Bishop, Jellinek, and Reede (1992) found that routine use of a brief screening measure (the Pediatric Symptom Checklist described later in this chapter) completed by parents at the time of well-child visits did increase the rate of referral for psychosocial problems to 12% from a baseline referral rate of 1.5%. When the routine screening procedure was discontinued, the referral rate dropped back down to 2%. Clearly, more research is needed to examine the consequences of screening practices in the primary care setting and to identify factors that facilitate or impede the ongoing use of screening procedures in pediatric primary care practices.

Behavioral checklists and rating scales have been used extensively in childhood psychopathology research to identify psychological disorders and to evaluate response to treatment, particularly psychotropic medication. For example, the Conners Rating Scale (Conners, 1969) was one of the first instruments developed to document stimulant drug efficacy in children with symptoms associated with ADHD. Advantages of rating scales and behavioral checklists include their simplicity in administration, their cost-effectiveness, and the ease with which information can be systematically gathered across multiple informants (i.e., parents, teachers, children). Rating scales and checklists are particularly valuable for pediatricians when behavior must be summarized for the purpose of identifying potential problems and determining if further evaluation is warranted (Stancin & Palermo, 1997).

Pediatricians have available an array of rating scales to use for screening and assessment, ranging from global assessments to the identification of more specific types of emotional and behavioral disturbances (e.g., anxiety, depression, attentional problems). Although an overview of these many rating scales is beyond the scope of this chapter, the reader is referred to Aman and Pearson (1999), Brown and Sawyer (1998), and a review by Stancin and Palermo (1997). The use of behavioral rating scales can assist practitioners in keeping pediatric records, soliciting and assessing caregivers' concerns about their child's behavior or development, providing information to other professionals, and quantifying symptoms associated with various psychopathologies. In selecting an instrument, Eisert, Sturner, and Mabe (1991) suggested that the pediatrician consider response format (i.e., presence or absence of a symptom versus placement along a severity continuum), whether the rating scale has acceptable psychometric properties like reliability and validity, scoring and completion time, and whether normative data are available when choosing behavioral rating scales for office use.

One measure that meets all of Eisert's criteria is the Pediatric Symptom Checklist (PSC) (Jellinek & Murphy, 1990), a 35-item parent questionnaire developed to screen for psychosocial dysfunction in school-age children. The reliability of this screening instrument has been demonstrated across a variety of settings, and the validity of this measure with more extensive psychiatric assessments has been established (Jellinek et al., 1988; Murphy, Arnett, et al., 1992; Murphy, Reede, Jellinek, & Bishop, 1992). Normative data are available for several relevant pediatric populations (e.g., military, health maintenance organizations, suburban pediatric practices). The questionnaire was developed specifically for use in pediatric practices. It takes approximately 5 minutes for parents to complete, so it can reasonably be completed by the parent in the waiting room. On this questionnaire, the parents rate impressions of the frequency ("often," "sometimes," "never") with which their children exhibit a variety of symptoms and behaviors. Total scores that fall above the cutoff suggest the child is at risk for emotional or behavioral disturbance and indicate the need for further evaluation.

For younger children, the Toddler Behavior Screening Inventory (Mouton-Simien, McCain, & Kelley, 1997) is easy to incorporate into a primary care setting. McCain, Kelley, and Fishbein (1999) examined the instrument in clinical and nonclinical samples. The measure was found reliable and valid, and it discriminated clinical from nonclinical participants.

A MODEL FOR ADDRESSING MENTAL HEALTH ISSUES

Typically, mental health services are provided on a consultation basis in which the primary care provider initiates a referral and requests that an independent mental health specialist evaluate and provide treatment services (Drotar, 1995; Roberts & Wright, 1982). As an alternative model, indirect consultation does not involve direct contact between the patient and the specialty mental health provider. Instead, primary care providers seek guidance and instruction so that they can more effectively manage the child's emotional disturbance without the initiation of outside referrals (Kush & Campo, 1998). This collaborative approach involves both the primary care practitioner and the mental health specialist working in concert to provide optimal management.

To make referrals more convenient for pediatric patients and their families, efforts to provide integrated services within the primary care practice setting have increased (Drotar, 1995; Hannemann, 1997; Schroeder, 1997, 1999). Minimally integrated primary care consists of a mental health professional, such as a pediatric or clinical psychologist, working in a primary care setting. This mental health provider offers services with the benefit of already being a member of the child's medical team. This professional may have primary responsibility for screening, assessing, and providing interventions to children seen by the physicians in the practice. Although pediatricians and psychologists have a long history of collaborative academic and research endeavors (Drotar, 1995), the integration of psychologists into pediatric primary care settings is more recent (Stancin, 1999). There are a number of examples of such successful collaborative efforts (e.g., Schroeder, 1997), but the inclusion of a psychosocial component in primary care settings remains the exception rather than a standard component of pediatric care.

An exemplar of collaborative primary care is the Chapel Hill Pediatrics practice developed and described by Schroeder (1997), which is a component of the interdisciplinary training program at the University of North Carolina at Chapel Hill. The program has existed for nearly 25 years and has been described as an outstanding example of programmatic collaboration between psychology and pediatrics and one that thoroughly embraces the spirit of the scientist-practitioner model (Drotar, 1995). Although similar programs have been described in the literature (Cunningham, Bremner, & Boyle, 1995; Hurley, 1995; Wertlieb, 1999), the Chapel Hill program is reviewed here because the program received the American Academy of Ambulatory Pediatrics Teaching Excellence Award.

Design of the collaborative practice model began with a telephone survey of parents to inquire about problems they were having with their children and ways in which they would like these problems addressed (Schroeder, Goolsby, & Stangler, 1975). The goal of this survey was to develop a community practice in which parents would be provided with timely information, education, and intervention services around their children's development. Based on the data from their survey, the practitioners developed the following services: a call-in hour twice a week whereby caregivers were permitted the opportunity to ask a psychologist questions about behavior and development; a walk-in service for 2 hours per week, whereby caregivers were permitted to consult with psychologists pertaining to issues of behavior management and appropriate development; and parent groups that were held three evenings per month designed to provide support for caregivers as well as provide strategies for behavior management. The practice serves nearly 12,000 children and is considered to be particularly innovative because it provides clinical service within a primary care setting and also because it creatively integrates research and training activities (Drotar, 1995). Another innovative feature of this collaborative practice model is that it also provides consultation for community agencies such as schools, mental health departments, departments of social services, and the courts. It is hoped that such models will become more standard than exception, especially given its positive impact on the lives of children and families in the community. Clearly, payment for such services will not likely be derived from third-party payers; external funding sources, including federal and state models of program demonstration, will be necessary to augment the costs of these services.

SERVICE DELIVERY BARRIERS

A number of factors play a role in impeding the assessment and management of emotional and behavioral disturbances in primary care practice (Perrin, 1999). Barriers include training programs that do not provide pediatricians with adequate education, knowledge, training, and skills to address psychosocial disturbances in their patients. Pediatricians may be undertrained in recognizing the complex problems associated with mental health issues and may lack the necessary expertise to care for children who evidence psychopathology. With the constraints associated with managed care, physicians are often faced with time and financial pressures that impede their ability to devote sufficient efforts toward assessment and management of their patients' psychological functioning (American Academy of Pediatrics Committee on Psychosocial Aspects of Child and Family Health, 1993; American Academy of Pediatrics, 2000; Perrin, 1999). In fact, the average office visit in a pediatric practice for both well-child visits and sick visits is less than 15 minutes (Ferris et al., 1998), barely sufficient time to assess and manage physical needs.

Primary care physicians also may be faced with inadequate resources to manage emotional disturbances in their patients. For example, they may practice in a community where services to address emotional disturbances among children and families are inadequate (Drotar, 1995). Also, primary care providers may face cumbersome impediments when referring patients to other specialty providers (American Academy of Pediatrics, 2000). Even in the case where a child is identified by the primary care physician and referred to a mental health specialist for further evaluation and treatment, families may be reluctant for a number of reasons to follow through with recommended services. Reasons may include financial issues, long wait lists, and the stigma associated with labeling and receiving services at a psychiatric or mental health clinic (Armstrong et al., 1999). As Perrin observed, the stigma associated with receiving mental health services will diminish when these services are provided in pediatric offices. This also will facilitate access to mental health services.

Armstrong and associates (Armstrong et al., 1999) delineated barriers to the mental health care environment. A general unfamiliarity with the nature and benefits of psychological services by other health care providers, children, and their caregivers hinders use of services. So do environmental barriers such as limited office space and schedules that overlap medical appointments. Patient barriers may include resources for travel, increased time demands on patients due to multiple medical appointments, and factors associated with serving an ethnically diverse population. Armstrong and colleagues (1999) argue that if specialty psychological services typically provided in tertiary care settings are integrated into primary care settings, some barriers associated with provision of services can be overcome, both for health care providers and for families.

Another factor that may play a role in the identification and management of psychosocial problems in primary care settings is the extent to which the primary care provider adheres to a dualistic model that views physical and mental health as very distinct entities. For some, the incorporation of mental health issues into one's scope of practice may reflect a paradigm shift. McLennan, Jansen-Williams, Comer, Gardner, and Kelleher (1999) found that primary care providers' psychosocial orientation was associated with their practice of identifying and managing emotional and behavioral disturbances. Physicians' beliefs about their inability to manage psychosocial problems, coupled with their perceptions that patients would resist having psychosocial issues addressed in the primary care setting, were associated with primary care providers' practice methods.

There has been some interest in determining the degree to which pediatricians regard specific treatments as acceptable and whether they actually follow treatment guidelines (Tarnowski, Kelly, & Mendlowicz, 1987). Interventions applied to severe behavioral problems (e.g., suicidal concerns) were rated as more acceptable than those interventions applied to more minor behavioral problems (e.g., temper tantrums). The severity of the children's medical condition did not contribute to the outcome of acceptability ratings. Although these findings are important in understanding the acceptability of psychological treatments among pediatric primary care providers, much more research in this area is necessary before formulating any definitive conclusions.

Consistent patterns of referral problems for primary care practitioners have included externalizing behavioral problems (e.g., oppositional defiant disorder, tantrums, demanding behaviors), toileting problems (e.g., enuresis, encopresis), developmental delays, and learning problems (Charlop et al., 1987; Finney et al., 1991; Roberts, 1986). Differences also have been identified in referral patterns to mental health specialty clinics versus pediatric primary care clinics where there are mental health providers (Drotar, 1995). For example, somatic complaints, including stomachaches and headaches, were frequently referred to pediatric clinics in children's hospitals but were rarely referred to pediatric primary care practices.

FUTURE DIRECTIONS AND RESEARCH IMPLICATIONS

Primary care settings have long been sites for collaboration between pediatricians and psychologists (Drotar, 1995; Perrin, 1999). Although conducting research in primary care settings has proven arduous because of the high clinical demands (Cunningham et al., 1995; Hurley, 1995), emphasis on the scientist-practitioner model has integrated research with practice activities. Examples of research activities include children's memory for physical examinations (Baker-Ward, Gordon, Omstein, Larus, & Clubb, 1993), courses on child development for new parents (Christophersen, 1993), prevention of accidents and injuries (Christophersen, Sosland-Edelman, & LeClaire, 1985), evaluation of behavioral management techniques to enhance compliance in difficult to manage children (Finney et al., 1990), and the assessment of techniques to enhance adherence to various medical therapies (Finney, Friman, Rapoff, & Christophersen, 1996).

Clearly, additional and important studies that take place in the primary care setting need to be on the empirical horizon, including investigations designed to evaluate the cost, efficacy, and acceptability of various screening methods and consumer satisfaction from assessment and management of mental health problems. Over the past several years, the American Academy of Pediatrics (2000) has developed a number of clinical practice guidelines designed to provide evidenced-based data for the diagnosis and management of specific diseases. Recently, the Academy has promulgated a clinical practice guideline for both the evaluation and management of ADHD in the primary care setting. This guideline is designed to assist primary care clinicians by providing a framework for both diagnostic decision making and managing the disorder. The guideline also contains a clinical algorithm providing decision trees to derive an appropriate diagnosis. Such a guideline is not intended to replace clinical judgment or to establish a protocol for all children with the disorder, but rather to assist the primary care practitioner identify and manage behavioral and emotional difficulties. Future research will need to assess the long-term efficacy of such a clinical practice guideline and to evaluate the viability of such a prototype in diagnosing and managing other psychiatric disorders within the pediatric primary care arena.

It will be important to learn how pediatricians benefit from additional training in the identification and management of emotional and behavioral disturbances. There may be appropriate periods in residency curriculum for training in identification and management of emotional problems in the primary care setting. Both the immediate and long-term effect of mental health service delivery in the primary care setting needs to be addressed in research. Whether increased detection rates of specific psychopathologies in the primary care setting are associated with concomitant increases in psychosocial interventions or psychotropic medications also remains an important research question.

The effect of early-intervention programs that are delivered in the primary care setting must be assessed, along with health care use and the long-term financial effect of such program efforts. Immediate improvements of early-intervention programs designed to enhance the mental health of children and adolescents may have some short-term positive economic consequences, including increased caregiver work productivity, less absenteeism, and less use of general medical services (American Academy of Pediatrics, 2000). Investigation of the long-term impact of these programs is likely to prove fruitful, particularly reduction in negative outcomes in later childhood and adolescence, reduction of health care use, and economic cost savings.

The pediatric setting is a very appropriate venue from which to consider developmental variations as they influence the identification and treatment process of emotional disorders. It is well known that current psychiatric nomenclature falls short of including a developmental perspective in the diagnosis of child psychiatric disorders. The use of the *DSM-PC* allows for a better developmental perspective for many emotional and behavioral problems and also enables a consideration of subthreshold disorders. Whether the identification of psychological disorders in the primary care clinic results in a greater frequency of children receiving psychological services remains an important question.

SUMMARY

Up to 1 in 5 children has emotional or behavioral disturbances. Even so, many providers of primary care do not feel adequately trained, do not have time, or cannot afford to address psychosocial problems in their practices. We argue that it is imperative and well within the domain of primary care to train pediatric practitioners to address mental health and psychosocial issues. In fact, there are increasing opportunities between psychologists and primary care pediatricians as a result of the shifts in the priority of the health care system from specialty care to primary care (Rabasca, 1999). As Roberts (1986) observed over a decade ago, an increasing number of roles for psychologists may be available in primary care settings. In addition, many inner-city parents value working with primary care providers to enhance their own knowledge of developmental and behavioral issues (Schultz & Vaughn, 1999). Only 8% of these caregivers were in need of medical information, but nearly one half wanted specific information about developmental and behavioral issues.

An important advance in recognizing and facilitating the examination of mental health problems in primary care settings has occurred with the development of the *DSM-PC.* Two other important steps forward in meeting the mental health needs of children include improving the detection of emotional and behavioral disturbances in primary care settings and building more integrated primary care settings in which mental health professionals can work alongside pediatricians and family physicians in children's primary medical homes. There are advantages associated with the provision of psychosocial services in the primary care setting. The stigma associated with emotional disturbances and psychological services may be diminished when care is received in the pediatricians' offices. Also, in-house services ameliorate the myriad of pragmatic issues associated with accessing outside mental health services. A wealth of research opportunities are likely to emerge from multidisciplinary collaborations between primary care pediatricians and psychologists that are related to health care use, consumer satisfaction, and access to mental health services. It is hoped that the clinical and research collaborations between primary care pediatricians and psychologists will thrive, thus improving the quality of life for children and adolescents with emotional disturbances.

REFERENCES

Aman, M. G., & Pearson, D. A. (1999). Rating scales. In J. S. Werry & M. G. Aman (Eds.), *Practitioner's guide for psychoactive drugs for children and adolescents.* New York: Plenum.

American Academy of Pediatrics. (1996). *Diagnostic and Statistical Manual for Primary Care (DSM-PC), Child and Adolescent Version.* Elk Grove Village, IL: Author.

American Academy of Pediatrics. (2000). Insurance coverage of mental health and substance abuse services for children and adolescents: A consensus statement (RE0090). *Pediatrics, 106,* 860–862.

American Academy of Pediatrics Committee on Psychosocial Aspects of Child and Family Health. (1993). The pediatrician and the "new morbidity." *Pediatrics, 92,* 731–733.

American Academy of Pediatrics Committee on Quality Improvement, Subcommittee on Attention-Deficit/Hyperactivity Disorder. (2000). Clinical practice guideline: Diagnosis and evaluation of the child with attention-deficit/hyperactivity disorder. *Pediatrics, 105,* 1158–1170.

American Psychiatric Association. (1994). *Diagnostic and statistical manual of mental disorders* (4th ed.). Washington, DC: American Psychiatric Press.

American Psychiatric Association. (1999). *Issues affecting mental health coverage for children.* Washington, DC: Author.

Armstrong, F. D., Harris, L. L., Thompson, W., Semrad, J., Jensen, M. M., Lee, D. Y., Miloslavich, K., & Garcia, A. (1999). The outpatient developmental services project: Integration of pediatric psychology with primary medical care for children infected with HIV. *Journal of Pediatric Psychology, 24,* 381–391.

Baker-Ward, L., Gordon, B. N., Omstein, P. S., Larus, D. M., & Clubb, P. A. (1993). Young children's long-term retention of a pediatric examination. *Child Development, 64,* 1519–1533.

Bradbury, K., Janicke, D. M., Riley, A. W., & Finney, J. W. (1999). Predictors of unintentional injuries to school-age children seen in pediatric primary care. *Journal of Pediatric Psychology, 24,* 423–433.

Brown, R. T., & Sawyer, M. G. (1998). *Medications for school-age children.* New York: Guilford.

Burns, B. J., Costello, E. J., Angold, A., Tweed, D., & Stangl, D. (1995). Children's mental health service use across service sectors. *Health Affairs, 14,* 147–159.

Cadman, D., Boyle, M., Szatmari, P., & Offord, D. R. (1987). Chronic illness, disability, and mental and social well-being: Findings of the Ontario Child Health Study. *Pediatrics, 79,* 805–813.

Chang, G., Warner, V., & Weissman, M. M. (1988). Physicians' recognition of psychiatric disorders in children and adolescents. *American Journal of Disabled Children, 142,* 736–739.

Charlop, M. H., Parrish, J. M., Fenton, L. R., & Cataldo, M. J. (1987). Evaluation of hospital-based pediatric psychology services. *Journal of Pediatric Psychology, 12,* 485–503.

Christophersen, E. R. (1993). Pediatric compliance: A guide for the primary care physician. New York: Plenum Press.

Christophersen, E. R., Sosland-Edelman, D., & LeClaire, S. (1985). Evaluation of two comprehensive infant car seat loaner programs with 1-year follow-up. *Pediatrics, 76,* 36–42.

Conners, C. K. (1969). A teacher rating scale for use in drug studies with children. *American Journal of Psychiatry, 126,* 884–888.

Costello, E. J., Angold, A., Burns, B. J., Erkanli, A., Stangl, D. K., & Tweed, D. L. (1996). The Great Smoky Mountains study of youth. Functional impairment and serious emotional disturbance. *Archives of General Psychiatry, 53,* 1137–1143.

Costello, E. J., Burns, B. J., Costello, A. J., Edelbrock, C., Dulcan, M., & Brent, D. (1988). Service utilization and psychiatric diagnosis in pediatric primary care: The role of the gatekeeper. *Pediatrics, 82,* 435–441.

Coury, D. L., Berger, S. P., Stancin, T., & Tanner, J. L. (1999). Curricular guidelines for residency training in developmental-behavioral pediatrics. *Journal of Developmental and Behavioral Pediatrics, 20,* S1–S38.

Cunningham, C. E., Bremner, R. B., & Boyle, M. (1995). Large group community-based parenting programs for preschoolers at risk for disruptive behavior disorders: Utilization, cost effectiveness, and outcome. *Journal of Child Psychology and Psychiatry and Allied Disciplines, 36,* 1141–1159.

Drotar, D. (1995). *Consulting with pediatricians: Psychological perspectives.* New York: Plenum Press.

Drotar, D. (1999). The diagnostic and statistical manual for primary care (DSM-PC), child and adolescent version: What pediatric psychologists need to know. *Journal of Pediatric Psychology, 24,* 369–380.

Dulcan, M. K., Costello, E. J., Costello, A. J., Edelbrock, C., Brent, D., & Janiszewski, S. (1990). The pediatrician as gatekeeper to mental health care for children: Do parents' concerns open the gate? *Journal of the American Academy of Child and Adolescent Psychiatry, 29,* 453–458.

Durlak, J. A. (1997). Successful prevention programs for children and adolescents. *Issues in Clinical Child Psychology.* New York: Plenum.

Eisert, D., Sturner, R. A., & Mabe, A. P. (1991). Questionnaires in behavioral pediatrics: Guidelines for selection and use. *Journal of Developmental and Behavioral Pediatrics, 12,* 42–50.

Ferris, T. G., Saglam, D., Stafford, R. S., Causino, N., Starfield, B., Culpepper, L., & Blumenthal, D. (1998). Changes in the daily practice of primary care for children. *Archives of Pediatric and Adolescent Medicine, 152,* 222–225.

Finney, J. W., Brophy, C. J., Friman, C. J., Golden, A. S., Richman, G. S., & Ross, A. F. (1990). Promoting parent-provider interaction during young children's health supervision visits. *Journal of Applied Behavioral Analysis, 23,* 207–213.

Finney, J. W., Friman, P. C., Rapoff, M., & Christophersen, E. R. (1996). Improving compliance with antibiotic regimens for otitis media: Randomized clinical trial in a pediatric clinic. *American Journal of Diseases of Children, 139,* 89–95.

Finney, J. W., Lemanek, K., Cataldo, M. E., Katz, H. P., & Fuqua, R. W. (1989). Pediatric psychology in primary health care: Brief targeted therapy for recurrent abdominal pain. *Behavior Therapy, 20,* 283–293.

Finney, J. W., Riley, A. W., & Cataldo, M. F. (1991). Psychology in primary care: Effects of brief targeted therapy on children's medical care utilization. *Journal of Pediatric Psychology, 16,* 447–461.

Garralda, M. E., Bowman, F. M., & Mandalia, S. (1999). Children with psychiatric disorders who are frequent attenders to primary care. *European Child and Adolescent Psychiatry, 8,* 34–44.

Gortmaker, S. L., Walker, D. K., Weitzman, M., & Sobol, A. M. (1990). Chronic conditions, socioeconomic risks, and behavioral problems in children and adolescents. *Pediatrics, 85,* 267–276.

Graham, P., & Rutter, M. (1973). Psychiatric disorders in the young adolescent: A follow-up study. *Proceedings from the Royal Society of Medicine, 66,* 1226–1229.

Hannemann, R. (1997). *Pediatrics and pediatric psychology: A relationship poised for growth.* Invited address at the Annual Meeting of the American Psychological Association, Chicago, IL.

Hickson, G. B., Altemeier, W. A., & O'Connor, S. (1983). Concerns of mothers seeking care in private pediatric offices: Opportunities for expanding services. *Pediatrics, 66,* 619–624.

Hurley, L. K. (1995). Developing a collaborative pediatric psychology practice in a pediatric primary care setting. In D. Drotar (Ed.), *Consulting with pediatricians: Psychological perspectives.* New York: Plenum Press.

Jellinek, M. S., & Murphy, J. M. (1990). The recognition of psychosocial disorders in pediatric office practice: The current status of the Pediatric Symptom Checklist. *Journal of Developmental and Behavioral Pediatrics, 11,* 273–278.

Jellinek, M. S., Murphy, J. M., Robinson, J., Feins, A., Lamb, S., & Fenton, T. (1988). Pediatric Symptom Checklist: Screening school-age children for psychosocial dysfunction. *Journal of Pediatrics, 112,* 201–209.

Kanoy, K. W., & Schroeder, C. S. (1985). Suggestions to parents about common behavior problems in a pediatric primary care office: Five years of follow-up. *Journal of Pediatric Psychology, 10,* 15–30.

Kazdin, A. E., Bass, D., Ayers, W. A., & Rodgers, A. (1990). Empirical and clinical focus of child and adolescent psychotherapy research. *Journal of Consulting Clinical Psychology, 58,* 729–740.

Kelleher, K. J., McInerny, T. K., Gardner, W. P., Childs, G. E., & Wasserman, R. C. (2000). Increasing identification of psychosocial problems: 1979–1997. *Pediatrics, 105,* 1313–1321.

King, G. A., Rosenbaum, P. L., & King, S. M. (1996). Parents' perceptions of caregiving: Development and validation of a measure of processes. *Developmental Medicine in Child Neurology, 38,* 47–62.

Kinsman, A. M., Wildman, B. G., & Smucker, W. D. (1999). Brief report: Parent report about health care use: Relationship to child's and parent's psychosocial problems. *Journal of Pediatric Psychology, 24,* 435–439.

Kush, S. A., & Campo, J. V. (1998). Consultation and liaison in the pediatric setting. In R. T. Ammerman & J. V. Campo (Eds.), *Handbook of pediatric psychology and psychiatry: Psychological and psychiatric issues in the pediatric setting* (pp. 23–40). Boston: Allyn & Bacon.

Lavigne, J. V., Arend, R., Rosenbaum, D., Binns, H. J., Christoffel, K. K., Burns, A., & Smith, A. (1998). Mental health service utilization among young children receiving pediatric primary care. *Journal of the American Academy of Child and Adolescent Psychiatry, 37,* 1175–1183.

Lavigne, J. V., Gibbons, R. D., Arend, R., Rosenbaum, D., Binns, H., & Christoffel, K. K. (1999). Rational service planning in pediatric primary care: Continuity and change in psychopathology among children enrolled in pediatric practices. *Journal of Pediatric Psychology, 24,* 393–403.

Lavigne, J. V., Binns, J. H., Christoffel, K. K., Rosenbaum, D. L., Arendt, R., Smith, K., Hayford, J. R., & McGuire, P. A. (1993). Behavioral and emotional problems among preschool children in pediatric primary care: Prevalence and pediatricians' recognition. *Pediatrics, 91,* 649–655.

Lynch, T. R., Wildman, B. G., & Smucker, W. D. (1997). Parental disclosure of child psychosocial concerns: Relationship to physician identification and management. *Journal of Family Practice, 44,* 273–280.

McCain, A. P., Kelley, M. L., & Fishbein, J. (1999). Behavioral screening in well child care: Validation of the Toddler Behavioral Screening Inventory. *Journal of Pediatric Psychology, 24,* 415–422.

McLennan, J. D., Jansen-Williams, L., Comer, D. M., Gardner, W. P., & Kelleher, K. J. (1999). The Physician Belief Scale and psychosocial problems in children: A report from the Pediatric Research in Office Settings and the Ambulatory Sentinel Practice Network. *Journal of Developmental and Behavioral Pediatrics, 20,* 24–30.

Morris, J. (1996). *Rural mental health.* Washington, DC: American Psychological Association.

Mouton-Simien, P., McCain, A. P., & Kelley, M. I. (1997). The development of the Toddler Behavior Screening Inventory. *Journal of Abnormal Child Psychology, 2,* 59–64.

Murphy, J. M., Arnett, H. L., Bishop, S. J., Jellinek, M. S., & Reede, J. Y. (1992). Screening for psychosocial dysfunction in pediatric practice. A naturalistic study of the Pediatric Symptom Checklist. *Clinical Pediatrics, 31,* 660–667.

Murphy, J. M., Reede, J., Jellinek, M. S., & Bishop, S. J. (1992). Screening for psychosocial dysfunction in inner-city children: Further validation of the Pediatric Symptom checklist. *Journal of the American Academy of Child and Adolescent Psychiatry, 31,* 1105–1111.

National Advisory Mental Health Council. (1990). *National plan for research on child and adolescent mental health disorders* (DHHS Publication No. 1990-724-785/20509). Washington, DC: U.S. Government Printing Office.

National Center for Education in Maternal and Child Health. (2000). *Bright futures in practice: Mental health.* Washington, DC: Georgetown University.

Perrin, E. C. (1998). Ethical questions about screening. *Journal of Developmental and Behavioral Pediatrics, 19,* 350–352.

Perrin, E. C. (1999). Commentary: Collaboration in pediatric primary care: A pediatrician's view. *Journal of Pediatric Psychology, 24,* 453–458.

Rabasca, L. (1999, April). Looking for opportunities? Network with physicians. *APA Monitor, 26.*

Richardson, L. A., Keller, A. M., Selby-Harrington, M. L., & Parrish, R. (1996). Identification and treatment of children's mental health problems by primary care providers: A critical review of research. *Archives of Psychiatric Nursing, 10,* 293–303.

Riekert, K. A., Stancin, T., Palermo, T. M., & Drotar, D. (1999). A psychological behavioral screening service: Use, feasibility, and impact in a primary care setting. *Journal of Pediatric Psychology, 24,* 405–414.

Roberts, M. C. (1986). *Pediatric psychology: Psychological interventions and strategies for pediatric problems.* New York: Pergamon Press.

Roberts, M. C. & Wright, L. (1982). The role of the pediatric psychologist as consultant to pediatricians. In J. M. Tuma (Ed.), *Handbook for the practice of pediatric psychology* (pp. 251–289). New York: Wiley & Sons.

Safer, D. J., Zito, J. M., & Pine, E. M. (1996). Increased methylphenidate usage for attention deficit disorder in the 1990s. *Pediatrics, 98,* 1084–1088.

Schroeder, C. S. (1999). Commentary: A view from the past and a look to the future. *Journal of Pediatric Psychology, 24,* 447–452.

Schroeder, C. S. (1997). The changing practice paradigm in pediatric settings. In R. J. Illback, C. Cobb, & H. Joseph Jr. (Eds.), *Integrated services for children and families: Opportunities for psychological practice.* Washington, DC: American Psychological Association.

Schroeder, C. S., Goolsby, E., & Stangler, S. (1975). Preventive services in a private pediatric practice. *Journal of Clinical Child Psychology, 4,* 32–33.

Schultz, J. R., & Vaughn, L. M. (1999). Brief report: Learning to parent: A survey of parents in an urban pediatric primary care clinic. *Journal of Pediatric Psychology, 24,* 441–445.

Sharpe, L., Pantell, R. H., Murphy, L. O., & Lewis, C. C. (1992). Psychosocial problems during child health supervision visits: Eliciting, then what? *Pediatrics, 89,* 619–623.

Simonian, S. J., Tarnowski, K. J., Stancin, T., Friman, P. C., & Atkins, M. S. (1991). Disadvantaged children and families in pediatric primary care settings: II. Screening for behavior disturbance. Special section: Disadvantaged children and their families. *Journal of Clinical Child Psychology, 20,* 360–371.

Stancin, T. (1999). Introduction. *Journal of Pediatric Psychology, 24,* 367–368.

Stancin, T., & Palermo, T. M. (1997). A review of behavioral screening practices in pediatric settings: Do they pass the test? *Journal of Developmental and Behavioral Pediatrics, 18,* 183–194.

Starfield, B., Hoekelman, R. A., McCormick, M., Benson, P., Mendenhall, R. C., Moynichan, C., & Radecki, S. (1984). Who provides health care to children and adolescents in the United States? *Pediatrics, 74,* 991–997.

Tarnowski, K. J., Kelly, P. A., & Mendlowitz, D. K. (1987). Acceptability of behavioral pediatric interventions. *Journal of Consulting and Clinical Psychology, 55,* 435–436.

Wertlieb, D. (1999). Society of Pediatric Psychology Presidential Address—1997: Calling all collaborators, advancing pediatric care. *Journal of Pediatric Psychology, 24,* 77–83.

Wolraich, M. L. (1997). Diagnostic and statistical manual for primary care (DSM-PC) child and adolescent version: Design, intent, and hopes for the future. *Journal of Developmental and Behavioral Pediatrics, 18,* 171–172.

Young, K. T., Davis, K., Schoen, C., & Parker, S. (1998). Listening to parents: A national survey of parents with young children. *Archives of Pediatric and Adolescent Medicine, 152,* 255–262.

Chapter 24

CHILDREN, ADOLESCENTS, AND PSYCHOTROPICS: A PRIMER FOR THE NONPRESCRIBING MENTAL HEALTH PROFESSIONAL

JOHN D. GAVAZZI

Psychopharmacology has made significant advances in the past 20 years. These advances include the availability of medications with less potential lethality, a wider range of medications for specific disorders, and psychotherapeutics with fewer and less severe adverse effects. In spite of the advances in psychopharmacology, there are currently controversies about prescribing psychotropic medication to children and adolescents and about the role of the nonprescribing mental health professional in managing psychoactive medication. The intent of the chapter is to help the mental health professional (MHP) gain more knowledge in order to practice more ethically and effectively. The following topics are addressed: current controversies and economic realities; the various roles of the nonprescribing MHP; essential components of high-quality treatment; and important issues regarding classes of medication, such as antidepressant, antihypertensive, and neuroleptic agents.

CURRENT CONTROVERSIES AND ECONOMIC REALITIES

In spite of the improvements made in psychopharmacology, controversy grows about psychotropic medication in general (Glenmullen, 2000; Valenstein, 1998) and about the use of psychotropic medication with children and adolescents (Waters, 2000; Zito et al., 2000). The prevalence of psychotropic use raises questions regarding how individuals in American culture understand the causes and "cures" of emotional and behavioral difficulties (Duncan, Miller, & Sparks, 2000). General concerns are raised about the cultural expectations reflected in asking for a pill rather than modifying behavior, mobilizing internal resources, restructuring unhelpful cognitive patterns, garnishing social support, or finding healing in faith and spirituality. In addition, serious concerns are prompted by the lack of research on psychoactive medications for children and adolescents (Jensen et al., 1999). The lack of research leads to few approved uses of psychoactive substances for young patients, although the number of prescriptions for psychotropic medication continues to rise. In one retrospective study (Zito et al., 2000), the use of clonidine (which is not FDA approved for use in children) increased over 200% in children ages 2 to 4 from 1991 to 1995.

The economic reality is that psychoactive medications are part of a multibillion-dollar-per-year industry. From 1994 to 1998, revenues generated from psychotherapeutics quadrupled to $15.3 billion; by 2003, revenues for psychotherapeutics are expected to reach $27.7 billion (Kalorma Information, 2000). The pharmaceutical industry planned to spend $6 billion in 2000 on research and development of psychotropic medications (Pharmaceutical Research and Manufacturers of America, 2000). There are currently 103 medications in clinical testing for a variety of emotional and behavioral disorders. For instance, there are 10 medicines in development for attention-deficit/hyperactivity disorder (ADHD). The pharmaceutical industry promotes a medical model of healing; that is, the cause and the cure of emotional and behavioral difficulties are best treated through biological interventions. The money devoted to advertising psychotherapeutics far outweighs advertising for psychotherapies. Of the 84 Internet sites dedicated to pharmaceutical products, 11 sites for psychoactive medications made the top 20 most visited in 1998 (Sussman, 1999). Research clearly indicates that psychological and behavioral interventions are at least as effective as psychotropic medications for many emotional and behavioral disorders. Psychological and behavioral interventions demonstrate effectiveness with depression (Keller et al., 2000), panic disorder (Black, Wesner, Bowers, & Gabel, 1993), and obsessive-compulsive disorder (O'Connor, Todorov, Robillard, Borgeat, & Brault, 1999). Some psychological interventions have yielded neurochemical alterations (Schwartz, Stoessel, Baxter, Martin, & Phelps, 1996). Given cultural expectations, current controversies, and an industry that promotes a biological model for emotional and behavioral health, MHPs need to make a decision about their role in the use of psychoactive substances by children and adolescents.

ROLES OF THE NONPRESCRIBING MENTAL HEALTH PROFESSIONAL

The roles of the nonprescribing MHP can be unclear, depending on the relationship established with the prescribing professional. Sederer, Ellison, and Keyes (1998) suggest guidelines for psychiatrists in terms of their consultative and collaborative relationships with MHPs. Although these suggestions are for prescribing professionals, it may be helpful for the MHP to contemplate the roles, responsibilities, and boundaries in collaborative and consultative relationships.

First, the boundaries and definition of the role of the MHP varies with the prescribing professional's level of education and training. The prescribing professional may be a psychiatrist, pediatrician, internist, family practitioner, nurse practitioner, or physician's assistant. Some prescribers feel more comfortable and are more familiar with psychotropic medications than others. Second, prescribers have varied interest in mental health and family-systems issues. On one end of the continuum, emotional and behavioral issues fascinate some prescribers, whereas others find these issues confusing, annoying, and downright bothersome. Third, the collaborative relationship between the

MHP and the prescriber is essential to high-quality treatment. It is a truism that the greater the collaboration and respect, the more each professional will value the relationship and what the other professional has to offer. Given these factors, the role of the MHP can vary from the assessment specialist, to consultant, to a physician extender.

Role of the Assessment Specialist

MHPs have expertise in cognitive, behavioral, emotional, interpersonal, existential, psychodynamic, and family systems models of treatment. As experts, MHPs develop a diagnostic formulation and a treatment plan to aid the patient and family. Because many diagnoses overlap and the dynamics of the individuals and families can be difficult, many prescribers prefer to have a mental health expert work with them. In many situations, of which ADHD is a prime example, the need for a thorough assessment is essential in order to make an appropriate diagnosis. For a professional to diagnose ADHD, a thorough interview augmented by behavioral rating scales from the child, parents, and teachers is essential. The MHP typically has that expertise. In the absence of a comprehensive assessment, a prescriber of medications for ADHD can sometimes do more harm than good.

The reverse can also be true for the MHP. If the MHP assesses an individual with an emotional or behavioral issue for which medication is indicated, an appropriate referral to a prescribing professional is essential to high quality of care. The prescribing professional will need to complete a full physical assessment, as physical disease processes can mimic or cause symptoms comparable to those of diagnoses found in the *Diagnostic and Statistical Manual, Fourth Edition* (*DSM-IV;* American Psychiatric Association [APA], 1994). For instance, thyroid disease can present as symptoms of depression. Similarly, the sensations of mitral valve prolapse can trigger symptoms of anxiety and panic. Thus, the prescribing professional needs to assess physical disease as a possible cause of symptoms. In addition, medications for other disease processes can create psychological symptoms. For example, the use of clonidine can create the subjective experience of depression.

Evaluation of substance use and abuse is an essential component of a thorough assessment. Just as physical causes and medication can create symptoms of a *DSM-IV* diagnosis, illicit drug use and inappropriate prescription use are of great concern. Substances such as steroids, "designer drugs," and inhalants need to be assessed. If substance use is not evaluated carefully, the use of psychotherapeutics can also create significant complications due to the combined effects of the psychotropics and the drugs of abuse. Substances such as alcohol and caffeine can affect the metabolism of psychotropics and interfere with the desired effects of the medication.

Role of the Consultant

The role of the MHP can be defined as that of a consultant in that the prescriber can ask for assistance and guidance in determining which medication and what titration schedule to follow with a specific patient. This situation becomes more complex ethically and legally because, although the MHP does not have the authority to prescribe, the MHP sometimes has better knowledge of psychotropic medication and the patient than the prescriber does. Preston and Ebert (1999) identify a number of difficult situations that may arise when acting in the role of consultant. For example, difficulties may arise when the prescriber recommends discontinuing medication from which a patient is benefiting. Another example is when the prescriber recommends using a subtherapeutic dose of the psychotropic medication. Concerns emerge when the prescriber is not following established treatment protocols, such as using imipramine as a first-line medication with ADHD without appropriate medical reasons. When these situations occur, the MHP can make significant positive contributions in the role of consultant by providing expertise. If necessary, the MHP can educate the prescriber on issues related to beneficial effects, dosing, titration schedules, and psychopharmacological guidelines.

Role of the Physician's Extender

The MHP can fill the role of a physician's extender. In this role, the MHP becomes the eyes and the ears of the prescribing professional. The MHP can provide information to the physician about the medication's beneficial and untoward effects and the progress of the individual and the family. Sometimes the patient may be too embarrassed to discuss difficult issues or adverse effects with the prescriber, such as sexual difficulties or diarrhea. Because the MHP usually develops a more intimate relationship, the patient and family are typically at greater ease to discuss uncomfortable issues. Alternatively, the MHP may provide information to the patient and family about medications' efficacy and adverse effects. As the MHP provides information and projects confidence about psychotropic medication as a viable and necessary component of the overall treatment, expectations of a positive outcome and compliance with the medication regimen increase.

In terms of communicating information to patients, an important cautionary note is necessary. The MHP is strongly discouraged from communicating dose changes from the prescriber to the patient. In those situations, it is more sensible, ethically and legally, to encourage the patient or legal guardians (depending on the developmental level of the patient) to discuss medication titration directly with the prescribing professional. Although MHPs want to be of assistance, the responsibility for starting, stopping, or adjusting medication falls specifically within the purview of the prescribing profession. Reducing potential liabilities and role confusion makes good ethical and risk management sense.

ESSENTIAL ELEMENTS FOR PHARMACOTHERAPY IN TREATMENT

One of the criticisms of psychotherapeutic medication is an overemphasis on the medical model as the *primary* mode of intervention. Although psychotropic medications are not always primary in treating emotional and behavioral disorders in childhood and adolescence, psychotropic medications are effective in treating disorders for which they are approved. Reducing the risk of harm is essential due to the lack of available research and the lack of approval by the Food and Drug Administration for many psychoactive drugs used to treat children and adolescents. Therefore, fundamental requirements are crucial to maximize treatment success and minimize harm when treating children and adolescents with psychotropics.

First, an appropriate diagnostic workup is essential to ethical and effective practice. A high degree of comorbidity exists with many *DSM-IV* diagnoses that are usually first diagnosed in childhood and adolescence. For example, symptom overlap is evident with ADHD, oppositional defiant disorder (ODD), learning disorders, anxiety disorders, and depressive disorders. In spite of a parent's request for medication to treat a "hyperactive" child, prescribing a stimulant can be detrimental. Psychostimulants may increase acting-out behavior, irritability and anger outbursts in children who do not have ADHD, and can trigger psychotic symptoms in some children.

A comprehensive assessment that incorporates behavior rating scales, clinical interviews, family history, developmental history, and current family dynamics is needed. As this often cannot be accomplished in a primary care setting, a complete evaluation can be completed by the MHP with such expertise. The diagnosis and target symptoms must be identified before the start of a medication regime. If not, prescribers run the risk of prescribing inappropriately and making a difficult situation worse.

Second, the MHP needs to communicate clearly about roles and boundaries in order to practice ethically and effectively. For example, if the MHP refers to a prescribing professional, issues surrounding informed consent can be communicated to patients and family members by the MHP. The elements of informed consent include the goals of the psychotropic intervention, the expected outcomes of the use of medication, and the length of time that the child or adolescent may need to be on the medication. It is important to emphasize that the prescribing professional will ultimately decide which medication, if any, will be prescribed. The responsibility for informed consent falls squarely on the shoulders of the prescribing professional; however, clear communication about these issues will enhance the likelihood of a solid relationship with the patient and the family.

Third, the necessity of behavioral, cognitive, interpersonal, family-systems, or psychodynamic interventions must be considered. The MHP is acutely aware of the value and effectiveness of nonpharmacological interventions in treating emotional and behavioral disorders. It is incumbent upon MHPs to continue to remind their prescribing colleagues as to the necessity and effectiveness of psychologically and behaviorally based interventions. The surgeon general's report (Satcher, 1999) on child and adolescent mental health issues specifically cites the need for psychological treatment in conjunction with psychopharmacological interventions.

IMPORTANT ISSUES IN PRESCRIBING MEDICATIONS TO CHILDREN AND ADOLESCENTS

There are important issues related to prescribing medications to children and adolescents. This section is not comprehensive, but it offers the clinician some helpful hints when thinking about the use of psychoactive medication to treat patients.

First, psychotropic medications do not cure disease; they reduce symptoms. Psychotropic medications have a valuable, yet limited, role in treatment. One way to conceptualize a general treatment model is to divide it into five phases: crisis intervention, diagnostic procedures, treatment planning, symptom reduction, and enhanced level of functioning. From this model, medications are only part of the overall plan. At the same time, treatment professionals need to realize that many psychotherapeutic strategies reduce symptoms as well. For example, diaphragmatic breathing aids in reducing the symptoms of panic and anxiety. Cognitive restructuring decreases symptoms of depression. With medication management, symptom reduction gives the patient and family more time, emotional resources, and flexibility to progress toward a greater level of healing. As symptoms begin to remit, the patient and family can work on issues such as communication skills, positive parenting, cognitive restructuring, social support, and relapse prevention.

As a side note, the goal of treatment in managed care systems is limited to symptom reduction in a biological framework. The term *medical necessity* captures the essence of the managed care philosophy. Unfortunately, this limited model is comparable to a battlefield mentality; that is, patch the wounded (reduce the symptoms quickly) and send the troops back to the war zone (move patients out of treatment as soon as possible). The symptom-reduction model is not sufficiently comprehensive to meet the emotional and behavioral needs of children, adolescents, and their families.

Second, psychotropic medications only have *effects;* however, there are certain adverse or unwanted effects that are labeled "side effects." The term *side effects* is only a reframing of how the drug affects the body. For example, the "main effect" of selective serotonin reuptake inhibitor (SSRI) antidepressants is to alleviate dysphoric mood. The "side effects" of the SSRIs include difficulties such as gastrointestinal distress, nausea, vomiting, agitation, weight gain, and sleep disturbance (*Physician's Desk Reference* [*PDR*], 2000). Therefore, it is more helpful to view medications as only having effects, some wanted and some adverse, in order to appreciate the need for caution in using psychotropic medication to treat children and adolescents.

Third, if a patient suffers with an adverse effect, it is a *real* effect. This is especially true with medications newly on the market. For example, in the early 1990s, the literature was silent on the adverse effect of weight gain with the use of fluoxetine (e.g., Green, 1991; Pirodsky & Cohn, 1992). Anecdotal stories and professional literature suggested that patients actually lost weight on fluoxetine (Green, 1991). While on SSRI medication, several adolescent female patients whom the author treated complained of weight gain as a negative effect and discontinued the psychotropic medication against medical advice because the prescribing provider did not believe that SSRIs caused weight gain. More recently, Fava (2000) concluded that weight gain is a common and serious adverse effect of the SSRIs. The lesson here is that if a patient *perceives* that a medication causes an intolerable effect, the MHP needs to practice proactively—that is, consult with the prescriber immediately to possibly modify the dosage amount, time of administration, or type of medication. Otherwise, the patient has a greater likelihood of noncompliance.

Finally, adult doses do not equal doses for children and adolescents. When the MHP makes psychotropic medication recommendations to a prescribing provider, the adult data on dosing levels may serve as a guide to help the prescribing professional determine at what dose to start the medication and what titration, if any, is needed. Dosing levels and schedules are easy to obtain (DeBattista & Schatzberg, 2000; *PDR,* 2000).

Since there is a lack of specific research with most psychotropics for persons under age 18, the principle of nonmaleficence reminds the ethical practitioner to do no harm. Therefore, a graded use of medication (i.e., "start low and go slow") is most wise.

IMPORTANT ISSUES WITH CLASSES OF MEDICATIONS

In order to practice effectively, the MHP needs to understand some simple issues related to psychotropic medication. The goal of this section is to review some basic issues related to psychotropic medications used in treating children and adolescents. Due to space limitations, certain classes of psychotropics and medications within some classes are not covered. The reader who wants a more comprehensive review is referred to other publications (Gitlin, 1990; Preston & Johnson, 2000; Preston, O'Neill, & Talaga, 1999; Stahl, 2000). Other sources of current information are *Child & Adolescent Psychopharmacology News* and *Primary Psychiatry.* These sources are helpful in providing updated information, case reviews, and timely articles.

ANTIDEPRESSANTS

Several general points regarding antidepressants are important to know when working with children and adolescents. First, there is an increase in the use of antidepressants to treat children and adolescents. For example, the use of antidepressants has more than doubled for preschoolers from 1991 to 1995 (Zito et al., 2000). In 1999, 6% of the total number of SSRI prescriptions were written for individuals under the age of 18 (Waters, 2000).

Second, antidepressant medications need a full trial; that is, a therapeutic dose needs to be administered for an adequate length of time. A *therapeutic dose* means an effective dose. For example, a therapeutic dose of sertraline (Zoloft) may be 75 mg, although a prescribing professional may start at 25 mg and gradually increase the dose. With slow increases, the patient may need several weeks to build up to a therapeutic dose. The time needed to evaluate the positive effects of the medication ranges from 2 to 4 weeks. If the patient is not experiencing sufficient symptom reduction after 2 to 4 weeks, the prescribing professional can wait for 2 more weeks *or* increase the dose and wait another 2 weeks. Again, the prescriber needs to inform patients and families of the time needed to reach effectiveness. A lack of symptom reduction is common when patients take medication intermittently. Without sufficient informed consent, patients and families may mistakenly believe that antidepressants are taken only when the patient feels depressed, much like aspirin is taken to alleviate a headache.

Third, along similar lines, it is helpful to discuss the expected duration of treatment with the antidepressant medication. In the author's experience, patients and their families sometimes expect to take psychotherapeutics for 7 to 10 days, much like a course of antibiotics. Some families are shocked to learn the guidelines on the length of treatment needed with antidepressants. It is helpful to prepare patients and families regarding the length of time that the antidepressant medication needs to be taken. Duration of antidepressant therapy is at least 6 months after symptom remission to prevent recurrences (National Institute of Mental Health, 2000).

Tricyclic Antidepressants (TCAs)

Tricyclic antidepressant (TCA) medications are so named because of the three rings in their chemical structure. TCAs include drugs such as amitriptyline (Elavil), imipramine (Tofranil), desipramine (Norpramin), and nortriptyline (Pamelor). The antidepressant mechanism of the TCAs is thought to operate by blocking the reuptake of serotonin and norepinephrine (Stahl, 1998). TCAs are prescribed for depression, ADHD, enuresis, and sleep disturbance for children and adolescents. However, a review of the literature on using TCAs in treating children and adolescents with depression indicates that there are few double-blind, placebo-controlled studies, and even fewer positive results (Geller, Reising, Leonard, Riddle, & Walsh, 1999). Even though TCAs have been an essential part of child and adolescent psychopharmacology, the use of TCAs as a first-line medication appears to be dwindling due to their adverse effects, their toxicity profile, the unresolved issue of sudden death in children taking TCAs, and the availability of newer antidepressant medications (Klee, Hack, & Green, 1998).

The Need for Heart Monitoring Before and During Treatment

Adverse cardiovascular effects are a concern when using TCAs at any age, but especially with children and adolescents. Children and adolescents are particularly vulnerable to the cardiotoxic effects of TCAs as higher doses are used. These adverse effects include cardiac arrhythmia, tachycardia, and heart block (Green, 1991). Therefore, an electrocardiogram (EKG) baseline is essential before TCA treatment. An EKG during TCA treatment is also recommended to monitor heart functioning and to ensure the welfare of the patient.

Adverse Effects

TCAs have a variety of adverse effects directly related to their chemical complexity. Stahl (1998) suggests that TCAs are actually five drugs in one: a serotonin reuptake inhibitor, a norepinephrine reuptake inhibitor, an anticholinergic and antimuscarinic drug, an alpha 1 antagonist, and an antihistamine. The first two mechanisms of action create the antidepressant effect, while the other actions create the untoward effects. By blocking the acethylcholine receptors, TCAs create constipation, blurred vision, dry mouth, and drowsiness. The antihistaminic effect causes weight gain and drowsiness.

Lethality

The lethality of TCAs is important to note, especially with those patients who present as suicidal. The MHP must be acutely aware that it is much easier for a patient to commit suicide with TCAs than with the newer antidepressants. Ingestion of as little as 1 week's dose of TCA medication can be lethal (Gitlin, 1990). The MHP must assess this risk in all patients and families.

Selective Serotonin Reuptake Inhibitors (SSRIs)

Fluoxetine (Prozac) started the revolution of selective serotonin reuptake inhibitors. Fluoxetine became a favored antidepressant medication because of comparable efficacy, increased safety, and fewer adverse effects. The FDA approves several other SSRIs for the treatment of depression as well as panic disorder, posttraumatic stress disorder (PTSD), obsessive-compulsive disorder (OCD), and social phobia. Other SSRIs are sertraline (Zoloft), paroxetine (Paxil), citalopram (Celexa), and fluvoxamine (Luvox). Blocking the reuptake of serotonin is thought to be the method of action that creates the antidepressant effect (Stahl, 1998). Because the SSRIs are not as selective as the name implies, these medications influence a number of receptor sites that cause some adverse effects, detailed later.

While the FDA has yet to approve these psychotropics for the treatment of depressive disorders in persons under age 18, sertraline and fluvoxamine are approved to treat symptoms of OCD in children as young as 6. Practitioners prescribe SSRIs to children and adolescents for more than just OCD. SSRIs are used for other anxiety disorders, such as panic disorder, depressive disorders, and eating disorders. Therefore, it is necessary to be aware of adverse effects, discontinuation syndrome, and dose issues relevant to SSRIs.

Myth: The SSRIs Do Not Have Significant Adverse Effects

SSRIs have far fewer adverse effects than TCAs, but they are not risk- or nuisance-free. Significant adverse effects associated with SSRIs are weight gain, agitation, sleep disturbance, diarrhea, gastrointestinal distress, and sexual dysfunction. The MHP may employ some strategies to enhance compliance in spite of multiple untoward effects. These strategies might include training the patient and family regarding possible negative effects, educating the provider about untoward effects, encouraging the provider to start with a low dose and increase gradually, and monitoring compliance. If an unwanted effect becomes intolerable, the MHP may either encourage the patient to explain this to the prescribing professional or contact the prescribing professional directly.

Myth: SSRI Medications Can Be Stopped Quickly

Abrupt discontinuation of an SSRI may lead to the emergence of other adverse effects. SSRI discontinuation syndrome can manifest as headache, dizziness, nausea and vomiting, electric shock sensations, tremor, lethargy, and anxious, irritable, or low mood (Rosenbaum, Fava, Hoog, Ascroft, & Krebs, 1998). This information must be communicated to patients and their families so they recognize the seriousness of stopping the medication quickly. Unwanted results can otherwise occur. For example, a child from a family with divorced parents who do not communicate well may spend a weekend with the noncustodial parent. If that parent is not in favor of psychotropic medication, the parent's uninformed decision to stop the medication can be detrimental to the child. Therefore, it is important that psychotropic medication information is distributed to all of the caregivers involved with the child or adolescent.

Myth: The Same Doses Work for All Patients

With most medications, there is a range in which the medication is effective. This can differ between and within patients. That is, patients who differ in height, weight, metabolism, and symptom severity will probably require somewhat different dosages. The MHP needs to be aware of these dose ranges for the SSRI class of medication.

Prescribers sometimes use other antidepressants, which are not FDA approved for use in treating children and adolescents, such as bupropion (Wellbutrin), mirtazapine (Remeron), and venlafaxine (Effexor). Because of space limitations, the reader is referred to resources mentioned previously for additional information about these medications.

PSYCHOSTIMULANTS

Psychostimulants are one of the most studied medications in children and adolescents. These medications are amphetamine-like compounds. Psychostimulants are a class of psychotropic medications that stimulate dopamine and norepinephrine activity at the synaptic level. The effects are an increased autonomic response (increased heart rate, blood pressure, and muscle tension), a decrease in fatigue, and an increase in concentration capacities. The FDA has approved psychostimulants for the treatment of ADHD and narcolepsy. The effectiveness of the short-term use of psychostimulants for treating the symptoms of ADHD is clear (National Institutes of Health [NIH]; 1998). Methylphenidate (Ritalin, Concerta, and Metadate), dextroamphetamine (Dexedrine), dextroamphetamine plus amphetamine (Adderall), and pemoline (Cylert) are most likely familiar names to MHPs who work with children and adolescents.

Although research demonstrates their effectiveness, it is important to understand and monitor the adverse effects of the psychostimulants. Potential adverse physiologic effects include stomachache, decreased appetite, weight loss, headache, growth suppression, sleep disturbance, increased perspiration, increased heart rate, and increased blood pressure. One of the most frequent concerns is weight loss; this adverse effect is easily measurable, and parents are readily able to see this result. Taking stimulants with food can minimize decreased appetite and weight loss. The untoward cognitive effects of stimulants include mood alterations, irritability, delayed processing, sedation, and nervousness. Some basic issues related to psychostimulants include their abuse potential, dosing issues, and the rebound effect.

Psychostimulants and Abuse Potential

There are no data to indicate that therapeutic use of psychostimulants is harmful or leads to substance abuse. As with most potentially addictive substances, any person who misuses psychostimulants can become dependent. However, one study indicates that adolescents treated with stimulants for symptoms of ADHD have a lower incidence of substance abuse than adolescents with untreated ADHD (Biederman, Wilens, Mick, Spencer, & Faraone, 1999).

Two issues related to psychostimulants involve the family system. First, it is possible that the motivation to have a child diagnosed with ADHD may be a function of a parent's addiction or desire to sell medications to make money. Although this view may seem extreme, police reports, television news shows, and clinical practice indicate that such behavior occurs. Unfortunately, no research data exist about the extent of parents' inappropriate attempts to obtain psychostimulants. Second, the availability and the addictive nature of psychostimulants can also create use and abuse issues with siblings. Situations arise in which siblings inappropriately use psychostimulants or sell or give them to other children. Warning signs of inappropriate use include "lost" prescriptions and "stolen" bottles of medication. One method of curbing medication-seeking behavior is to complete a comprehensive assessment of the child that incorporates multiple sources of data. If the child is acting out only in the prescriber's office, then an issue other than ADHD may be present. If the symptoms do not remit with appropriate doses of stimulant medication and several stimulant medications have been tried, then concerns about potential inappropriate use by family members may be considered.

Dosing Levels Based on Weight

Prescribers use the weight of the patient to determine the initial and subsequent doses of a psychostimulant. For example, the initial starting range of methylphenidate is 0.3 to 0.6 mg/kg. Using this formula with a child weighing 84 lb (38.2 kg), the starting dose of methylphenidate could be 10 to 20 mg/day. A medication trial should start with the lower dose in the range and then gradually increase until sufficient symptom reduction is achieved. As children and adolescents gain weight, the effectiveness of psychostimulants may decrease. Therefore, monitoring the relationship between weight, dosing, and effectiveness is important.

Psychostimulant Rebound

Psychostimulant rebound occurs as the body rapidly eliminates the medication and efficacy is lost. Rebound presents as a return of ADHD symptoms, such as increased activity and negative mood. Rebound appears more frequently with the shorter-acting forms of psychostimulants and is more common in younger children. Any signs of rebound must be reported to the prescribing professional. Two strategies to reduce the effects of rebound are to change the dose or to alter the schedule of the stimulant administration. A third strategy is to use an extended-release form of the medication. An extended-release tablet gradually introduces the medication into the body and tapers more slowly than regular tablets, thus reducing the likelihood of rebound.

ANTIHYPERTENSIVE MEDICATIONS

The antihypertensive medications clonidine (Catapres) and guanfacine (Tenex) are used to treat children and adolescents with emotional and behavioral concerns. This section reviews only clonidine. Clonidine is a centrally acting adrenergic-stimulating agent that inhibits brain noradrenergic activity and creates a calming effect on the patient. Prescribers use clonidine to treat symptoms related to impulse control disorders (such as ADHD), tic disorders, sleep disturbance, and aggression. Although prescribers use clonidine because of its sedating effects, the FDA approves clonidine solely for adults suffering with hypertension (*PDR,* 2000).

It takes approximately 30 to 60 minutes for clonidine to exert a change in behavior, which then typically lasts from 3 to 6 hours. Some children and adolescents are extremely sensitive to clonidine, meaning that lower doses are needed for effectiveness and that adverse effects are greater even at the lower doses. However, higher doses of clonidine are often needed to reduce sleep difficulties.

Between 1994 and 1998, the use of clonidine increased 200% in preschool children (Zito et al., 2000). In 1994, roughly 125,000 prescriptions were written for children and adolescents to treat symptoms of ADHD (Kutcher, 1999). Only half of the prescriptions were written in combination with methylphenidate, dexedrine, or pemoline. This fact indicates that many prescribers use clonidine as the primary biological treatment for ADHD. These numbers are surprising given the limited research, the lack of FDA approval for use in children, complications with compliance, and the adverse effects associated with clonidine.

Limited Research on Effectiveness

The research on the use of clonidine with ADHD is quite limited. A literature search revealed only six placebo-controlled studies with fewer than 500 patients. That same search revealed there are no controlled studies using clonidine and methylphenidate in combination to treat ADHD. The lack of literature is both surprising and unsettling given the number of prescriptions written to treat symptoms of ADHD in children and adolescents. Other research involving clonidine to treat Tourette's syndrome, conduct disorder, sleep disturbance, PTSD, and autism shows limited effectiveness. Kutcher (1999) concluded that the beneficial effect derived from an antihypertensive medication is a function of sedation.

Adverse Effects

Children and adolescents with preexisting cardiovascular disease or syncope (dizziness and fainting) do not appear to be good candidates for this medication (Kutcher, 1999). Regular blood pressure assessment is also essential to good clinical practice. A common unwanted effect with clonidine is oversedation. Sedation is most intensely experienced during the first 2 to 4 weeks of use. Because it is an antihypertensive medication, reduced blood pressure and heart rate are expected. Other common adverse effects include headache and dizziness. Less common negative effects are night awakenings, nightmares, depression, and constipation.

Compliance and Abrupt Discontinuation

Because the effectiveness of clonidine lasts from 3 to 6 hours, clonidine is typically prescribed in multiple doses. Depending on the family and school system, multiple dosing can be problematic. Clonidine is also available as a patch, which can aid with compliance. As a cautionary note, discontinuation of the medication needs to occur over a period of 2 to 4 days (Green, 1991). Abrupt withdrawal can cause a hypertensive crisis, agitation, nervousness, and headache (*PDR*, 2000). A hypertensive crisis can be lethal. Therefore, informed consent, close monitoring by a prescriber, and caution are prudent when using clonidine.

MOOD-STABILIZING AGENTS

Mood stabilizers are a class of medications used to treat bipolar disorder as well as intermittent explosive disorder. Lithium and valproic acid (valproate and divalproex sodium) are FDA approved to treat bipolar disorder and mania in adults. However, prescribers use mood stabilizers to treat a variety of disorders in children and adolescents, such as mood disturbance, aggression, conduct problems, anger outbursts, and hyperactive behavior. Other mood stabilizers include carbamazapine (Tegretol), gabapentin (Neurontin), and lamotrigine (Lamictal). Due to space limitations, lithium and valproic acid are the focus of this section.

Lithium

Lithium carbonate is a metallic element that is commonly found in natural springs and seawater. Since the 1870s, physicians have prescribed this highly soluble salt to treat numerous emotional difficulties. Although this psychotropic has been used for a long period, no conclusive evidence exists as to how lithium works (Gitlin, 1990). The FDA approves lithium for the treatment of mania and bipolar disorder in persons over 12 years of age. Adverse effects, toxic reactions, and the need for blood level monitoring are essential elements to consider when working with lithium.

Adverse Effects

Common adverse effects of lithium include nausea, diarrhea, tremor, ataxia, cognitive slowing, frequent urination, thirst, and weakness (*PDR*, 2000). Although less frequent, the other adverse effects are usually more important to adolescents. For example, weight gain, rash, hair loss, and acne are untoward effects that may negatively influence compliance and may complicate treatment.

Toxic Levels

Lithium has a low therapeutic index. The *therapeutic index* is the difference between the therapeutic dose and the toxic dose of the medication. As a result, lithium can become lethal if misused or taken in overdose. The signs of lithium toxicity include vomiting, increased muscle weakness, extreme tremor, sedation, drowsiness, slurred speech, and impaired coordination. The most serious and lethal effects of lithium involve cardiac arrhythmia, stupor, impaired consciousness, and coma.

Blood Work

Blood work is essential when using lithium. The need for blood work adds another variable to the compliance equation. Lithium is the only psychotropic that the body excretes without metabolization (Gitlin, 1990). Thus, any water or salt imbalance can lead to dangerous levels of lithium in the body. A number of situations arise in which blood levels should be checked (Gitlin, 1990). First, it should be obvious that suspected signs of lithium toxicity (listed previously) warrant laboratory work. Second, major changes in weight may alter the therapeutic effectiveness as well as the toxicity of lithium. A decrease in weight may increase the risk of toxicity, whereas an increase in weight may decrease effectiveness. Third, the use of diuretics will alter lithium levels. Diuretics decrease the water level in the body. Diuretics include medications such as furosemide (Lasix) and everyday substances such as caffeine. A substantial increase or decrease in caffeine use has implications for therapeutic and toxic effects when taking lithium. For example, decreasing caffeine use after an effective dose of lithium is reached can increase the possibility of lithium toxicity. Fourth, dehydration can be a potentially dangerous situation. For example, children who experience an intense illness like the flu are at greater risk for dehydration. Playing or working outdoors in extreme heat can negatively affect a person taking lithium. These issues highlight the need for caution and close monitoring of lithium. Many prescribers are hesitant to work with lithium for these reasons. Nonpsychiatric physicians write only 30% of the total prescriptions for lithium (Beardsley, Gardocki, Larsen, & Hidalgo, 1988).

Valproic Acid (Valproate and Divalproex Sodium)

Valproic acid is an anticonvulsant that is chemically different from other anticonvulsants. The anticonvulsant properties of valproic acid were discovered in the early 1960s, and FDA approval for seizures was made in 1978. The FDA approved valproic acid for the treatment of bipolar disorder in 1995. In March 1996, the FDA approved valproate for prevention of migraine headaches. Valproic acid is currently more commonly prescribed than lithium for bipolar disorder. Prescribers are using valproate for mood disturbance and behavioral disturbance in children and adolescents. The method of action appears to be an inhibition of central nervous system (CNS) activity by increasing gamma-aminobutyric acid (GABA). In more simple language, valproic acid slows the electrical activity of the brain.

Recent research with children and adolescents who display mood variability and temper outbursts shows promise in terms of symptom reduction (Donovan et al., 2000). Although the research used a limited number of subjects, the study demonstrated effectiveness in reducing specific target symptoms. In spite of this demonstrated effectiveness and promise, several concerns remain, including adverse effects, hepatotoxicity, polycystic ovaries, and pancreatitis.

Adverse Effects

The adverse effects created by valproic acid are numerous. Common untoward gastrointestinal effects include nausea, diarrhea, and constipation. Because valproic acid inhibits CNS functioning, patients may experience depression and lethargy. In terms of motor systems, valproic acid may cause agitation, tremors, and ataxia. Although weight gain is not a common side effect, this untoward effect is important, especially for adolescents. An increase in weight may prompt noncompliance in spite of symptom reduction. Other negative effects related to appearance, such as rashes and hair loss, are likewise important and should be monitored.

Drug-Induced Hepatotoxicity

Hepatotoxicity is a toxic state of the liver that can be caused by valproic acid. Other psychotropics have the potential for hepatotoxicity; however, valproic acid presents a greater risk. Patients have died as a result of liver failure caused by valproic acid. Hepatotoxicity appears in a small but variable number of patients (*PDR,* 2000). Malaise, weakness, lethargy, facial swelling, anorexia, and vomiting are the nonspecific symptoms that precede hepatotoxicity. Liver function tests before and at regular intervals during pharmacotherapy are essential. As with lithium, blood work is another factor that influences compliance. Children are at particular risk for drug-induced hepatotoxicity.

Drug-Induced Pancreatitis

In July 2000, Abbott Laboratories (the manufacturer of Depakote and Depakene) issued a new warning regarding pancreatitis when using valproic acid (Pizzuti, 2000). Life-threatening pancreatitis has been reported in children who were administered valproate. Abdominal pain, vomiting, and anorexia can be symptoms of pancreatitis. Pancreatitis occurred in both initial and long-term use of valproic acid. Prompt medical attention is essential when these symptoms occur.

Polycystic Ovary Syndrome (PCOS)

It is known that valproic acid can have a significant effect on the endocrine system. A controversy exists with polycystic ovary syndrome (PCOS) because this syndrome is associated with the long-term use of valproate. Currently, there is no identified cause of PCOS. The clinical symptoms of PCOS are menstrual irregularities, excessive hair growth, lack of ovulation, and obesity (Legro, 1998). PCOS is a common cause of infertility. Although a causal link between long-term use of valproic acid and PCOS has yet to be established, a low positive correlation exists between them. Because of its effects on the endocrine system, hormonal disturbances must be considered when valproic acid is used to treat adolescent females (Vainionpaa et al., 1999).

NEUROLEPTICS

Neuroleptic medications are also known as *antipsychotic medications* and *major tranquilizers.* Neuroleptic medications have a long history in the treatment of emotional and behavioral disorders. Newer types of neuroleptic medications were developed in the past 15 years. Some of the older neuroleptic medications are haloperidol (Haldol), thioridazine (Mellaril), and chlorpromazine (Thorazine). Several of the newer neuroleptics are quetiapine (Seroquel), olanzapine (Zyprexa), risperidone (Risperdal), and ziprasidone (Zeldox). Current theories suggest that the therapeutic mechanism of action of the neuroleptics involves the blocking of dopamine receptors in the central nervous system. By blocking postsynaptic dopamine receptors, the neuroleptics decrease CNS activity. These medications decrease the positive symptoms of psychosis (i.e., hallucinations and delusions). Because the neuroleptics are not specific to a certain portion of the CNS, multiple complications are a product of this global effect on the CNS.

Although these medications are used in the treatment of psychotic disorders in adults, they have been prescribed to children and adolescents for other reasons. Physicians prescribe neuroleptics to treat symptoms of childhood and adolescent onset of schizophrenia; to reduce symptoms of severe aggression, autistic disorders, and conduct disorder; and to prevent self-injurious behavior in youth with mental retardation. Prescribers also employ neuroleptics to treat more severe symptoms of OCD and psychotic symptoms associated with mood disorders. In spite of the multiple off-label uses, these medications should be used only with great caution because of the potential for severe adverse effects. Informed consent is an important component in this psychopharmacological intervention. The MHP and prescriber need to have respect for the neuroleptics because, in spite of their effectiveness, a higher risk of harm exists with these psychotropics. Extrapyramidal symptoms, other untoward effects, and the need for expert management are key points.

Extrapyramidal Symptoms

Extrapyramidal symptoms (EPSs) result from the neuroleptic medication's effect on the extrapyramidal motor system. The MHP must document any abnormal movement and communicate these to the prescriber immediately. The types of EPS vary in terms of onset, course, and severity.

Tardive dyskinesia (TD) is a rare but *irreversible* side effect that affects motor movement. The risk of TD increases significantly with higher doses and longer duration of treatment. Symptoms of TD commonly involve the involuntary movements of the face, tongue, jaw, and neck muscles. These behaviors take the form of sucking or smacking of the lips and tongue. The involuntary trunk and extremity movements appear as arrhythmic, rapid, and jerky actions. Although lower doses and shorter duration reduce the risk of TD, children and adolescents are more sensitive to the medications.

TD must be distinguished from the motor restlessness (akasthisia) that presents as a more common adverse effect. Subjectively, akathisia is extremely uncomfortable and disconcerting. Akasthisia presents as the inability to sit still, pacing, foot tapping, and a strong urge to move (Green, 1991). Akasthisia needs to be distinguished from anxiety. A thorough interview conducted by an MHP with sufficient clinical expertise can assist in differentiating between anxiety and akasthisia. Prescribers can lower the dose of the medication or employ other medications (beta blockers and clonazepam) to ameliorate these symptoms. As would be expected, the persistent experience of akathisia can negatively influence compliance.

Parkinson-like symptoms (muscle rigidity, tremor, and slowed motor response) and acute dystonias (muscle spasms and prolonged muscle contractions) are also part of the extrapyramidal effects of neuroleptics. Space limitations constrain discussion of these negative effects.

Multiple Side Effects and Syndromes

Although movement disorders occur, other adverse effects and syndromes are part of working with neuroleptics. Some of these adverse outcomes are a function of anticholinergic effects, as outlined in the discussion of TCAs. Untoward anticholinergic effects include dry mouth, blurred vision, drowsiness, and weight gain. Other unwanted outcomes not directly related to anticholinergic effects include sedation, low blood pressure, photosensitivity, and constipation.

Agranulocytosis is an acute febrile syndrome created by a significant decrease in granulocyte-producing bone marrow. Tachycardia, extreme exhaustion, high fever, chills, swollen neck, and sore throat (sometimes accompanied by local ulceration) characterize this condition. Treatment for agranulocytosis includes discontinuing the medications and controlling any infection with antibiotics until the bone marrow can regenerate.

Neuroleptic malignant syndrome (NMS) can be life threatening. NMS can occur abruptly and without warning. NMS is characterized by fever, severe muscle rigidity, altered state of consciousness, stupor, and catatonia. NMS can continue after the neuroleptic is discontinued.

Psychiatric Consultation Required

Because of the intricacies and adverse effects of the neuroleptics, psychiatric consultation is important in order to act in the patient's best interest. As stated previously, informed consent, close monitoring by the prescribing professional, and expert evaluation of negative effects is essential when working with neuroleptics.

CONCLUSION

In summary, prescribers will continue to use psychoactive medications to treat children and adolescents with emotional and behavioral disorders. MHPs need to determine the roles in which they feel most comfortable when collaborating with prescribing professionals. The responsibilities of the MHP can vary among the roles of assessment specialist, consultant, and physician's extender. A comprehensive evaluation is necessary before referring for medication consultation. Psychotropic medications for children and adolescents are appropriate when certain diagnostic criteria are met, a viable treatment plan is developed, and specific symptoms are identified. Diagnostic services, individual psychotherapy, and family therapy remain essential ingredients of high-quality treatment. To practice ethically, the nonprescribing MHP needs to have a psychopharmacology knowledge base, which helps the practitioner to understand the benefits and the limitations of psychotropic medications.

REFERENCES

American Psychiatric Association. (1994). *Diagnostic and statistical manual* (4th ed.). Washington, DC: Author.

Beardsley, R. S., Gardocki, G. J., Larsen, D. B., & Hidalgo, J. (1988). Prescribing psychotropic medication by primary care physicians and psychiatrists. *Archives of General Psychiatry, 45,* 1117–1119.

Biederman, J., Wilens, T., Mick, E., Spencer, T., & Faraone, S. V. (1999). Pharmacotherapy of attention-deficit hyperactivity disorder reduces risk for substance abuse disorder. *Pediatrics, 104,* 293–297.

Black, D. W., Wesner, R., Bowers, W., & Gabel, J. (1993). A comparison of fluvoxamine, cognitive therapy, and placebo in the treatment of panic disorder. *Archives of General Psychiatry, 50,* 44–50.

DeBattista, C., & Schatzberg, A. F. (2000). Current psychotropic dosing and monitoring guidelines. *Primary Psychiatry, 7*(1), 26–64.

Donovan, S. J., Stewart, J. W., Nunes, E. V., Quitkin, F. M., Parides, M., Daniel, W., Susser, E., & Klein, D. F. (2000). Divalproex treatment with youth with explosive temper and mood liability: A double-blind, placebo-controlled crossover design. *American Journal of Psychiatry, 157*(5), 818–820.

Duncan, B., Miller, S., & Sparks, J. (2000, March/April). Exposing the mythmakers: How soft cell has replaced hard science. *The Family Therapy Networker,* 24–34, 53.

Fava, M. (2000). Weight gain during short- and long-term treatment of antidepressants. *Primary Psychiatry, 7*(5), 28–32.

Geller, B., Reising, D., Leonard, H. L., Riddle, M. A., & Walsh, B. T. (1999). Critical review of tricyclic antidepressant use in children and adolescents. *Journal of the American Academy of Child and Adolescent Psychiatry, 38*(5), 513–516.

Gitlin, M. J. (1990). *The psychotherapists guide to psychopharmacology.* New York: Free Press.

Glenmullen, J. (2000). *Prozac backlash: Overcoming the dangers of Prozac, Zoloft, Paxil, and other antidepressants with safe, effective alternatives.* New York: Simon & Schuster.

Green, W. H. (1991). *Child and adolescent clinical psychopharmacology.* Baltimore: Williams and Wilkins.

Jensen, P. S., Bhatara, V. S., Vitiello, B., Hoagwood, K., Feil, M., & Burke, L. B. (1999). Psychoactive medication prescribing practices for U.S. children: Gaps between research and clinical practice. *Journal of the American Academy of Child and Adolescent Psychiatry, 38,* 557–565.

Kalorama Information. (2000, March 9). *Psychotherapeutic drug market experiences record growth* [Press release]. New York: Market Research.

Keller, M. B., McCullough, J. P., Klein, D. N., Arrow, B., Dunner, D. L., Gelenberg, A. J., Markowitz, J. C., Nemeroff, C. B., Russell, J. M., Thase, M. E., Trivedi, M. H., & Zajecka, J. (2000). A comparison of nefazadone, the cognitive behavioral-analysis system of psychotherapy and their combination for the treatment of chronic depression. *The New England Journal of Medicine, 342*(20), 1462–1470.

Klee, B. J., Hack, S., & Green, W. H. (1998). Tricyclic antidepressants in child and adolescent psychiatry: Indications, use, and safety. *Primary Psychiatry, 5*(7), 86–90.

Kutcher, S. P. (1999). Clonidine and guanfacine in the treatment of children with ADHD and associated conditions. *Child & Adolescent Psychopharmacology News, 4*(3), 1–6.

Legro, R. S. (1998). Polycystic ovary syndrome: current and future treatment paradigms. *American Journal of Obstetrics and Gynecology, 179,* 101–108.

National Institutes of Health. (1998). Diagnosis and treatment of attention deficit hyperactivity disorder. *NIH Consensus Statement, 16*(2), 1–37.

National Institutes of Mental Health. (2000). *Depression in children and adolescents: A fact sheet for physicians.* Bethesda, MD: Author.

O'Connor, K., Todorov, C., Robillard, S., Borgeat, F., & Brault, M. (1999) Cognitive-behaviour therapy and medication in the treatment of obsessive compulsive disorder. *Canadian Journal of Psychiatry, 44*(1), 64–71.

Pharmaceutical Research and Manufacturers of America. (2000). *Survey 2000: New medications in development for mental illnesses.* Washington, DC: PhRMA Foundation.

Physician's desk reference (54th ed.). (2000). Mountvale, NJ: Medical Economics.

Pirodsky, D. M., & Cohn, J. S. (1992). *Clinical primer of psychopharmacology* (2nd ed.). New York: McGraw-Hill.

Pizzuti, D. J. (2000). *Important drug warning communication.* Abbott Park, IL: Abbott Laboratories.

Preston, J., & Ebert, B. (1999, October). Psychologists' role in the discussion of psychotropic medication with clients: Legal and ethical considerations. *California Psychologist,* 34–35.

Preston, J., & Johnson, J. (2000). *Clinical psychopharmacology made ridiculously simple* (4th ed.). Miami, FL: MedMaster.

Preston, J., O'Neill, J. H., & Talaga, M. C. (1999). *Handbook of clinical psychopharmacology for therapists* (2nd ed.). Oakland, CA: New Harbinger Publications.

Rosenbaum, J. F., Fava, M., Hoog, S. L., Ascroft, R. C., & Krebs, W. B. (1998). Selective serotonin reuptake inhibitor discontinuation syndrome: A randomized clinical trial. *Biological Psychiatry, 44,* 77–87.

Satcher, D. (1999). *Mental health: A report of the surgeon general.* Bethesda, MD: National Institute of Mental Health.

Schwartz, J. M., Stoessel, P. W., Baxter, L. R., Martin, K. M., & Phelps, M. E. (1996). Systematic changes in cerebral glucose metabolic rate after successful behavior modification treatment of obsessive-compulsive disorder. *Archives of General Psychiatry, 53*(2), 109–113.

Sederer, L. I., Ellison, J., & Keyes, C. (1998). Guidelines for prescribing psychiatrists in consultative, collaborative, and supervisory relationships. *Psychiatric Services, 49*(9), 1197–1203.

Stahl, S. M. (2000). *Essential psychopharmacology: Neuroscientific basis and practical applications* (2nd ed.). New York: Cambridge University Press.

Stahl, S. M. (1998). *Psychopharmacology of antidepressants.* London: Martin Dunitz.

Sussman, N. (1999). Managing a popular science: The internet and clinical trials. *Primary Psychiatry, 6*(8), 12.

Vainionpaa L. K., Rattya, J., Knip, M., Tapanainen, J. S., Pakarinen, A. J., Lanning, P., Tekay, A., Myllyla, V. V., & Isojarvi, J. I. (1999). Valproate-induced hyperandrogenism during pubertal maturation in girls with epilepsy. *Annals of Neurology, 45*(4), 444–450.

Valenstein, E. S. (1998). *Blaming the brain: The truth about drugs and mental health.* New York: Free Press.

Waters, R. (2000, March/April). Generation Rx: The risk of raising our kids on pharmaceuticals. *The Family Therapy Networker,* 35–43.

Zito, J. M., Safer, D. J., dosReis, S., Gardner, J. F., Boyles, M., & Lynch, F. (2000). Trends in the prescribing of psychotropic medications to preschoolers. *Journal of the American Medical Association, 283,* 1025–1030.

Author Index

Subject Index

ABOUT THE EDITORS

Diane T. Marsh, PhD, is a professor of psychology at the University of Pittsburgh at Greensburg and has many years of experience as a therapist, consultant, and workshop presenter. She is chair of the American Psychological Association Task Force on Serious Mental Illness (SMI) and Serious Emotional Disturbance (SED). She is the author or editor of numerous books, including *Families and Mental Illness: New Directions in Professional Practice* (Praeger, 1992), *Families and Mental Retardation: New Directions in Professional Practice* (Praeger, 1992), *New Directions in the Psychological Treatment of Serious Mental Illness* (Praeger, 1994), *Ethical and Legal Issues in Professional Practice with Families* (Wiley, 1997), *Troubled Journey: Coming to Terms with the Mental Illness of a Sibling or Parent* (Tarcher/Putnam, 1997), *Serious Mental Illness and the Family: The Practitioner's Guide* (Wiley, 1998), and *A Family-Focused Approach to Serious Mental Illness: Empirically Supported Interventions* (Professional Resource Press, 2001). She has received many awards for her work as a mental health advocate.

Mary A. Fristad, PhD, ABPP, is a professor of psychiatry and psychology at the Ohio State University in Columbus, Ohio. She is the director of research and psychological services in the Division of Child & Adolescent Psychiatry. She is also a member of the American Psychological Association Task Force on Serious Mental Illness (SMI) and Serious Emotional Disturbance (SED) and is chair of the SED committee. In addition, she serves on the executive board of Division 53, Society of Clinical Child and Adolescent Psychology, of the American Psychological Association and the editorial board of the Journal of Clinical Psychology, and she has served on numerous review committees for the National Institute of Mental Health (NIMH). She has been the principal investigator or coprincipal investigator on numerous NIMH, state, local, and industry grants. She has authored or coauthored more than 95 scientific articles and book chapters on the assessment and treatment of childhood mood disorders. She has also published a structured diagnostic interview for children. She maintains a clinical practice working with children, adolescents, and their families in addition to her teaching, research, and administrative duties.